AIRBRUSH ACTION 2

The Best New Airbrush Illustration

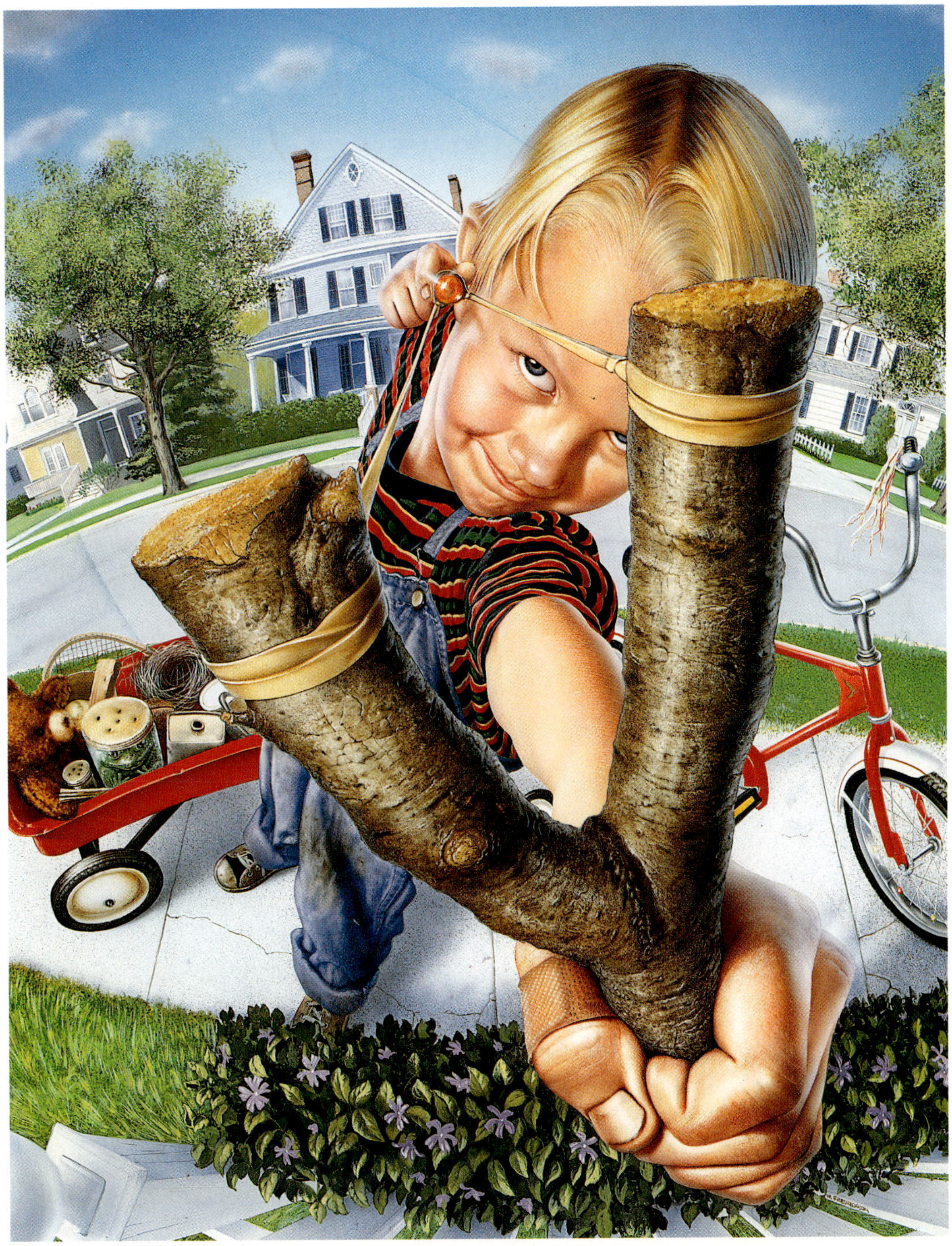

MARK FREDRICKSON

Rockport Publishers, Inc. • Rockport, Massachusetts
Distributed by North Light Books, Cincinnati, Ohio

Designer: Thom Lewis
Editor: Rosalie Grattaroti
Production Manager: Barbara States
Production Assistant: Pat O'Maley
Cover Illustration: Bill Mayer
Cover Design: Sara Day

First published in the United States of America by:
Rockport Publishers, Inc.
146 Granite Street
Rockport, Massachusetts 01966
Telephone: (508) 546-9590
Fax: (508) 546-7141
Telex: 5106019284 ROCKORT PUB

Distributed to the book trade and art trade in the U.S. and Canada by:
North Light, an imprint of
F & W Publications
1507 Dana Avenue
Cincinnati, Ohio 45207
Telephone: (513) 531-2222

Other Distribution by:
Rockport Publishers, Inc.
Rockport, Massachusetts 01966

0 9 8 7 6 5 4 3 2

Printed in Singapore

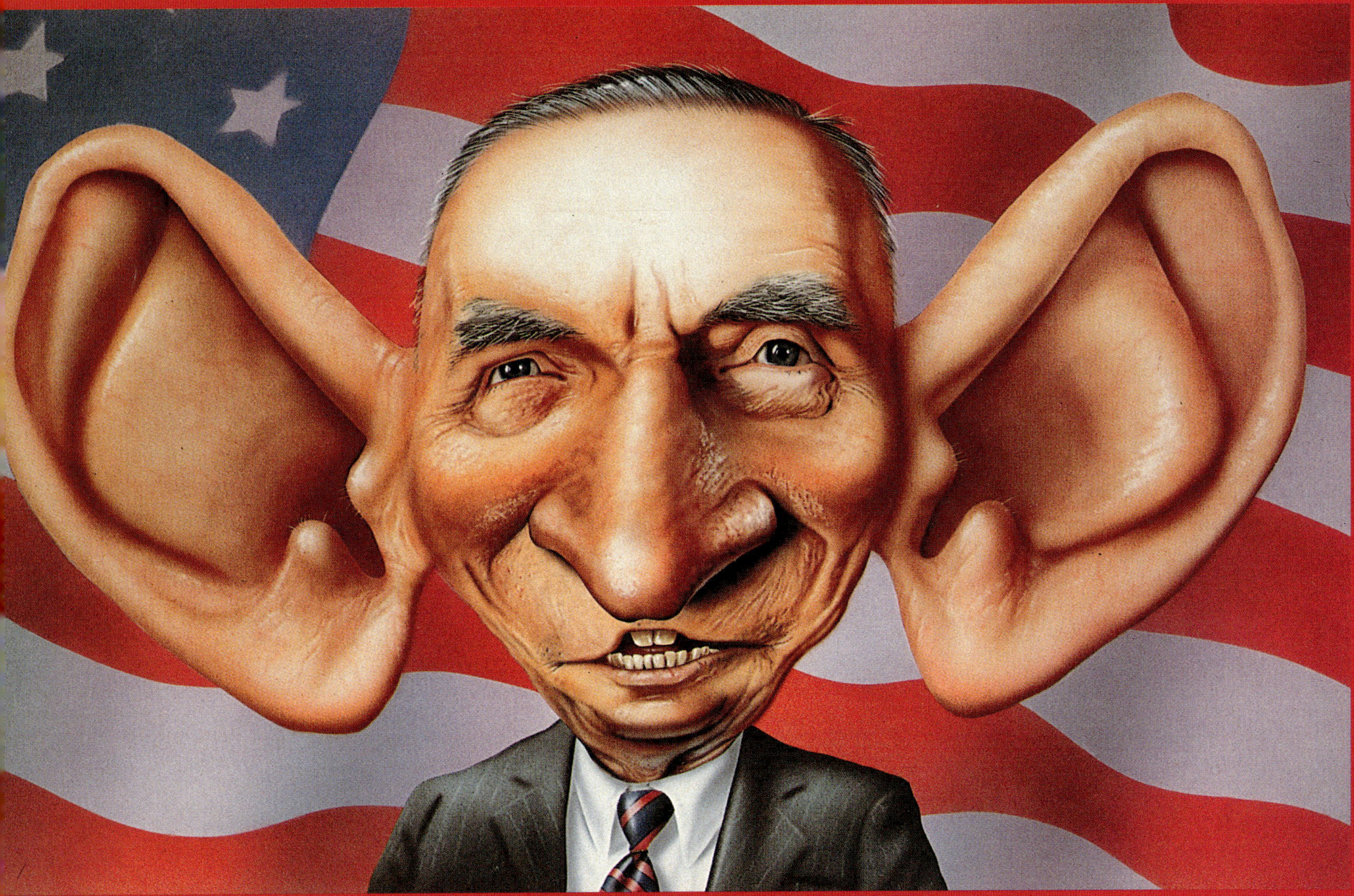

KEN WESTPHAL

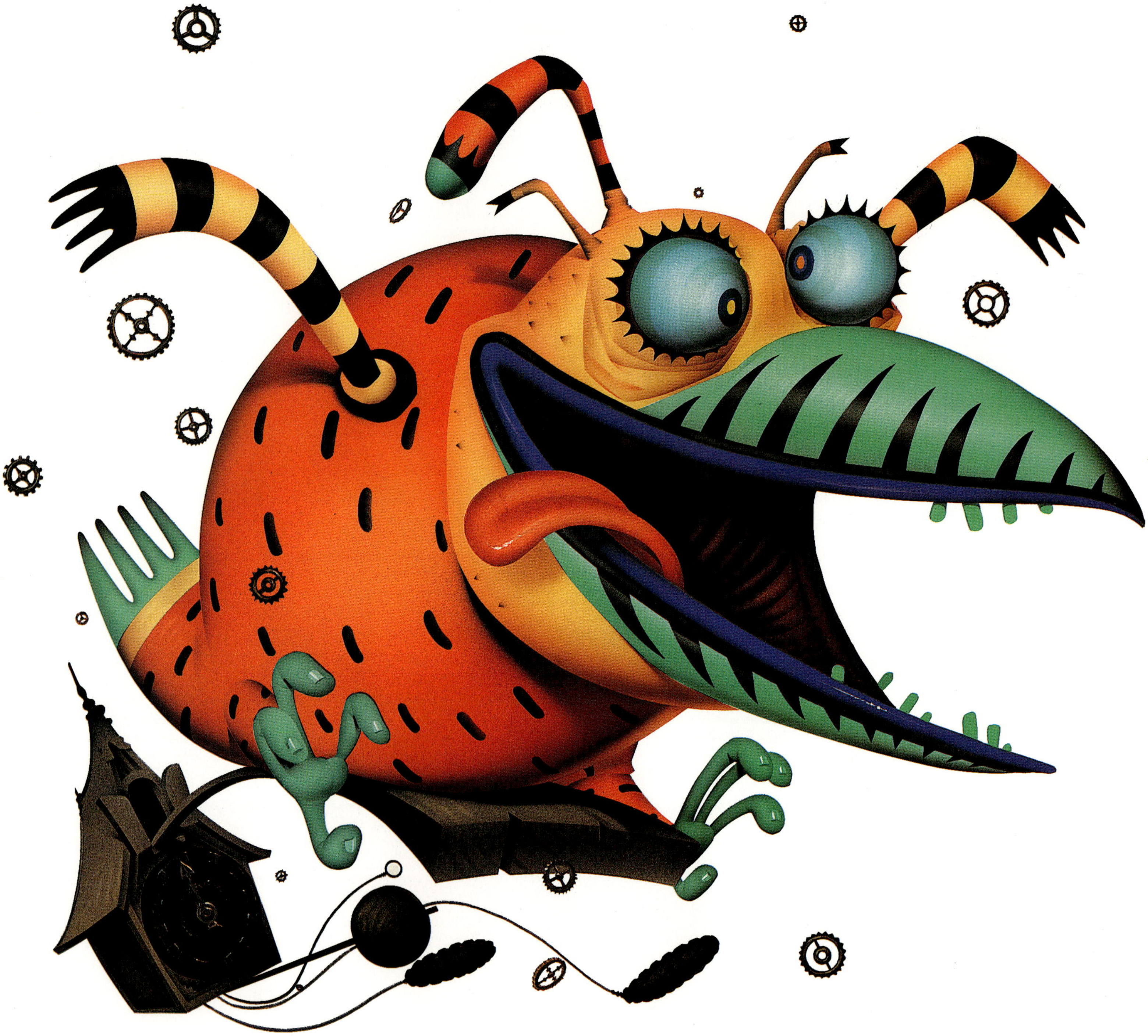

BILL MAYER

Contents

Angel	9
Lori Anzalone	9
Chris P. Apostolou	10
Craig Attebery	10
Peter Bartczak	11
Leslie Bates	11-12
Rodino R. Bautista	13
Dennis Bayuzick	13
Scott Beckley	13-14
Doron Ben-Ami	15
Mark A. Bender	15-17
Anita S. Bice	18-21
Kurt Bittle	21-22
Brian Blair	22-24
Tim Blough	24
John M. Booth	25-28
Steven Boswick	28-29
Marty Braun	30-37
Robert Brun	38
Todd Buck	39
Hank Buffington	40
Lonnie Busch	40-45
Thomas Cain	46-49
Philip H. Campbell	56
Kurt Carloni	49-51
Martin Castillo	51
Gary Ciccarelli	51-53
Mick Coulas	54-55
David Crowe	56-59
Tom Daly	60-61
Richard Daskas	62
Ruben Deanda	62
Catherine Dittmer	63
Jim Durk	63
Jim Effler	64-65
Dave Ekman	66
Brian Evans	66
Alan Flinn	66-67
Mark A. Fredrickson	68-74
Brian Fujimori	75
Pedro Gamero	75
Mike Gardner	76-78
Ben Garvie	79
Scott T. Gee	79
Alan Giana	80-81
Gary Glover	82-84
Stuart Hall	85
Andy Hickes	85-88
Michael Holguin	88
Reggie Holladay	89-91
Tom Hoover	92
Robert L. Horwath	93
Ron Houghton, Jr.	93
Thomas J. Humpert	93-95
Michael W. Hunt, Jr.	95
Stephen M. Hunter	96-99
Greg Hurley	100-101
Christopher Iorillo	102
Jake Jones	102
Albert Juarez	102
Nicholas Kendysh	103
Brian Kim	104
Robert A. Kling	105
Andrew Kong Knight	105-106
David Kovach	106-107
Dave Kuhn	108
Vincent Lacava	109-110
Andy Lackow	110
Jim Langman	111
Jorgen Larsson	111
Pete LaSalle, Jr.	111-112
Samuel Laterza	112
Robert Leverette	113
Jerry Lofaro	113-117
Travis A. Louie	118
Shannon Mac Donald	118
Farley Magadia	119-121
Joseph Martin	121-122
Trent Martin	123
Bill Mayer	123-131
Craig McKay	132-133
Richard O. Menchaca	133
Jim Mendillo	134-136
Doug Meythaler	137
Richard Mollo	137
Gerard Mooney	138-141
Clark Most	141
Peggy Mozley	142-145
Eric Oliver	146
Osni Omena	146
Mark Otnes	147-148
Christopher Palmer	149-150
Thomas Peiffer	150
Gary Penca	150-151
Stephen Peringer	152
Eric Perrotta	153
Thom Peterson	154-155
Myles Pinkney	156
Oscar Quarles	156
Roberto Ramirez	156-157
Kathleen Regan	157
Robert Revels	158
Mark V. Robinson	158
David Salazar	159
Samuel Salfino III	159-160
Dr. William C. Schneider	161
Greg Schooley	161
Steve Shamburger	161
Mary A. Shafer	162
Steve Singer	163
Timothy Stafford	163
William R. Stewart	164
Winston Sturgen	164
Ian Suk	164
Michael Takagi	165
Daniel K. Tennant	165-168
John E. Thies	169-170
Carlos Torres	171-173
Jimmie Turner	173
Mark Villarta	173
Patrick C. Wanebo	174
Tobie Warren	174
Wayne Watford	175-176
Tom Watters	176-177
Michael E. Weaver	177
Ken Westphal	178
June Workman	179
Gary Yealdhall	179-180
Eddie Young	181-184
Andy Zito	184-189
Boris Zlotsky	189

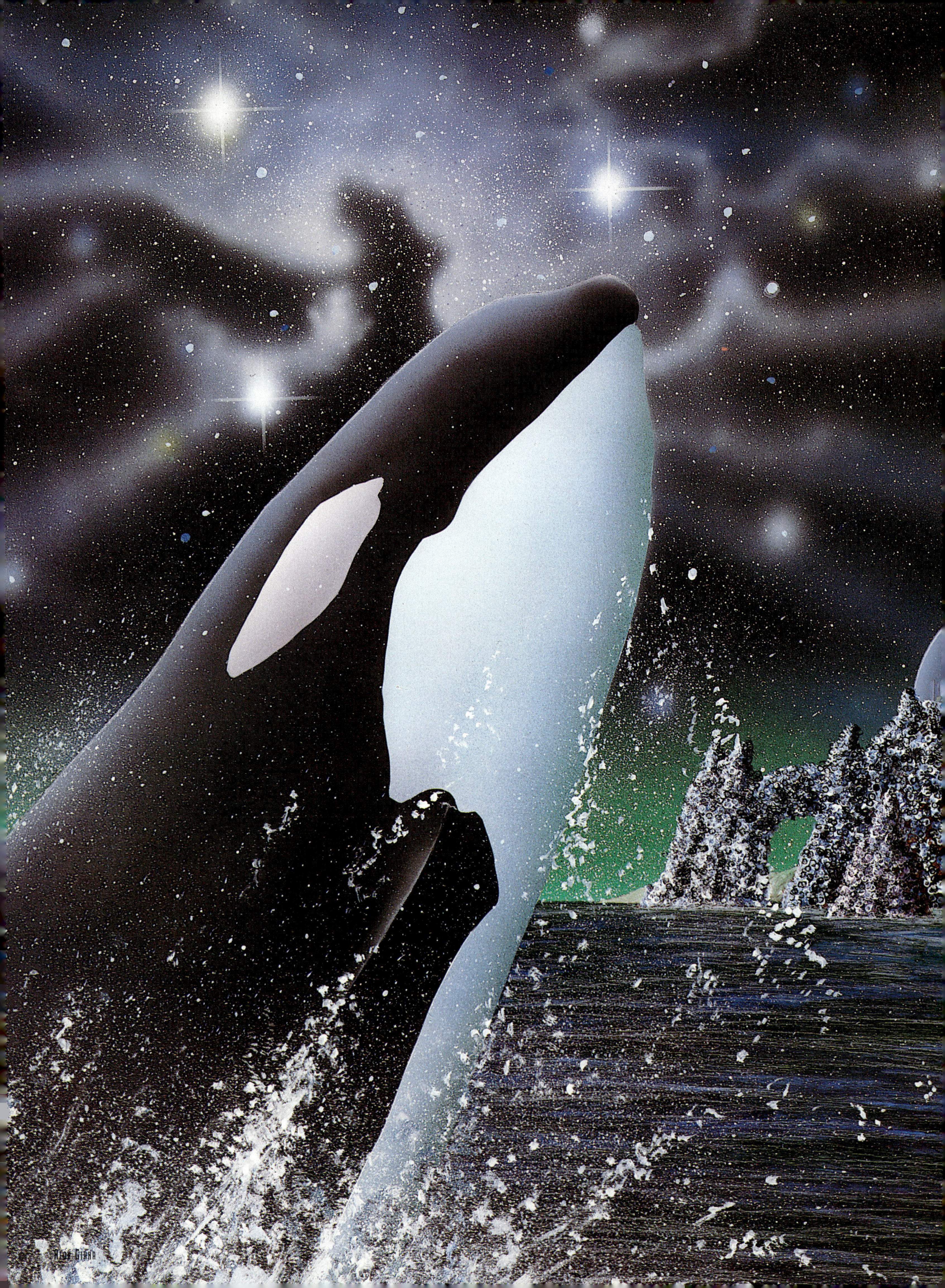

INTRODUCTION

When I started airbrushing in the early 1980's, few educational or product resources were available: an intermittently published magazine, Airbrush Digest (defunct since 1984); a couple of books on airbrushing; no seminars or videos. Even airbrush-related supplies, especially ready-to-spray paints, were hard to come by.

Ten years later, the influence of the airbrush at both school and professional levels has exploded. The popularity of Airbrush Action magazine grows each year, workshop programs are held across the country, books and videos abound, and new airbrushes, paints, and compressors are introduced each year.

This spiraling growth is impressive despite repeated attempts by industry observers to write the airbrush's epitaph. Stan Patey, Rockport's president, was originally advised against producing last year's first Airbrush Action book because of the erroneous perception that airbrushing was waning, perhaps falling prey to computing.

Thanks to Stan's keen business sense-and personal intuition-he printed Airbrush Action anyway. As a result of the first edition being successful, here is its sequel.

Although the computer has overtaken hand photo-retouching and is beginning to compete with technical illustration, I believe that it will be a long time, if ever, before the hand in art is totally eclipsed by the computer-if indeed that day ever comes.

Airbrush Action, as a book and as a magazine, is an important reflection of the growth, popularity, and high standard of airbrush art as we know it today. These publications serve to promote the high standards that new and less experienced users can aspire to and experienced artists can stay abreast of.

In our drive to showcase the best, we've been criticized from time to time for being a bit lofty, or as someone put it, "hoity toity," showing the best at the expense of the down-to-earth. To us, it's a simple matter: Artists cannot improve with mediocrity as their model. And it is in this spirit of striving for the best that the Airbrush Action book exists.

Today, there are 12 airbrush manufacturers, 23 paint manufacturers, and 9 compressor manufacturers and distributors catering to the U.S. market alone.

The fervent activity of airbrushed-related manufacturing and consumption is the most accurate and dependable indicator of airbrushing's bright future. In fact, I'd predict that airbrushing's peak is yet to come.

I am proud of the success of the Airbrush Action book and am grateful for Rockport's demonstrated belief in the vitality and excitement of airbrushing.

Clifford S. Steiglitz, Publisher
AIRBRUSH ACTION MAGAZINE

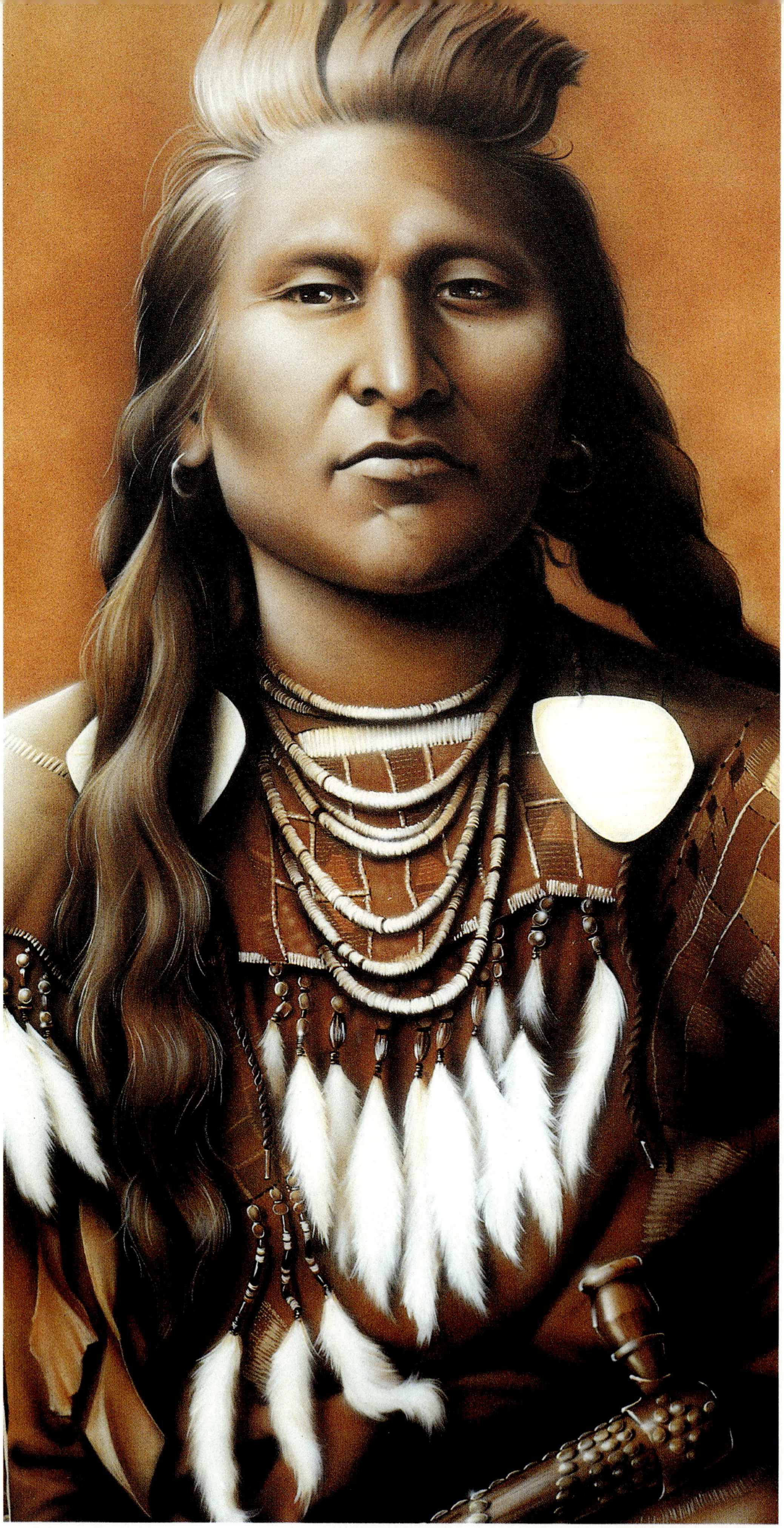

1

1
Artist Angel
Title Fierce Warrior
Usage Fine Art
Media Used Acrylic

2
Artist Angel
Title Glamour Girl
Client Private Home Owner
Usage Fine Art
Media Use Acrylic

3
Artist Angel
Title Reproduction (Botticelli)
Usage Fine Art
Media Used Acrylic

4
Artist Lori Anzalone
Title Jungle
Art Director Lori Anzalone
Usage Commercial Art
Media Used Acrylic

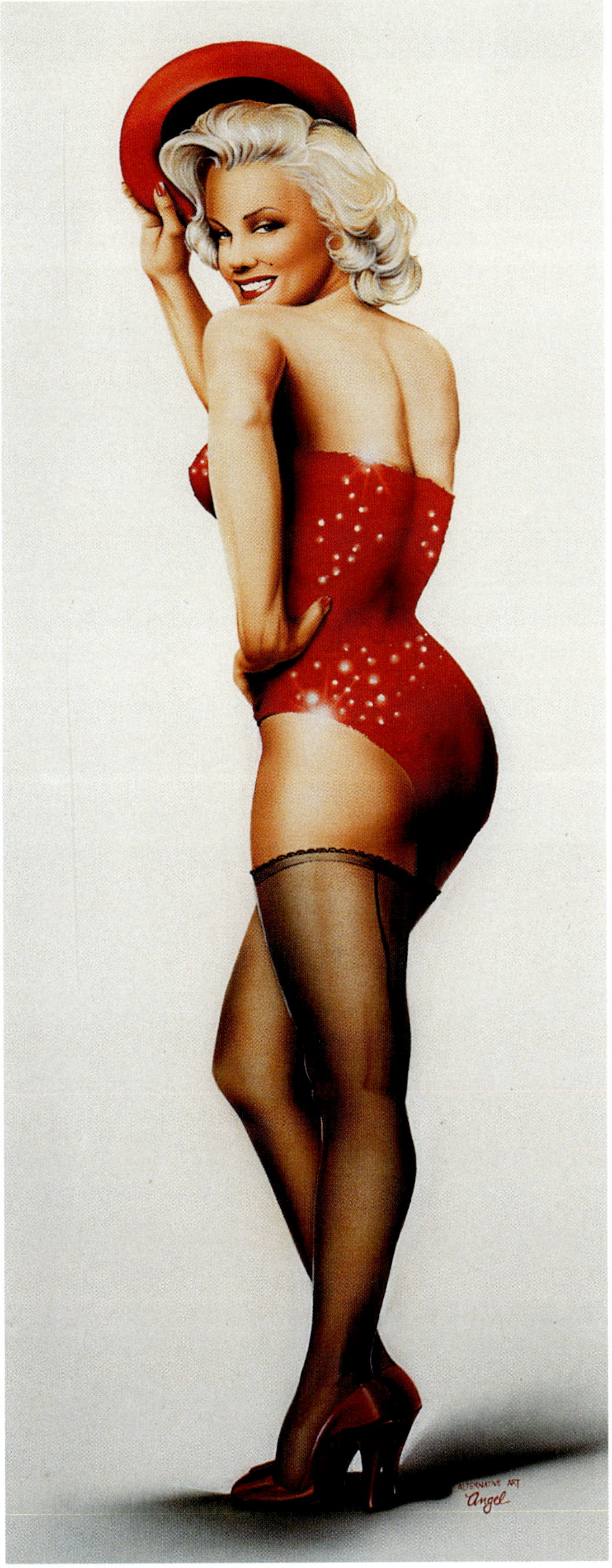

2

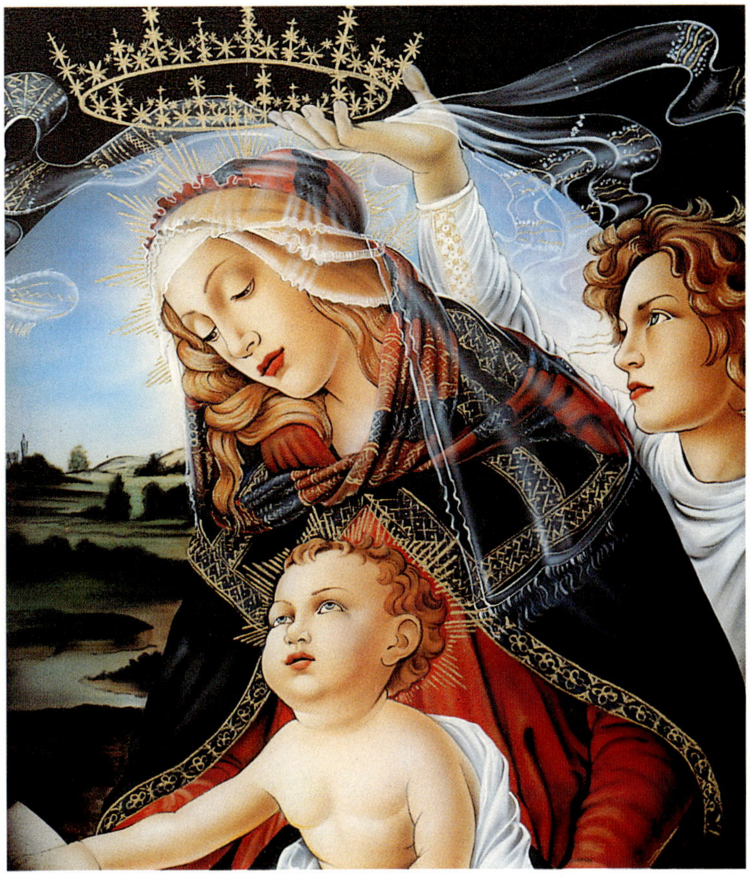

3

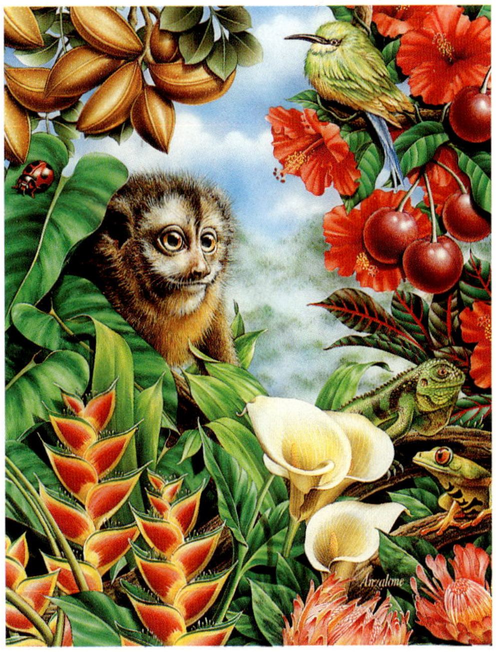

4

1
Artist Chris P. Apostolou
Title Lifeblood
Client Blind (Band)
Usage Commercial Art
Media Used Badger Acrylics

2
Artist Craig Attebery
Title HRMS Antenna Signal Path
Client Jet Propulsion Laboratory
Usage Technical Illustration
Media Used Gouache

1

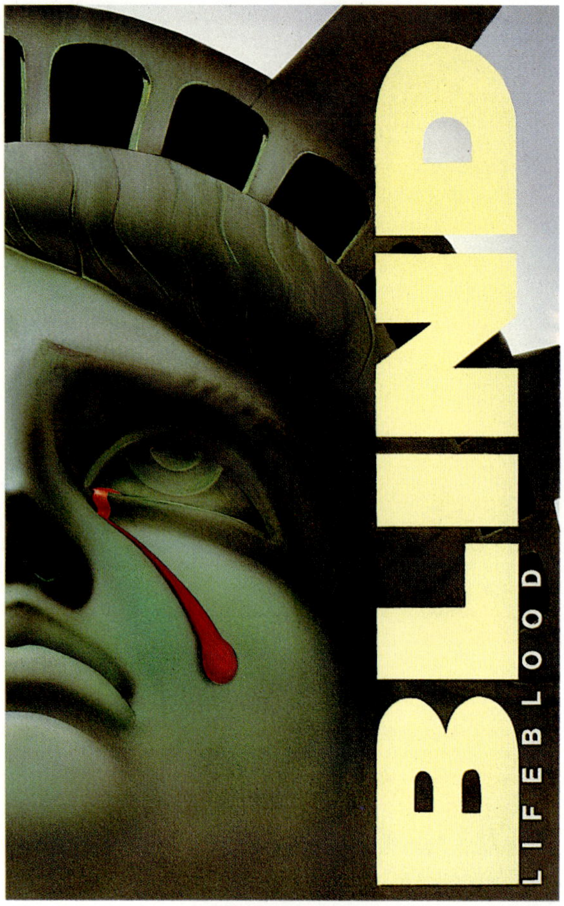

2

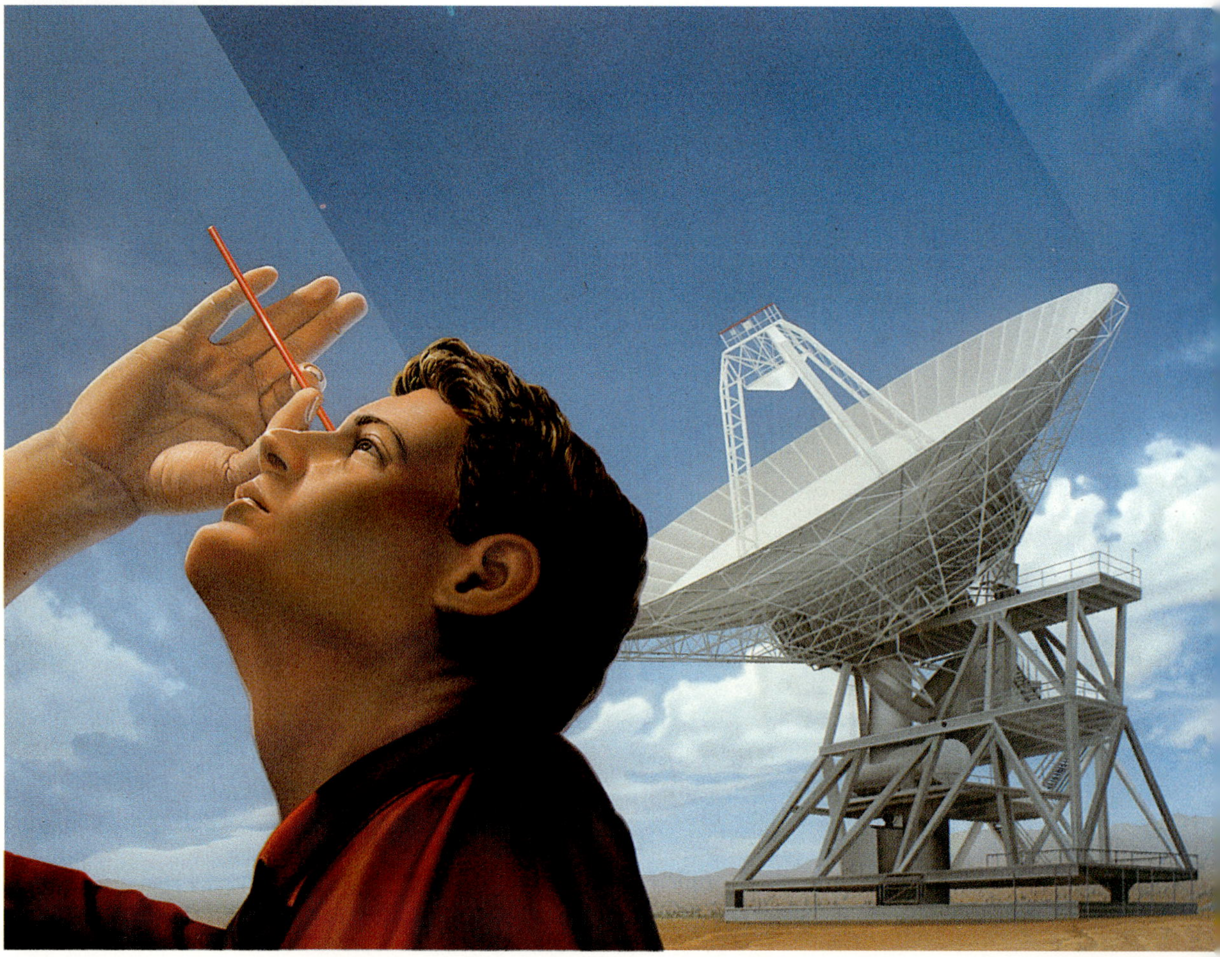

1
Artist Peter Bartczak
Title Ballerina
Client Hi-Tech Software
Media Used Airbrushed Badger Opaque Colors

2
Artist Peter Bartczak
Title Pig's Squeals & Ferris Wheels
Client Santa Cruz County Fair
Usage Poster
Media Used Gouache

3
Artist Leslie Bates
Title Journey From Krypton
Usage Self Promotion
Media Used Acrylic on Gessoed Masonite

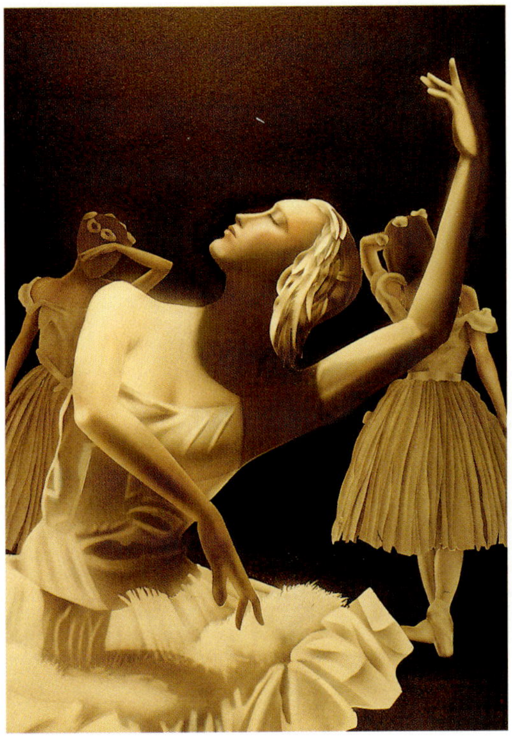

1

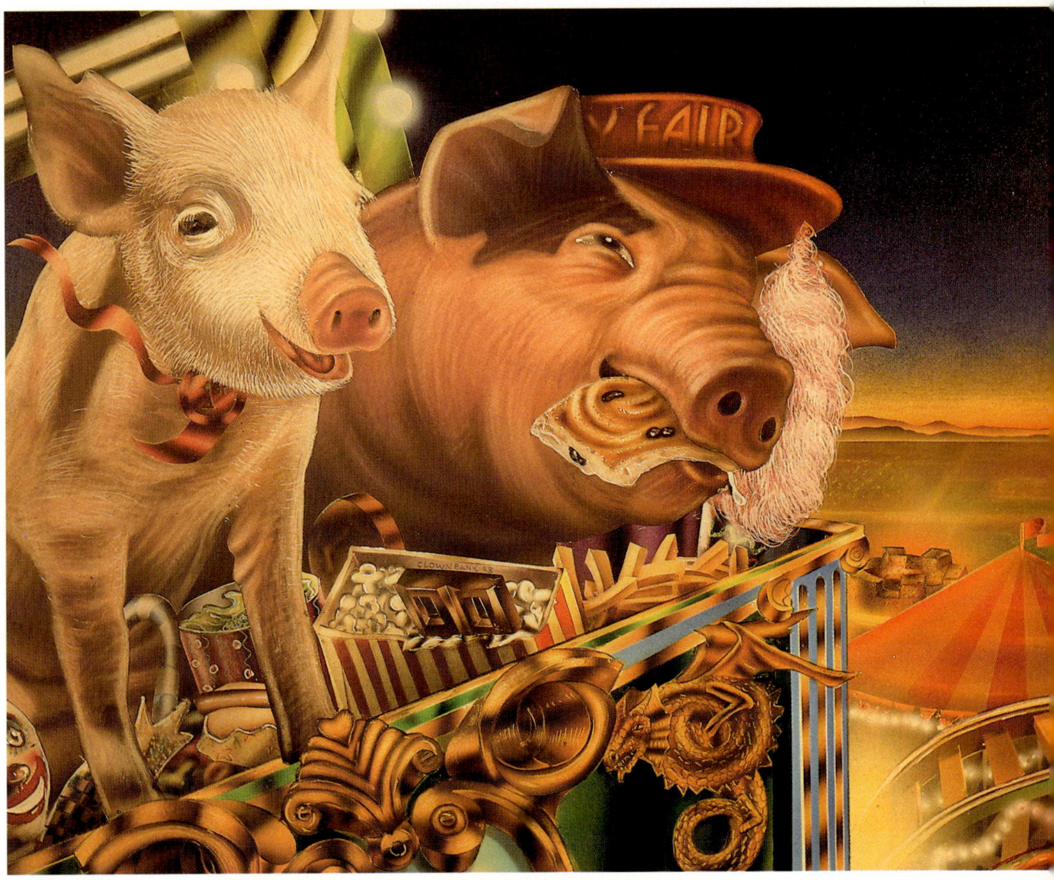

2

3

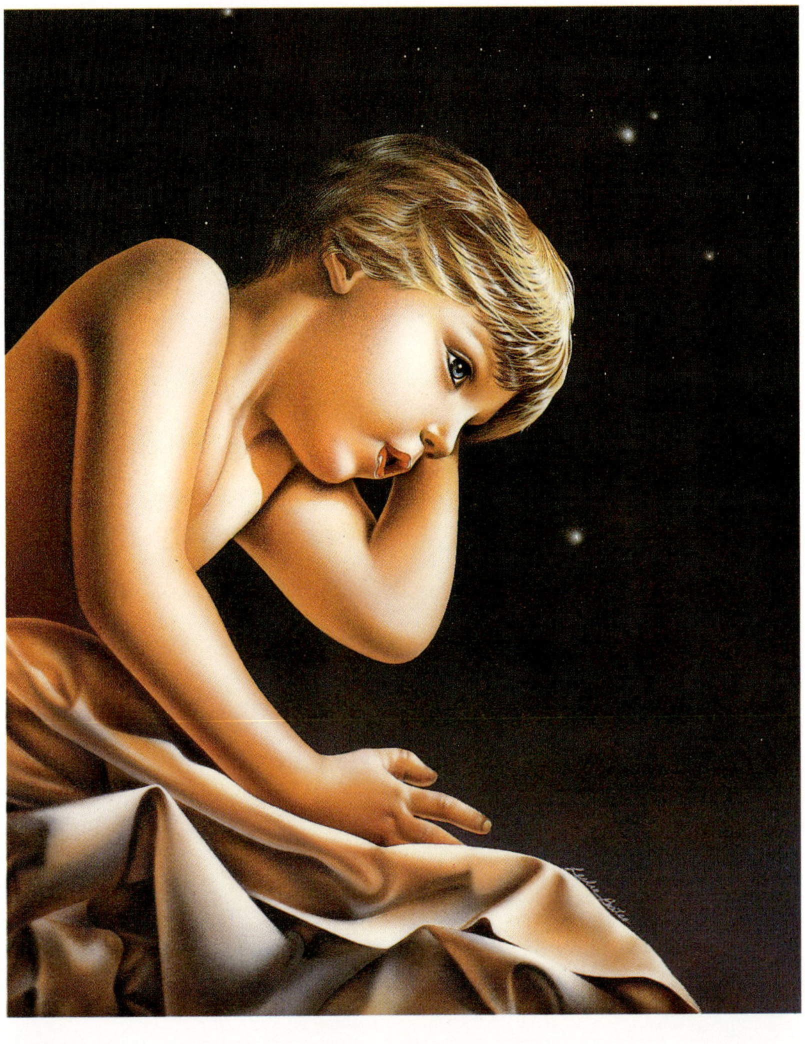

1
Artist Leslie Bates
Title Transparency #3
Usage Self Promotion
Media Used Acrylic on Gessoed Masonite

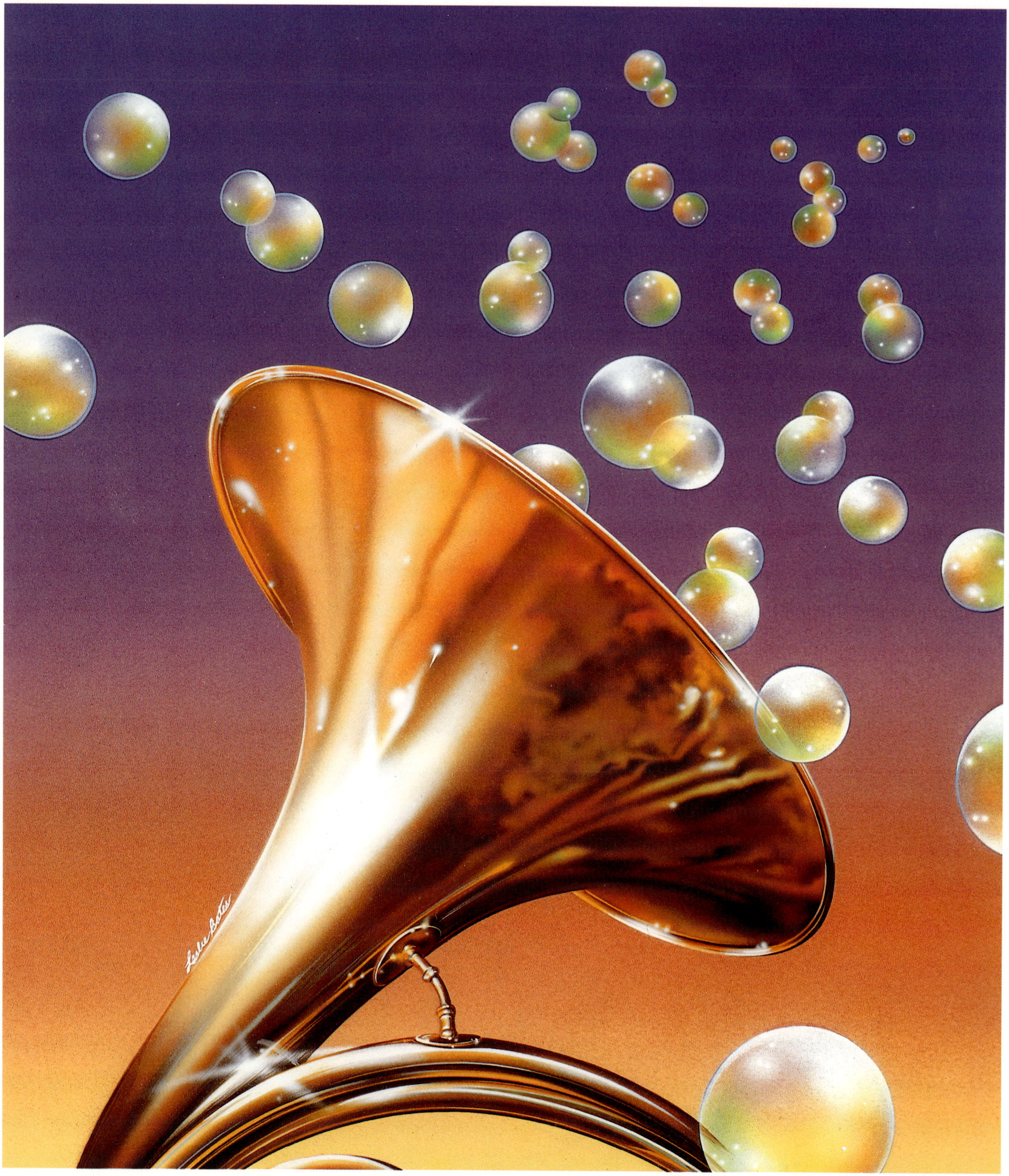

1

1
Artist Rodino R. Bautista
Title RWD Source
Client R.W.D. Rod-Water Design
Media Used Comart, Dr. Martins Spectalite

2
Artist Dennis Bayuzick
Title Painters Parable
Usage Fine Art
Media Used Acrylic

3
Artist Scott Beckley
Title Untitled
Client Radio Shack
Usage Brochure Cover
Media Used Gouache

4
Artist Scott Beckley
Title Colors
Usage Fine Art
Media Used Gouache

1

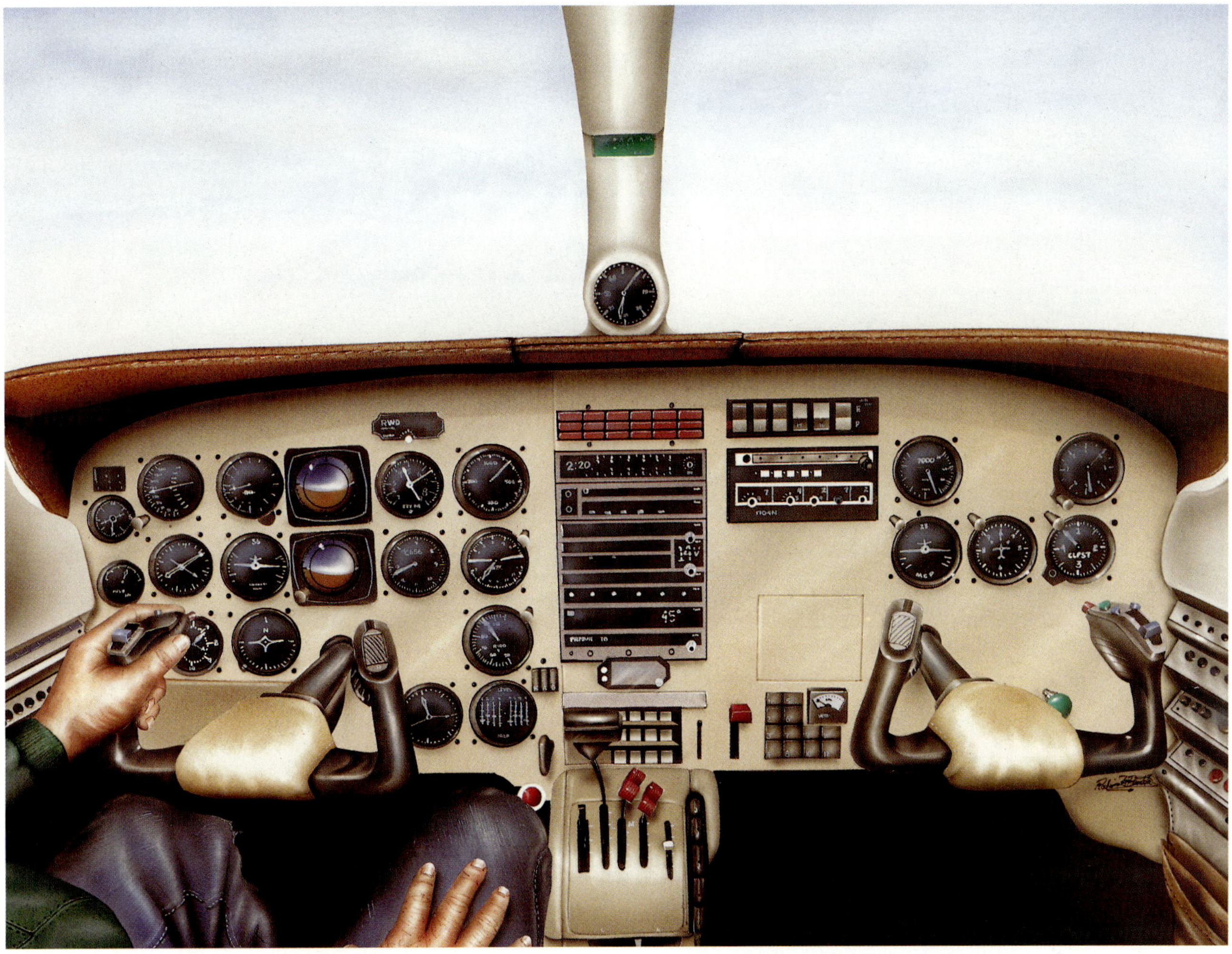

2

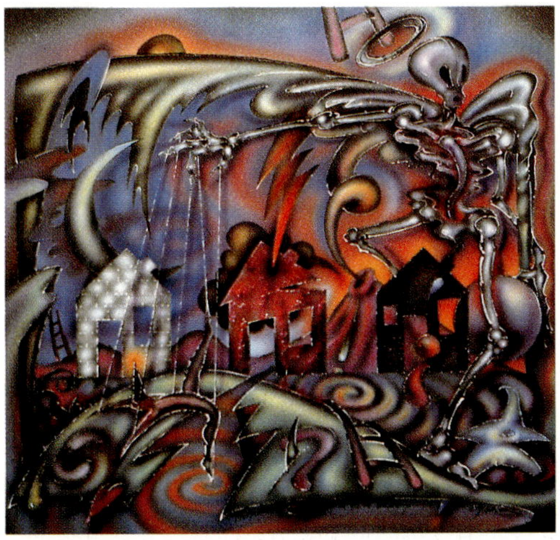

3

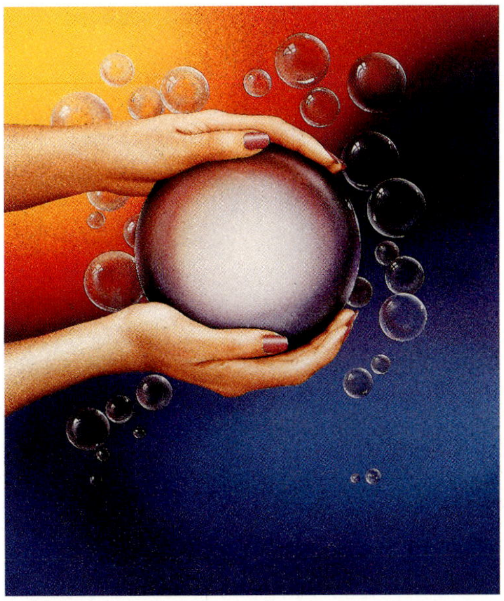

4

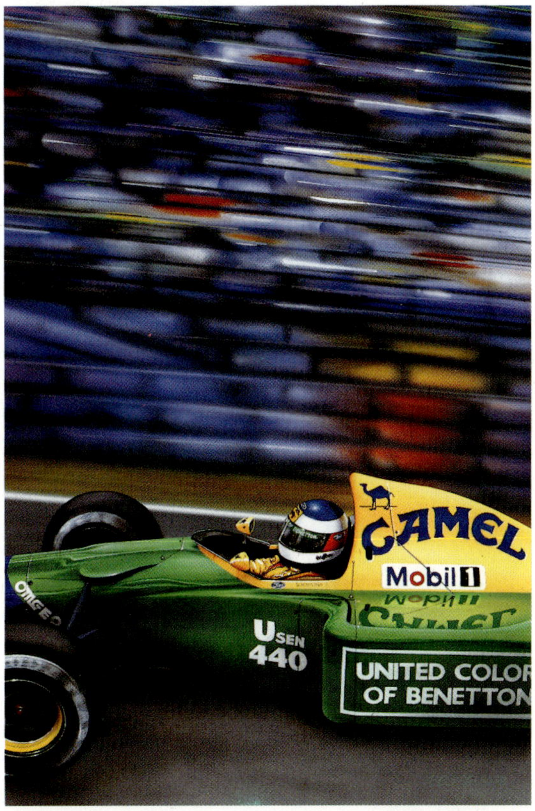

1
Artist Scott Beckley
Title Lion Heart
Usage Fine Art
Media Used Acrylic

2
Artist Scott Beckley
Title Untitled
Client Texas Instruments
Usage Magazine Advertisement
Media Used Gouache

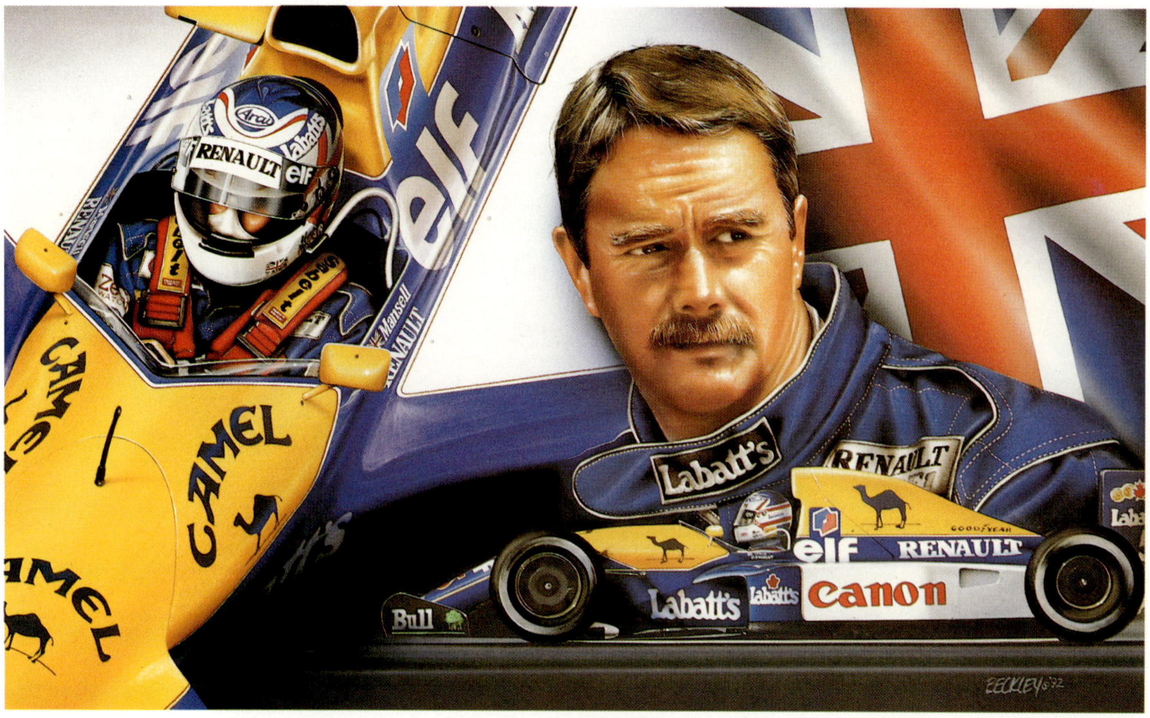

1

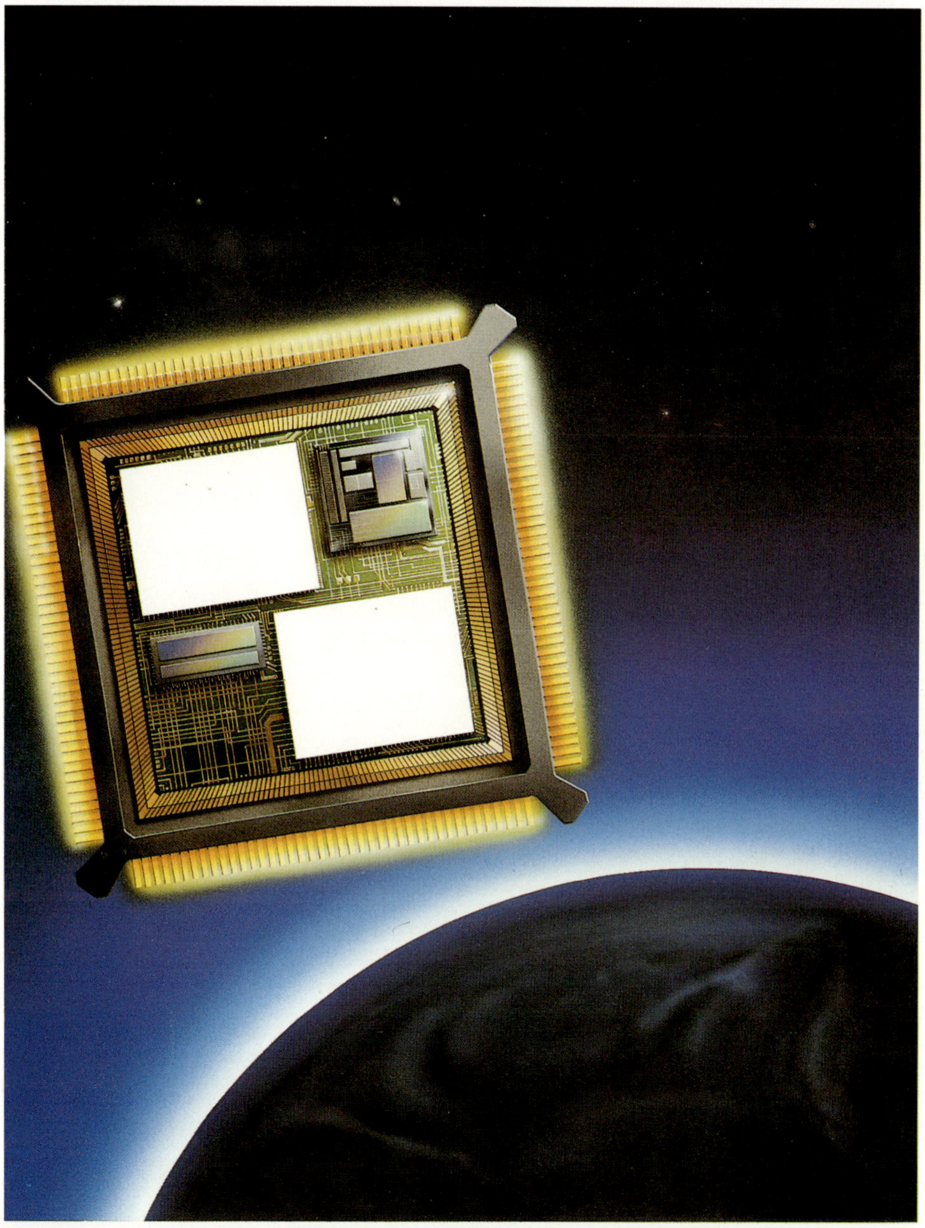
2

1
Artist Doron Ben-Ami
Title Little People, Big Pressures
Client Southwest Airlines/Spirit Magazine
Media Used Acrylic, Colored Pencil

2
Artist Mark A. Bender
Client McDonalds
Usage Calendar for Month of Febuary
Media Used Gouache

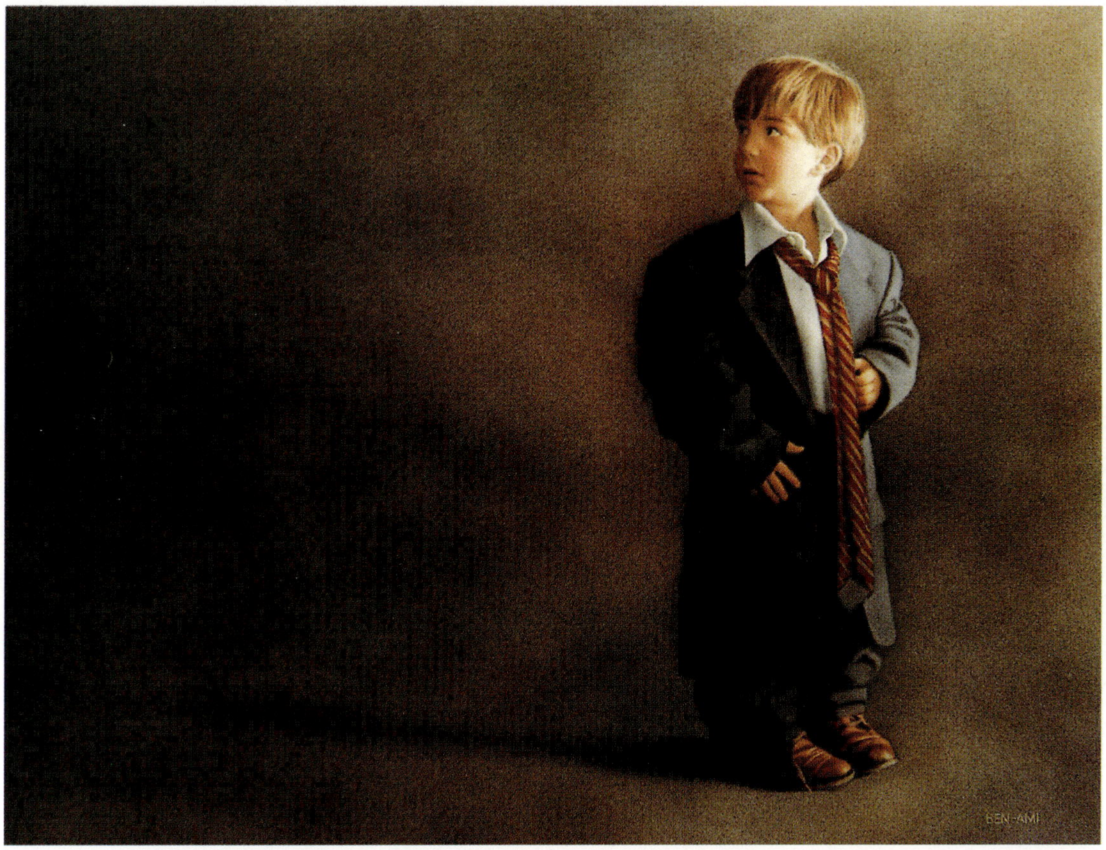

1

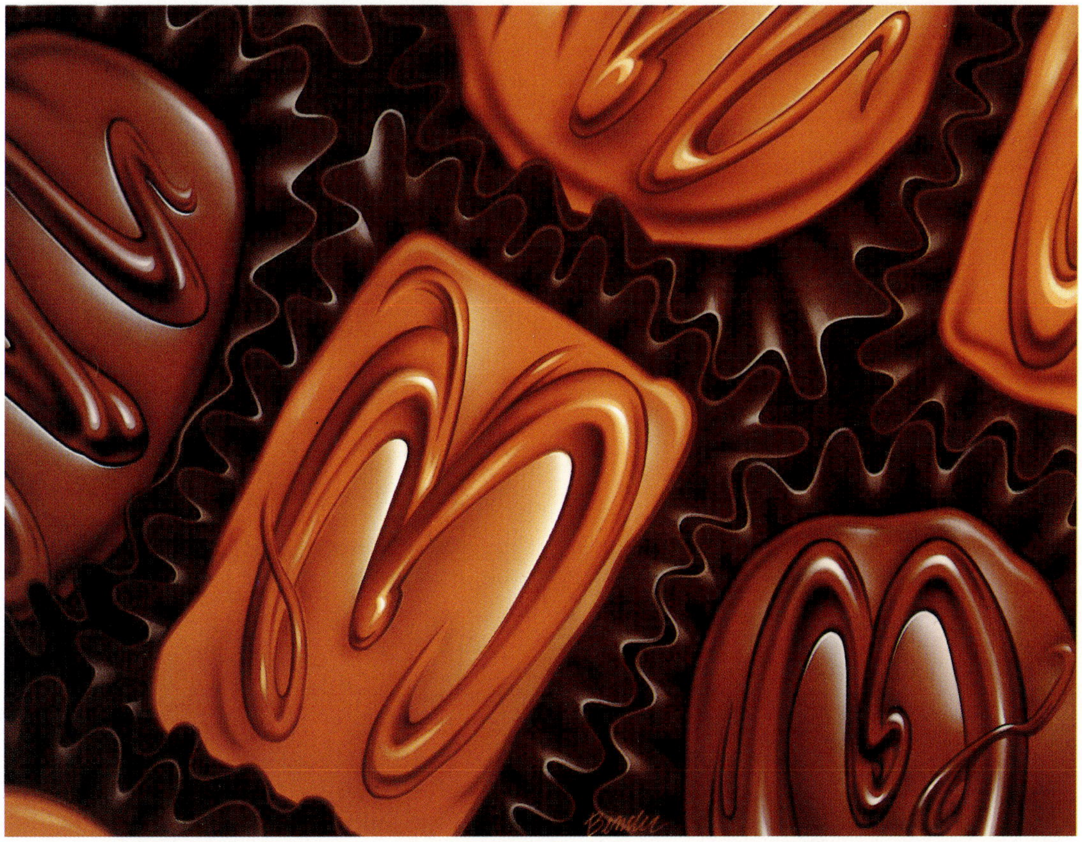

2

1
Artist Mark A. Bender
Client Public Relations Society of America
Art Director Alan Boarts
Usage Call for Entries - Renaissance Awards
Media Used Gouache

1

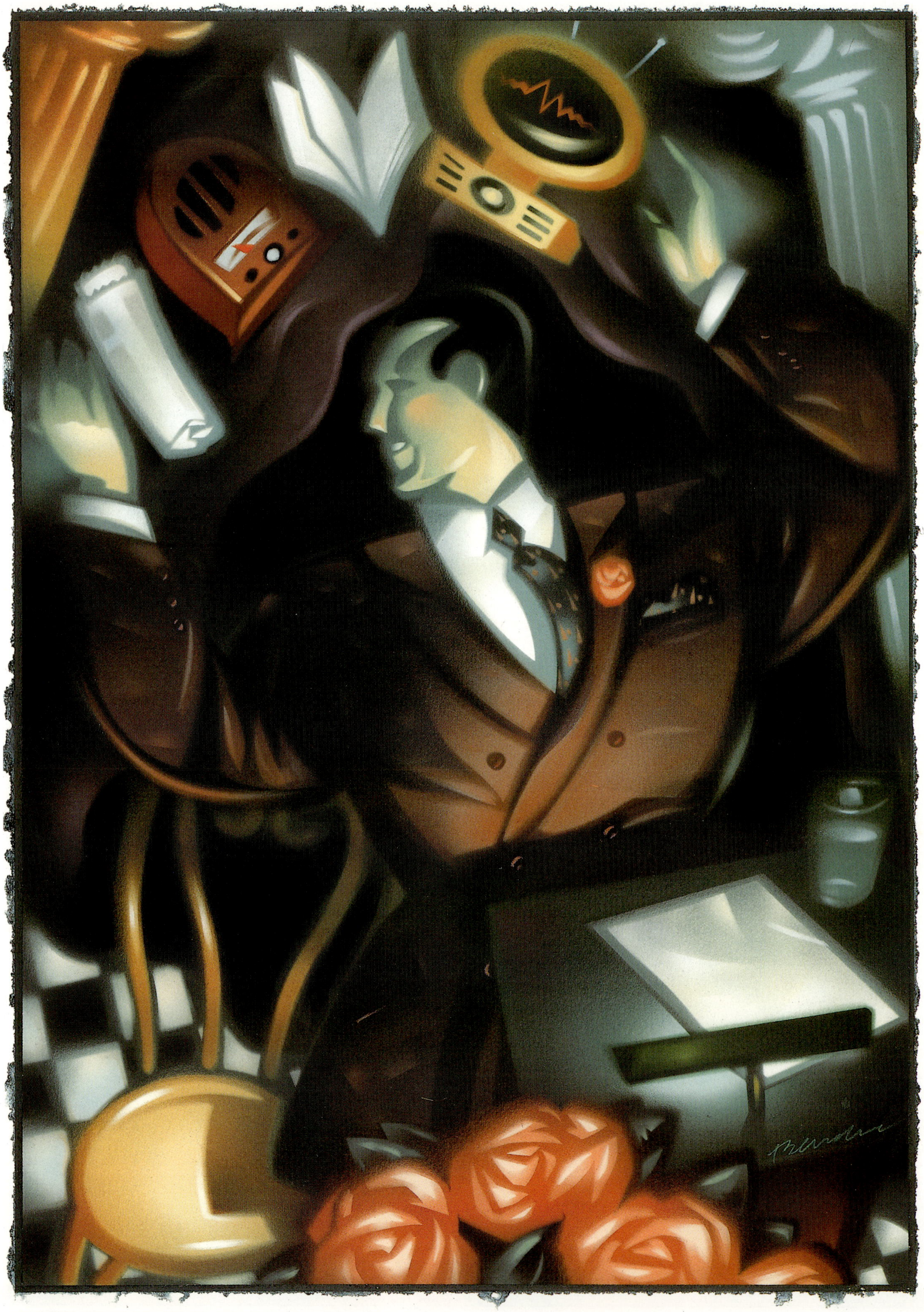

1
Artist Mark A. Bender
Title Brooklyn Bridge
Client CNG
Art Director Karen Burns
Usage Poster/Invitation
Media Used Gouache

2
Artist Mark A. Bender
Client Vance Wright Adams & Associates
Usage Capabilities Book
Media Used Gouache

3
Artist Mark A. Bender
Title Catch Hardball
Client Pittsburgh Pirates
Art Director Patti Ingold / Jeff Woods
Usage Billboard
Media Used Gouache

4
Artist Mark A. Bender
Client Self Promotion
Media Used Gouache

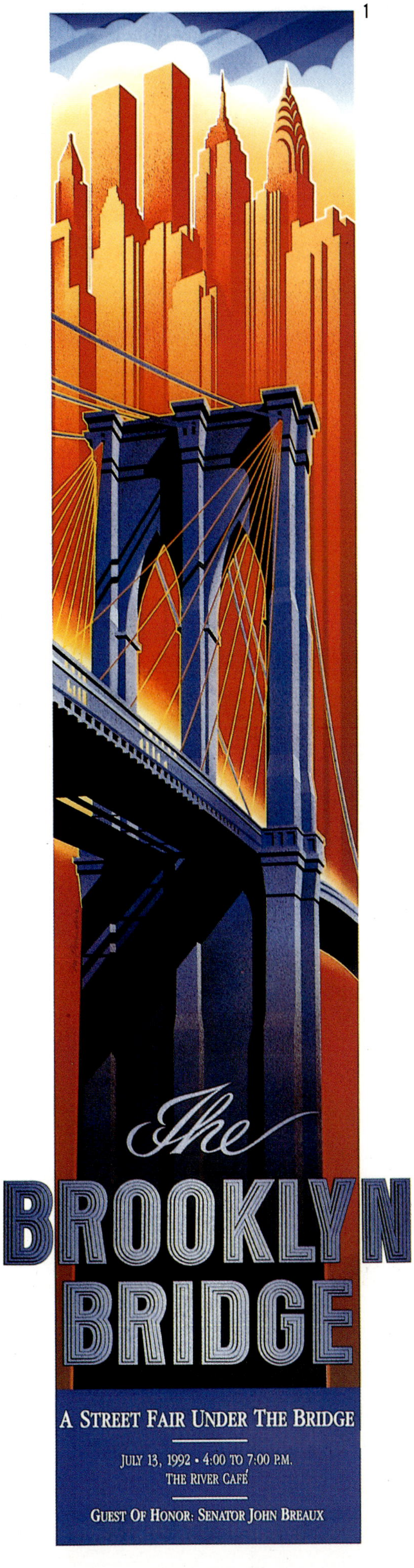

1

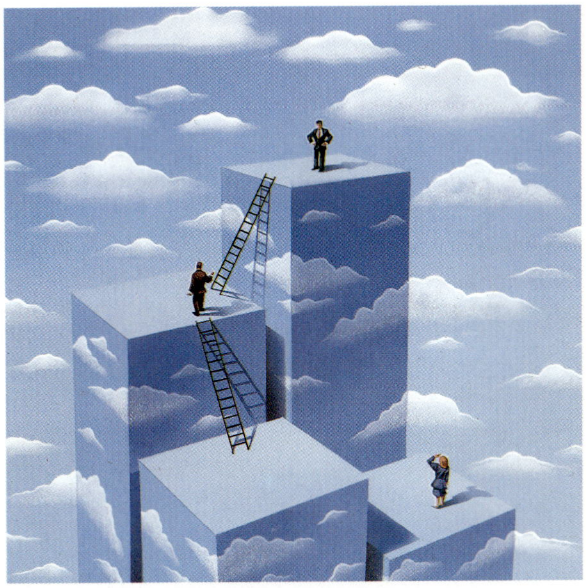
2

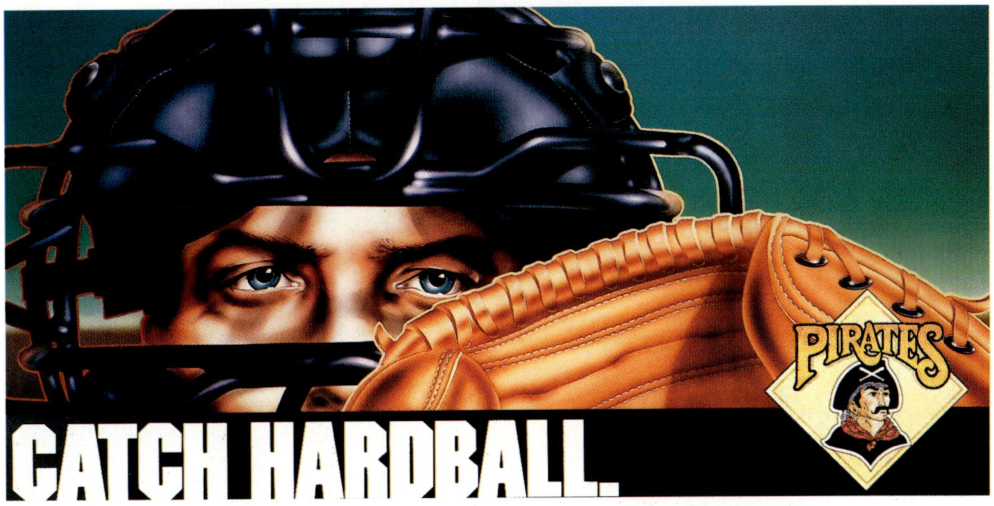

3

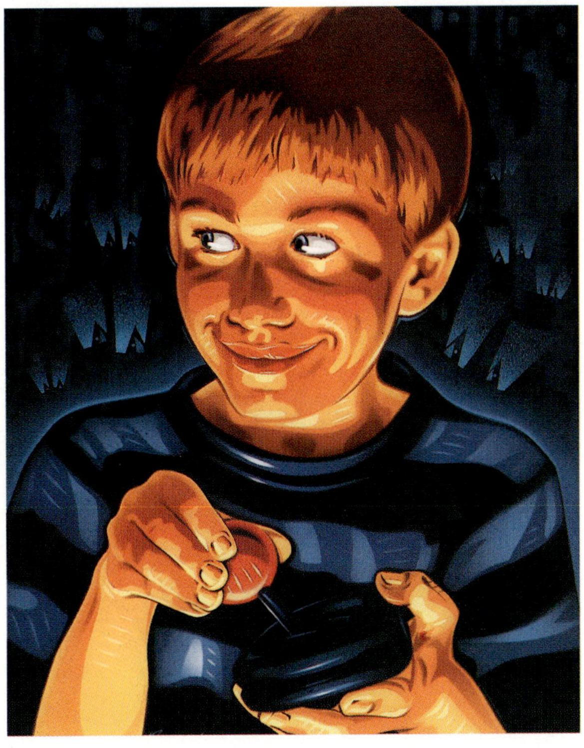
4

1
Artist Anita S. Bice
Title On the Drawing Board
Art Director Nina Lowry
Usage Editorial Illustration
Media Used Acrylic

2
Artist Anita S. Bice
Title Working Back from Injury
Art Director Nina Lowry
Media Used Acrylic

3
Artist Anita S. Bice
Title The Quadrangle - Harvard Medical School
Client New Horizons Limited
Usage Fine Art
Media Used Mixed

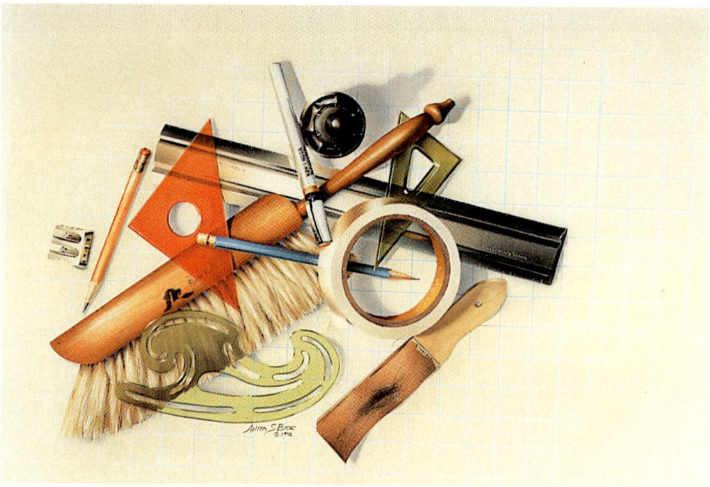

1

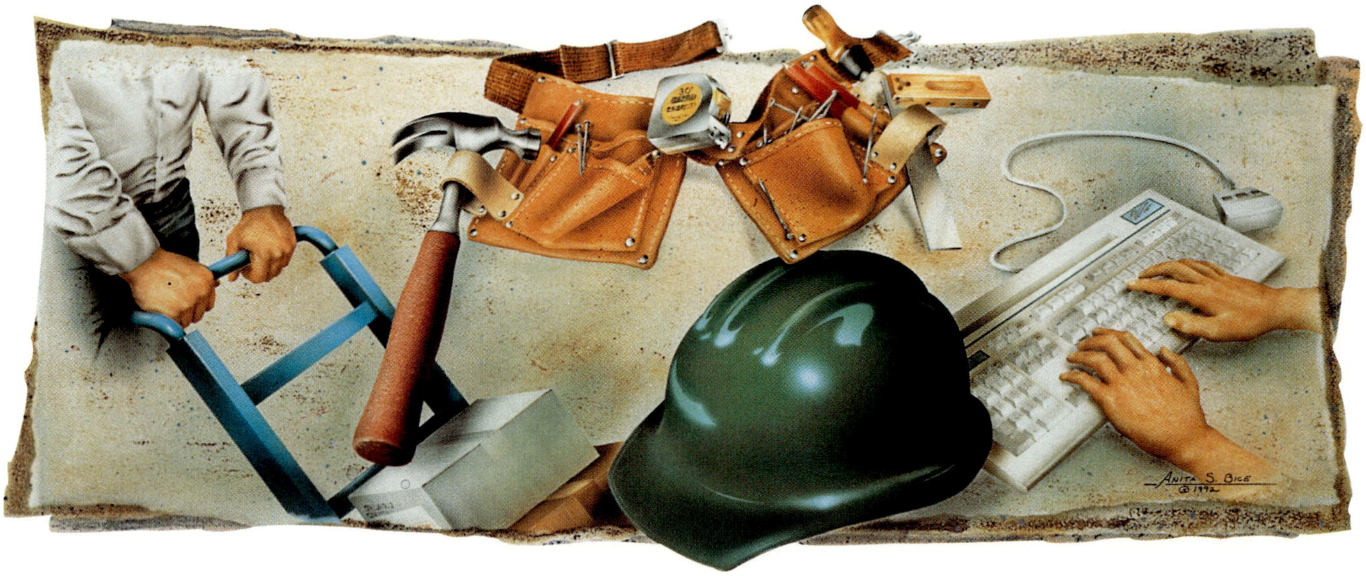

2

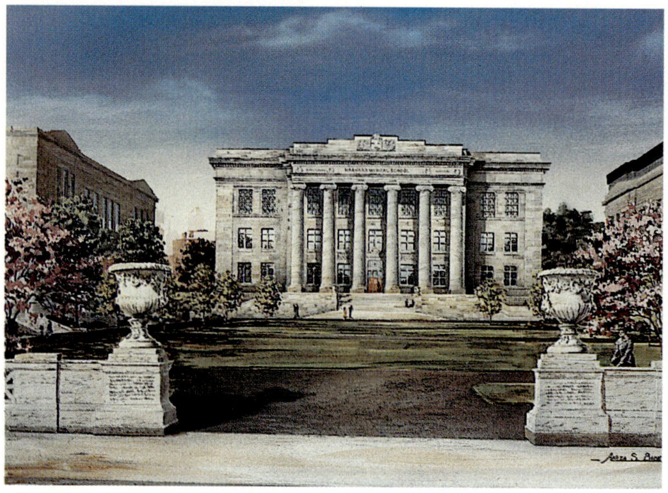

3

1
Artist Anita S. Brice
Title Marsh Chapel - Boston University
Client New Horizons Limited
Usage Fine Art
Media Used Mixed

2
Artist Anita S. Bice
Title Advancement with New Labor-Delivery-Recovery Suites **Art Director** Nina Lowry
Usage Editorial Illustration
Media Used Acrylic

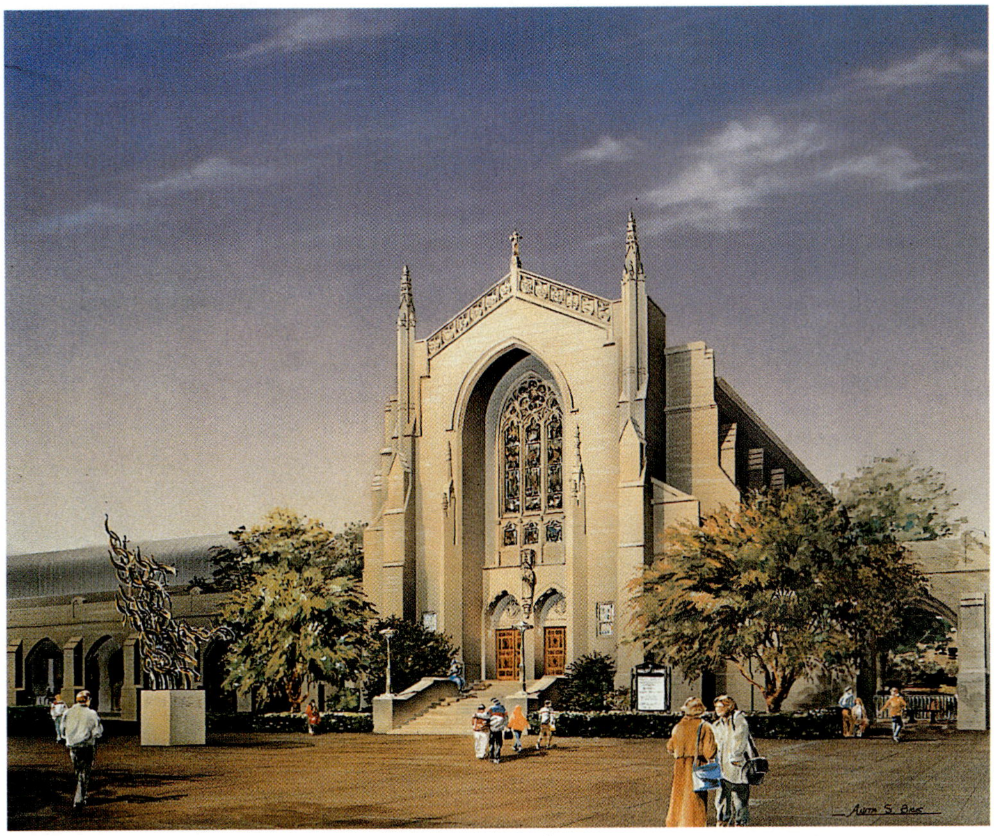

1

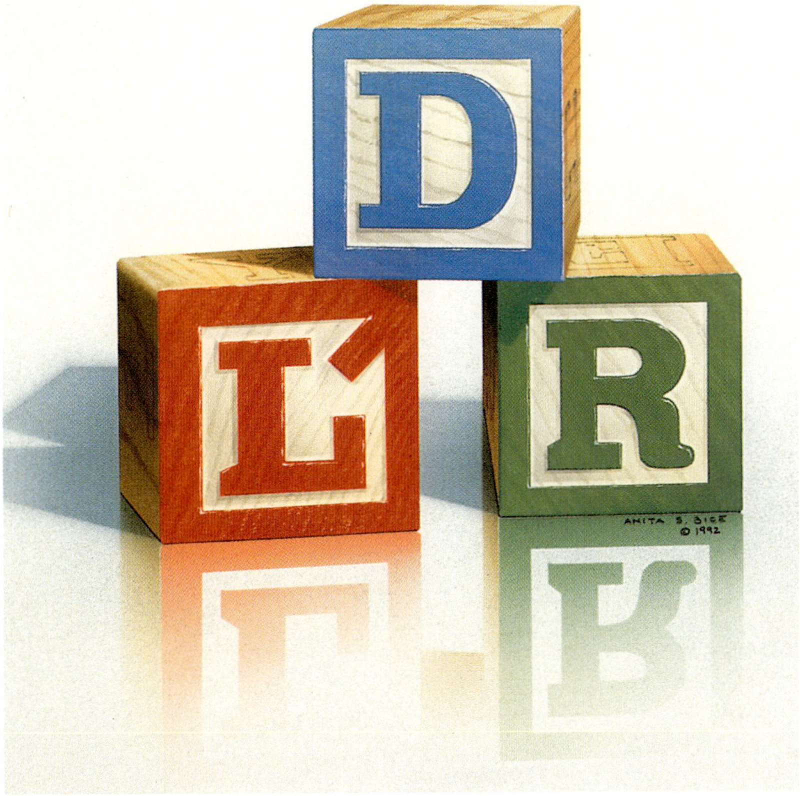

2

1
Artist Anita S. Bice
Usage Photo-Retouching (before)
Media Used Acrylic, Photo Oils

2
Artist Anita S. Bice
Usage Photo-Retouching (before)
Media Used Acrylic, Photo Oils

3
Artist Anita S. Bice
Usage Photo-Retouching (after)
Media Used Acrylic, Photo Oils

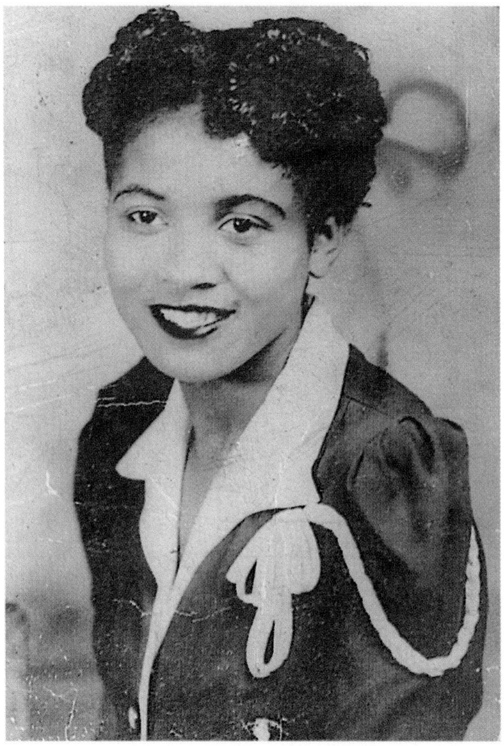

1

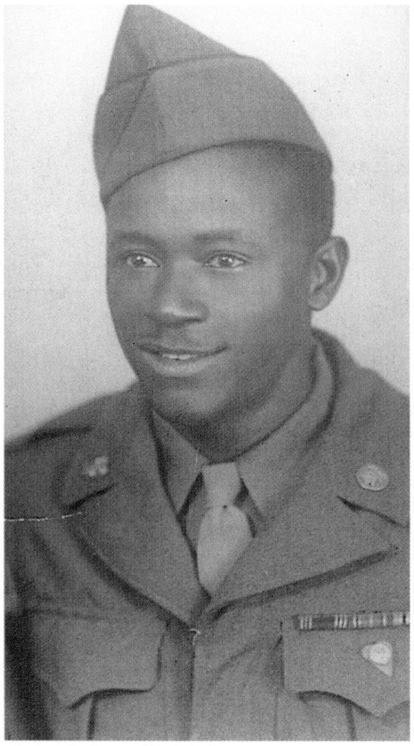

2

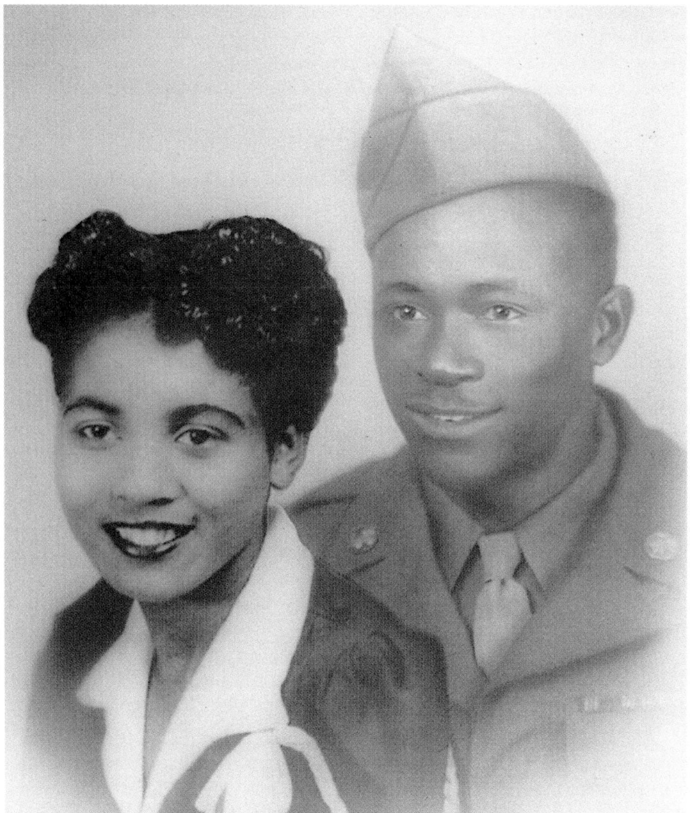

3

1
Artist Anita S. Bice
Usage Photo-Retouching (before)
Media Used Acrylic, Photo Oils

2
Artist Anita S. Bice
Usage Photo-Retouching (after)
Media Used Acrylic, Photo Oils

3
Artist Kurt Bittle
Title Watching You, Looking for Me
Art Director Kurt Bittle
Usage Fine Art
Media Used Graphite Pencil, Air Opaques

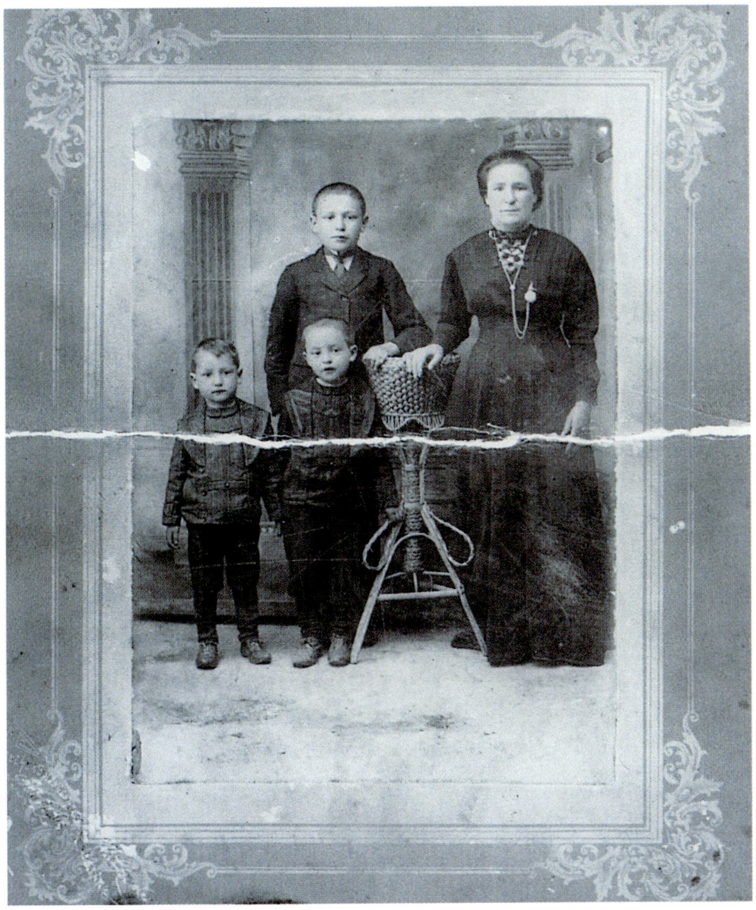

1

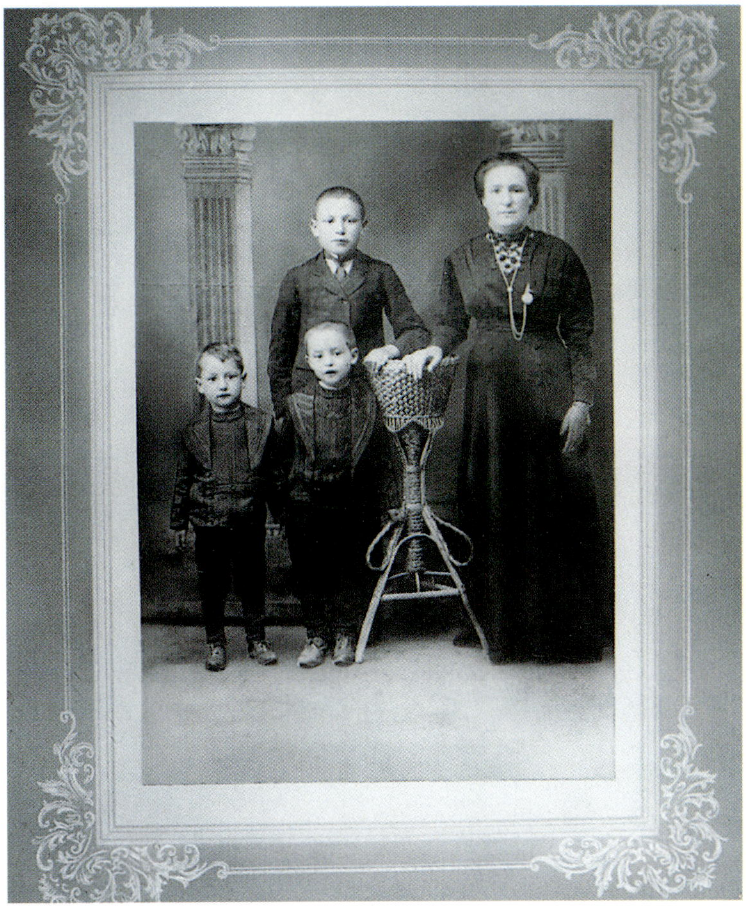

2

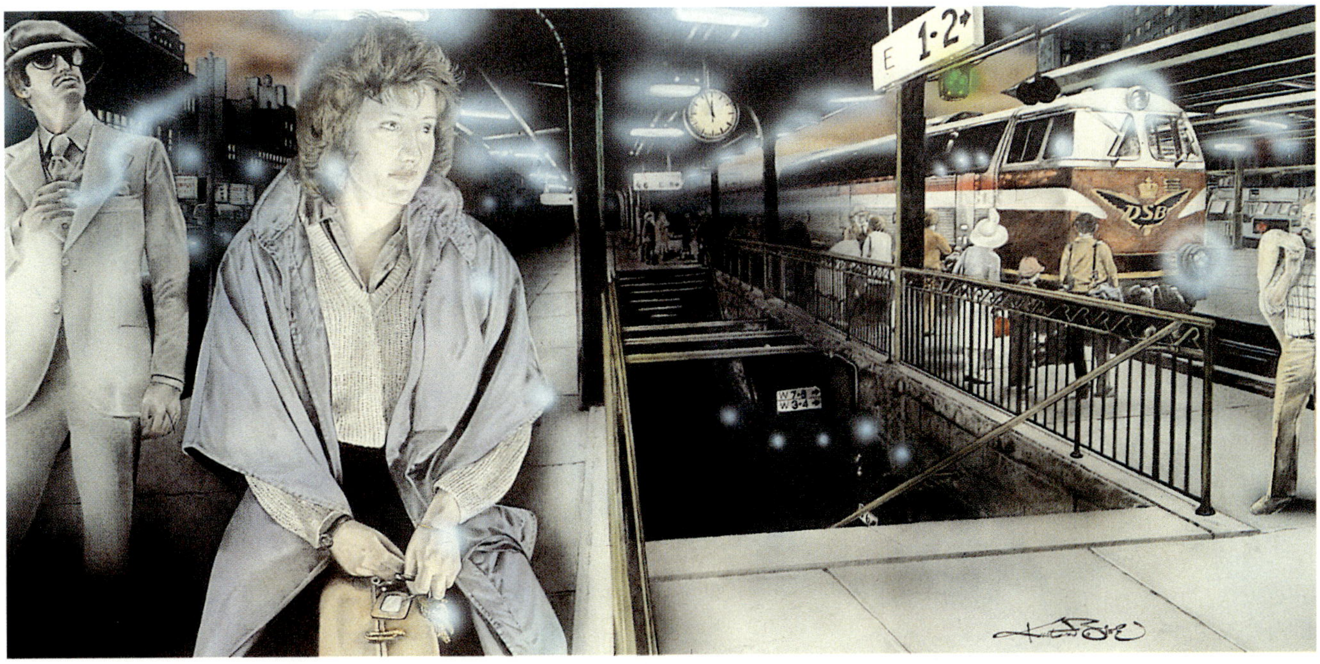

3

1
Artist Kurt Bittle
Title Our Vision
Client U.S.D.E.H.A.
Art Director Norman Pospisil
Usage Editorial Illustration
Media Used Badger Air Opaques, Berol Prismacolor

2
Artist Brian Blair
Title Ma Kelley
Client Ma Kelley (Rock Band)
Usage Commercial Art
Media Used Acrylic

3
Artist Brian Blair
Title Drug Monster
Client "Don't Do Drugs" Campaign
Usage Poster
Media Used Acrylic

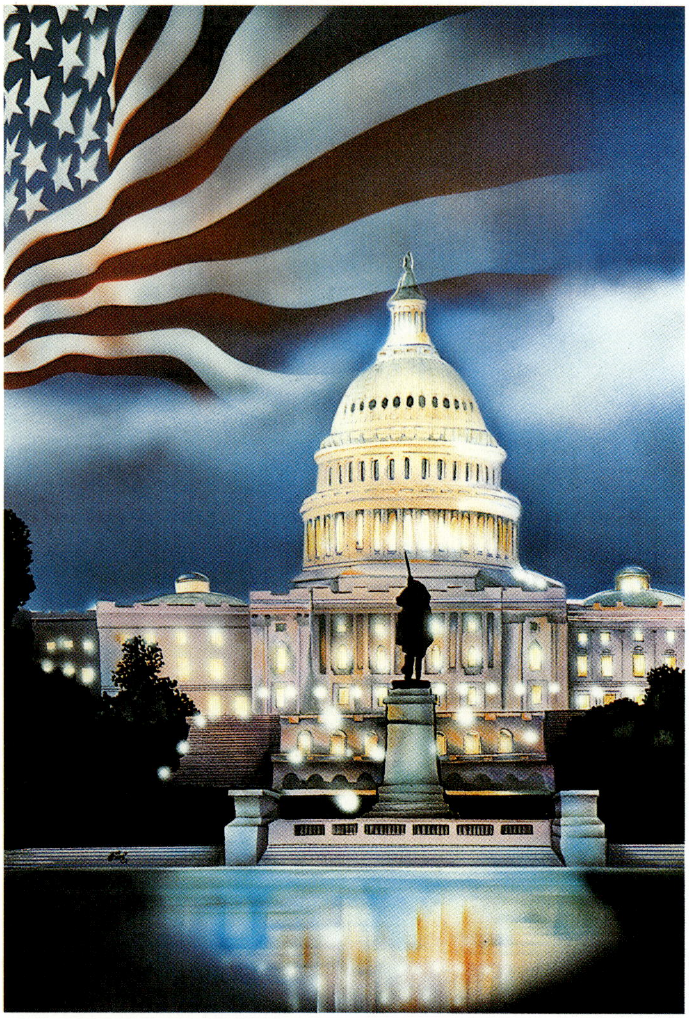

1

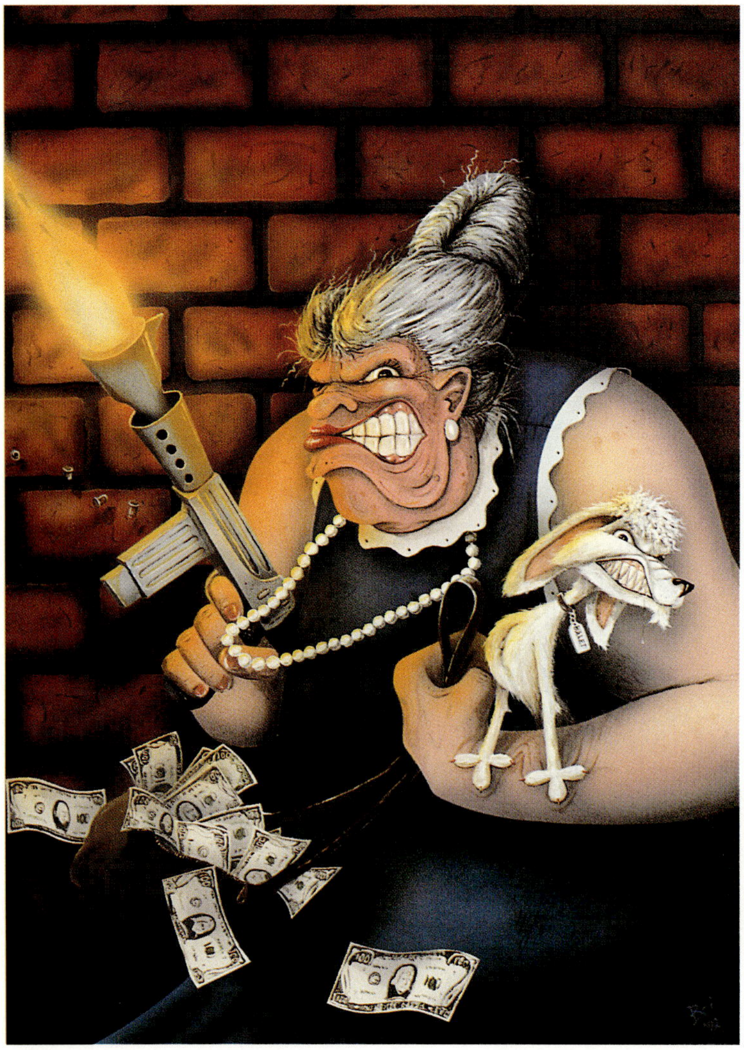

2

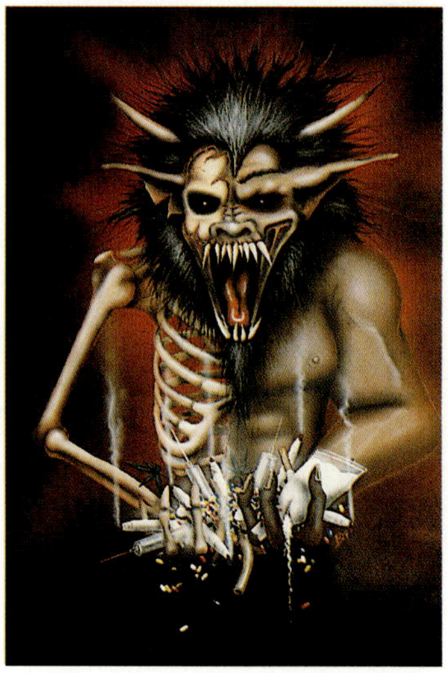

3

1
Artist Brian Blair
Title Open Season
Usage Children's Book
Media Used Acrylic

2
Artist Brian Blair
Title Dino bait
Usage Children's Book
Media Used Acrylic

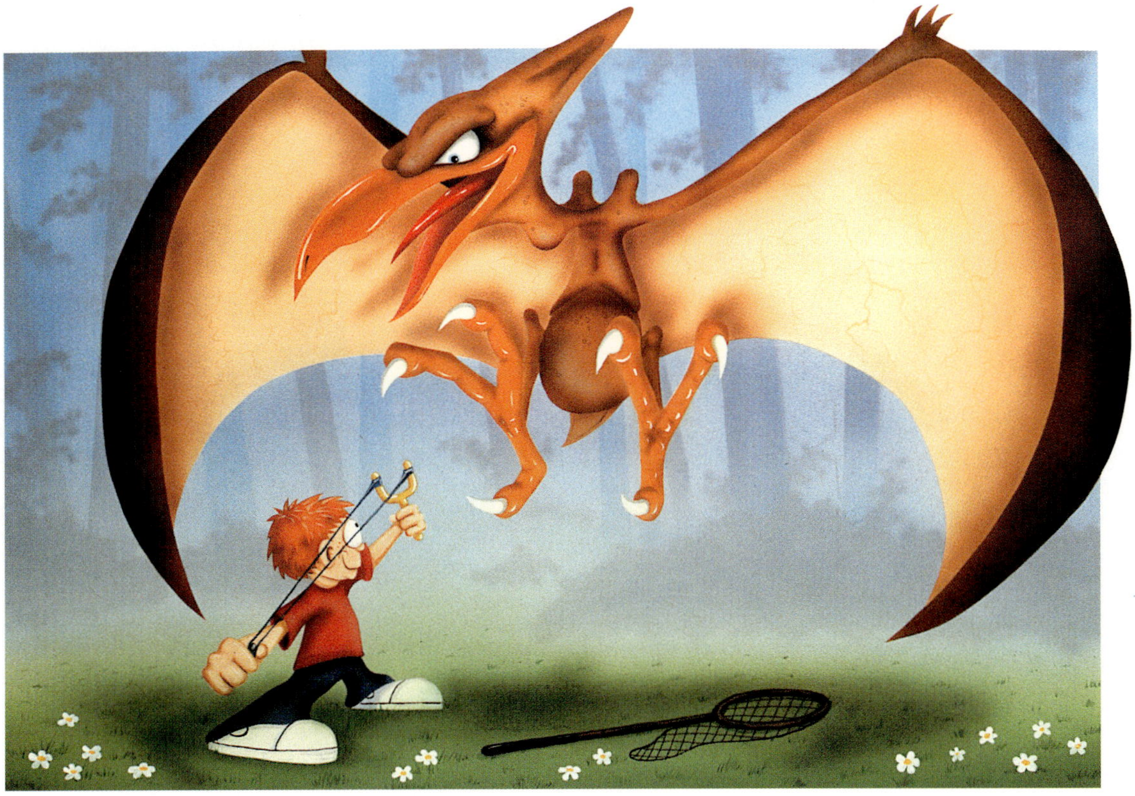

1

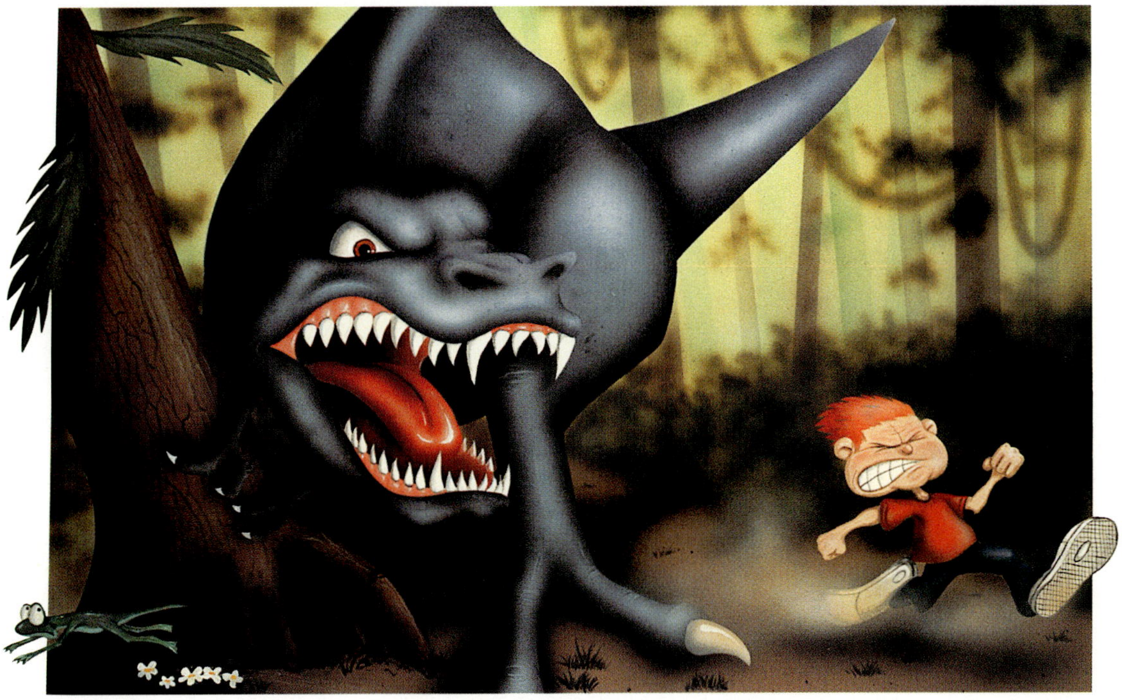

2

1
Artist Brian Blair
Title C.T. Peppers
Client C.T. Peppers Nightclub
Usage Poster
Media Used Acrylic

2
Artist Tim Blough
Title Minneapolis
Art Director Tim Blough
Usage Commercial Art
Media Used Comart

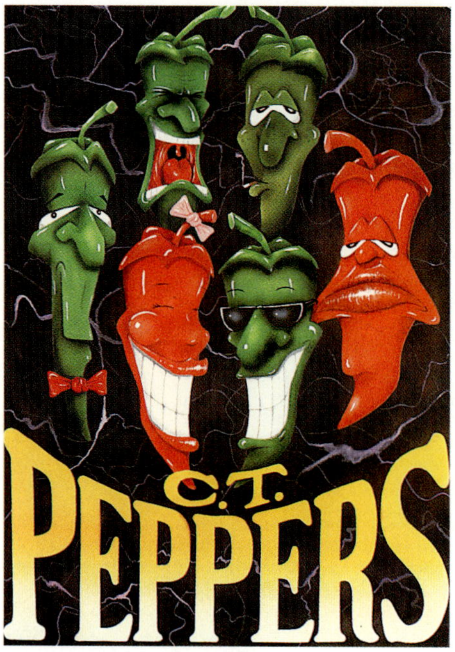

1

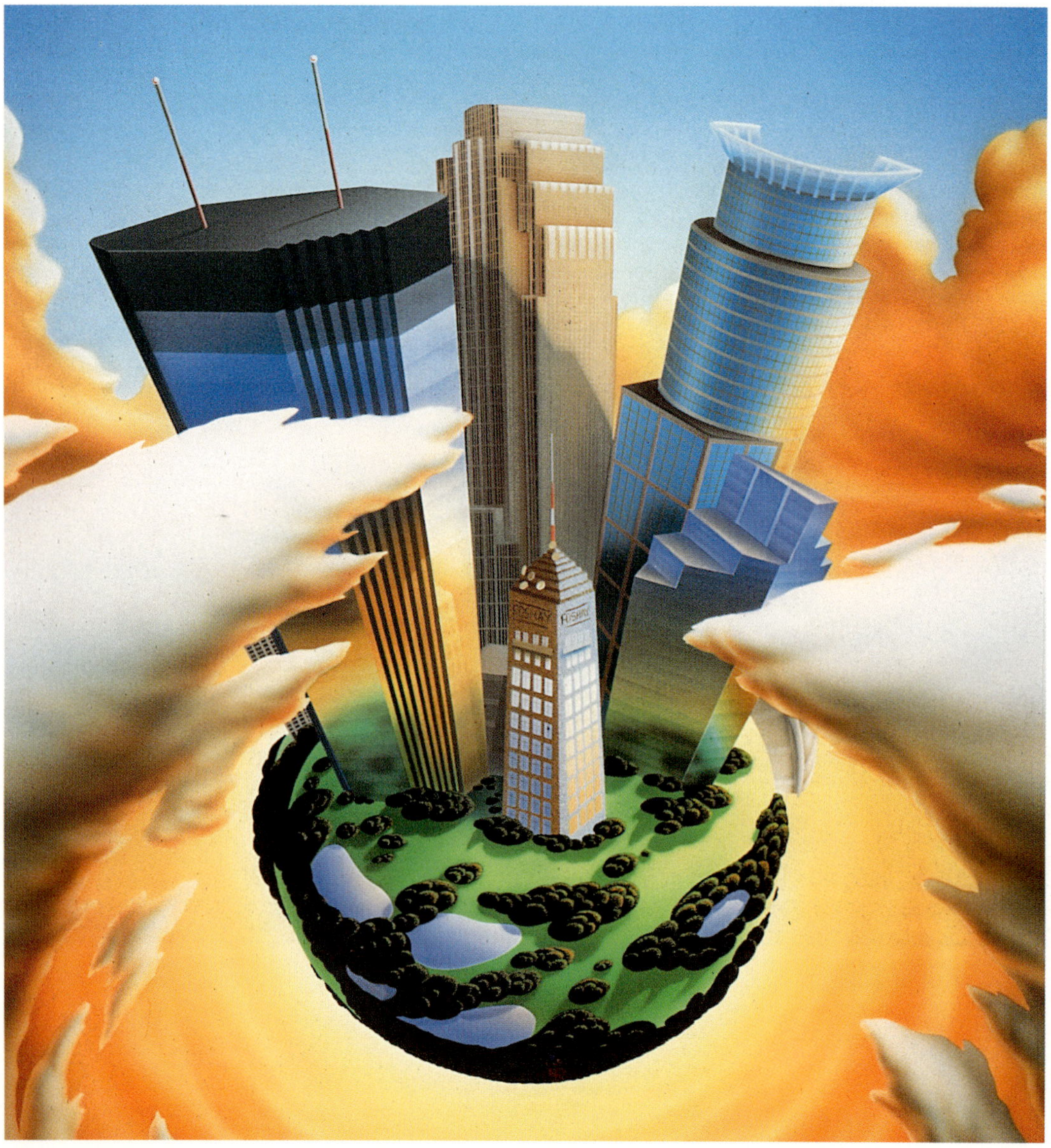
2

1
Artist John M. Booth
Title The Jungle
Usage Fine Art
Media Used Acrylic Paint on Illustration Board

2
Artist John M. Booth
Title Hey Diddle Diddle, the Cat and the Fiddle
Usage Fine Art
Media Used Acrylic Paint on Illustration Board

3
Artist John M. Booth
Title Save the World
Usage Fine Art
Media Used Acrylic on Illustration Board

4
Artist John M. Booth
Title The Fish Want to Play with the Pig Too
Usage Fine Art
Media Used Acrylic Paint on Illustration Board

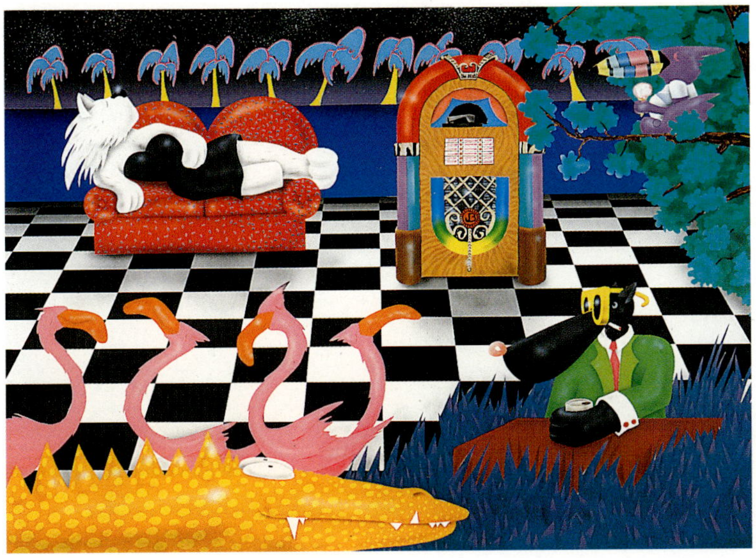

1

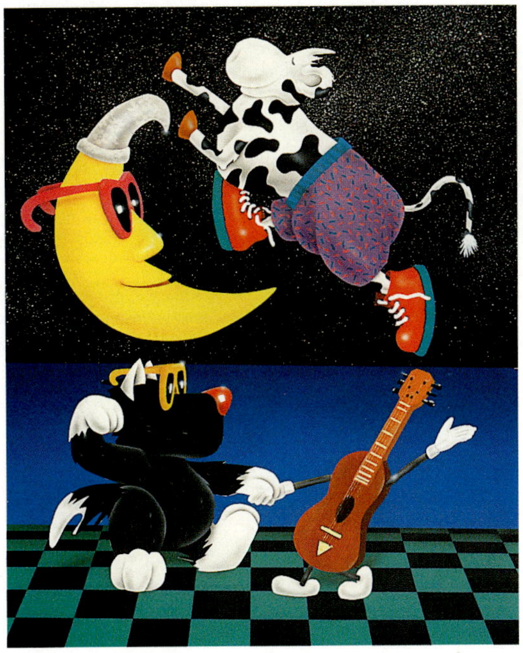

2

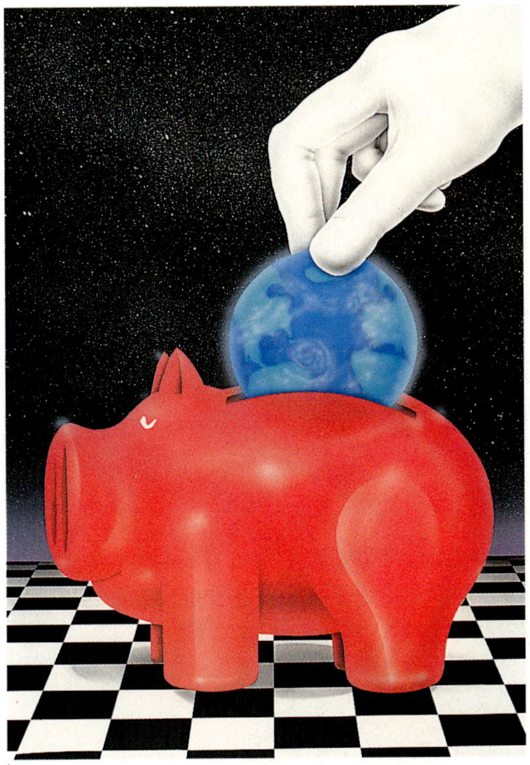

3

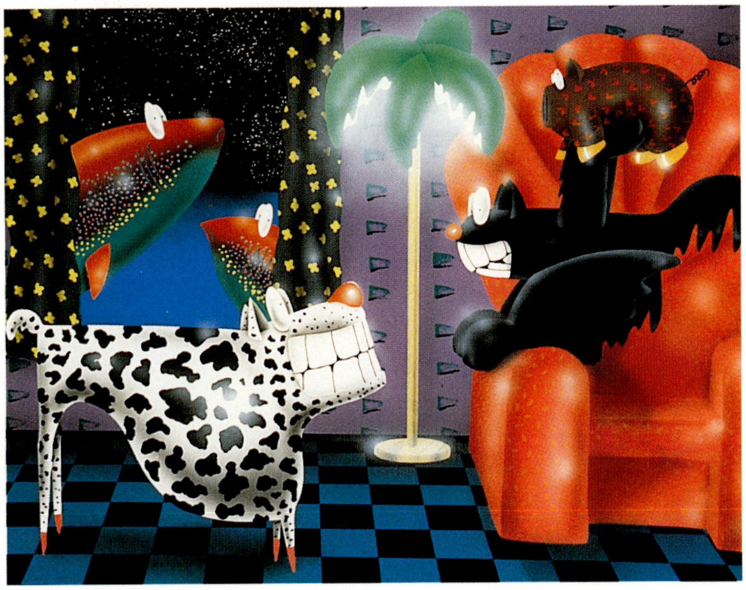

4

1
Artist John M. Booth
Title Flying Pigs
Usage Fine Art
Media Used Acrylic on Illustration Board

2
Artist John M. Booth
Title Dancing Chairs
Usage Fine Art
Media Used Acrylic on Illustration Board

3
Artist John M. Booth
Title Flying Cats
Usage Fine Art
Media Used Acrylic on Illustration Board

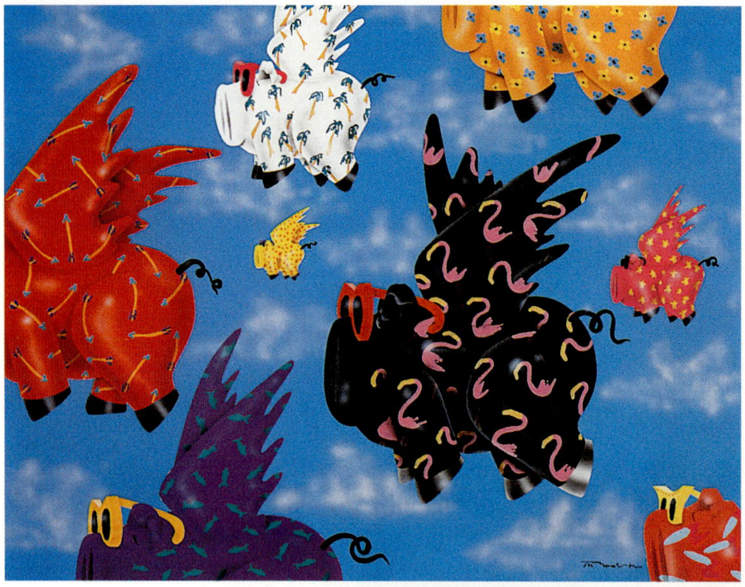

1

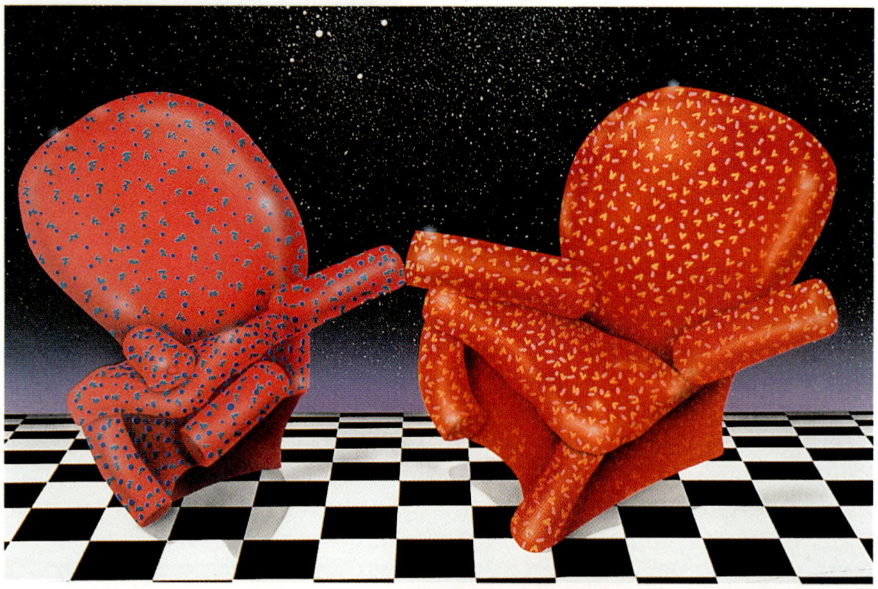

2

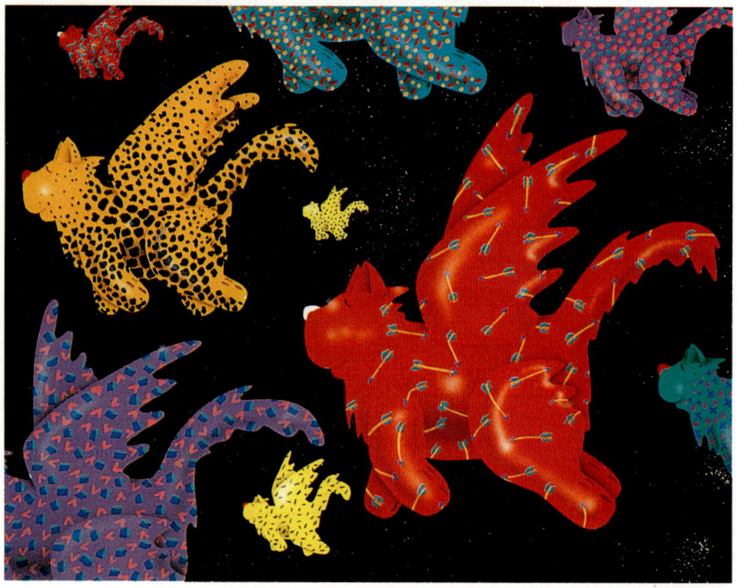

3

1
Artist John M. Booth
Title Cat on a Dolphin
Usage Fine Art
Media Used Acrylic on Illustration Board

2
Artist John M. Booth
Title Cats on Carphones
Usage Fine Art
Media Used Acrylic on Illustration Board

3
Artist John M. Booth
Title Fishin
Usage Fine Art
Media Used Acrylic on Illustration Board

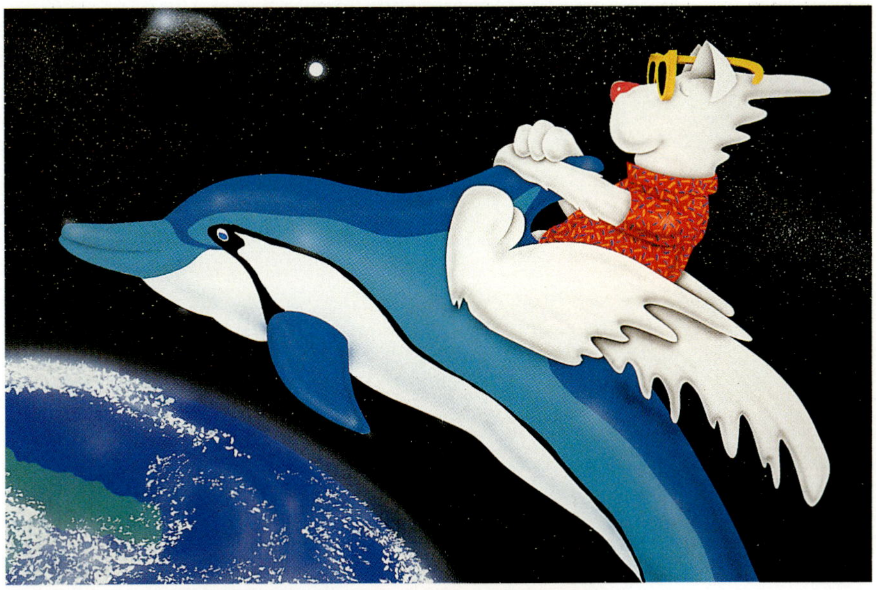

1

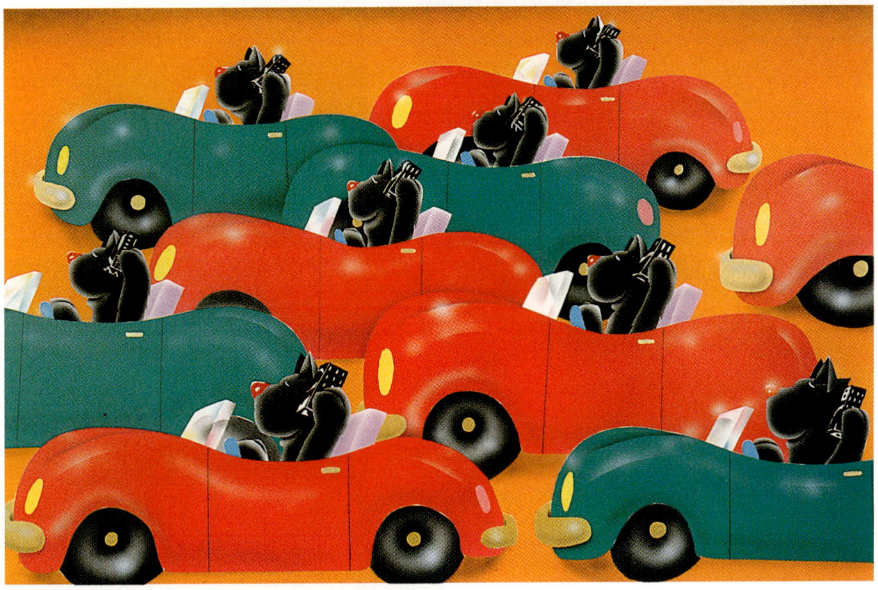

2

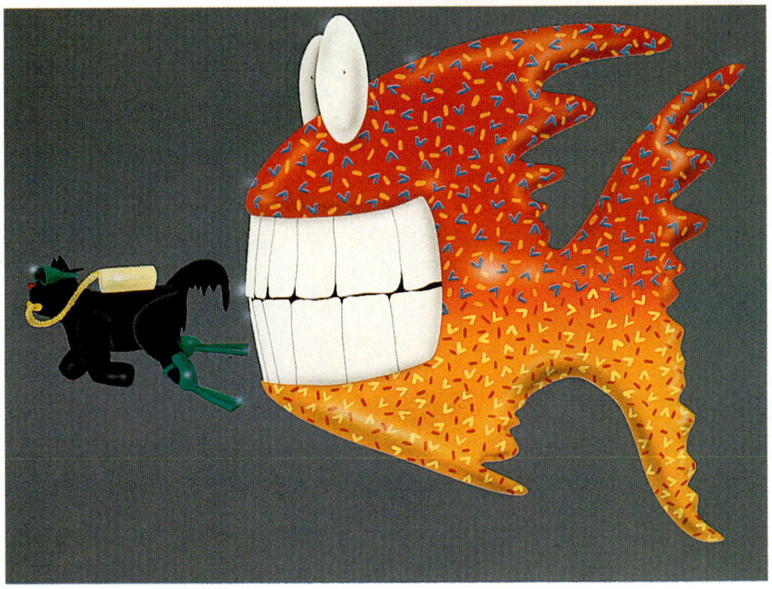

3

1
Artist John M. Booth
Title Trust Me
Usage Fine Art
Media Used Acrylic on Illustration Board

2
Artist John M. Booth
Title Blues Cat
Usage Fine Art
Media Used Acrylic on Illustration Board

3
Artist Steve Boswick
Title 60 Years of Advertising Age
Client Crains Communications
Art Director Geof Shives
Usage Feature Editorial
Media Used Gouache

4
Artist Steve Boswick
Title Modern Art
Client GHGO Sourcebook 10
Art Director Steve Boswick
Usage Cover for Sourcebook 10
Media Used Gouache

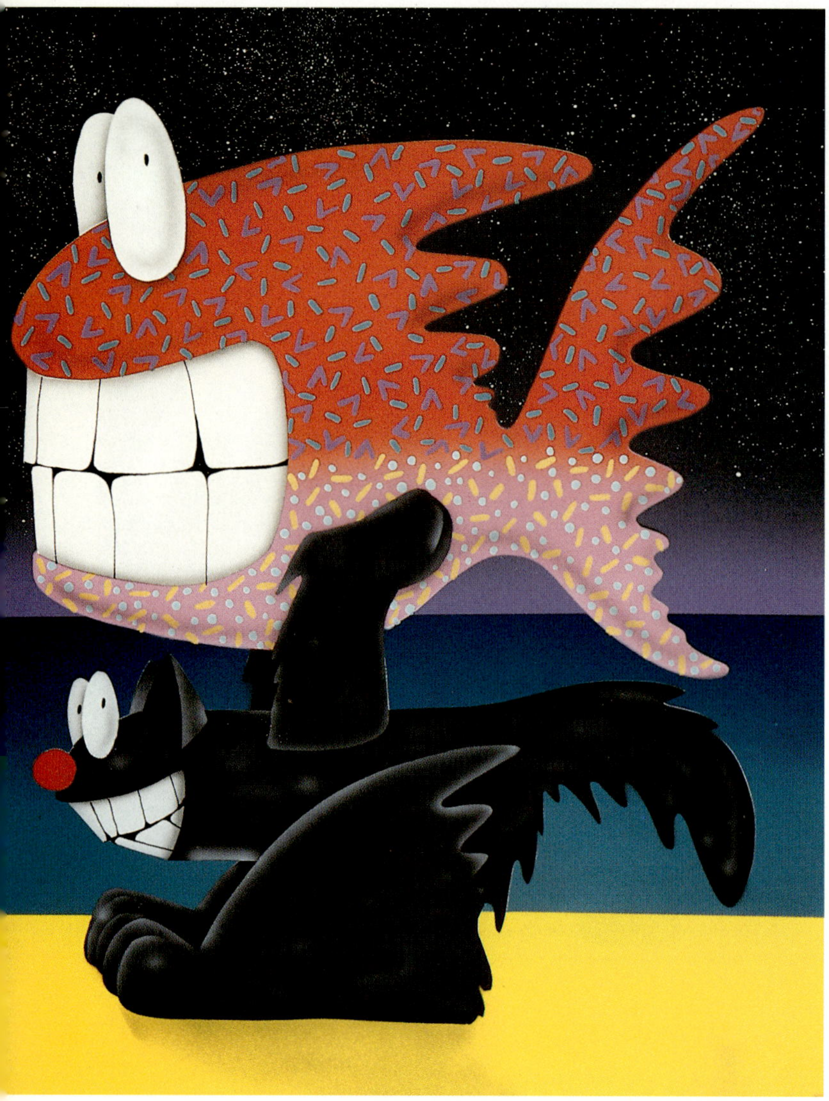

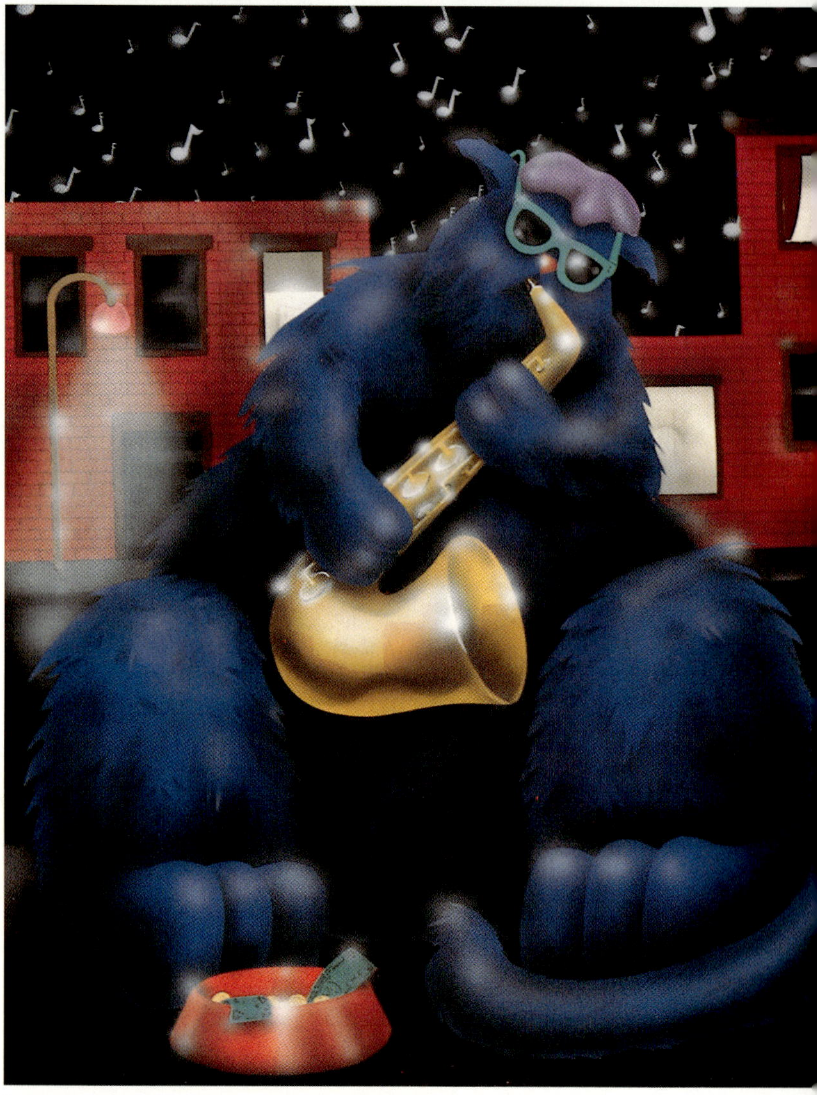

1 2

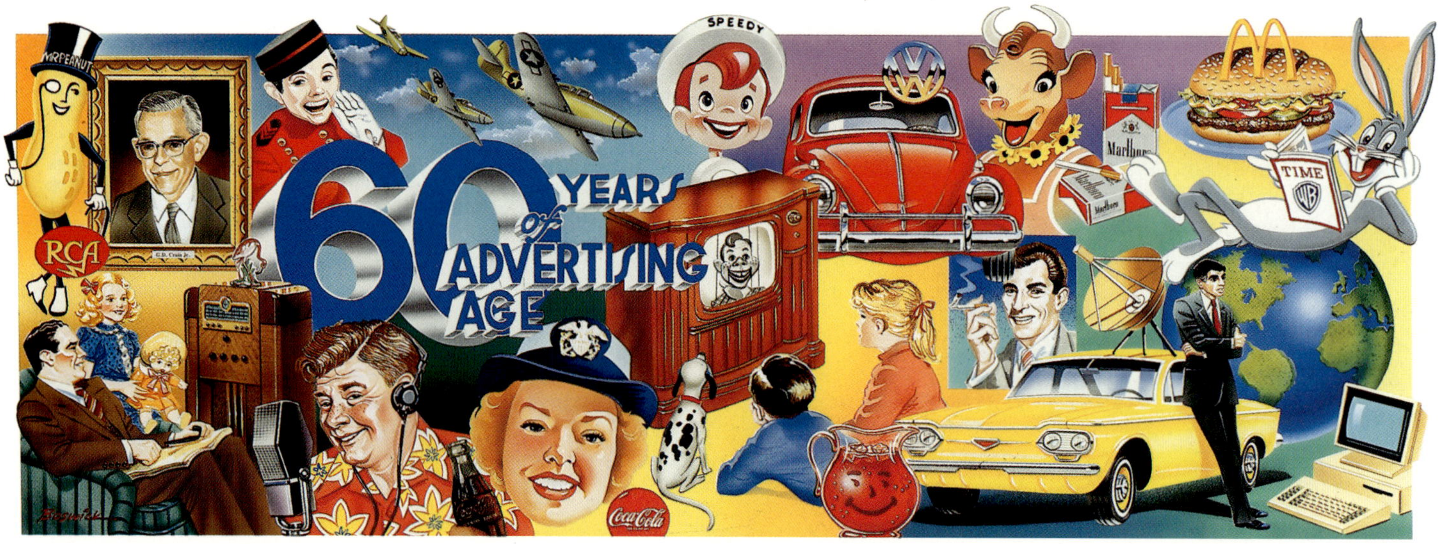

3

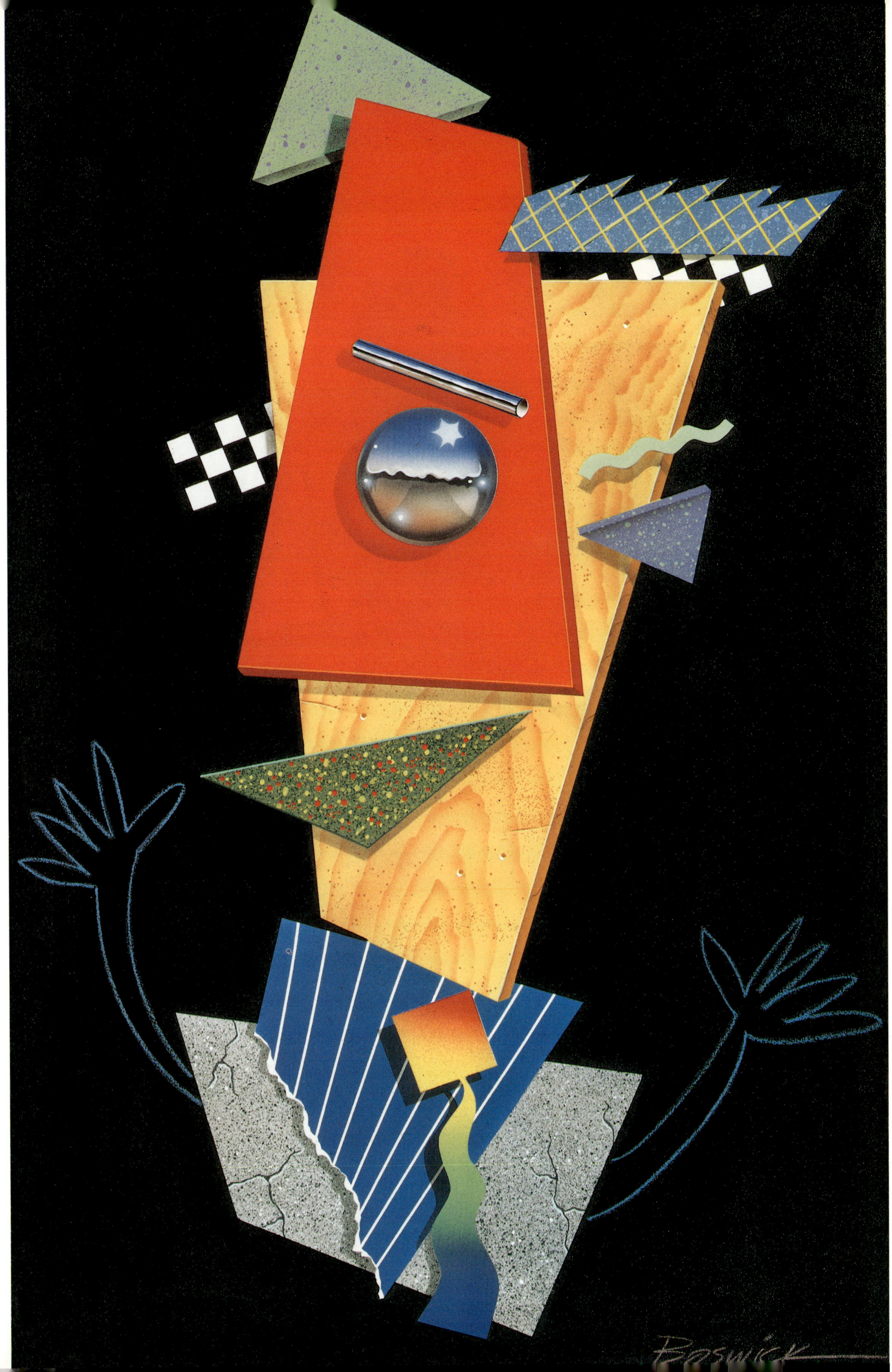

4

1
Artist Marty Braun
Title Pop Quiz
Client The Baltimore Sun
Art Director Donna Crivello
Usage Maryland Live Cover
Media Used Acrylic

2
Artist Marty Braun
Title Cherry Blossom Festival
Client The Washington Post
Art Director JoEllen Murphy
Usage Weekend Section
Media Used Acrylic

3
Artist Marty Braun
Title Pagemaker
Client M & T Publishing
Art Director Lauren Smith
Usage Book Cover
Media Used Acrylic

4
Artist Marty Braun
Title U.S. Ski Team Preview
Client Snow Country
Art Director Julie Curtis
Usage Editorial
Media Used Acrylic

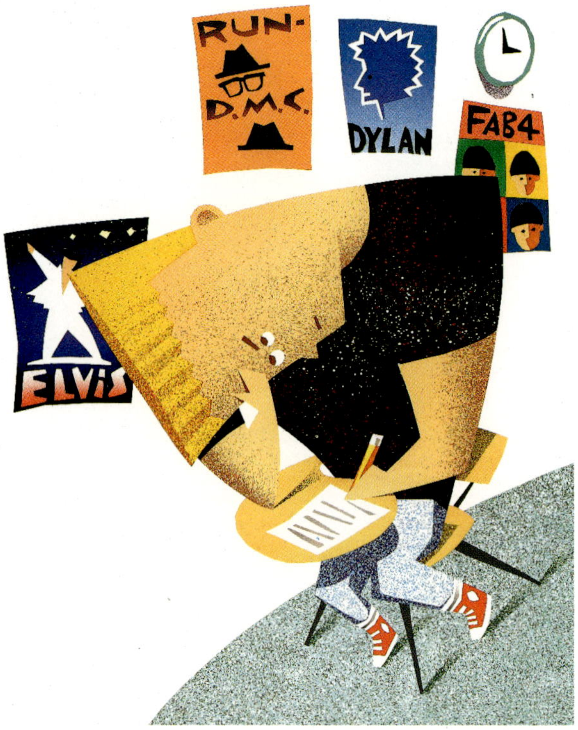

1

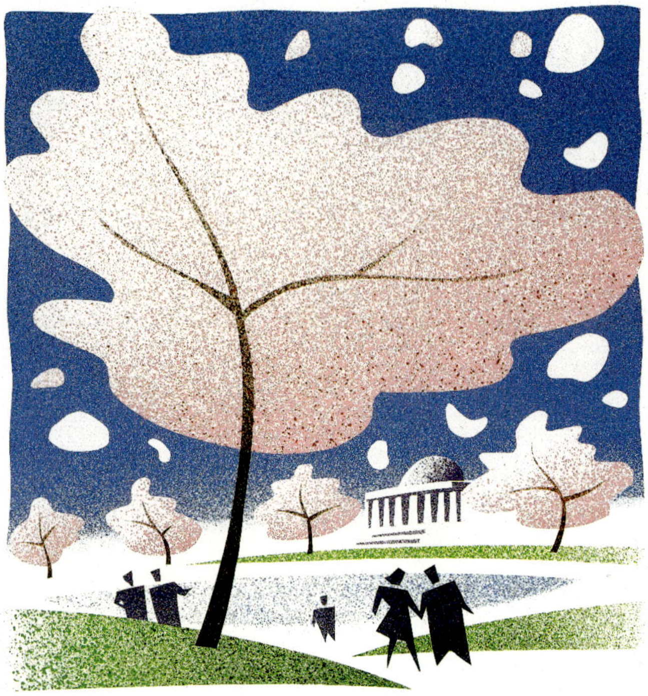

2

3

4

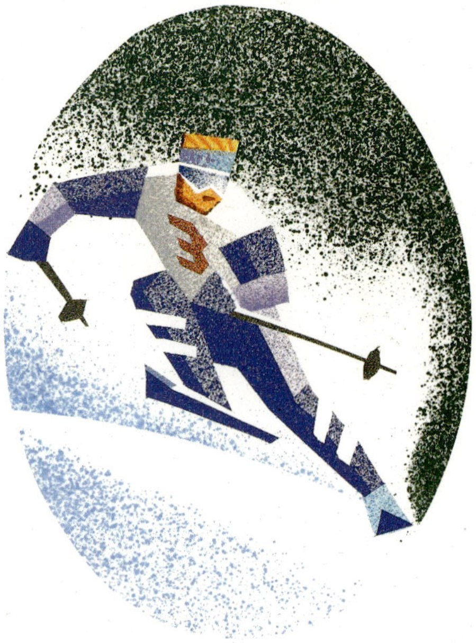

1
Artist Marty Braun
Title Alberobello, Itlay
Usage Self Promotion
Media Used Acrylic

2
Artist Marty Braun
Title Summer Festivals
Client Ford Motor Co. / The Atlantic
Art Director Karen Wesolowski
Usage Magazine Advertorial
Media Used Acrylic

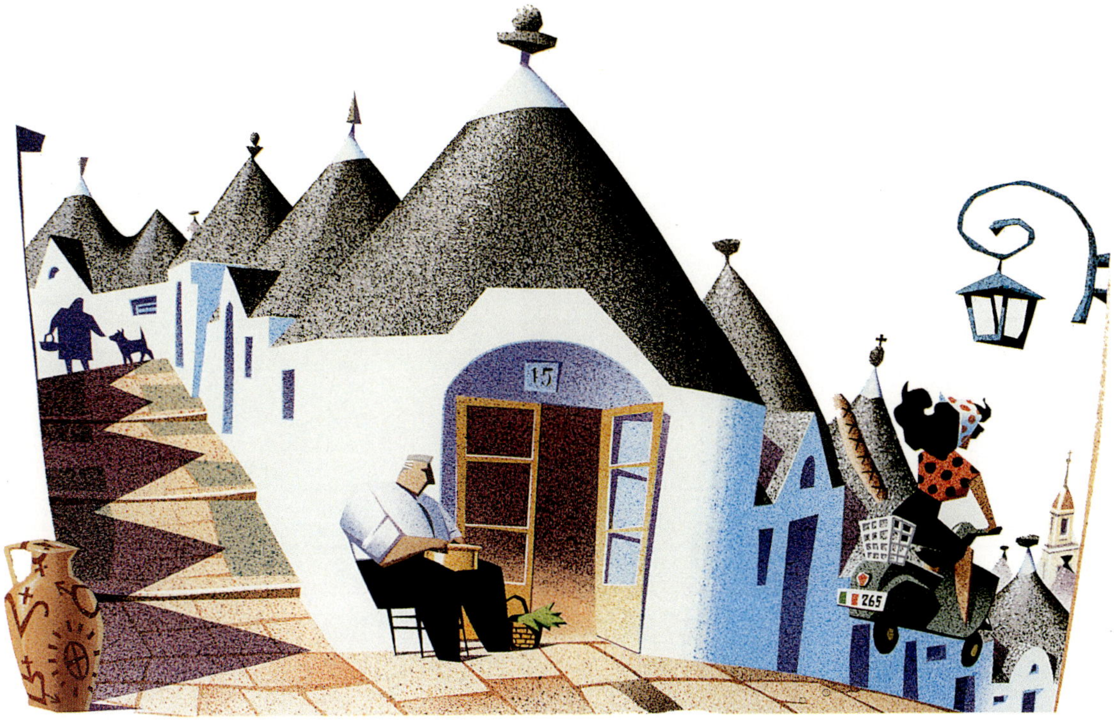

1

2

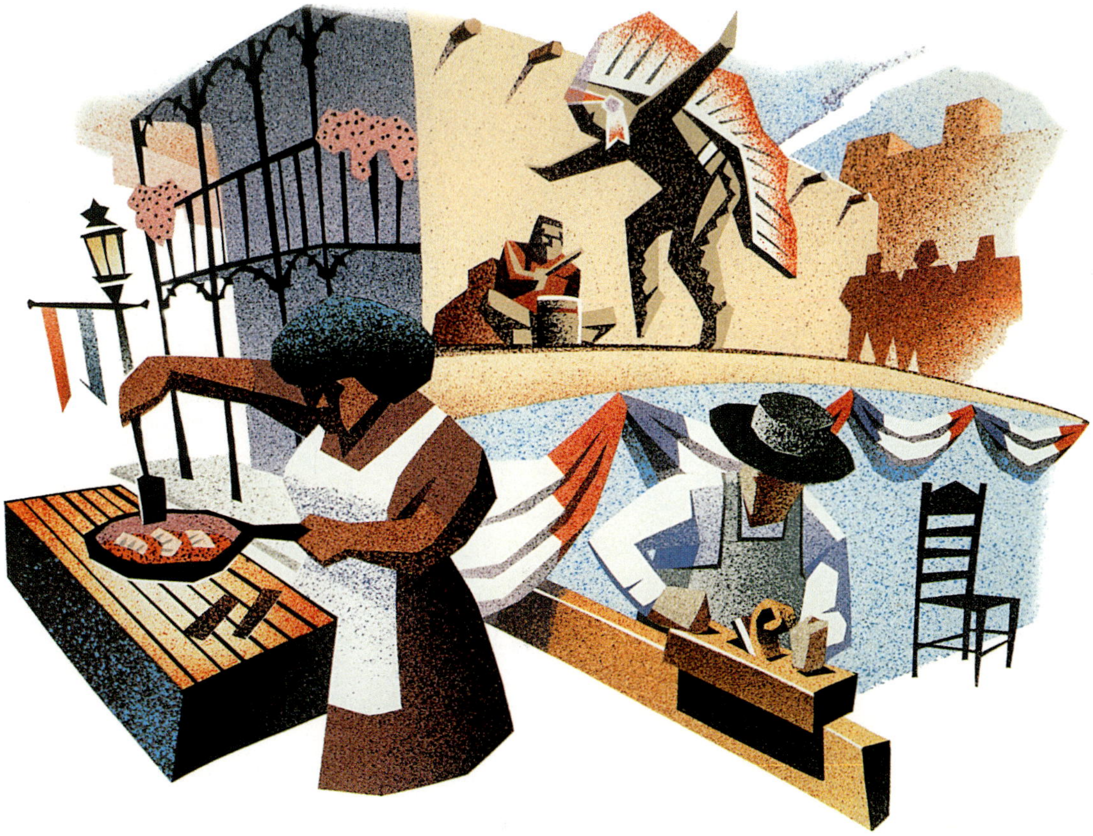

1
Artist Marty Braun
Title On the Edge of Technology
Client Communications Week International
Art Director Arch Carey
Usage Magazine Cover
Media Used Acrylic

2
Artist Marty Braun
Title Biking in Vermont
Client American Airlines
Art Director Marilyn Calley
Usage In-Flight Magazine Column
Media Used Acrylic

3
Artist Marty Braun
Title Only til Death
Client American Airlines
Art Director Alisann Marshalls
Usage In-Flight Magazine Fiction
Media Used Acrylic

4
Artist Marty Braun
Title Valentine's Date
Client The Washington Post
Art Director JoEllen Murphy
Usage Weekend Section Cover
Media Used Acrylic

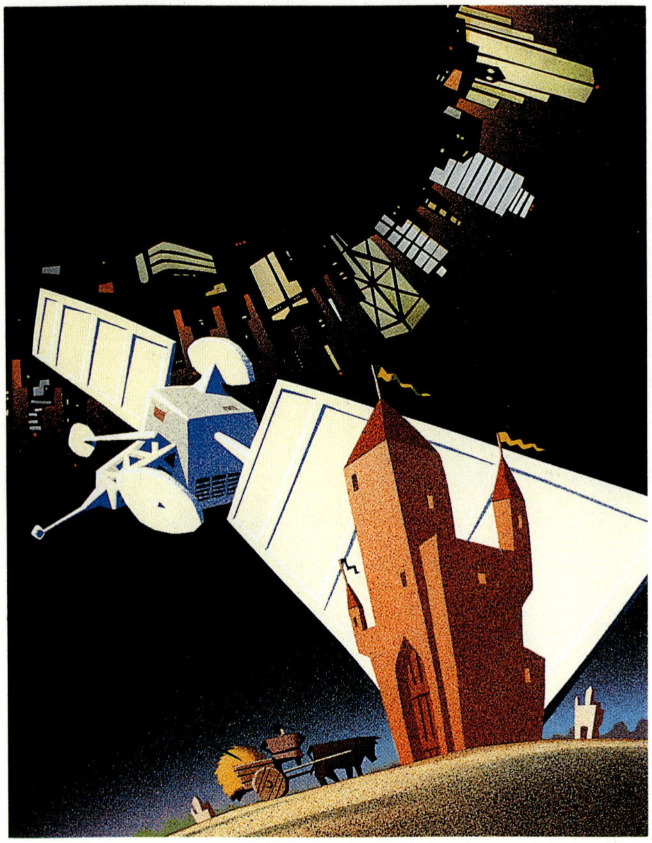
1

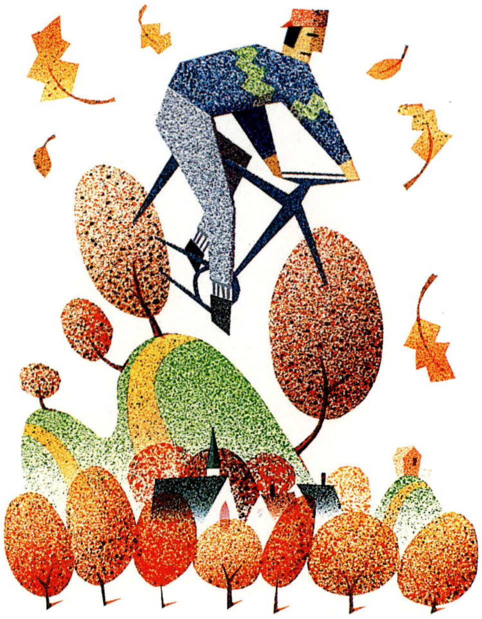
2

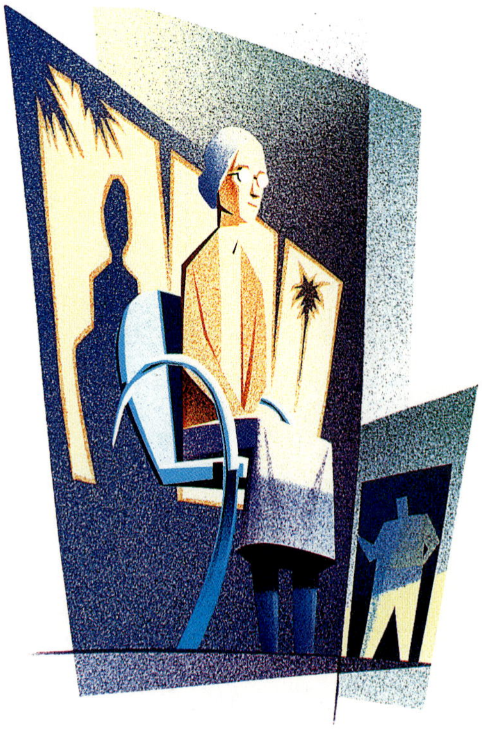
3

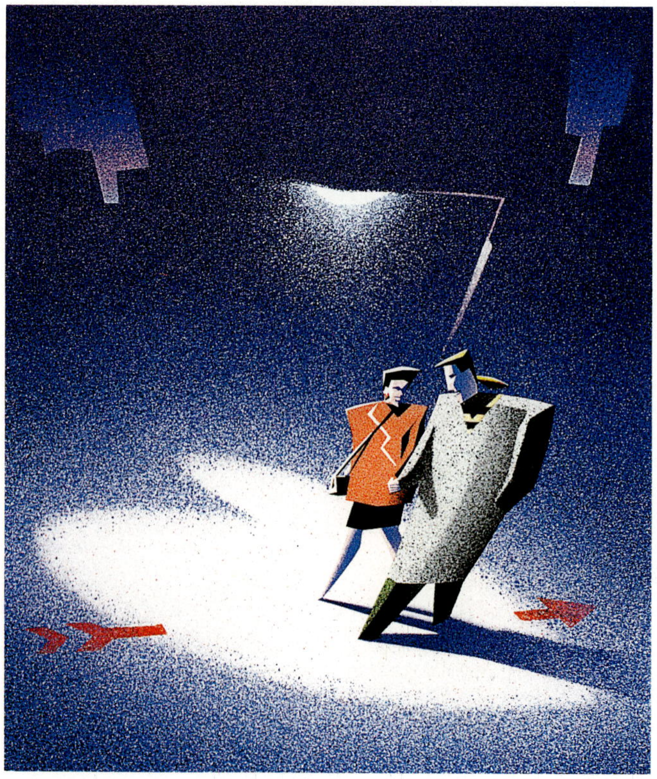
4

1
Artist Marty Braun
Title Budget Cuts at Dupont
Client Delaware Today
Art Director Ingrid Hansen Lynch
Usage Magazine Cover
Media Used Acrylic

2
Artist Marty Braun
Title The Blue Bikes of Amsterdam
Client European Travel and Life
Art Director Andrea Karman
Usage Editorial
Media Used Acrylic

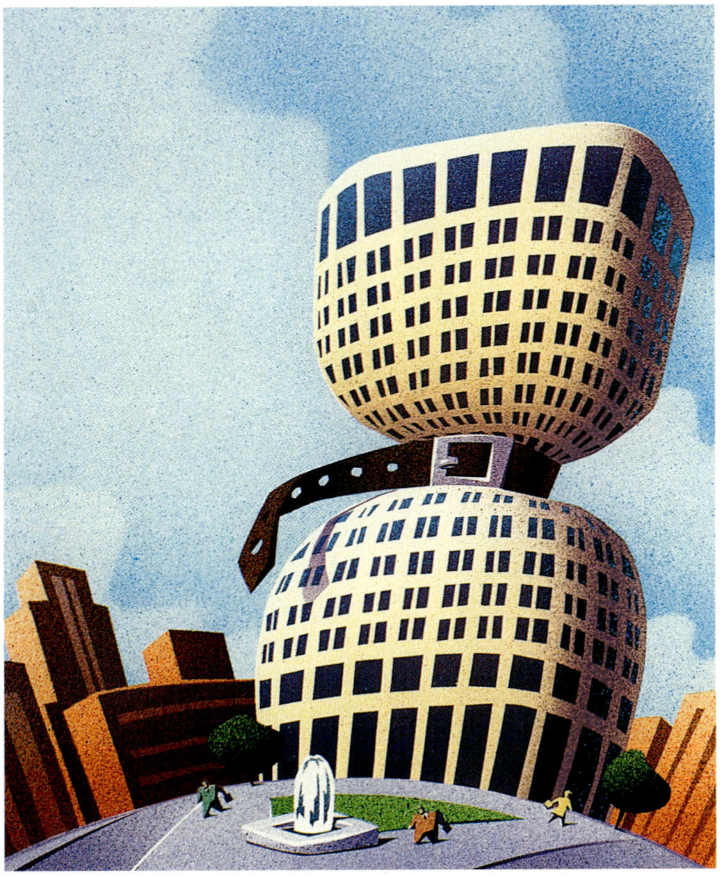
1

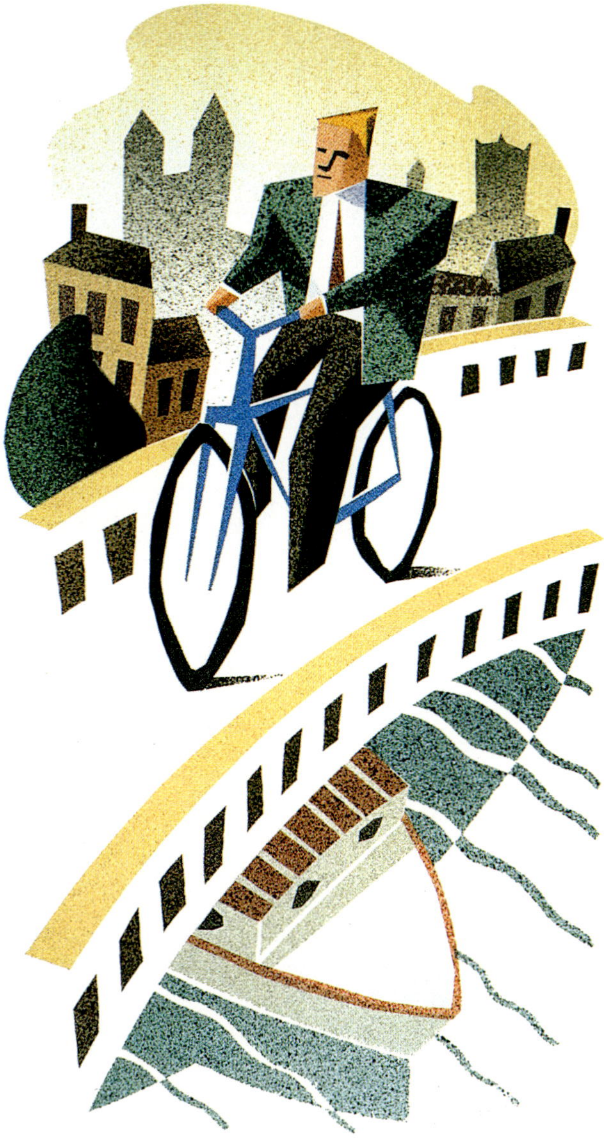
2

1
Artist Marty Braun
Title Dreams
Client Uniforum
Art Director Sylvia Dahlgren
Usage Magazine Spread
Media Used Acrylic

2
Artist Marty Braun
Title Autumn Hiking
Client The Washington Post
Art Director JoEllen Murphy
Usage Weekend Section Cover
Media Used Acrylic

3
Artist Marty Braun
Title Cross-Country Skiing
Client The Washington Post
Art Director JoEllen Murphy
Usage Weekend Section Cover
Media Used Acrylic

2

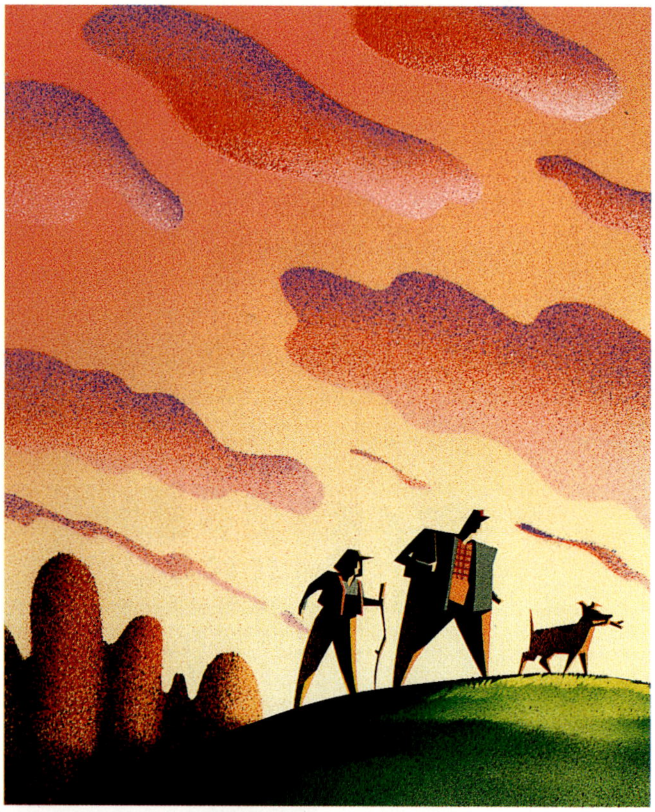

1

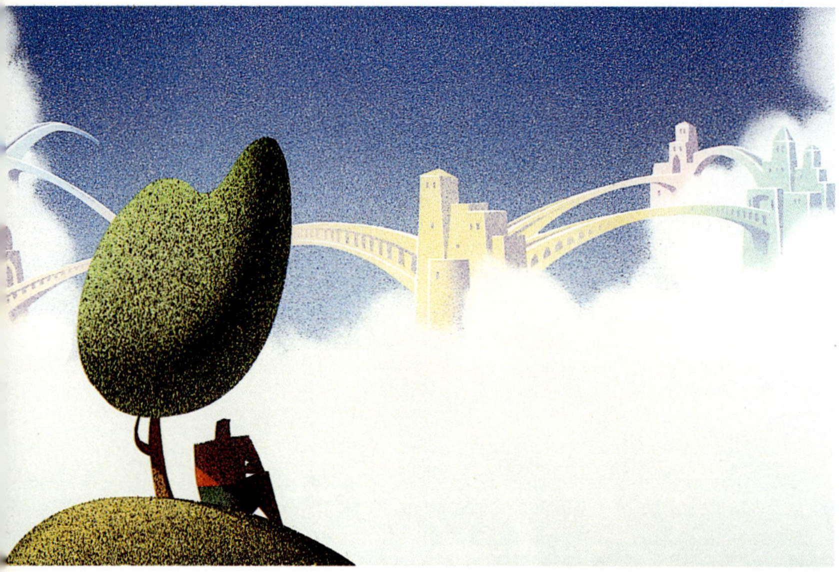

3

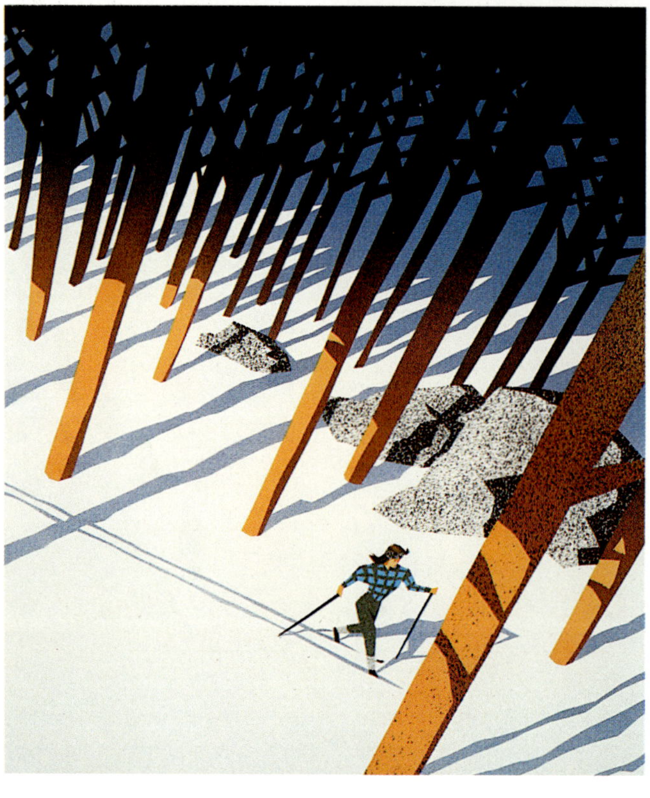

1
Artist Marty Braun
Title Whale Watching
Client The Boston Globe
Art Director Aldona Charlton
Usage Calendar Section Cover
Media Used Acrylic

2
Artist Marty Braun
Title Maggie at the Ball Field
Usage Christmas Card
Media Used Acrylic

3
Artist Marty Braun
Title Tucker
Client The Washington Post
Art Director Richard Baker
Usage Auto Column Movie Review
Media Used Acrylic

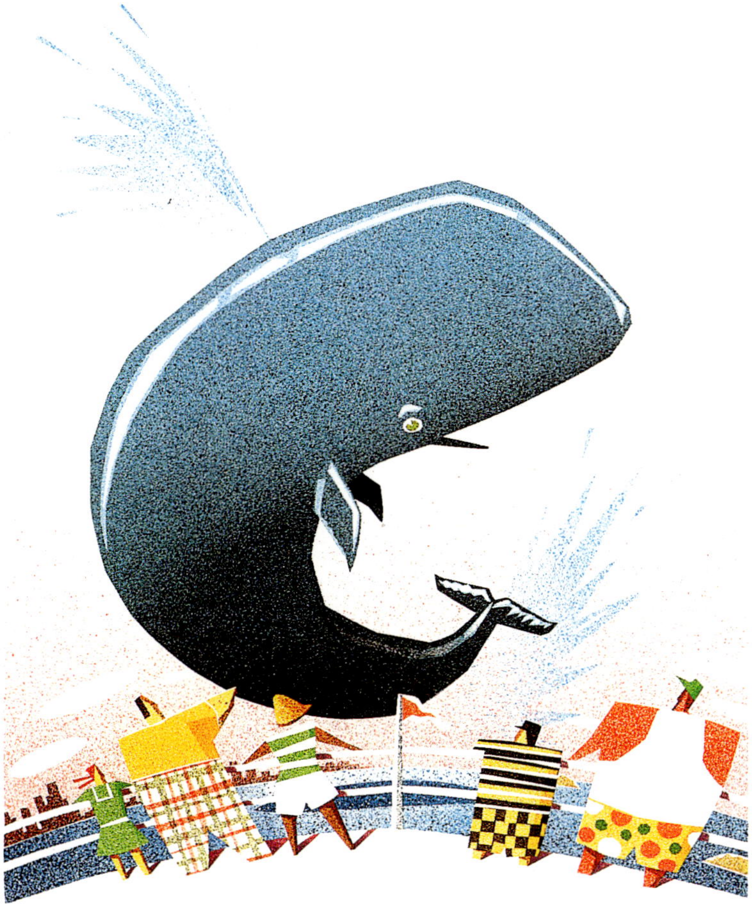

1

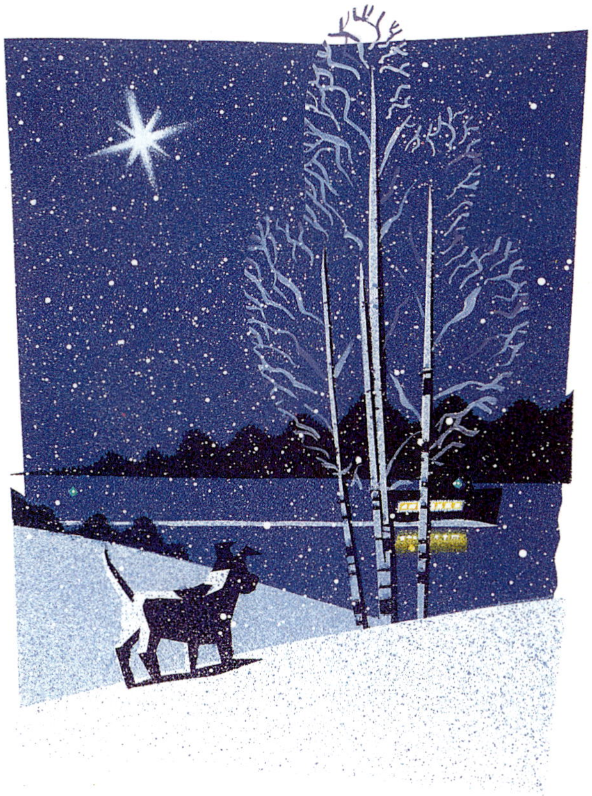

2

3

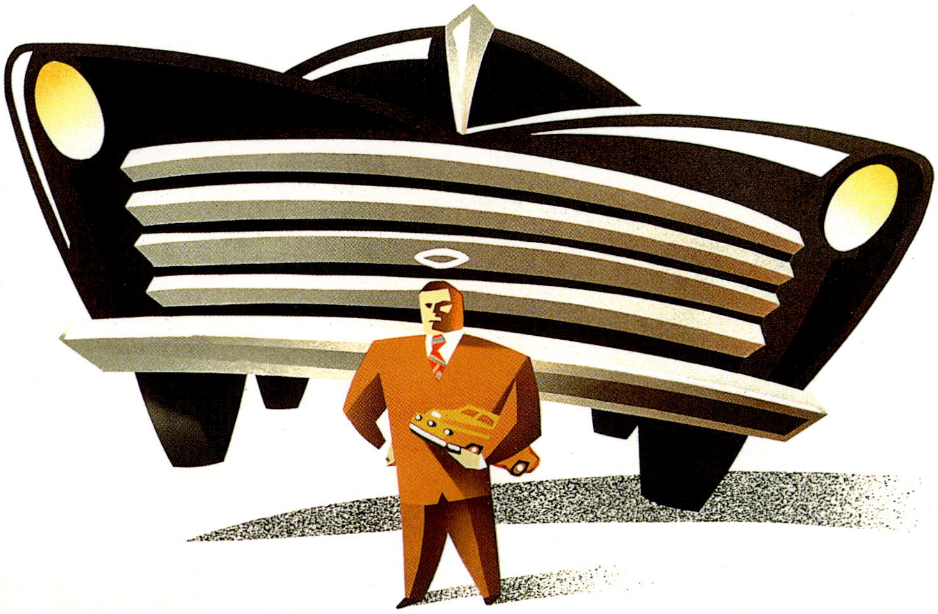

1
Artist Marty Braun
Title City of the Future
Client American Airlines
Art Director Marilyn Calley
Usage In-Flight Magazine Spread
Media Used Acrylic

2
Artist Marty Braun
Title The Real Estate Market
Client Diablo Business
Art Director Derek Davalos
Usage Magazine Section Cover
Media Used Acrylic

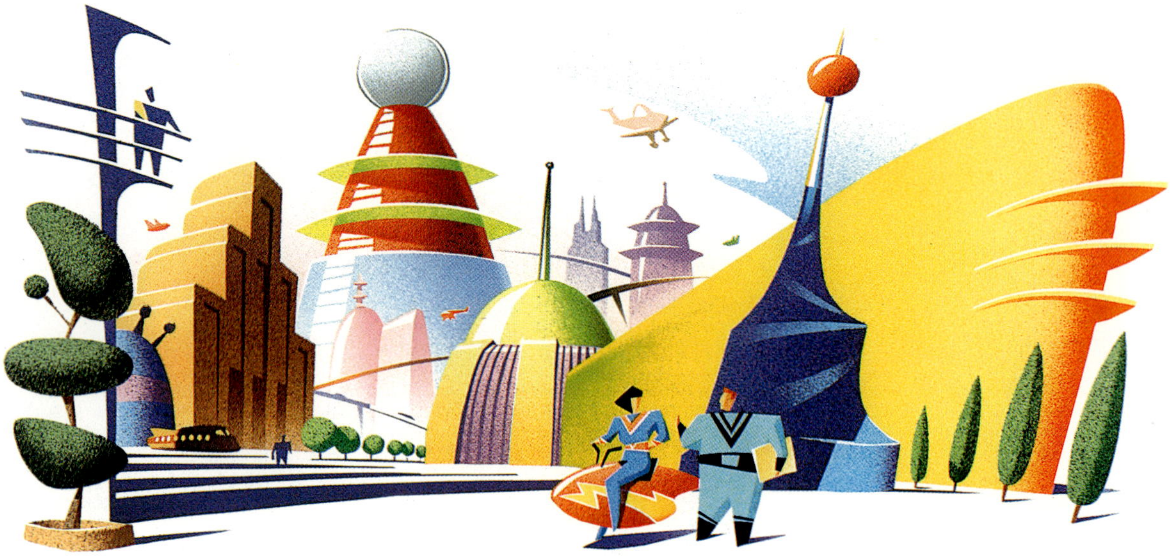

1

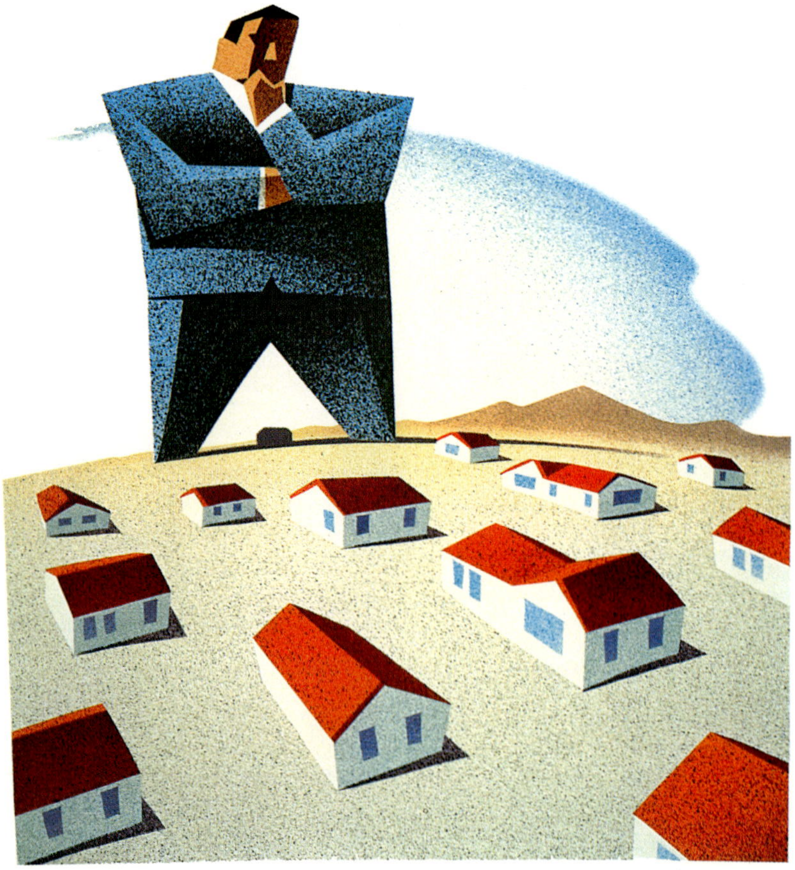

2

1
Artist Marty Braun
Title The Runner
Client The Boston Globe Sunday Magazine
Art Director Catherine Aldrich
Usage Health Column Illustration
Media Used Acrylic

2
Artist Marty Braun
Title Summer Cruise
Client New England Living
Art Director Ken Silvia
Usage Editorial
Media Used Acrylic

3
Artist Marty Braun
Title Tracing Family Roots
Client The Washington Post Sunday Magazine
Art Director Richard Baker
Usage Travel Section Opener
Media Used Acrylic

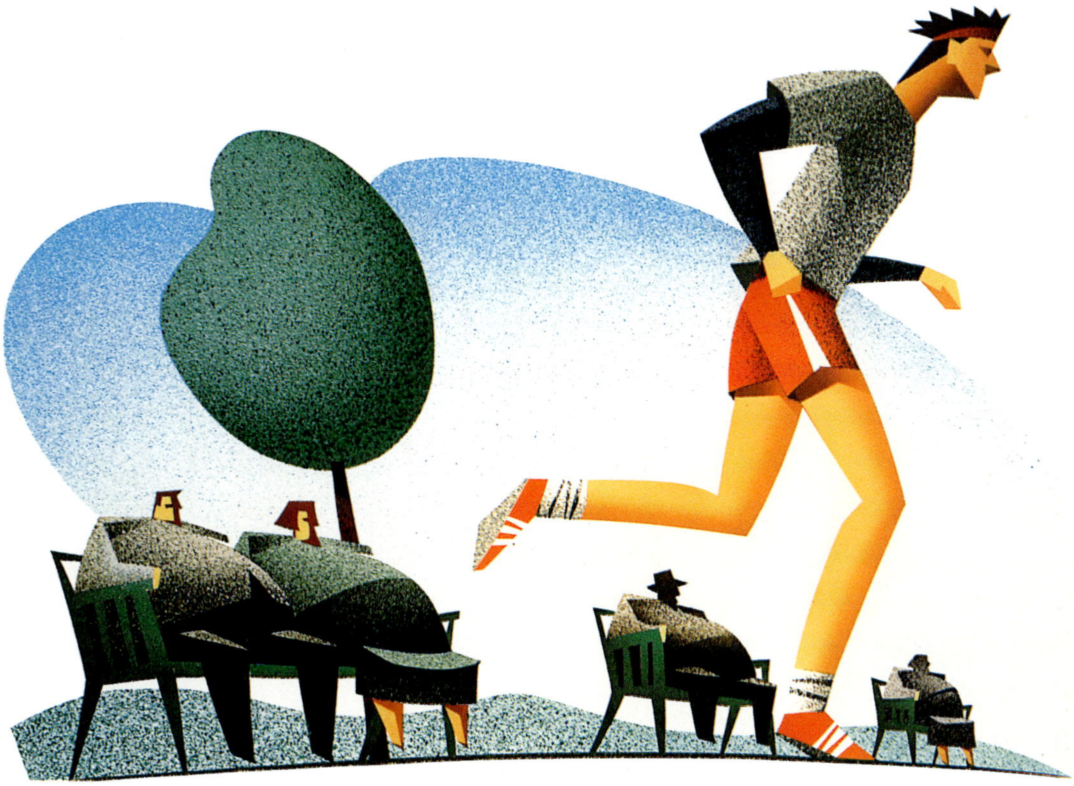

1

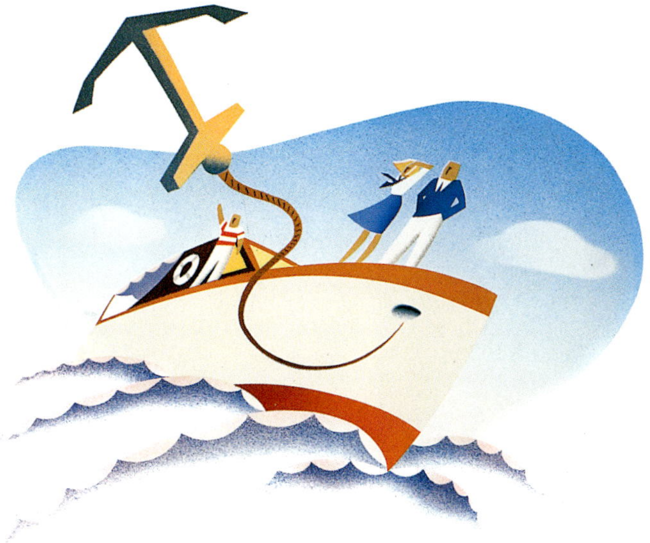

2

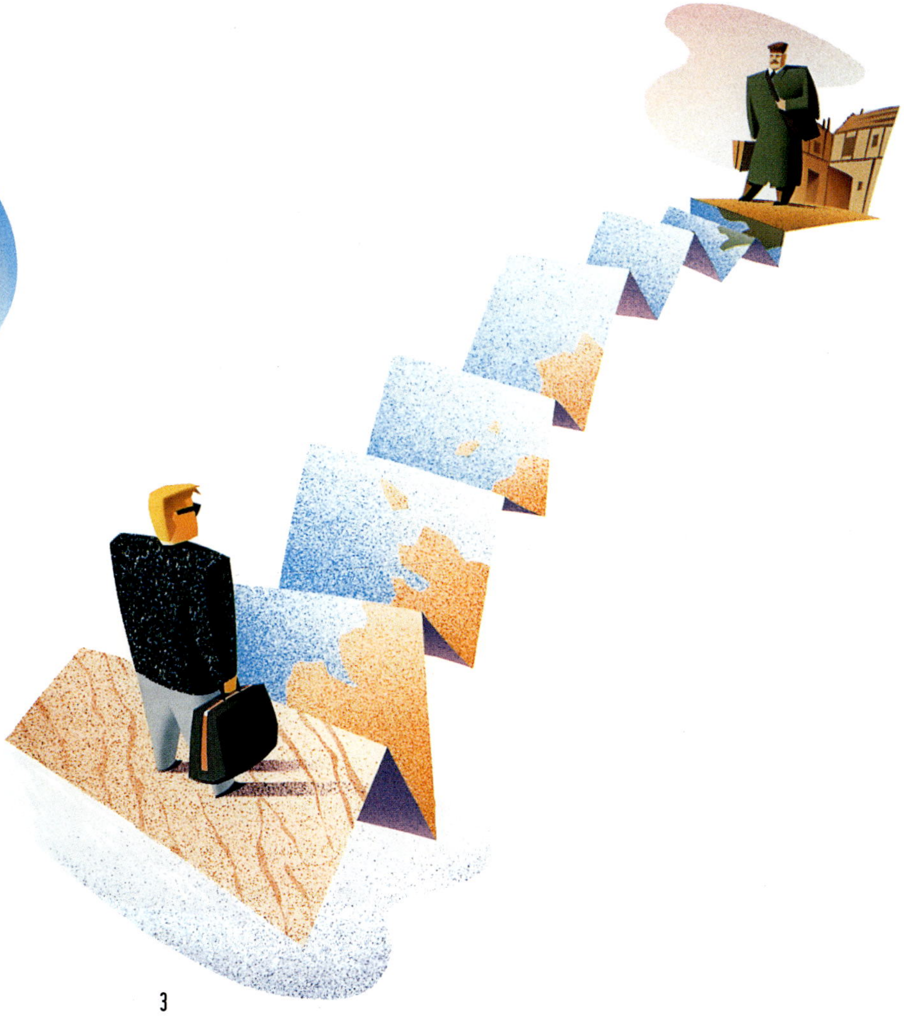

3

1
Artist Robert Brun
Client Ulvav Corporation
Art Director Kristi Borst
Usage Sales Brochure
Media Used Gouche on Vellum

2
Artist Robert Brun
Client Country Kitchen
Art Director Tom Morse
Usage Discount Coupon
Media Used Gouache

3
Artist Robert Brun
Title Downsizing
Client Network News
Art Director Micki Amick
Usage Magazine Cover
Media Used Gouache on Bristol

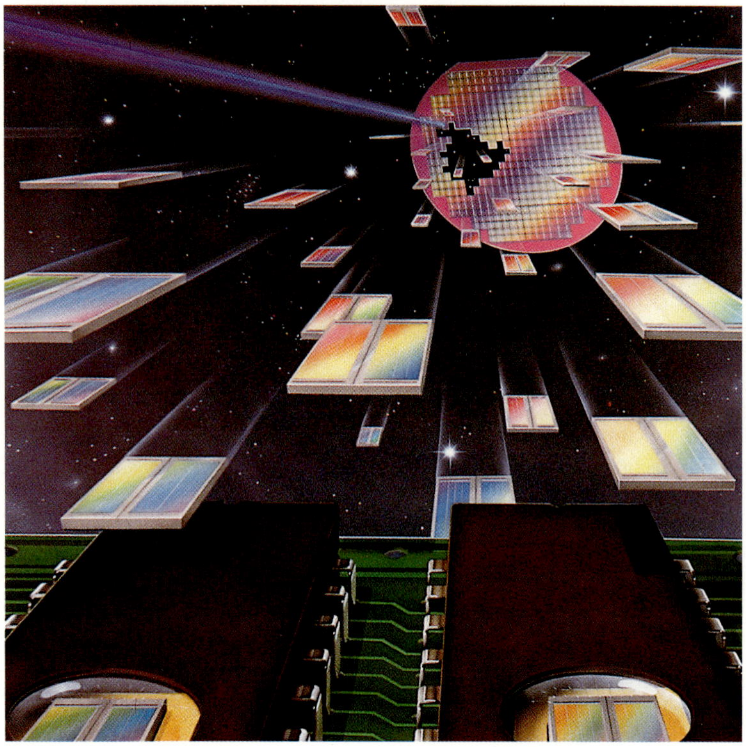

1

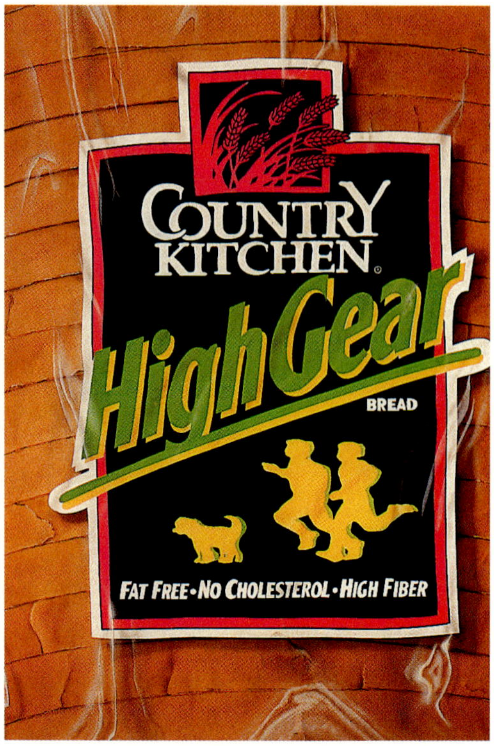

2

3

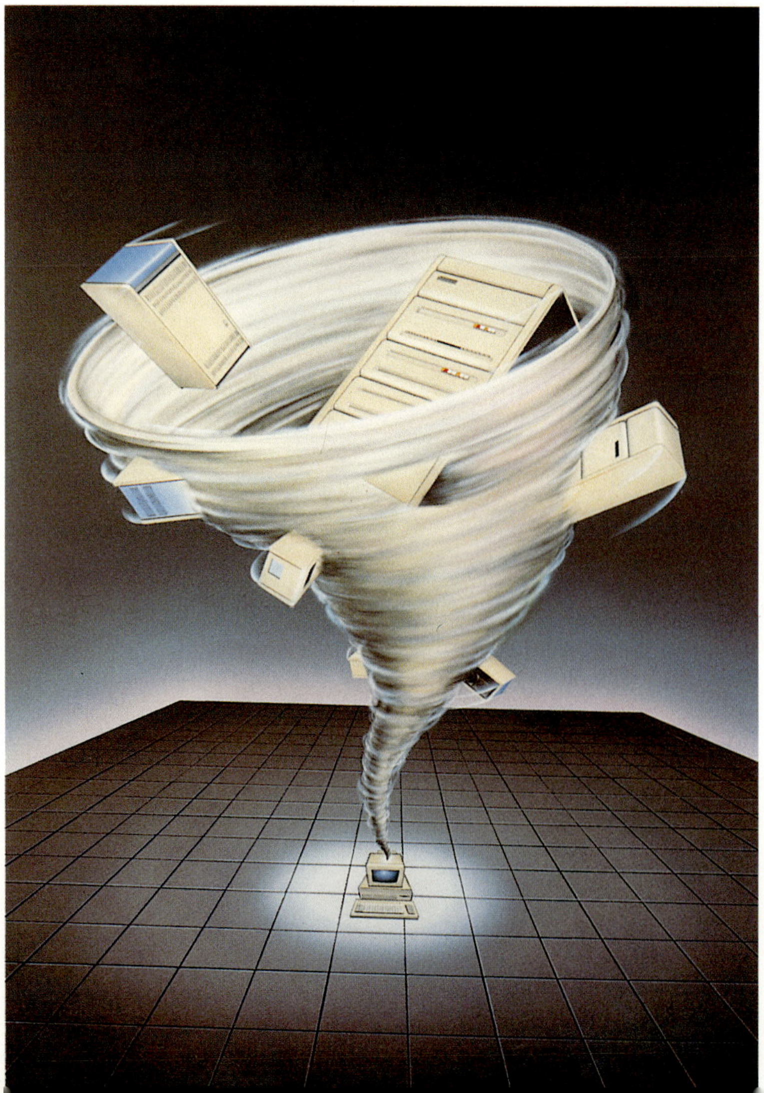

1
Artist Todd Buck
Title Streptococcus Infections in Children
Art Director Mary L. Jerrell of Slack Inc.
Usage Editorial Illustration
Media Used Acrylic

2
Artist Todd Buck
Title Why Some Children Refuse to Eat
Client Medical Economics Publishing
Art Director Michael Velthaus
Usage Editorial Illustration
Media Used Acrylic

3
Artist Todd Buck
Title Calcium & Bone Growth in Children
Art Director Mary L. Jerrell of Slack Inc.
Usage Editorial Illustration
Media Used Acrylic

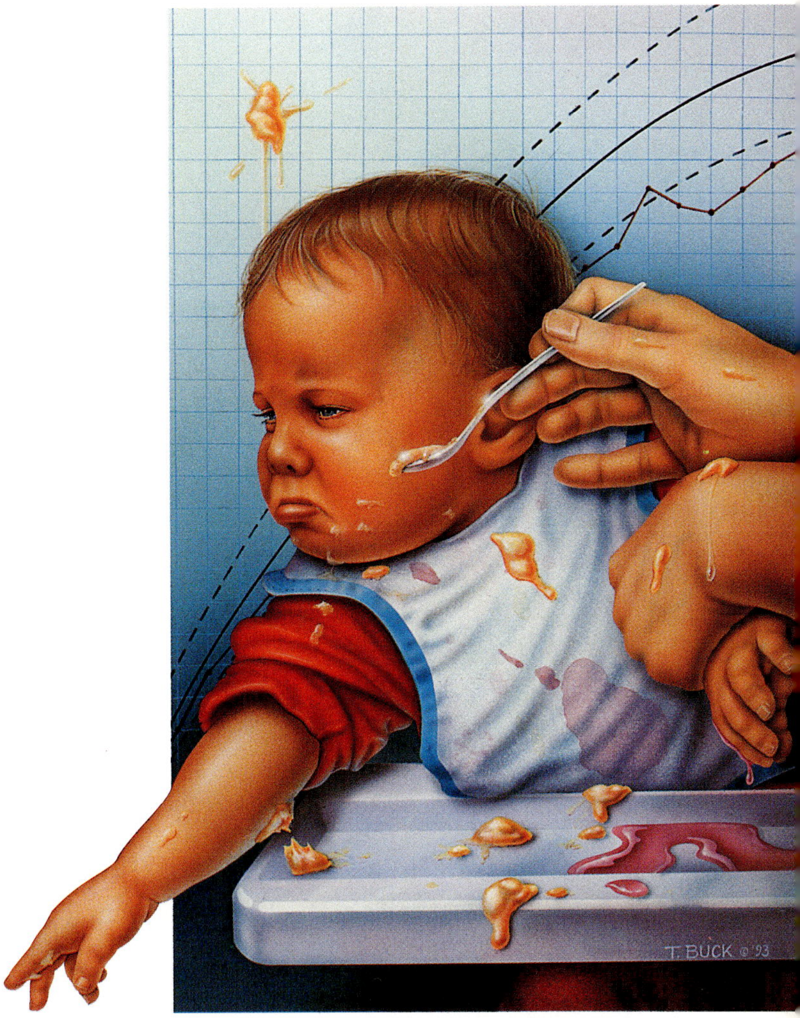

2

1

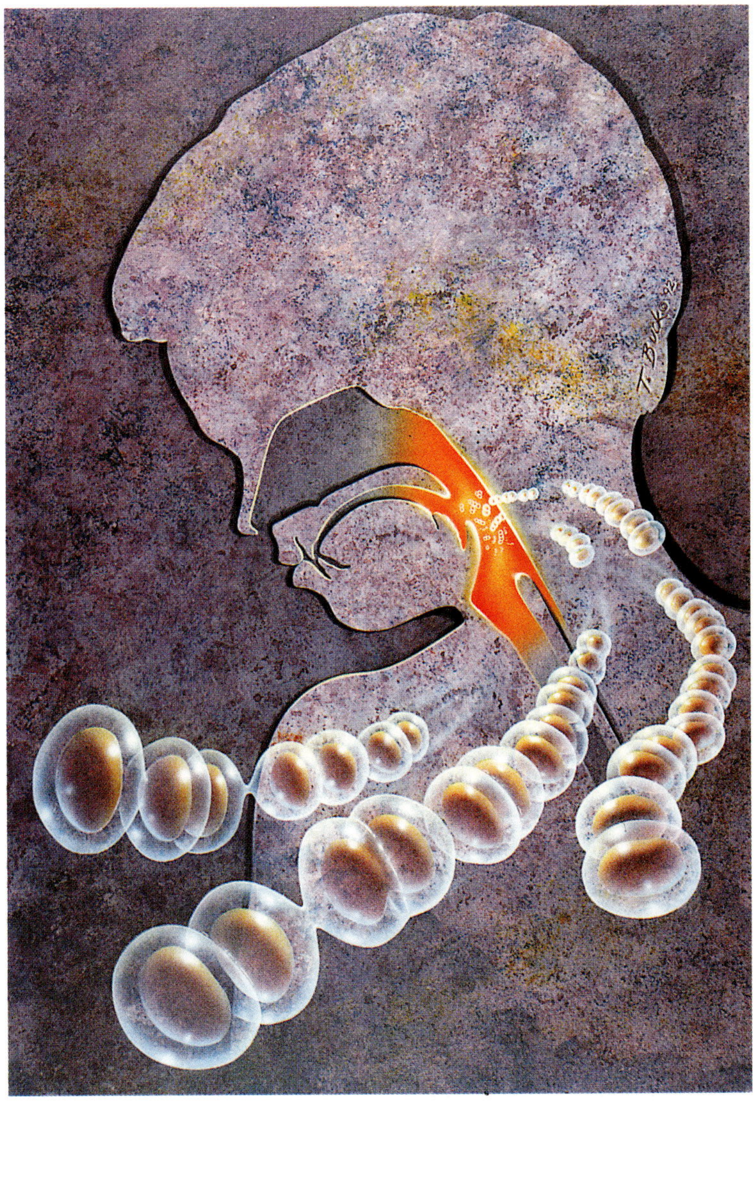

3

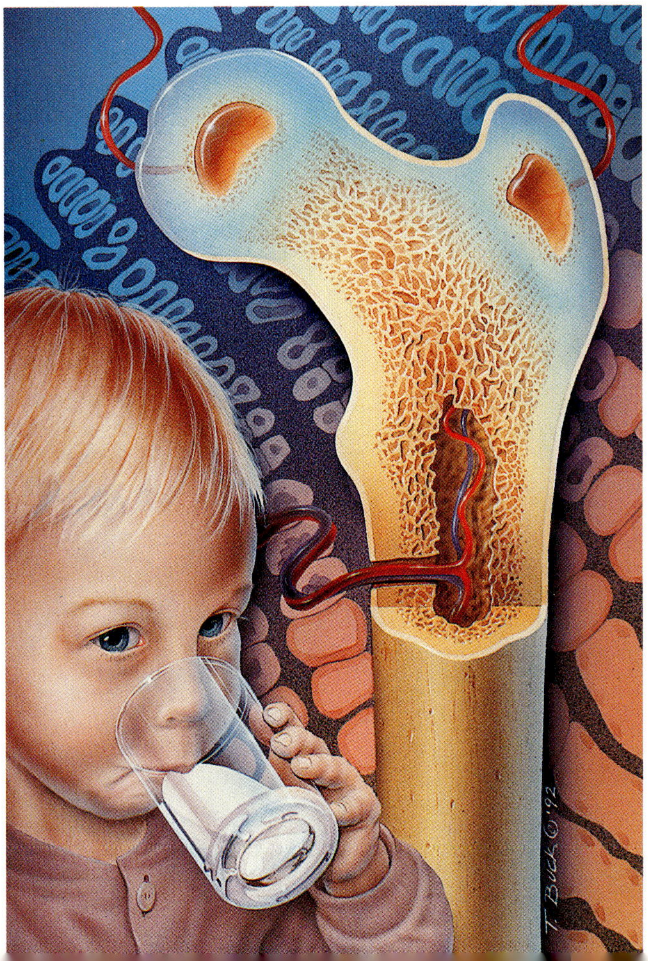

1
Artist Hank Buffington
Usage Student Art
Media Used Rotring Artist Color

2
Artist Lonnie Busch
Title White Mountain Cooler
Media Used Acrylic

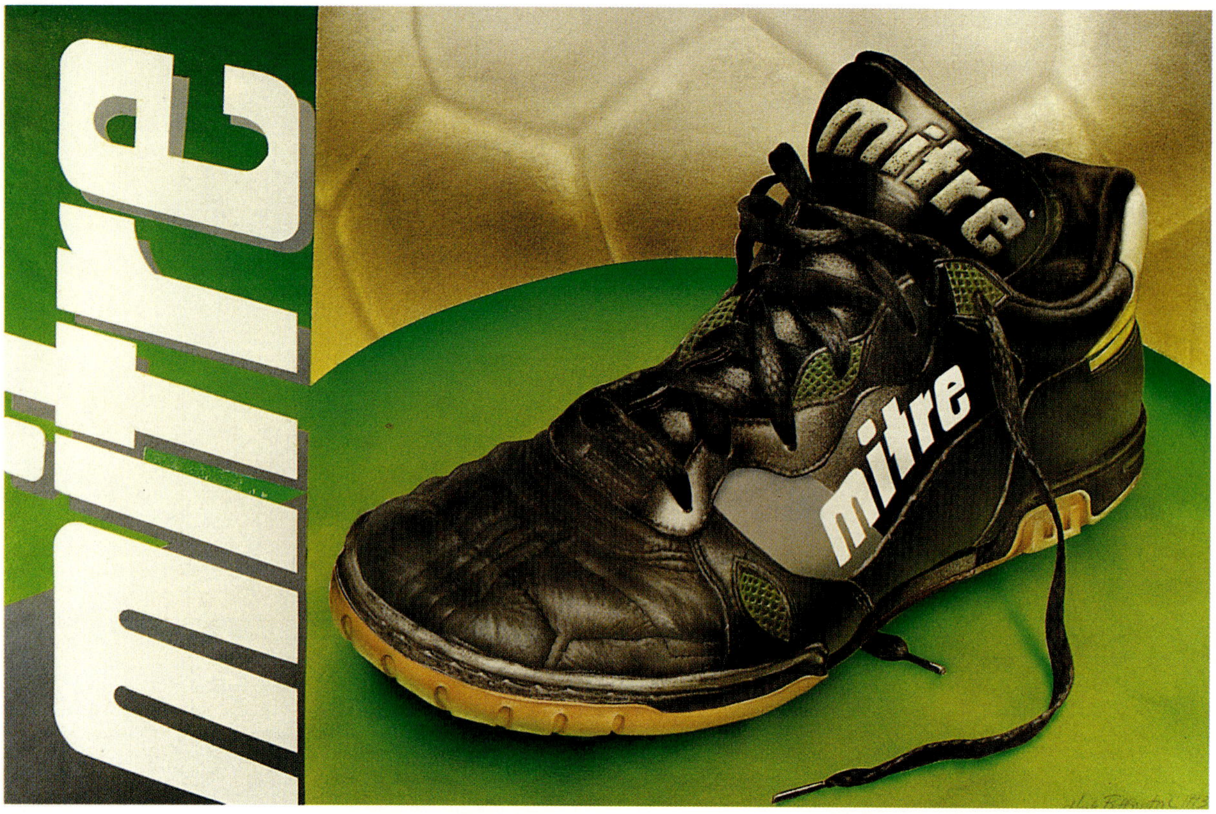

1

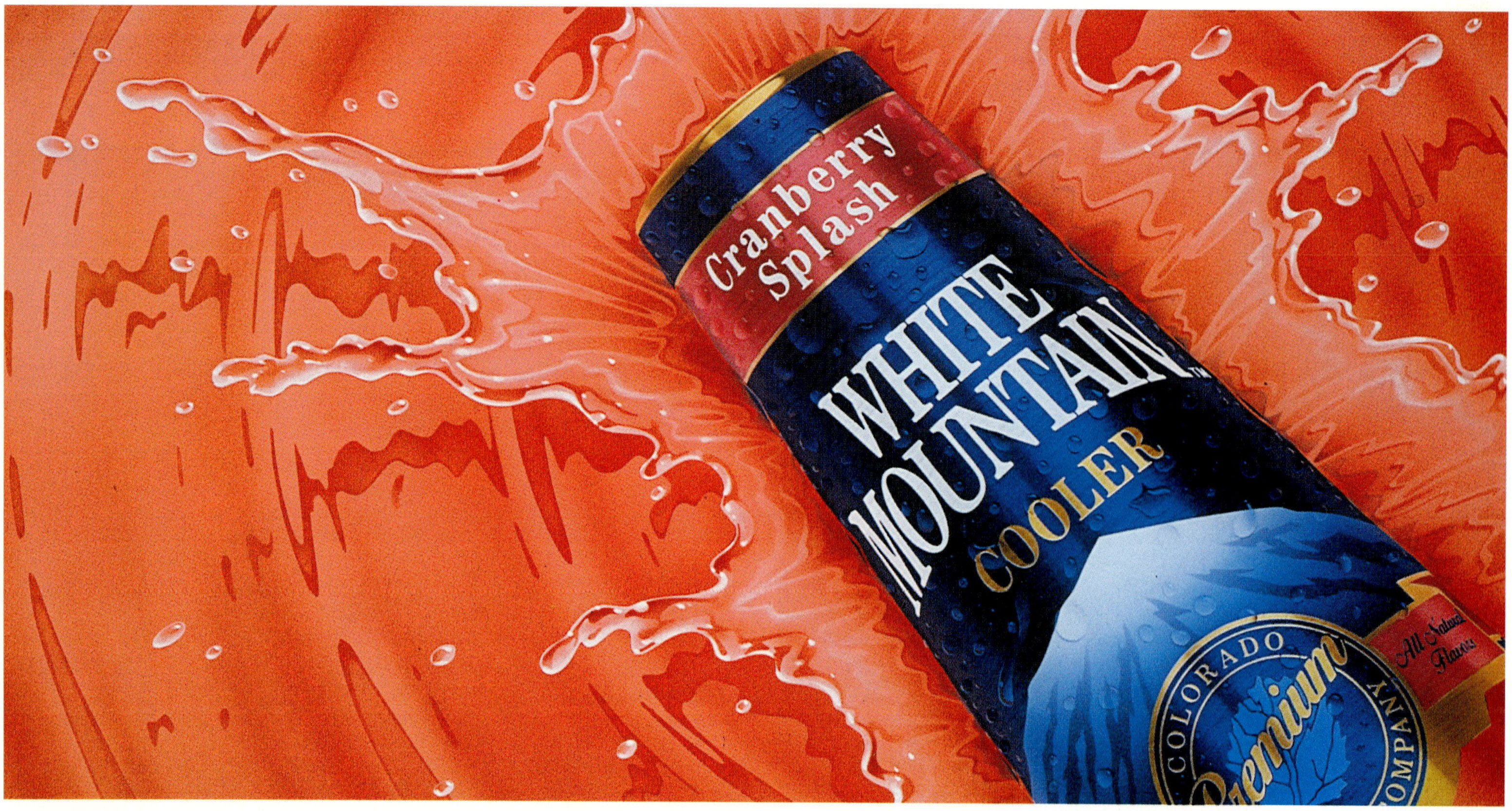

2

1
Artist Lonnie Busch
Title Mastercard Dishes
Media Used Acrylic

2
Artist Lonnie Busch
Title Bud Surfers
Media Used Acrylic

3
Artist Lonnie Busch
Title 7.UP Fountain
Media Used Acrylic

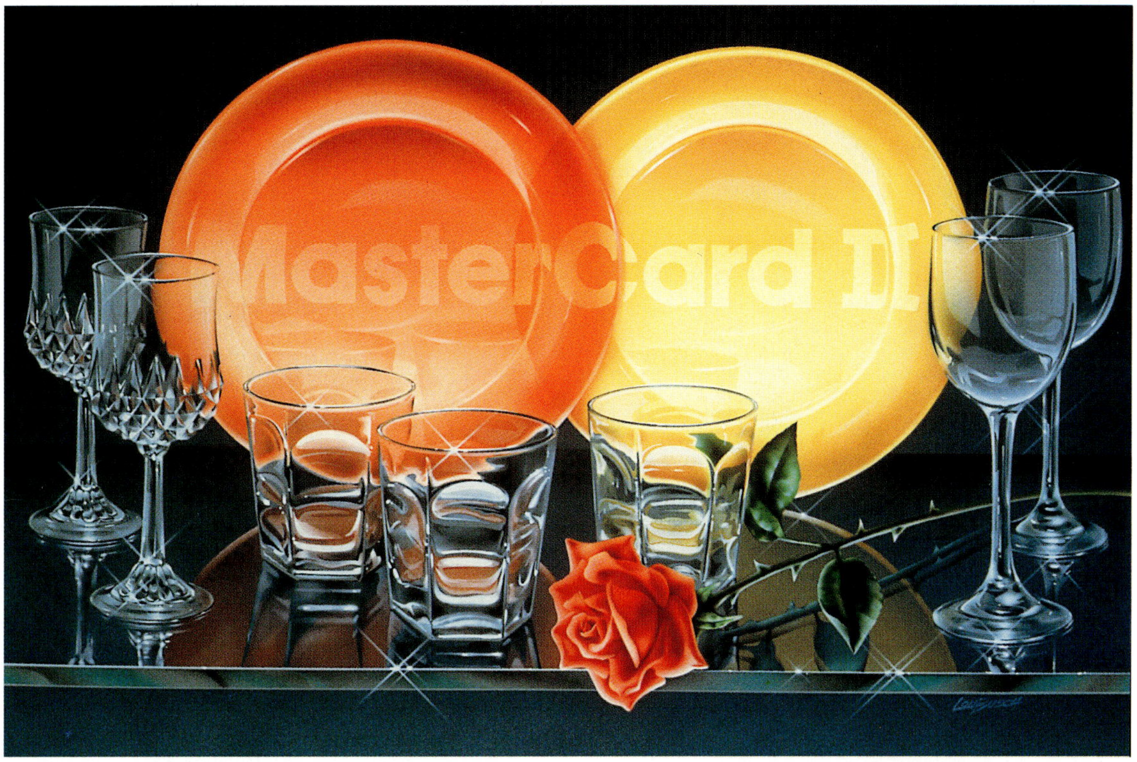

1

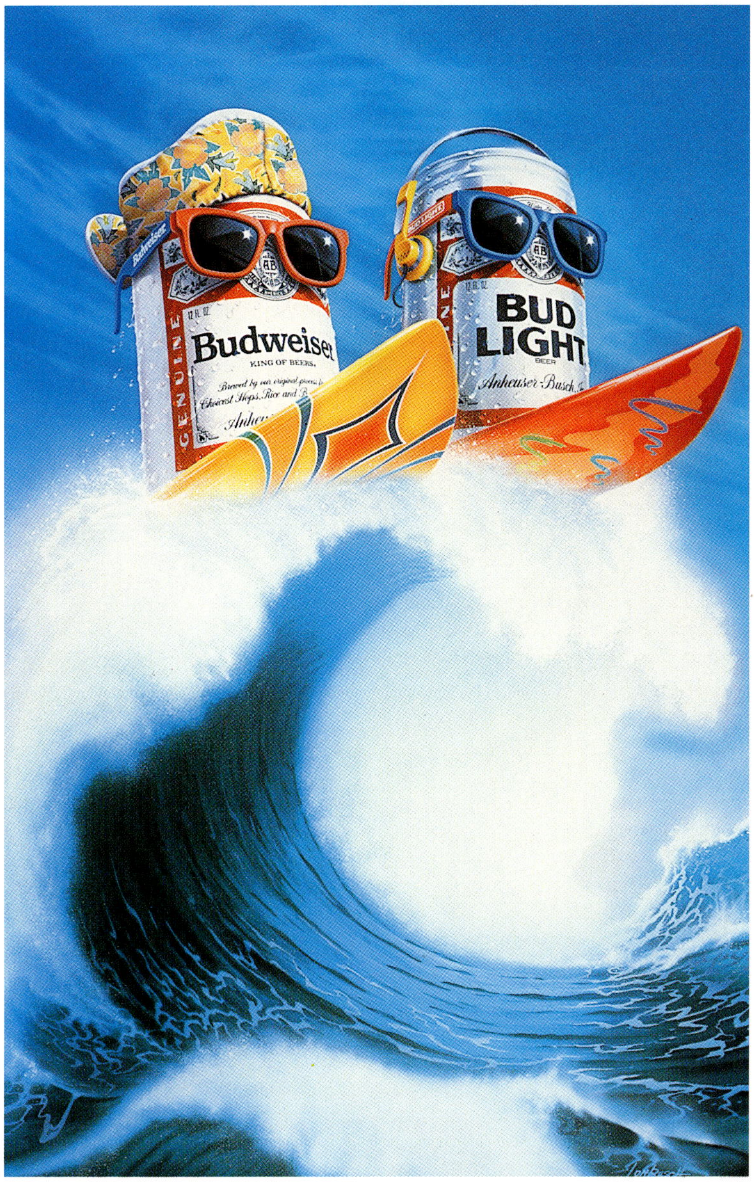

2

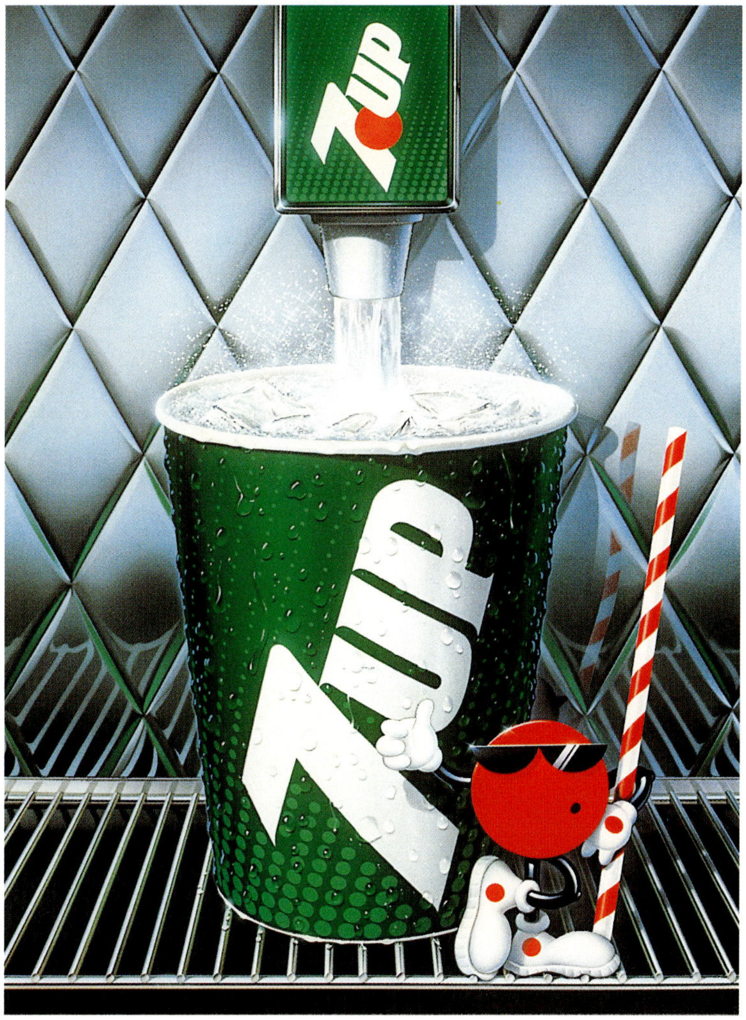

3

1
Artist Lonnie Busch
Title Humpty-Dumpty
Media Used Acrylic

2
Artist Lonnie Busch
Title Jars & Boxes
Media Used Acrylic

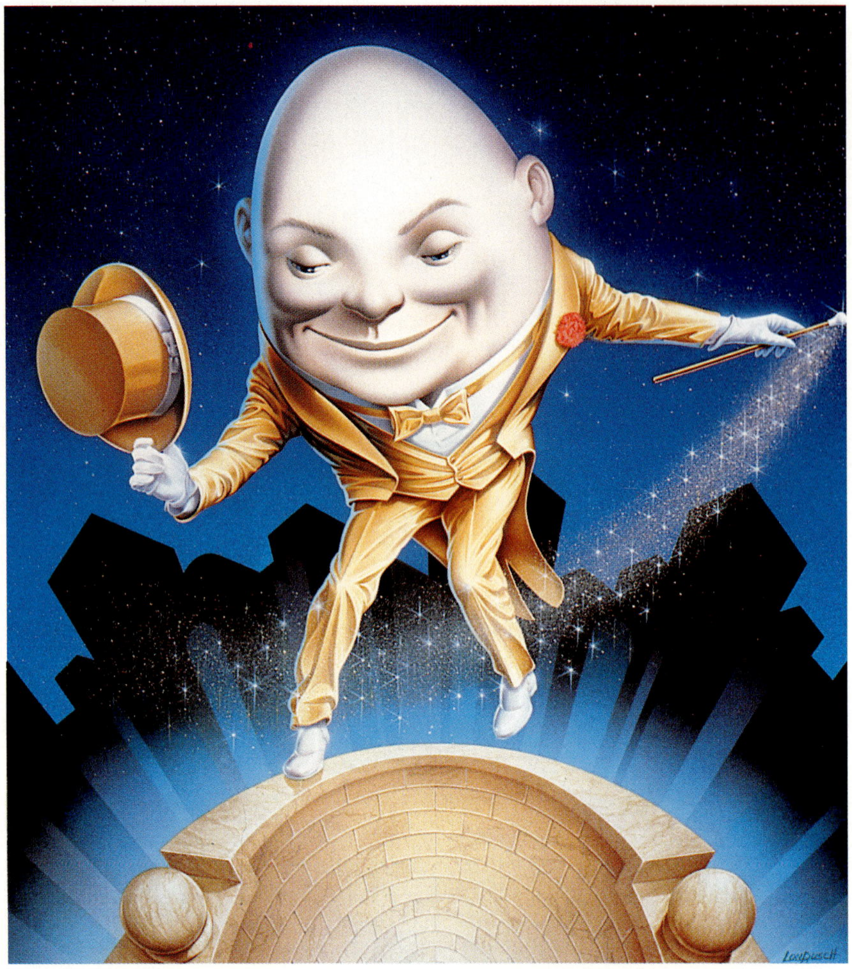

1

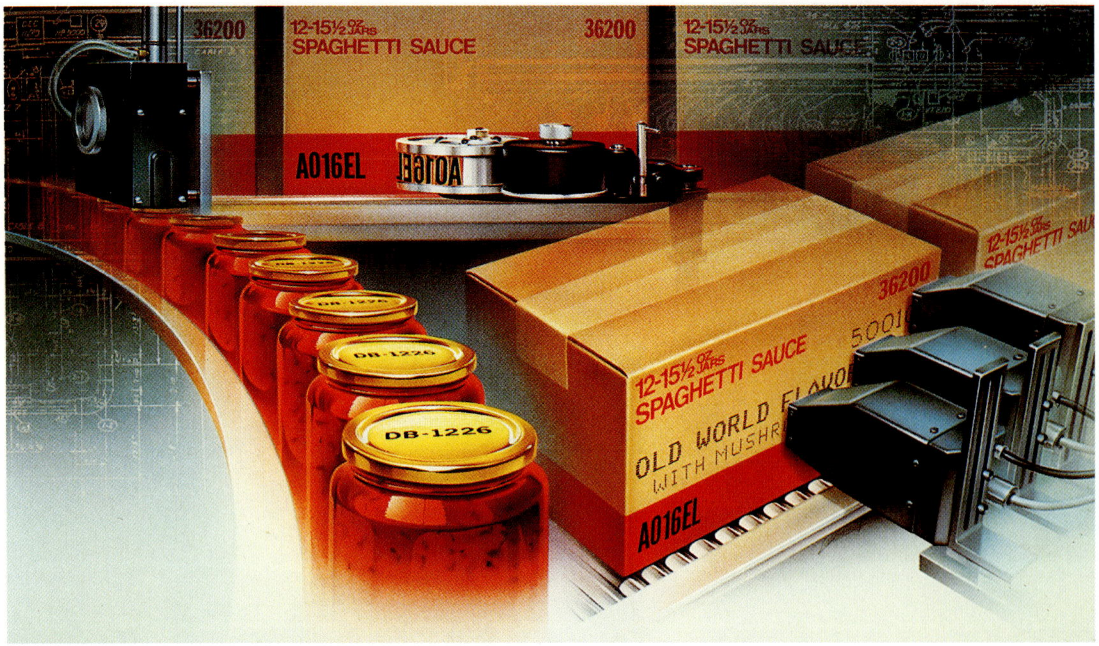

2

1
Artist Lonnie Busch
Title Mug Float
Media Used Acrylic

2
Artist Lonnie Busch
Title Miller Guitar
Media Used Acrylic

3
Artist Lonnie Busch
Title Bud Light Sand Castle
Media Used Acrylic

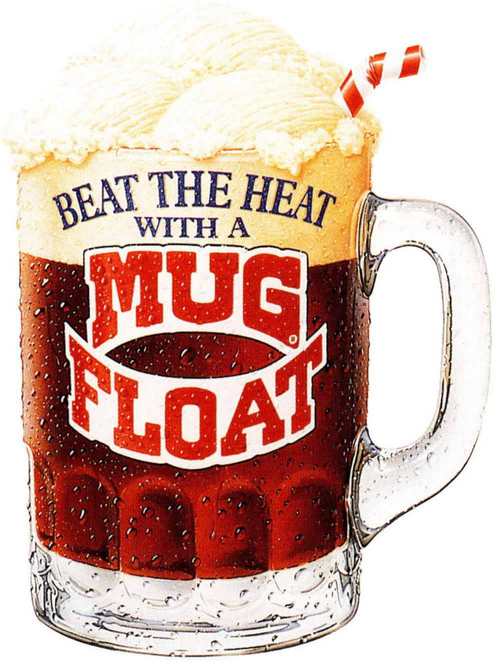

1

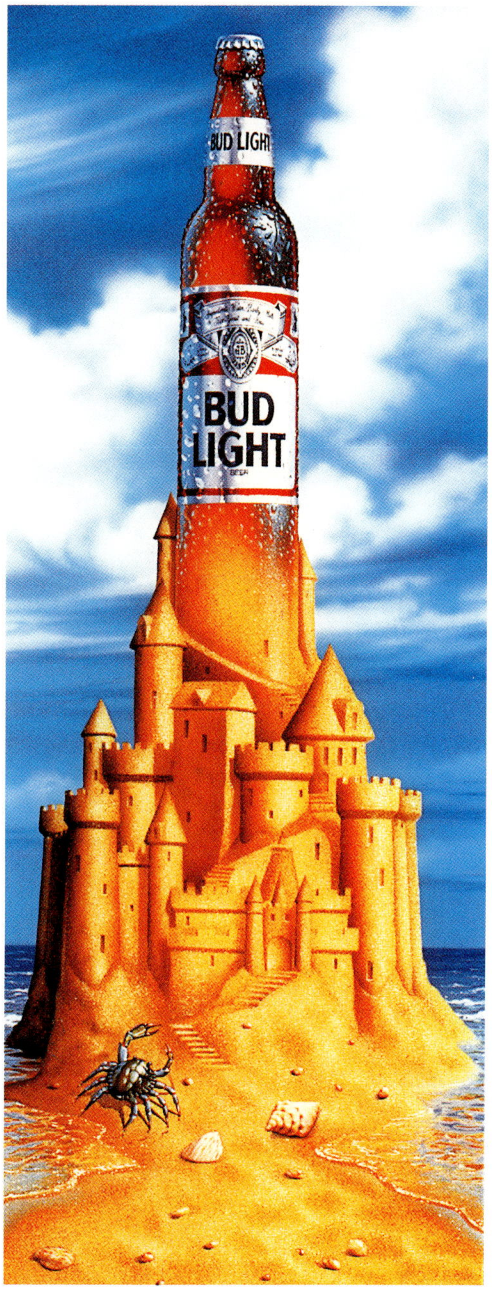

3

2

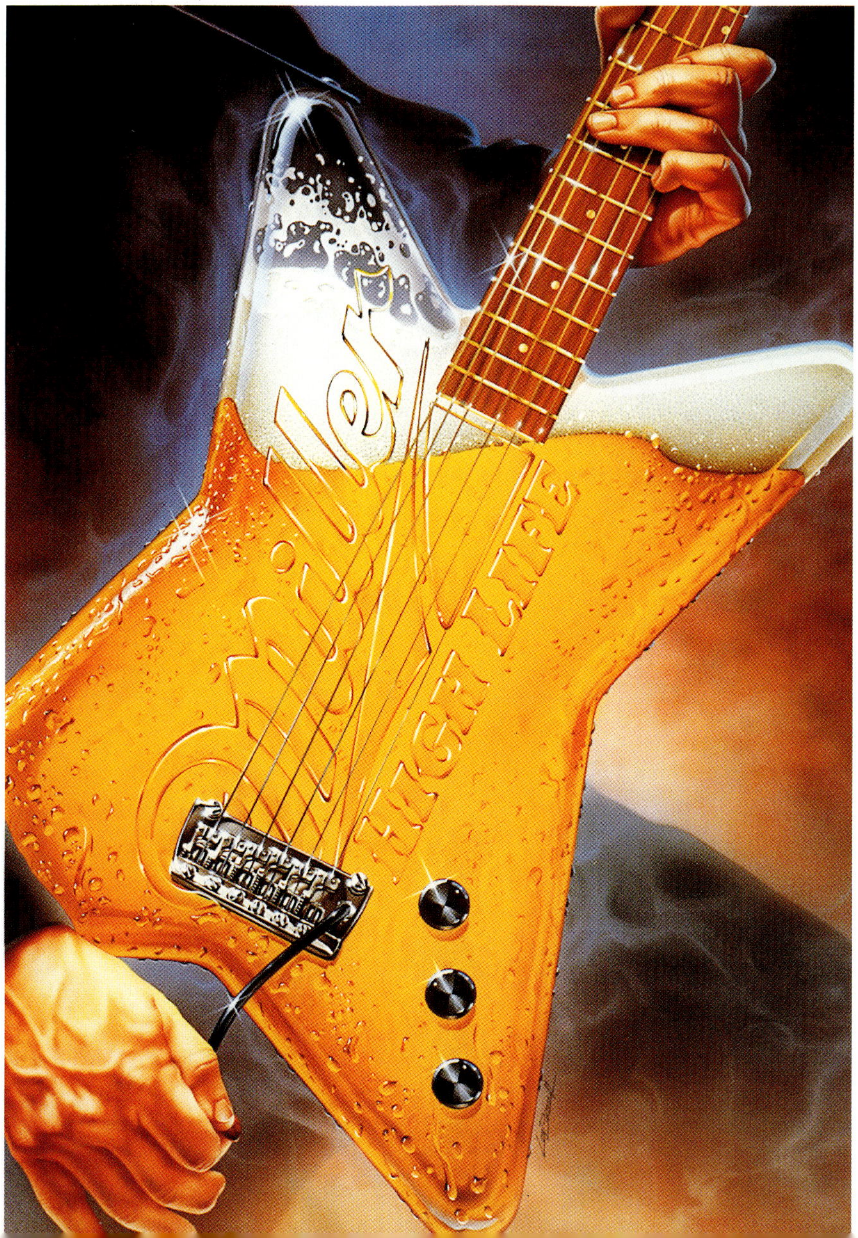

1
Artist Lonnie Busch
Title Elephant Malt Liquor
Media Used Acrylic

2
Artist Lonnie Busch
Title 7 UP Skier
Media Used Acrylic

1

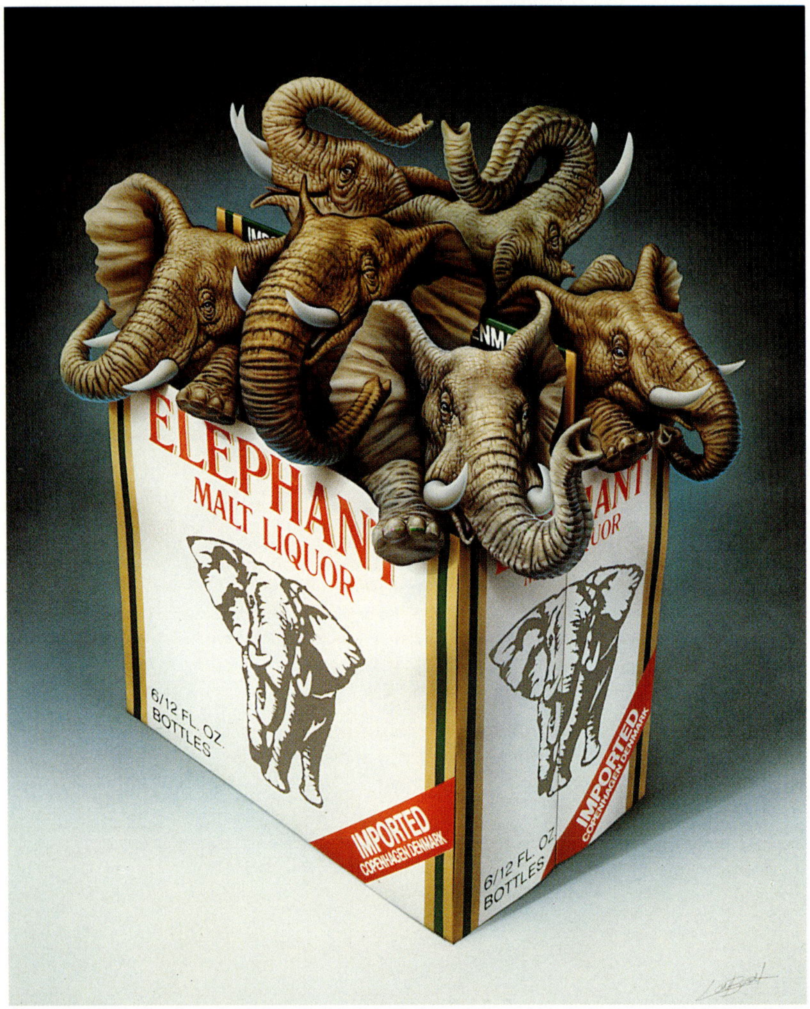

2

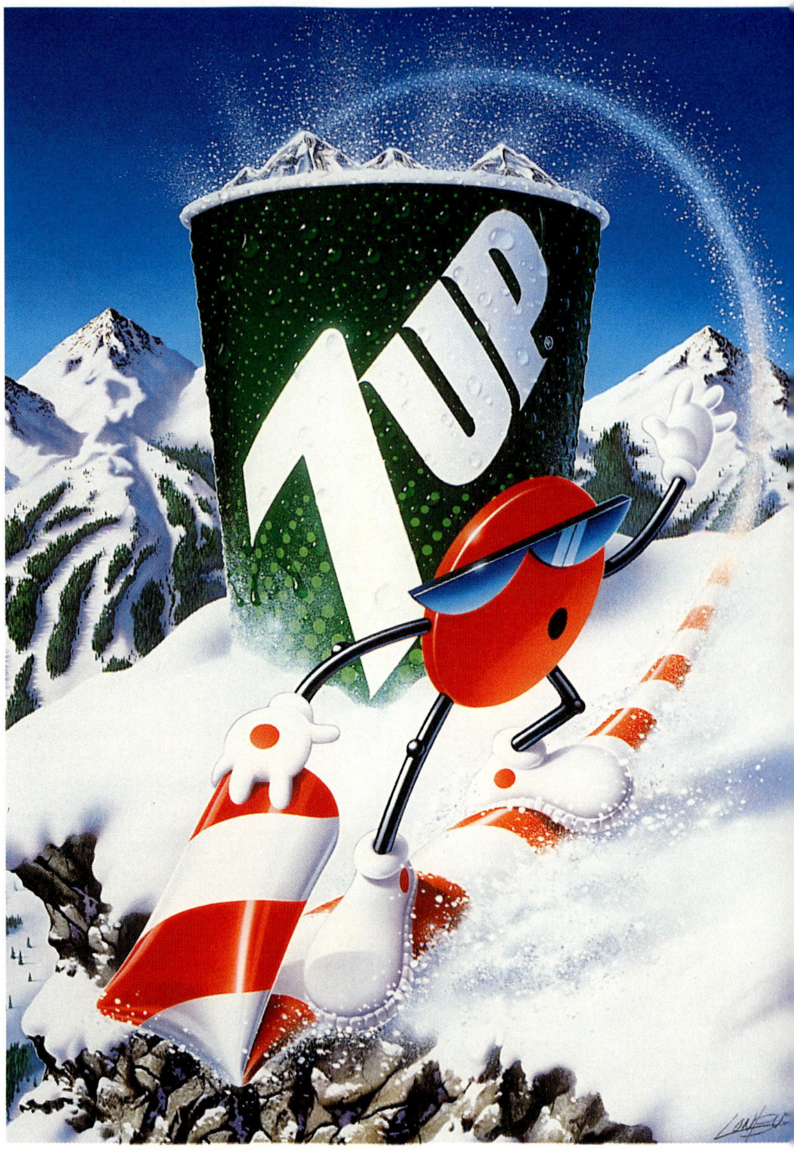

1
Artist Lonnie Busch
Title Pinnochio
Media Acrylic

2
Artist Lonnie Busch
Title Miller Genuine Draft
Media Used Acrylic

3
Artist Lonnie Busch
Title Taco Salad
Media Acrylic

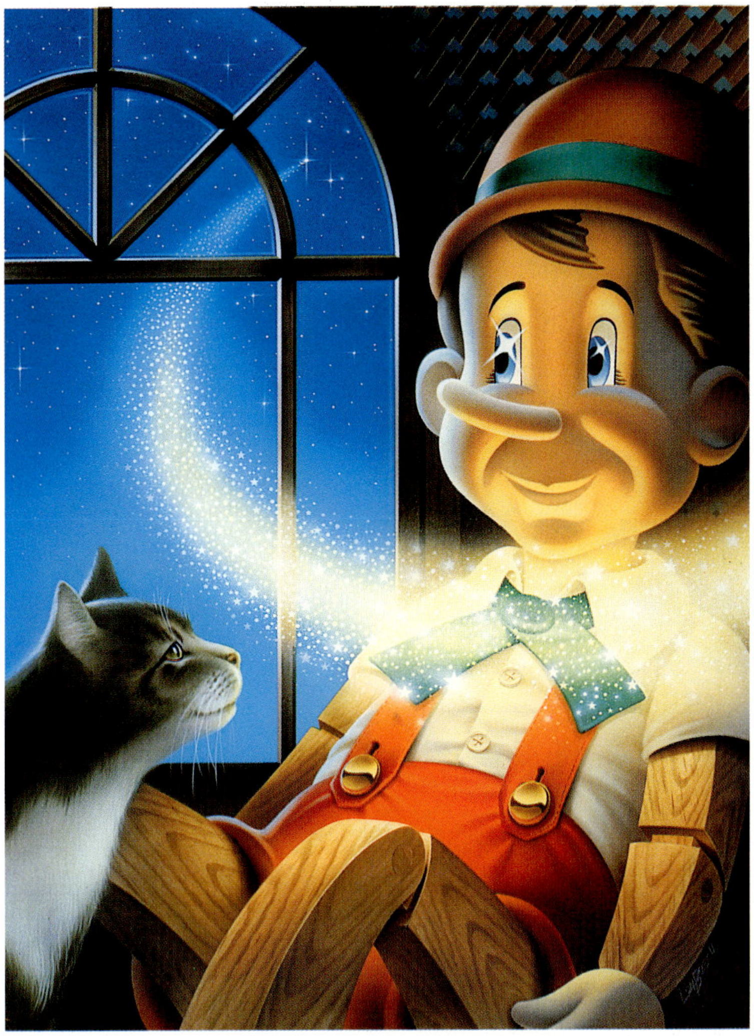

1

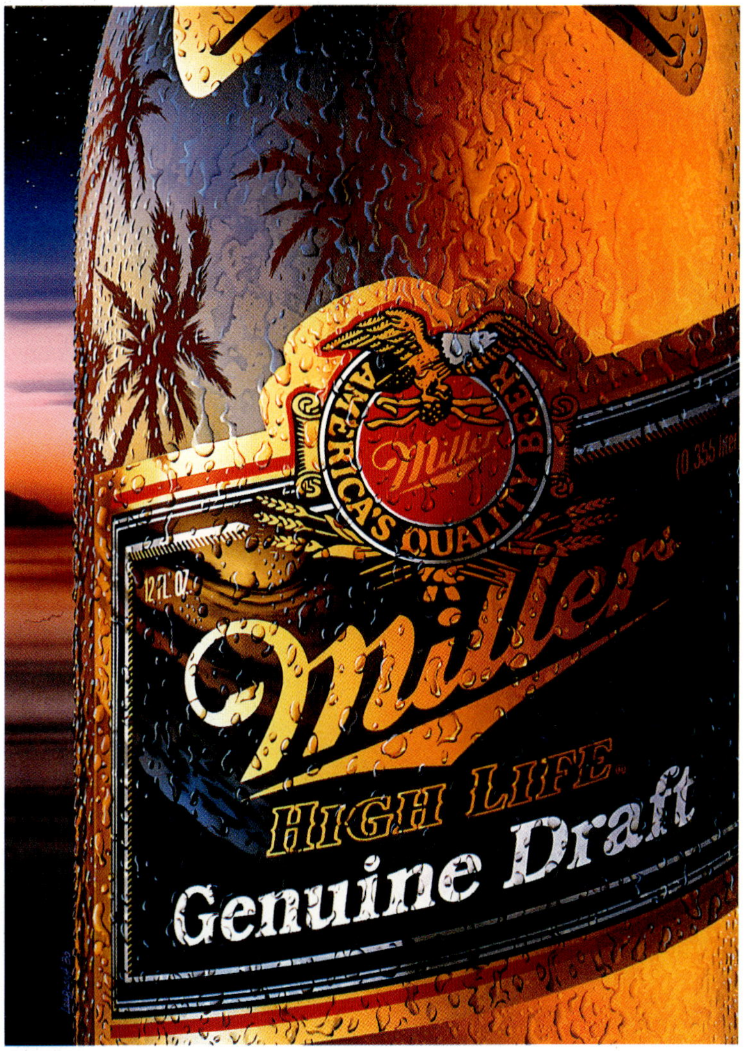

2

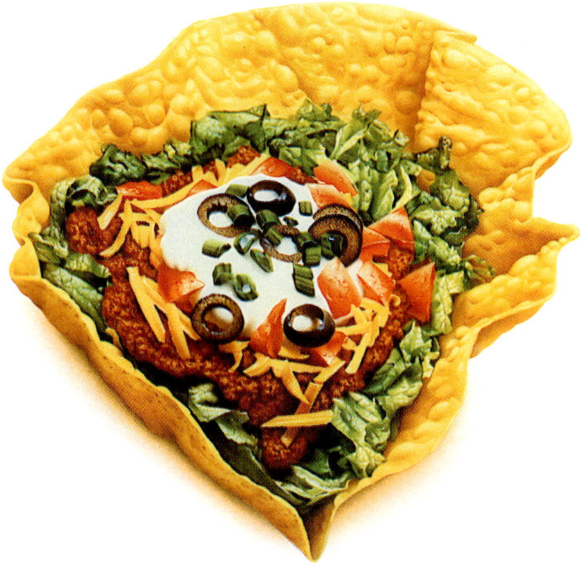

3

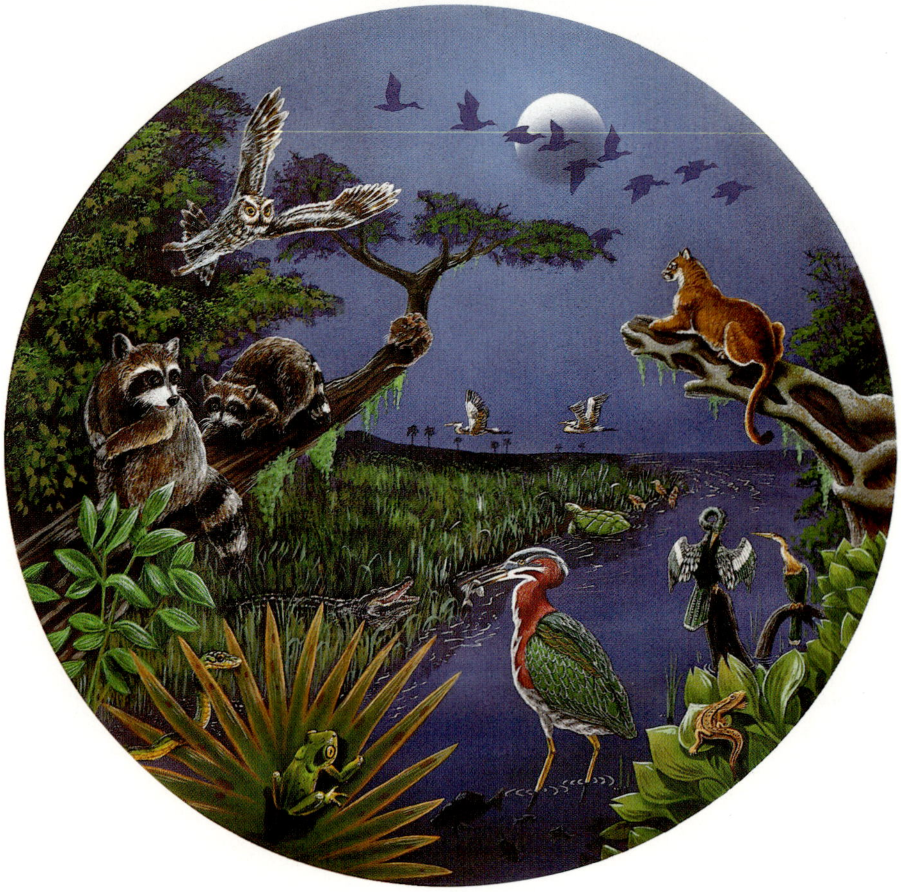

1

2

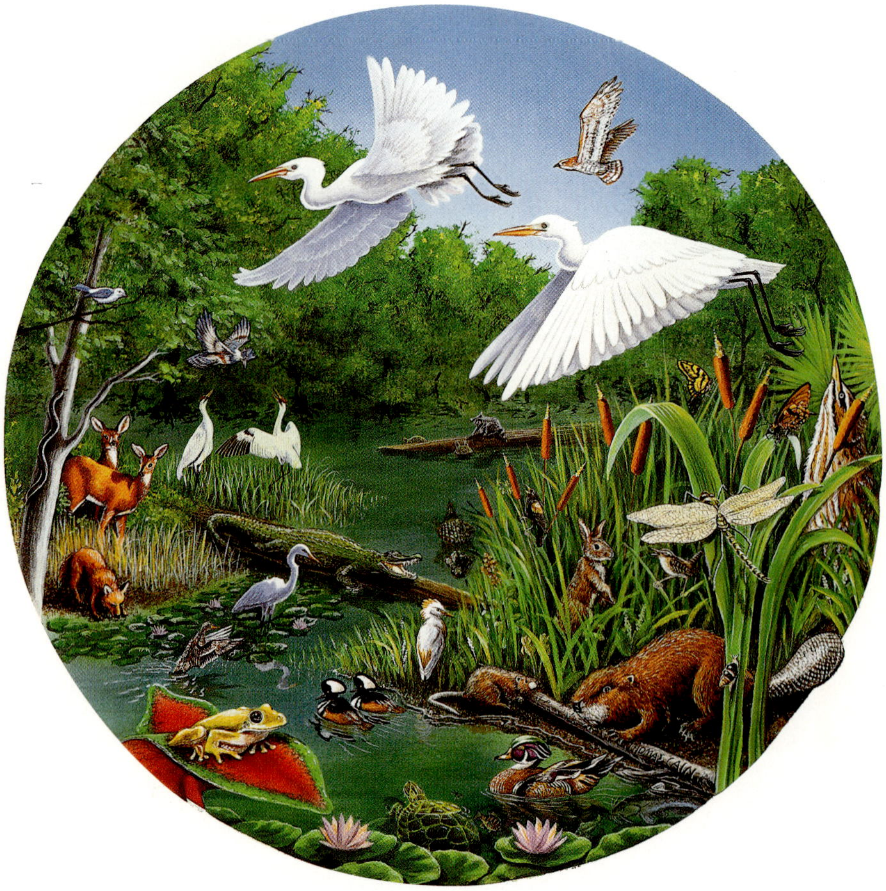

1
Artist Thomas Cain
Title Wetlands
Client Supply America, Inc.
Usage Round Tin - Inside of Lid, Night Scene
Media Used Acrylic

2
Artist Thomas Cain
Title Wetlands
Client Supply America, Inc.
Usage Round Tin - Inside & Outside of Lid Day Scene/Night Scene
Media Used Acrylic

3
Artist Thomas Cain
Client Albin-Pumps
Art Director Ian Greathead
Usage Brochure Cover
Media Used Acrylic

4
Artist Thomas Cain
Client Weyerhaeuser Paper Co.
Usage Crate for Strawberries
Media Used Acrylic

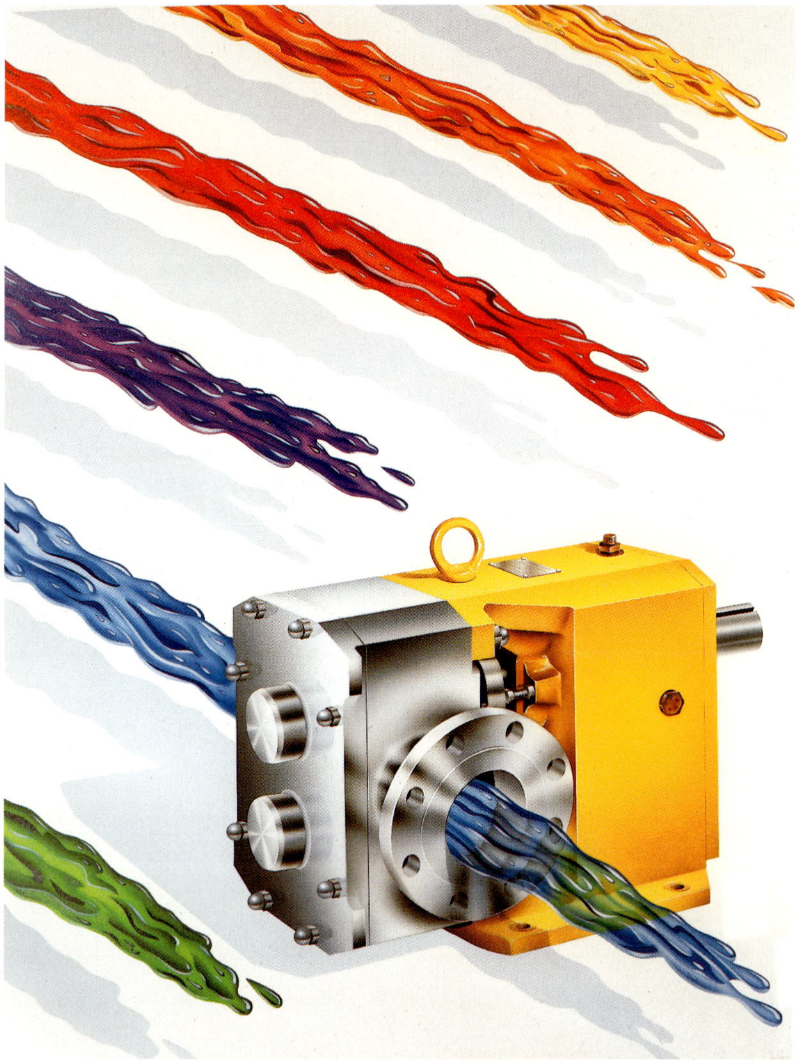

3

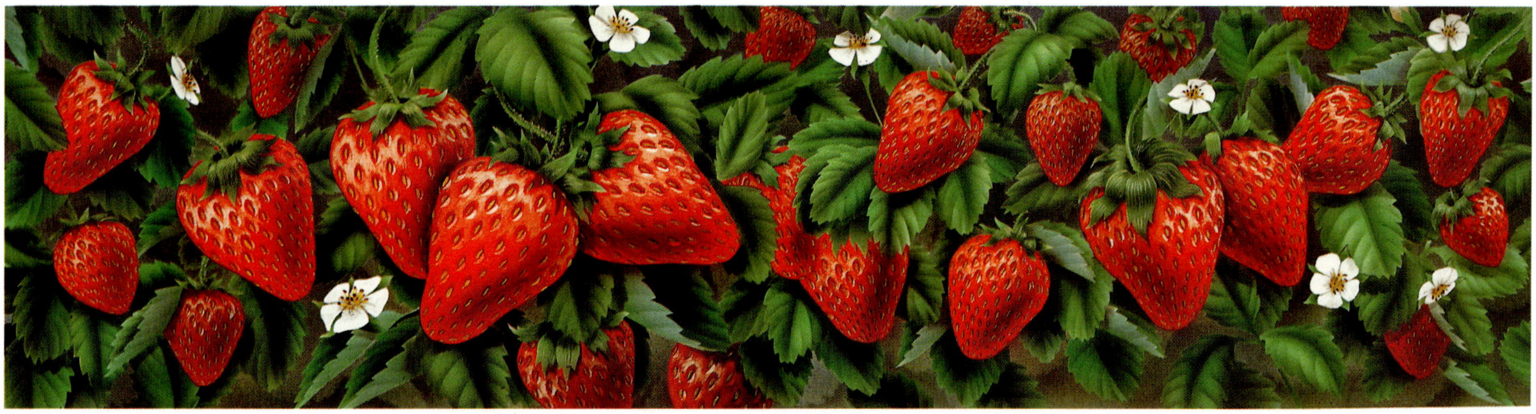

4

1
Artist Thomas Cain
Title BCFX (Breakstone Cain Special Effects)
Client Breakstone Cain Printing Co.
Art Director Trousdell Design
Usage Promotion for Printing Co.
Media Used Acrylic

2
Artist Thomas Cain
Client J.L. Clark
Usage TIN (Top & Sides)
Media Used Acrylic

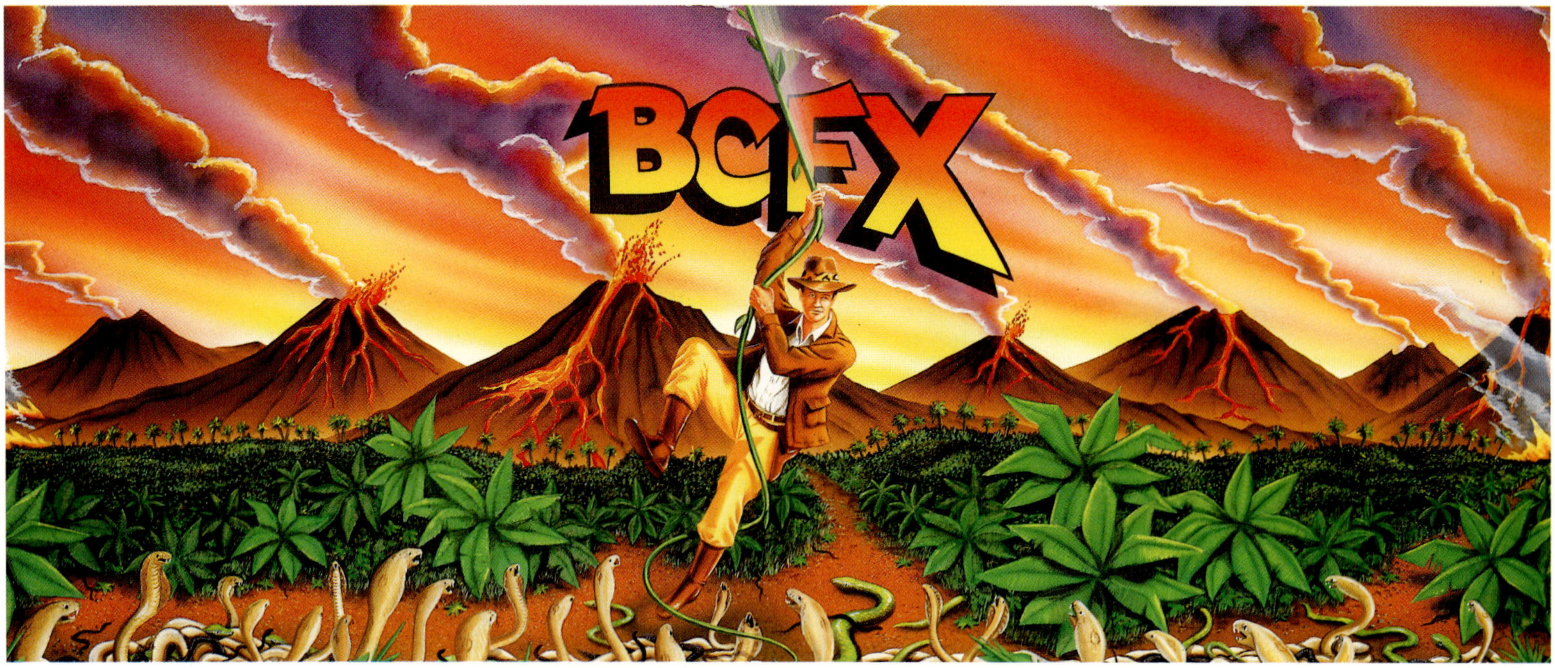

1

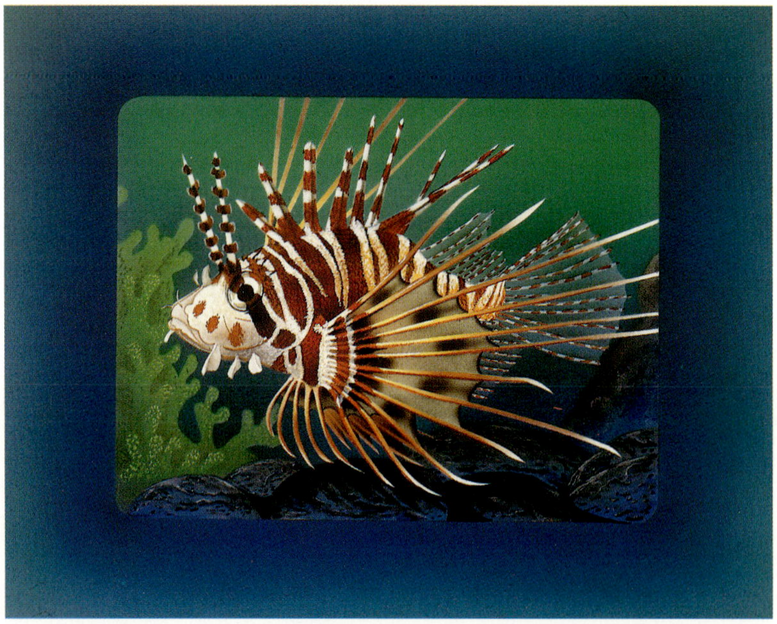

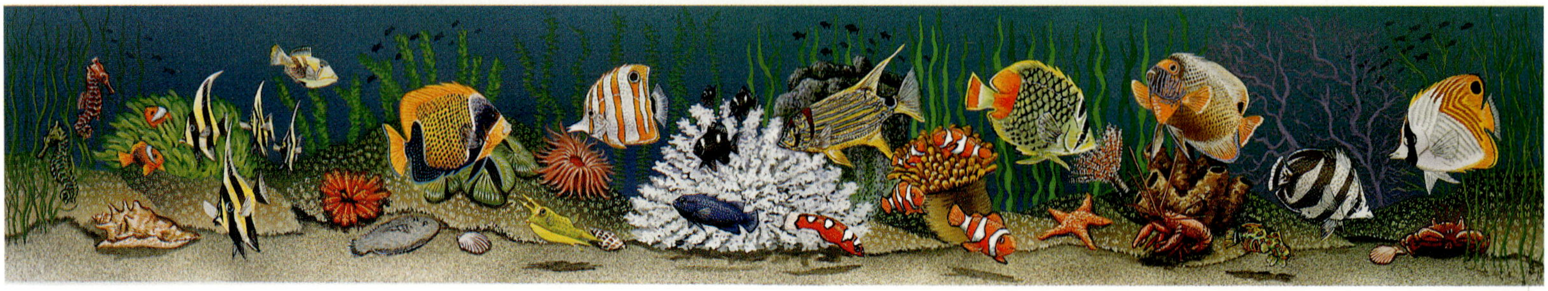

2

1
Artist Thomas Cain
Client Coca-Cola
Art Director Trousdell Design
Usage Promo for Magic Cup Game
Media Used Acrylic

2
Artist Thomas Cain
Title Canadian Rock & Roll
Usage Editorial
Media Used Acrylic

3
Artist Kurt Carloni
Client Centercom
Art Director Jurgen Strigenz
Usage Video Box Cover
Media Used Spectralite Airbrush Color

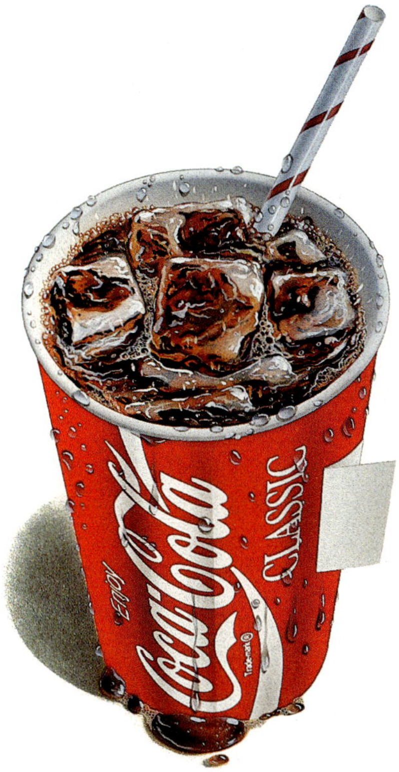

1

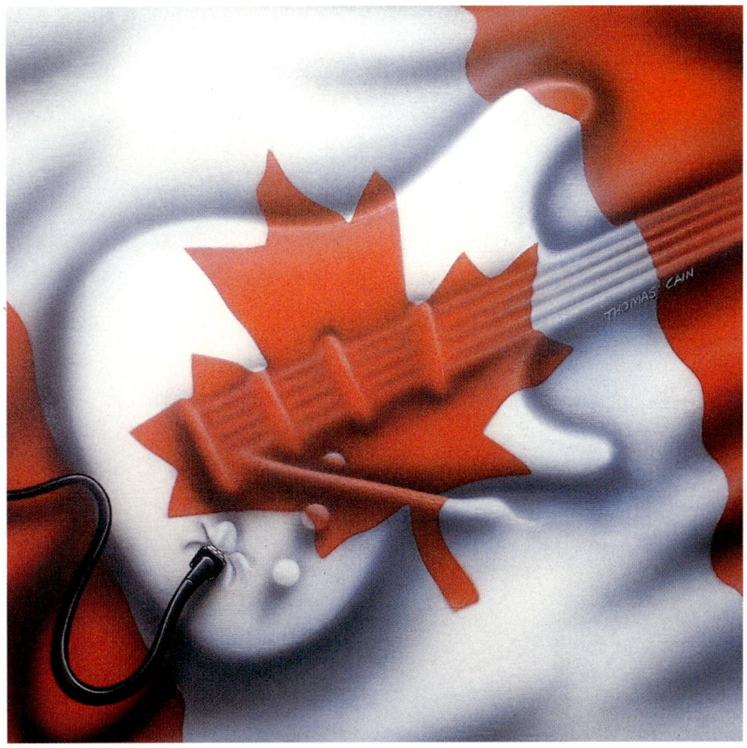

2

3

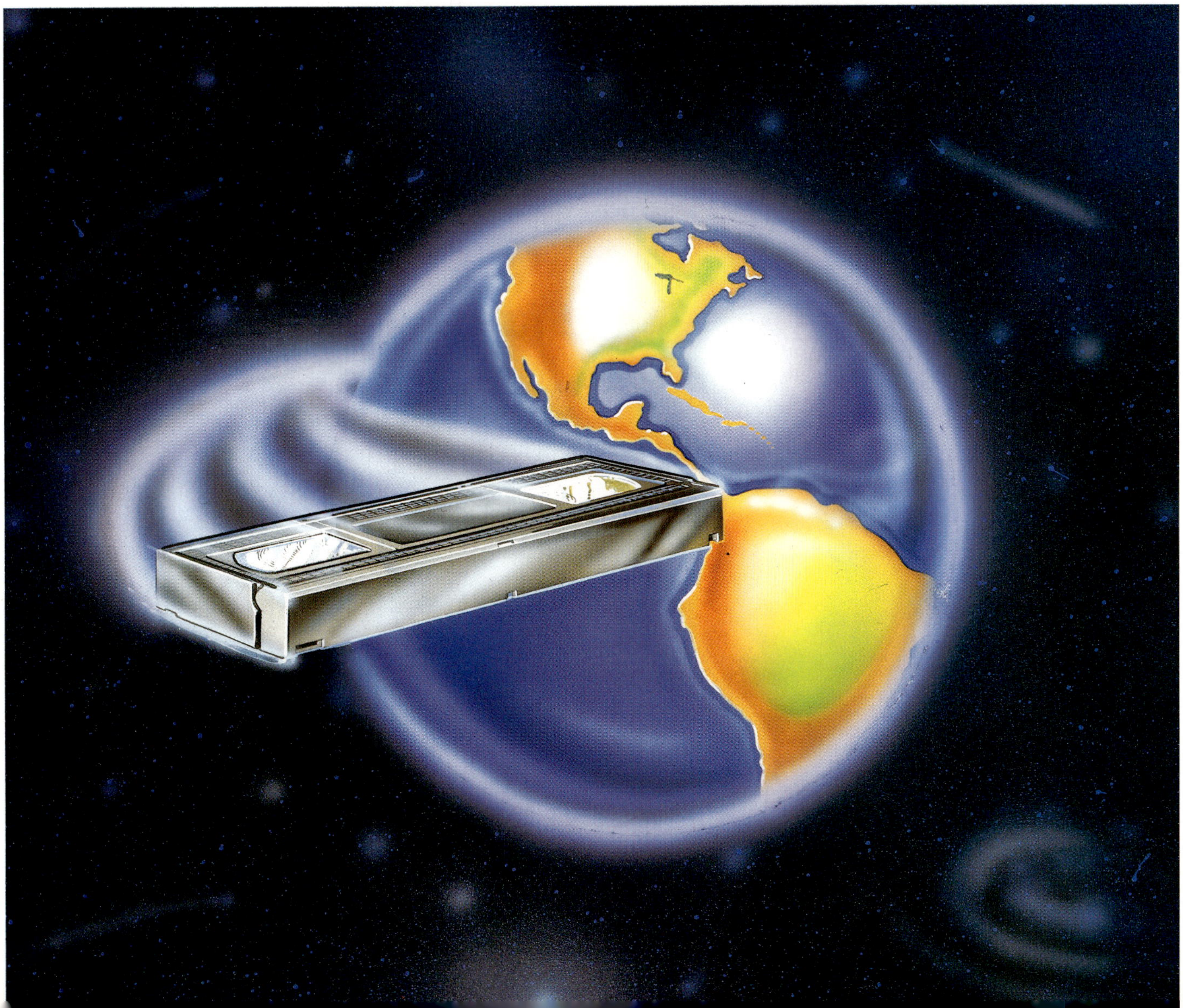

1
Artist Kurt Carloni
Usage Self Promotion
Media Used Spectralite Colors

2
Artist Kurt Carloni
Client Generac
Art Director Paul Wold
Usage Advertising
Media Used Spectralite Colors

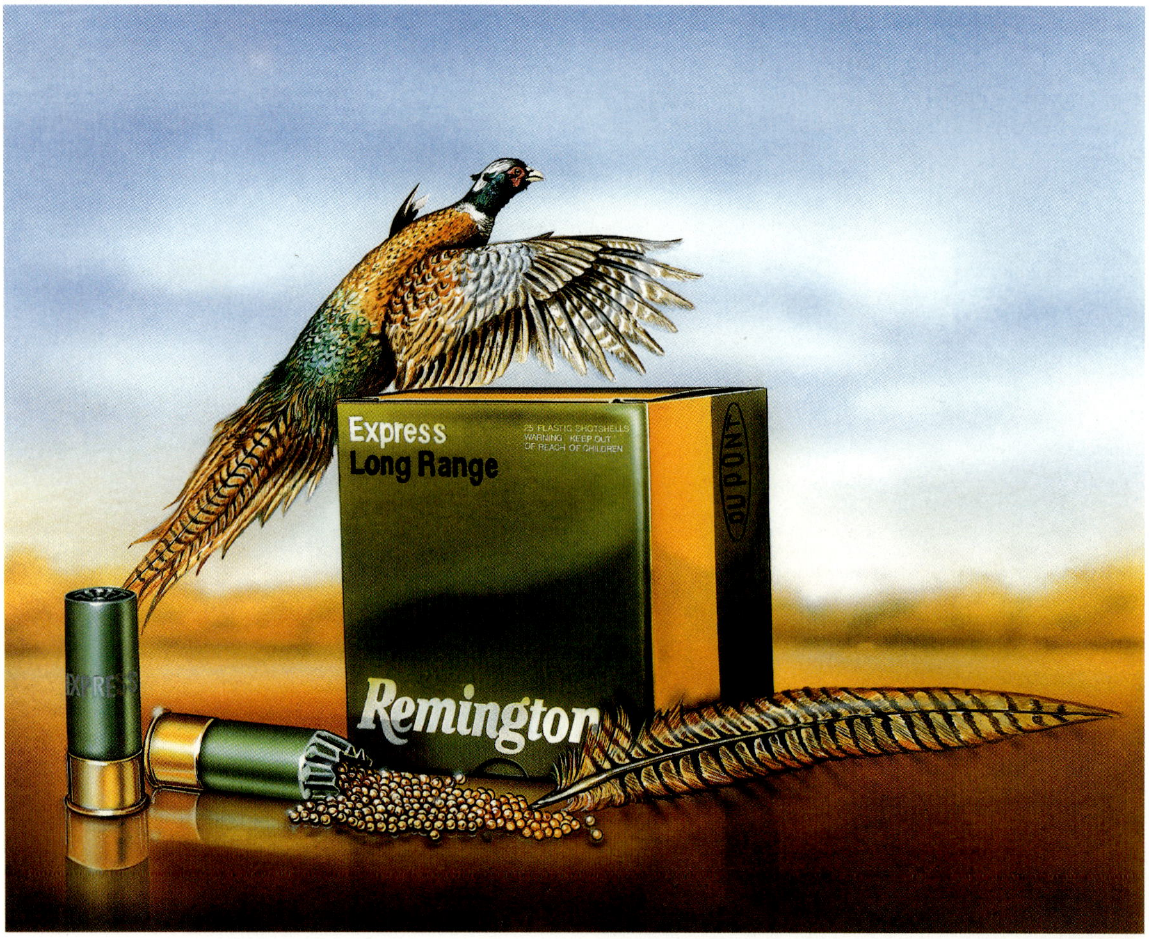

1

2

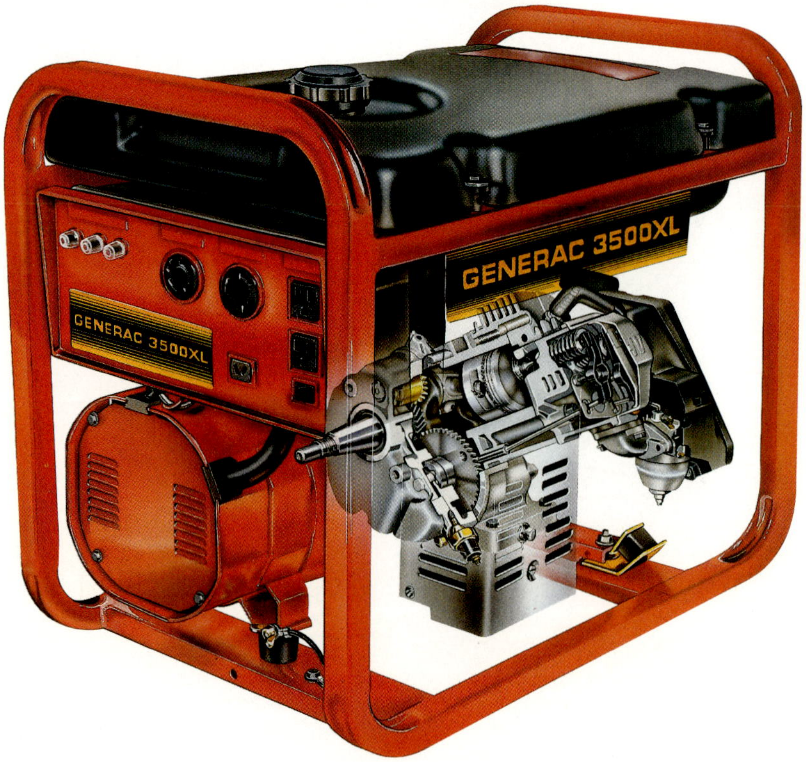

1
Artist Kurt Carloni
Title Harley Davidson Engine
Client Pholman Studio
Art Director Bob Mossle
Usage Display
Media Used Spectralite Colors

2
Artist Martin Castillo
Title Turkey Dinner
Instructor Mark Regalado
Usage Student Art
Media Used Acrylic

3
Artist Gary Ciccarelli
Title French & Indian War
Usage Self Promotion
Media Used Gouache, Colored Pencil

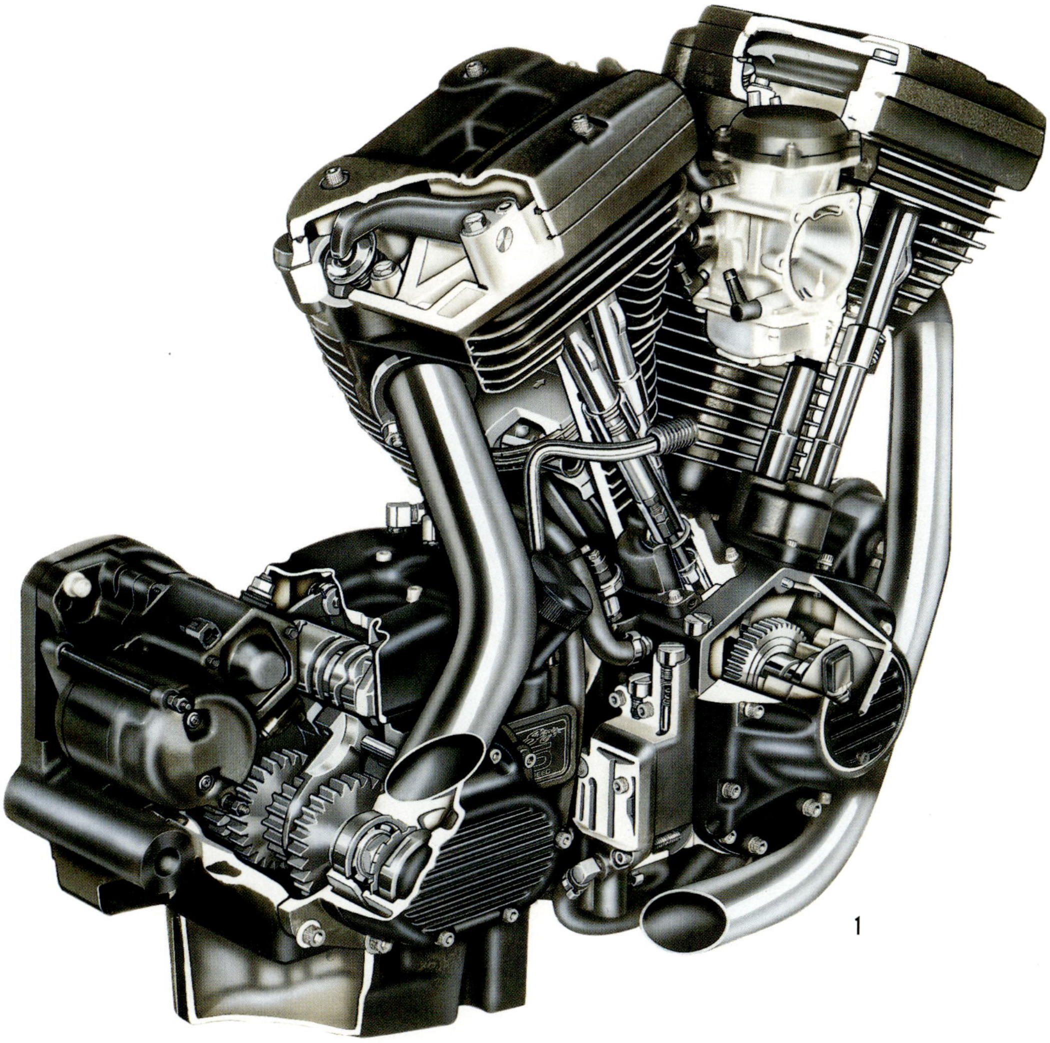

1

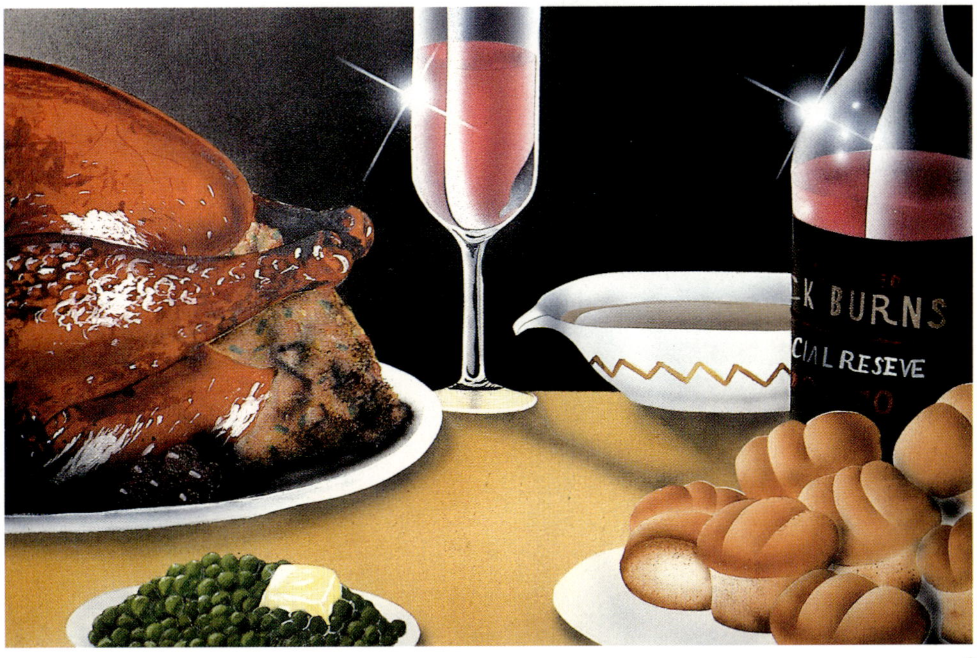

2

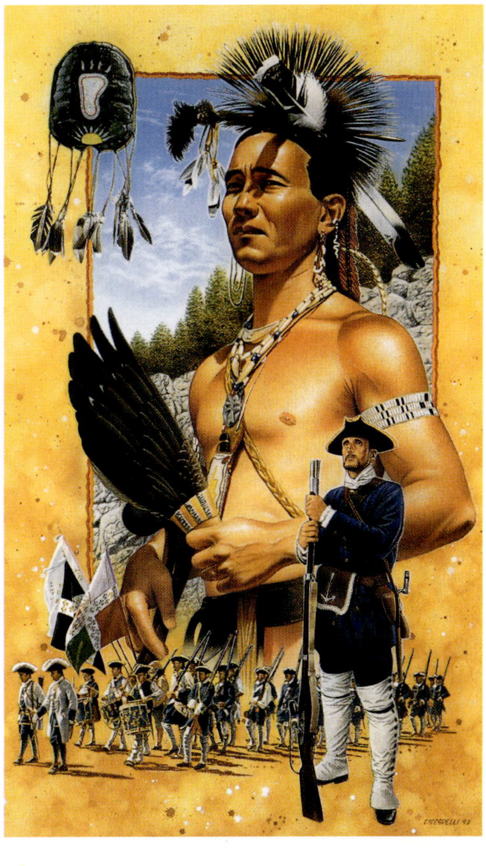

3

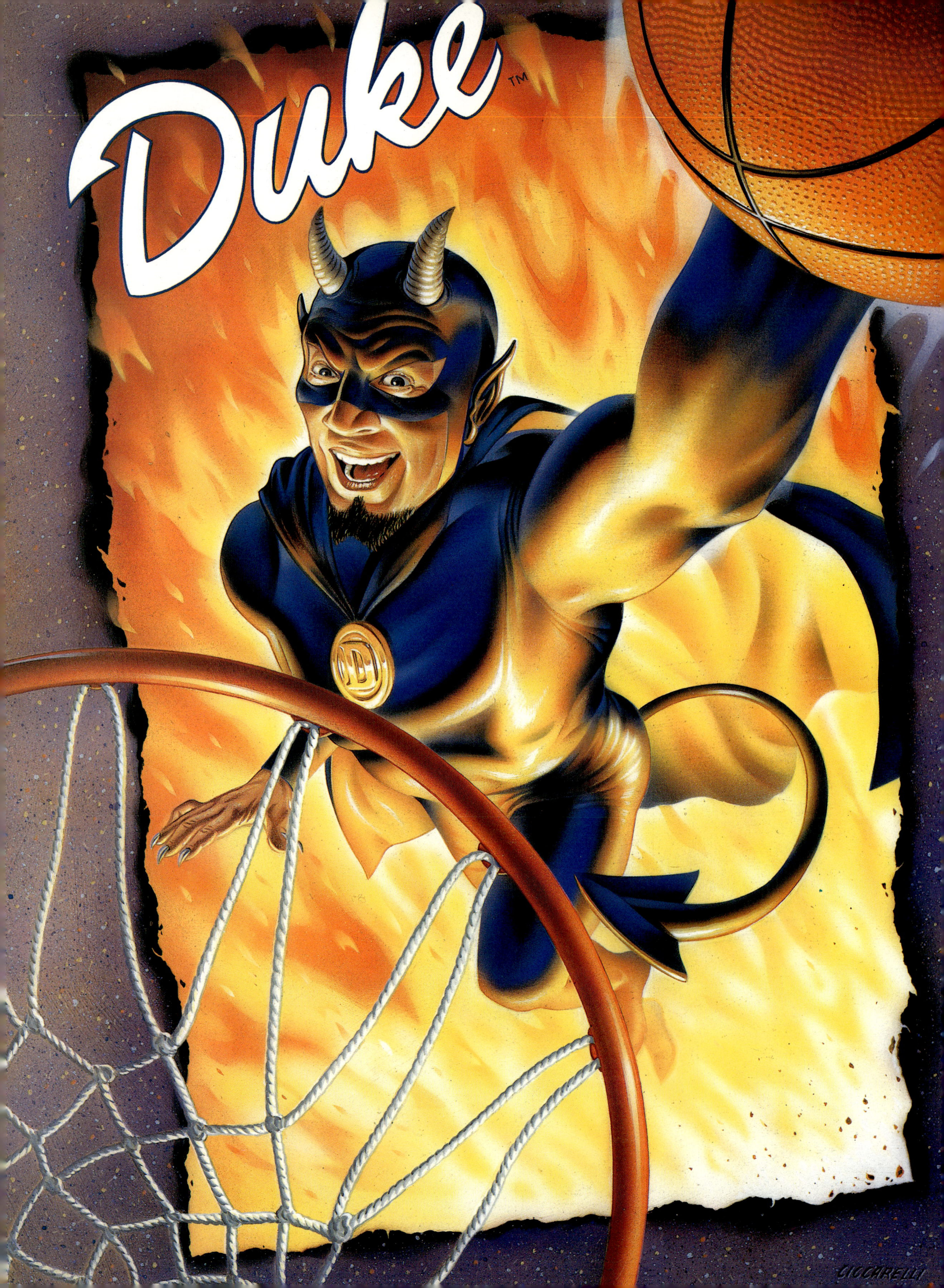
Duke™
CICCARELLI

1
Artist Gary Ciccarelli
Title Duke Blue Devils
Client Mascart
Art Director Mike Mendelsohn
Usage College Poster
Media Used Gouache

2
Artist Gary Ciccarelli
Title Tropical Fantasy
Client Brooklyn Bottling Co.
Art Director George Guinte
Usage Print Advertisment
Media Used Gouache, Colored Pencil

3
Artist Gary Ciccarelli
Title Brando
Client CBS Fox Video
Art Director Ron Rae
Usage Poster for Brando Videos
Media Used Gouache, Colored Pencil.

4
Artist Gary Ciccarelli
Title Elvis
Client River Group
Art Director Joe Mauro
Usage Elvis Cards Promotion
Media Used Gouache, Colored Pencil

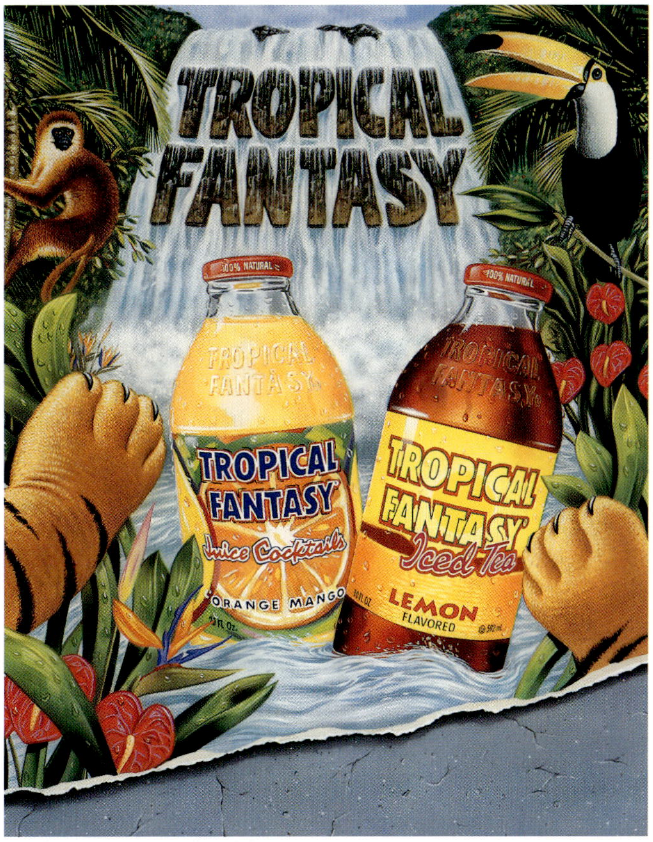

2

3

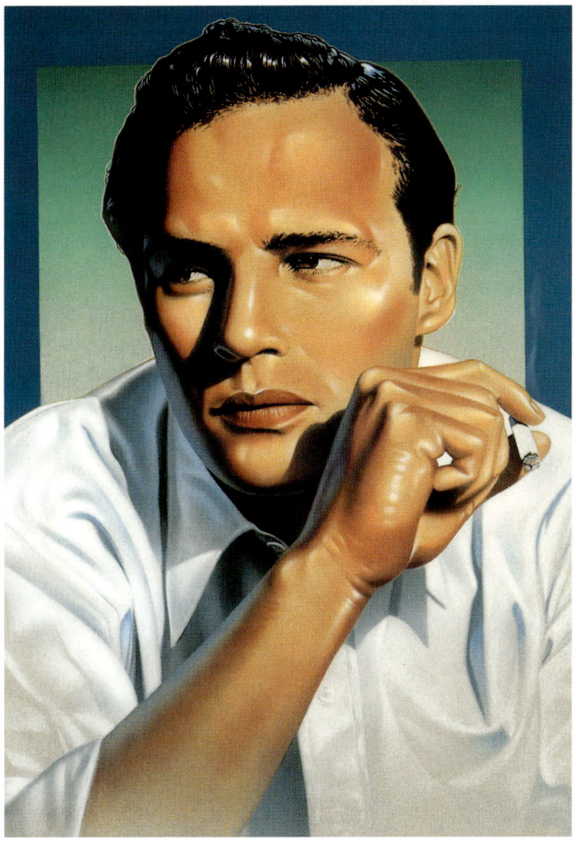

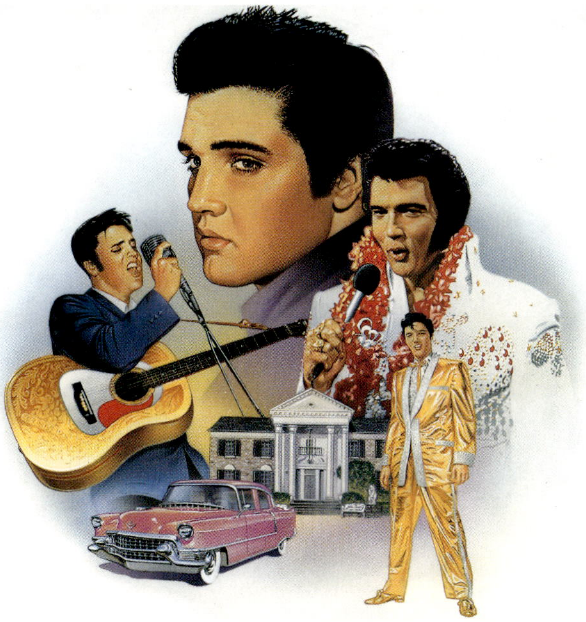

4

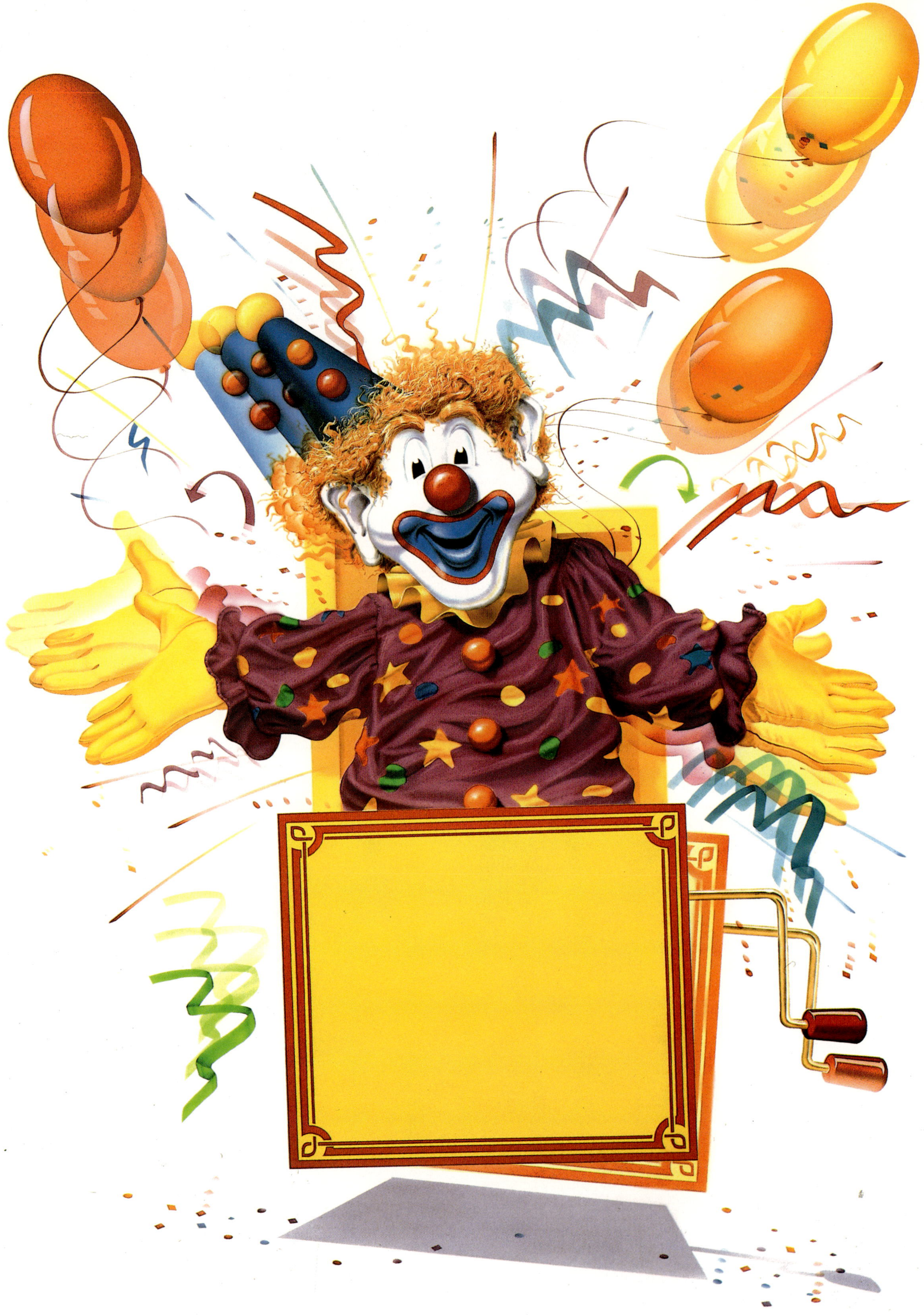

1
Artist Mick Coulas
Title Happy Humphry
Client National Trust
Art Director Ian Cruckshank
Usage Aniversary Poster

2
Artist Mick Coulas
Title The Brews Brothers TM.
Client Brews Brothers Coffee Corp
Art Director Andrew MauUsage Packaging & Logo

3
Artist Mick Coulas
Title Super Snack Team
Client Hostess Frito Way
Art Director Paul Galler
Usage Point of Sale

4
Artist Mick Coulas
Title Berry Blue
Client Kraft General Foods
Art Director Chue Parks / Micmael Paitich
Usage Jello Package

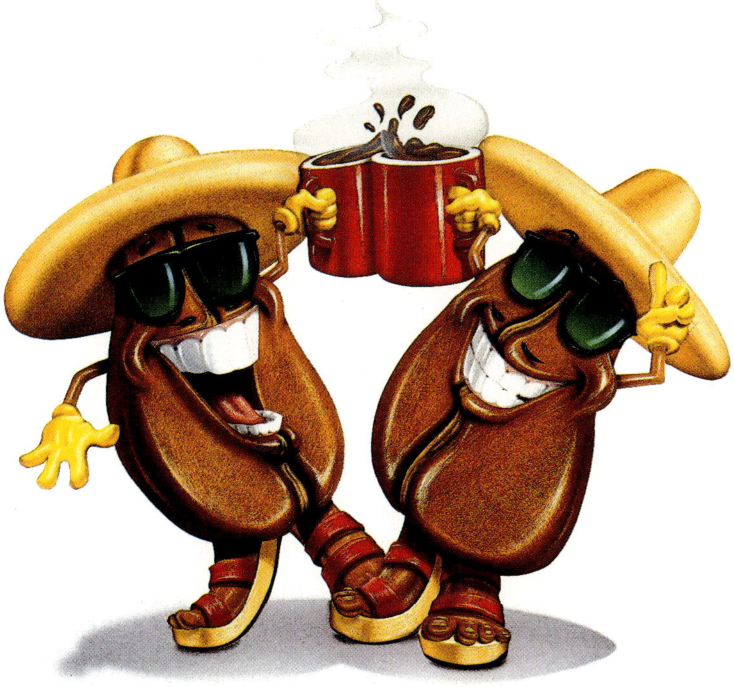

2

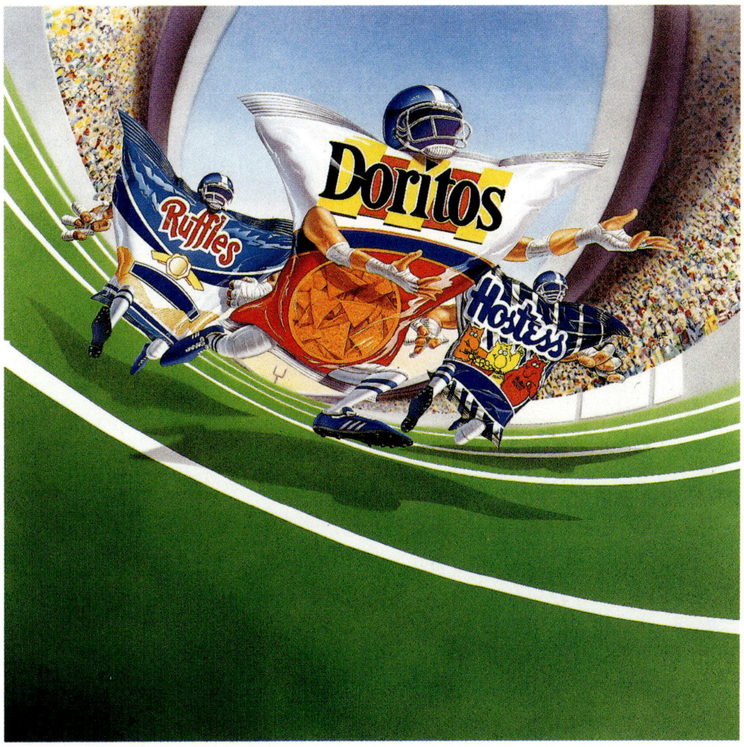

4

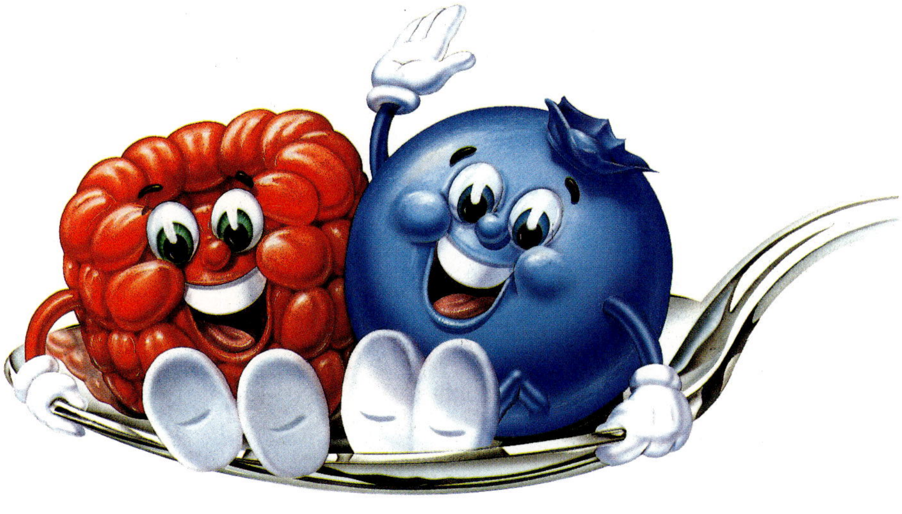

1
Artist Philip H. Campbell
Title Our New American Dream
Usage Fine Art
Media Used Liquitex & Badger Acrylics

2
Artist David Crowe
Title Subpopsublime
Usage Fine Art
Media Used Mixed

3
Artist David Crowe
Title Chemistry
Usage Fine Art
Media Used Mixed Acrylic

4
Artist David Crowe
Title Enigma
Usage Fine Art
Media Used Mixed

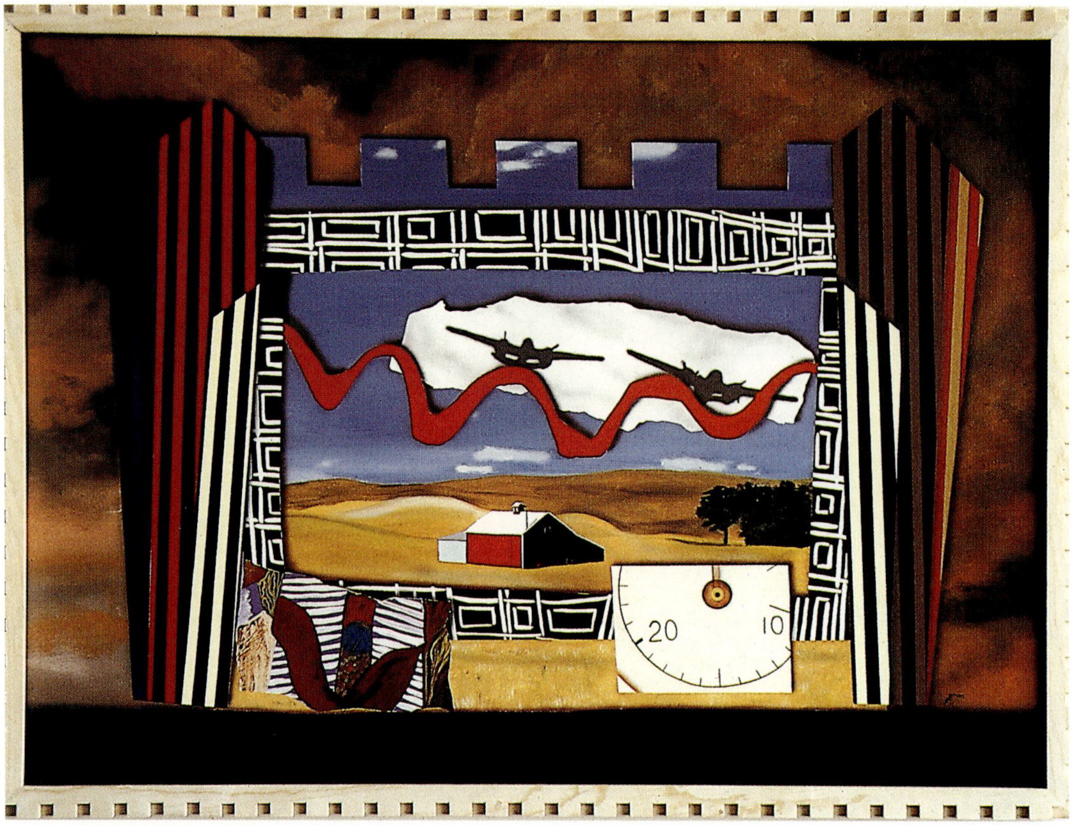

1

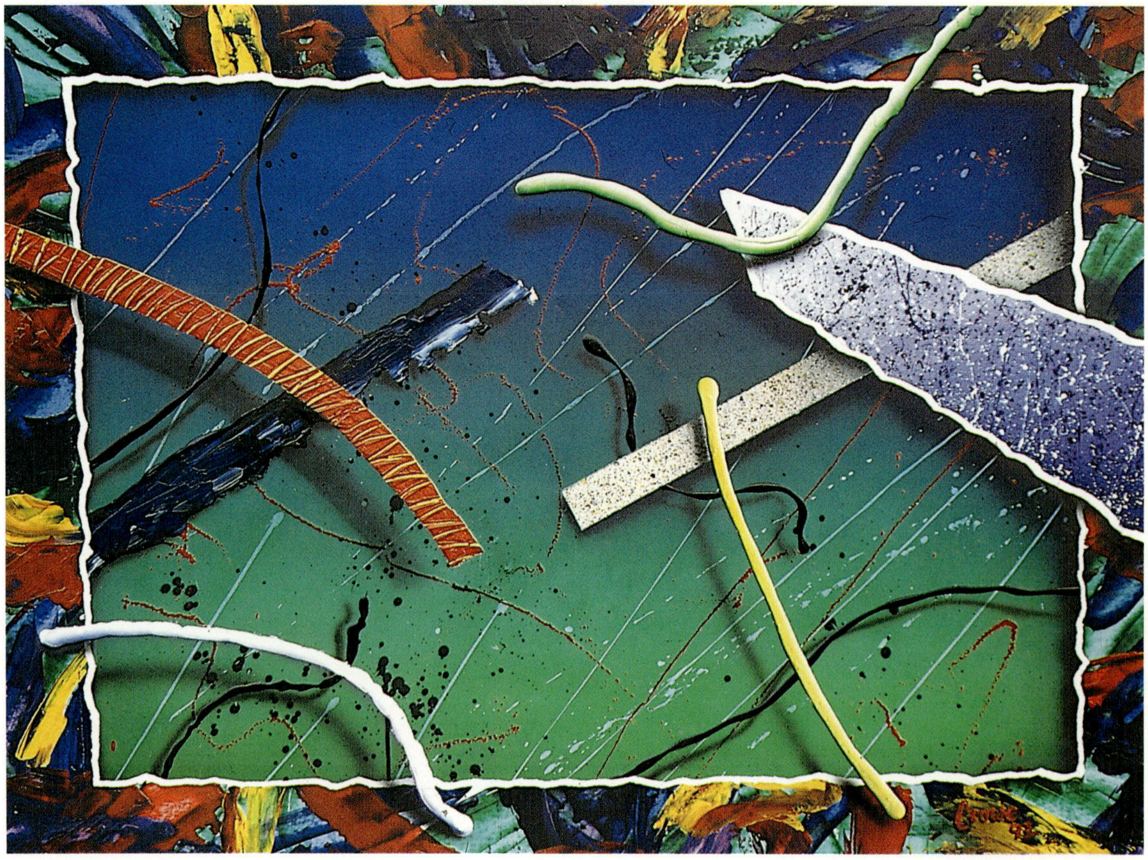

2

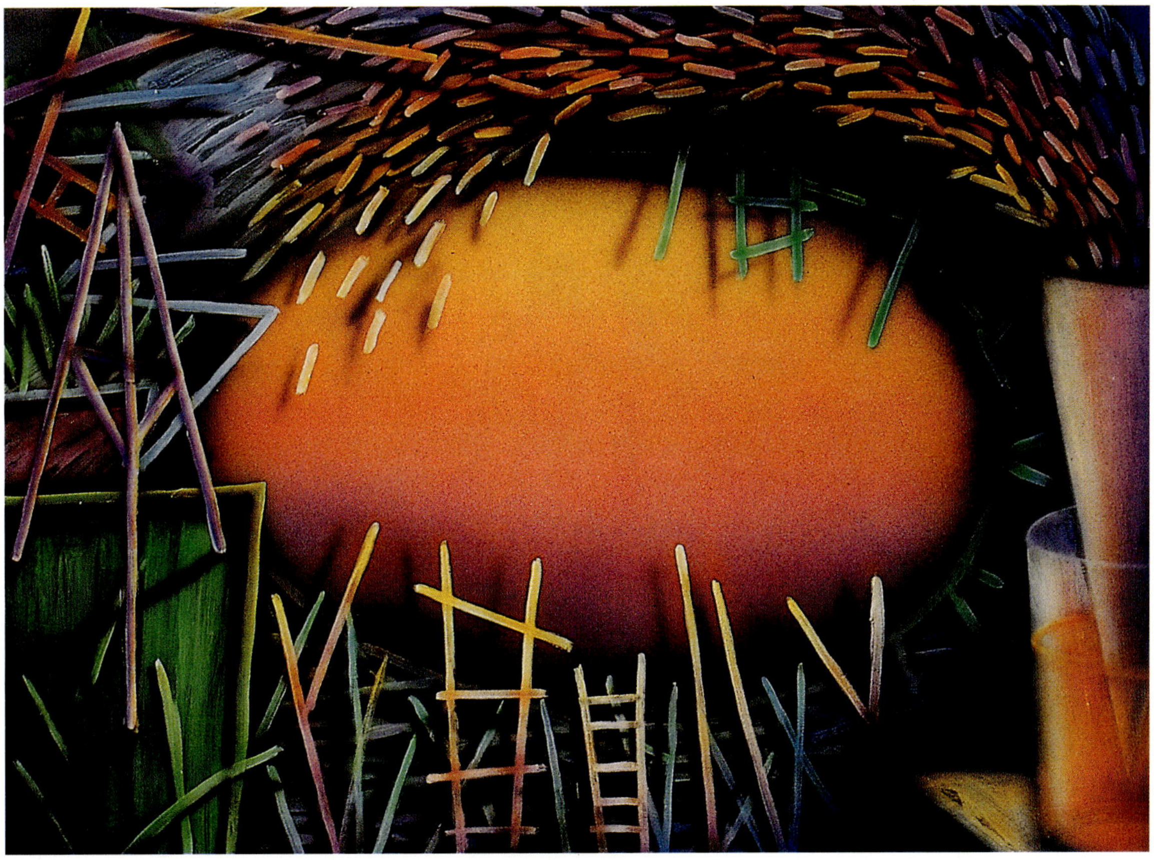

3

4

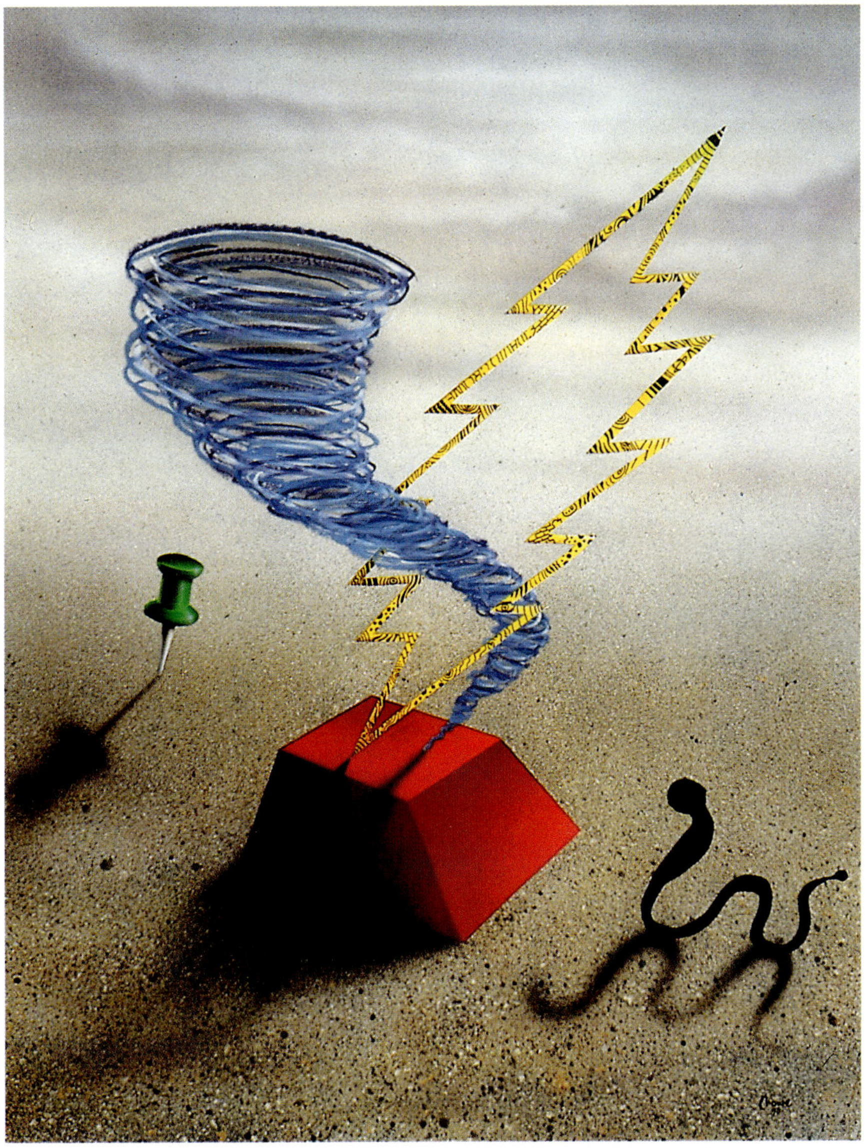

1
Artist David Crowe
Title Spontaneous Atmosphere
Client Private Collection
Usage Fine Art
Media Used Mixed

2
Artist David Crowe
Title Exploding Plastic Inevitable
Client Carmel Clay Schools Collections
Usage Fine Art
Media Used Mixed

3
Artist David Crowe
Title Don't Like It? I'm Crazy for It
Usage Fine Art
Media Used Mixed Acrylic, Enamel

4
Artist David Crowe
Title Spectre of Sex Appeal
Usage Fine Art
Media Used Mixed

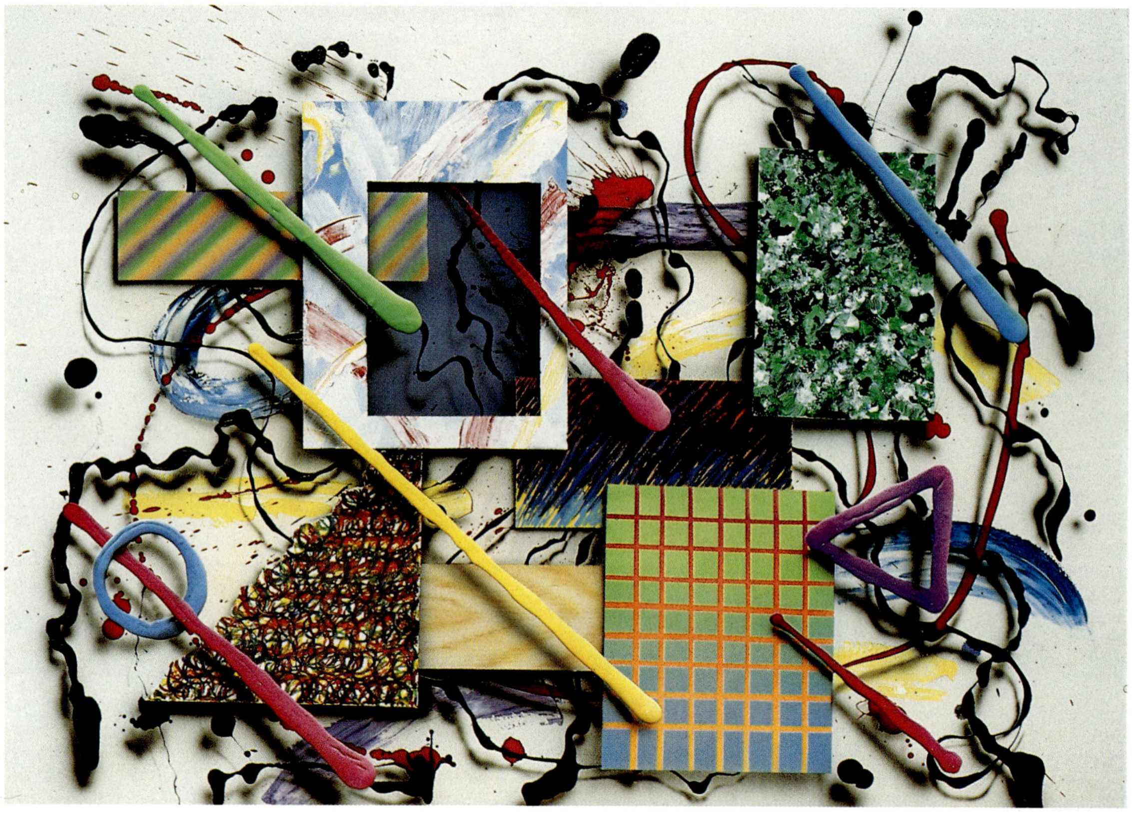

1

2

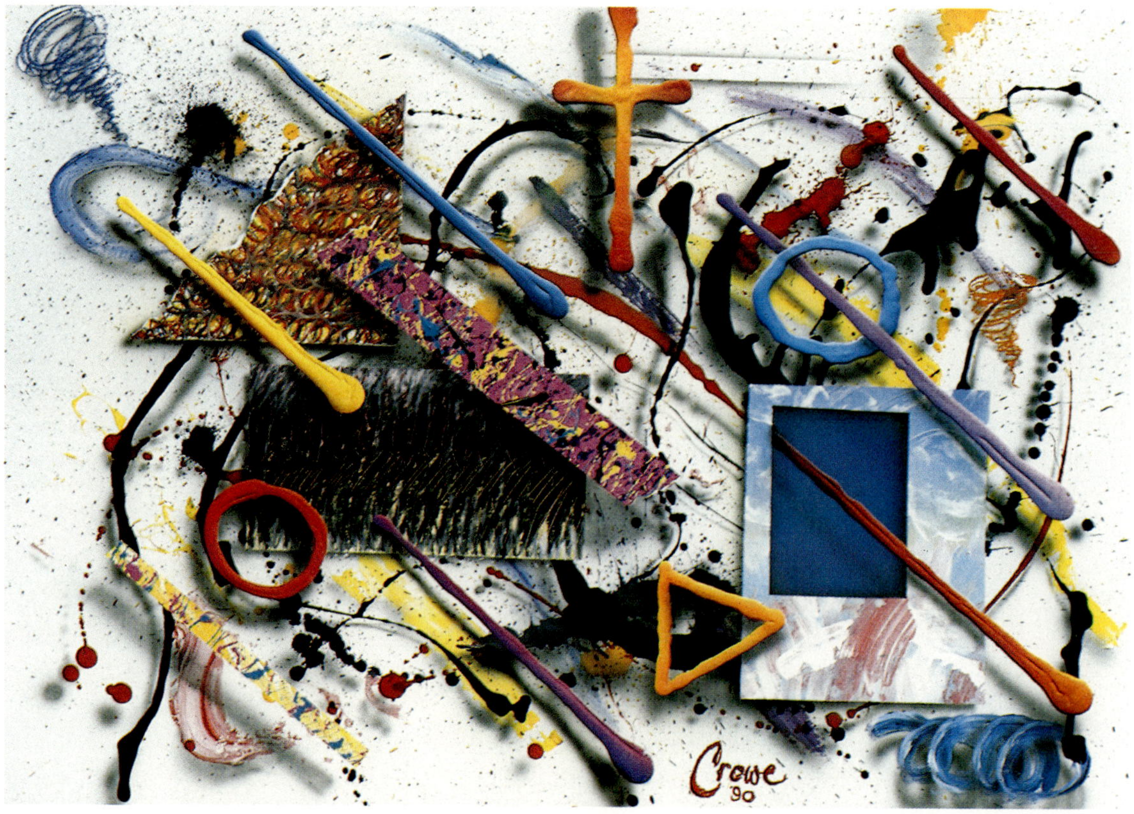

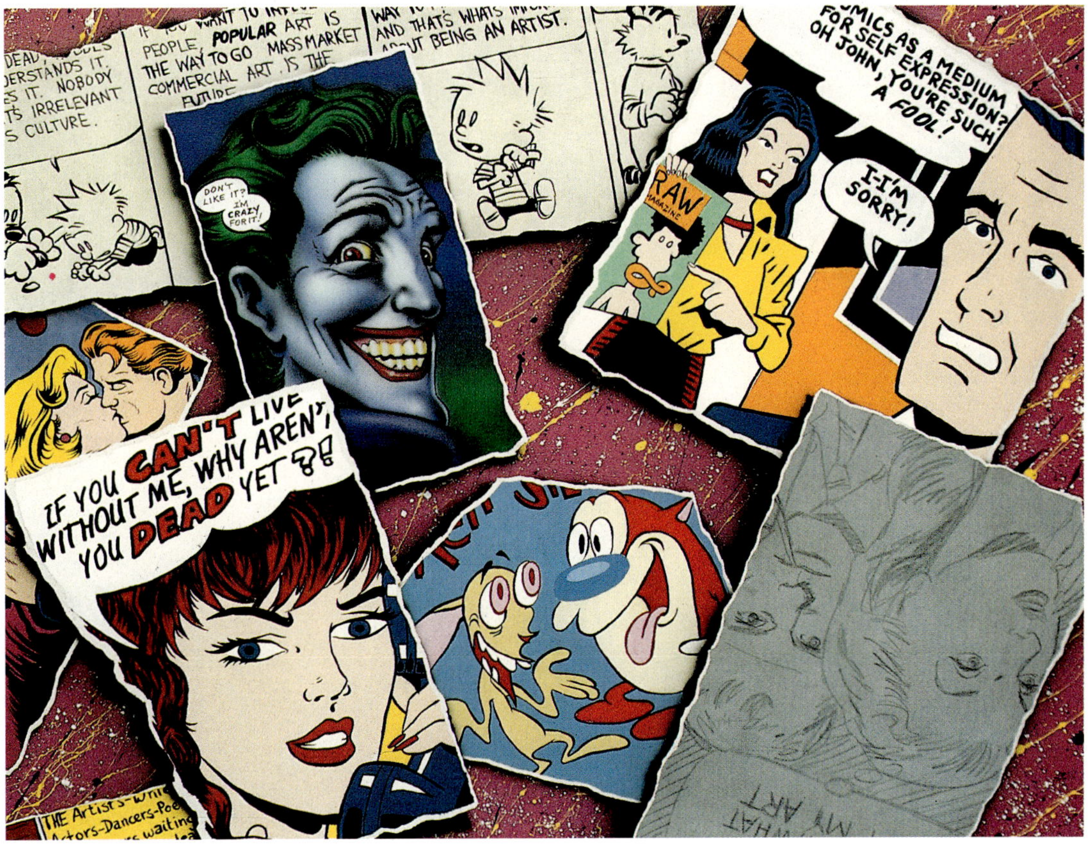
PEOPLE, POPULAR ART IS
THE WAY TO GO MASS MARKET
COMMERCIAL ART IS THE
DON'T LIKE IT? I'M CRAZY FOR IT!
FOR SELF EXPRESSION?
OH JOHN, YOU'RE SUCH
A FOOL!
I-I'M SORRY!
RAW
IF YOU CAN'T LIVE
YOU DEAD YET?!

3

4

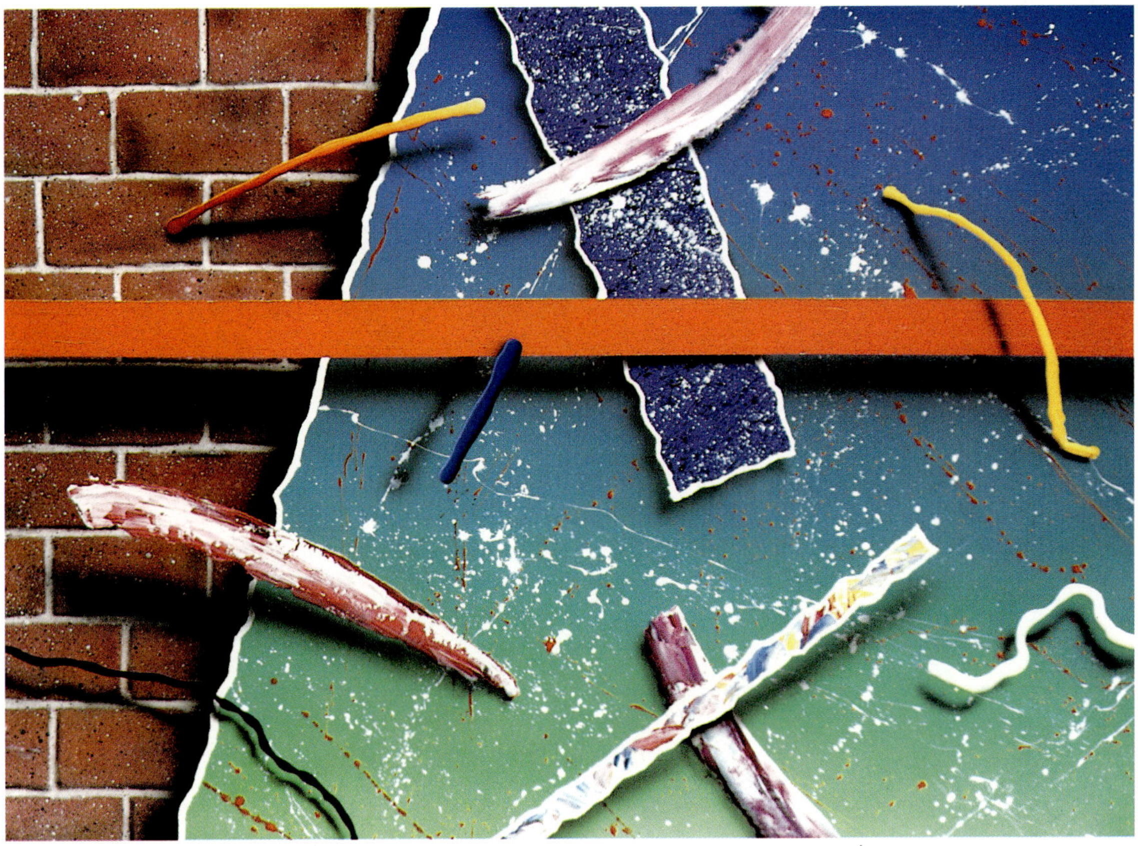

1
Artist Tom Daly
Title Russian Pepsi
Client Pepsi-Cola Co.
Art Director Tom Daly
Usage Poster
Media Used Gauche

2
Artist Tom Daly
Title Bellydancer
Client Image Bank
Art Director Tom Daly
Usage Stock
Media Used Gauche

1

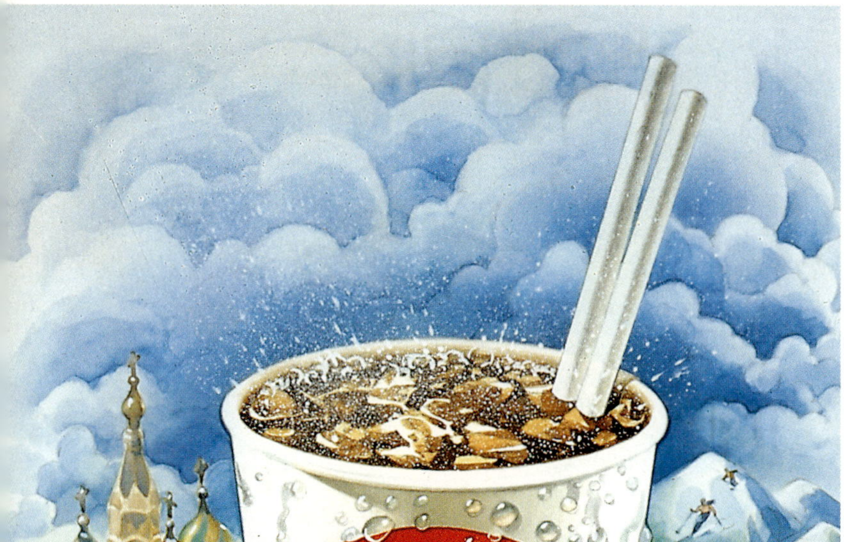

2

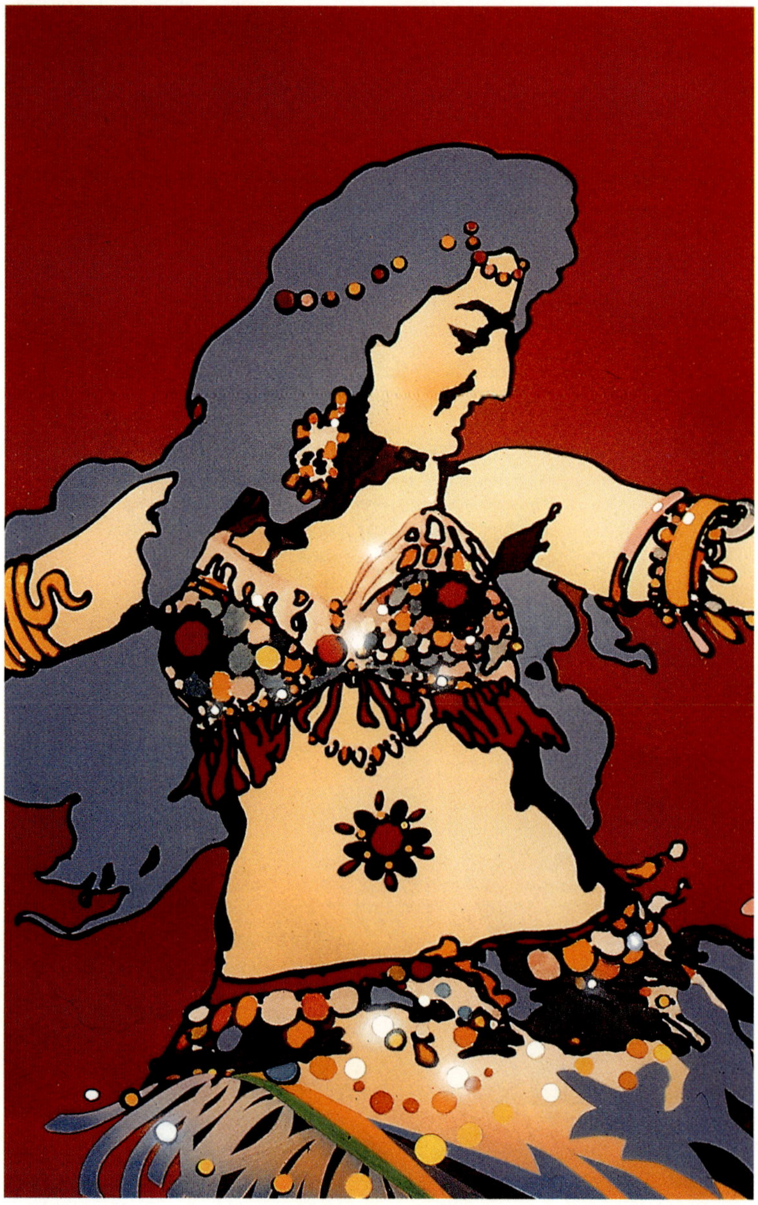

1
Artist Tom Daly
Title Hardee Boy
Client Hardee Restaurants
Art Director Jeff Cooper
Usage Store Poster
Media Used Gauche

2
Artist Tom Daly
Title Chef with Food
Client Restaurant Associates
Art Director Jack Auesh
Usage Poster
Media Used Gauche

3
Artist Tom Daly
Title Clown Pointing
Client Image Bank
Art Director Tom Daly
Usage Stock
Media Used Gauche

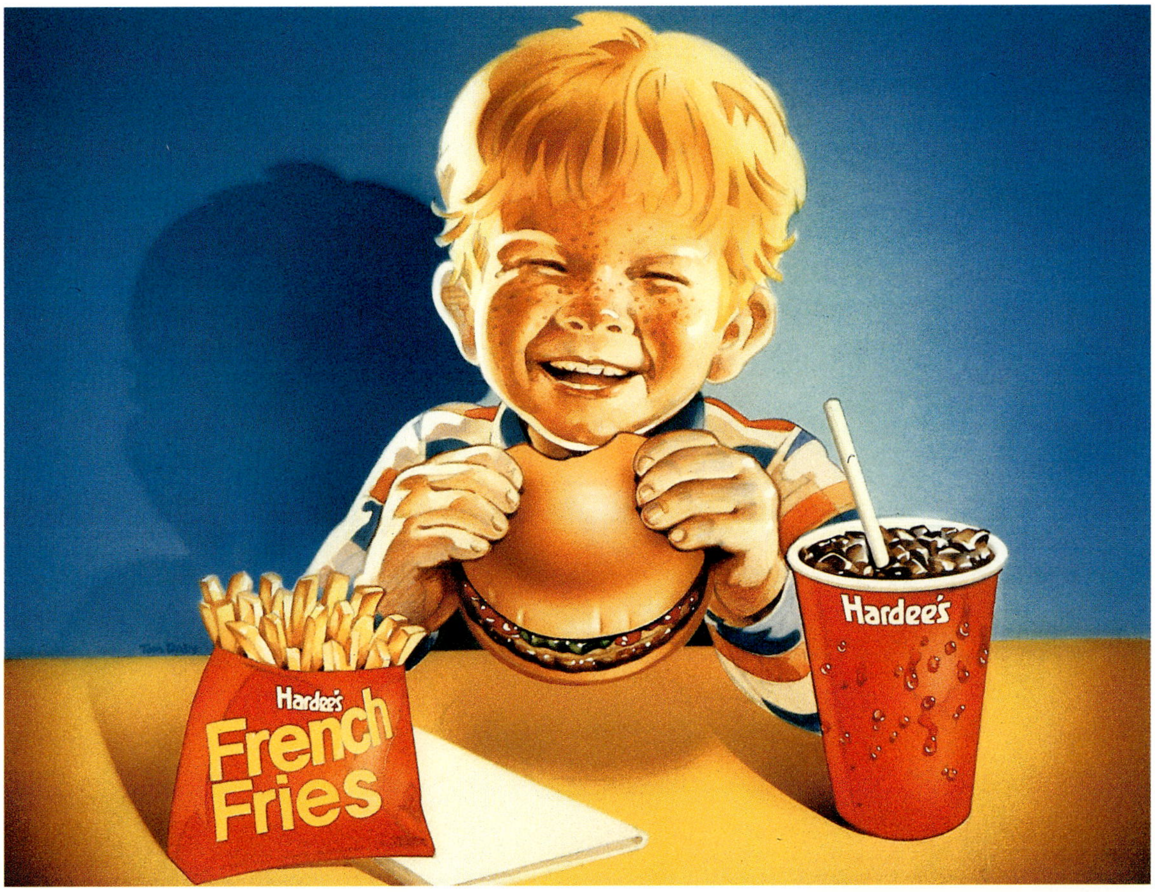

1

2

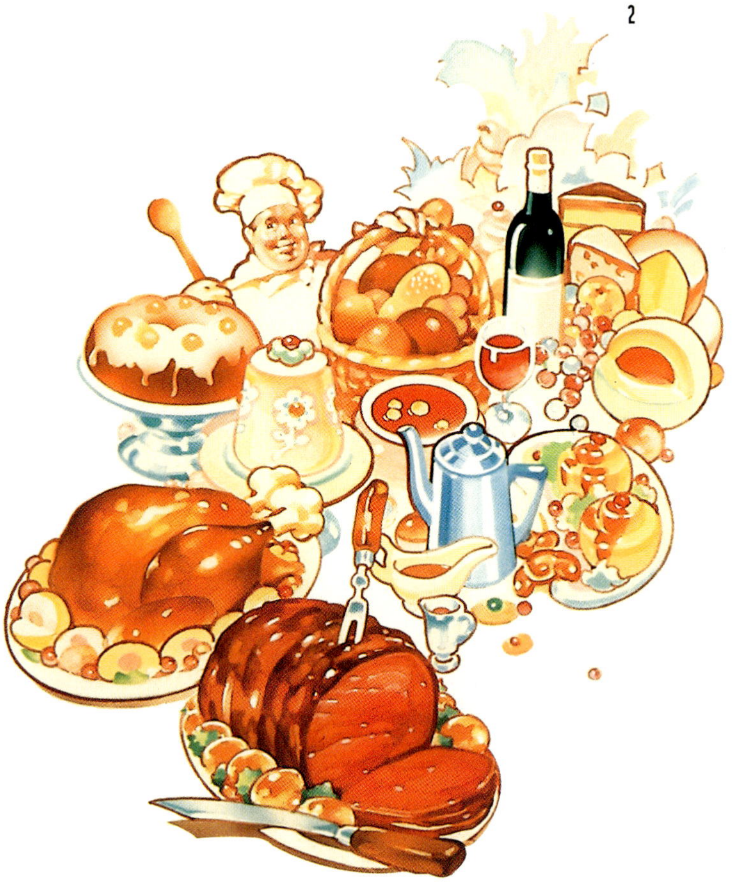

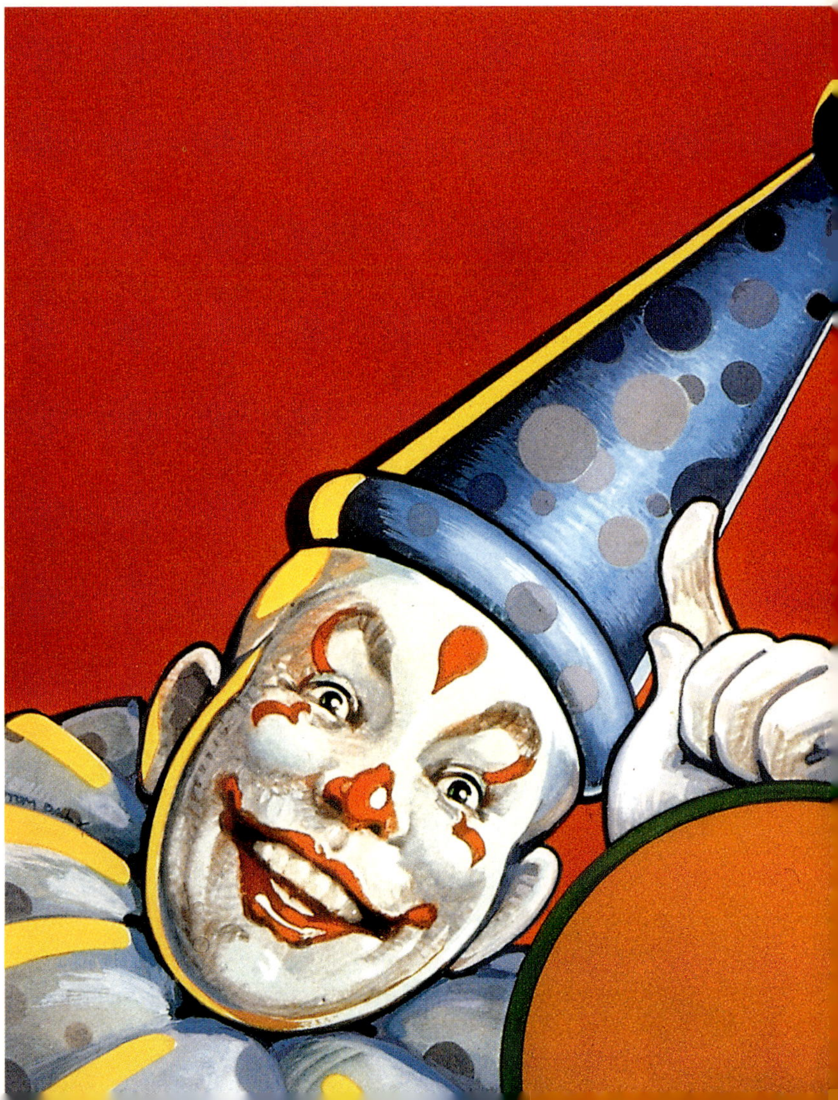

3

1
Artist Richard Daskas
Title Tark the Shark
Usage Commercial Art
Media Used Acrylic

2
Artist Ruben Deanda
Title Fiesta Gator
Art Director Ruben Deanda
Usage Commercial Art
Media Used Comart, Rotring, Acrylics

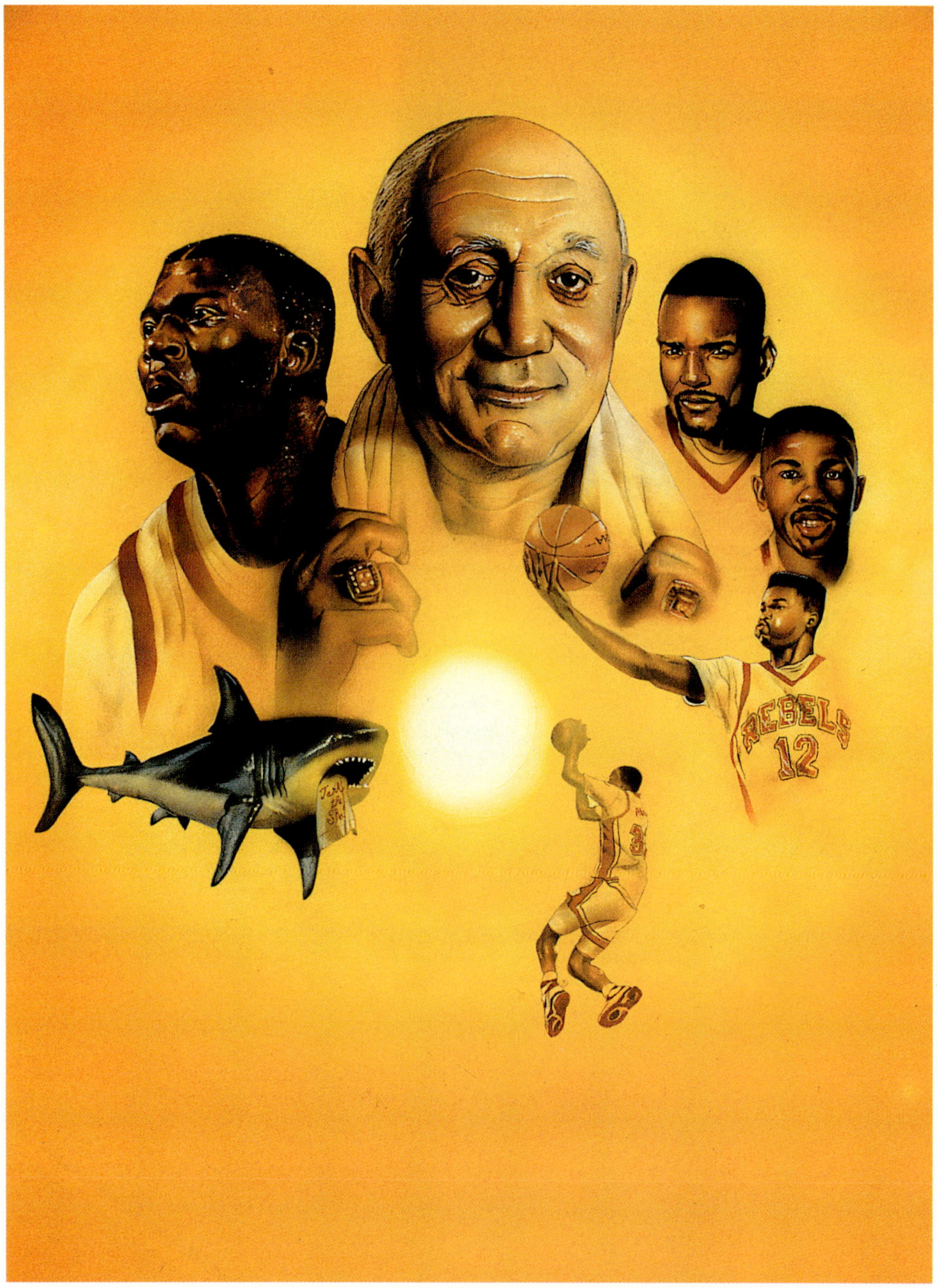

1

2

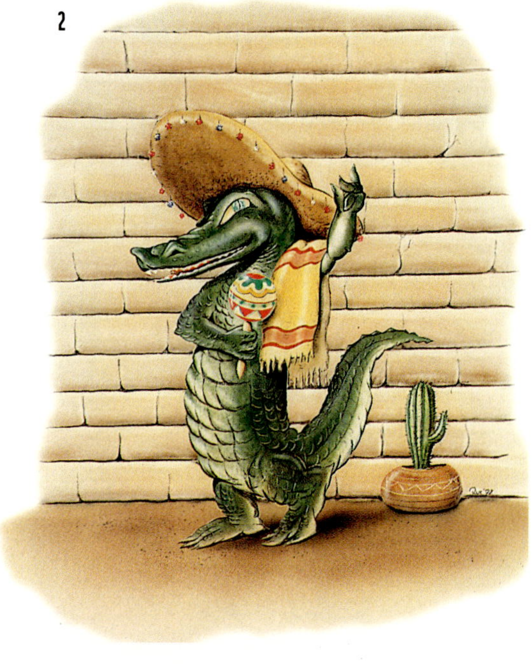

1
Artist Catherine Dittmer
Title A Frog Asks "HOW"?
Art Director C. Dittmer
Usage Commercial Art
Media Used Acrylic

2
Artist Jim Durk
Client Jim Durk
Usage Editorial Illustration
Media Used Comart & Opaque Transparencies

3
Artist Jim Durk
Client Jim Durk
Usage Editorial Illustration
Media Used Comart Opaque Transparencies

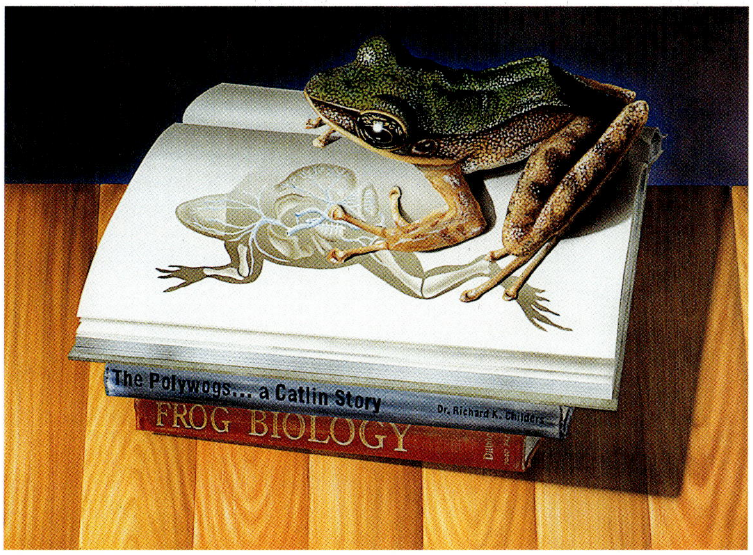

1

2

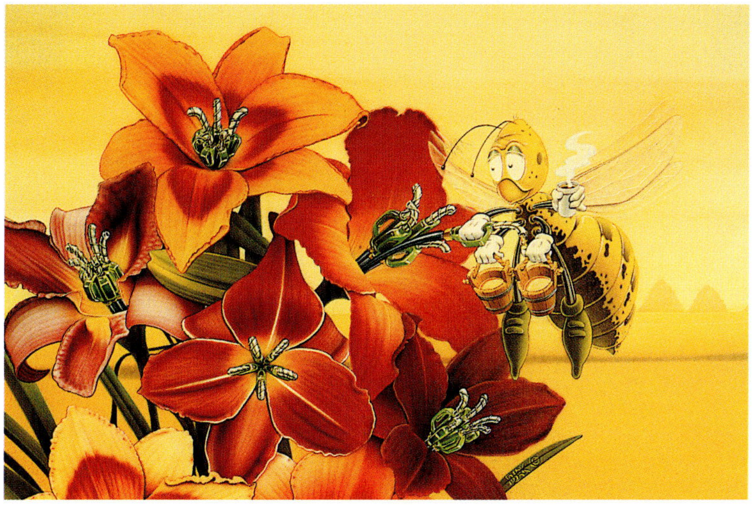

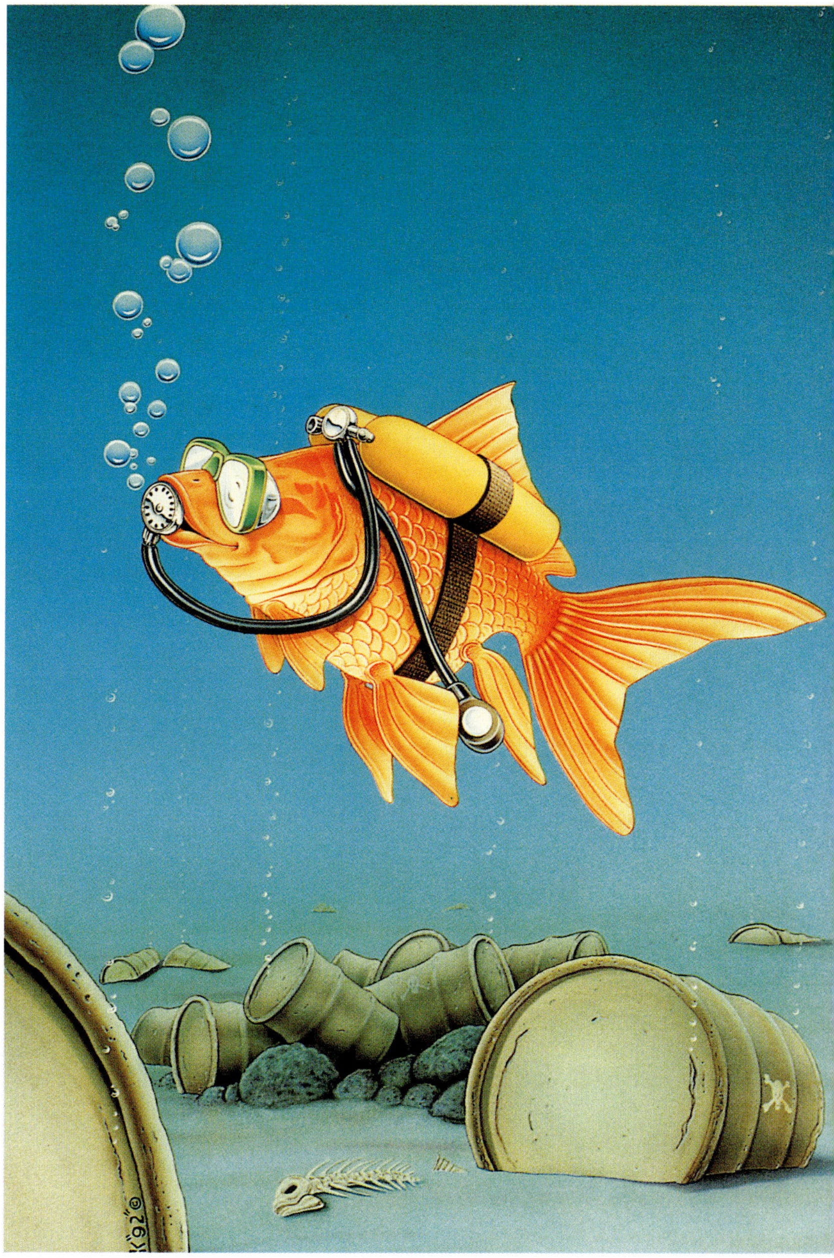

3

1

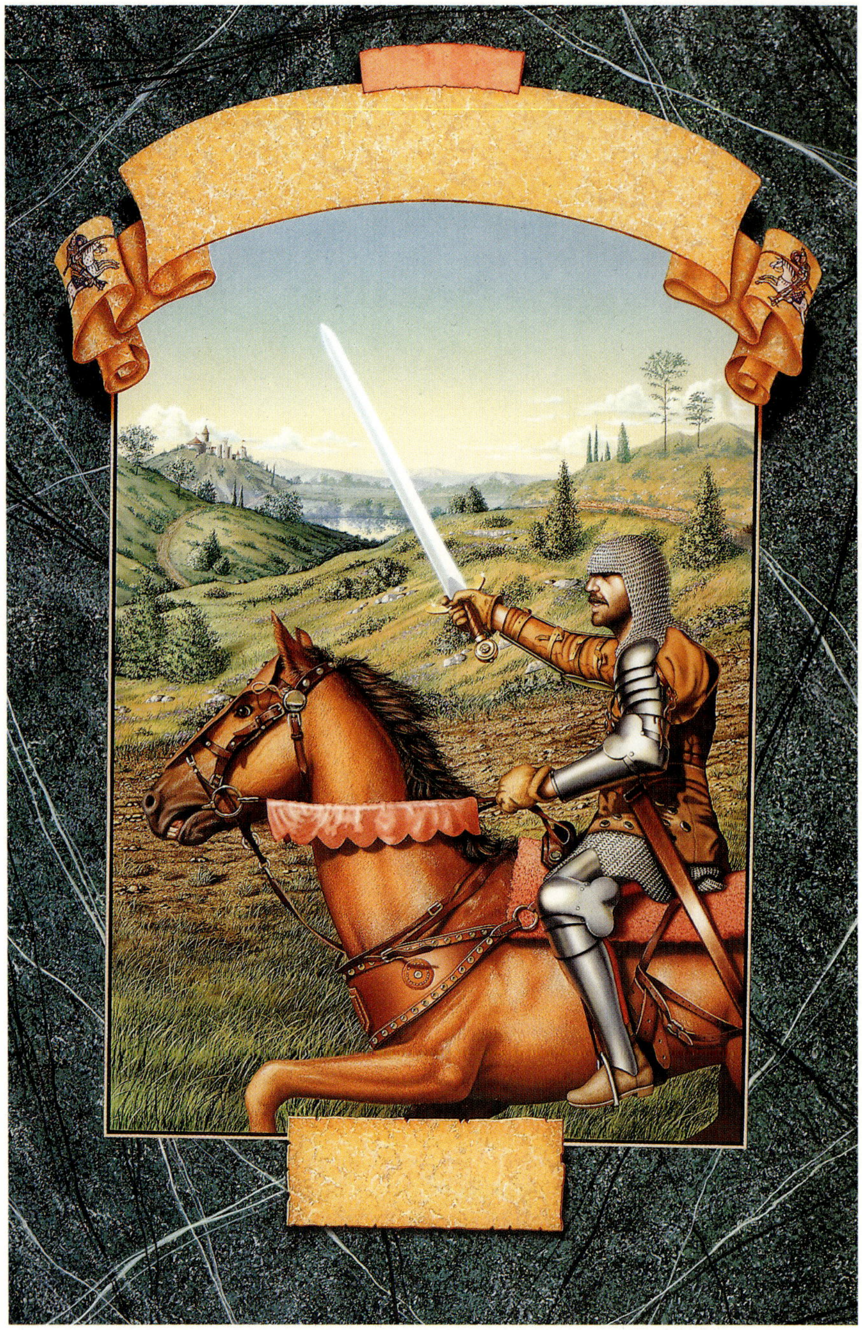

2

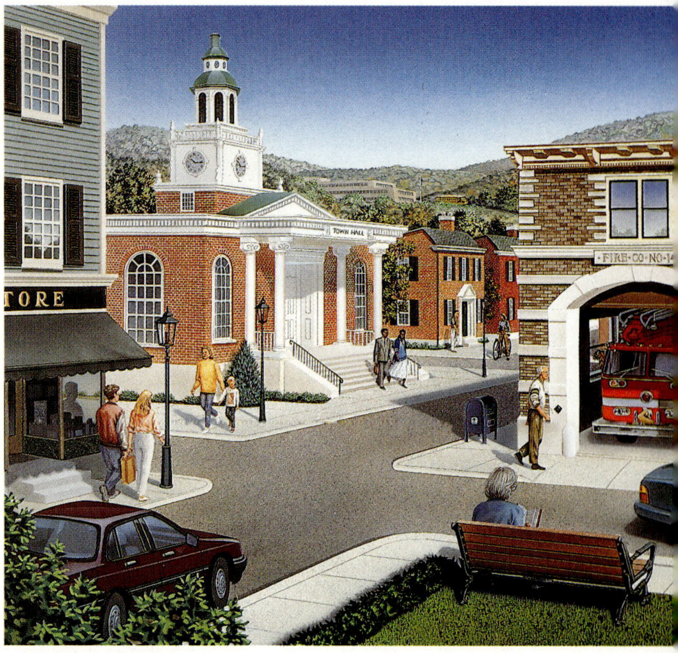

3

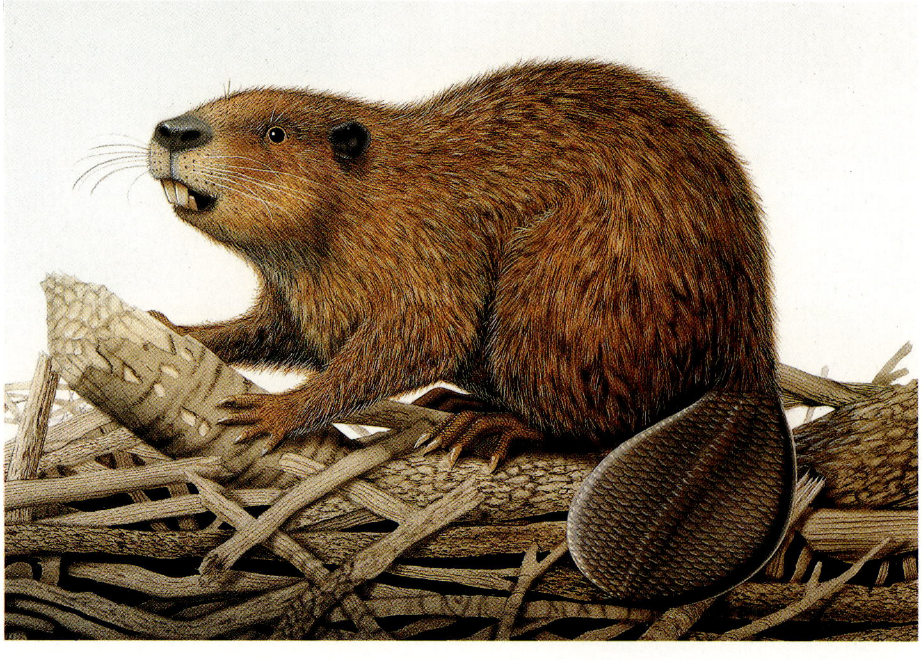

1
Artist Jim Effler
Title Renaissance Poster
Media Used Acrylic, Watercolor

2
Artist Jim Effler
Title New England Town
Client Graphic Expression for MBIA
Art Director Susan Muther
Usage Annual Report
Media Used Acrylics, Watercolor

3
Artist Jim Effler
Title Beaver
Client Shelly Berman Communicators
Art Director Brad Webb
Usage Outdoor Advertising
Media Used Watercolor-Airbrush & Dry Brush

4
Artist Jim Effler
Title Dark Castle
Client Clarion for Smirnoff
Art Director Ian Barribel
Usage Point of Purchase Display
Media Used Acrylics

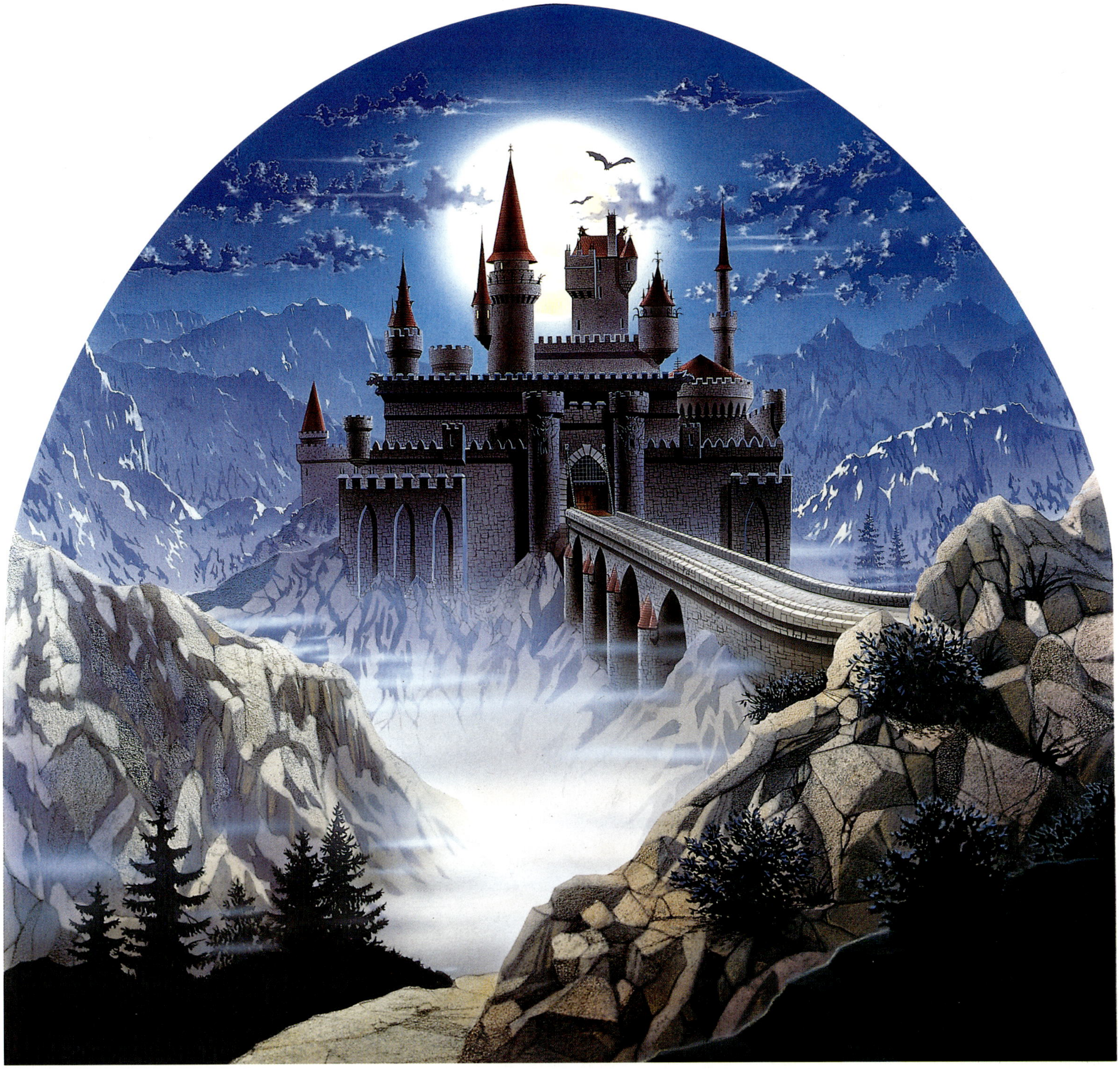

4

1
Artist David Ekman
Title Illustrator
Art Director Dave Ekman
Usage Commercial Art
Media Used Acrylic

2
Artist Brian Evans
Title Cirrhosis and Esophageal Varices
Art Director B. Evans
Usage Technical Illustration
Media Used Comart

3
Artist Alan Flinn
Title Outrageous Friendships Part 2
Client Breakaway Magazine
Art Director Jerry Price
Usage Editorial
Media Used Gouache

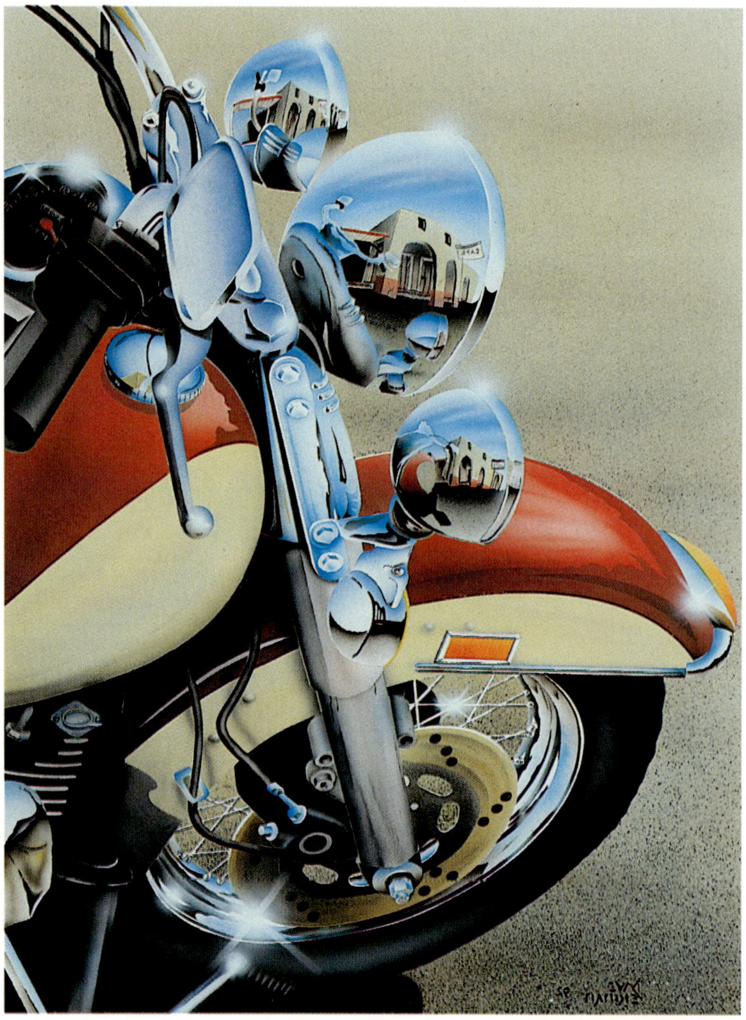

1

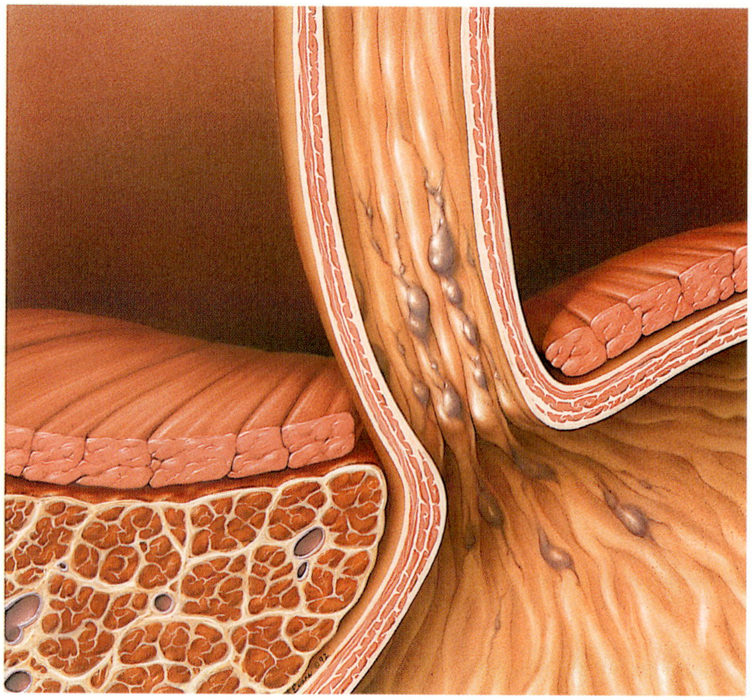

2

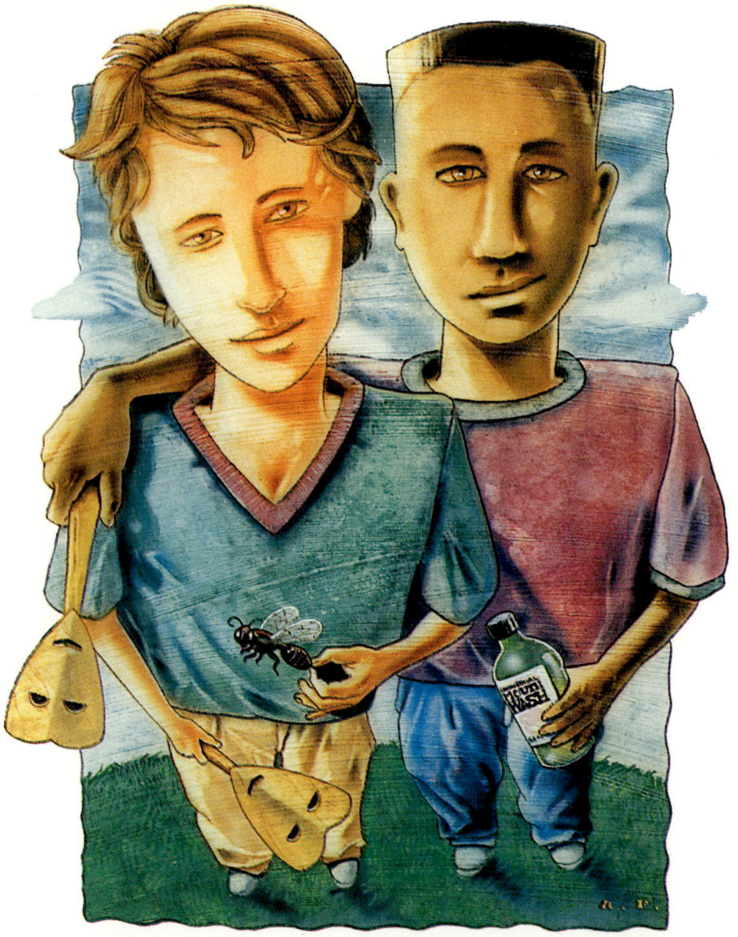

3

1
Artist Alan Flinn
Usage Self Promotion
Media Used Gouache

2
Artist Alan Flinn
Title Outrageous Friendships Part 1
Client Breakaway Magazine
Art Director Jerry Price
Usage Editorial
Media Used Gouache

3
Artist Alan Flinn
Client The Enviromental Film Festival
Art Director Alan Flinn
Usage Advertising
Media Used Gouache

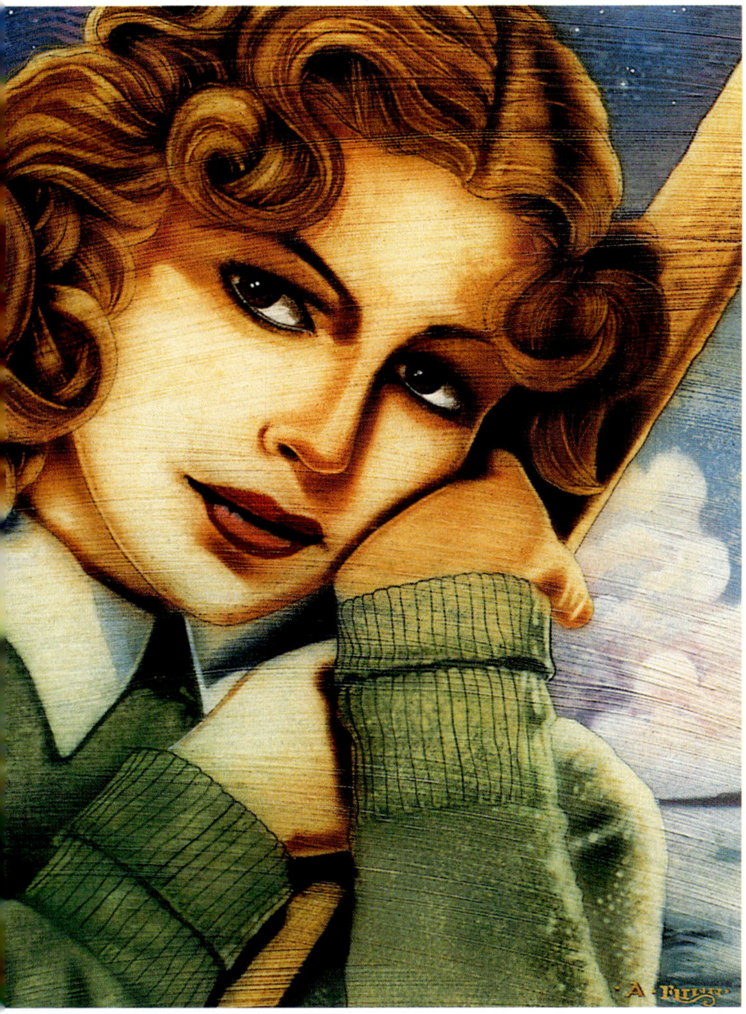

1

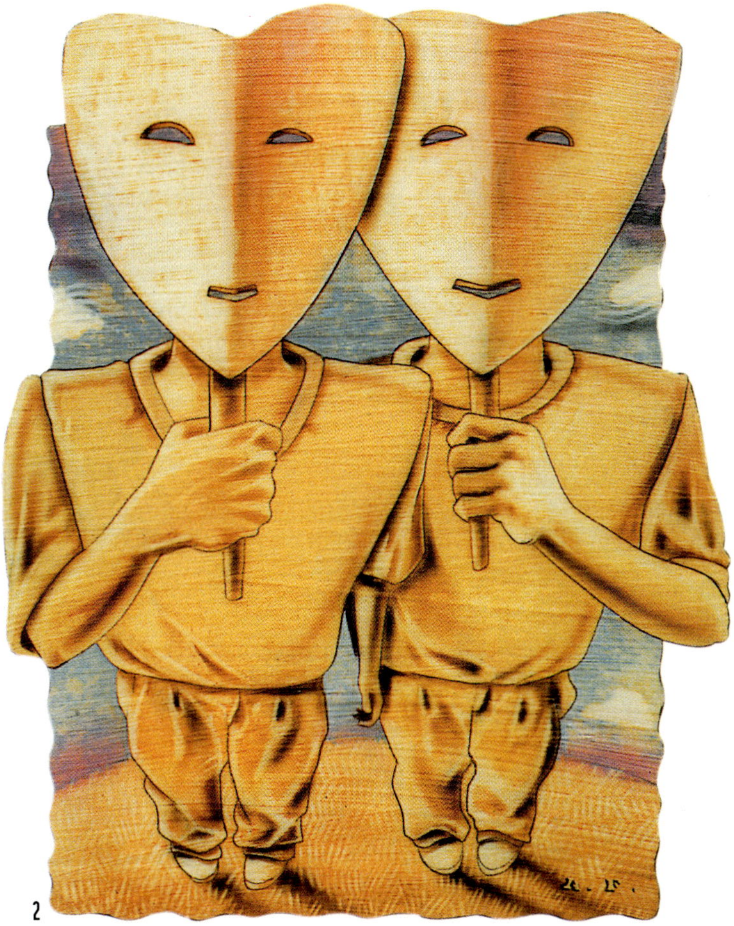

2

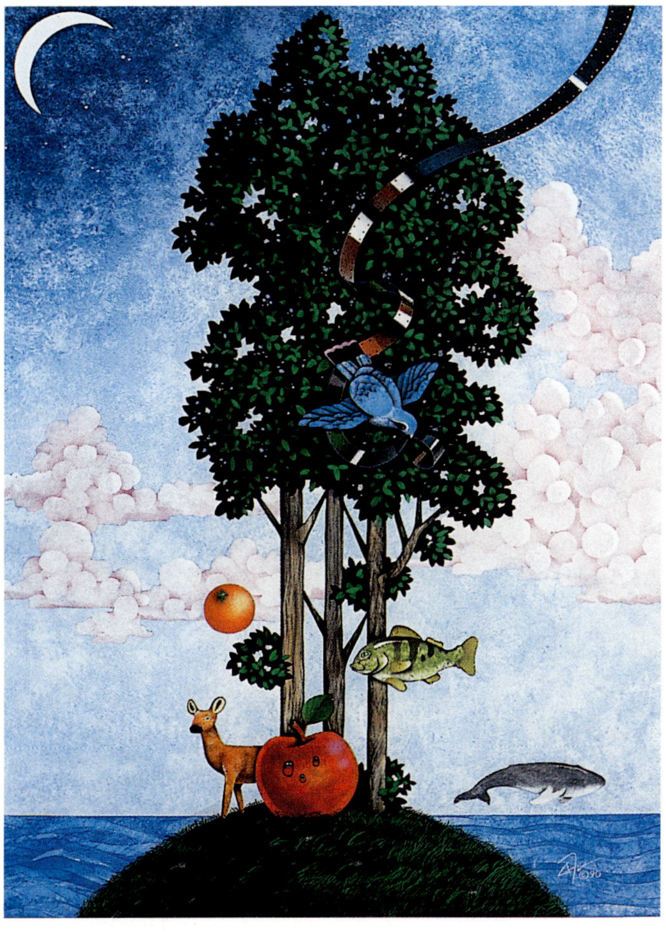

3

1
Artist Mark A. Fredrickson
Title On the Nature of Thing Erotic (Venus de Milo)
Client Arizona Portfolio
Art Director Ann Hubbard
Usage Divider Page for Creative Sourcebook
Media Used Acrylic

2
Artist Mark A. Fredrickson
Title Baseball Bear
Client Mead Products
Art Director Marna Henley
Usage Mead Portfolios
Media Used Acrylic

3
Artist Mark A. Fredrickson
Title Levi's Wild Creature (Skateboarder Leaving Flames)
Client Levi Strauss
Art Director Andrea Hyet
Usage Point of Purchase Poster
Media Used Acrylic

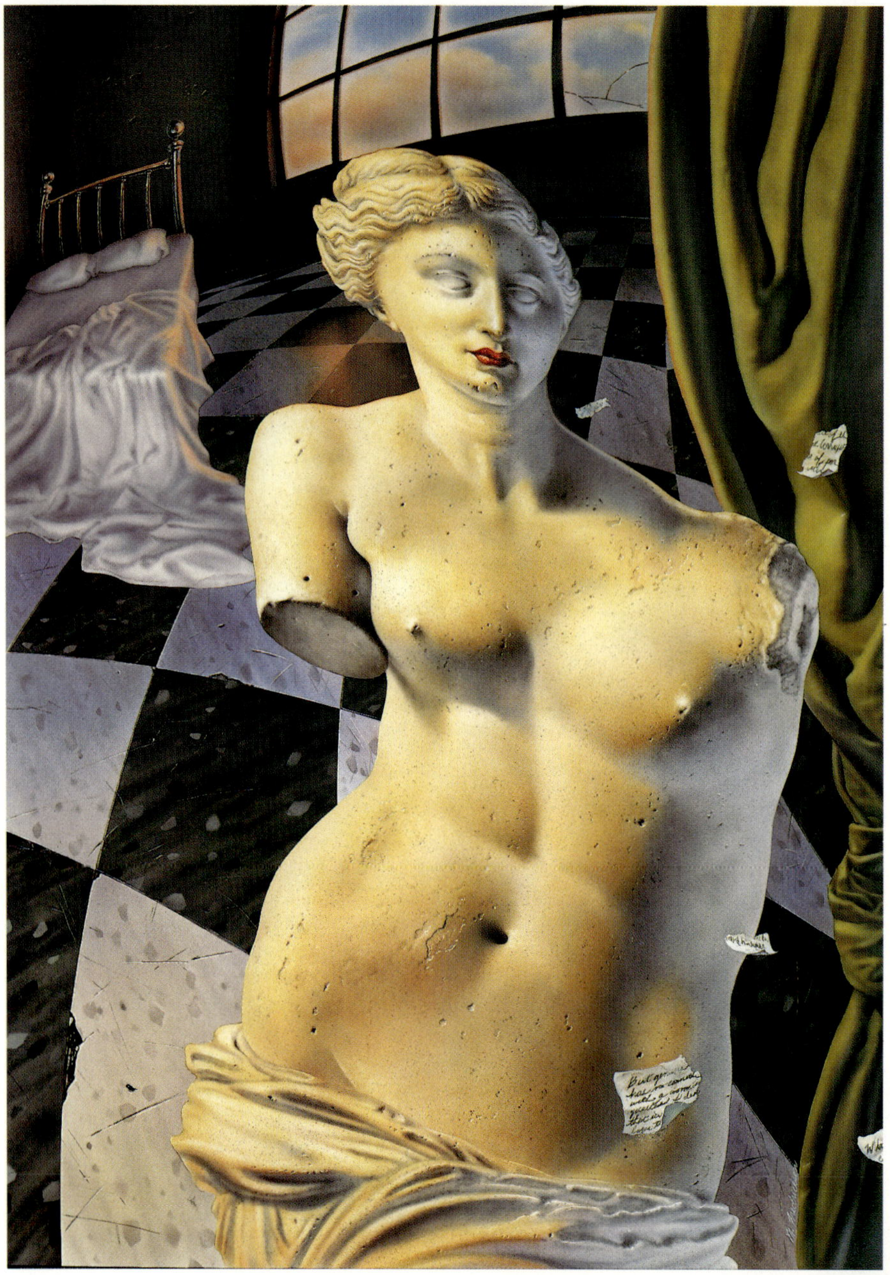

1

2

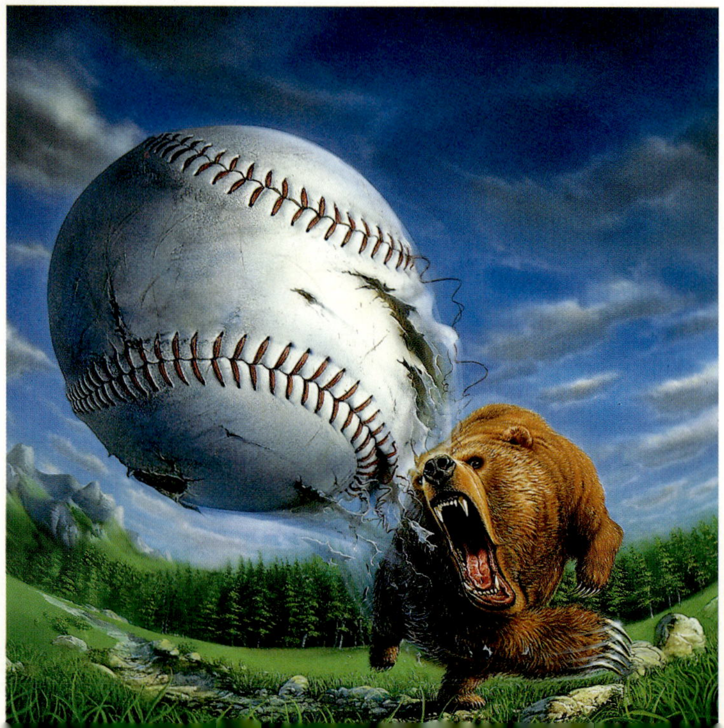

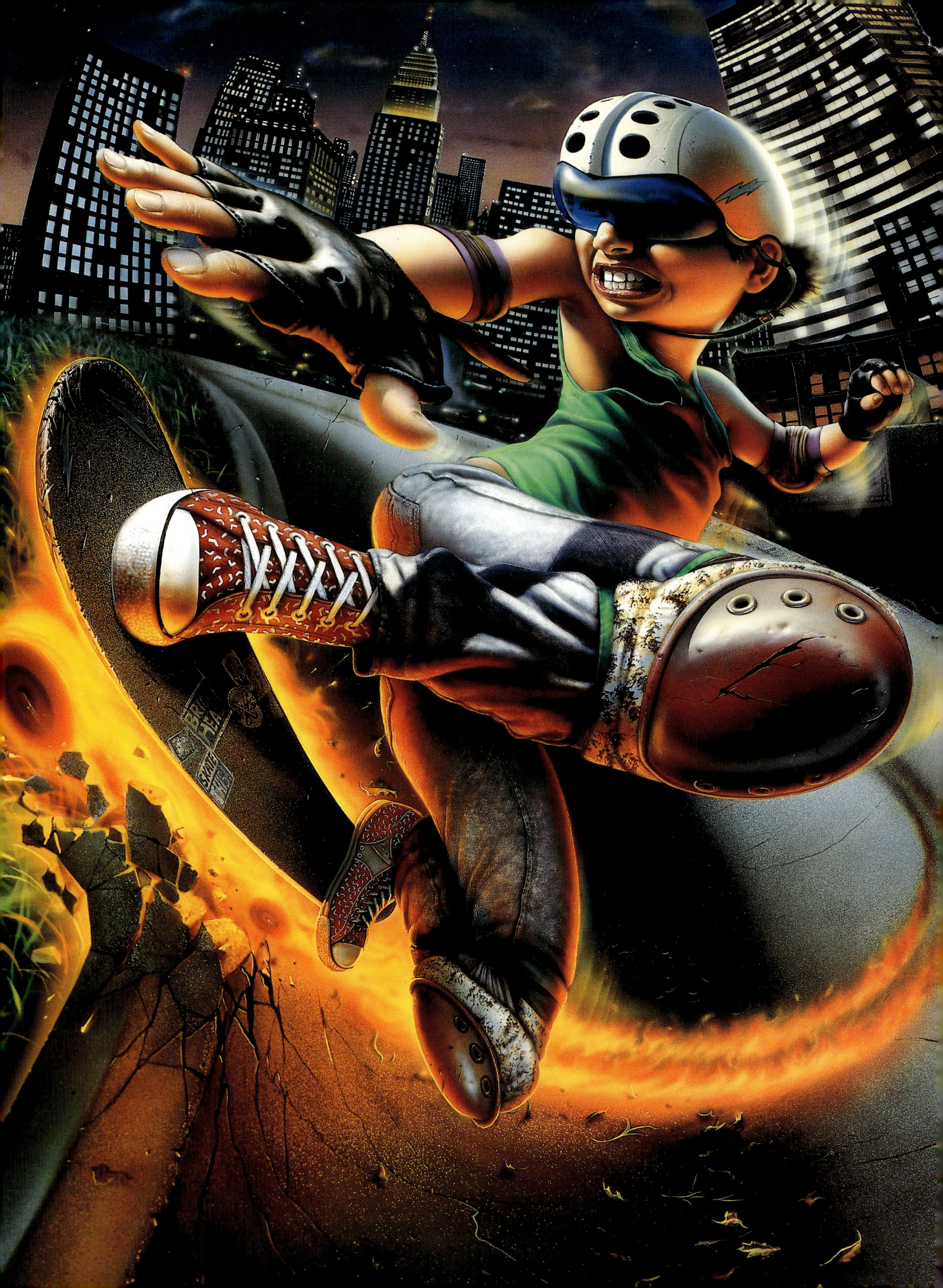

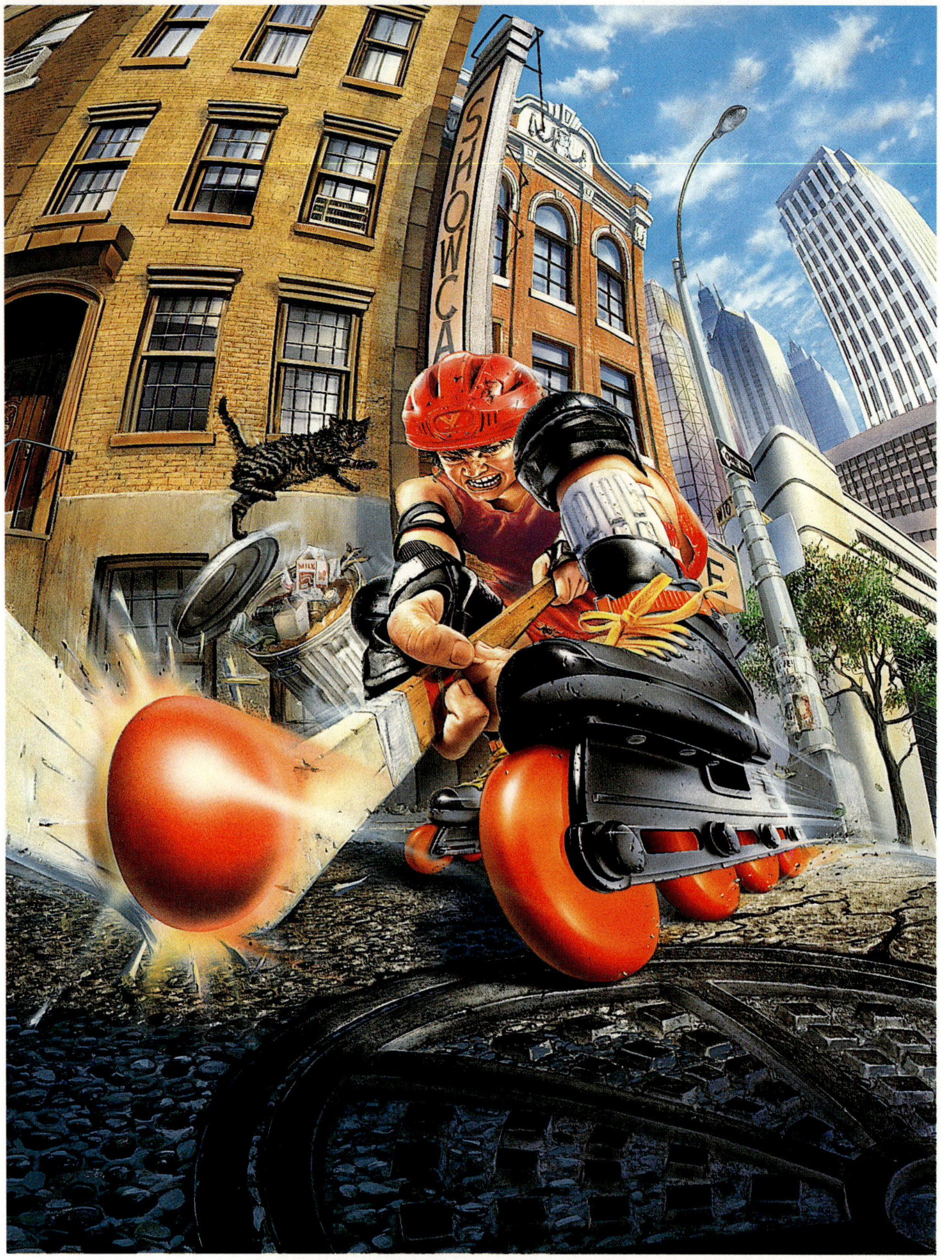

1

2

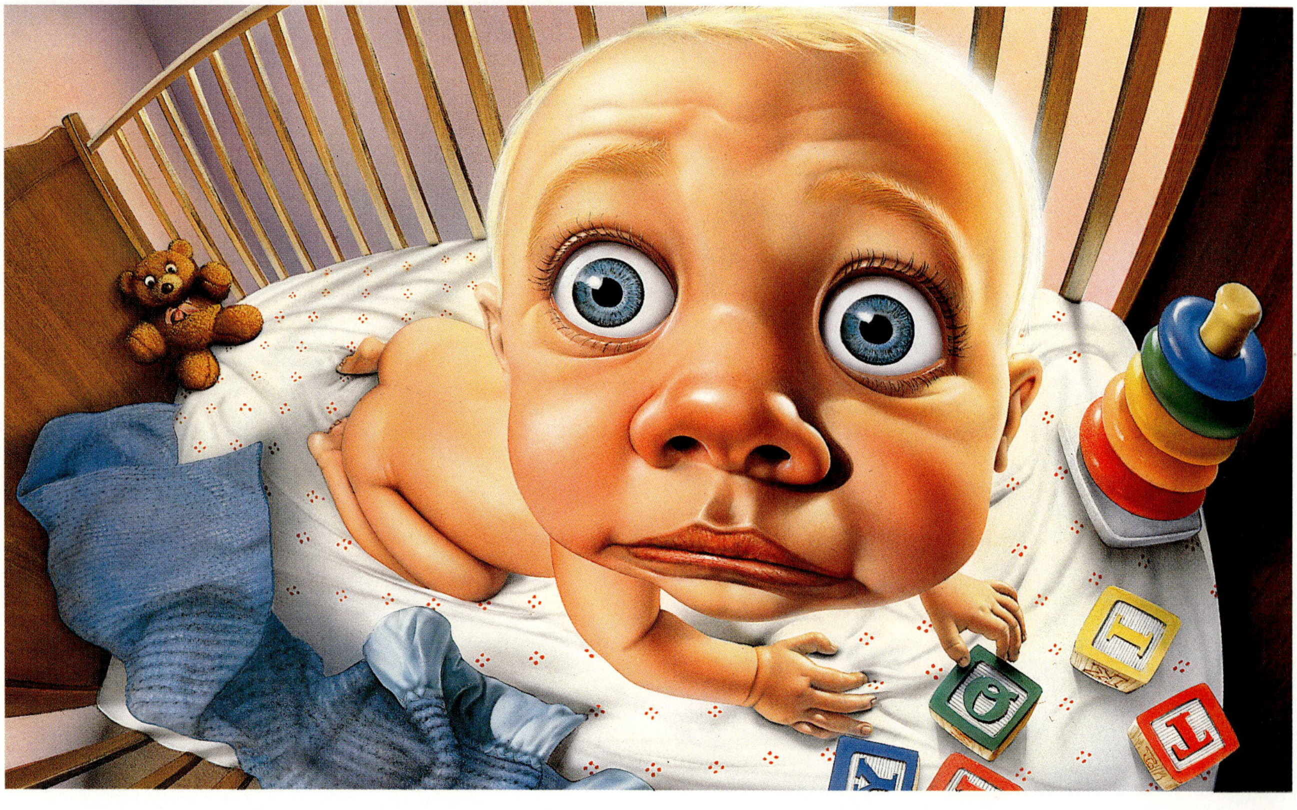

1
Artist Mark A. Fredrickson
Title Street Hockey Player
Client Mead Products
Art Director Marna Henley
Usage Mead Portfolios
Media Used Acrylic

2
Artist Mark A. Fredrickson
Title Thermoscan Baby (Baby in Crib)
Client Thermoscan
Art Director John Vitro
Usage Trade Publication Advertisement and Point of Purchase Poster
Media Used Acrylic

3
Artist Mark A. Fredrickson
Title Levi's Wild Creature (Black Rapper on Sidewalk)
Client Levi Strauss
Art Director Andrea Hyet
Usage Point of Purchase Poster
Media Used Acrylic

4
Artist Mark A. Fredrickson
Title Thermoscan Girl (Frightened Girl in Pajamas)
Client Thermoscan
Art Director John Vitro
Usage Trade Publication Advertisement and Point of Purchase Poster
Media Used Acrylic

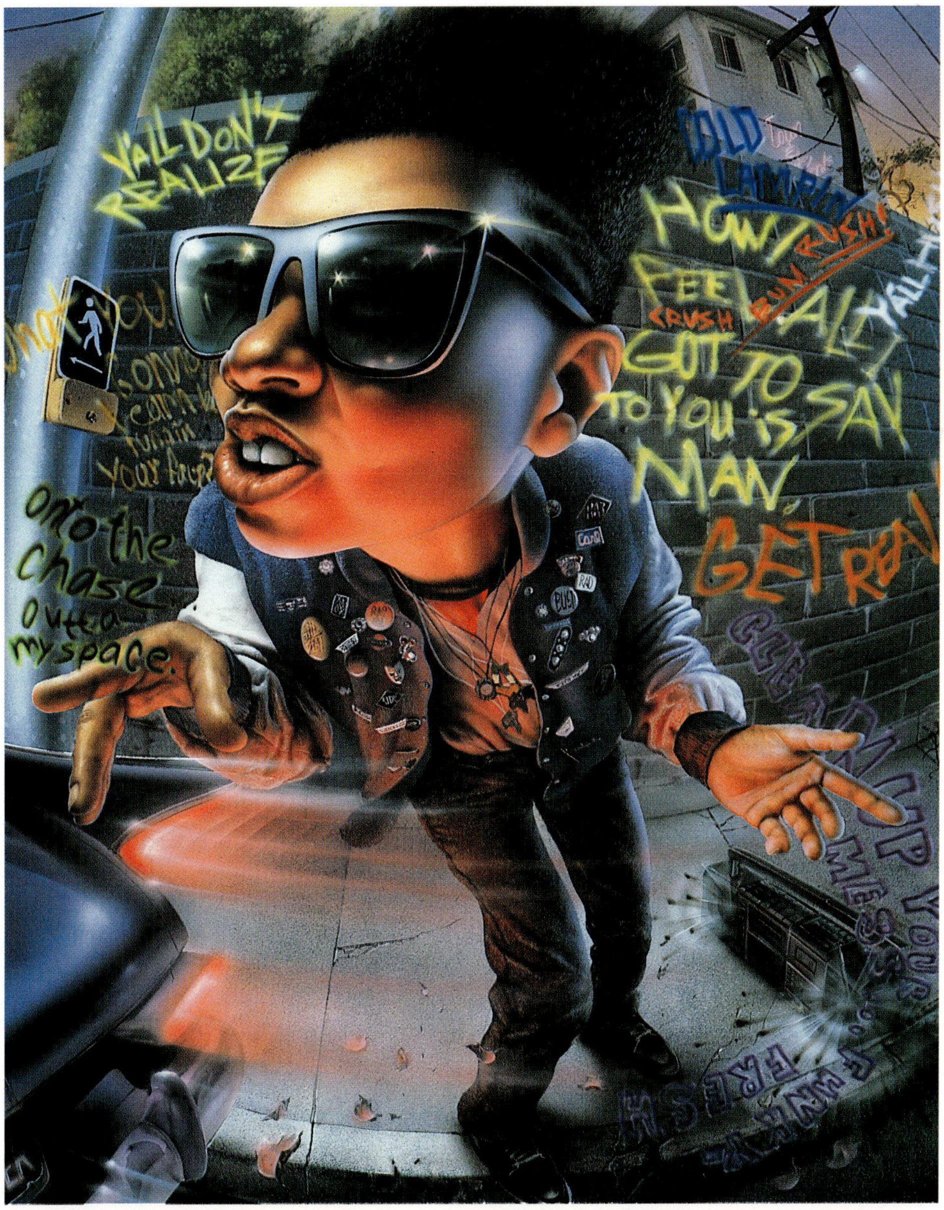

3

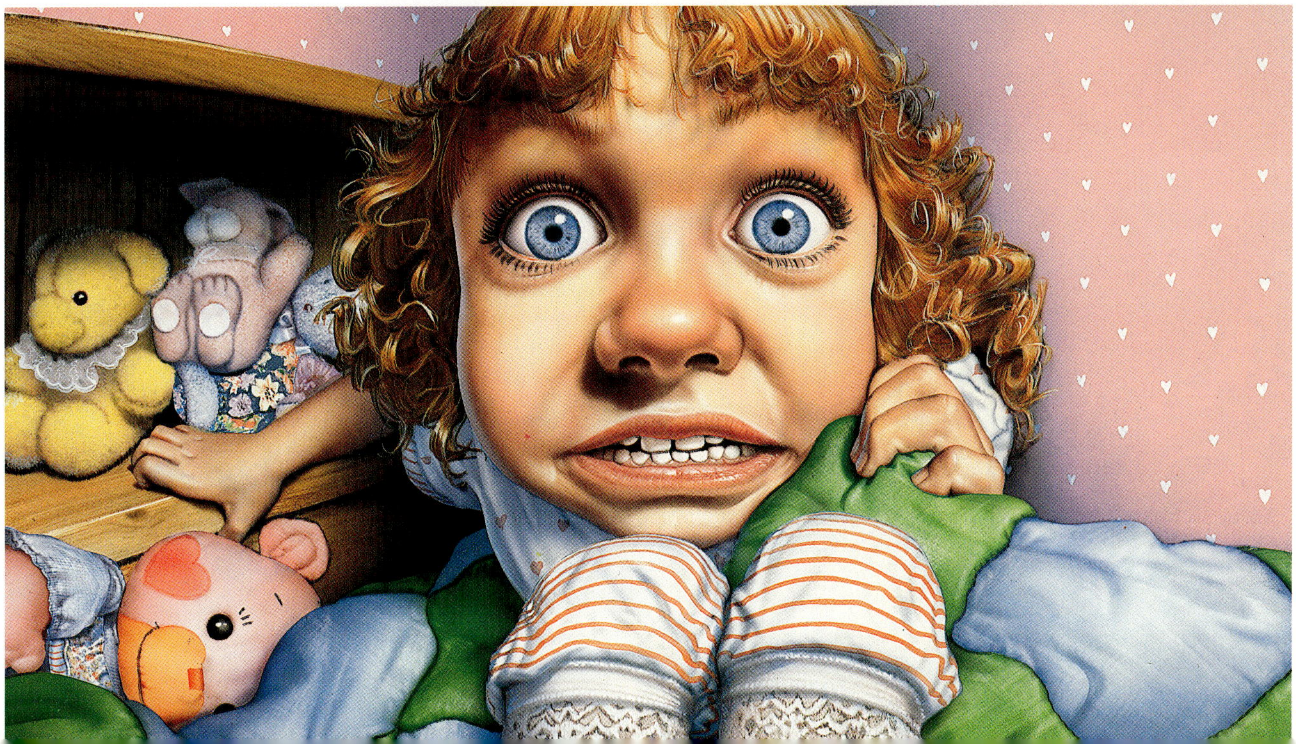

4

1
Artist Mark A. Fredrickson
Title Waxdex Bird Call
Client Bartels & Co.
Art Director David Bartels
Usage Poster for Tonight Show Competition
Media Used Acrylic

2
Artist Mark A. Fredrickson
Title Madalyn Murray O'Hair
Client Texas Monthly
Art Director D.J. Stout
Usage Magazine Editorial
Media Used Acrylic

3
Artist Mark A. Fredrickson
Title Levi's Wild Creature
Client Levi Strauss
Art Director Andrea Hyet
Usage Point of Purchase Poster
Media Used Acrylic

4
Artist Mark A. Fredrickson
Title Levi's Wild Creature
Client Levi Strauss
Art Director Andrea Hyet
Usage Point of Purchase Poster
Media Used Acrylic

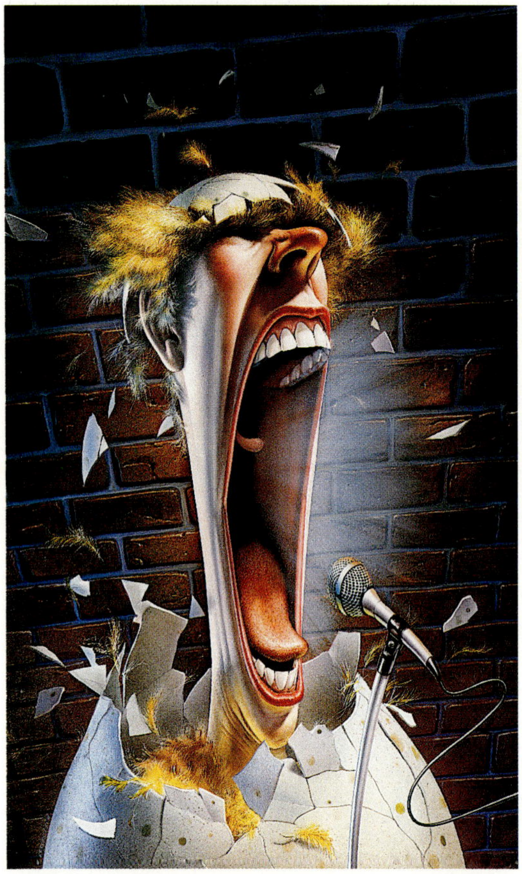

1

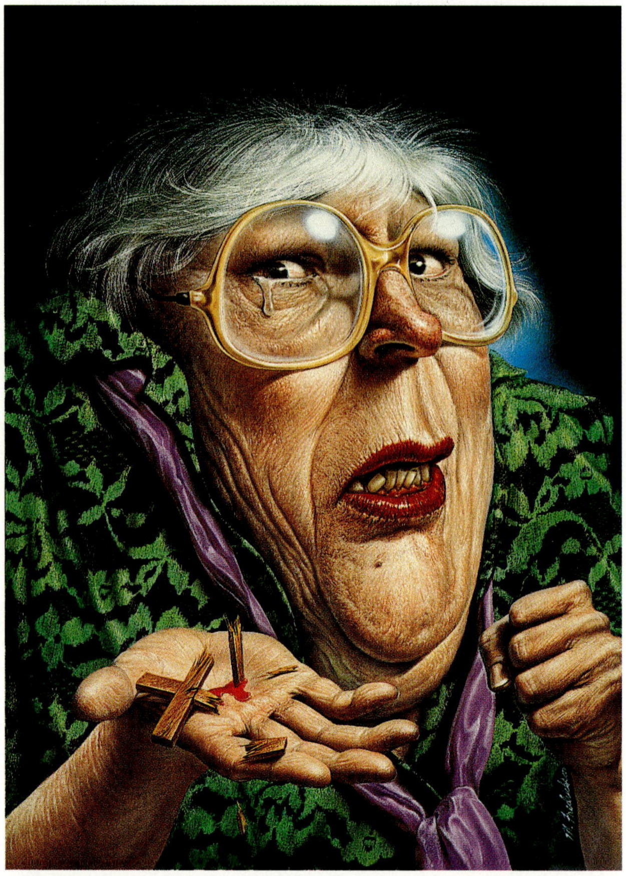

2

3

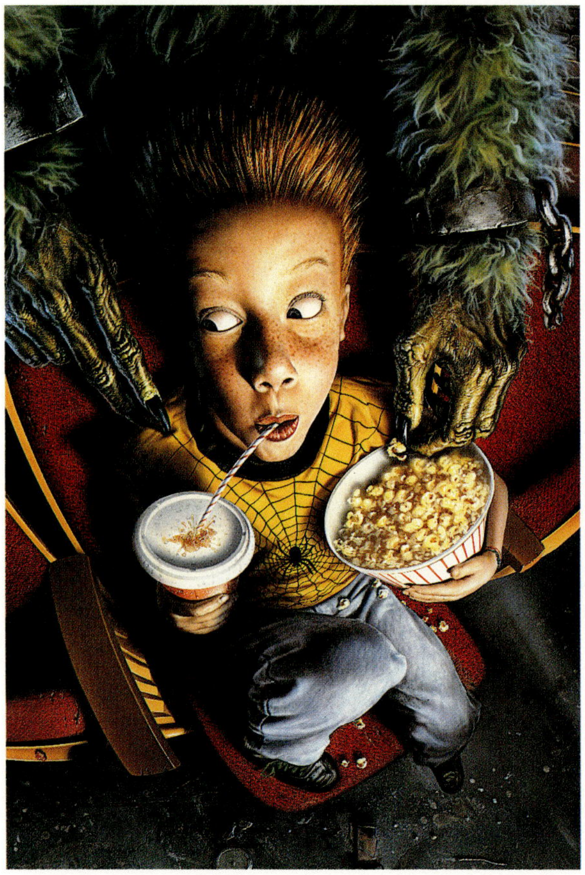

4

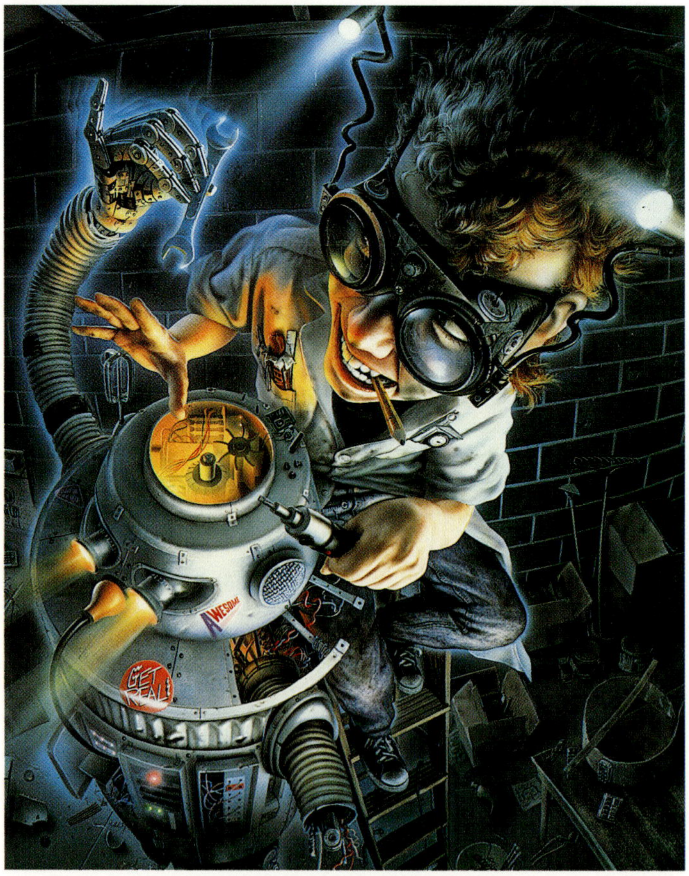

1
Artist Mark A. Fredrickson
Title Garrison Kellior
Client Atlantic Monthly
Art Director Judy Garlan
Usage Magazine Editorial
Media Used Acrylic

2
Artist Mark A. Fredrickson
Title Dennis the Menace
Client Warner Bros.
Art Director Steve Reaves
Usage Movie Promotion for "Dennis the Menace"
Media Used Acrylic

3
Artist Mark A. Fredrickson
Title Lying Business Man
Client EDS
Art Director David Bartels
Usage Trade Publication Advertisement
Media Used Acrylic

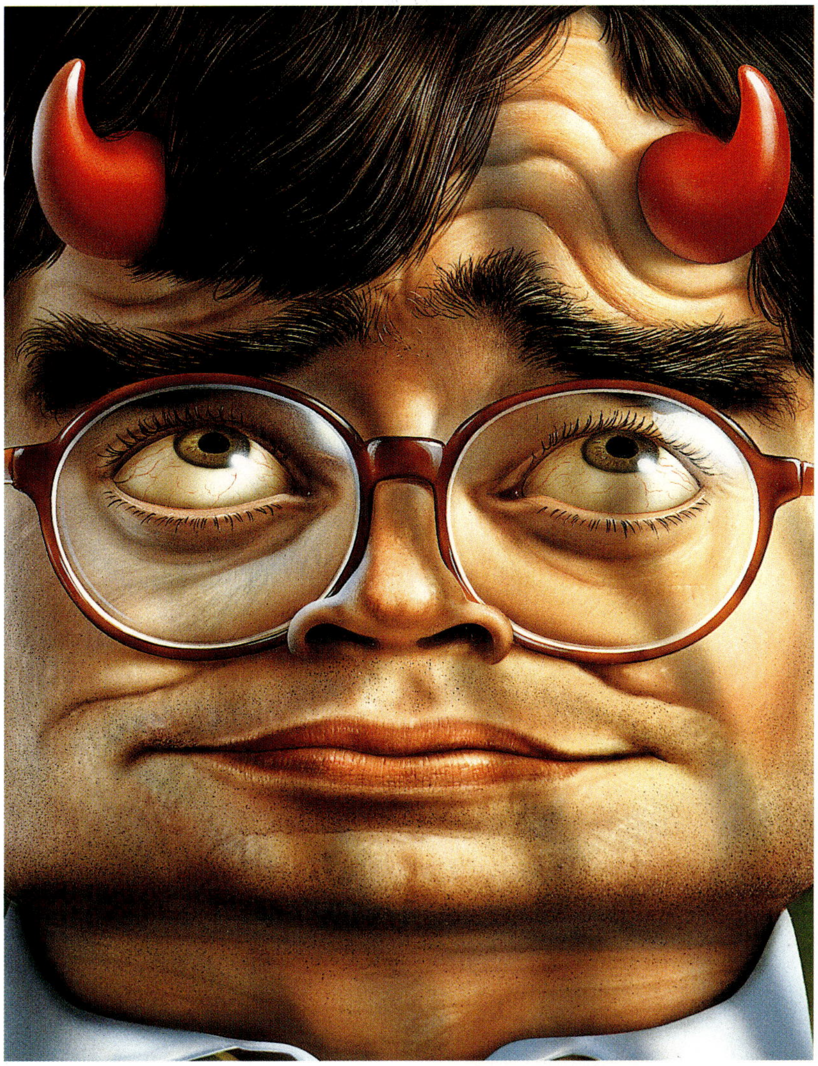

1

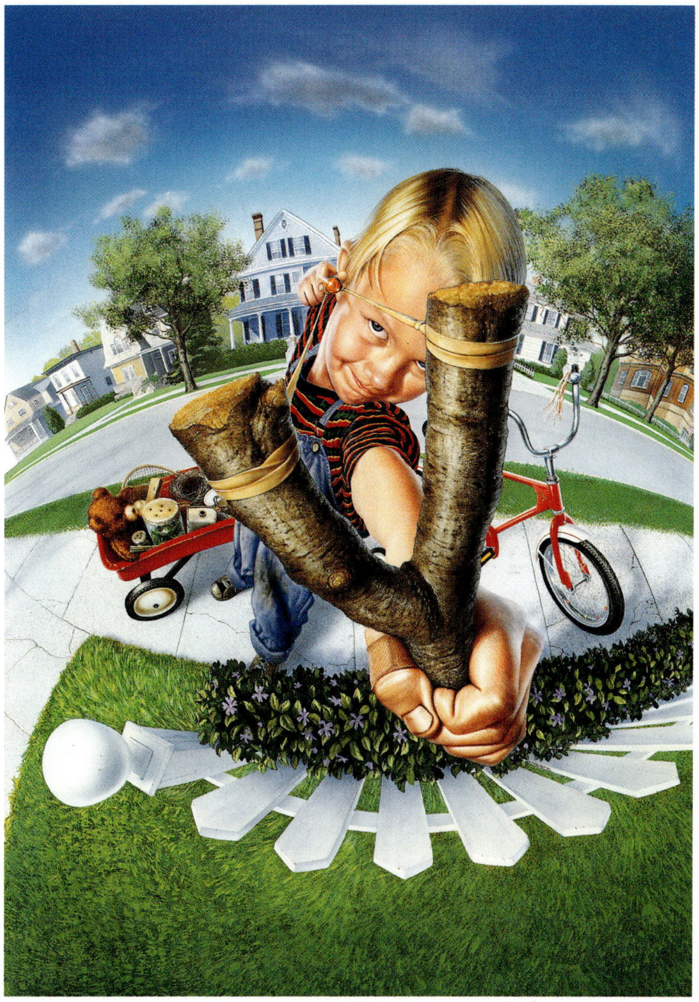

2

3

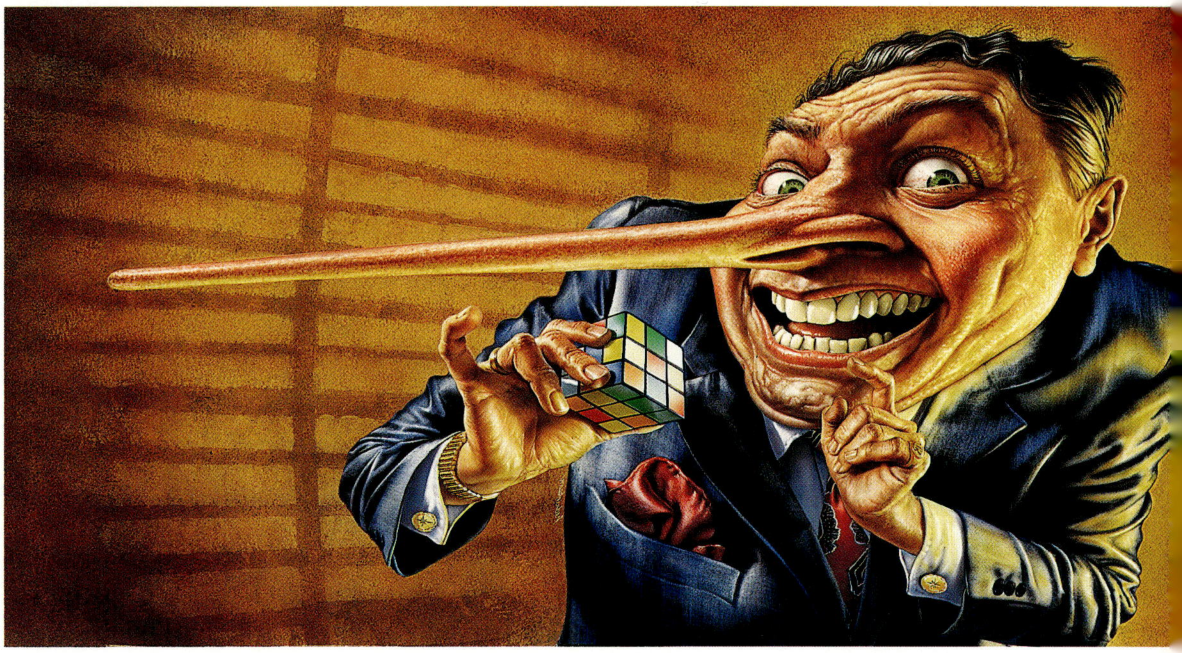

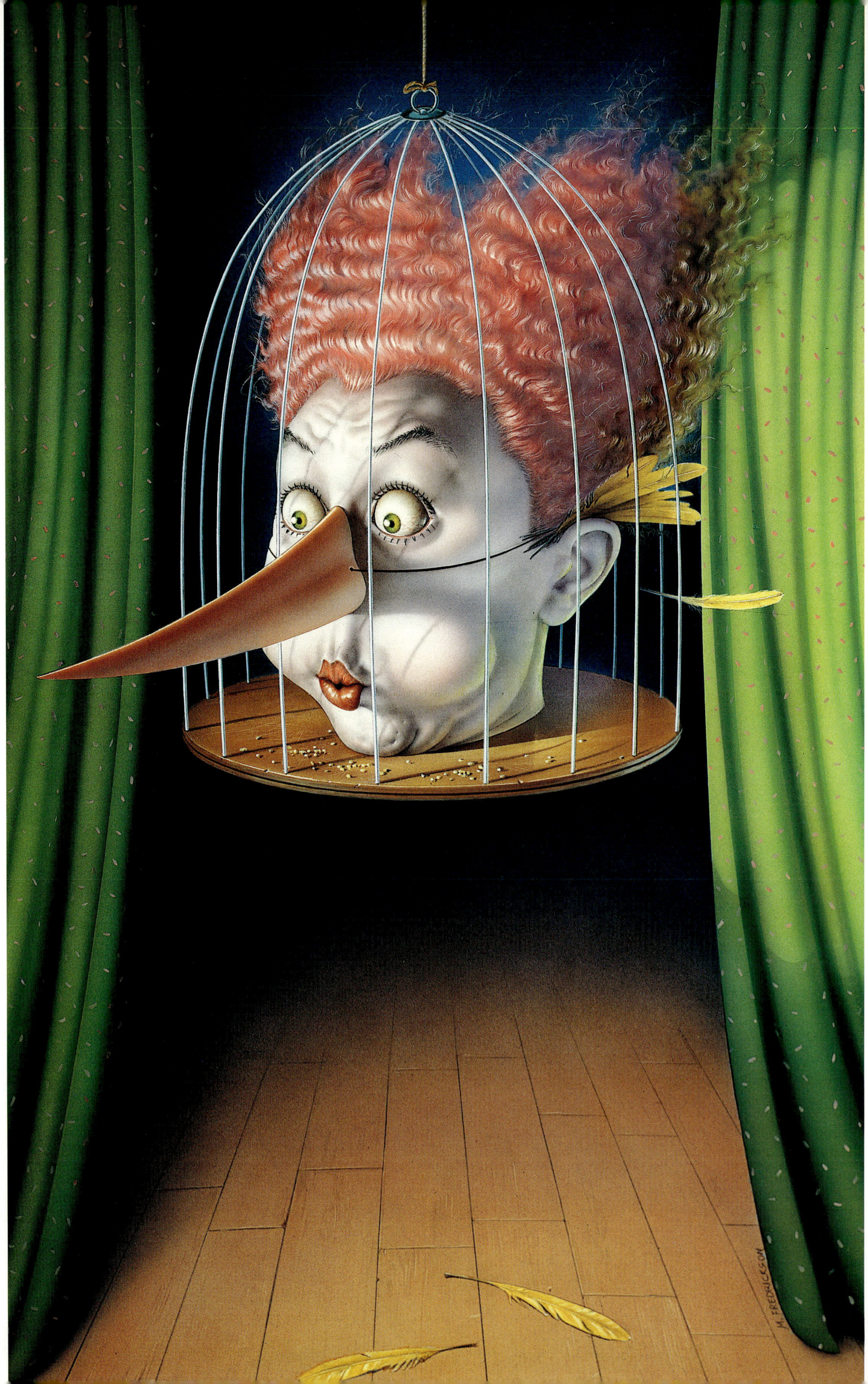

1

1
Artist Mark A. Fredrickson
Title Waxdex Bird Call Competition
Client Bartels & Co.
Art Director David Bartels
Usage Poster for Tonight Show Competition
Media Used Acrylic

2
Artist Brian Fujimori
Title Hammer
Client San Diego Union Tribune
Uasage Editorial Illustration
Art Director Amy Stirnkorb
Media Used Mixed

3
Artist Brian Fujimori
Title Santa
Usage Commercial Art
Media Used Mixed

4
Artist Pedro Gamero
Title Laurel
Usage Commercial Art
Media Used Acrylic

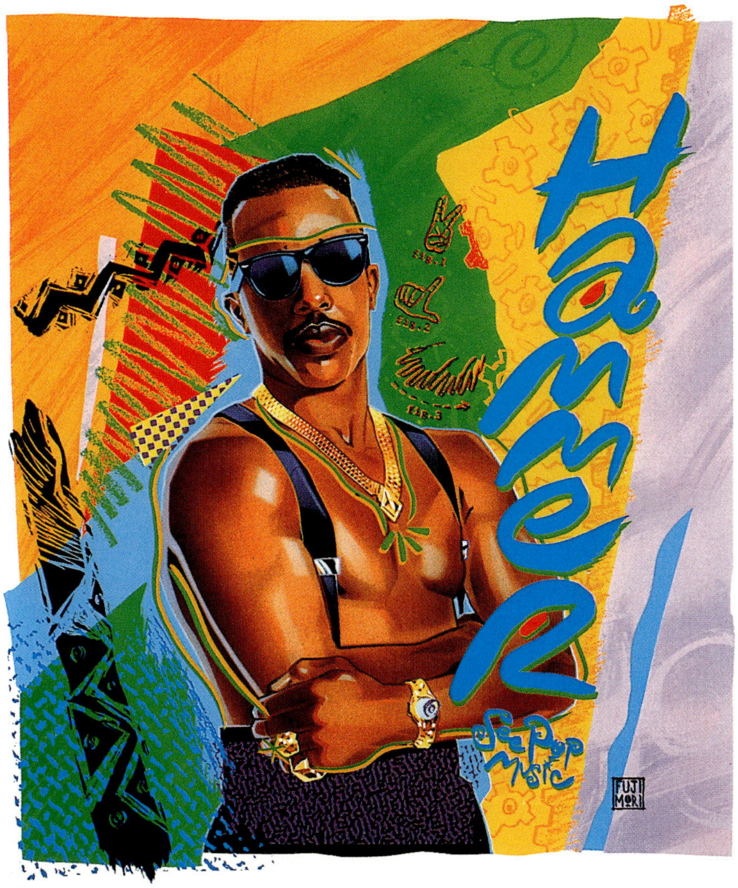

2

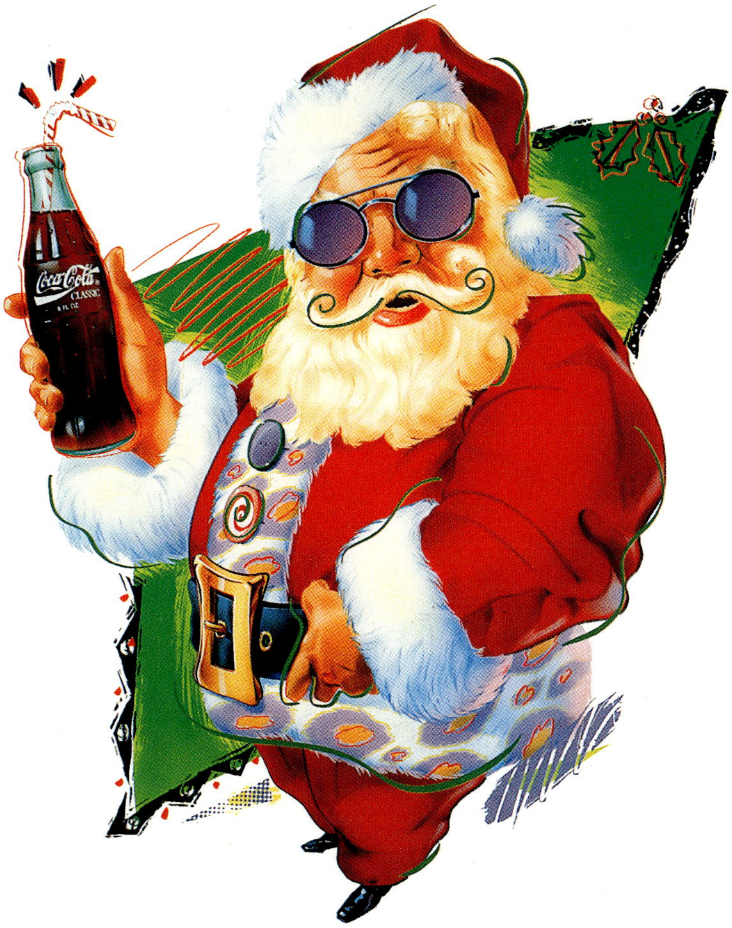

3

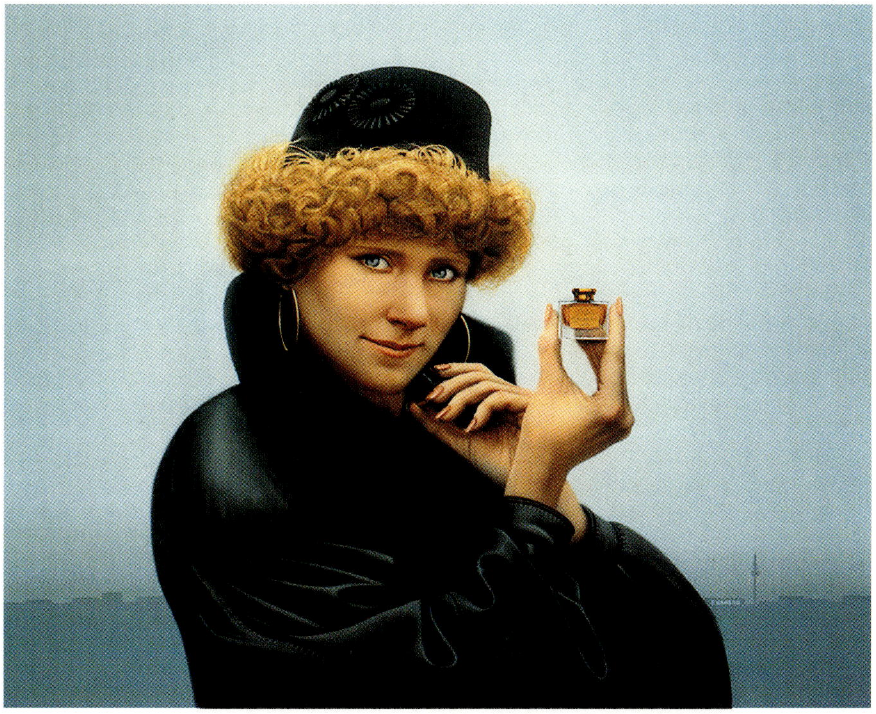

4

1
Artist Mike Gardner
Title Kirby Puckett
Client Legends Sports Memorabilia Inc.
Usage Sports Memorabilia Price Guide Cover
Media Used Acrylic

2
Artist Mike Gardner
Title Robin Yount
Client Legends Sports Memorabilia Inc.
Usage Sports Memorabilia Price Guide Cover
Media Used Acrylic

3
Artist Mike Gardner
Title The Shaq
Client Legends Sports Memorabilia Inc.
Usage Sports Memorabilia Price Guide Cover
Media Used Acrylic

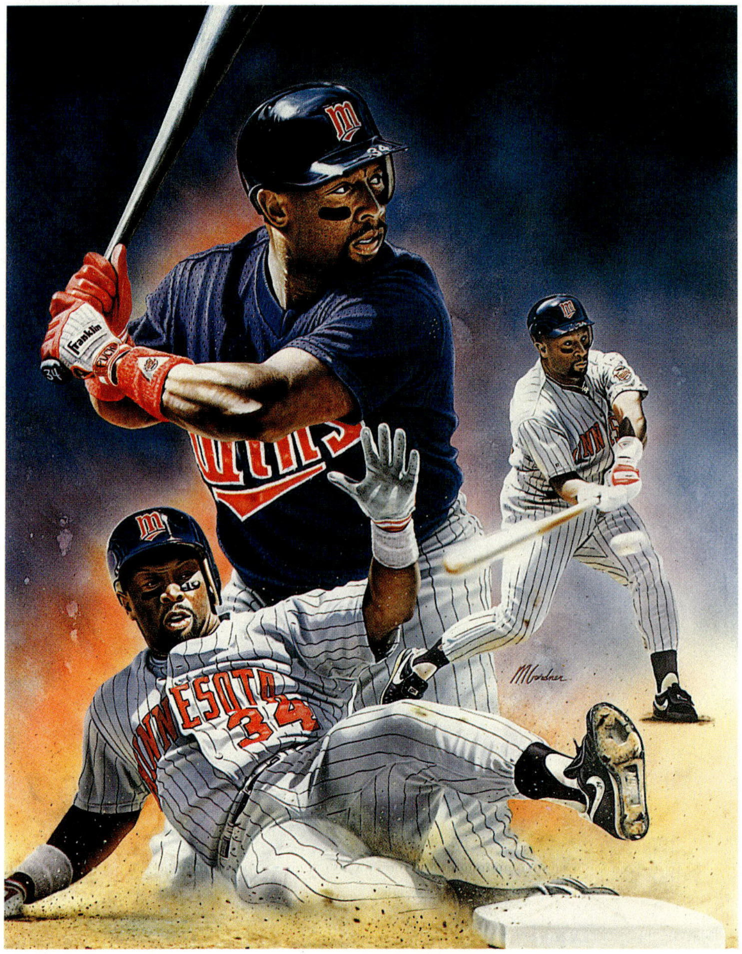

1

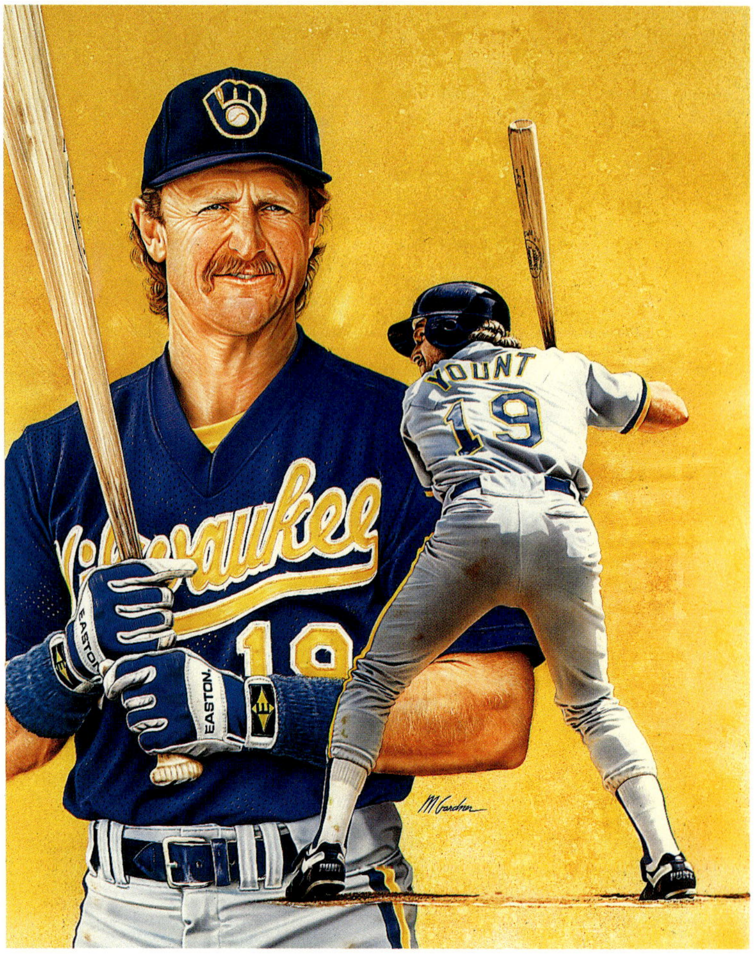

2

3

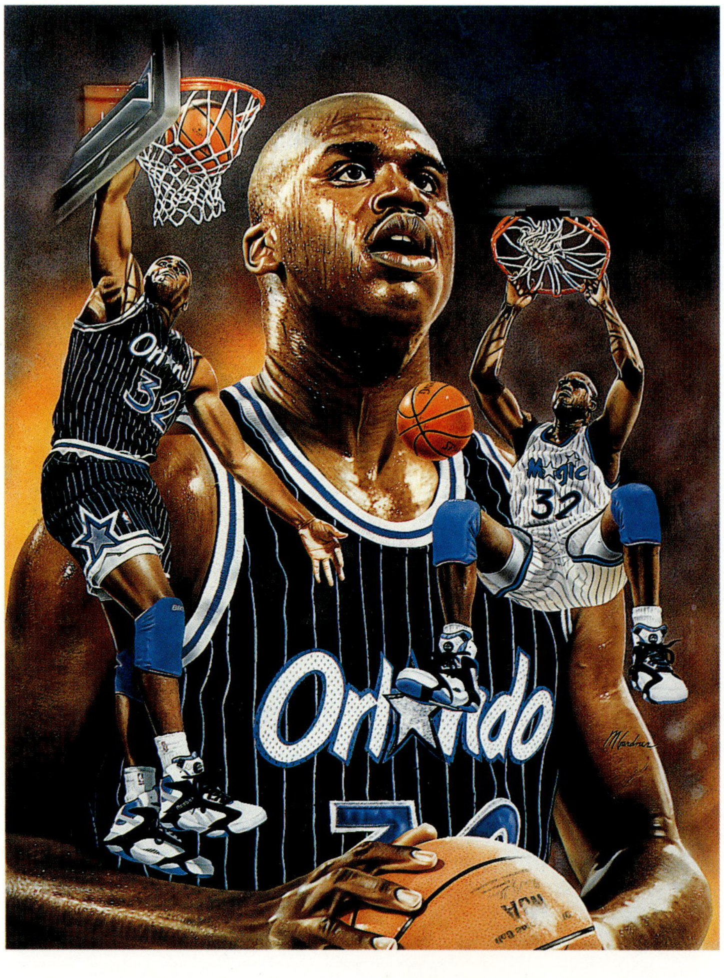

1
Artist Mike Gardner
Title Emmitt Smith
Client Legends Sports Memorabilia Inc.
Usage Sports Memorabilia Price Guide Cover
Media Used Acrylic

2
Artist Mike Gardner
Title Mark Messier
Client Legends Sports Memorabilia Inc.
Usage Sports Memorabilia Price Guide Cover
Media Used Acrylic

3
Artist Mike Gardner
Title Brooks Robinson
Client Legends Sports Memorabilia Inc.
Usage Sports Memorabilia Price Guide Cover
Media Used Acrylic

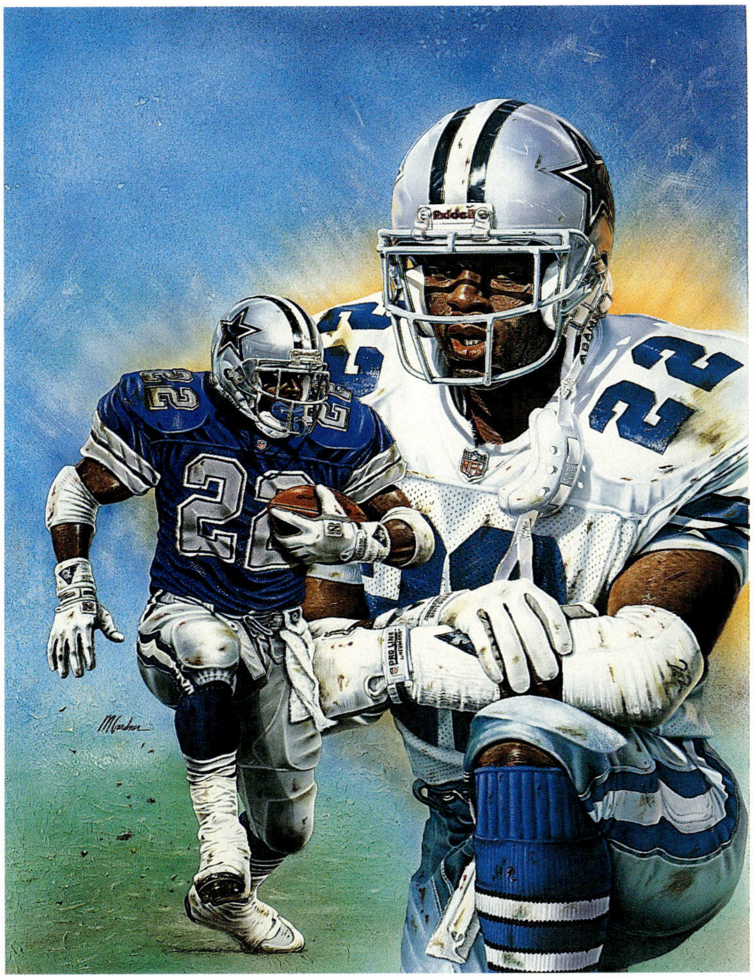

1

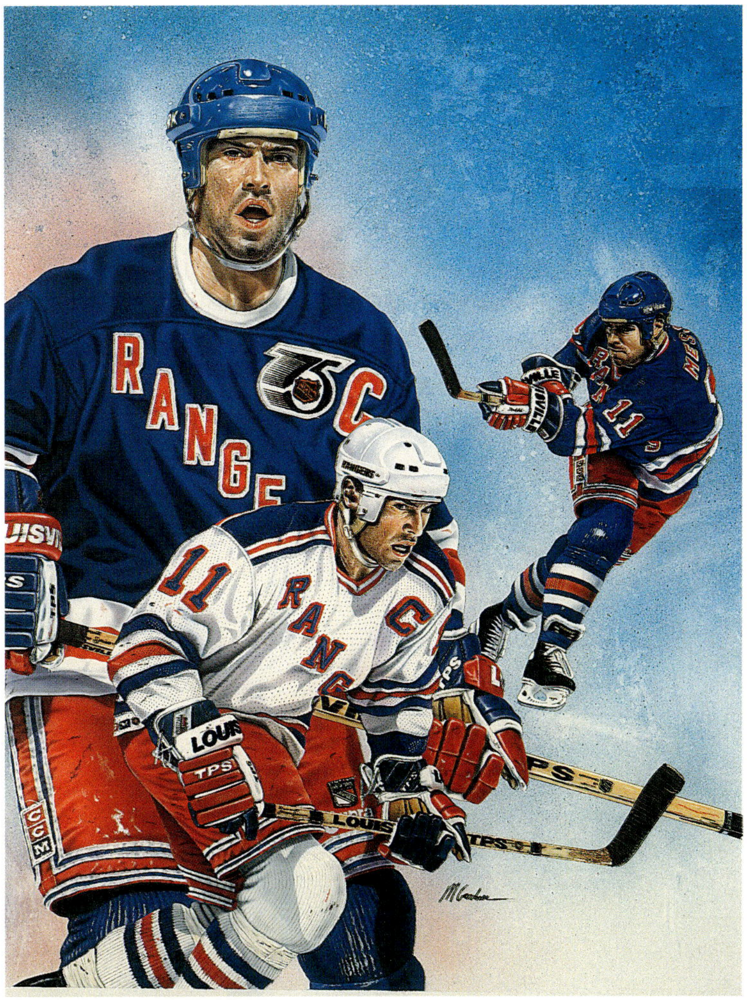

2

3

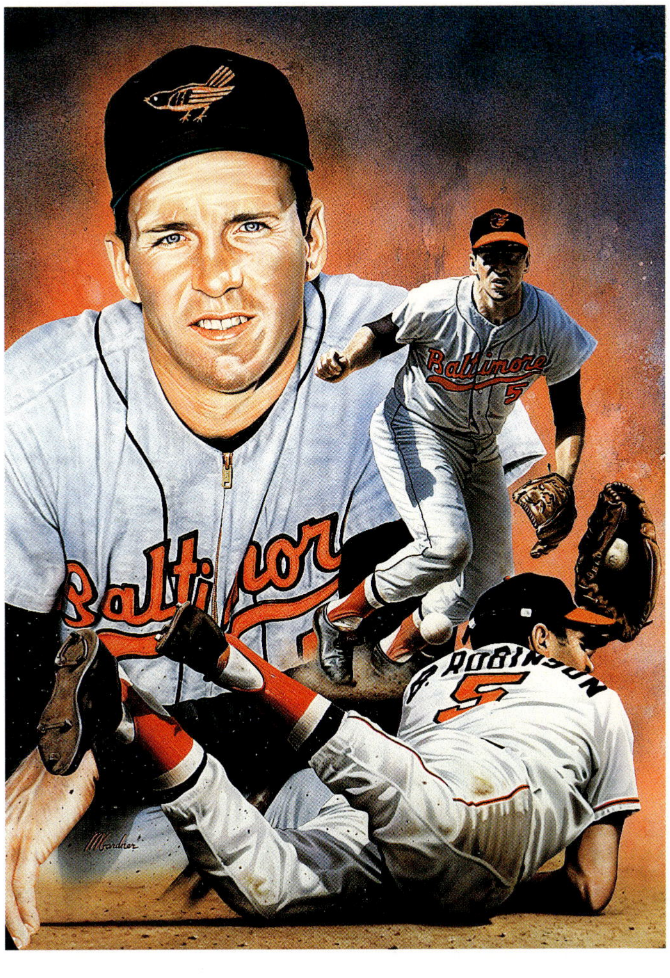

1
Artist Mike Gardner
Title Rollie Fingers
Client Legends Sports Memorabilia Inc.
Usage Limited Edition Lithograph
Media Used Acrylic

2
Artist Mike Gardner
Title Florida Marlins 1993 Inaugural Yearbook Cover
Client Sports Marketing Group
Art Director Faith Matorin
Usage Florida Marlins 1993 Inaugural Yearbook Cover
Media Used Acrylic

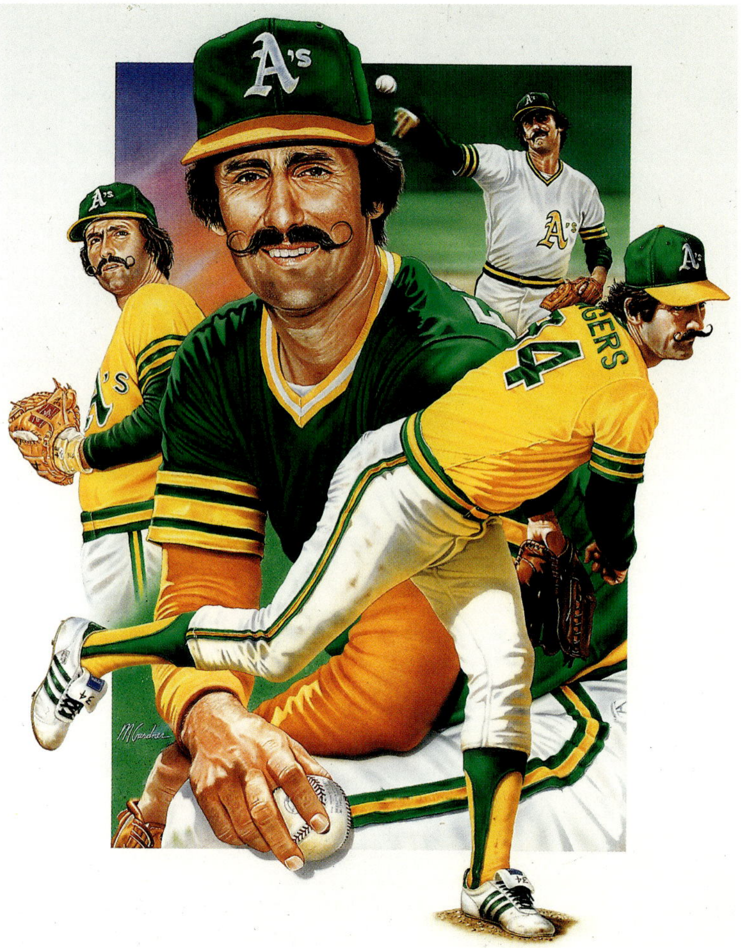

1

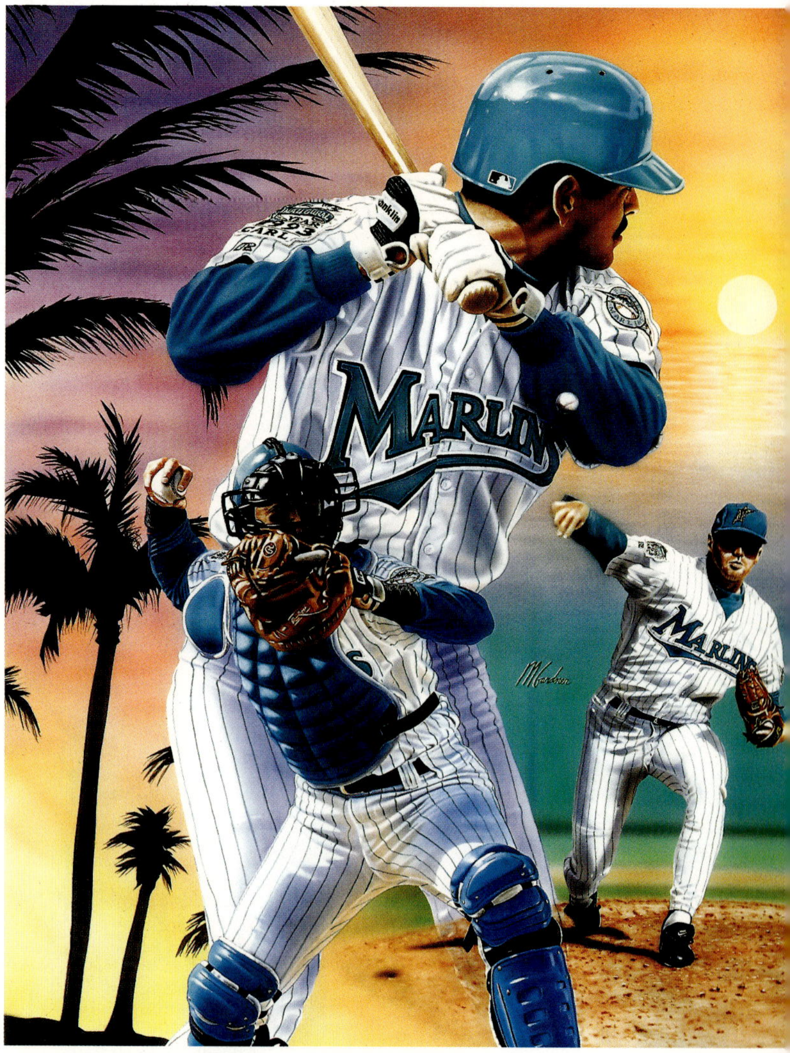

2

1
Artist Ben Garvie
Title Nestea
Client Nestea (Ram Group)
Usage Commercial Art
Media Used Acrylic

2
Artist Ben Garvie
Title Chocolate #26
Client Chronicle Books
Usage Editorial Illustration
Media Used Acrylic

3
Artist Scott T. Gee
Title Clown #2
Instructor Jerrold Bishop
Usage Student Art
Media Used Rotring Inks, Prismacolor

4
Artist Scott T. Gee
Title Self Portrait
Instructor Jerrold Bishop
Usage Student Art
Media Used Rotring Inks, Prismacolor

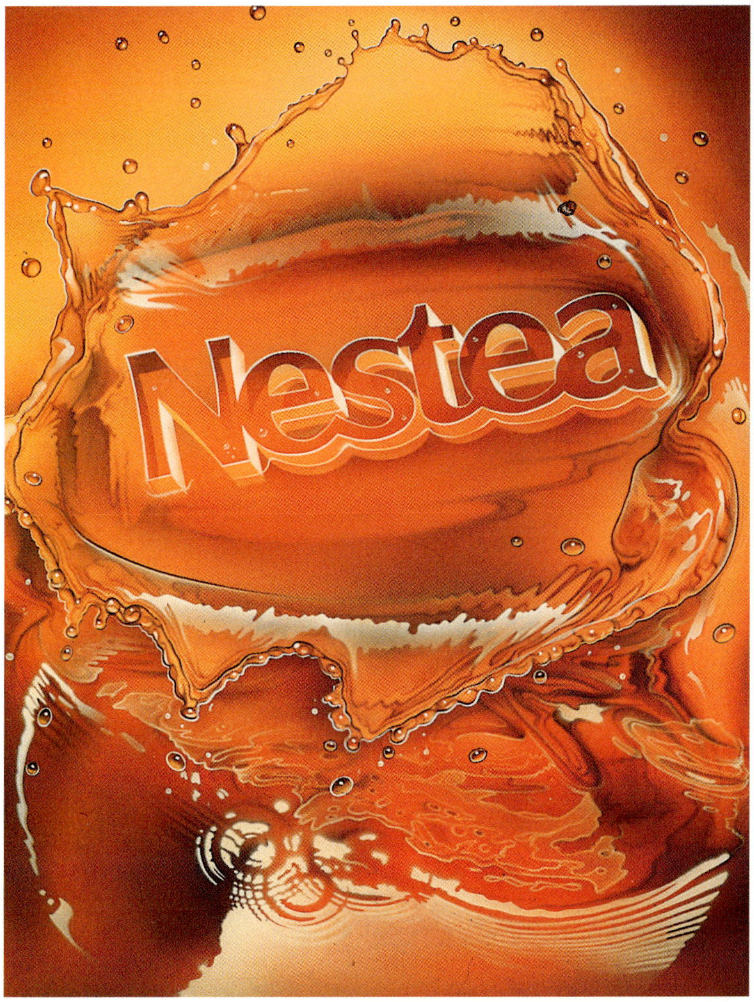

1

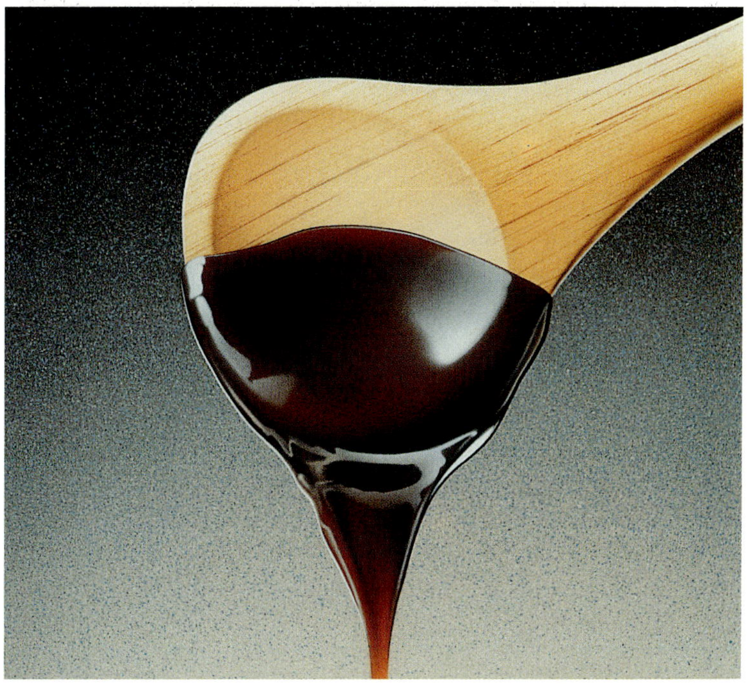

2

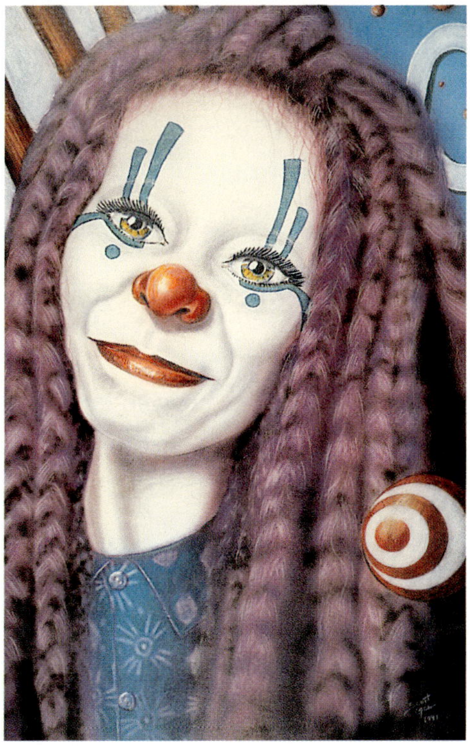

3

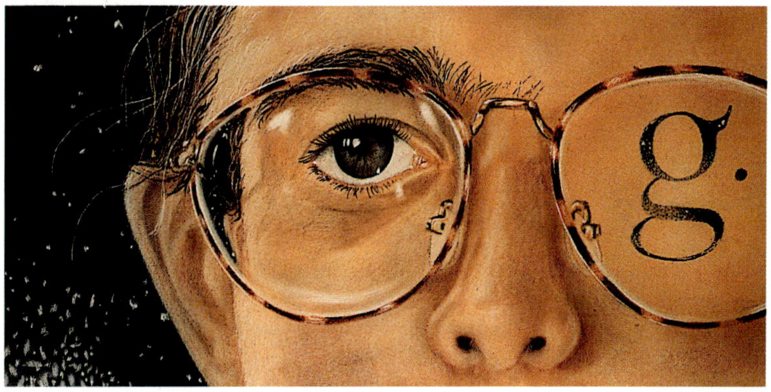

4

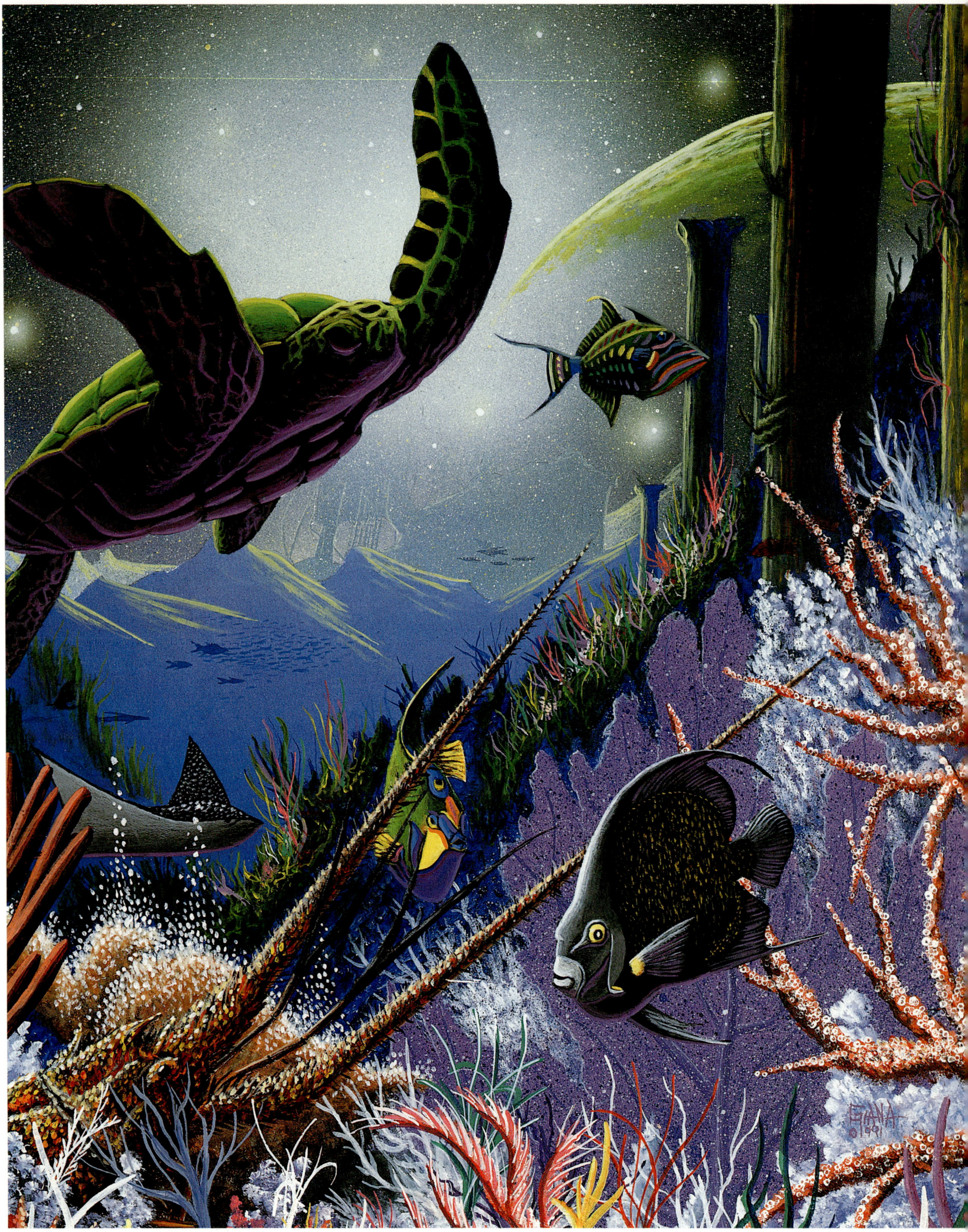

1

1
Artist Alan Giana
Title Tranquility Base
Usage Self Promotion
Media Used Acrylic

2
Artist Alan Giana
Title Breach of Peace
Usage Self Promotion
Media Used Acrylic

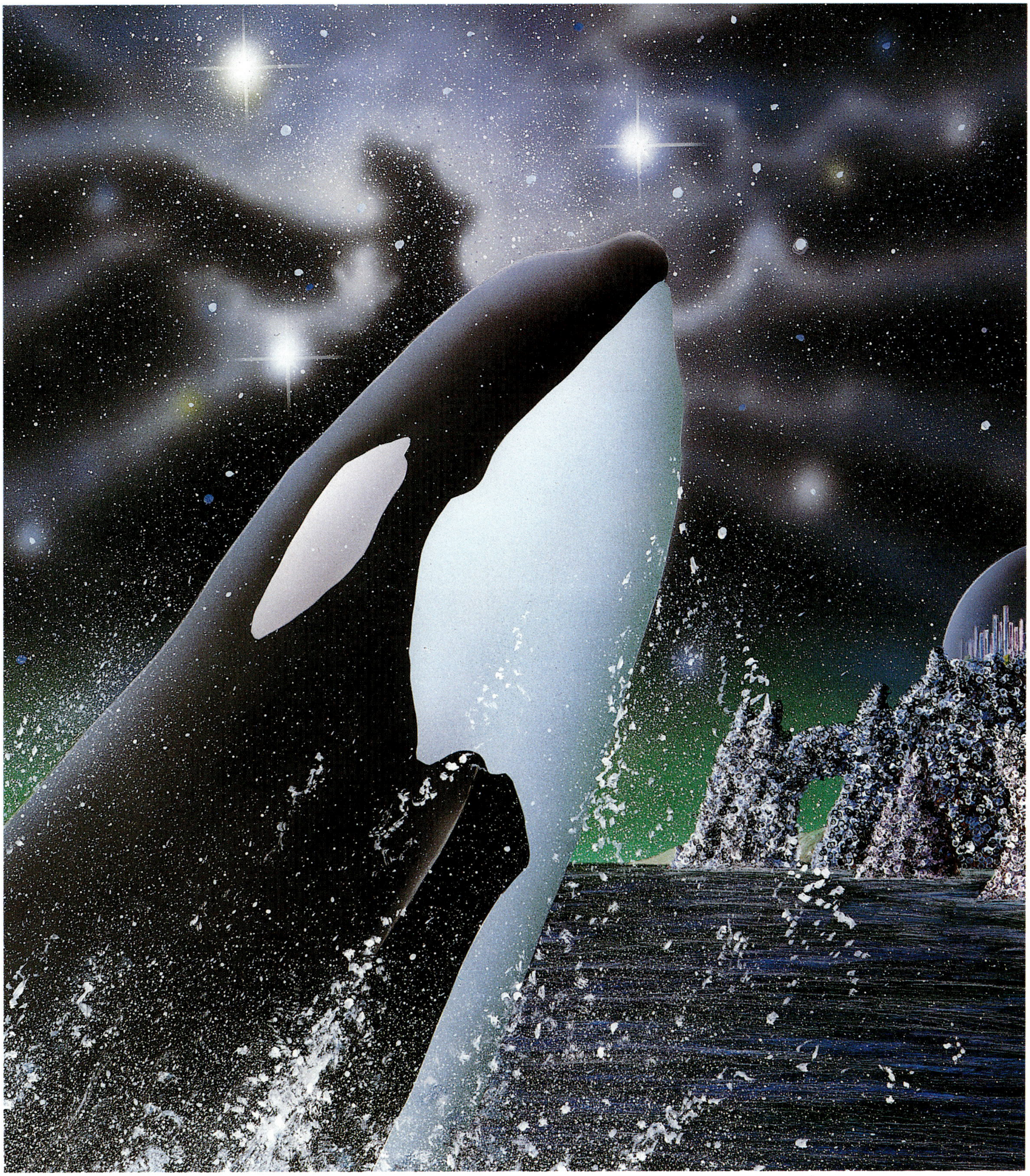

2

1
Artist Gary Glover
Title Misery
Usage Self Promotion
Media Used Acrylic

2
Artist Gary Glover
Title Hear the Children Calling
Client Nal/Penguin
Art Director George Cornell
Usage Book Cover
Media Used Acrylic, Oils

3
Artist Gary Glover
Title Dunc's Cannon
Client Dell Publishing
Art Director Lynn Andreozzi
Usage Book Cover
Media Used Acrylic

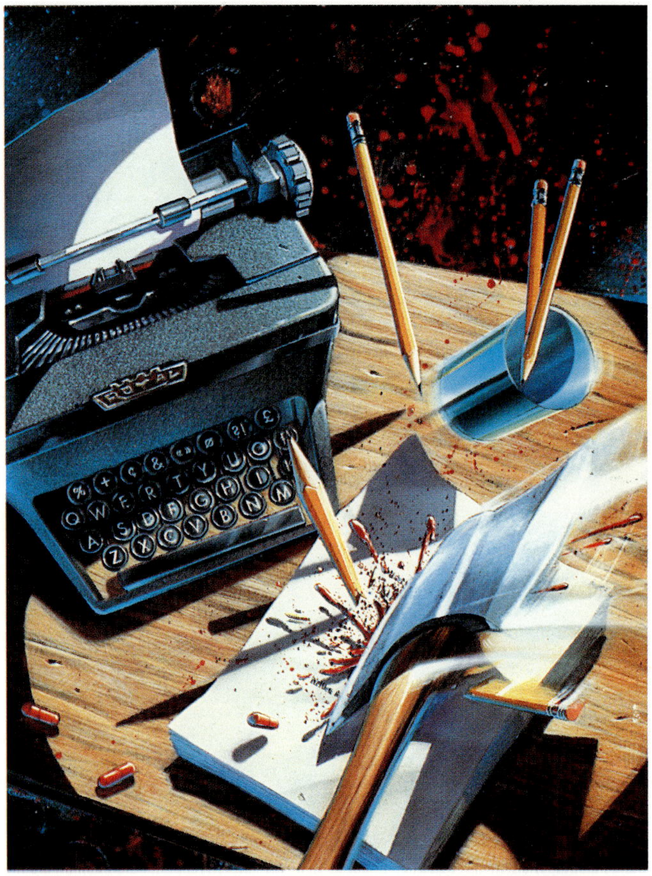
1

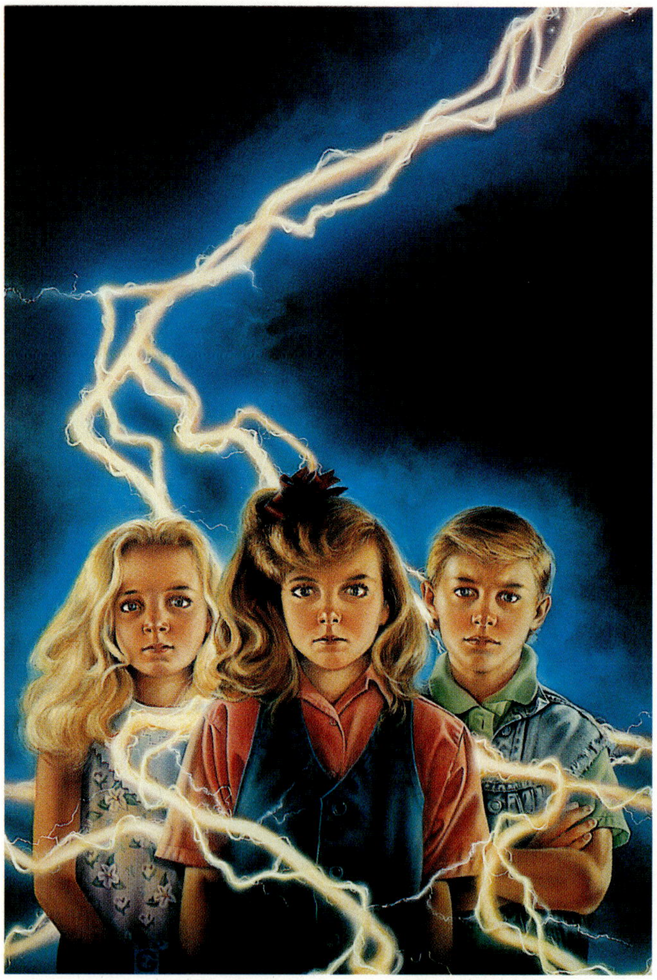
2

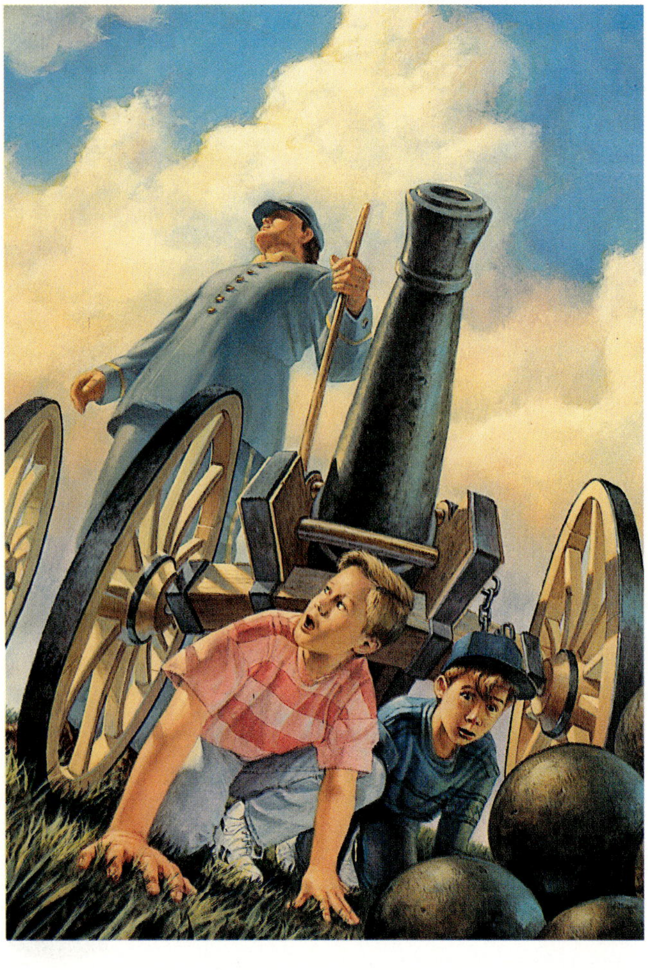
3

1
Artist Gary Glover
Title Dunc and Amos in the Big Top
Client Dell Publications
Art Director Lynn Andreozzi
Usage Book Cover
Media Used Acrylic

2
Artist Gary Glover
Title Dunc and the Flaming Ghost
Client Dell Publishing
Art Director Lynn Andreozzi
Usage Book Cover
Media Used Acrylic

3
Artist Gary Glover
Title Damn Fine Coffee
Usage Self Promotion
Media Used Acrylic, Oils

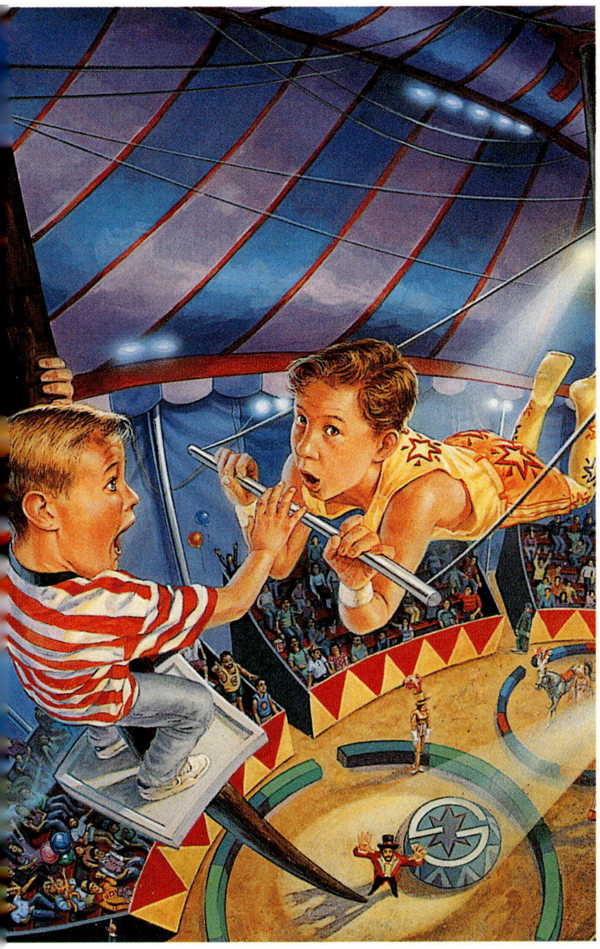

1

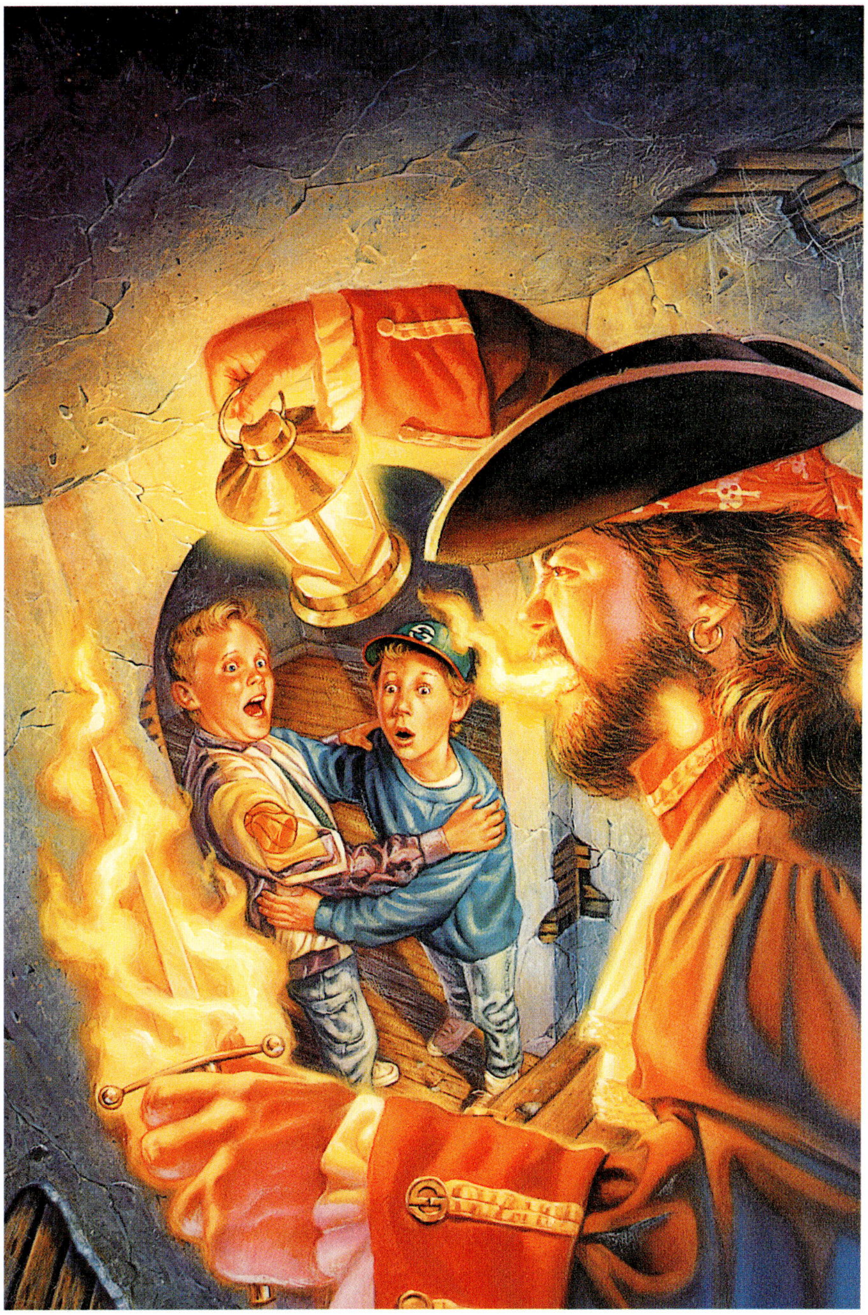

2

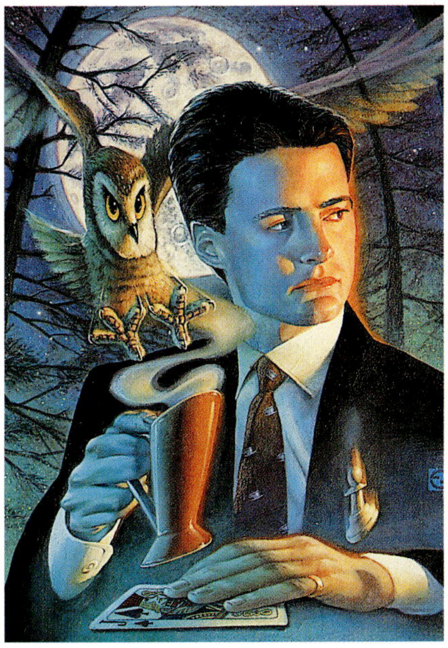

3

1
Artist Gary Glover
Title Easter Island
Usage Self Promotion
Media Used Acrylic

2
Artist Gary Glover
Title Worf
Client Universal Pictures/Statix
Usage Advertisement
Media Used Acrylic

3
Artist Stuart Hall
Title Zagra the Forbidden
Usage Editorial
Media Used Watercolor

4
Artist Andy Hickes
Title Interior IRS National Headquarters-Lobby
Client IRS
Architect Carlos Zapata for The Hiller Group
Usage Architectural Rendering
Media Used Mixed

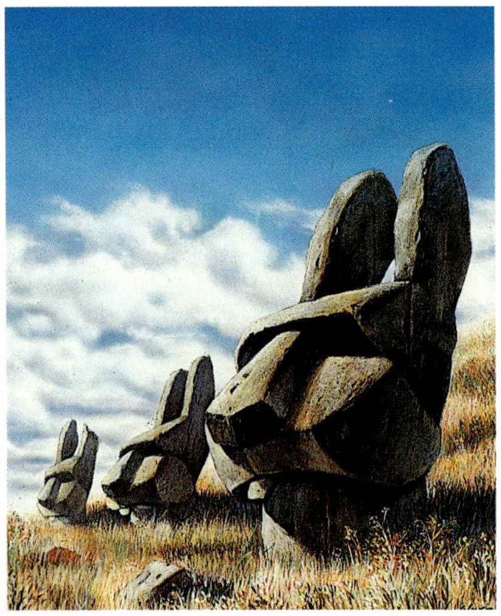

1

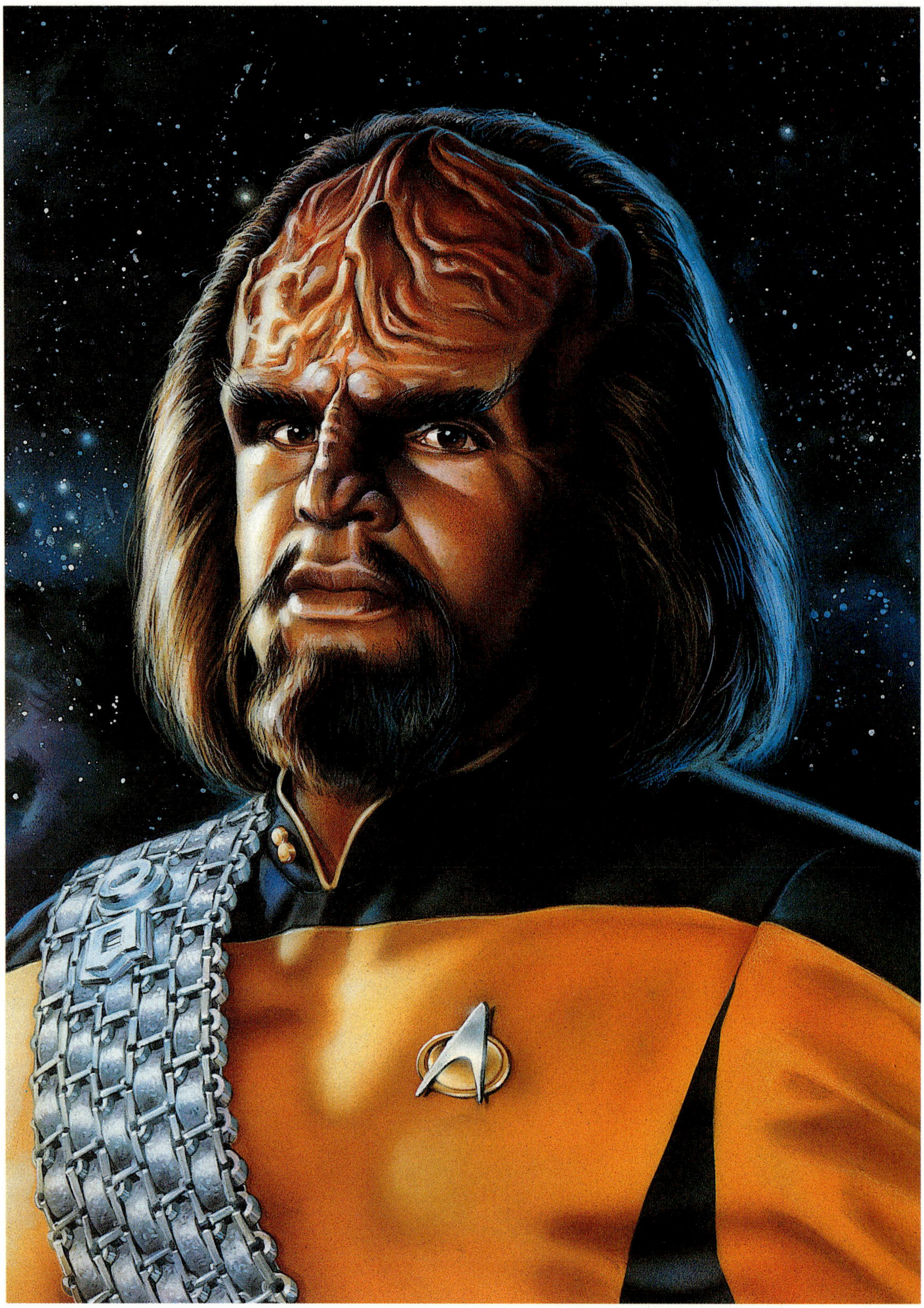

2

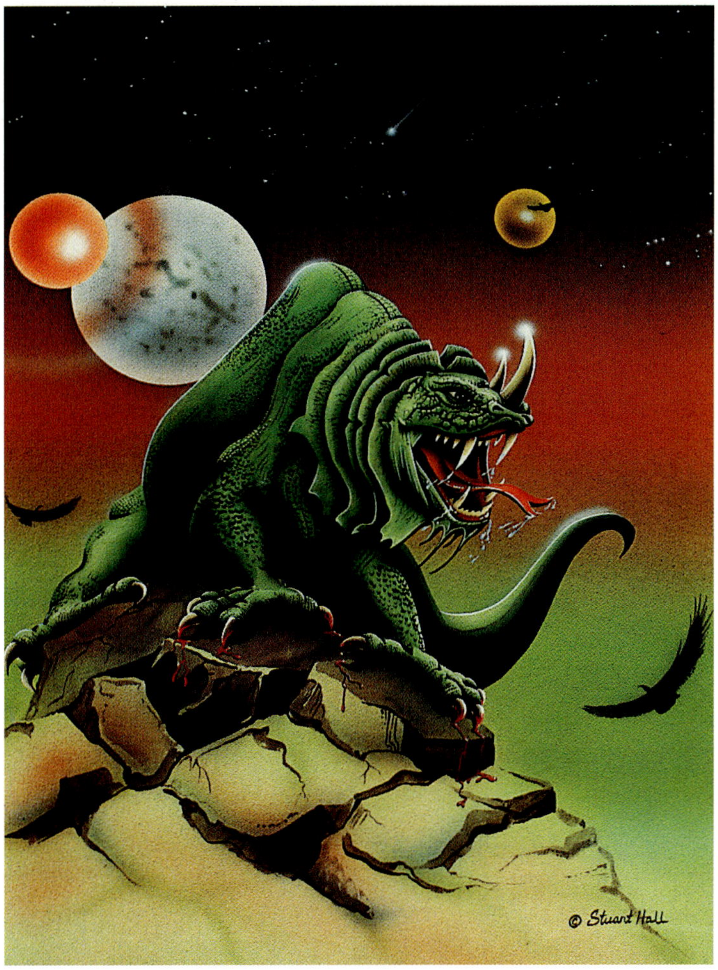

3

4

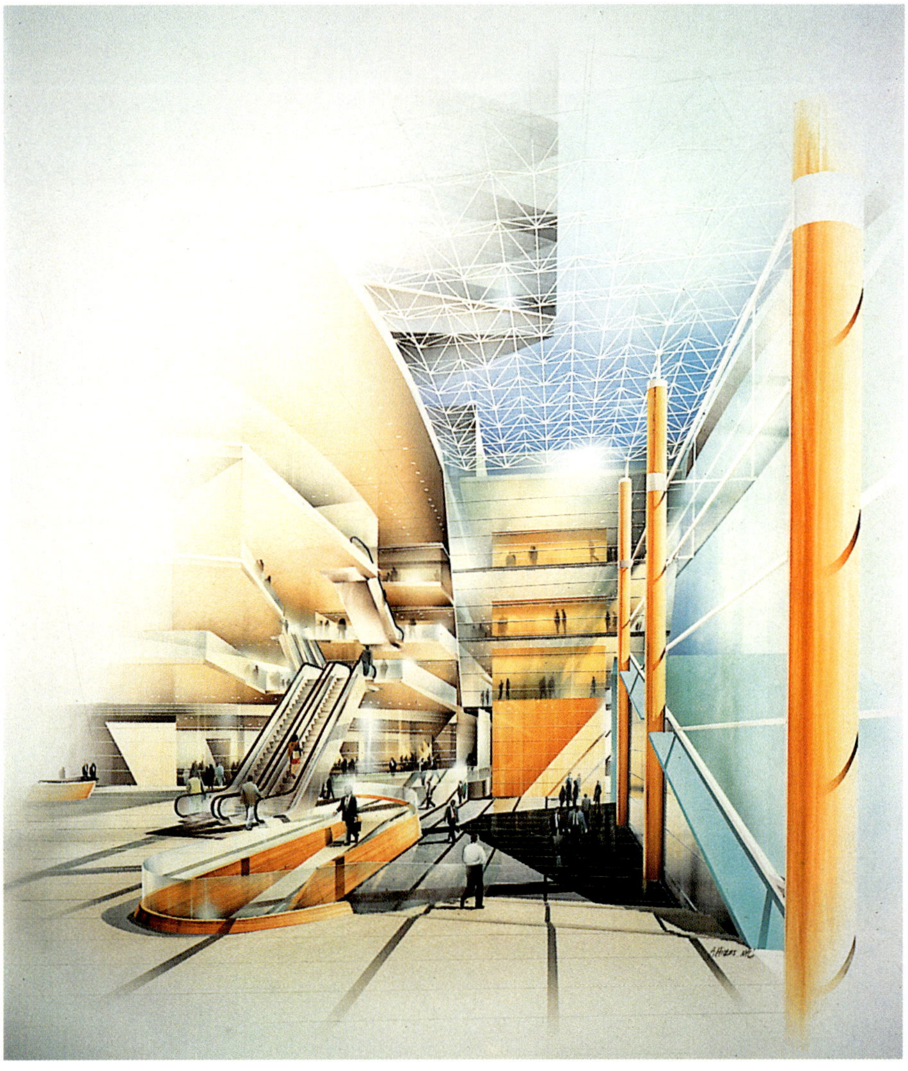

1
Artist Andy Hickes
Title North/South Section "House on a Hill," Bel Air, California
Art Director Thierry Despont
Media Used Dr. Martin's Acrylics, Pelican

2
Artist Andy Hickes
Title East/West "House on a Hill," Bel Air, California
Art Director Thierry Despont
Media Used Dr. Martin's Acrylics, Pelican

3
Artist Andy Hickes
Title Design Proposal for Coco Pazzo Restaurant, Chicago, Illinois
Client Harb Architects
Art Director Rosenblum
Media Used Dr. Martin's Acrylics, Pelican Ink

4
Artist Andy Hickes
Title Interior, Planet Hollywood, London
Client Planet Hollywood
Architect Haverson Rockwell Architects
Usage Architectural Rendering
Media Used Mixed

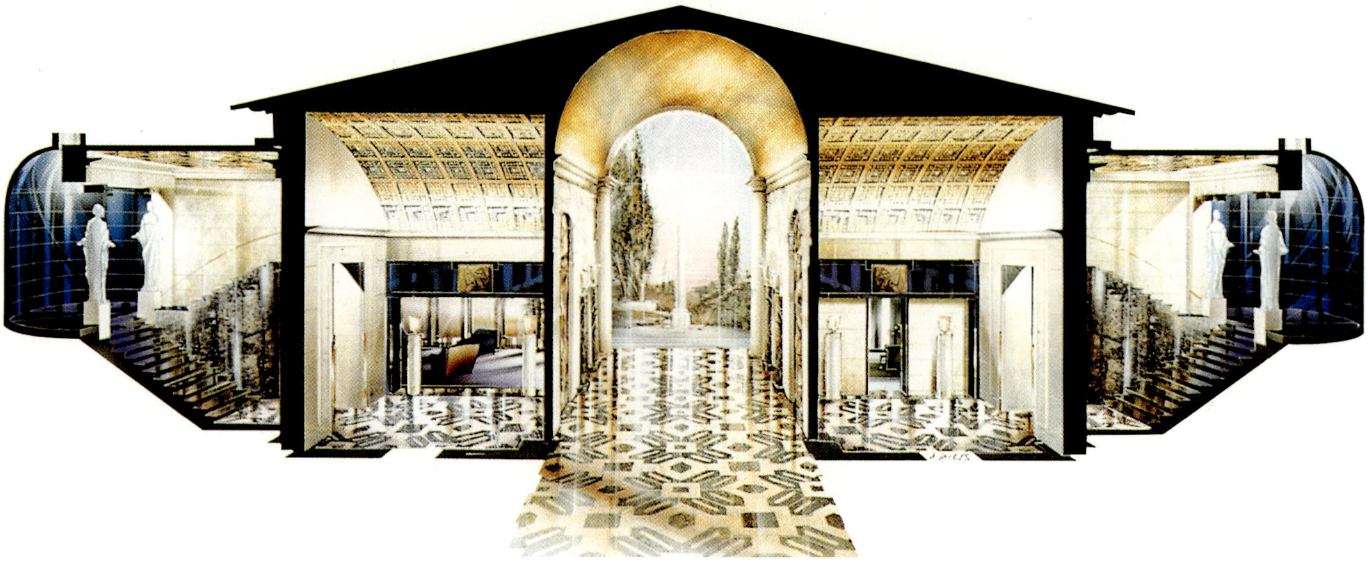

1

2

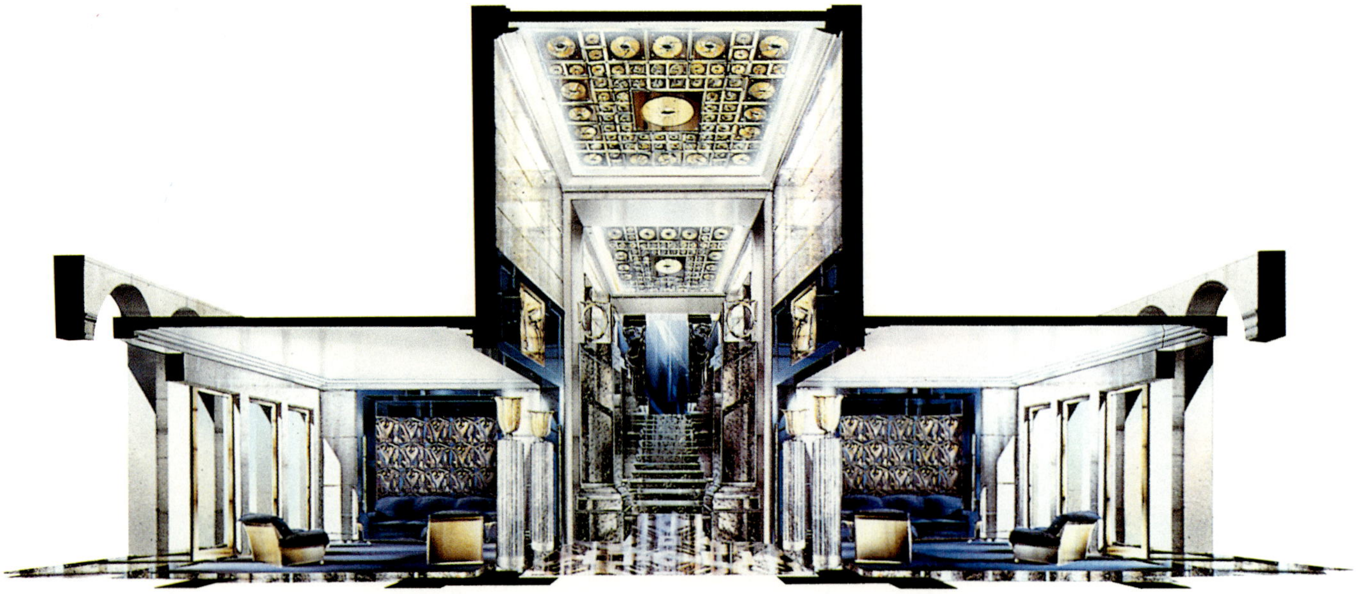

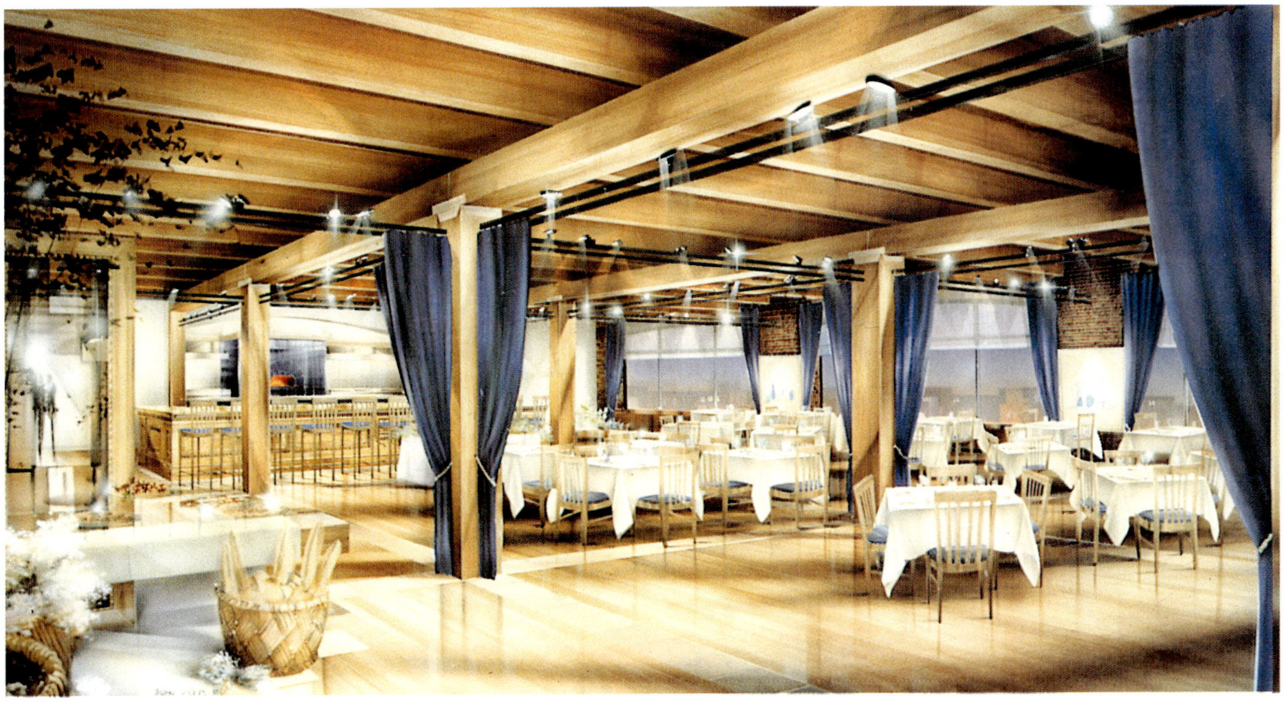

3

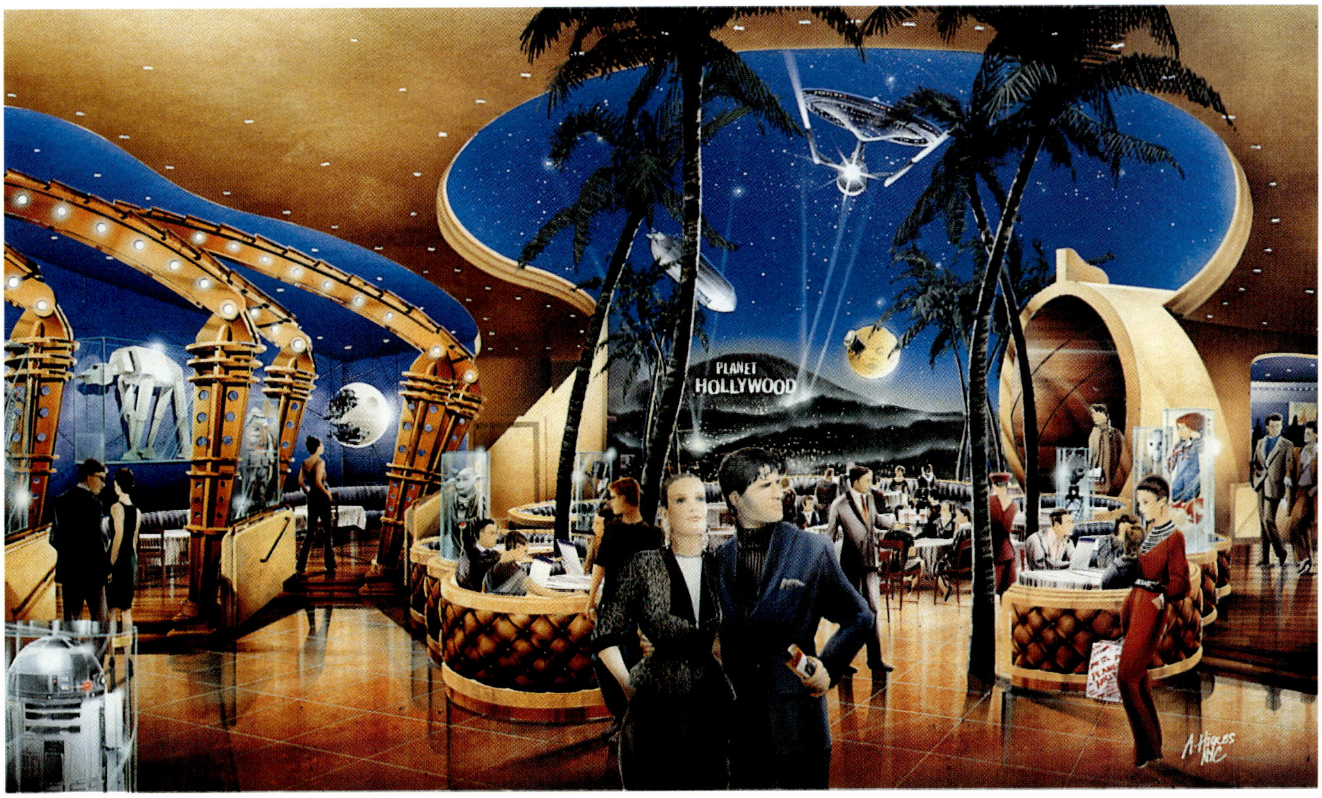

4

1
Artist Andy Hickes
Title Peter Wlodawski Aids Memorial
Art Director Andy Hickes
Media Used Mixed

2
Artist Andy Hickes
Title Exterior, Planet Hollywood, London
Client Planet Hollywood
Architect Haverson Rockwell Architects
Usage Architectural Rendering
Media Used Mixed

3
Artist Michael Holguin
Usage Self Promotion
Media Used Inks

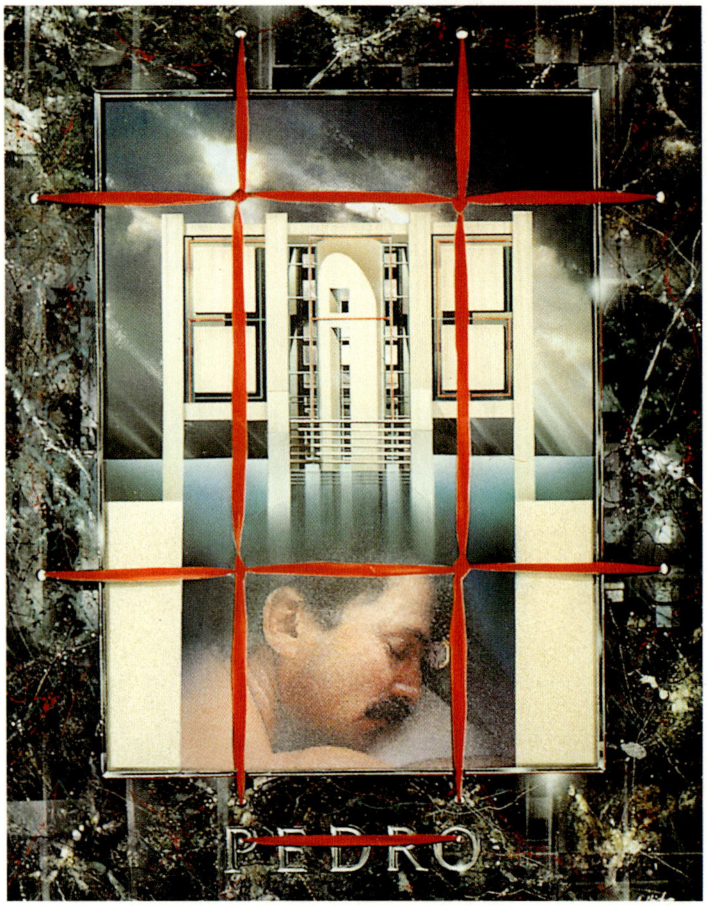

1

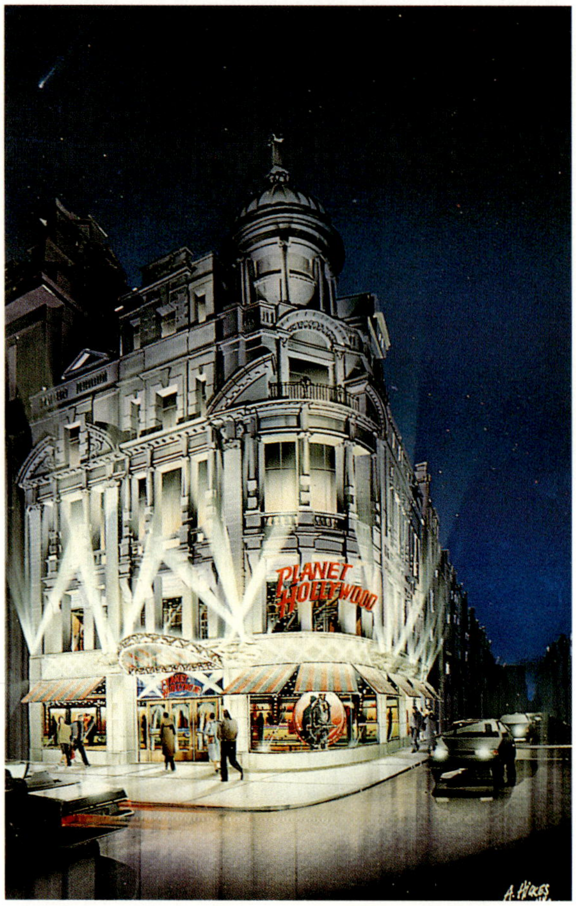

2

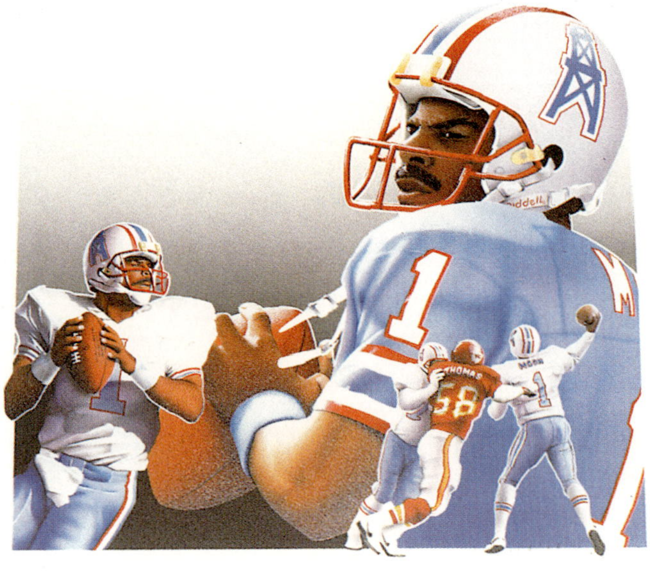
3

1
Artist Reggie Holladay
Title Cover Art A and Inside Art B
Client Florida Department of Citrus
Usage Brochure for Nutrition Music Video Contest for High School Students

2
Artist Reggie Holladay
Client Royal Carribean Cruise Lines
Art Director Christine Trani
Usage Trade Advertisement

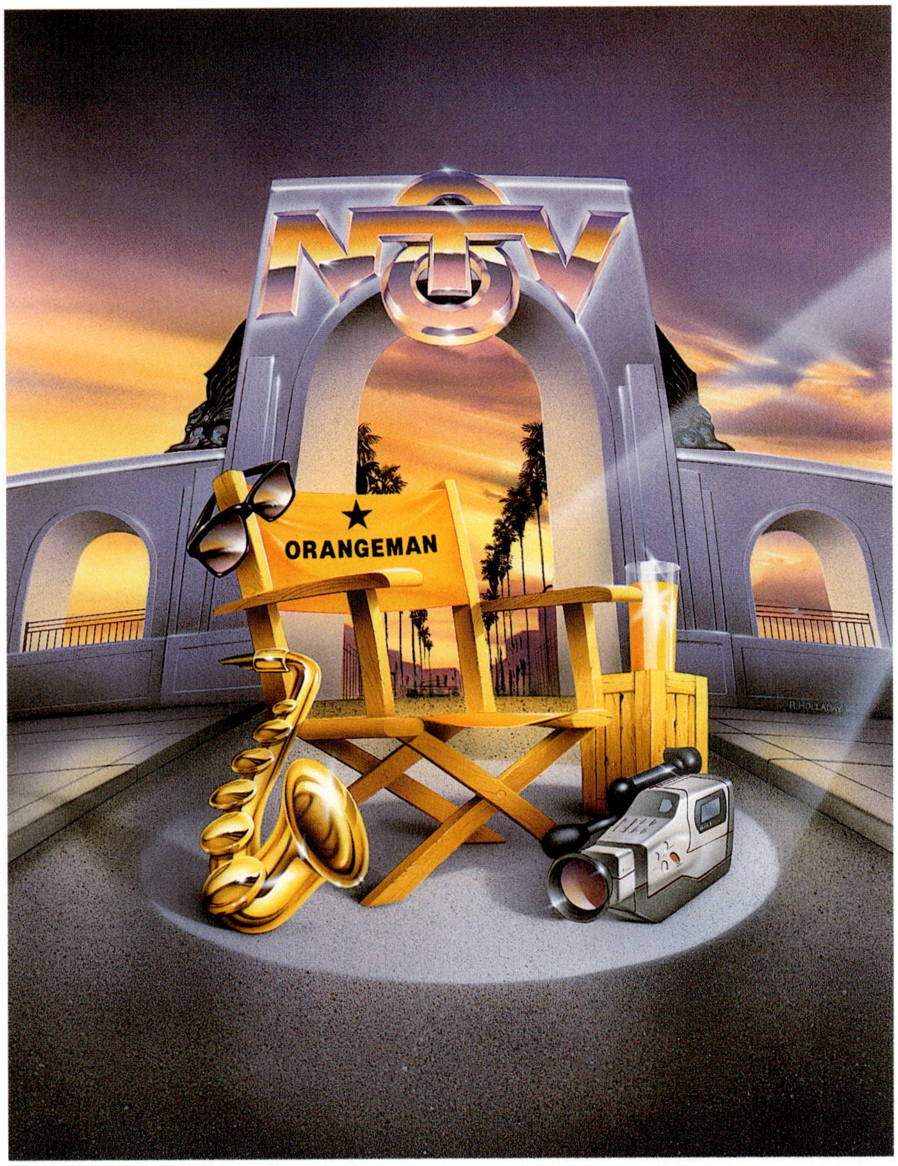

1

2

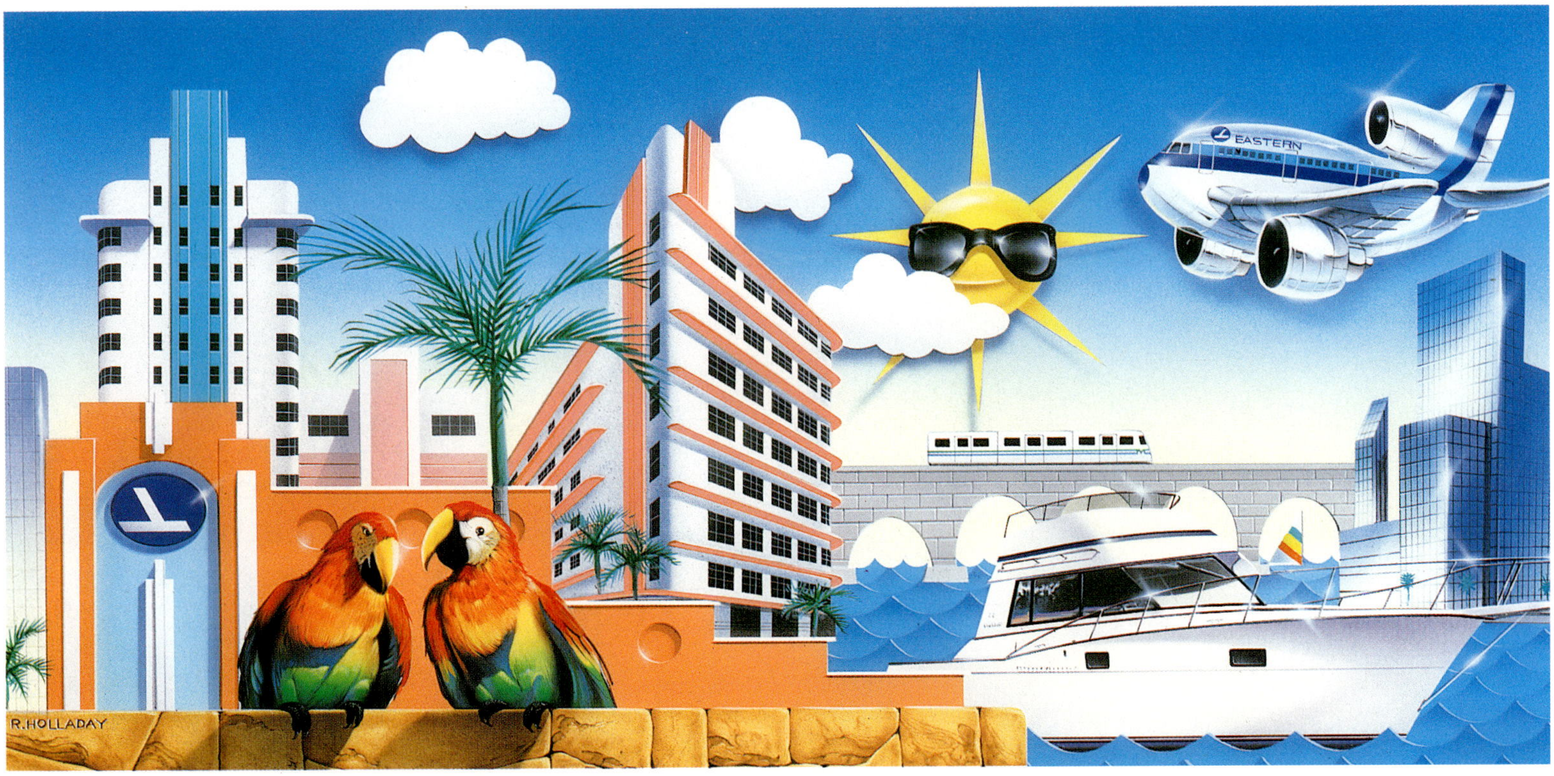

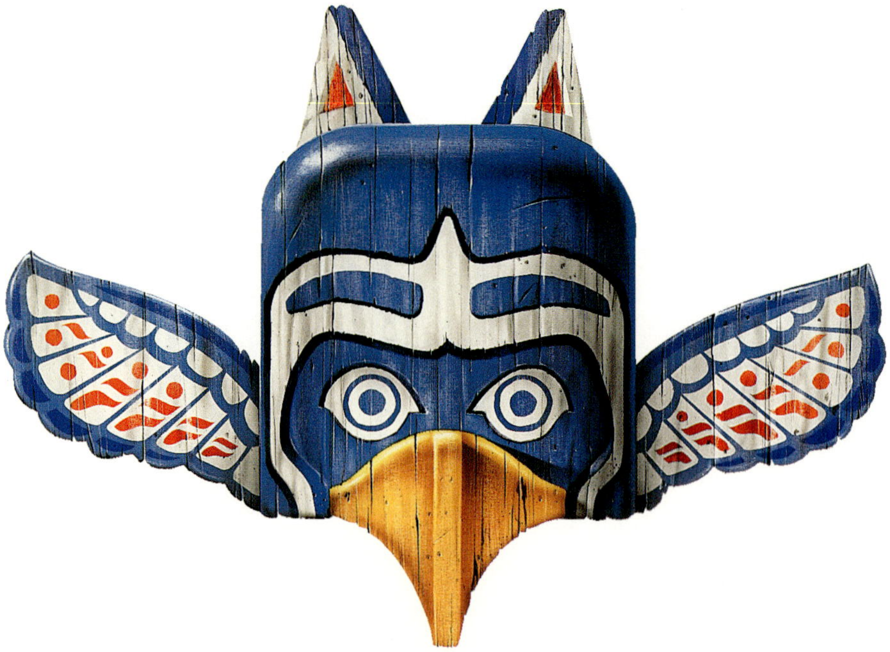

1

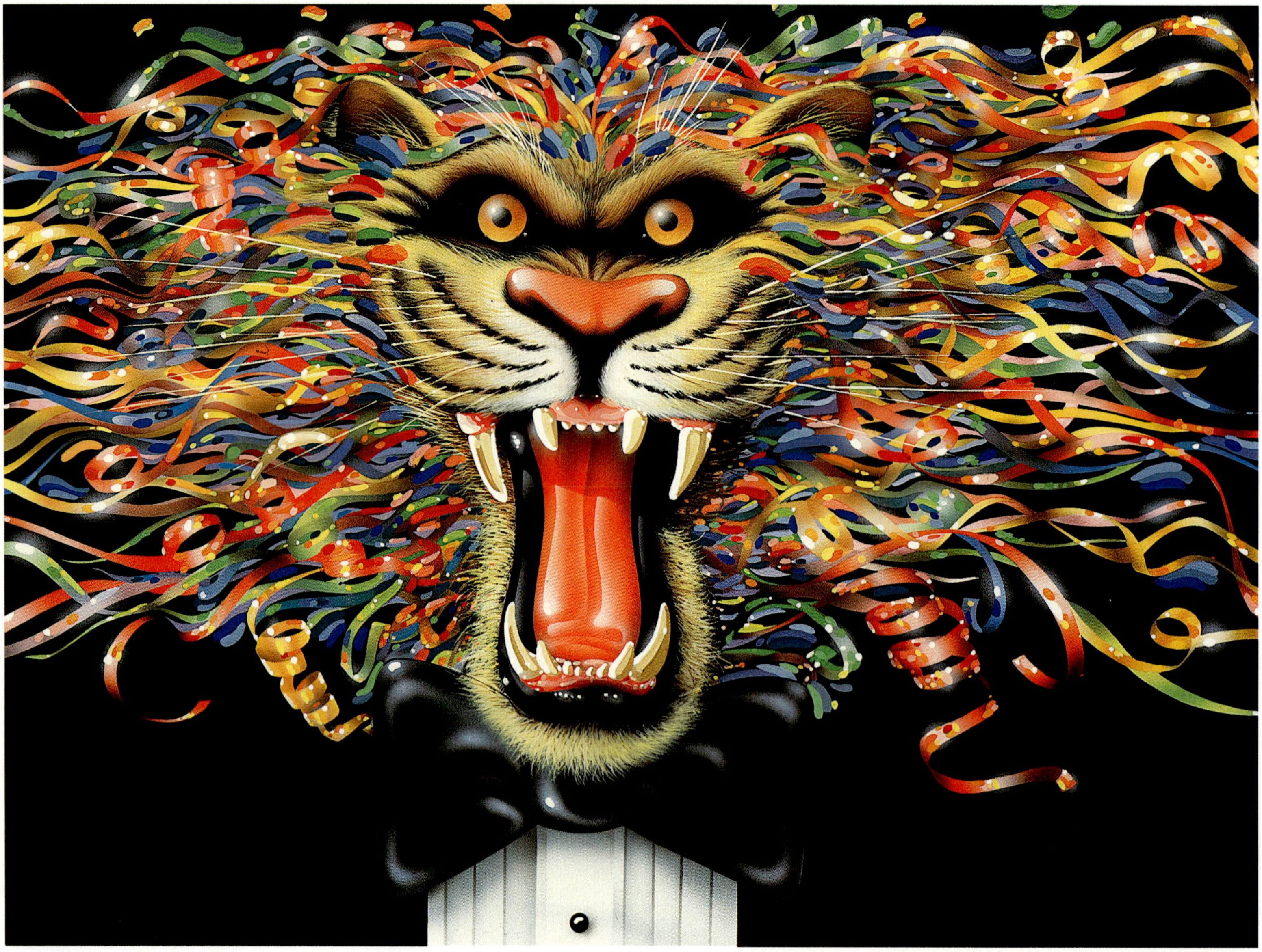

2

1
Artist Reggie Holladay
Client Eastern Airlines
Art Director Dennis Dunkelburger
Usage Trade Advertisement

2
Artist Reggie Holladay
Title Go Wild
Usage Self Promotion

3
Artist Reggie Holladay
Title Coolest Hits Summer Promotion, Promoting Bacardi and Lemon.
Client Bacardi
Art Director Ed Miller/Terry Coffy
Usage Tape Cassette Cover for "Bacardi's"

4
Artist Reggie Holladay
Title Cover Art
Client Florida Department of Citrus
Usage Brochure for Nutrition Music Video Contest

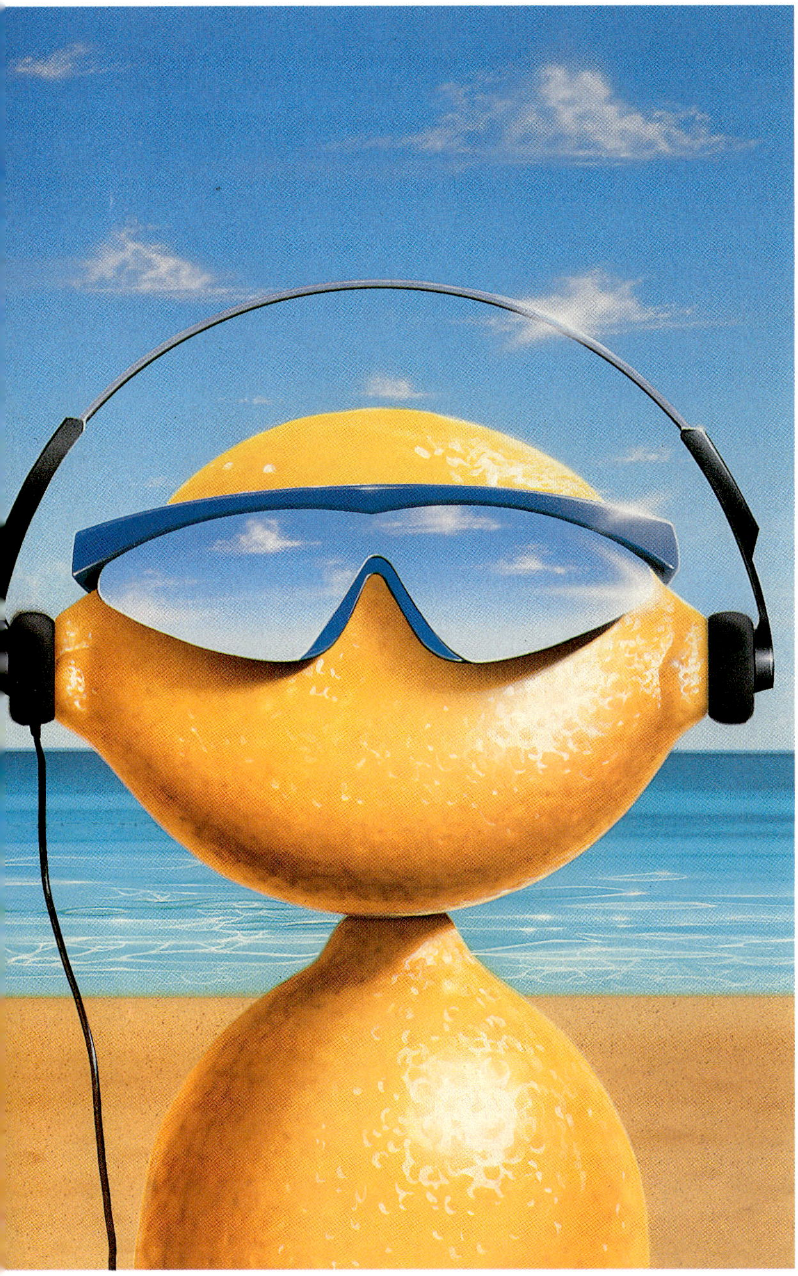

3

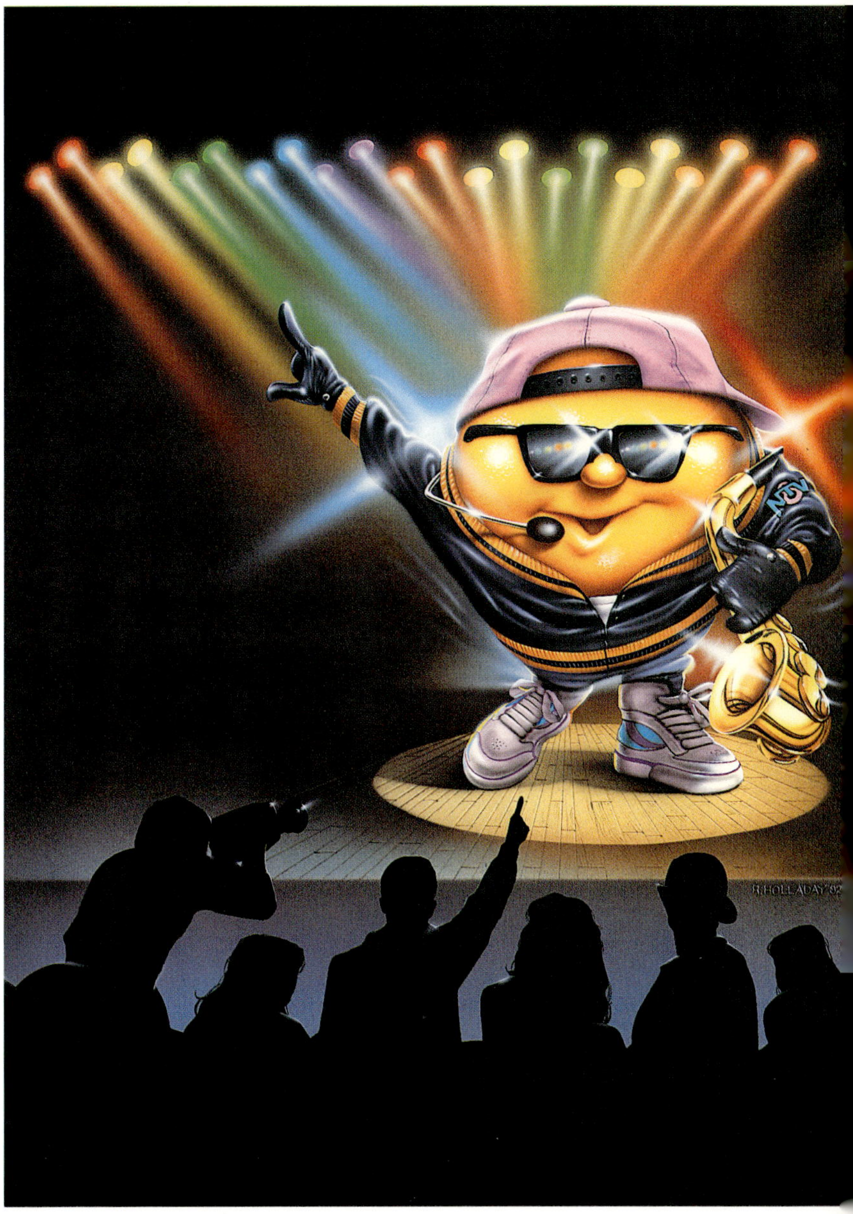

4

1
Artist Tom Hoover
Title Frank Raines
Client Private Commission
Media Used Acrylic

2
Artist Tom Hoover
Title Nigerian Nightmare
Client Self Promotion
Media Used Acrylic

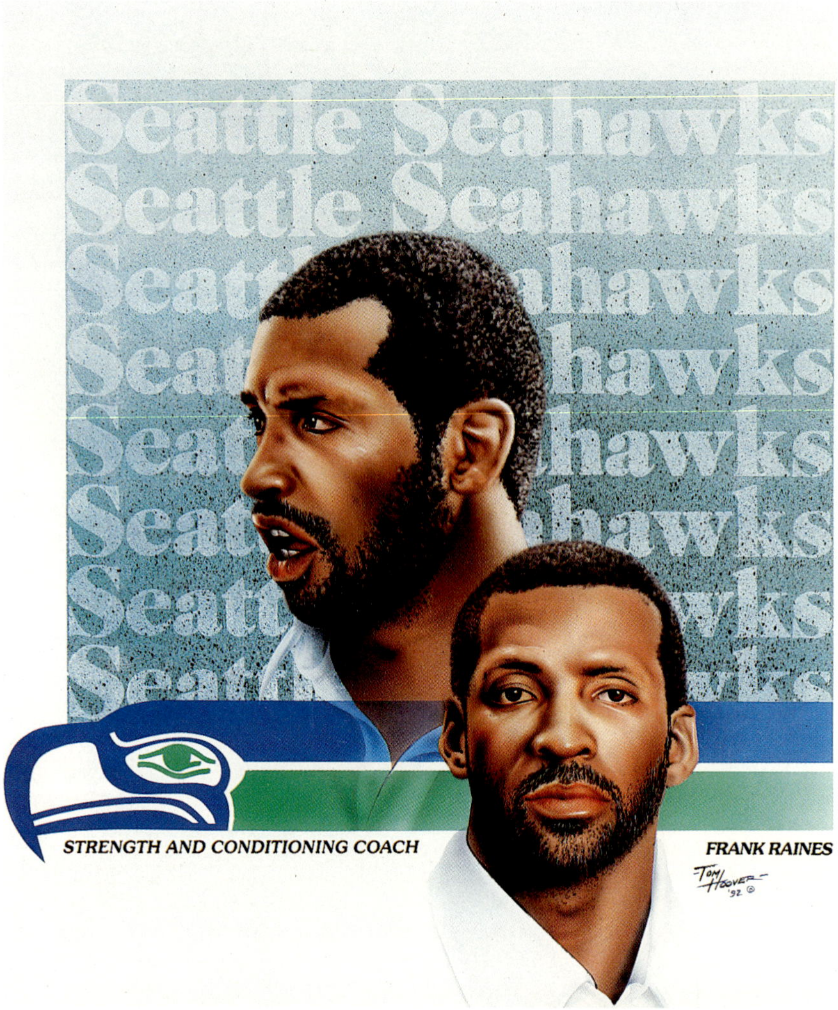

1

2

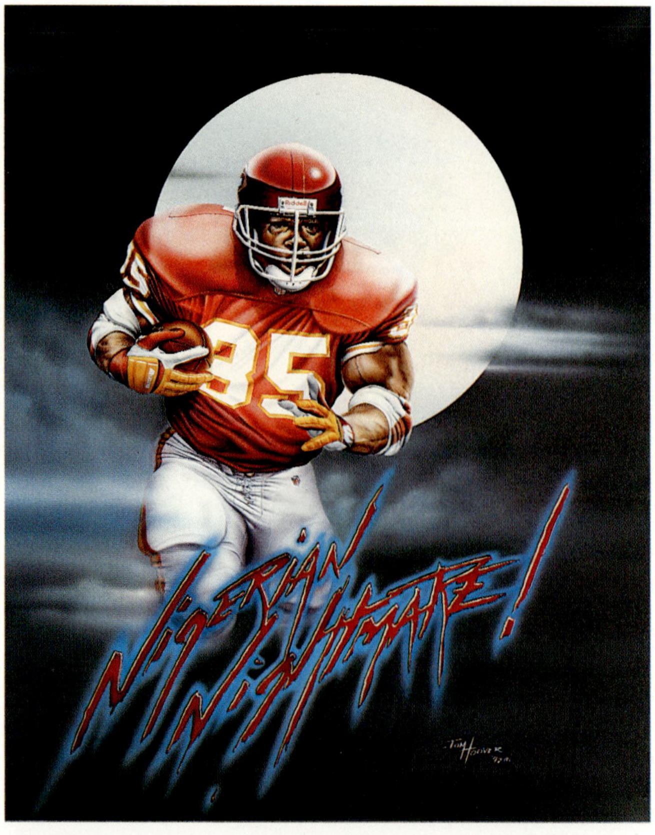

1
Artist Robert L. Horwath
Title AT&T Seabed Tractor
Art Director Frank Messina
Usage Technical Illustration
Media Used Comart, Acrylic

2
Artist Ron Houghton, Jr.
Title Endangered Species
Art Director Ron Houghton, Jr.
Usage Commercial Art

3
Artist Thomas J. Humpert
Title Nothing But Berries
Usage Self Promotion
Media Used Acrylic Comart Colors

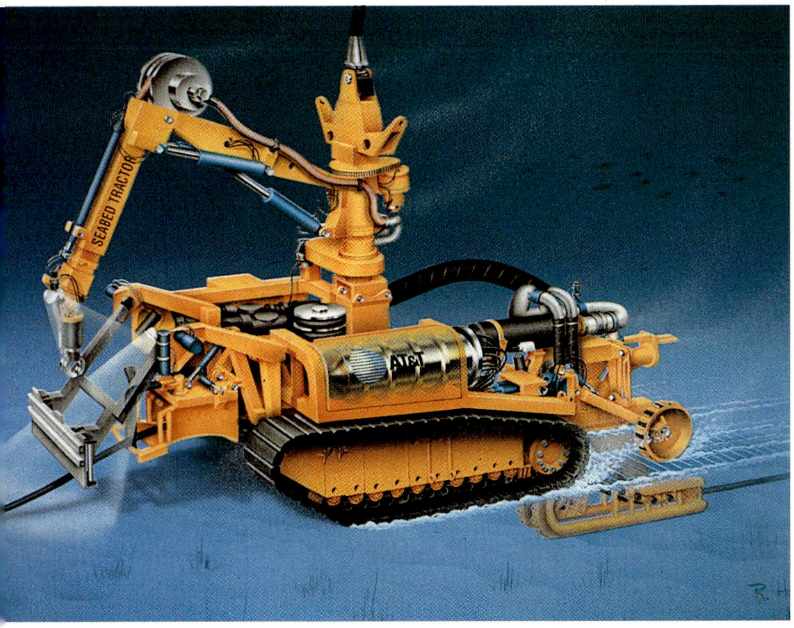

1

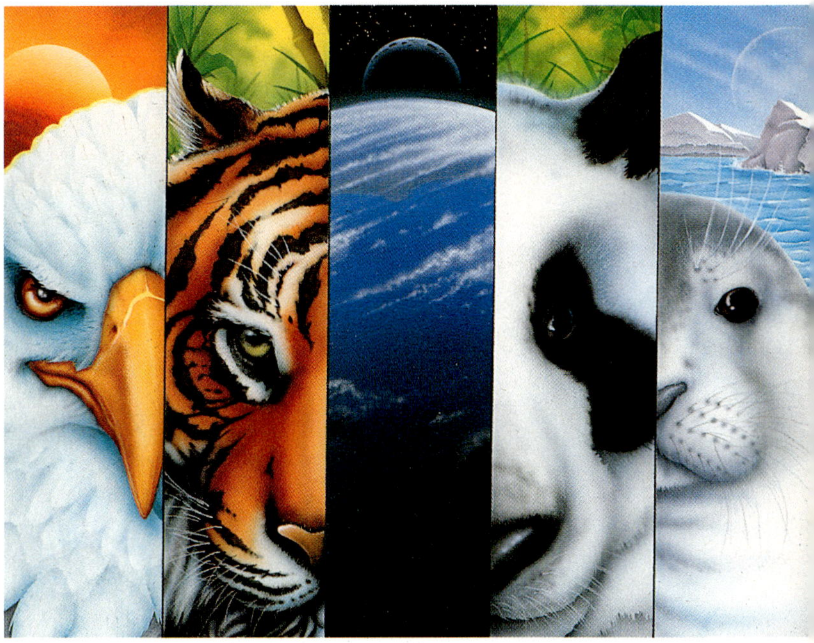

2

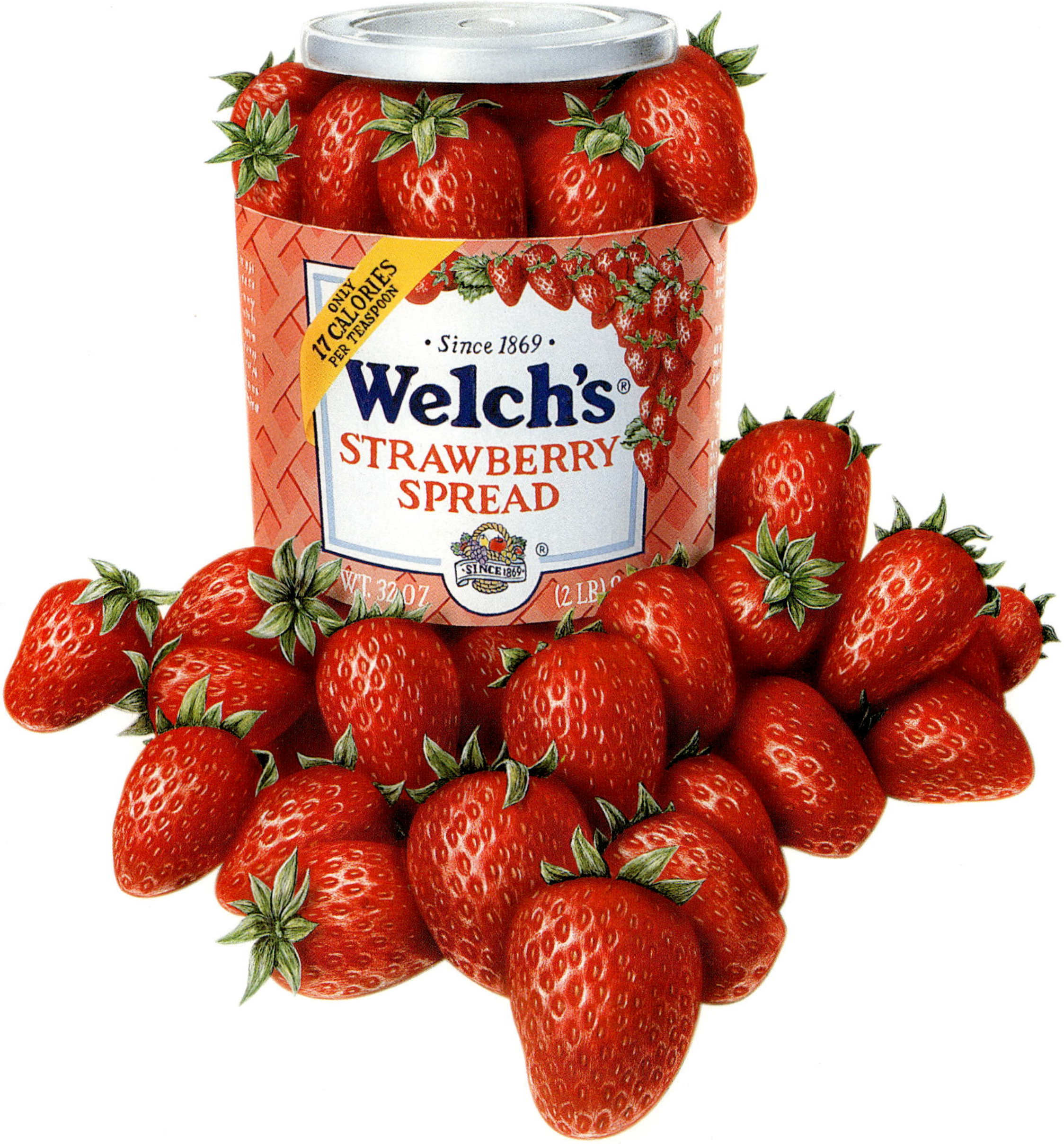

3

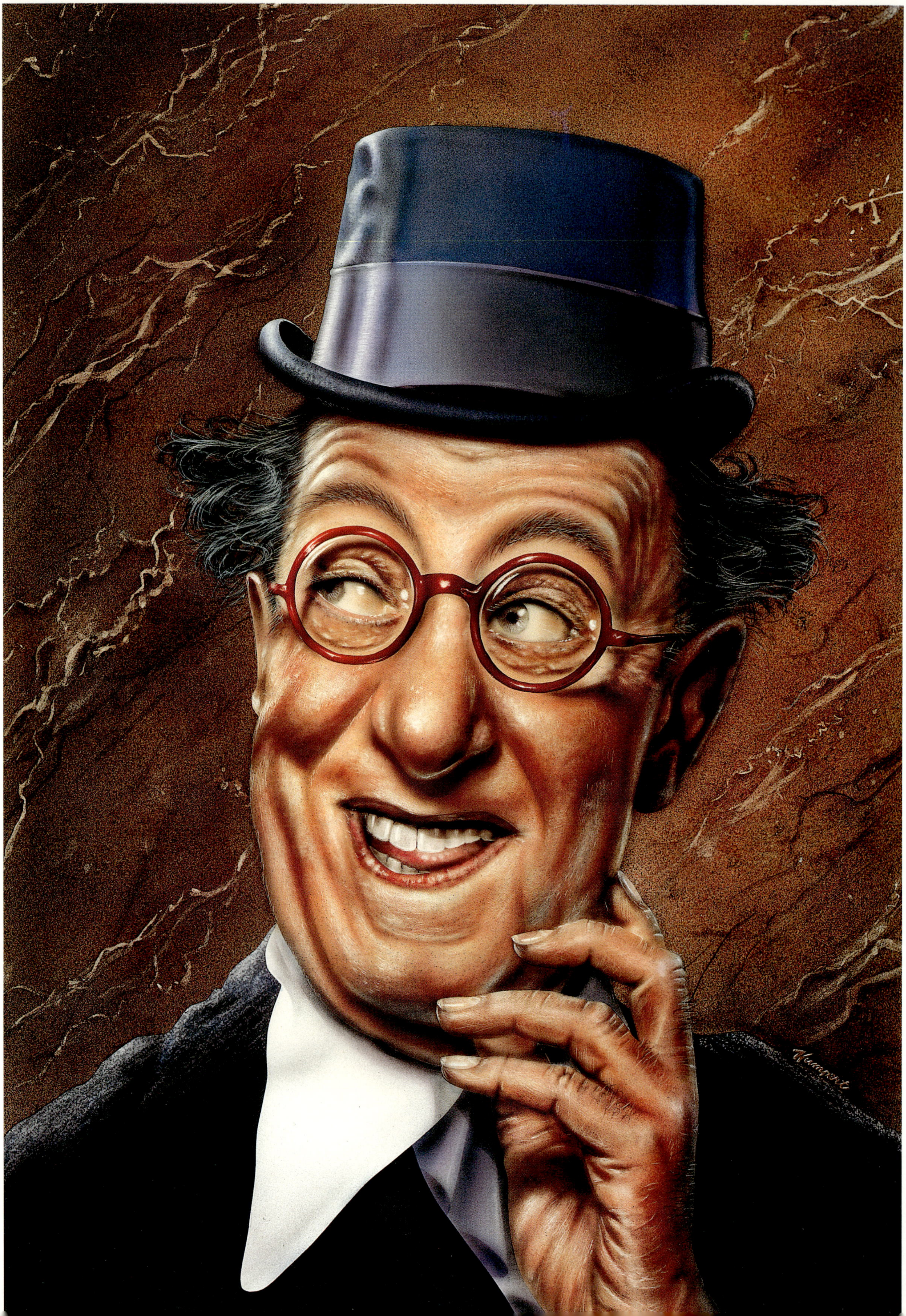

1

1
Artist Thomas J. Humpert
Title Ed Wynn
Usage Self Promotion
Media Used Acrylic

2
Artist Thomas J. Humpert
Title Quicksilver
Client Quicksilver Video
Art Director James Minor
Usage Logo, Business Cards, etc.
Media Used Acrylic

3
Artist Michael W. Hunt, Jr.
Title Mardi Gras '93
Client Mardi Gras '93
Art Director Michael W. Hunt, Jr.
Media Used Comart, Mixed

2

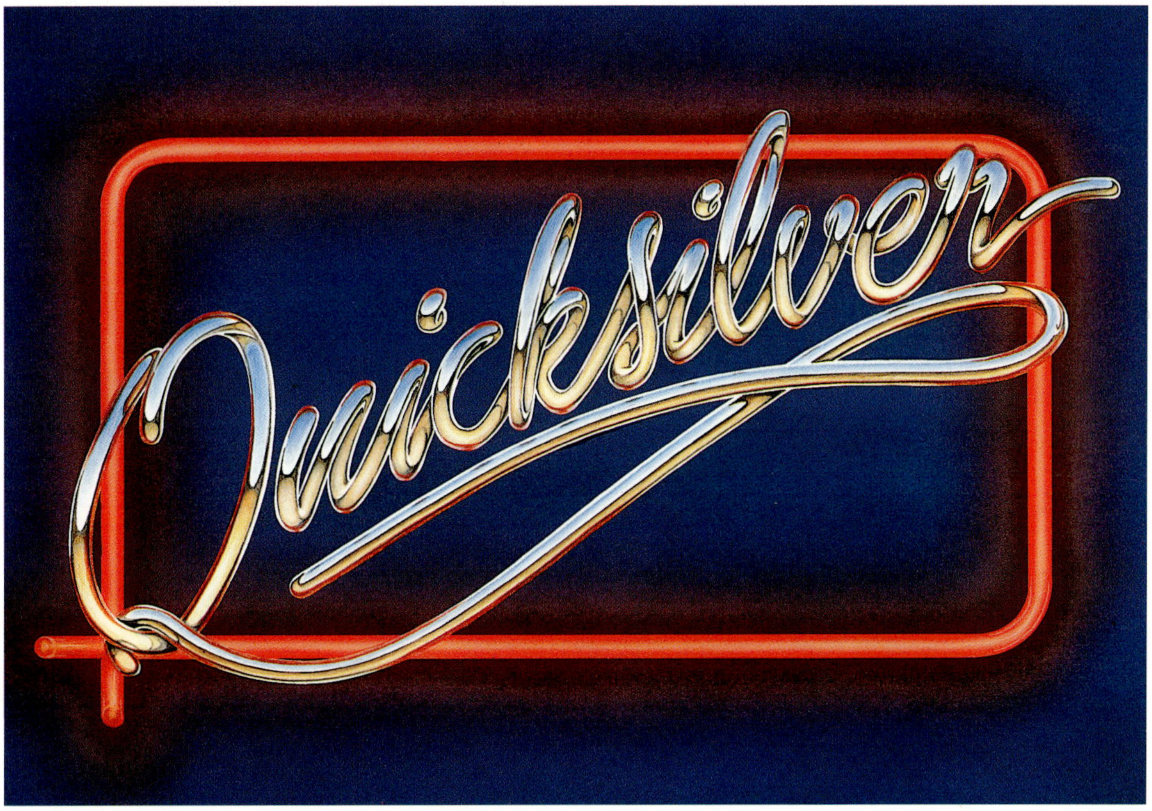

3

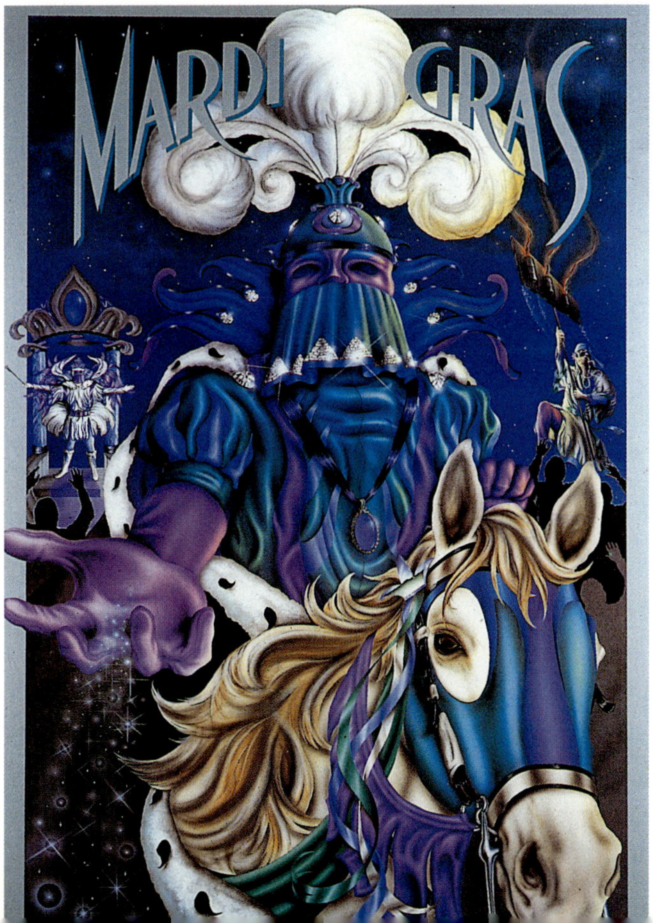

1
Artist Stephen M. Hunter
Title New Orleans
Client Holiday Inns International
Usage Promotional Calendar
Media Used Ink, Acrylic

2
Artist Stephen M. Hunter
Title Trio
Usage Self Promotion
Media Used Acrylic, Ink

3
Artist Stephen M. Hunter
Title Air Shows
Client Hellman Associates
Art Director Tom Roper
Usage Self Promotion
Media Used Acrylic

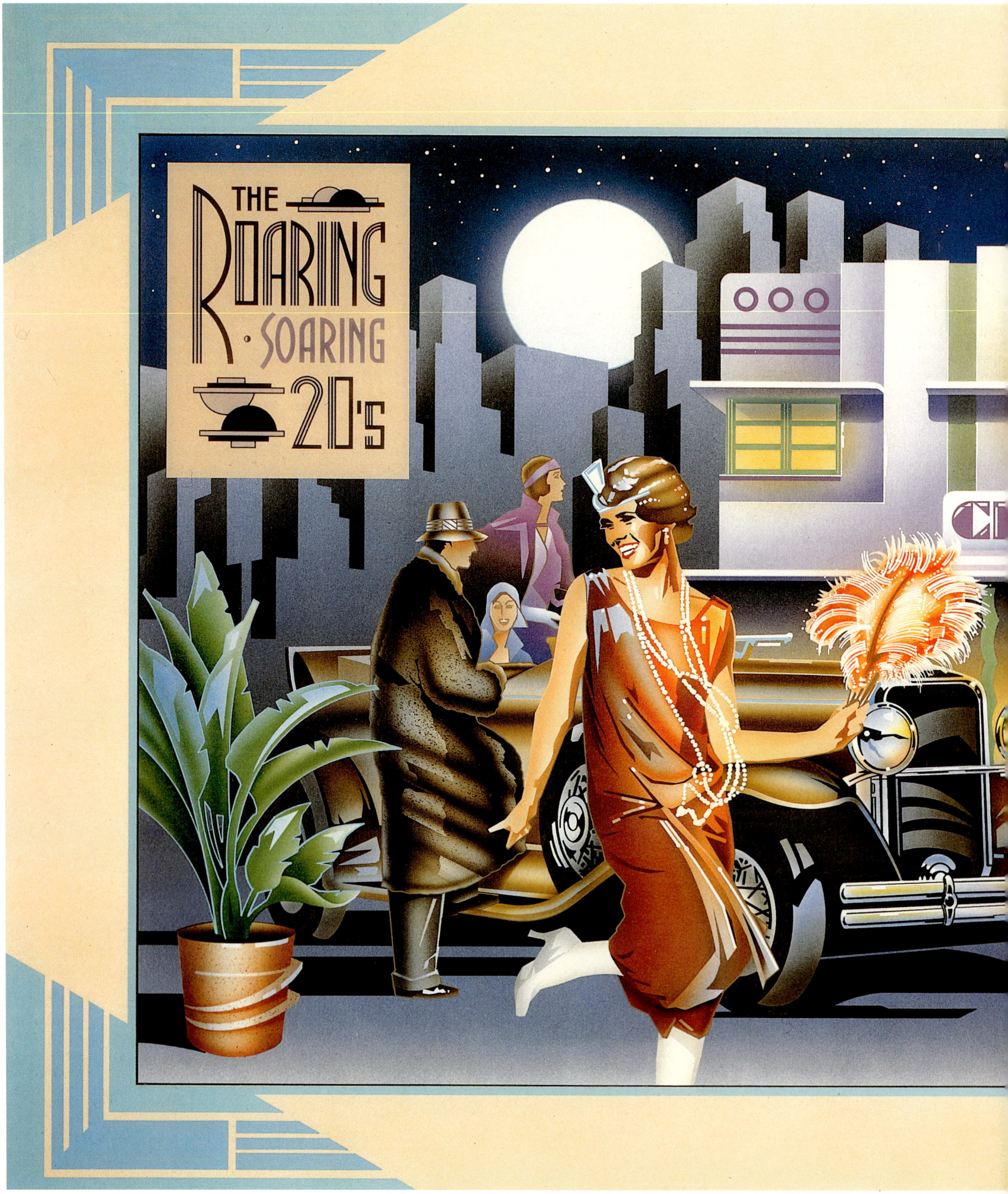

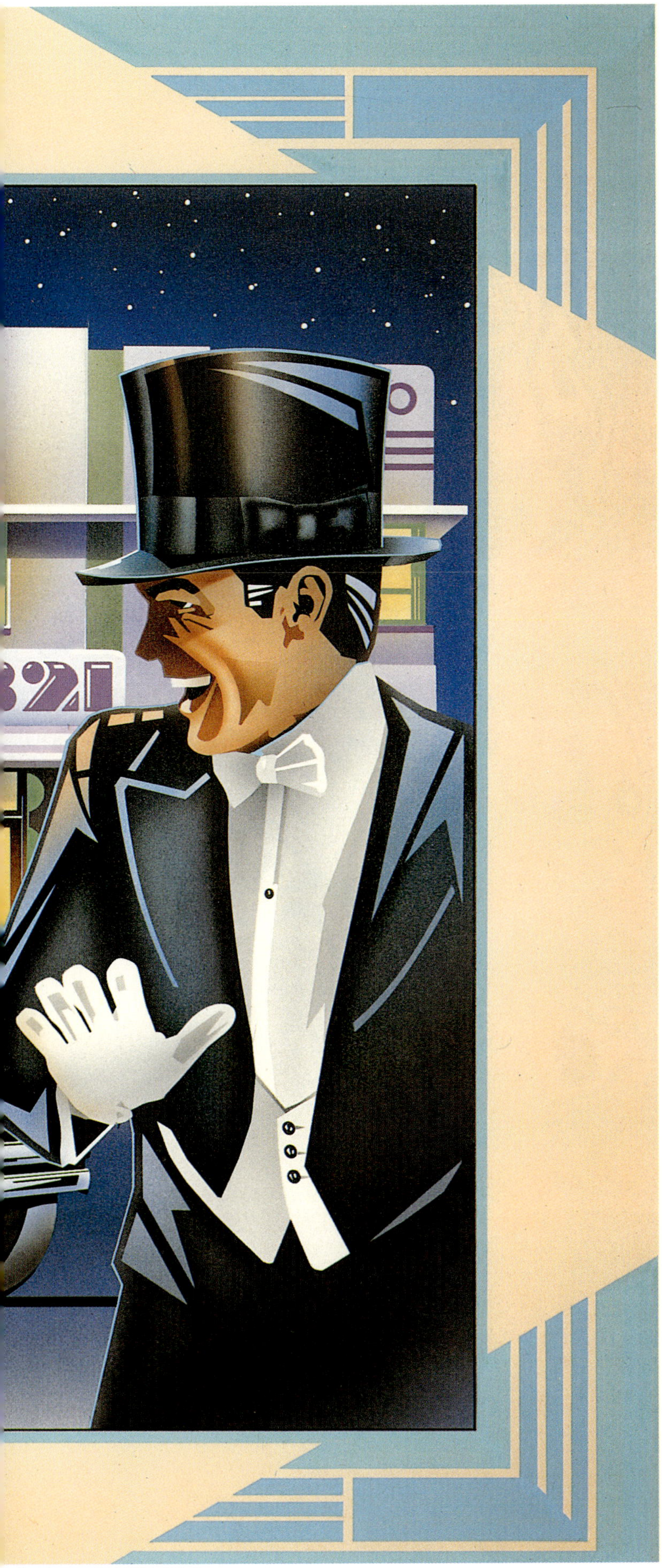
321

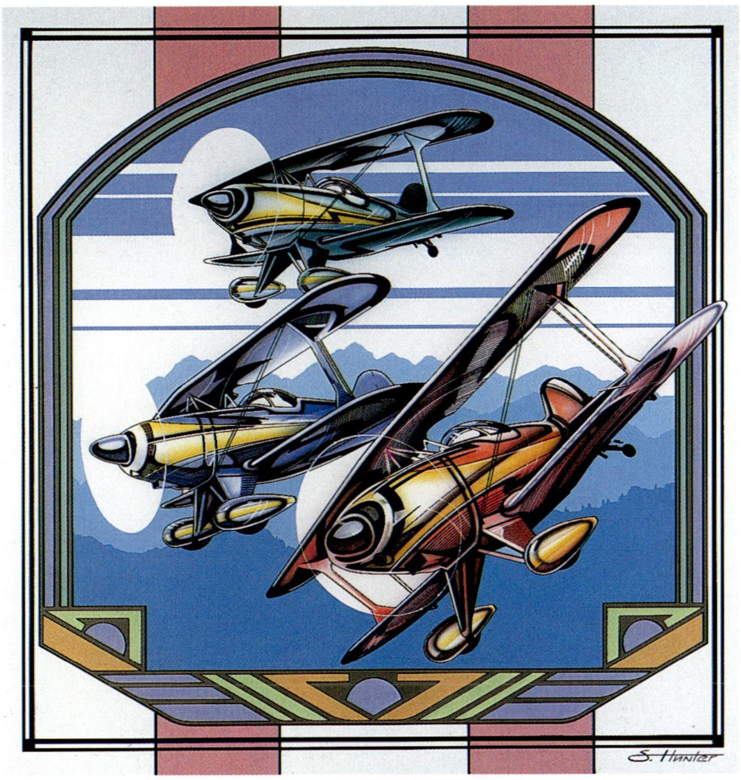
S. Hunter

2

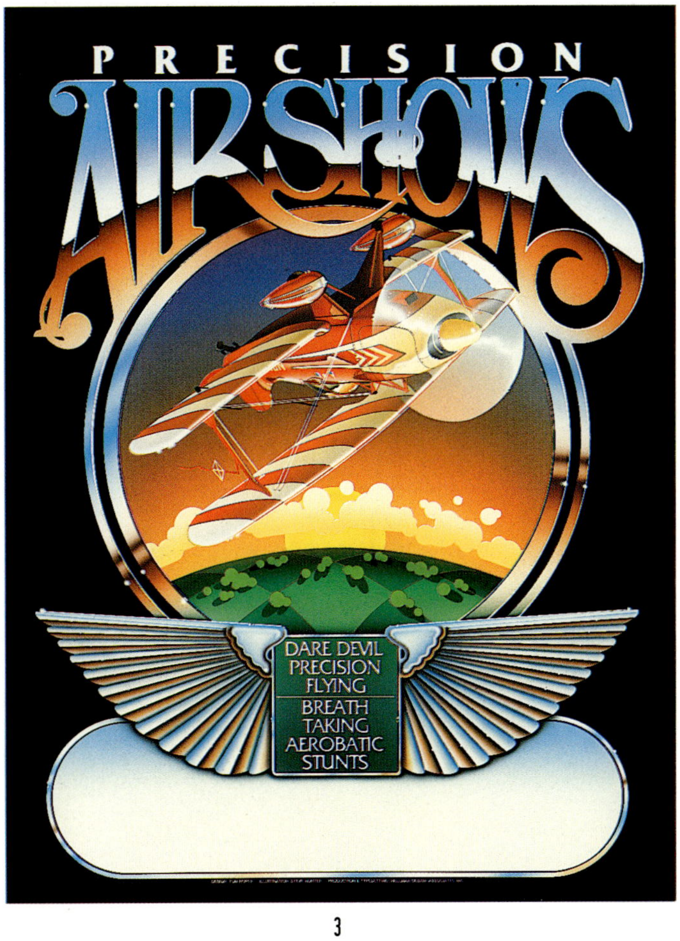
PRECISION
AIRSHOWS
DARE DEVIL
PRECISION
FLYING
BREATH
TAKING
AEROBATIC
STUNTS

3

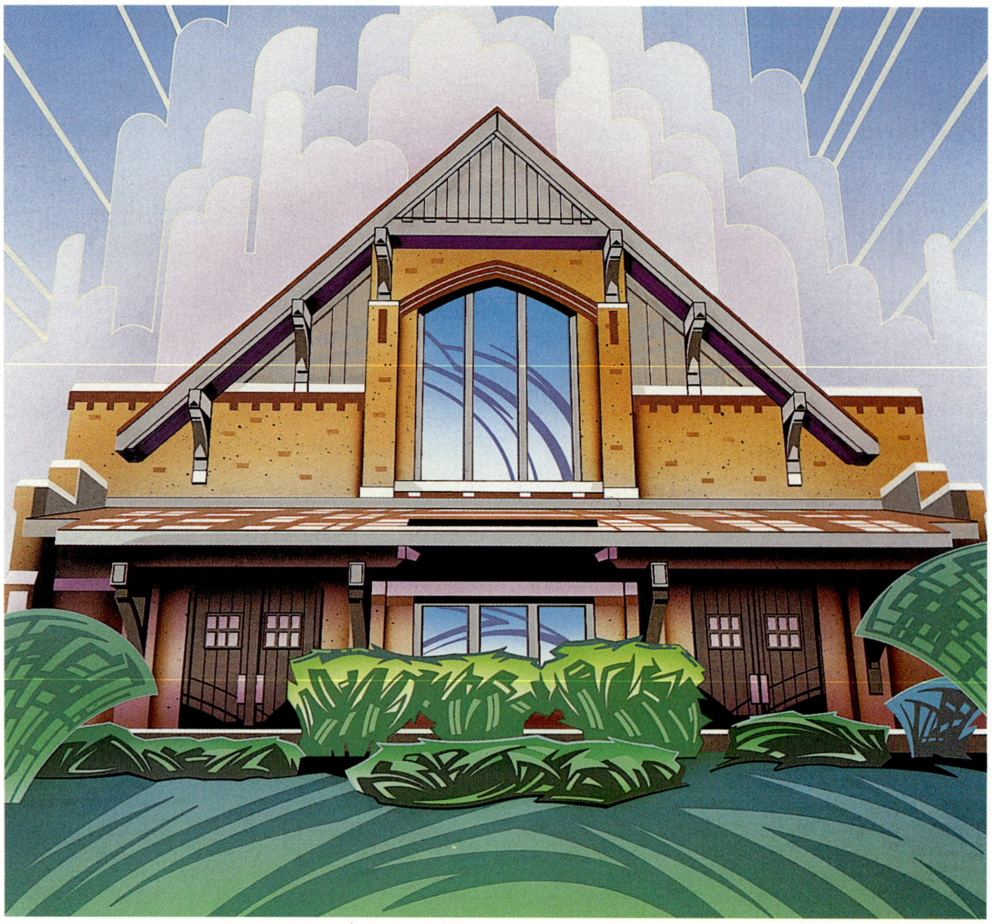

1

2

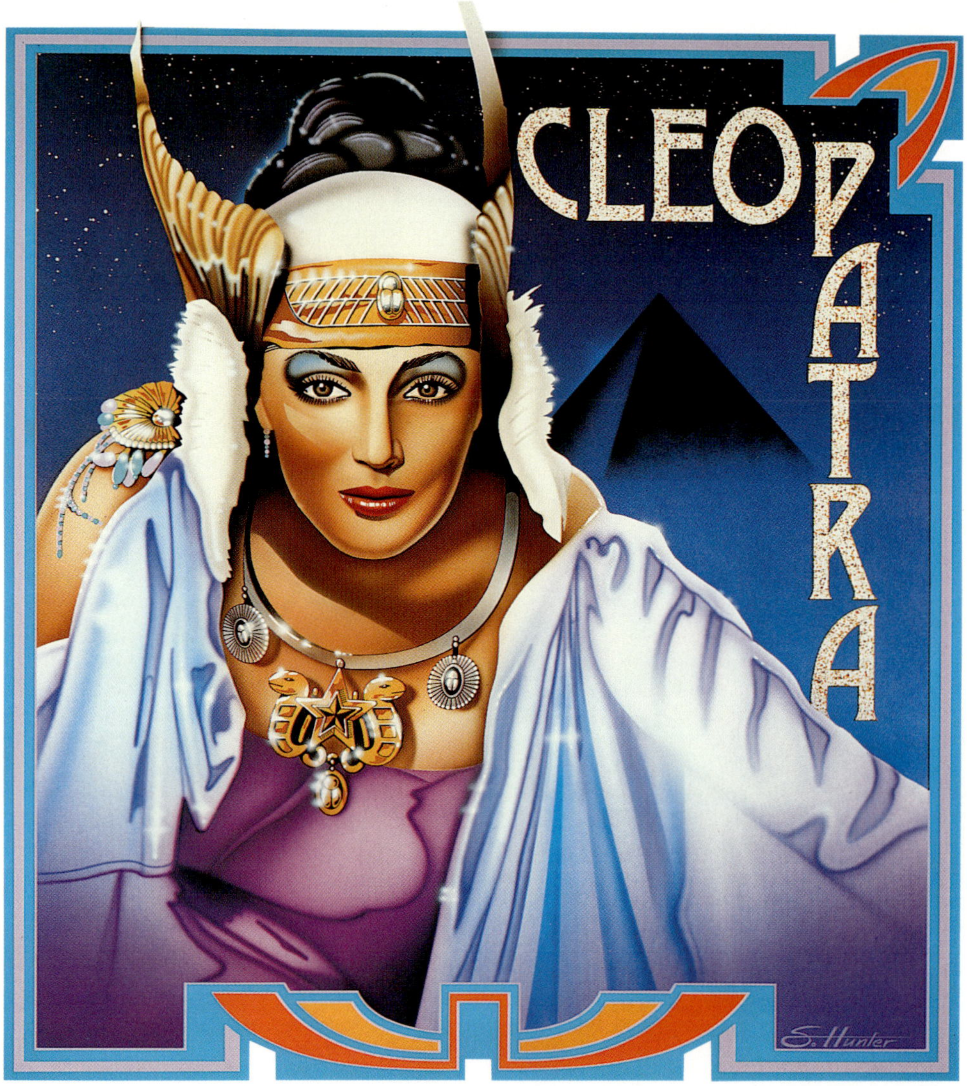

1
Artist Stephen M. Hunter
Title The Studio
Client Hellman Associates
Art Director Stephen M. Hunter
Usage Studio Promotion
Media Used Acrylic

2
Artist Stephen M. Hunter
Title Cleopatra
Client Hellman Associates
Usage Promotional Calendar
Media Used Acrylic

3
Artist Stephen M. Hunter
Title Zeppelin
Usage Self Promotion
Media Used Acrylic, Ink

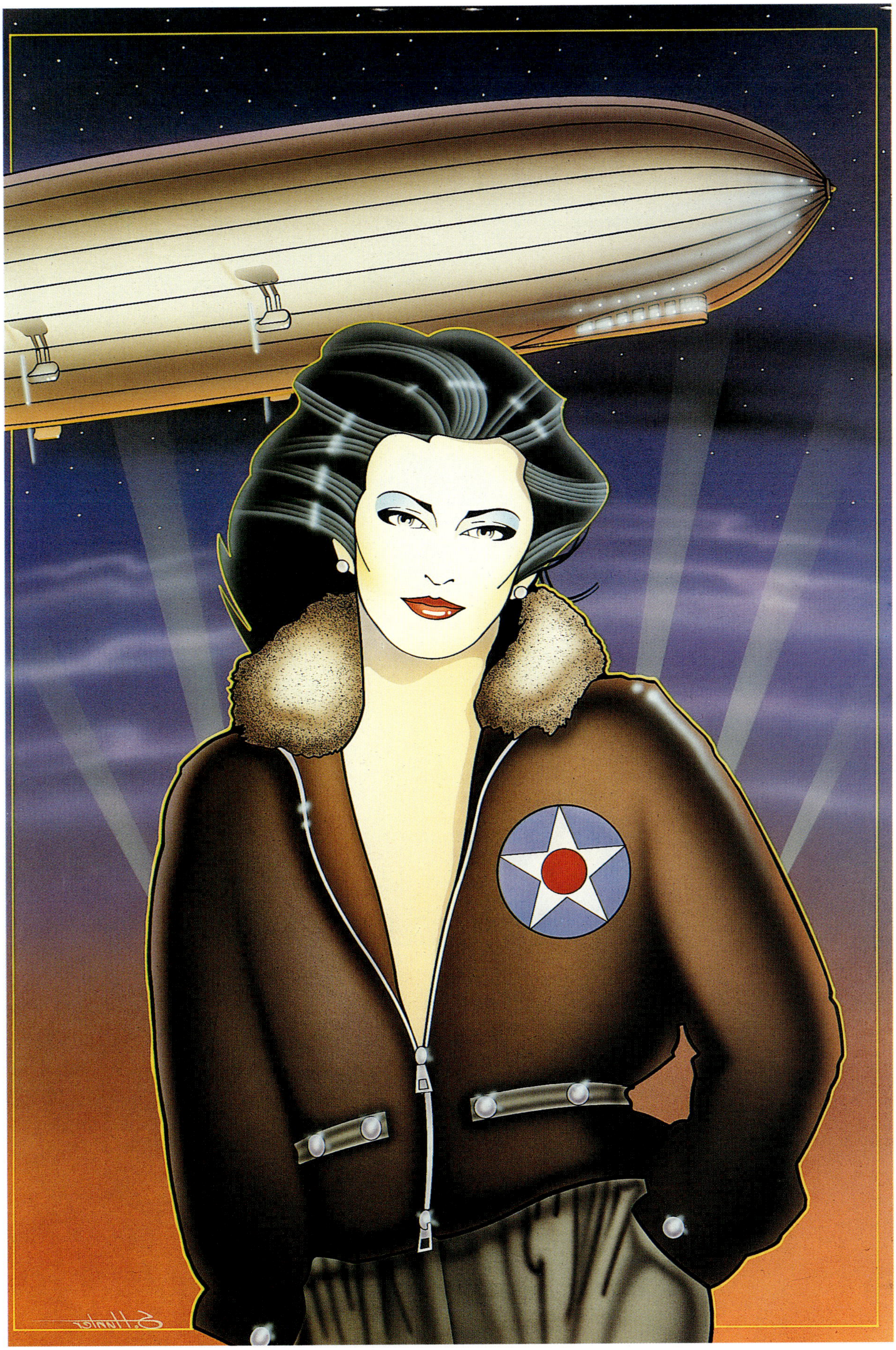

3

1
Artist Greg Hurley
Title Steven's Adventure (My Son)
Usage Conceptual Video Game Cover
Media Used Acrylic

2
Artist Greg Hurley
Title Power Surge
Client Robert Binkley
Usage CD/Album Cover
Media Used Acrylic

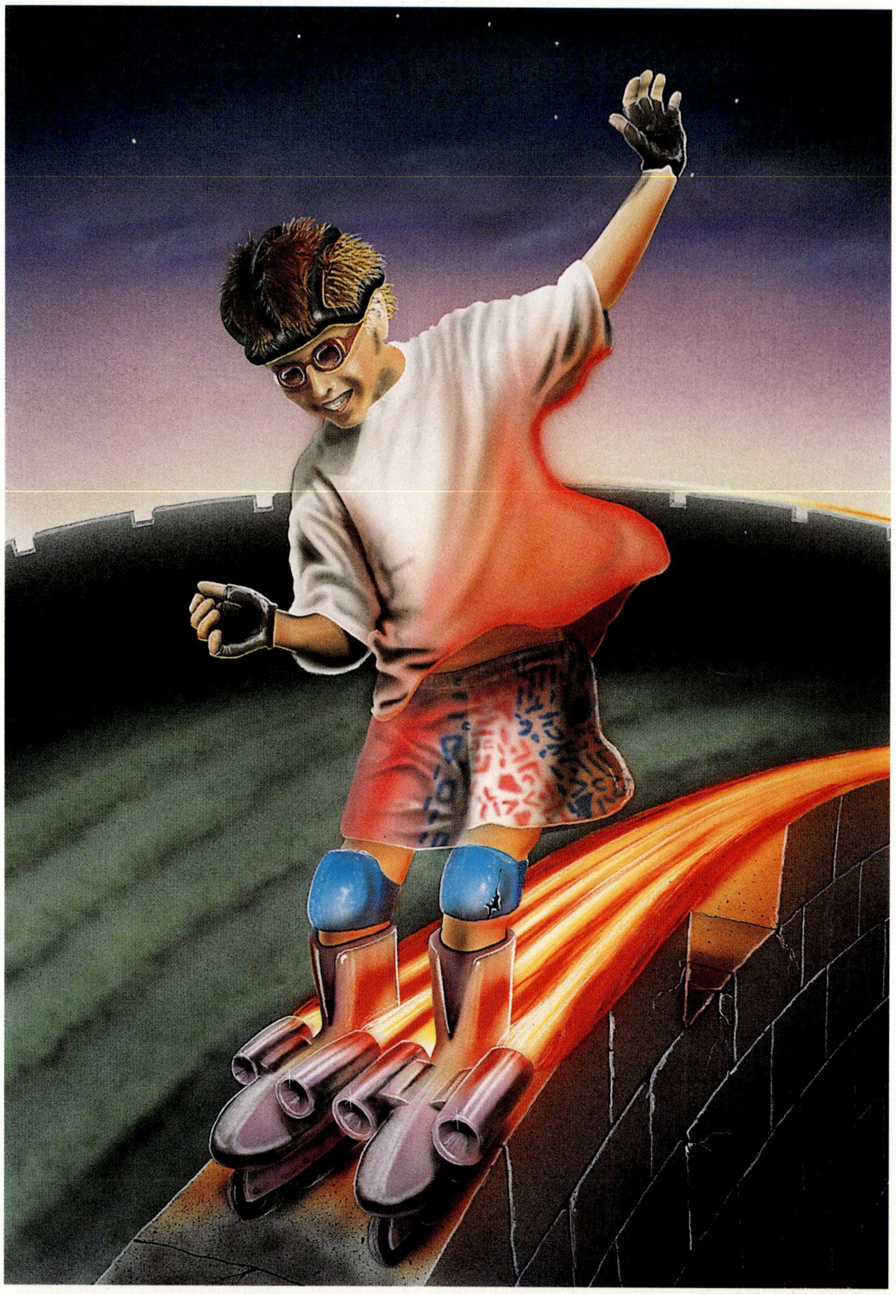

1

2

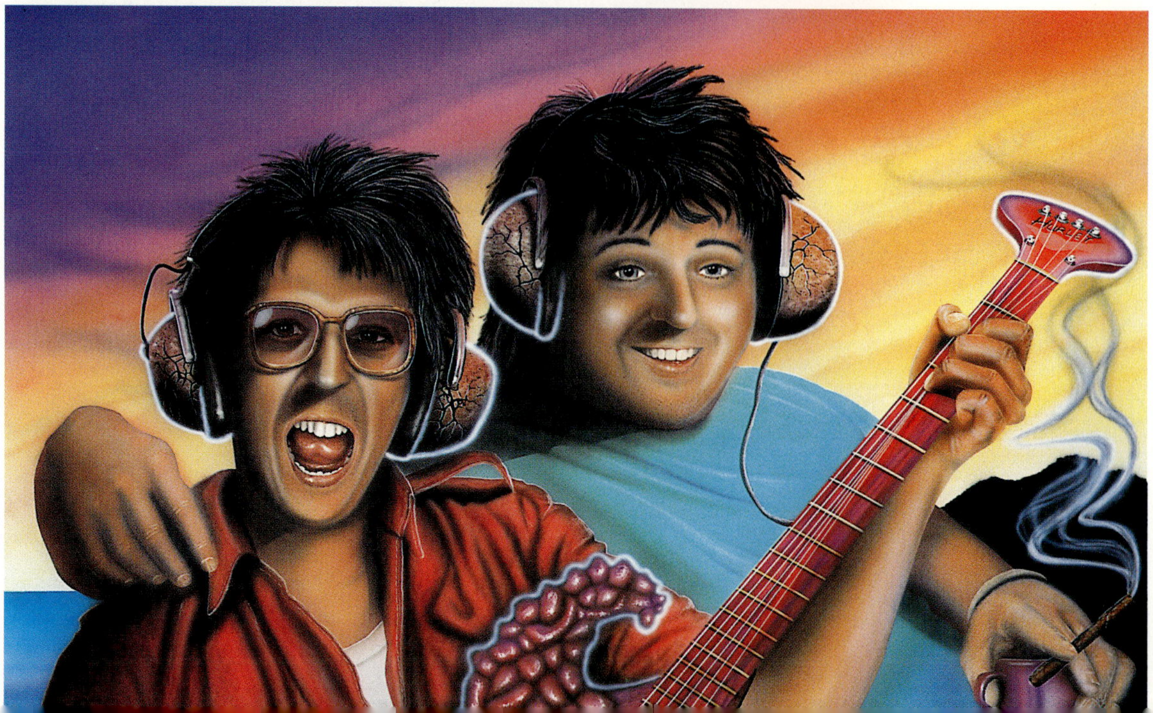

1
Artist Greg Hurley
Title The Wrath of Megan (My Daughter)
Usage Promotional
Media Used Acrylic

2
Artist Greg Hurley
Title Pain in the Neck
Usage Promotional
Media Used Acrylic

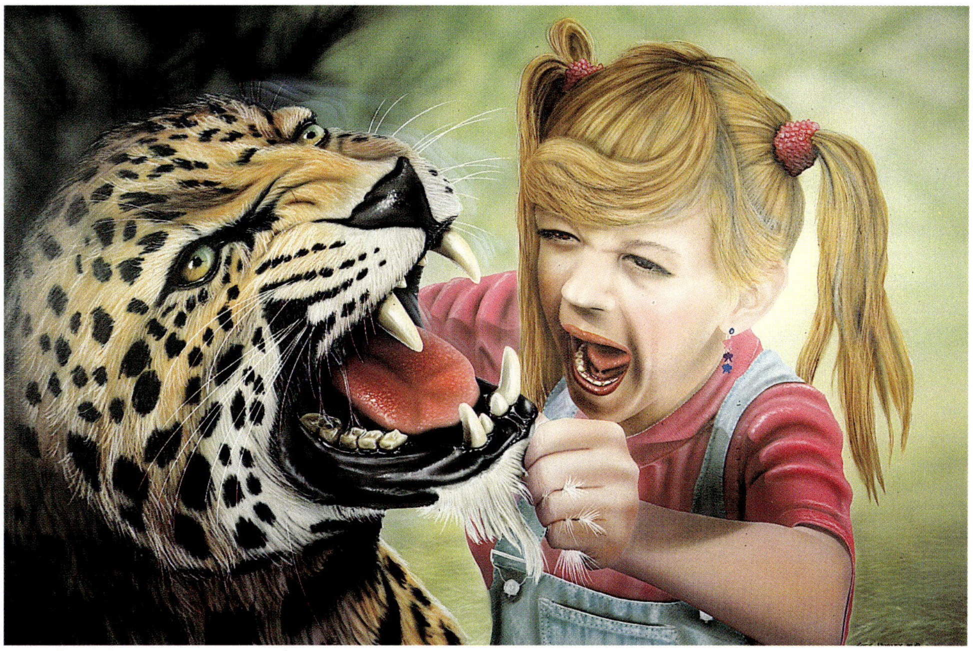

1

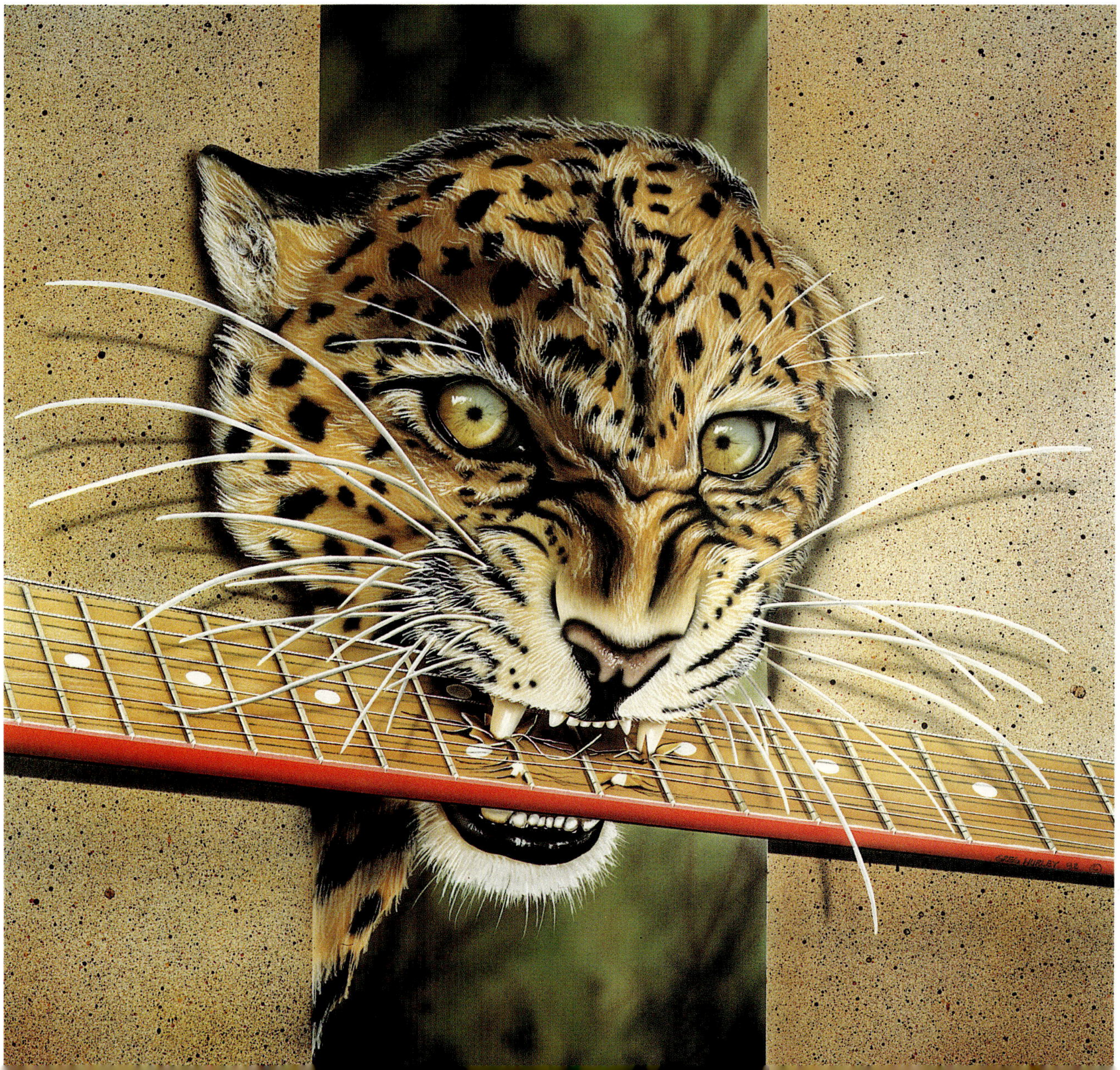

2

1
Artist Christopher Iorillo
Title Mitsubishi 3000 GT VR-4 Cut-Away
Client Christopher Iorillo
Usage Self Promotion
Media Used Acrylic, Both/Sides Film Positive, Colored Pencils, Technical Pen

2
Artist Jake Jones
Title Birthday
Client Naples Daily News
Art Director Joanne Mamenta
Usage Editorial Illustration
Media Used Transparent/Opaque Comart

3
Artist Albert Juarez
Title Dark Room
Client Sunset Color Graphics
Art Director Albert Juarez
Usage Door Poster
Media Used Comart Dyes

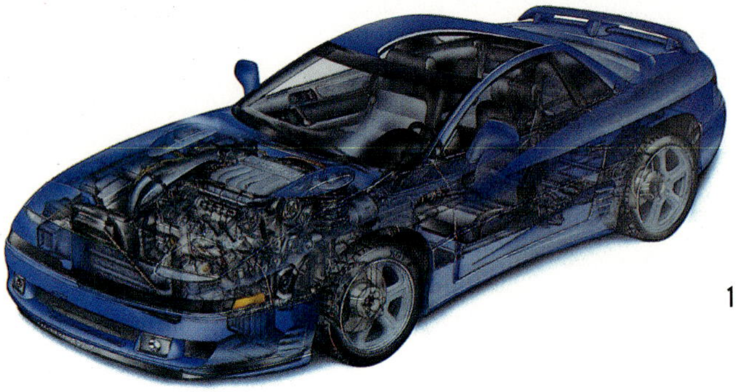

1

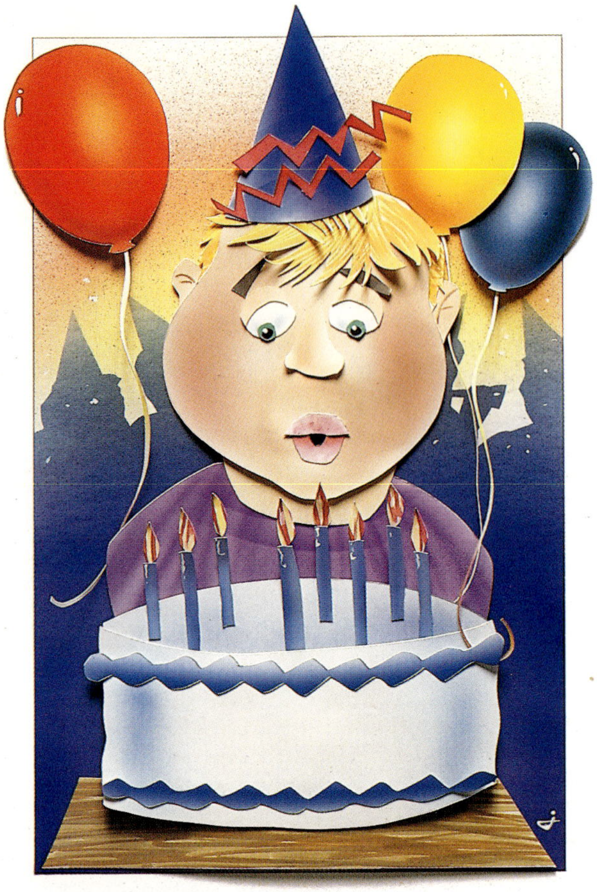

2

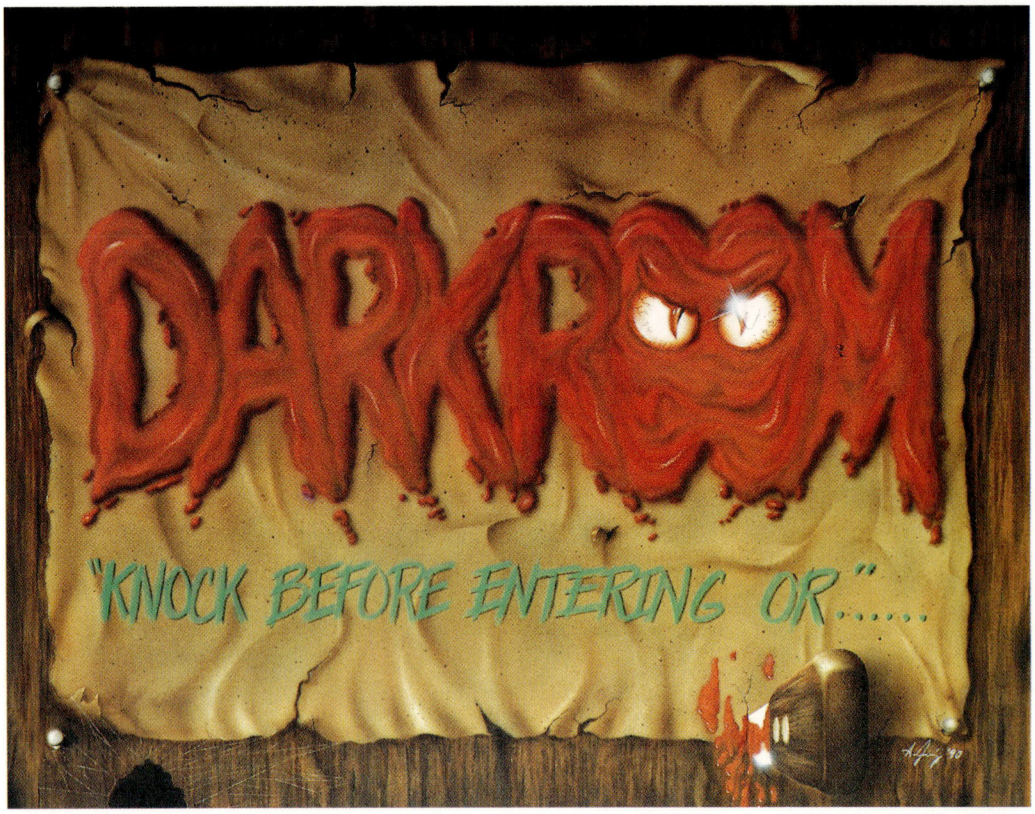

3

1
Artist Nicholas Kendysh
Title Arctic Hunters
Appraisor Fred Rash, Jr.
Usage Fine Art
Media Used Acrylic, Comart, Watercolors

2
Artist Nicholas Kendysh
Title A Moment in Time
Appraisor Fred Rash, Jr.
Usage Structure Art
Media Used Acrylic, Watercolor, Comart

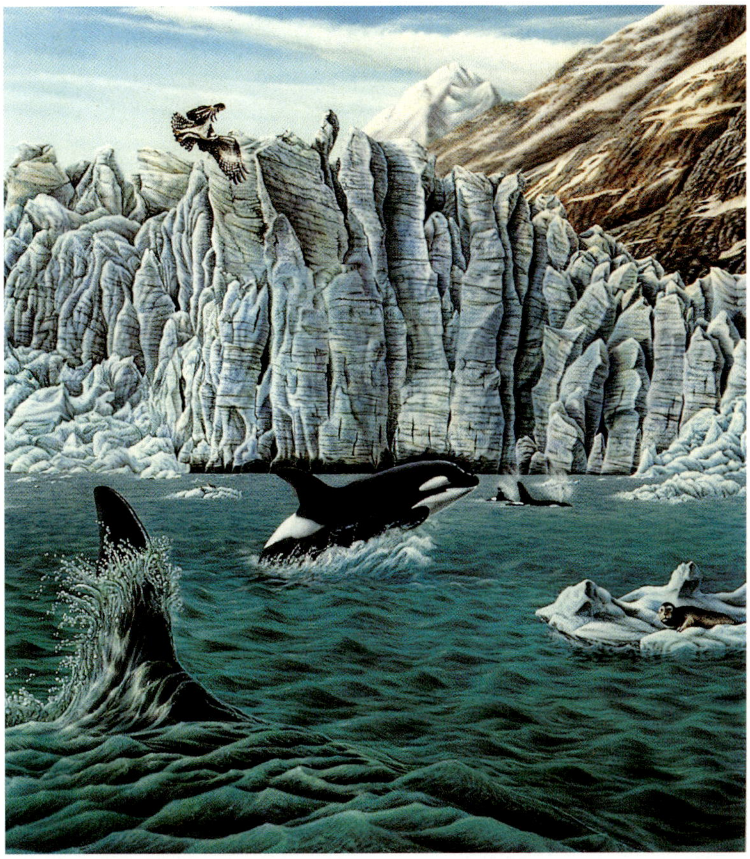

1

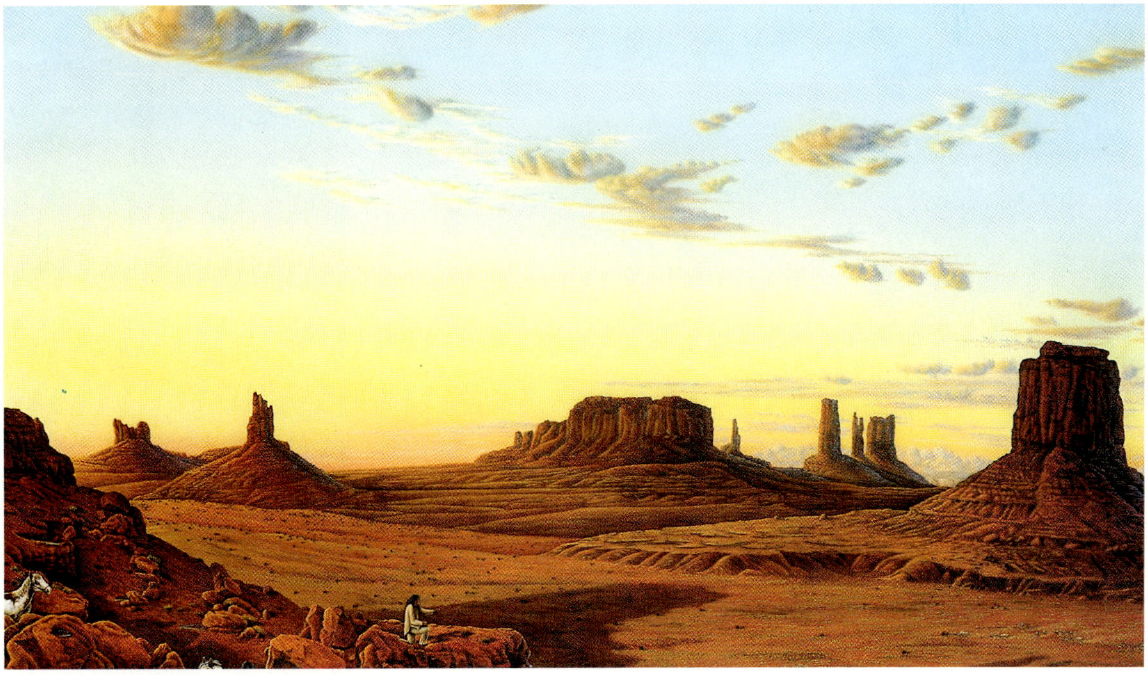

2

1
Artist Brian Kim
Media Used Watercolor, Comart

2
Artist Brian Kim
Usage Student Art
Media Used Watercolor, Acrylic

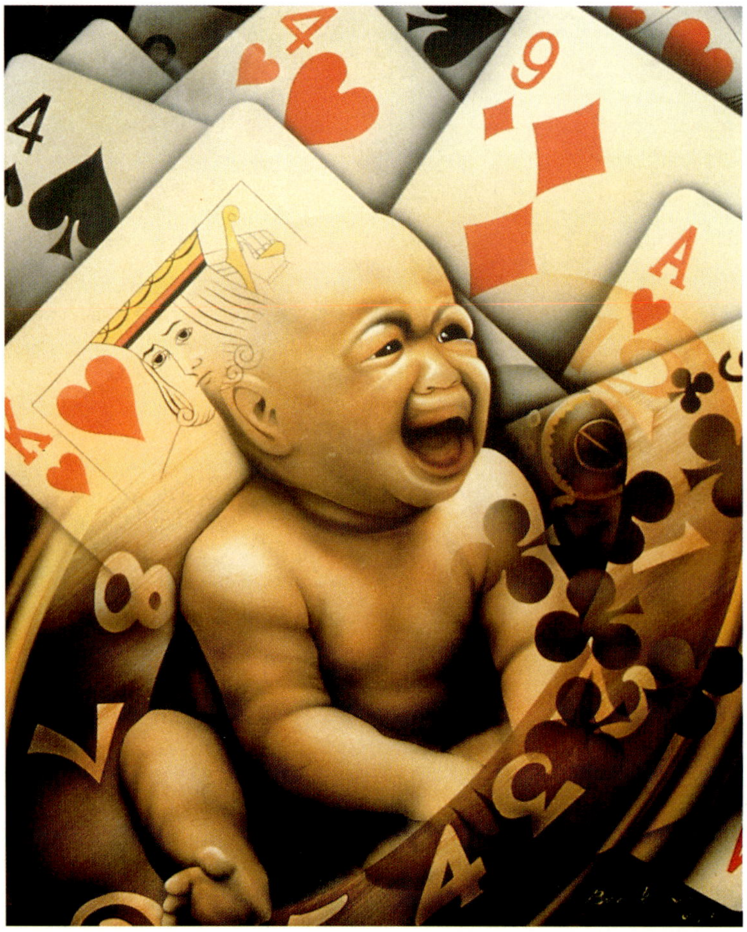

1

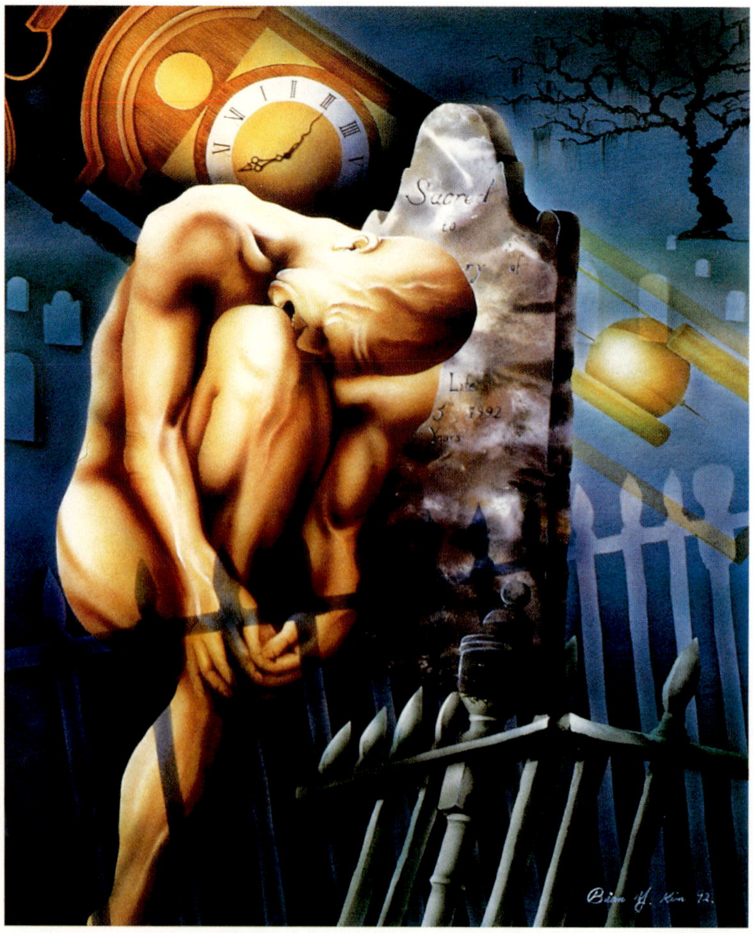

2

1
Artist Robert A. Kling
Title Nuthaus
Art Director Self Promotion
Usage Commercial Art
Media Used Watercolor Dyes

2
Artist Andrew Kong Knight
Title Not Guilty - E Pluribus Unum
Client Mondo 2000 Magazine
Art Director Andrew K. Knight
Usage Editorial Illustration
Media Used Acrylic, Sand

3
Artist Andrew Kong Knight
Title South Rim Sundown
Client W.A.E.L.
Art Director Julie McLean
Usage Commercial Art
Media Used Acrylic, Sand

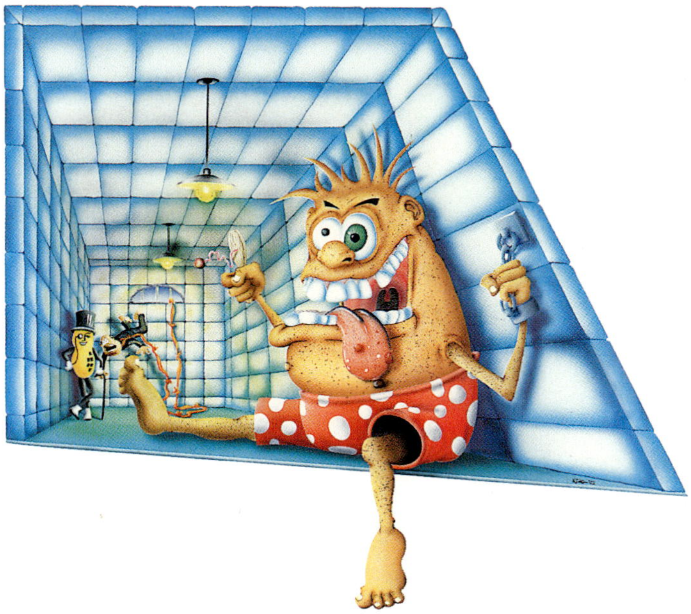

1

2

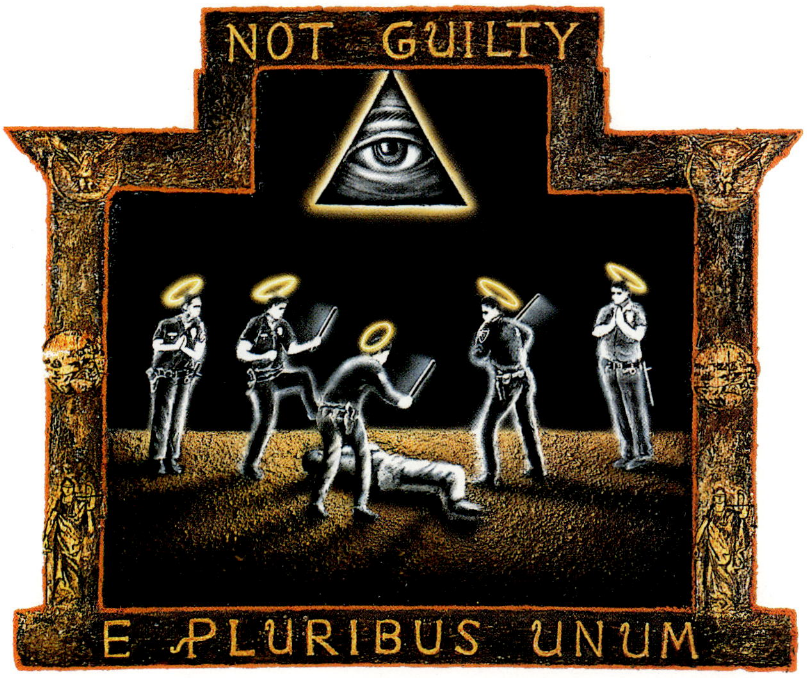

3

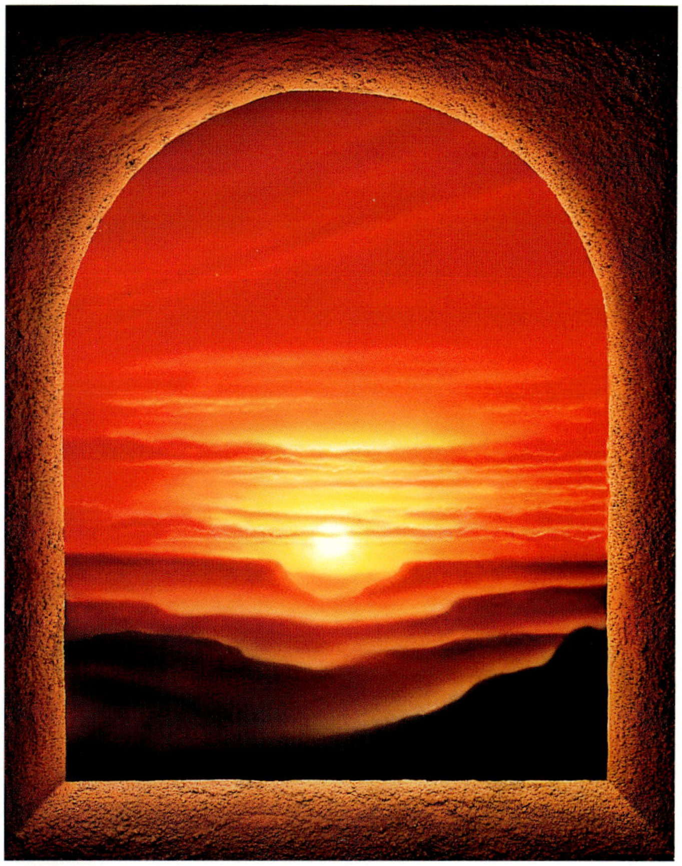

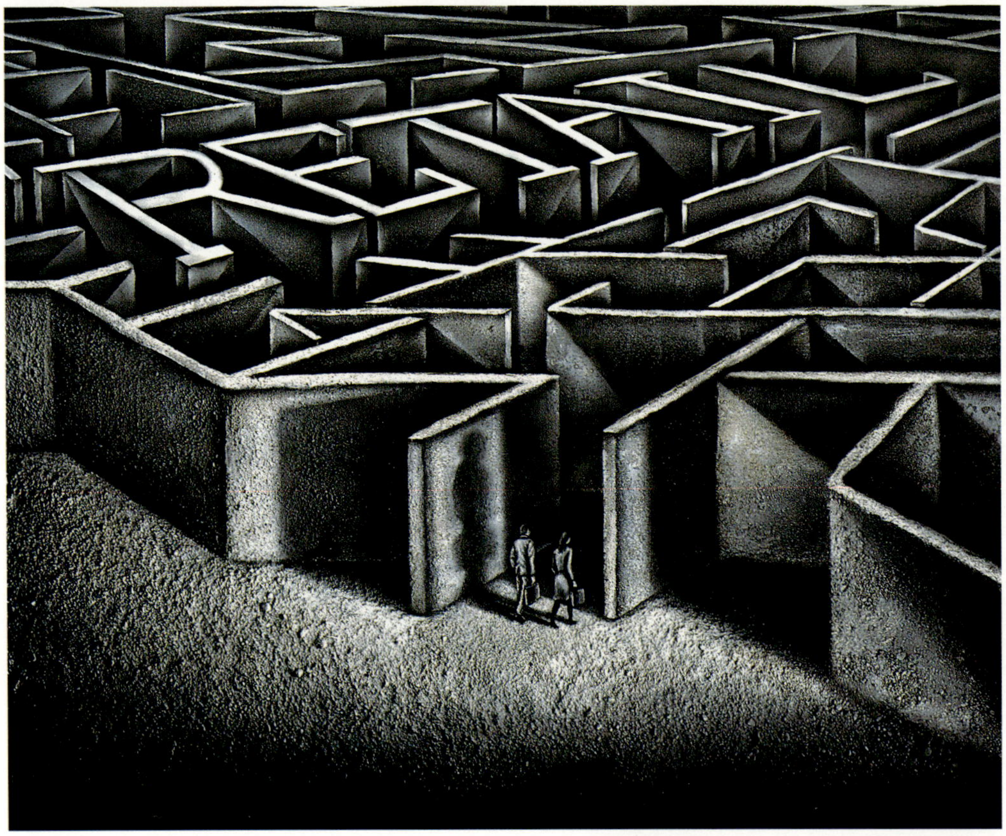

1

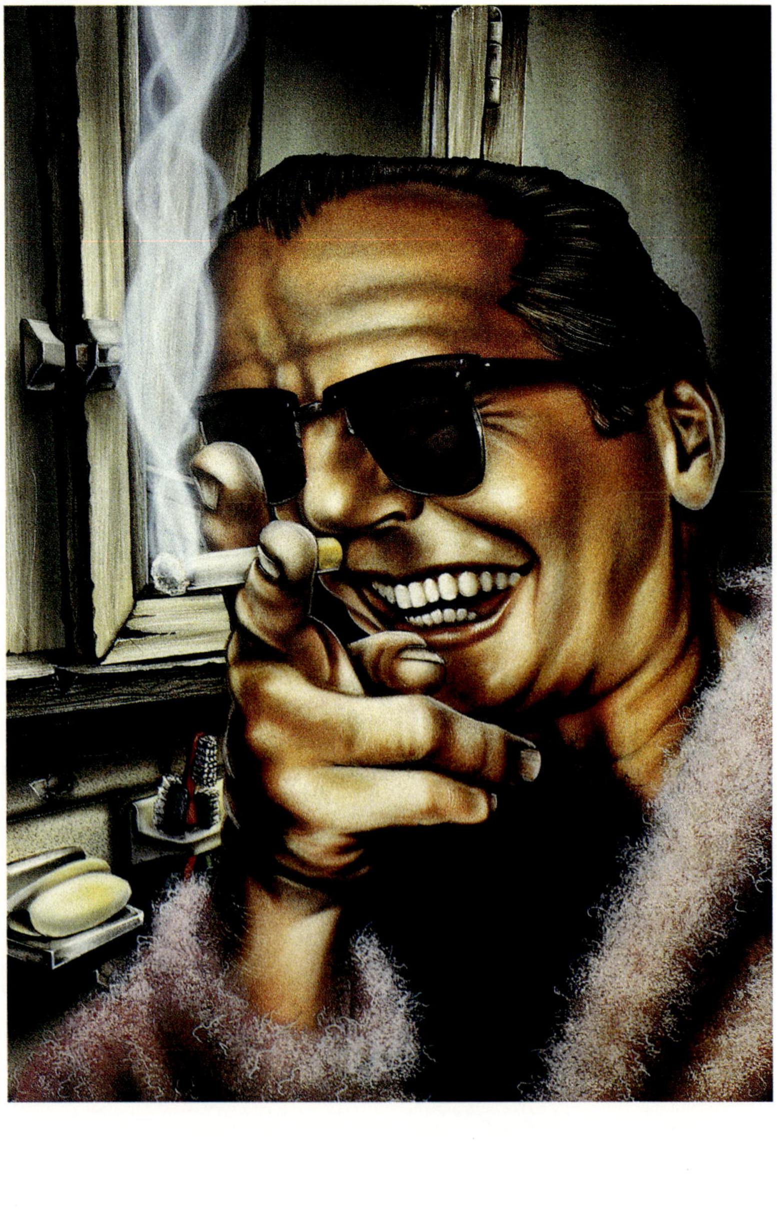

2

1
Artist Andrew Kong Knight
Title Retail Revealed
Client Retail Revealed, San Francisco
Art Director Andrew K. Knight
Usage Commercial Art
Media Used Acrylic, Sand

2
Artist David Kovach
Title Jack in My Bathroom
Art Director Self Promotion
Usage Student Art
Media Used Watercolor

3
Artist David Kovach
Title The Spirit of Cherokee
Client David Kovach
Art Director David Kovach
Usage Student Art
Media Used Watercolor, Oil

4
Artist David Kovach
Title Killing Time
Client David Kovach
Art Director David Kovach
Usage Student Art
Media Used Watercolor

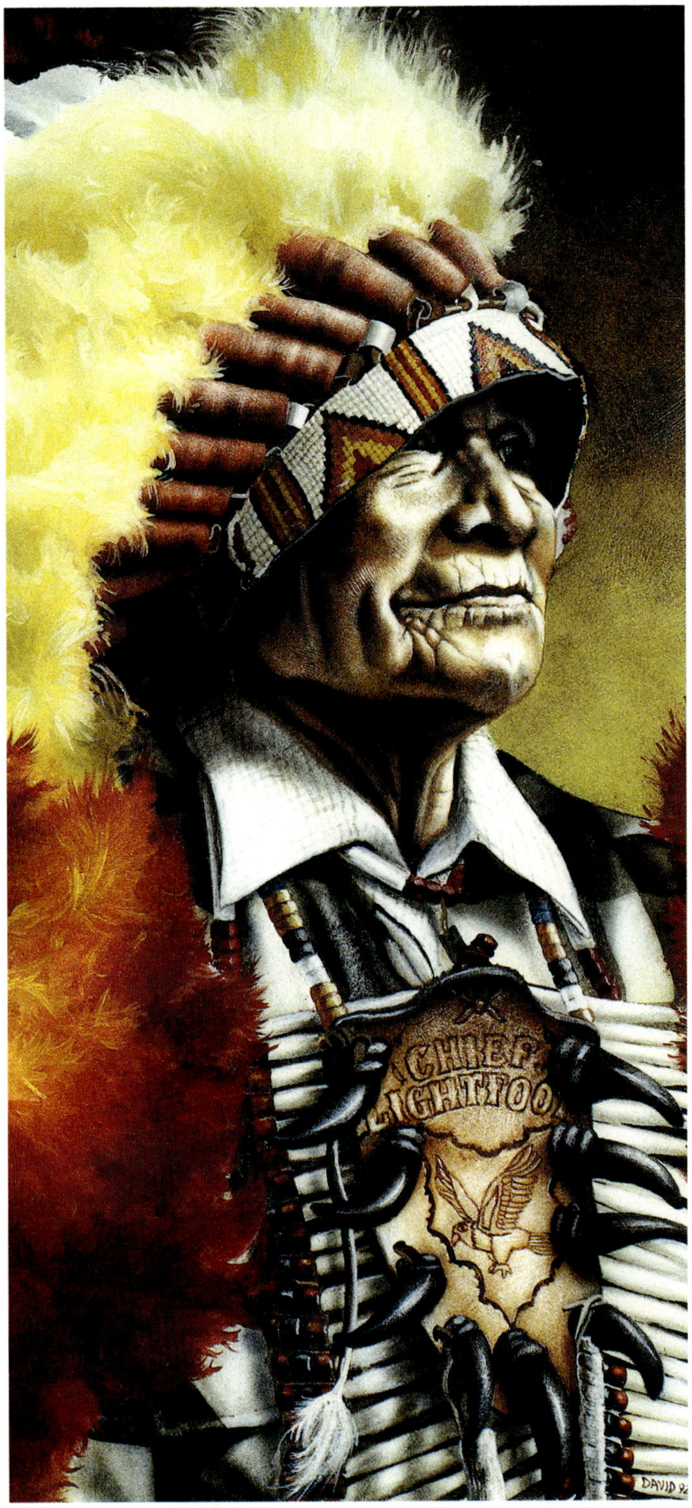

3

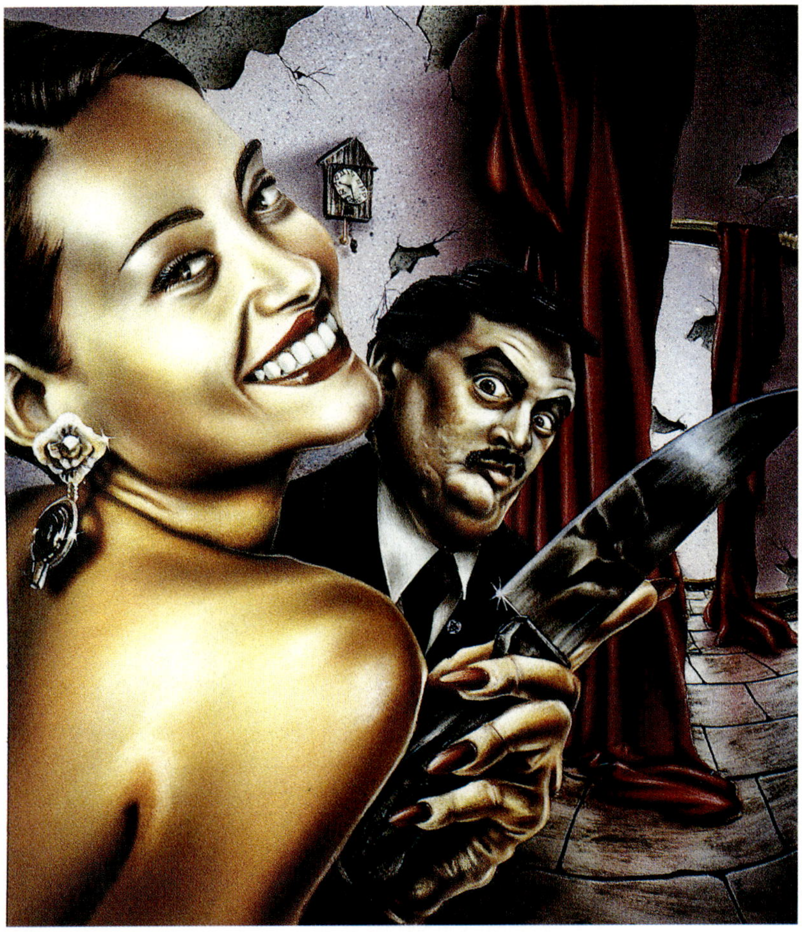
4

1
Artist Dave Kuhn
Title MZ. Strato 3000
Usage Fine Art
Media Used Acrylic on Cut-Out Board

2
Artist Dave Kuhn
Title Sarchophiguys
Usage Fine Art
Media Used Acrylic on Cut-Out Board

3
Artist Dave Kuhn
Title Wizard of #'s
Usage Fine Art
Media Used Acrylic on Cut-Out Board

4
Artist Dave Kuhn
Title Chic Sheik
Usage Fine Art
Media Used Acrylic on Cut-Out Board

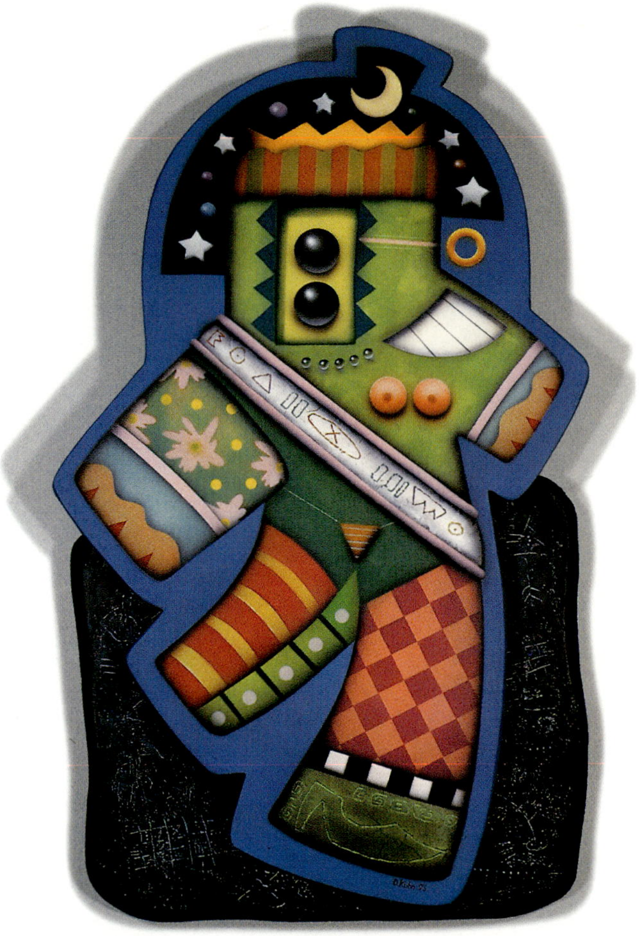

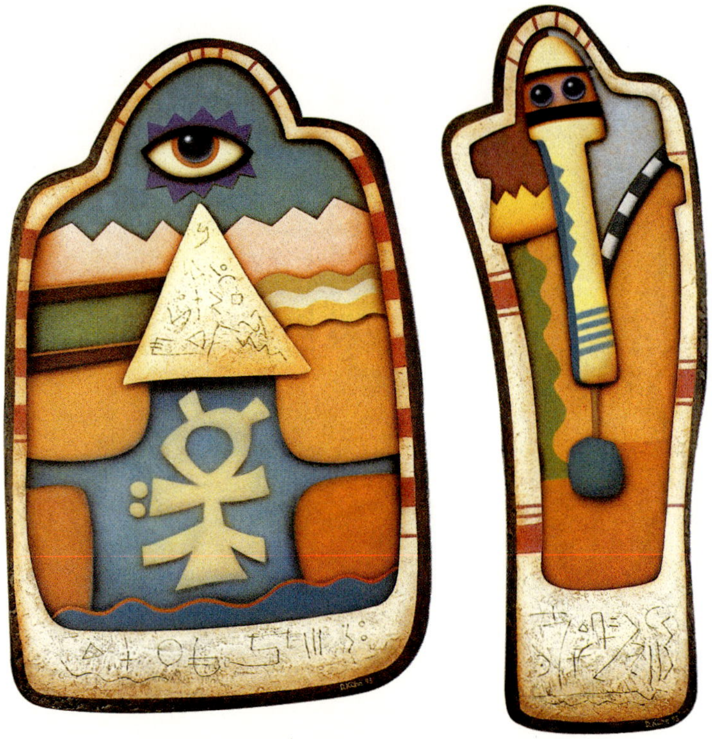

1 2

3 4

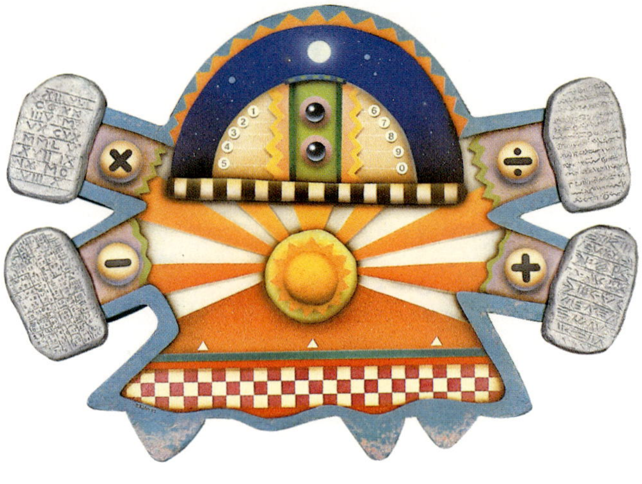

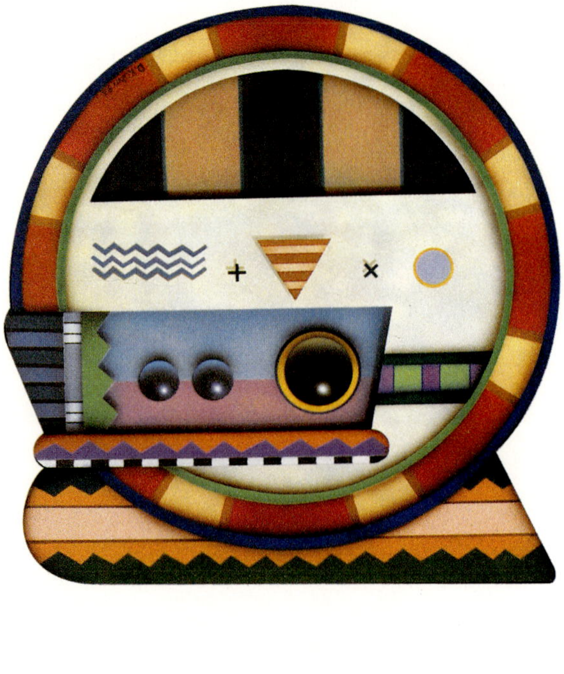

1
Artist Vincent Lacava
Title First Blood
Client Mixed Media Enterprises
Media Used Dr. Martin's

2
Artist Vincent Lacava
Title Naltrexone
Client Mixed Media Enterprises
Usage Editorial Illustration
Media Used Mixed, Dr. Martin's

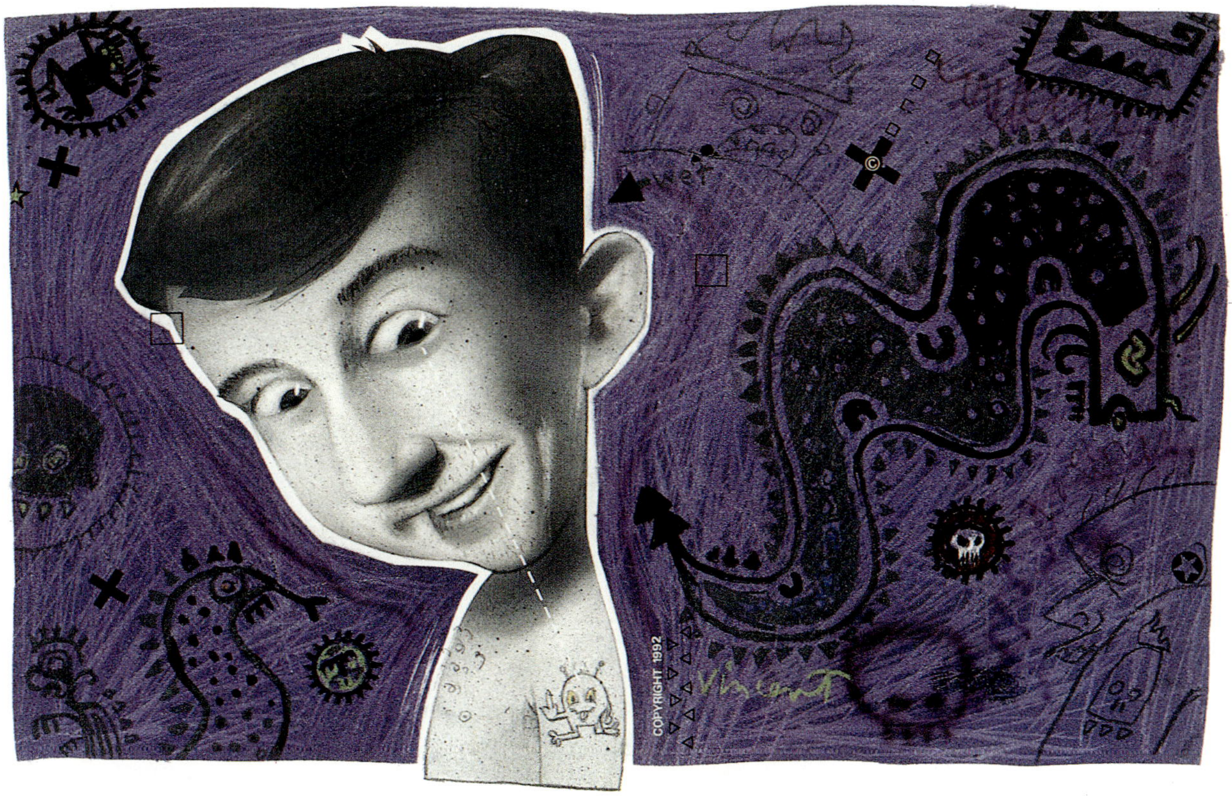

1

2

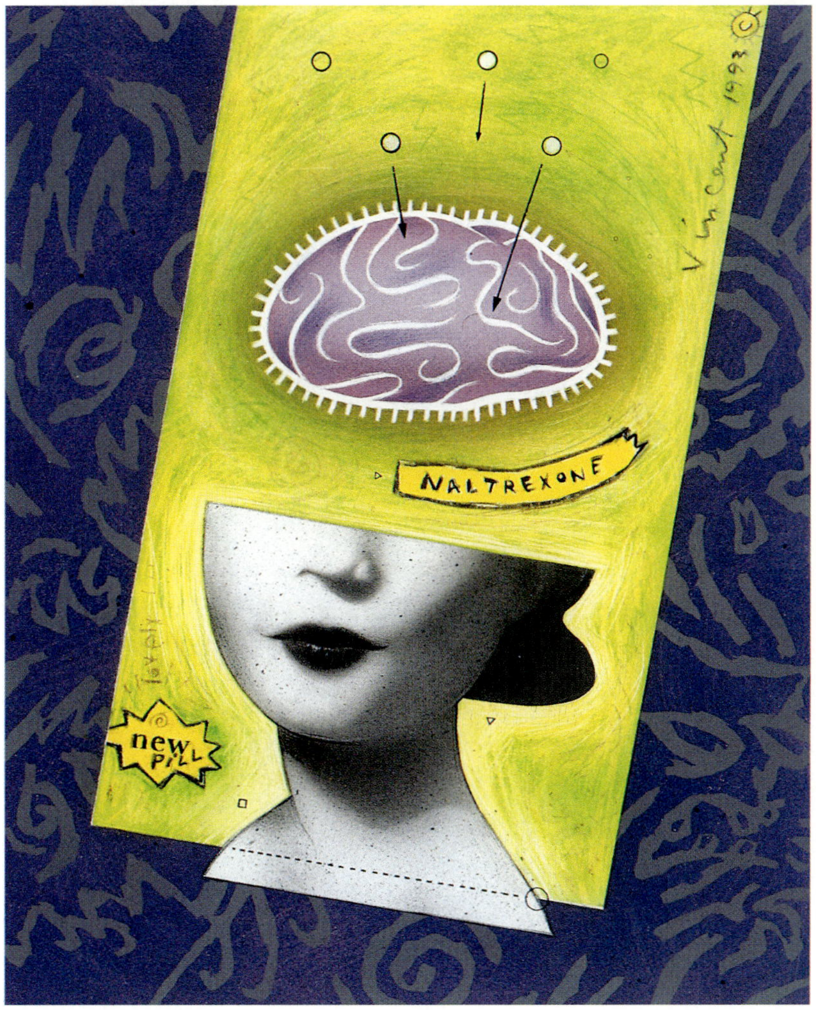

1
Artist Vincent Lacava & Mark T. Smith
Title Franken-Granny
Art Director Vincent Lacava & Mark T. Smith
Media Used Mixed, Dr. Martin's Liquitex

2
Artist Andy Lackow
Title Futuristic Car
Client Joint Armed Forces Recruitment Program
Art Director Glenn Batkin/Grey Advertising
Usage College Magazine
Media Used Gouache

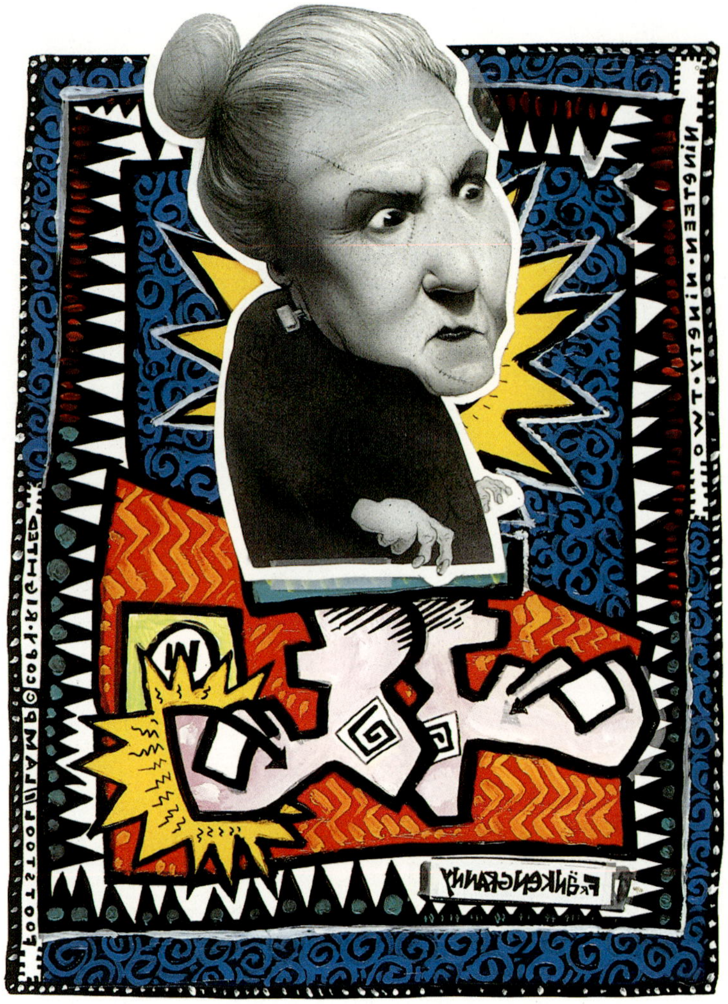

1

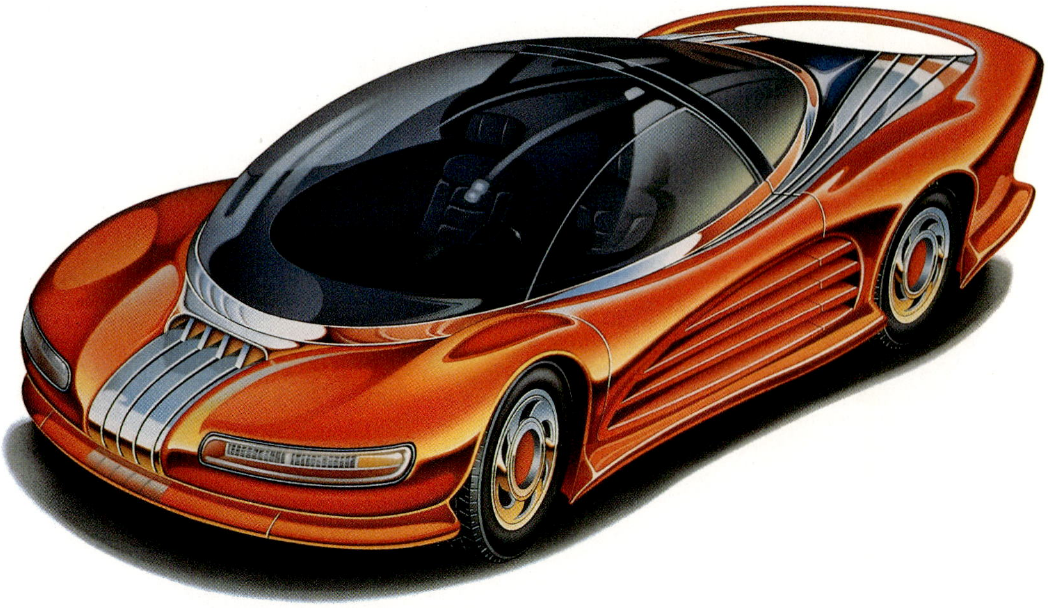

2

1
Artist Jim Langman
Title Obsession
Art Director Dave Ballangee, Instructor
Usage Student Art
Media Used Ink, Charcoal

2
Artist Jorgen Larsson
Title Self Promotion
Art Director Jorgen Larsson
Usage Commercial Art
Media Used Gouache, Watercolor

3
Artist Peter LaSalle, Jr.
Title Air Traffic Controller
Client Class Project
Usage Student Art
Media Used Acrylics, Colored Pencils

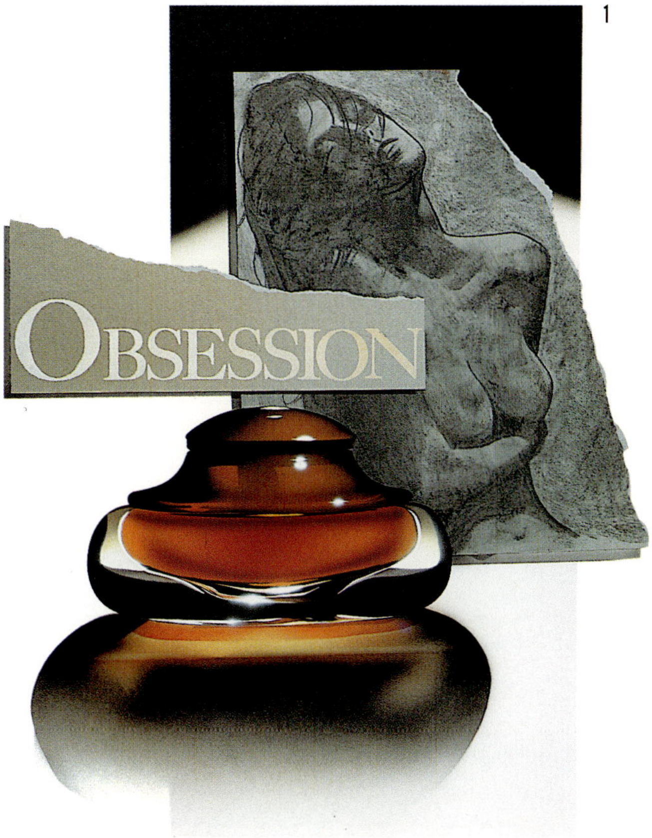

1

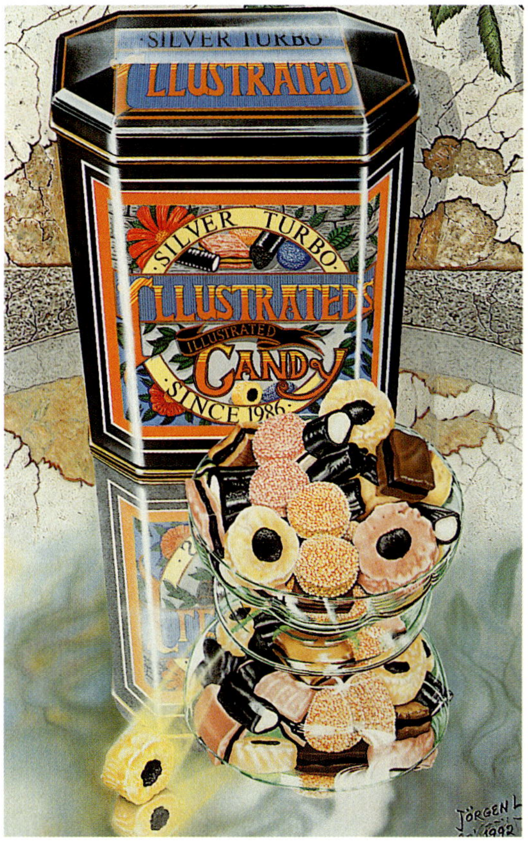

2

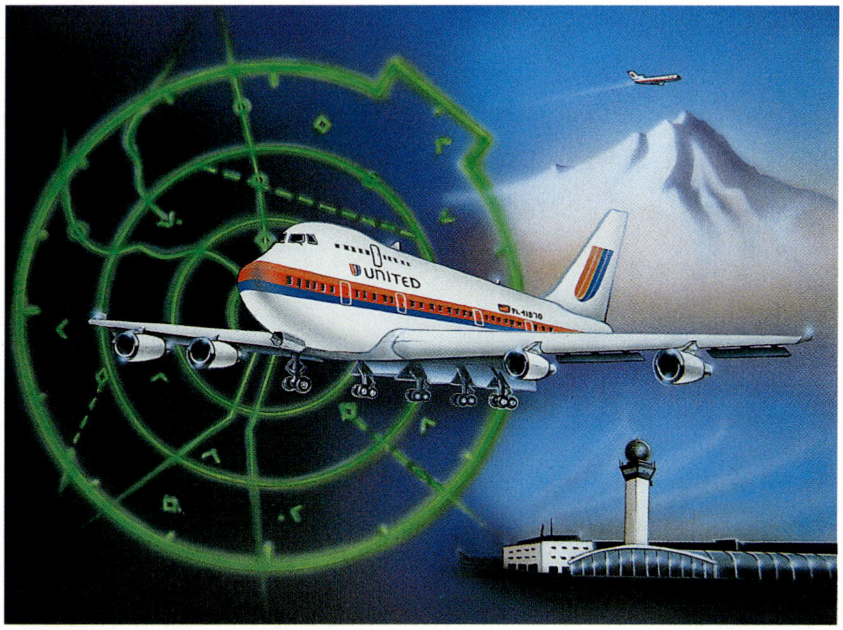

3

1
Artist Pete LaSalle, Jr.
Title Lizard
Client Class Project
Usage Student Art
Media Used Acrylics, Colored Pencil

2
Artist Samuel Laterza
Title Extinction
Usage Student Art
Media Used Watercolor

3
Artist Robert Leverette
Title Owner
Client Robert Leverette
Art Director Self Promotion
Usage Automotive Art & Student Art
Media Used Acrylic

4
Artist Jerry Lofaro
Title Love and Magic
Client Dell Books
Usage Book Cover
Media Used Acrylic

1
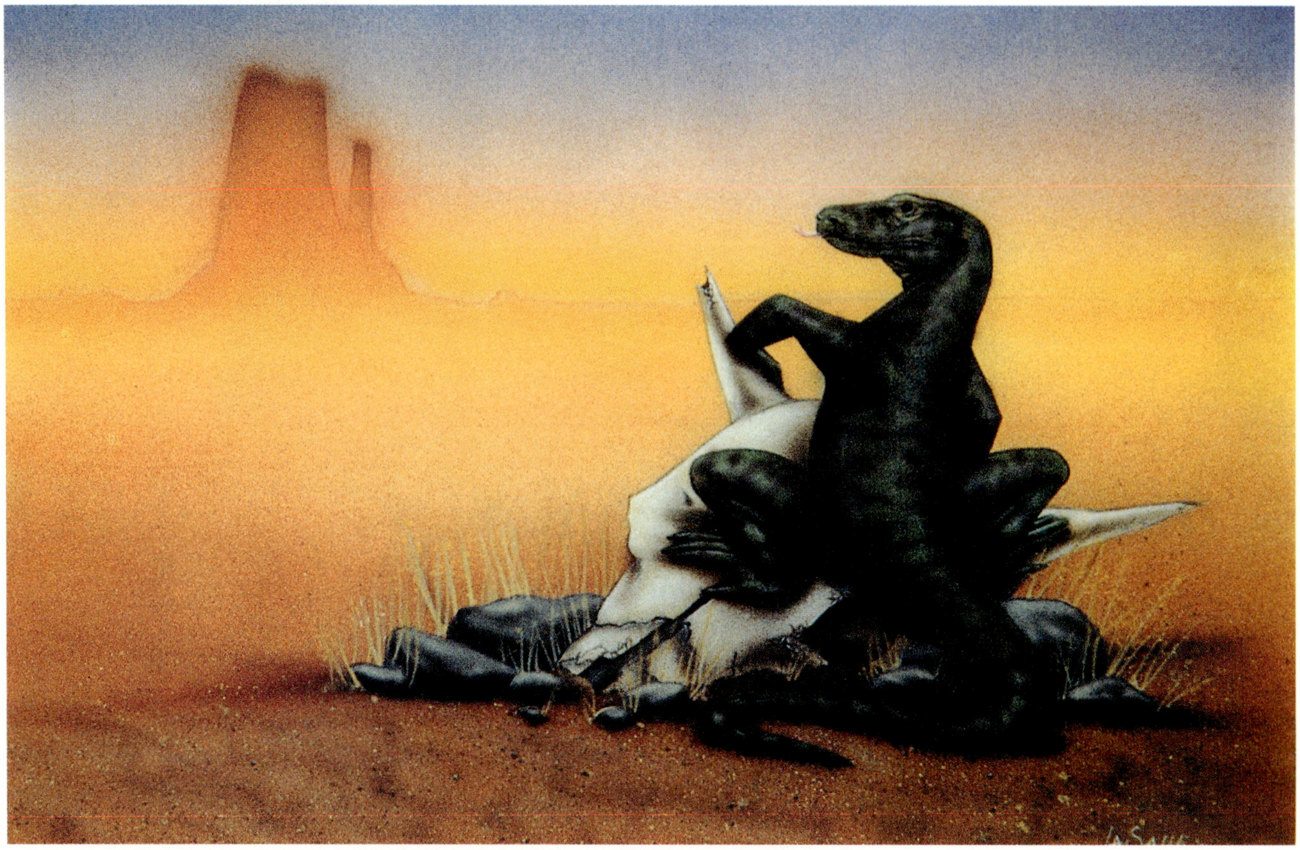

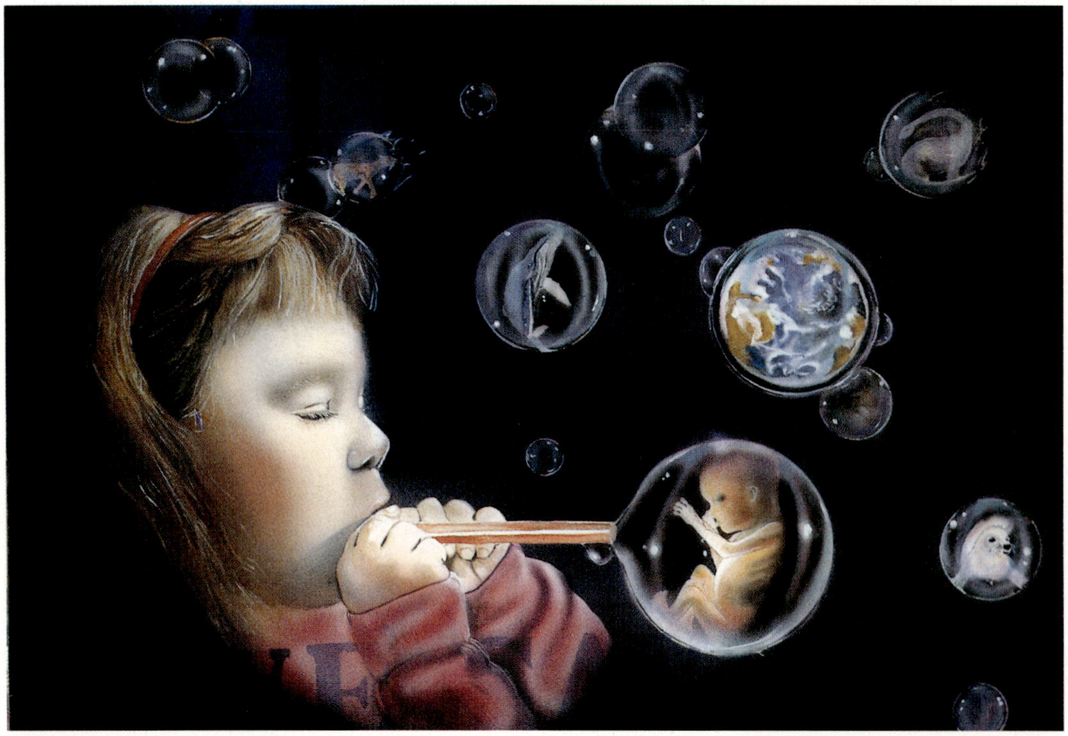
2

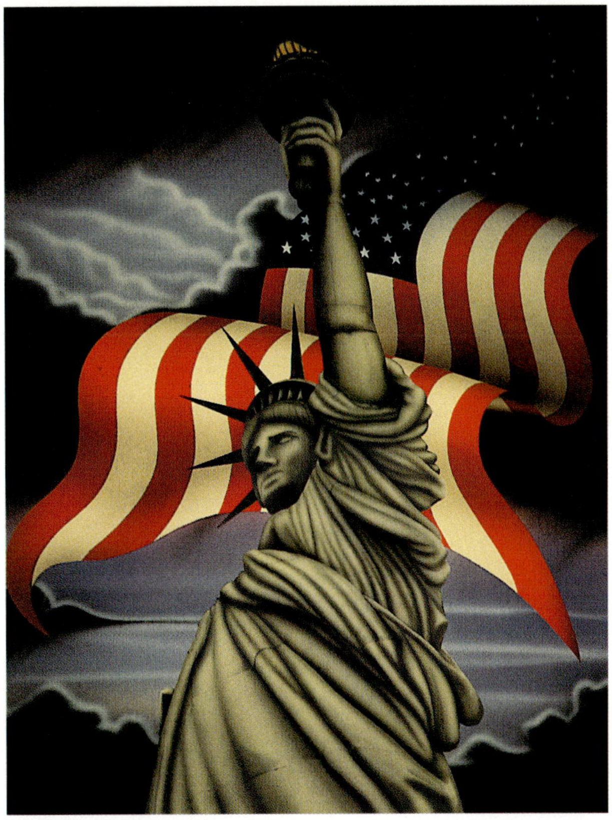
3

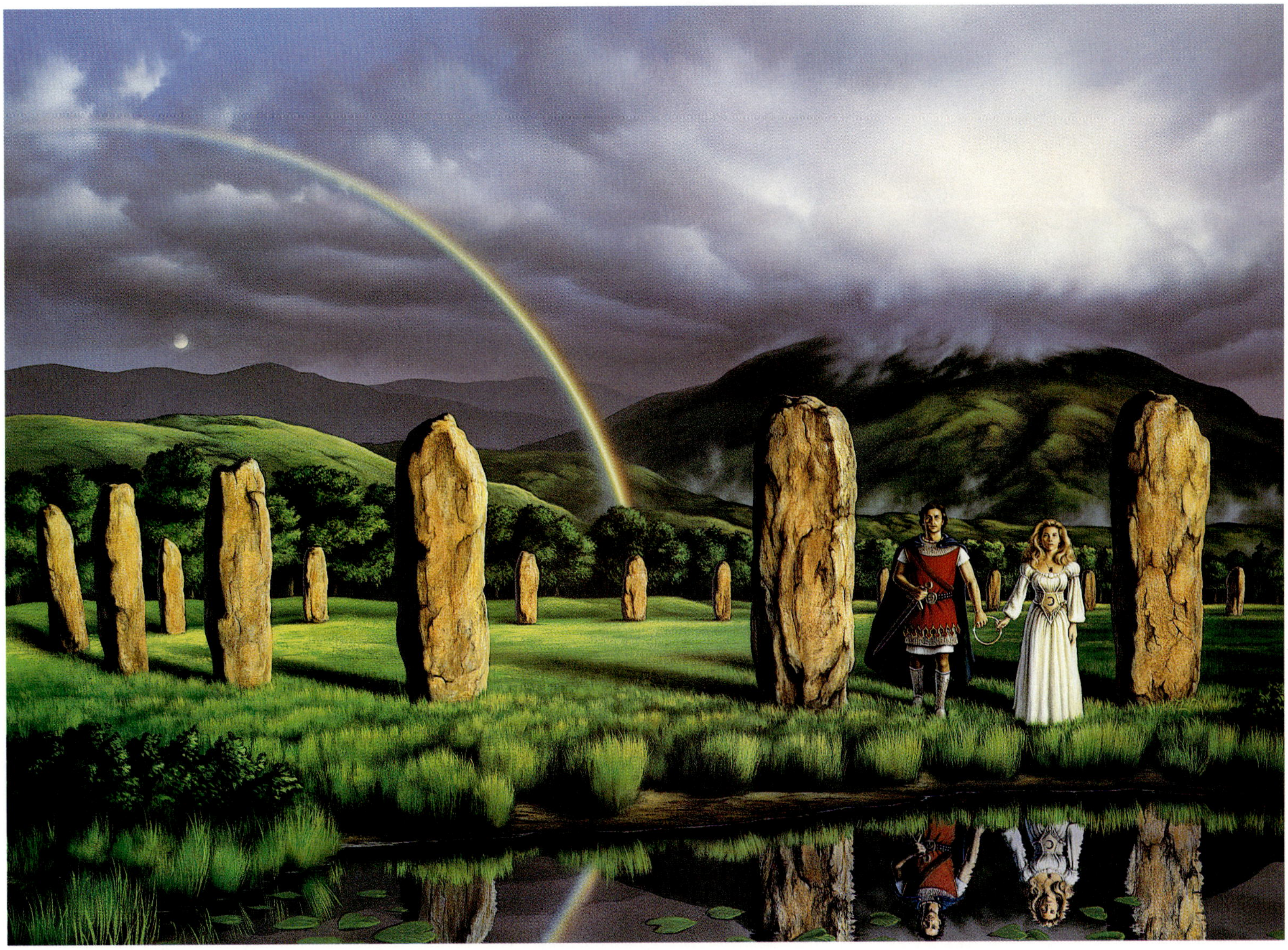
4

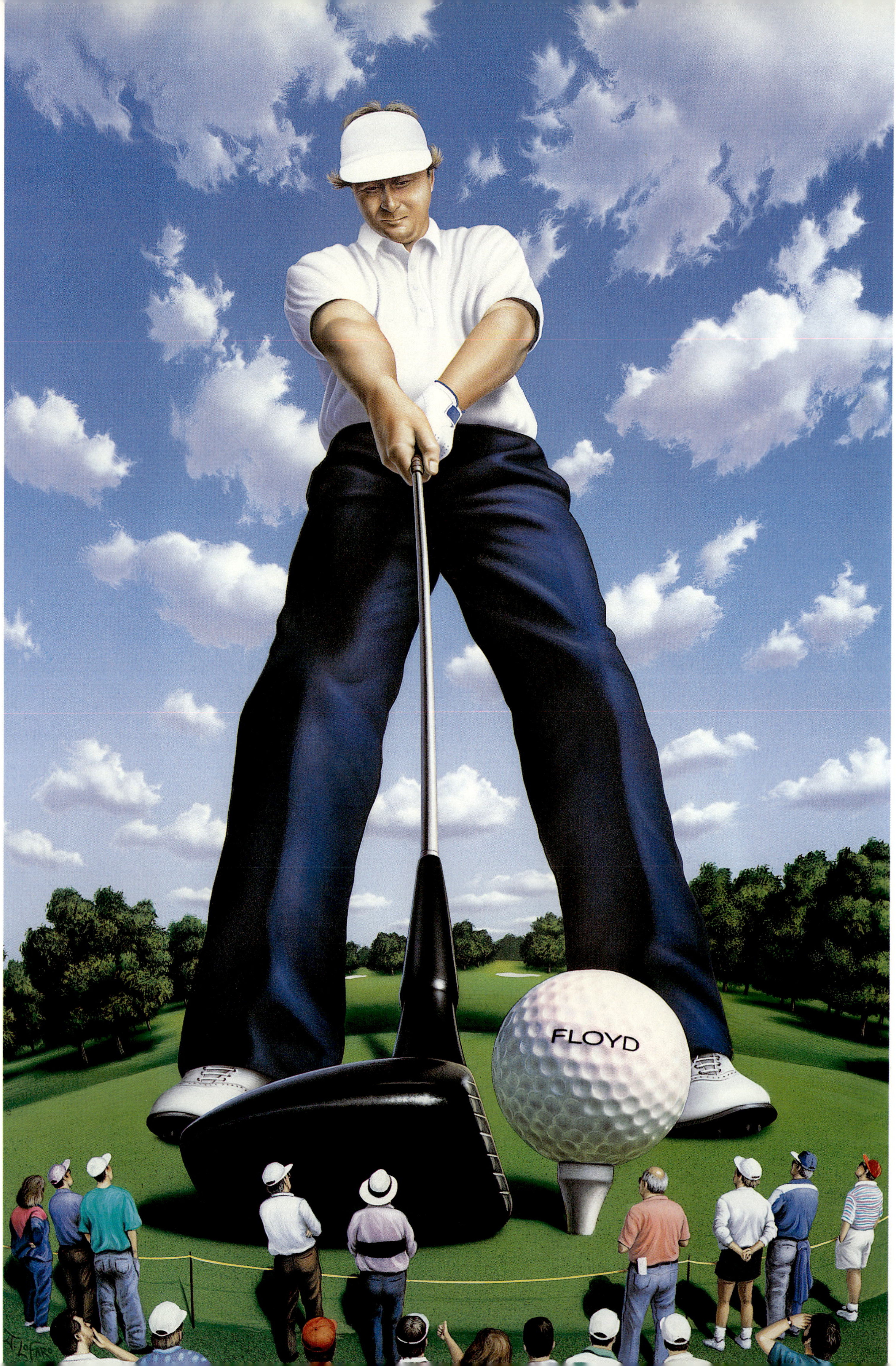

1

1
Artist Jerry Lofaro
Title Giants of Golfing - Ray Floyd
Client G.T.E. North Classic
Art Director Scott Willy
Usage Promotional Ads & Posters
Media Used Acrylic

2
Artist Jerry Lofaro
Title You Too Can Raise Your Level of Productivity
Client Minolta
Art Director Woody Litwhiler
Usage Print Advertisement
Media Used Acrylic

3
Artist Jerry Lofaro
Title Maybe the Best Way to Handle Risk Is to Avoid It Altogether
Client Minolta
Art Director Woody Litwhiler
Usage Print Advertisement
Media Used Acrylic

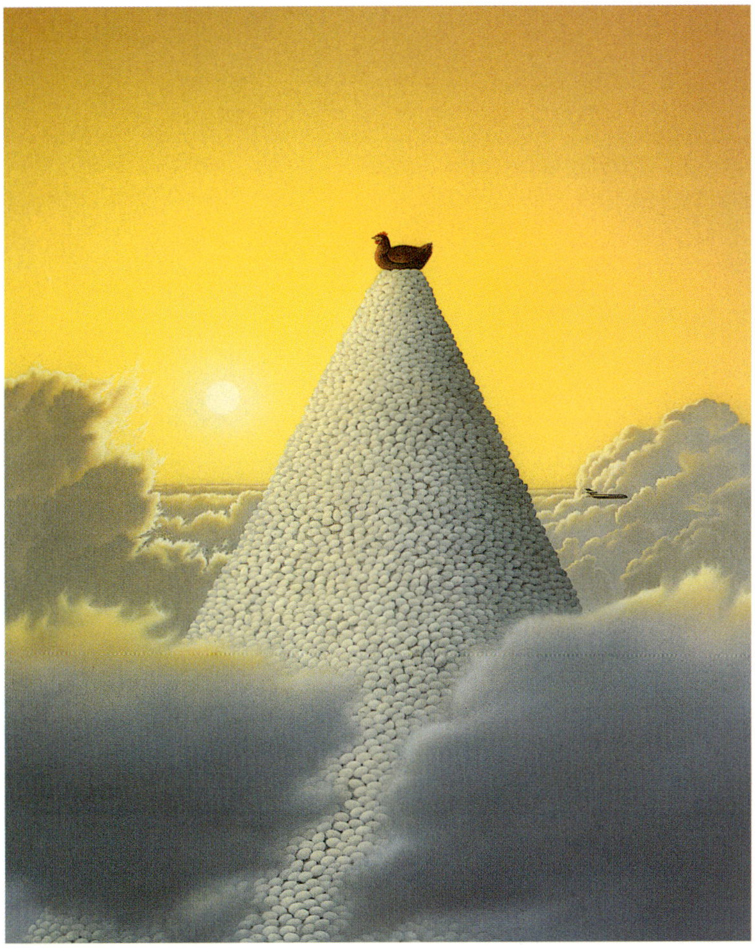

2

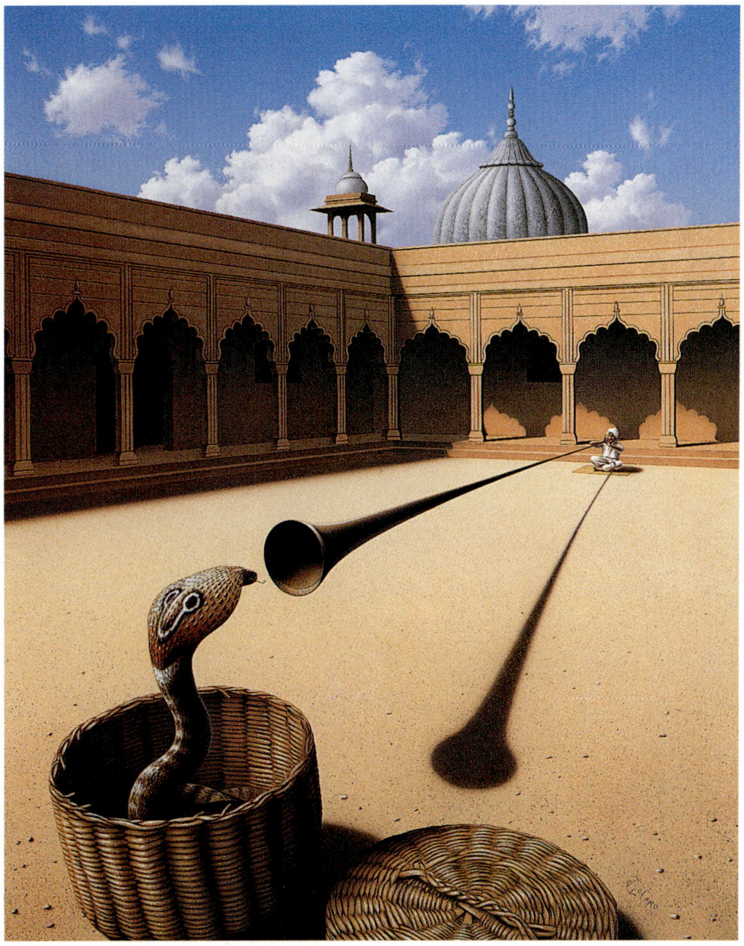

3

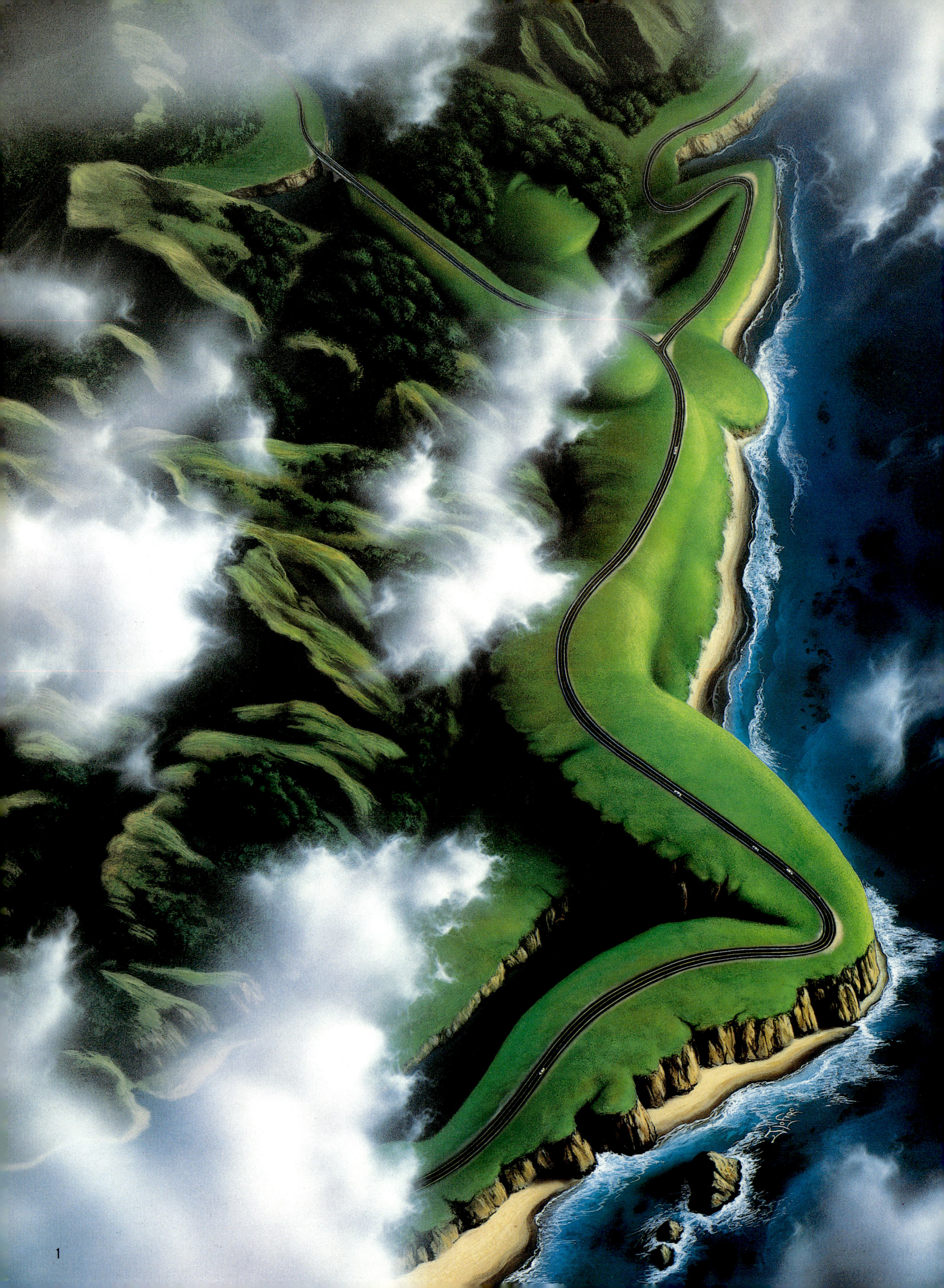

1

1
Artist Jerry Lofaro
Title World the Color of Salt
Client Avon Books
Usage Book Cover
Media Used Acrylic

2
Artist Jerry Lofaro
Usage Self Promotion
Media Used Acrylic

3
Artist Jerry Lofaro
Title Aunt Dimity's Death
Client Viking Penguin
Art Director Neil Stuart
Usage Book Cover
Media Used Acrylic

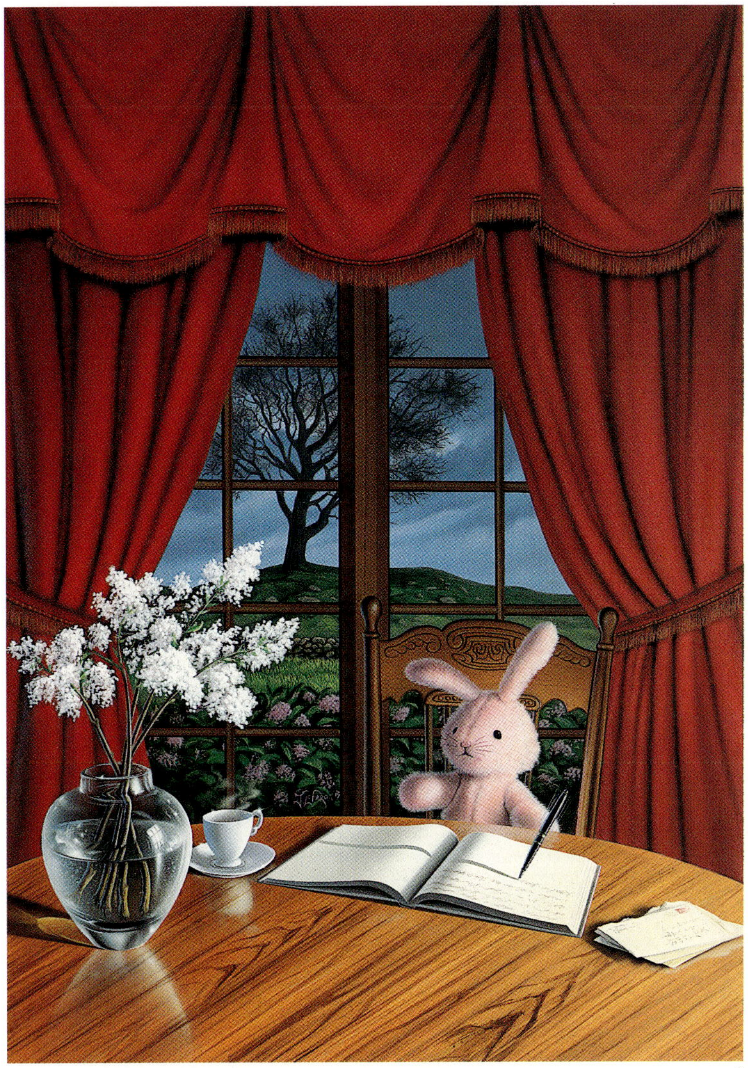

3

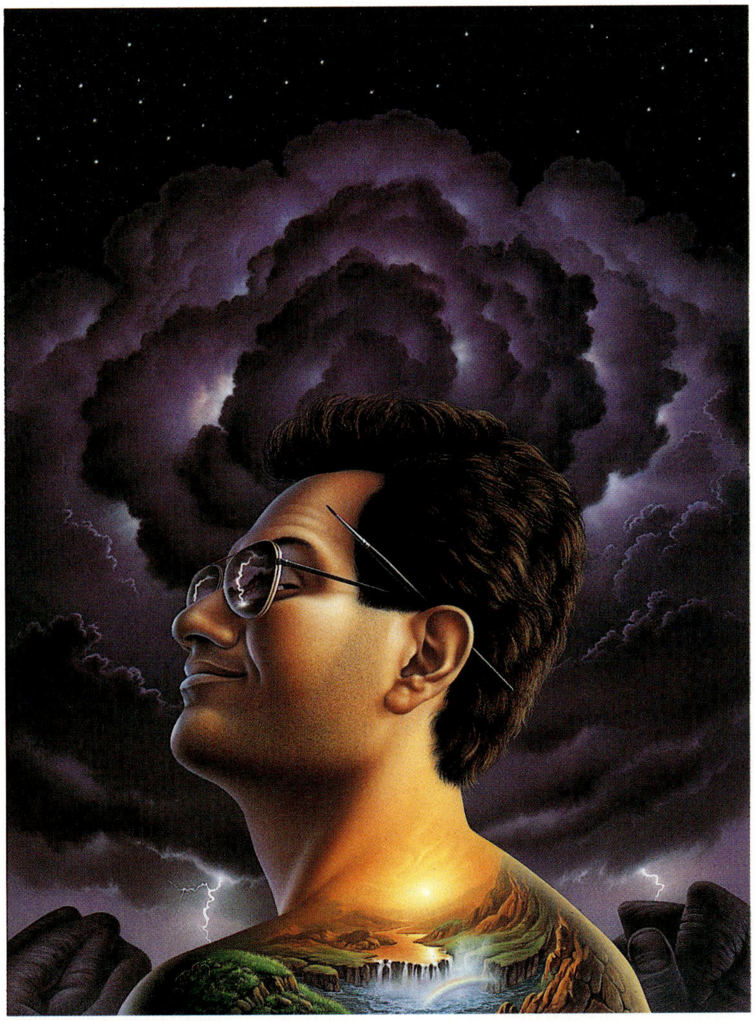

2

1
Artist Travis A. Louie
Title Fare Please
Art Director Douglas Mayfield
Usage Editorial Illustration
Media Used Acrylic

2
Artist Shannon Mac Donald
Title Monster Magic
Usage Fine Art
Media Used Enamel, Imron c/c

3
Artist Shannon Mac Donald
Title I'm Only Sleeping
Usage Fine Art
Media Used Enamel, Imron c/c

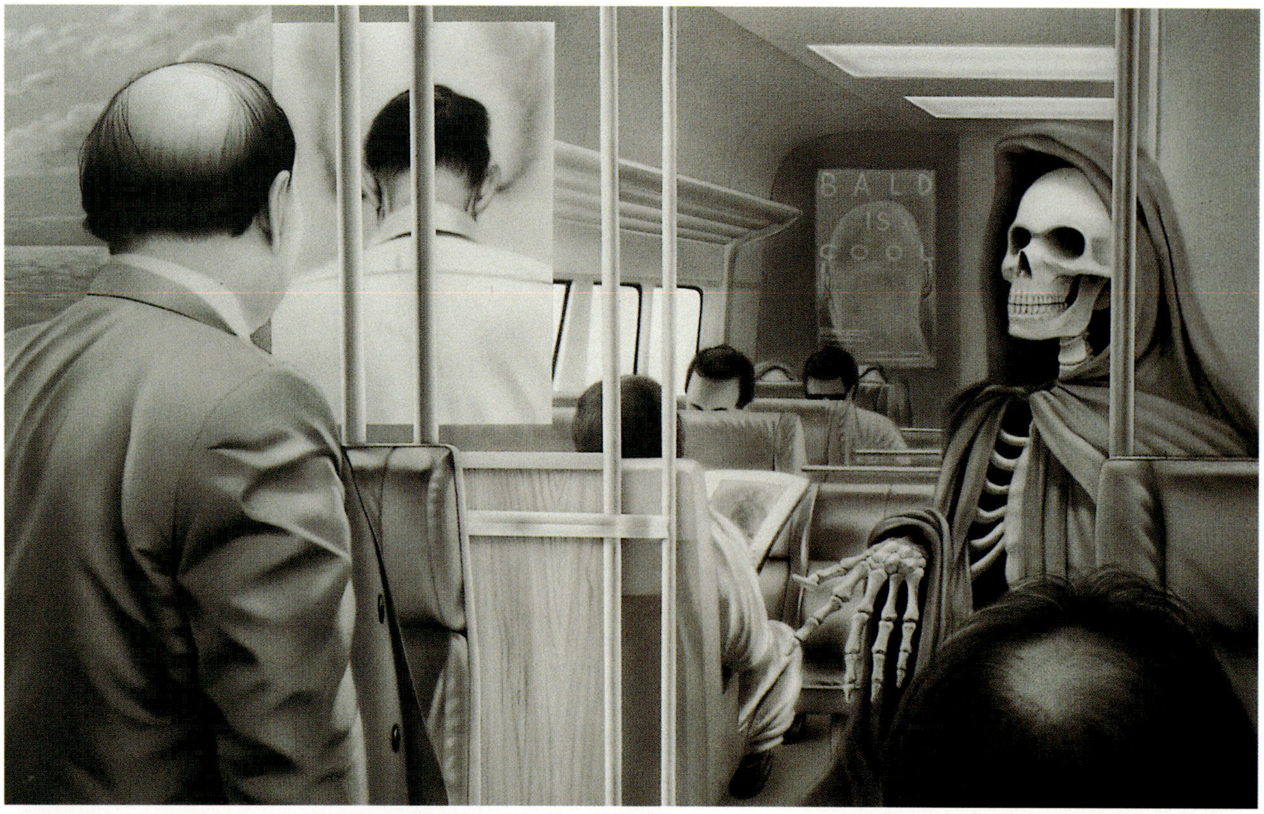

1

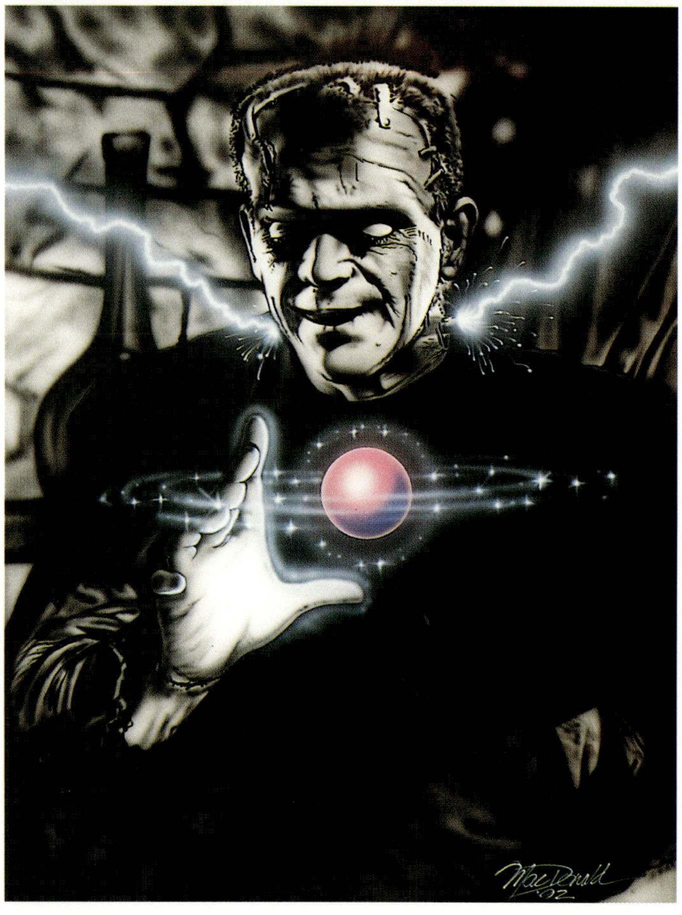
2

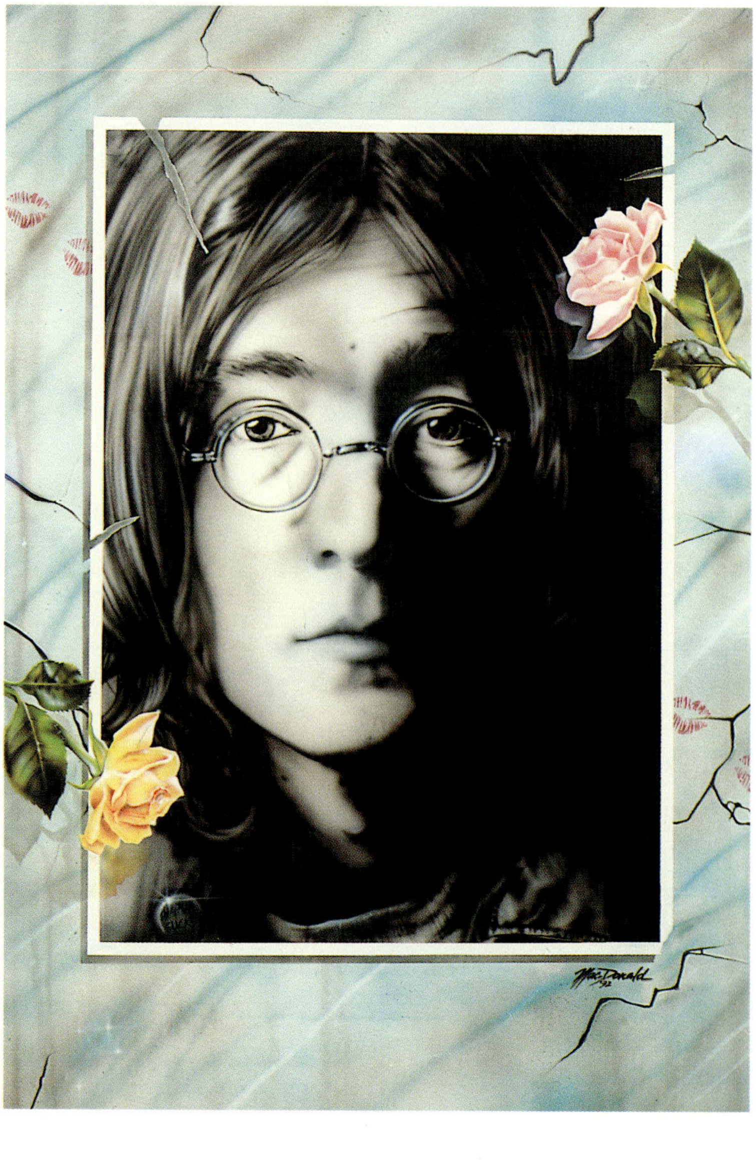
3

1
Artist Farley Magadia
Title Batman Returns (Catwoman)
Client Tower Video MTS Incorporated/Warner Home Video
Usage Home Video Release Teaser
Media Used Acrylic

2
Artist Farley Magadia
Title Batman Returns (The Penguin)
Client Tower Video MTS Incorporated/Warner Home Video
Usage Home Video Release Teaser
Media Used Acrylic

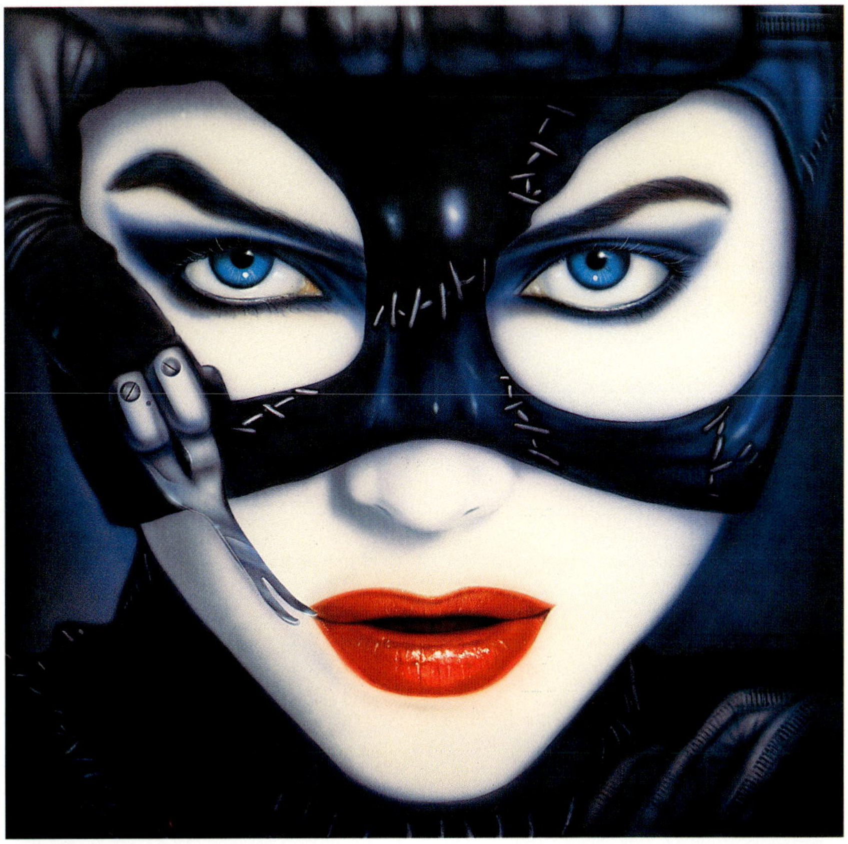

1

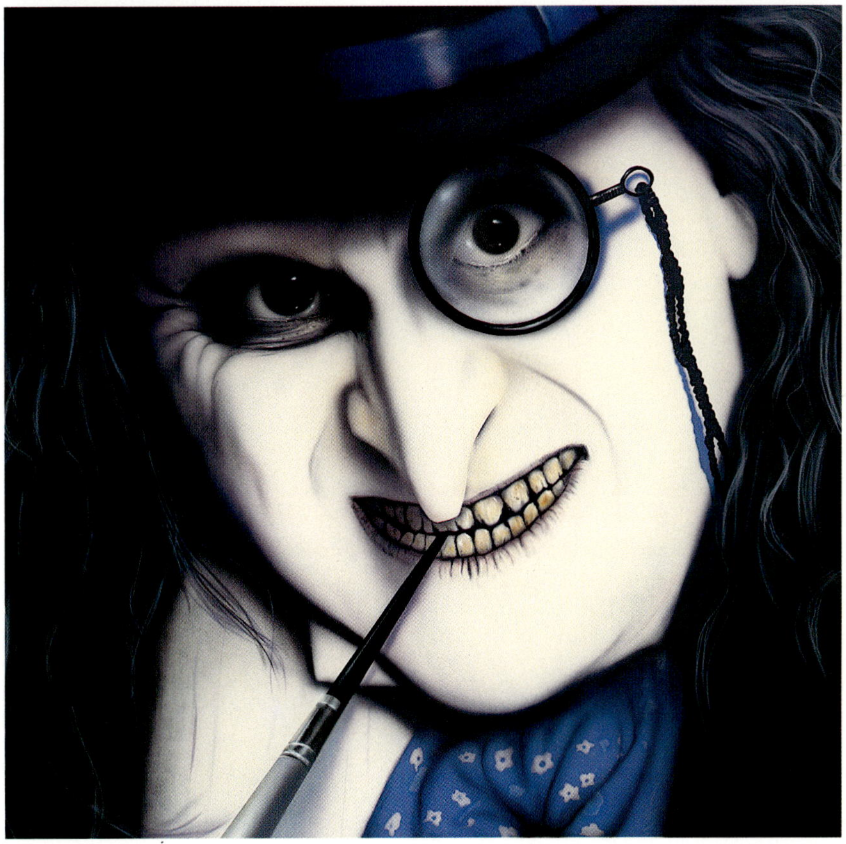

2

1
Artist Farley Magadia
Title Cape Fear
Client Tower Video MTS Incorporated/ Universal Pictures
Usage Home Video Release Teaser
Media Used Acrylic

2
Artist Farley Magadia
Title Cheryl
Client Farley Magadia
Art Director Farley Magadia
Usage Exhibited in a Body of Gallery Work of the Artist
Media Used Acrylic

3
Artist Farley Magadia
Title Jim Hensen's "Dog City"
Client Fox TV
Art Director Michelle Magat (Wallen Green Design)
Usage Fox Kids Club Magazine
Media Used Acrylic

4
Artist Joseph Martin
Title Cold Heart of Technology
Usage Fine Art
Media Used Acrylic

1

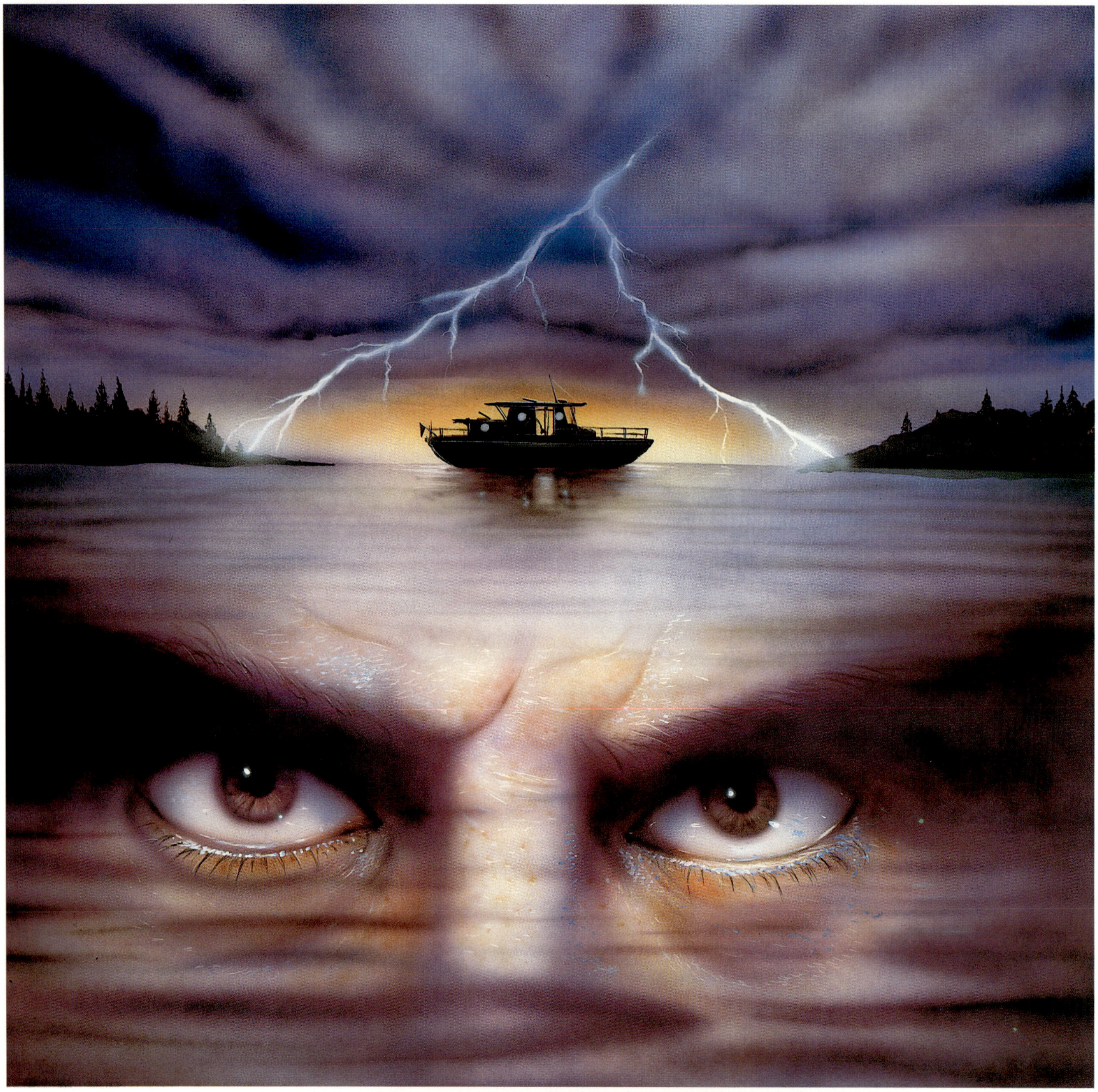

2

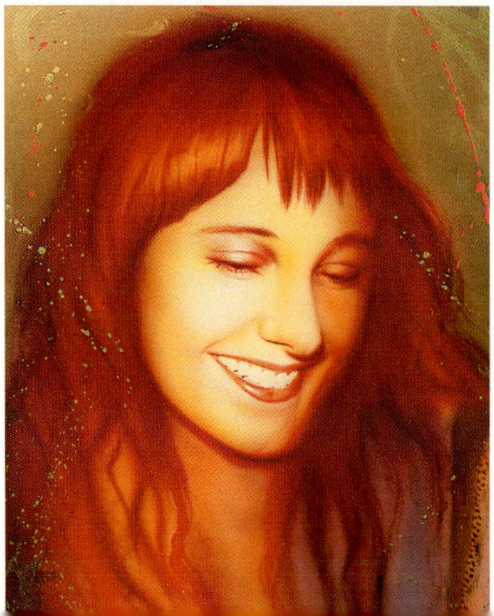

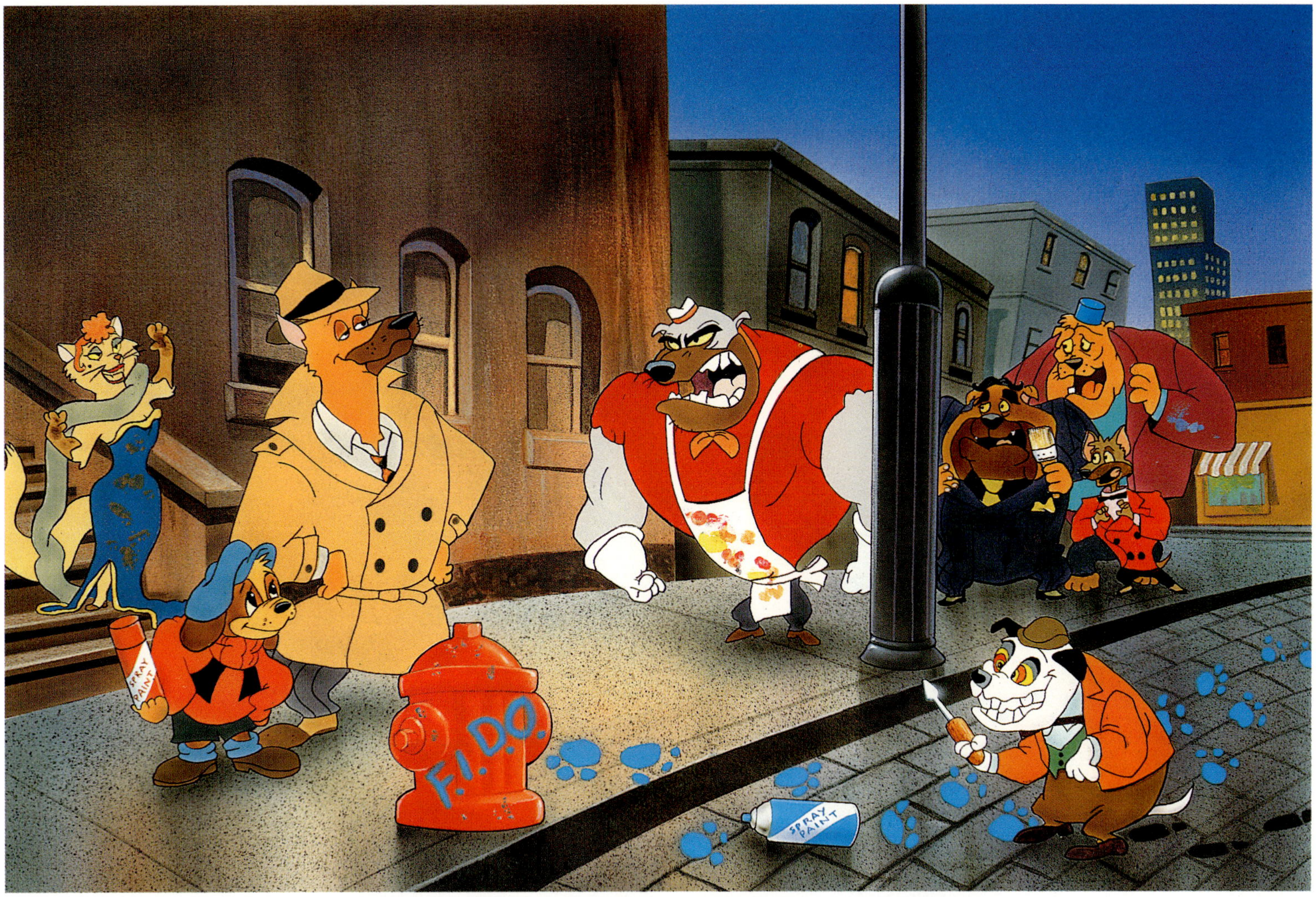

3

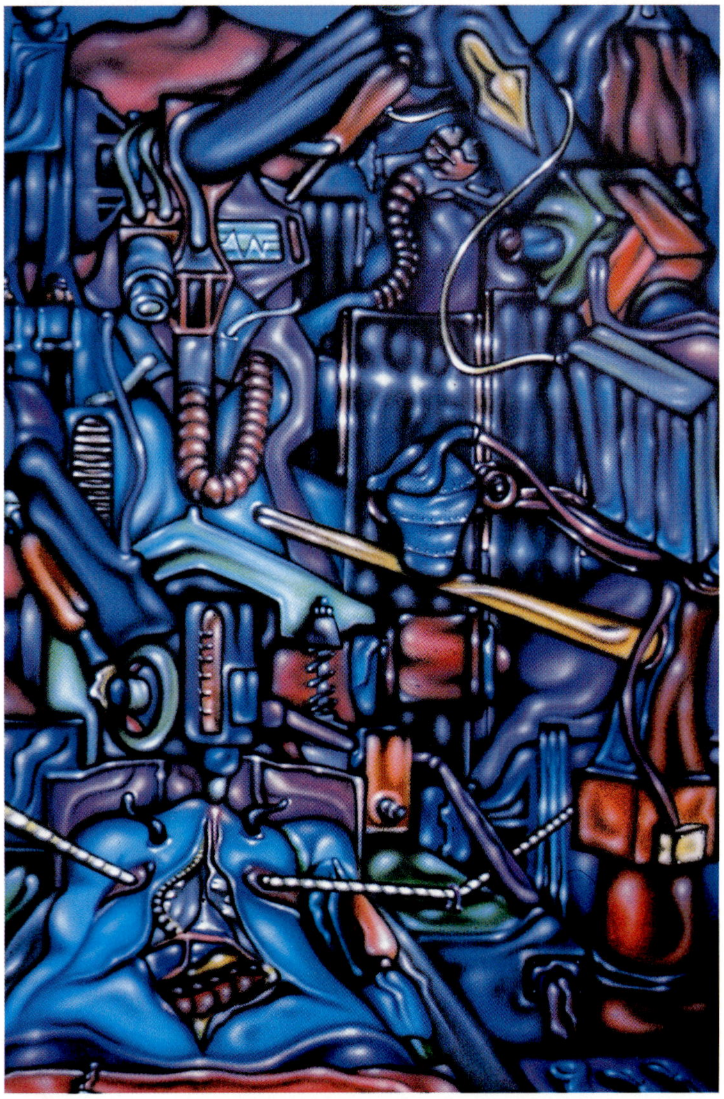

4

1
Artist Joseph Martin
Title Art of Censorship
Usage Fine Art
Media Used Acrylic

2
Artist Joesph Martin
Title Nuclear Waste Junkie
Usage Fine Art
Media Used Acrylic

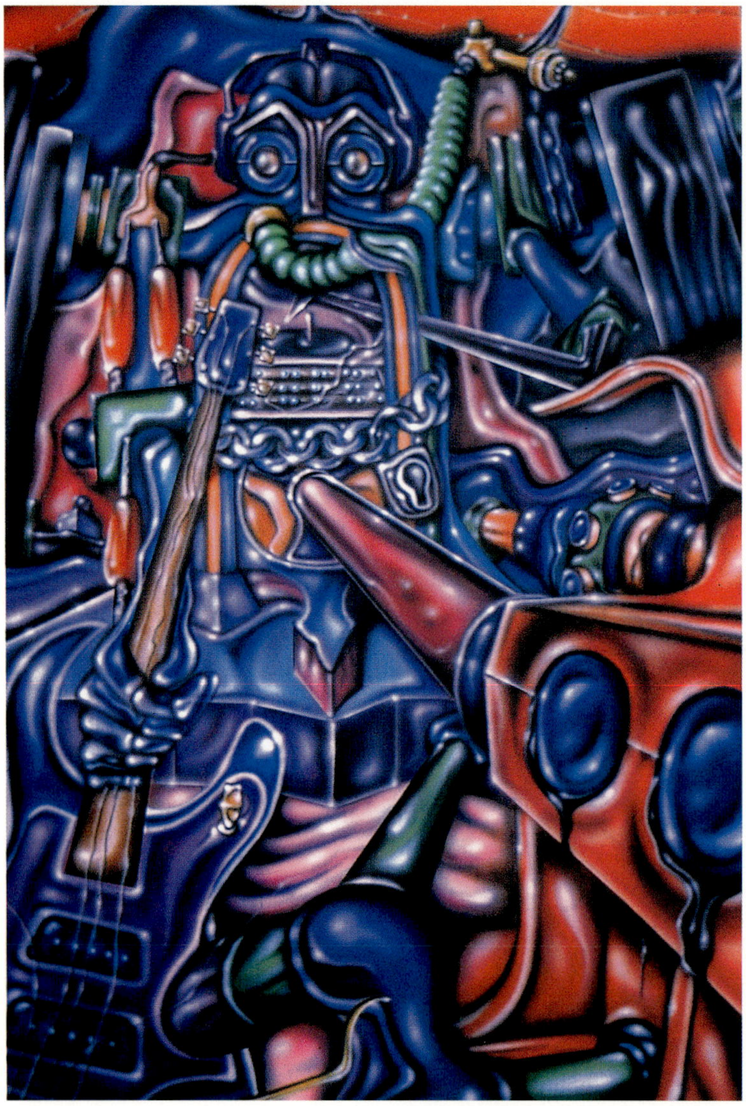

1

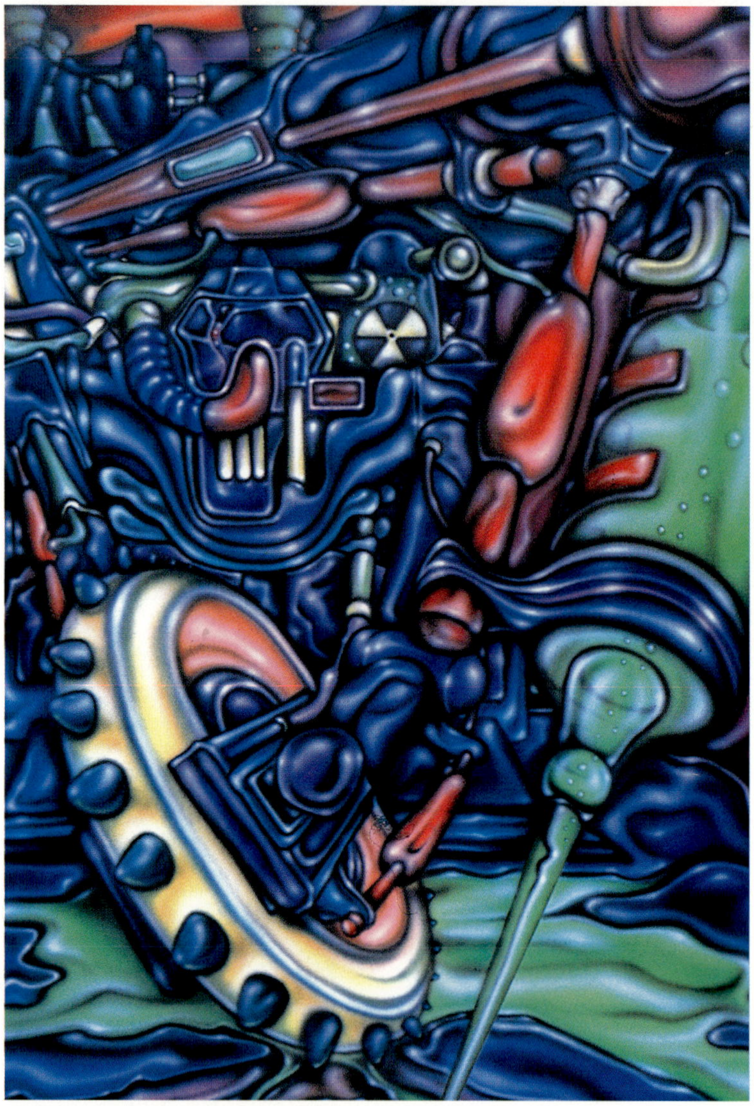

2

1
Artist Trent Martin
Title Airbrush Sickness
College Project Bob Blair
Usage Student Art
Media Used Liquitex Acrylic

2
Artist Bill Mayer
Client Scripto-Tokai
Art Director Bill Halfner
Usage Packaging
Media Used Gouache, Dyes

3
Artist Bill Mayer
Client Self Promotion
Art Director Bill Mayer
Usage Ad/Self Promotion
Media Used Gouache, Dyes

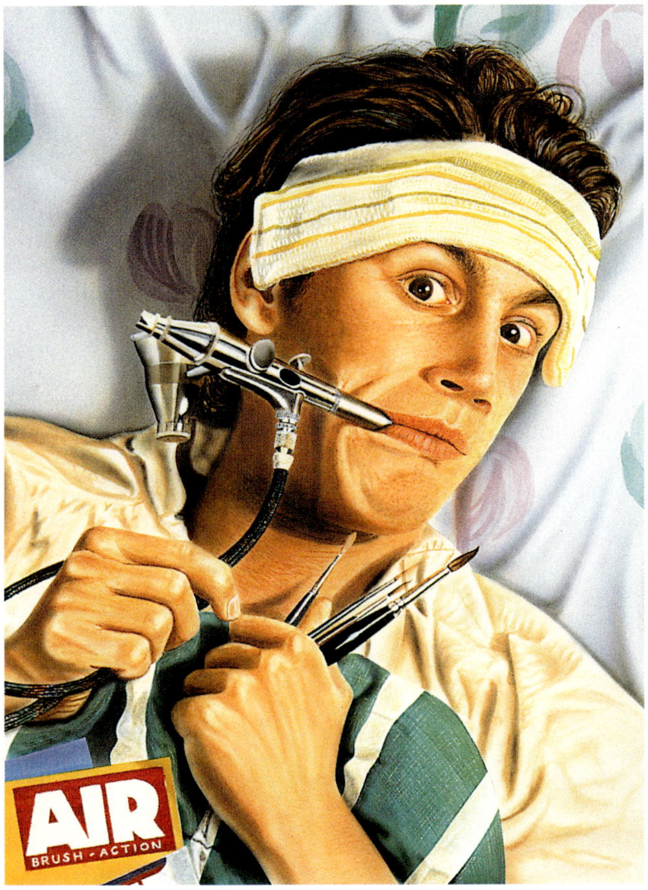

1

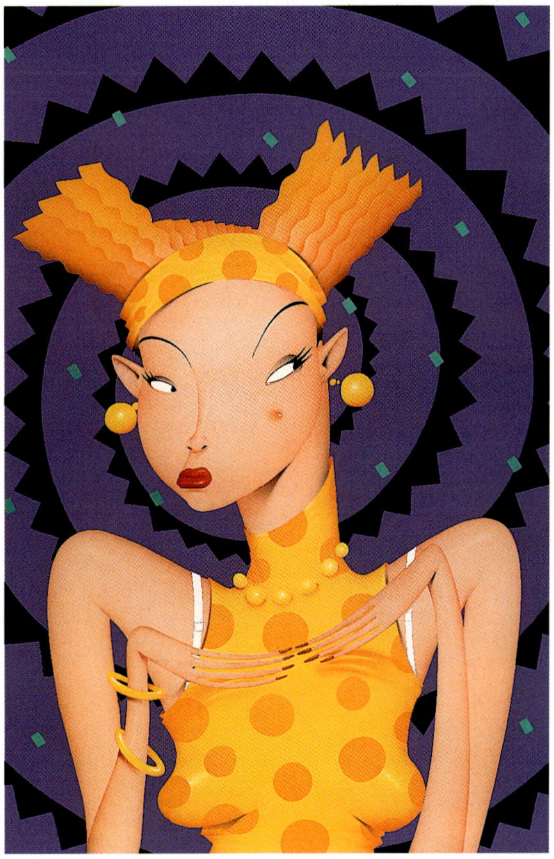
2

3

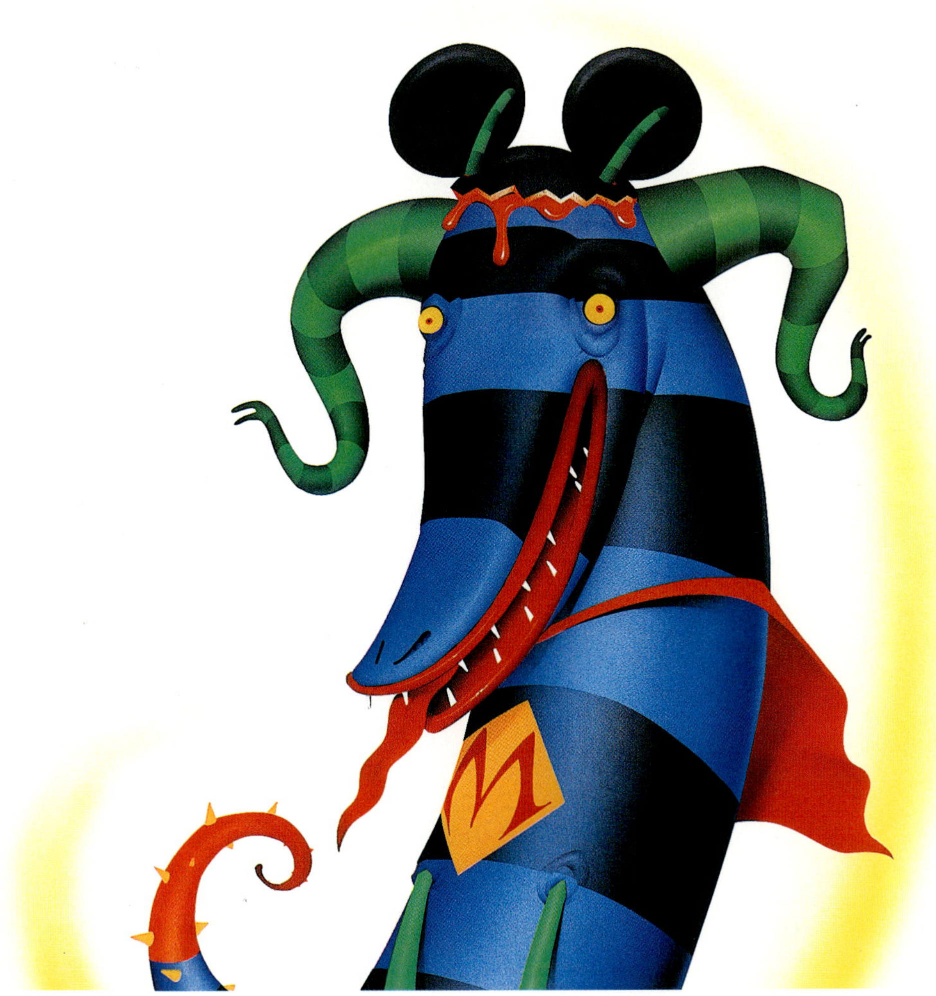

1
Artist Bill Mayer
Client Var Business
Art Director David Lowey
Usage Magazine Illustration
Media Used Gouache, Dyes

2
Artist Bill Mayer
Client Metro Mail
Art Director Bob Meyers
Usage Advertising Magazine Ad
Media Used Gouache, Dyes

3
Artist Bill Mayer
Client Scripto-Tokai
Art Director Bill Halfner
Usage Packaging
Media Used Gouache, Dyes

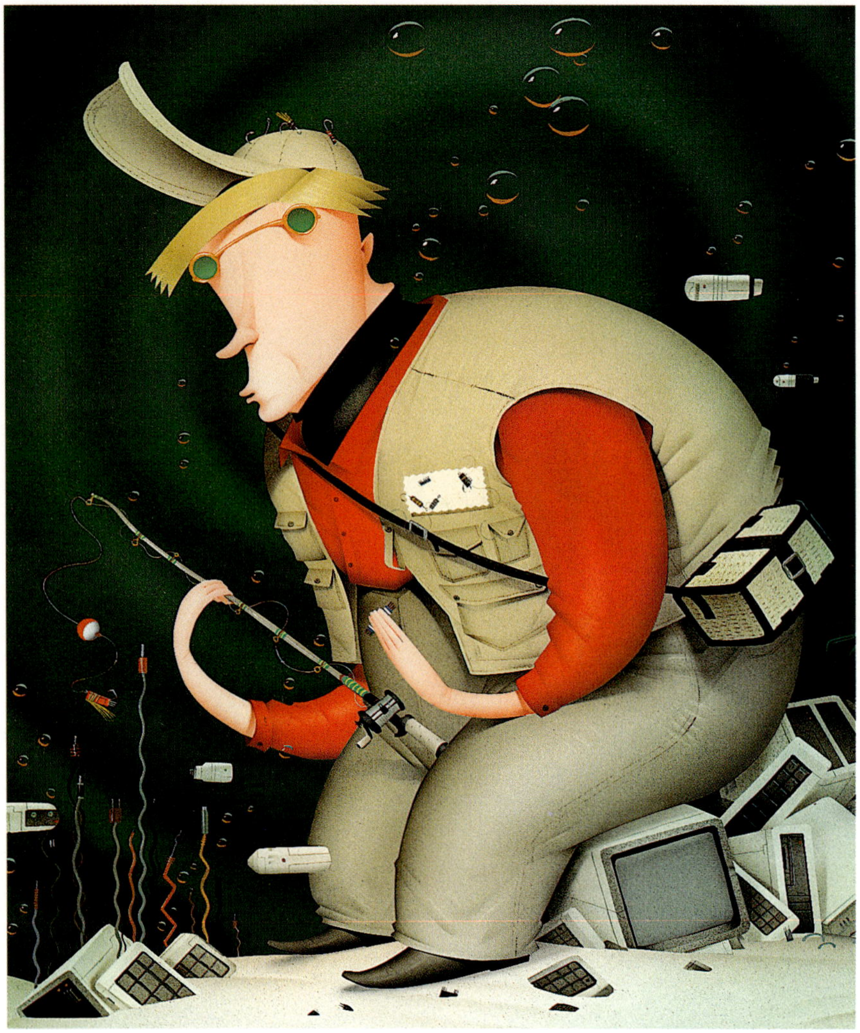

1

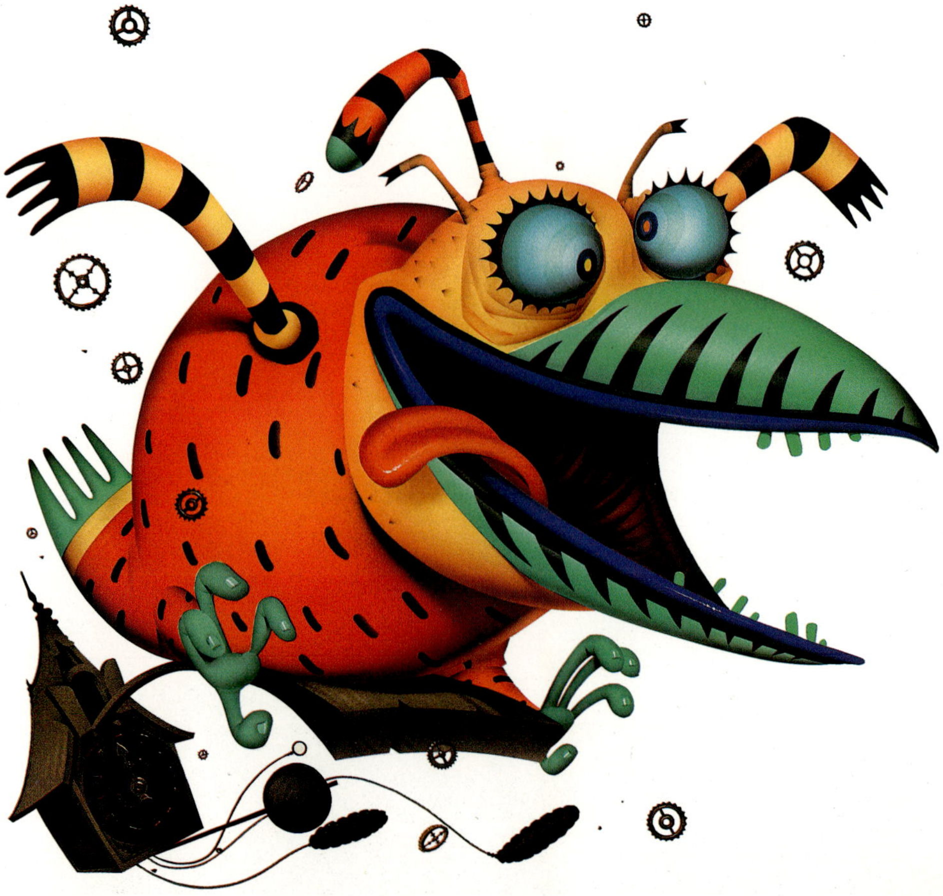

2

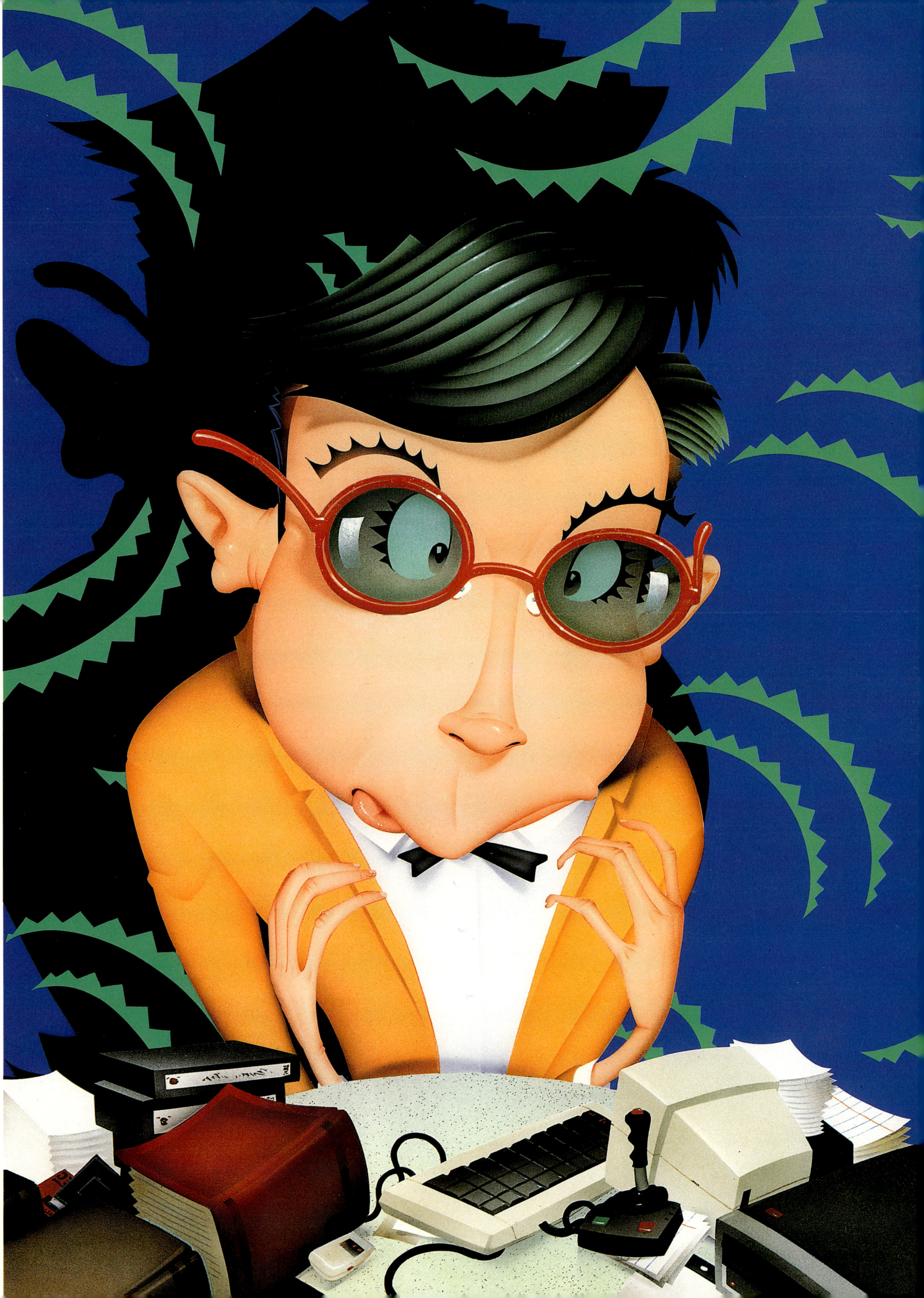

1
Artist Bill Mayer
Title Tilles Center for Performing Arts
Client Tilles Center
Art Director John Peterson
Usage Poster
Media Used Air Brush Gouache & Dyes

2
Artist Bill Mayer
Art Director Fred Martins
Usage Advertising
Media Used Gouache and Dyes

3
Artist Bill Mayer
Title They're Back
Client Woodridge Mall
Art Director Shirley Fee
Usage Poster
Media Used Gouache, Dyes

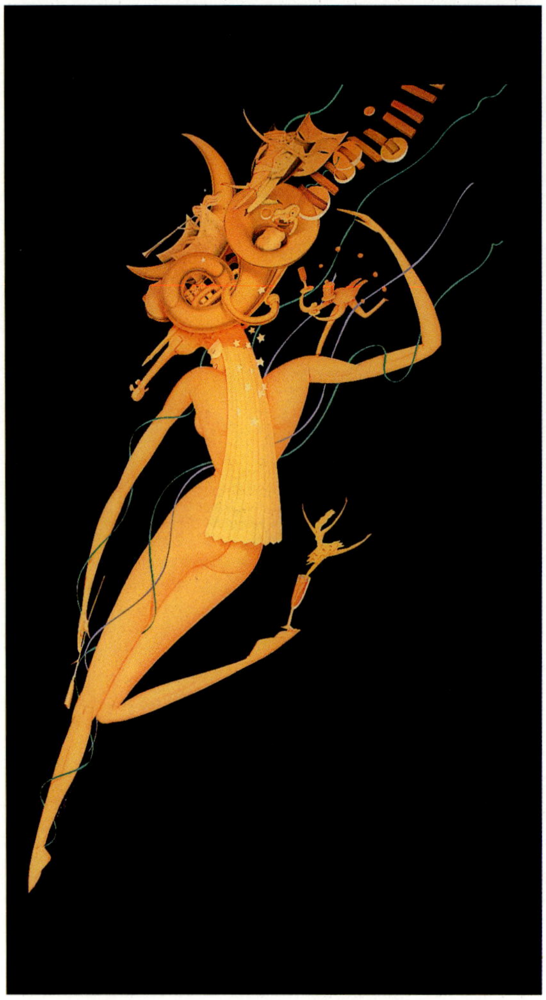

1

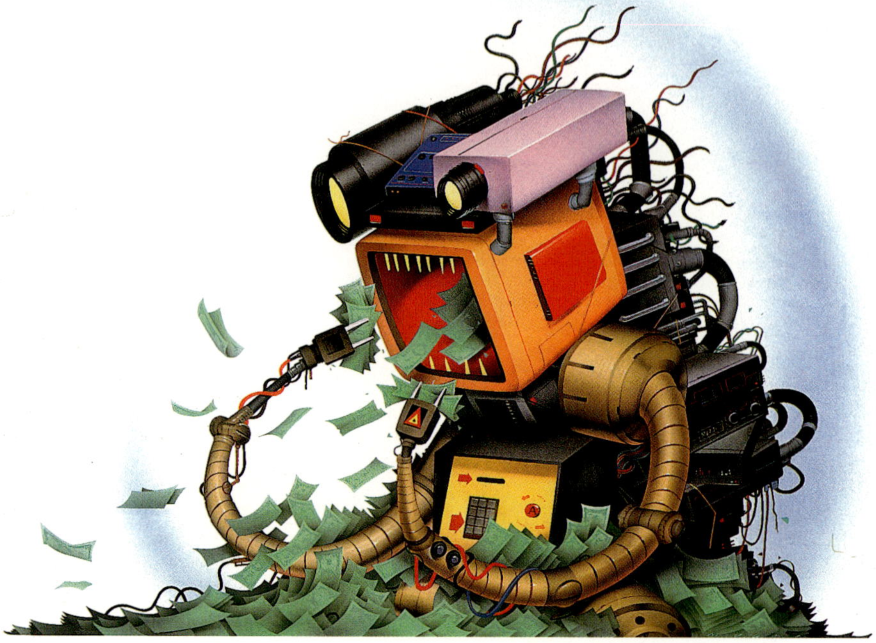

2

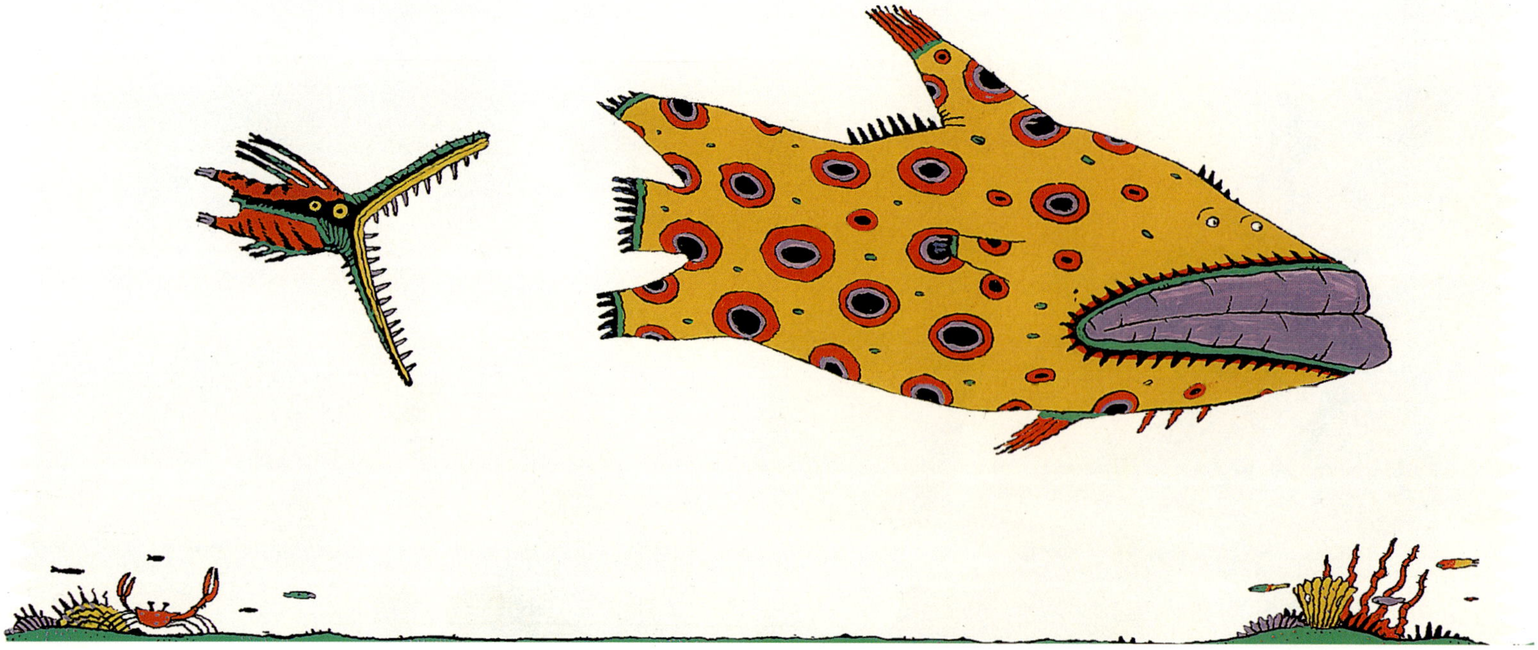

3

1
Artist Bill Mayer
Client Boston Children's Museum
Art Director Larry Bowdish
Usage Outdoor & Advertisement
Media Used Airbrush Gouache, Dyes

2
Artist Bill Mayer
Title Self Portrait
Client Frisk Artist Materials
Art Director Steve Rouseau
Usage Advertisement
Media Used Gouache, Dyes

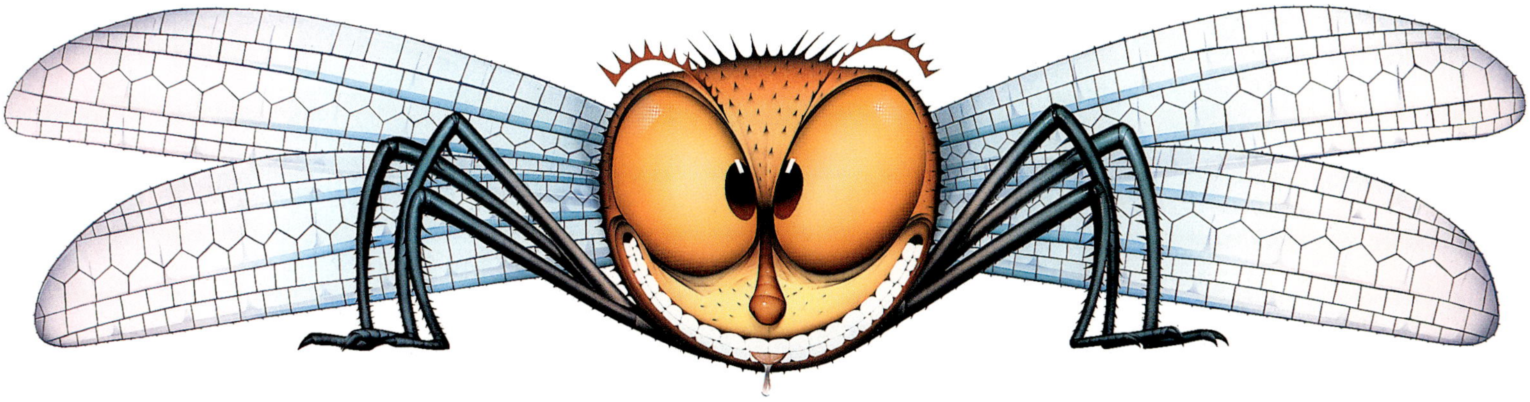

1

2

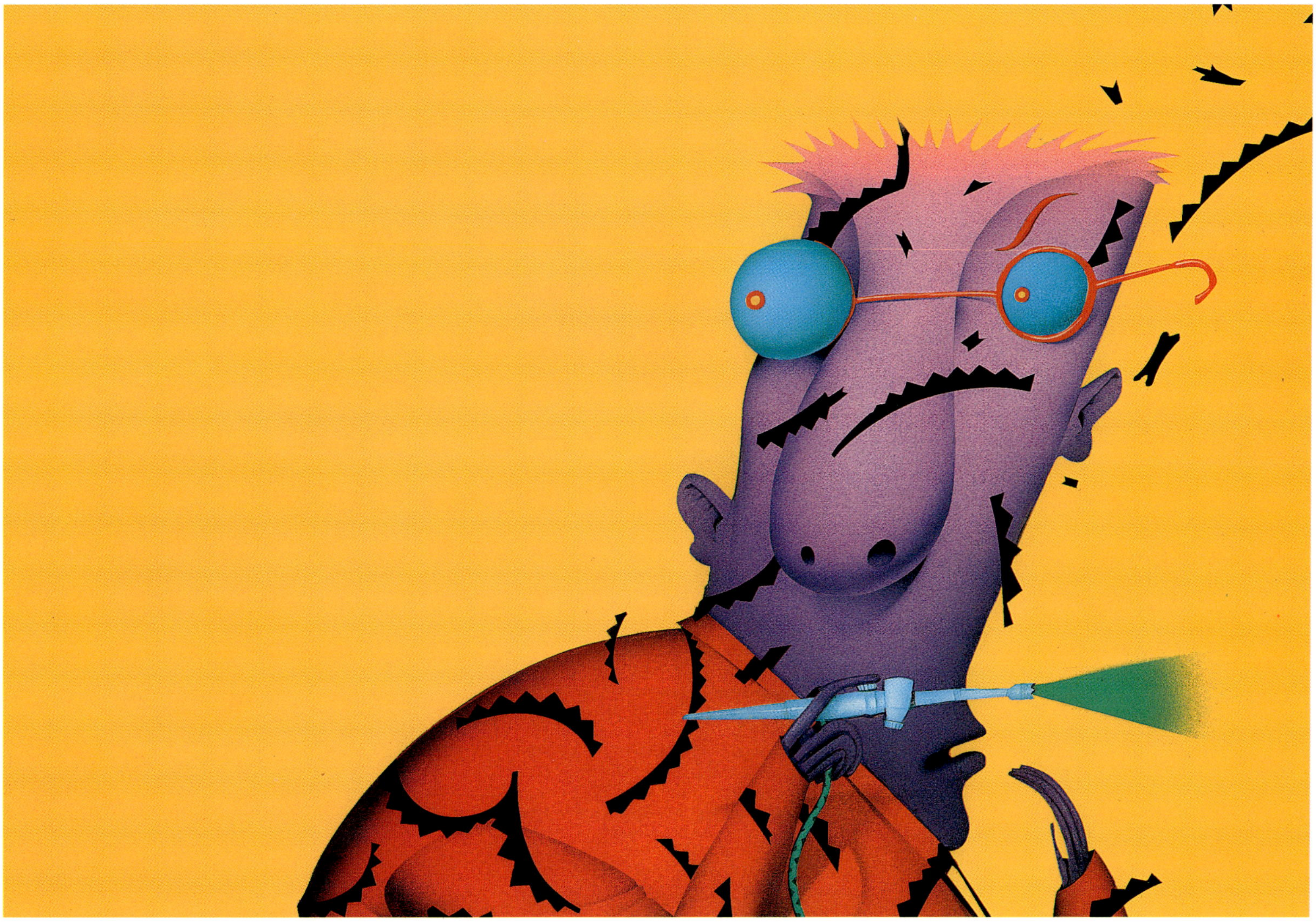

1
Artist Bill Mayer
Title Curves Ahead
Client Rippingtons/GRP Records
Art Director Andi Baltimore
Usage Audio File Cover
Media Used Gouache, Dyes

2
Artist Bill Mayer
Client NFL Properties
Art Director Victoria Eichinger
Usage Poster
Media Used Gouache, Dyes

3
Artist Bill Mayer
Title Software Made Simple
Client Business Week
Art Director Cynthia Friedman
Usage Cover
Media Used Gouache, Dyes

4
Artist Bill Mayer
Title Bull
Client Word Perfect
Art Director Ron Stuckie
Usage Spot/Magazine
Media Used Gouache, Dyes

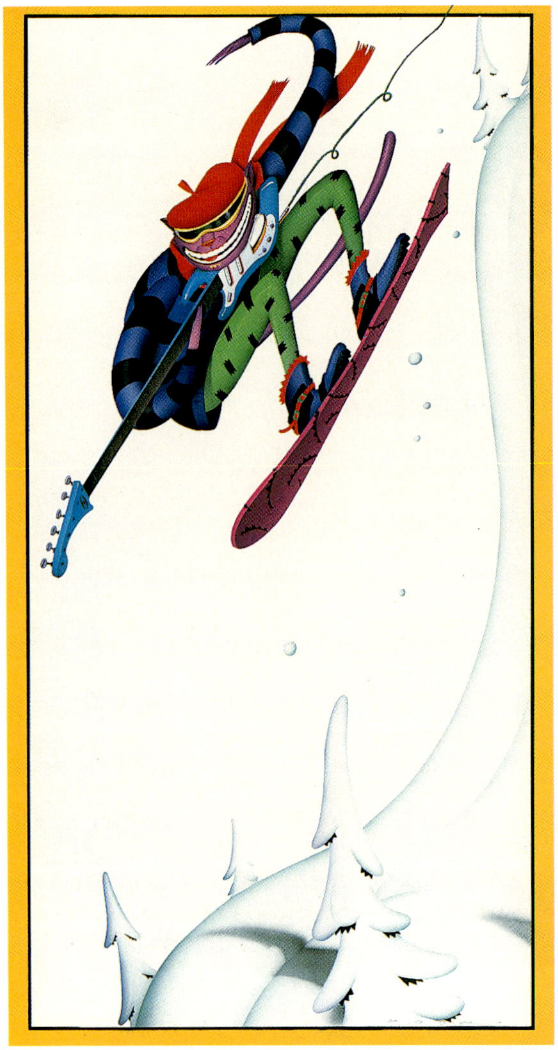

1

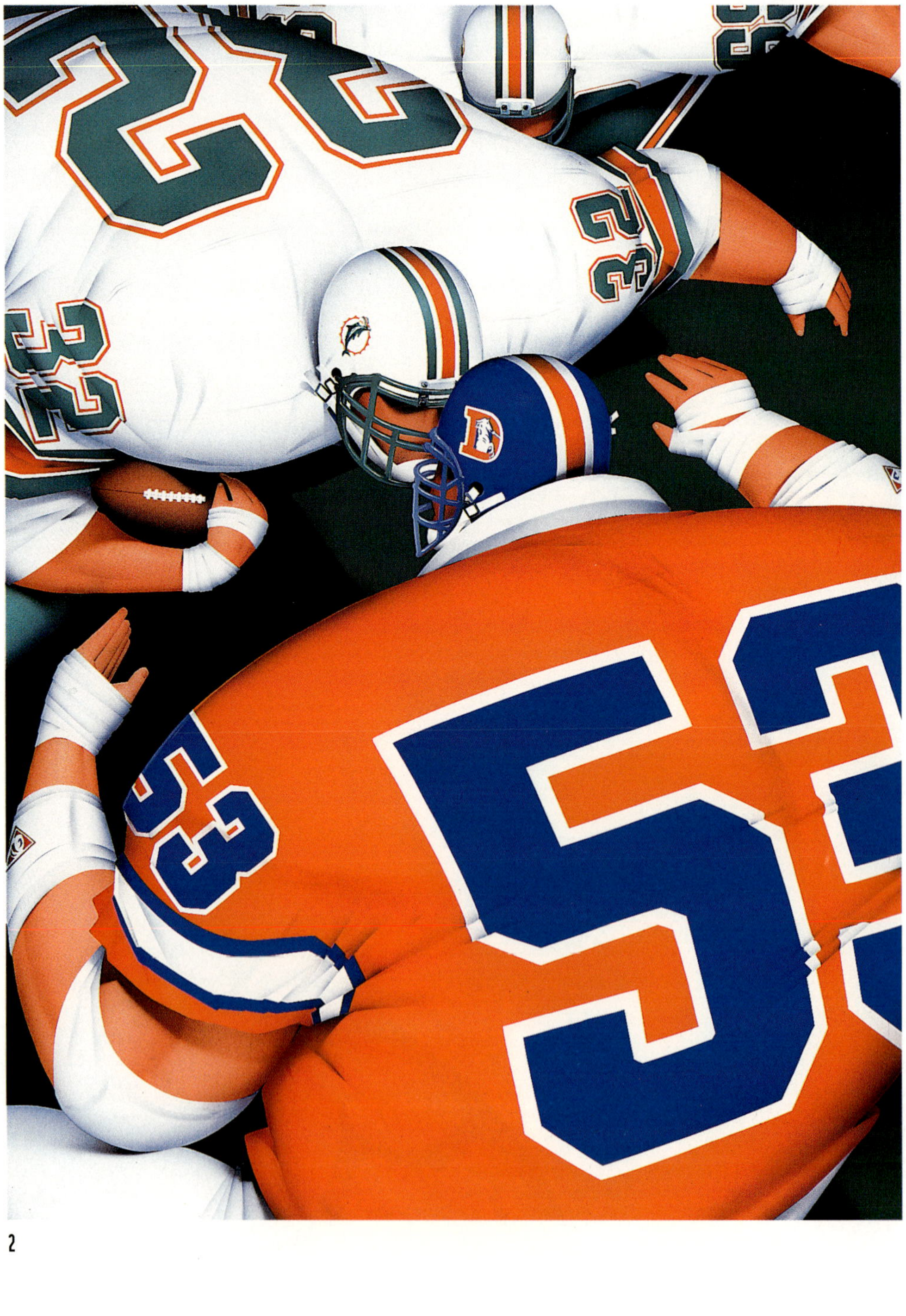

2

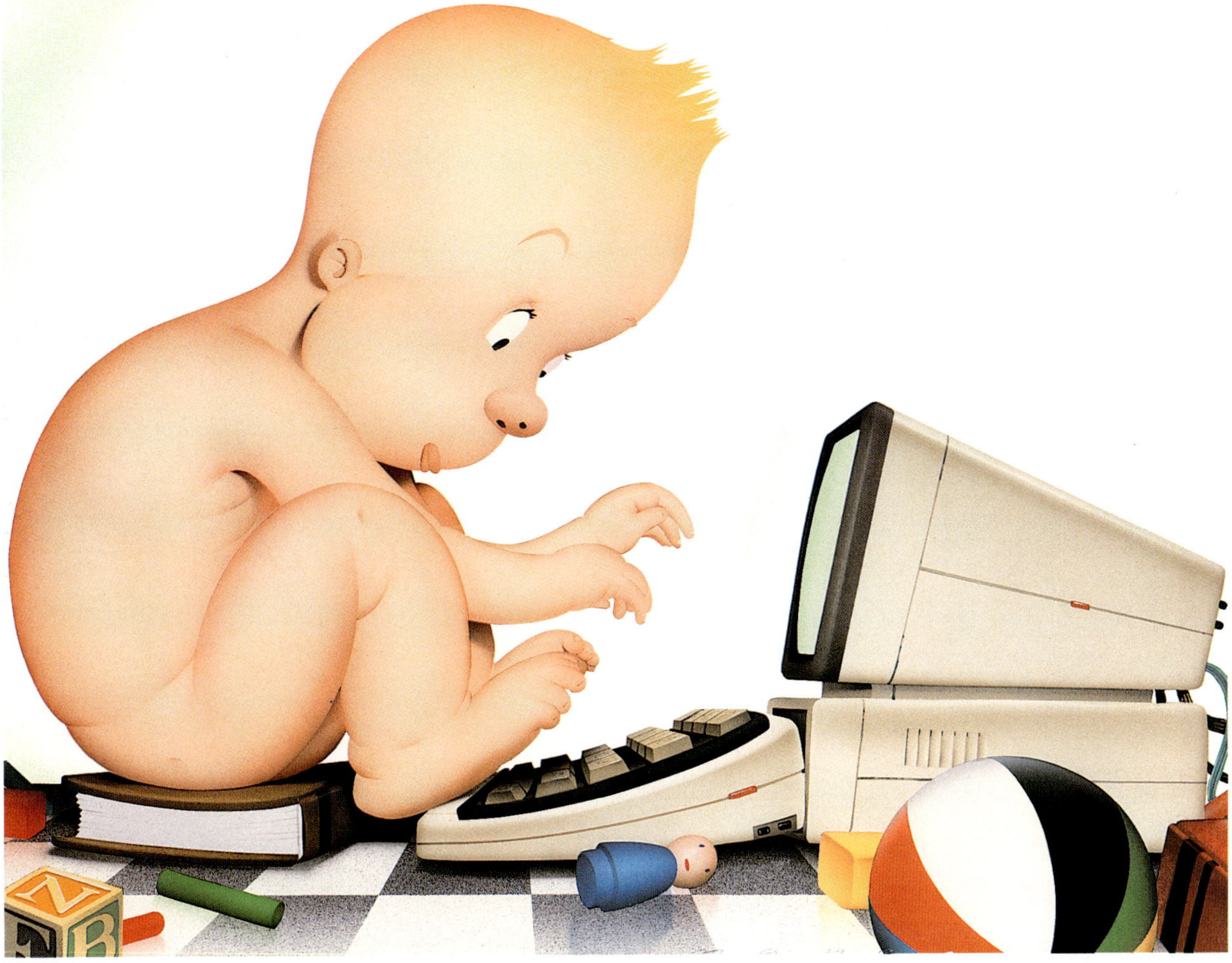

3

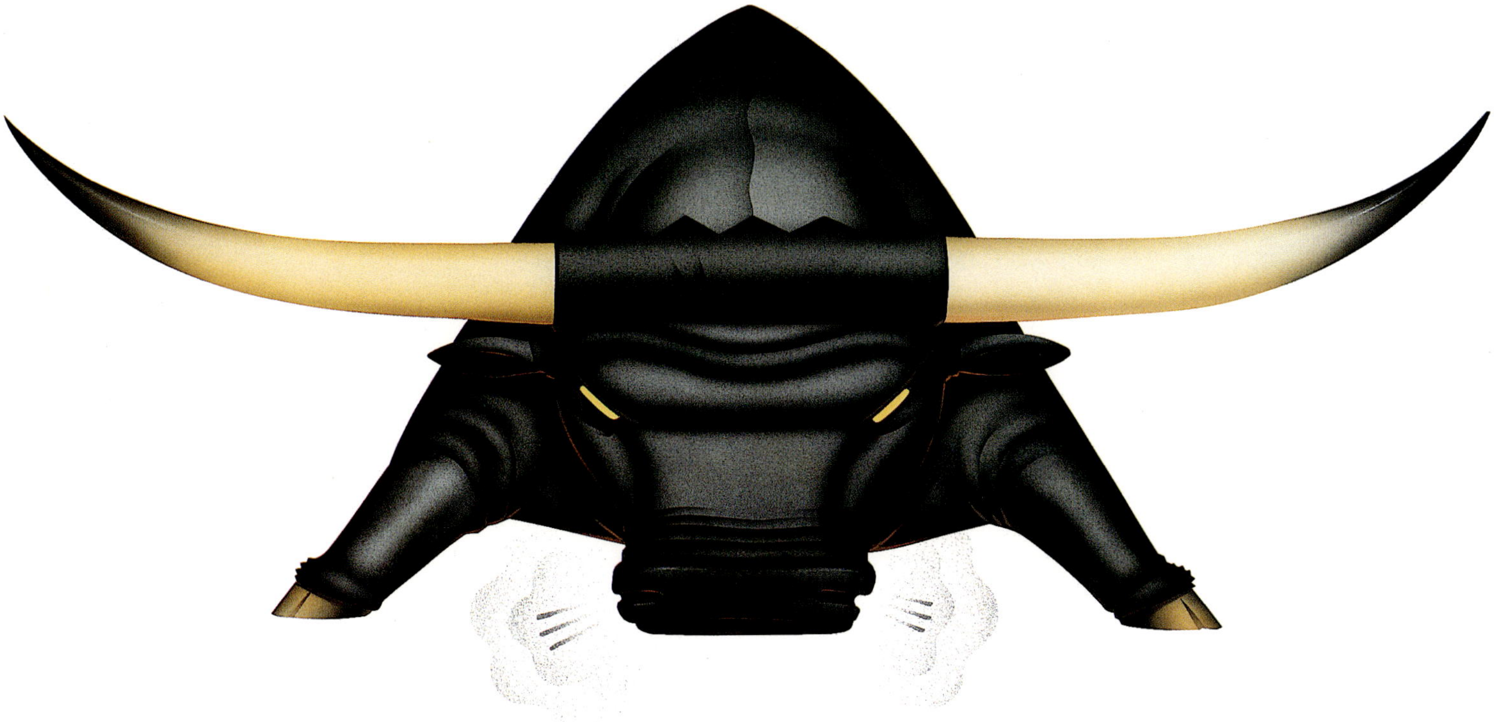

4

1
Artist Bill Mayer
Client Scripto-Tokai
Art Director Bill Halfner
Usage Packaging
Media Used Gouache, Dyes

2
Artist Bill Mayer
Title Adzooks
Client Williamson Printing
Art Director Alan Lidoi
Usage Poster
Media Used Gouache, Dyes

3
Artist Bill Mayer
Client Scripto-Tokai
Art Director Bill Halfner
Usage Packaging
Media Used Gouache, Dyes

4
Artist Bill Mayer
Client Scripto-Tokai
Art Director Bill Halfner
Usage Packaging
Media Used Gouache, Dyes

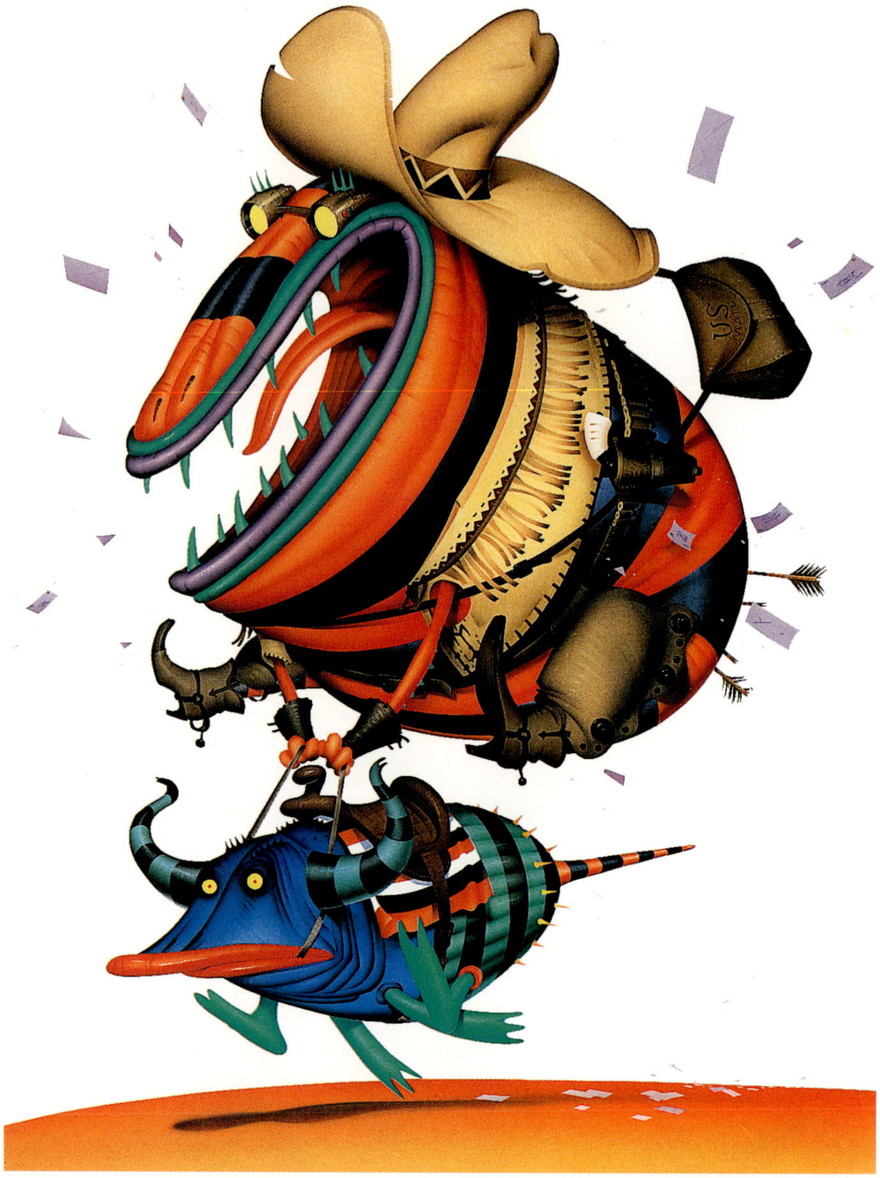

2

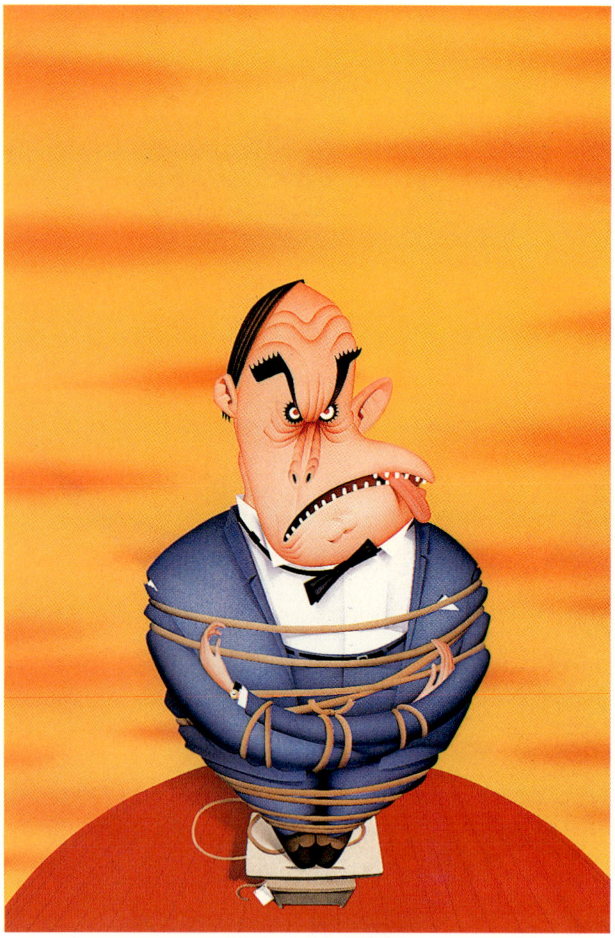

1

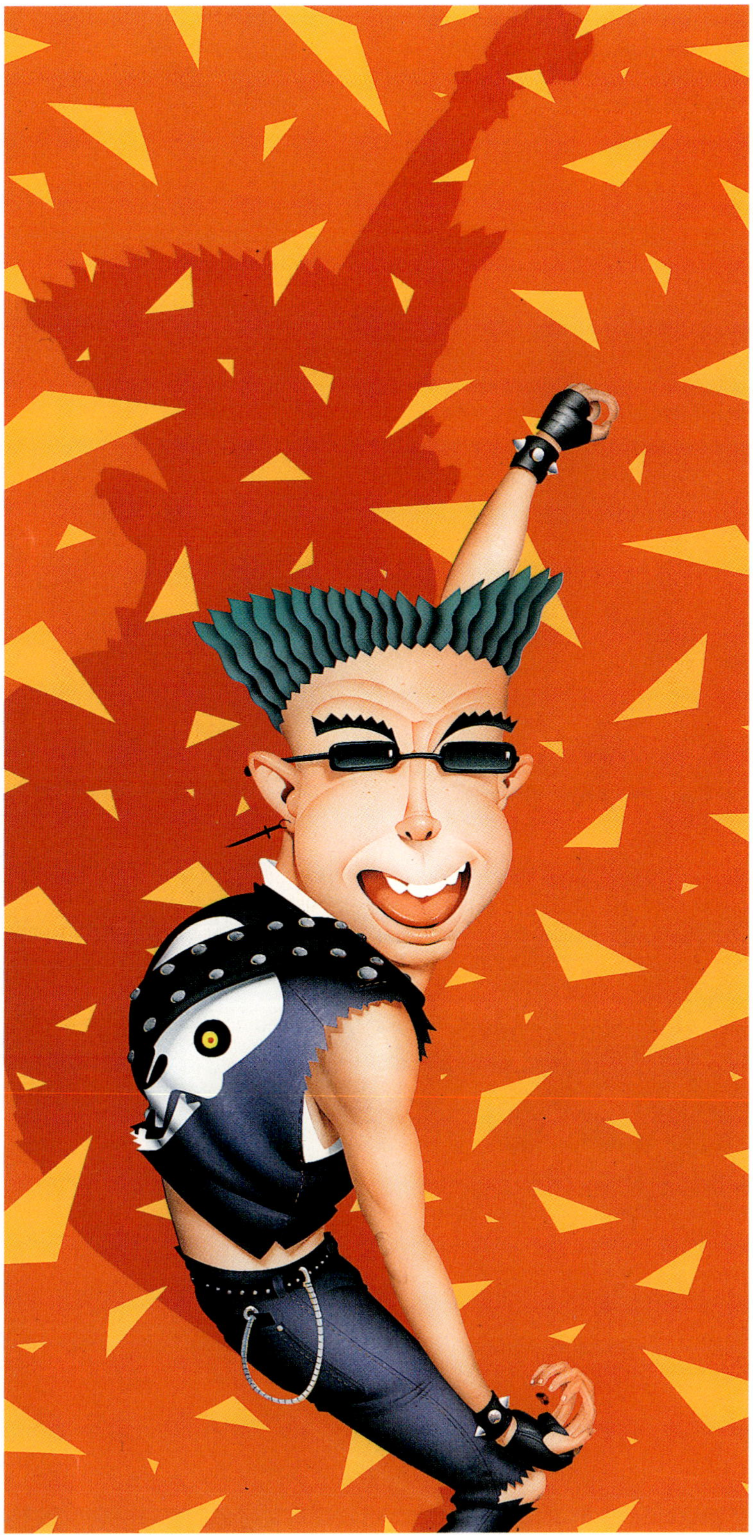

3

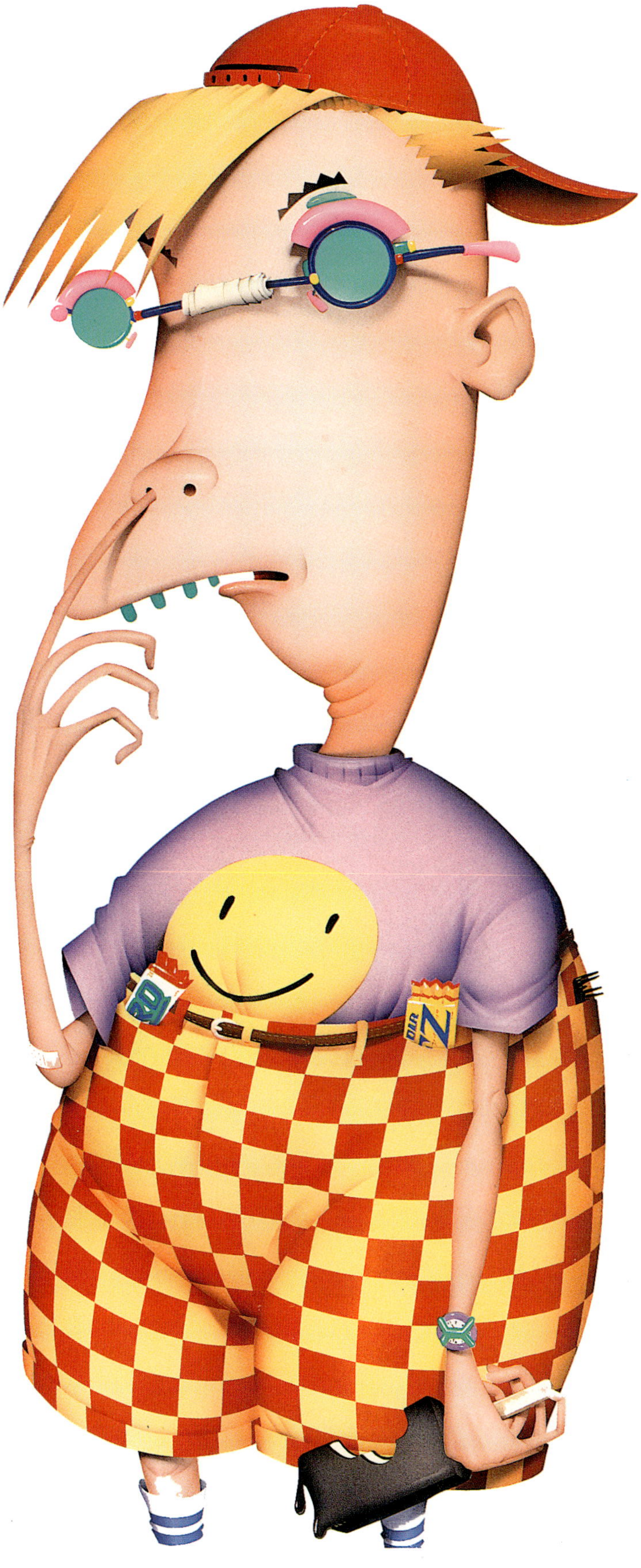

4

1
Artist Craig McKay
Client Turner Labels
Art Director Randy Shrout
Usage Sales Promotion Material
Media Used Mixed

2
Artist Craig McKay
Client Turner Labels
Art Director Randy Shrout
Usage Sales Promotion Material
Media Used Mixed

3
Artist Craig McKay
Title Rock-a-Billy Cafe
Client Rock-a-Billy Cafe
Art Director Randy Shrout
Usage Menu
Media Used Mixed

1

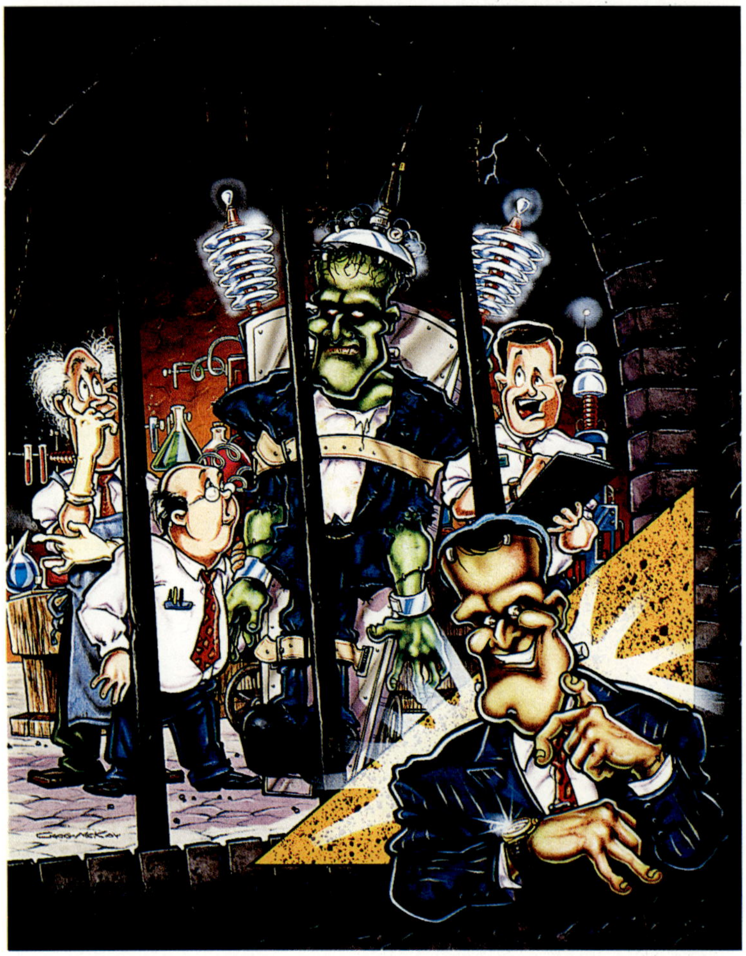

2

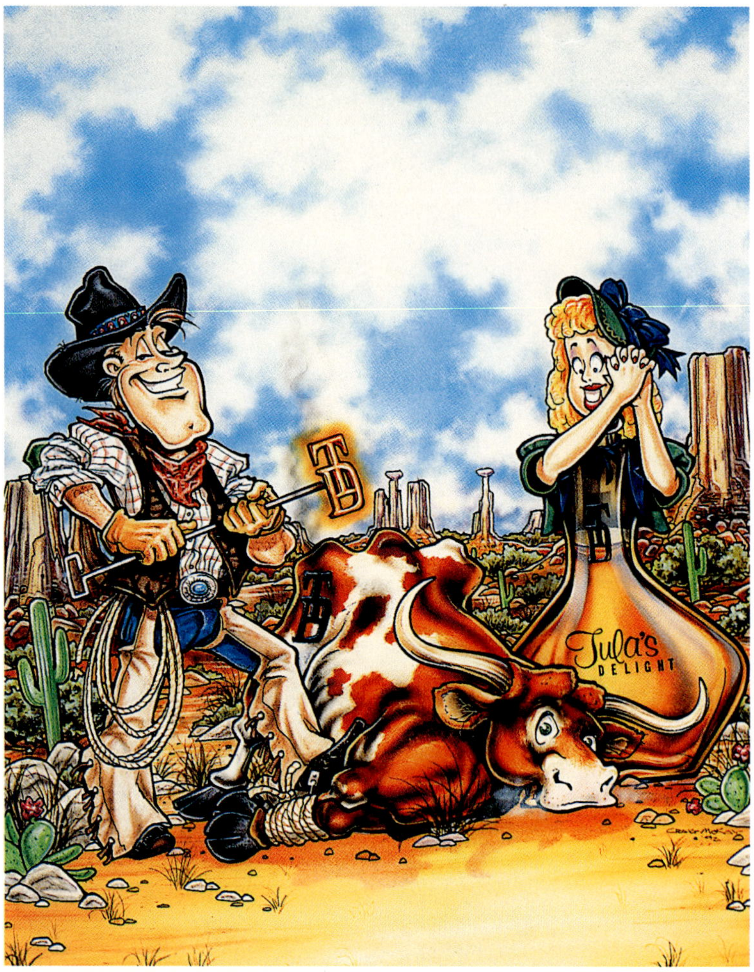

3

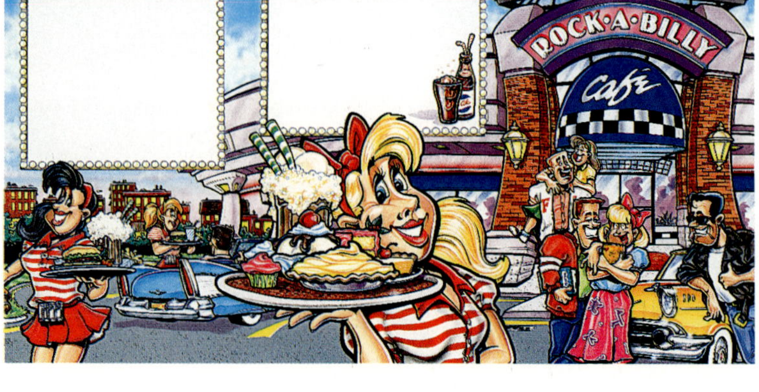

1
Artist Craig McKay
Title Margarits Bird
Client Doulde Q-WKQQ 98.1 FM (Lexington)
Art Director Linda Huston
Usage T-Shirt
Media Used Mixed

2
Artist Craig McKay
Title How to Make Money with Your Air Brush
Client North Light Books
Usage Book Cover
Media Used Mixed

3
Artist Richard O. Menchaca
Title General Blackjack Pershing
Media Used Gouache

1

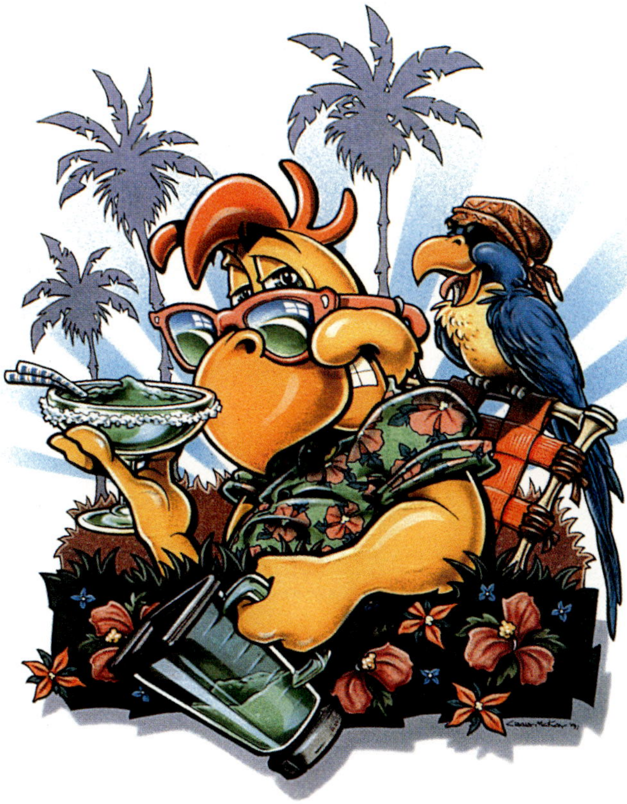

2

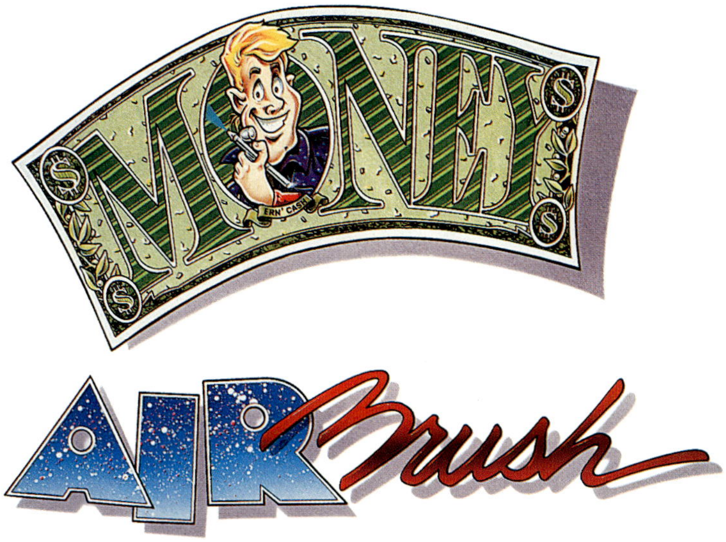

3

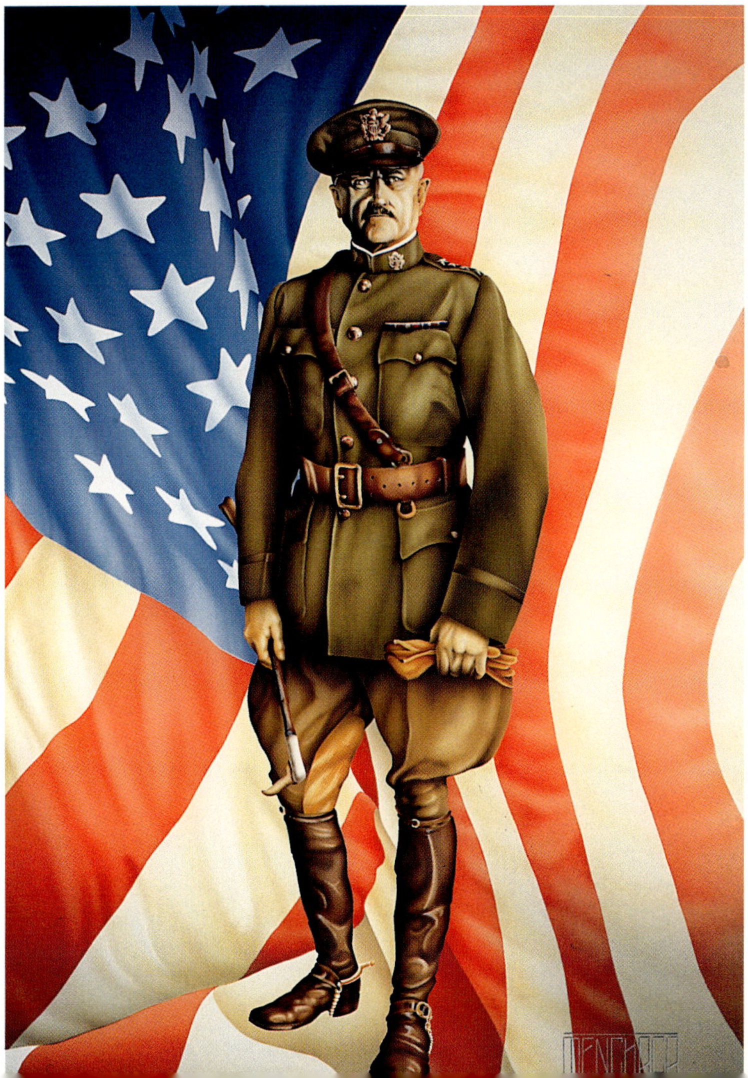

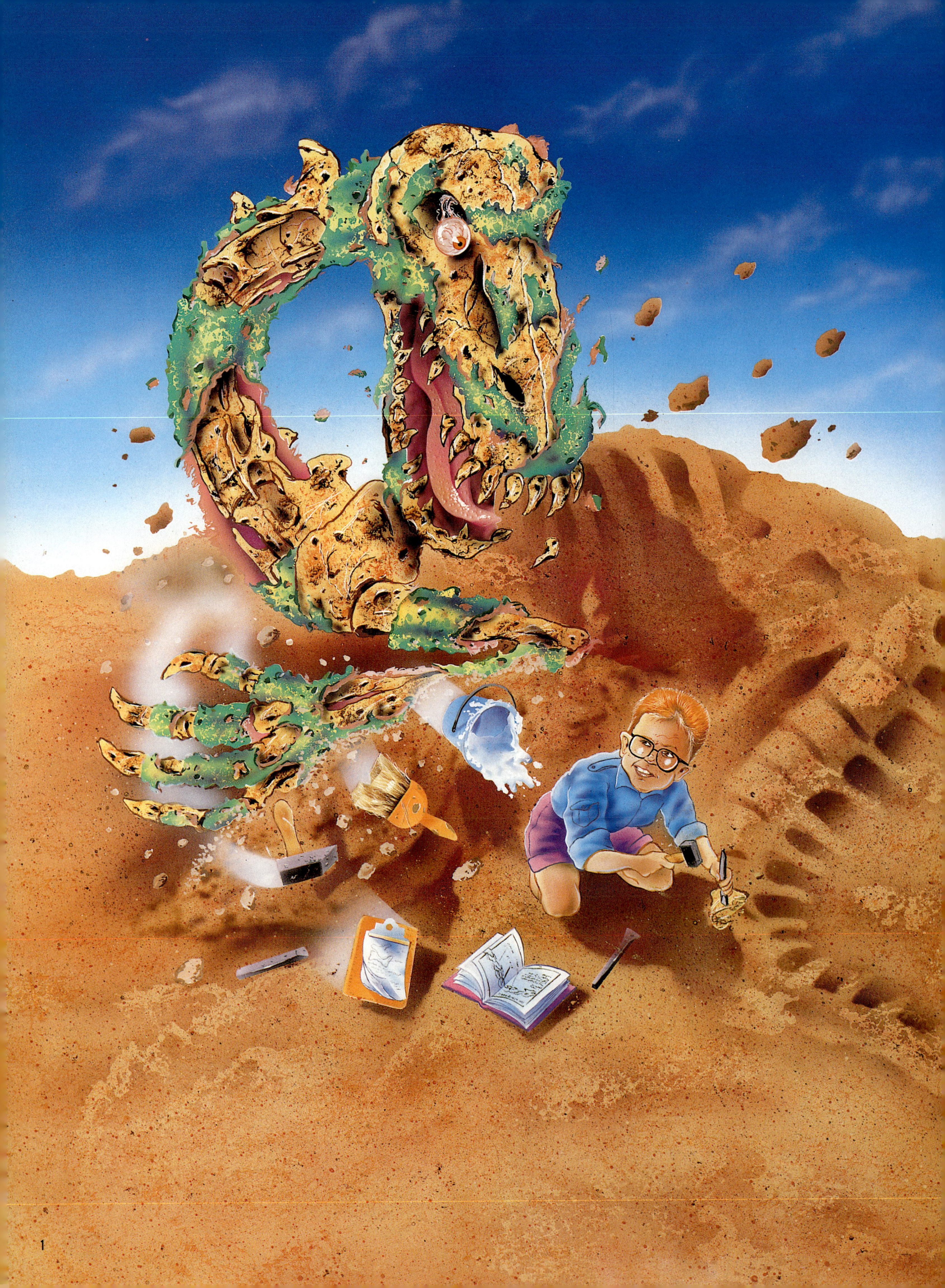

1
Artist Jim Mendillo
Title Breakthrough
Client Fasco
Usage Stationery Line
Media Used Comart Paint, Designer's Gouache

2
Artist Jim Mendillo
Title Saturday Matinee
Client Fasco
Usage Stationery Line
Media Used Comart Paint, Designer's Gouache

3
Artist Jim Mendillo
Title Early Bird Special
Client Fasco
Usage Stationery Line
Media Used Comart, Designer's Gouache

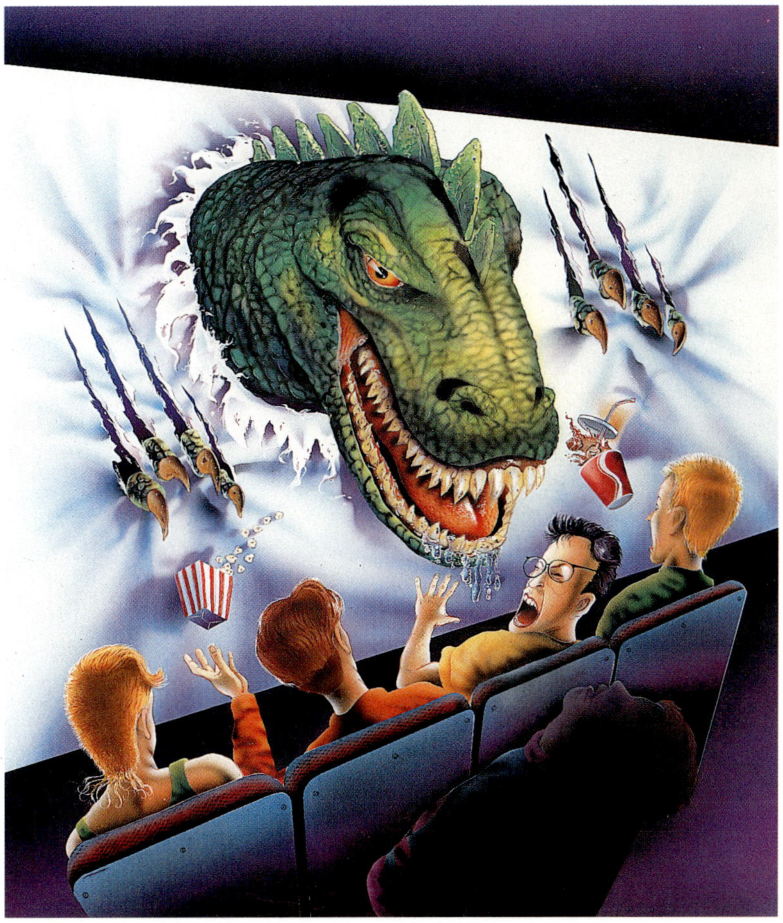

2

3

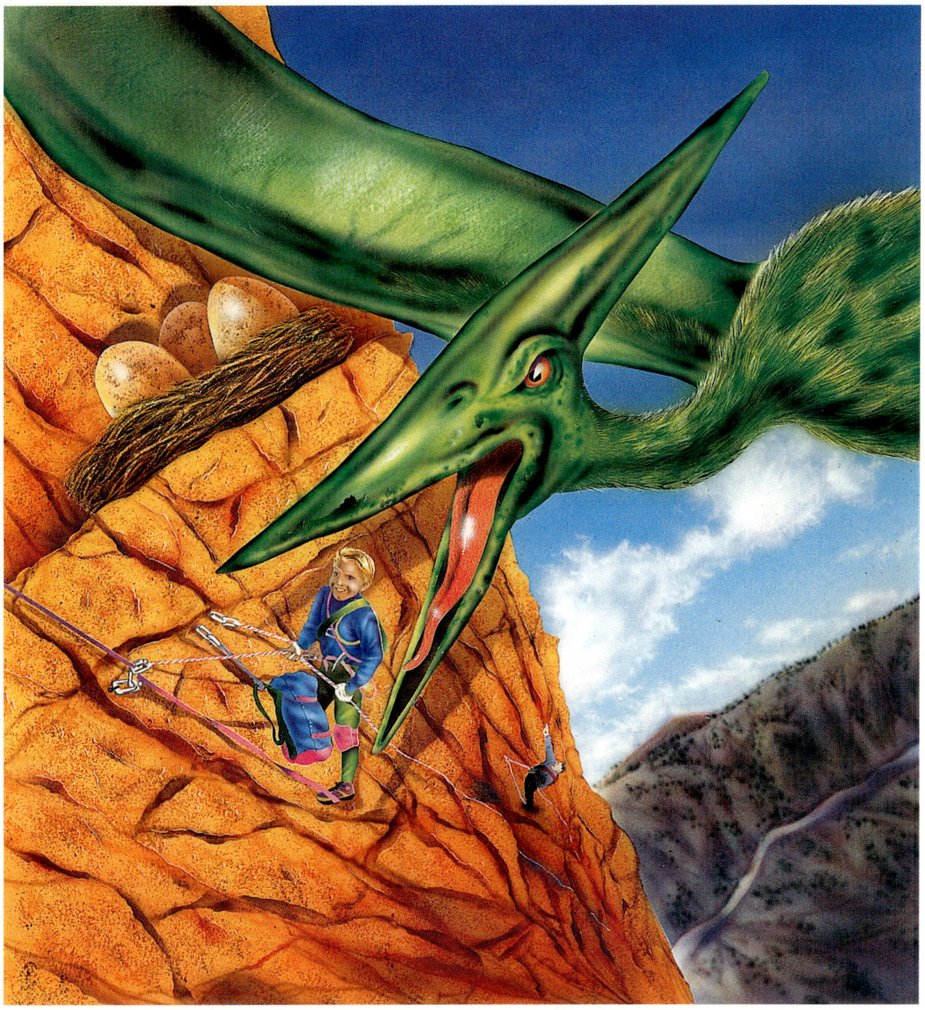

1
Artist Jim Mendillo
Title Dr. Drill N' Fill
Client Tyco Toys
Art Director Tom Watters
Usage Toy Package
Media Used Comart, Paint, Designer's Gouache

2
Artist Jim Mendillo
Title Crash Dummies
Client Tyco Toys
Usage Toy Package
Media Used Comart, Paint, Designer's Gouache

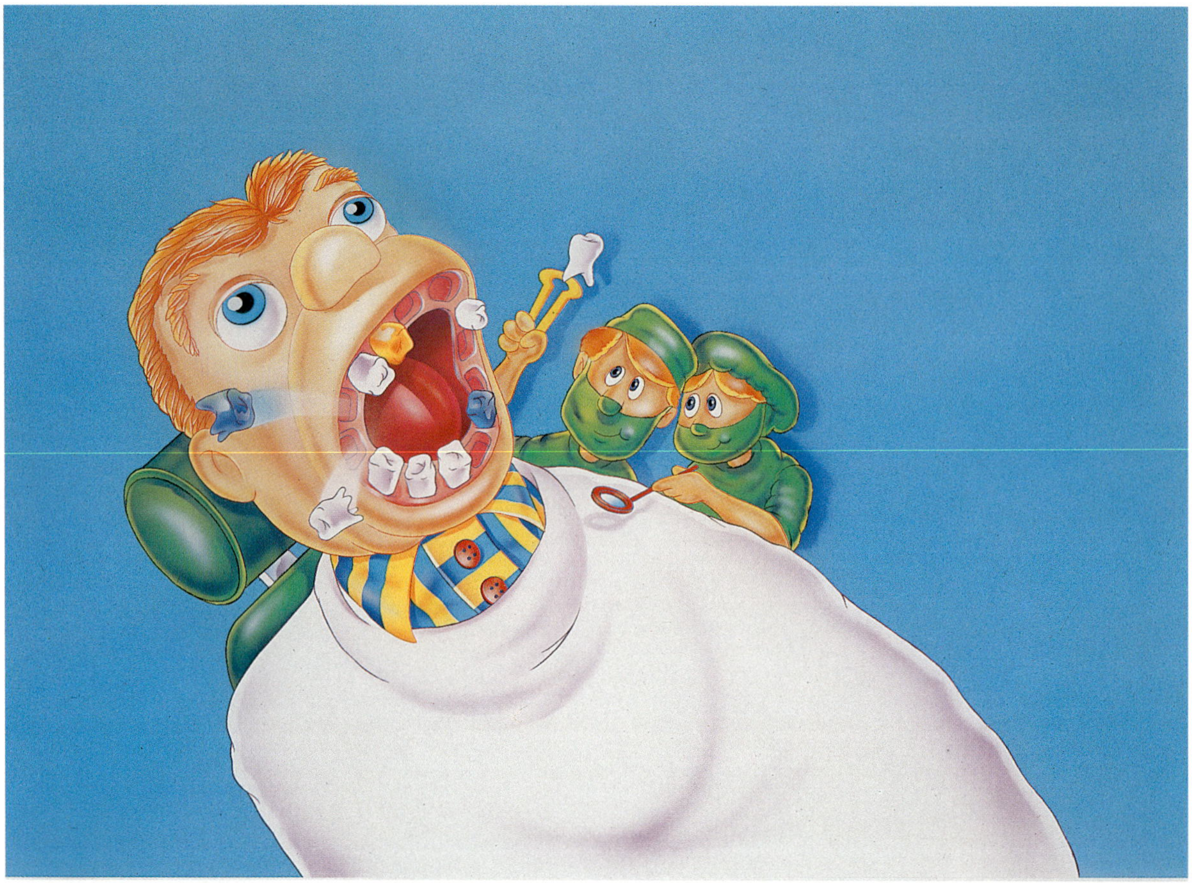

1

2

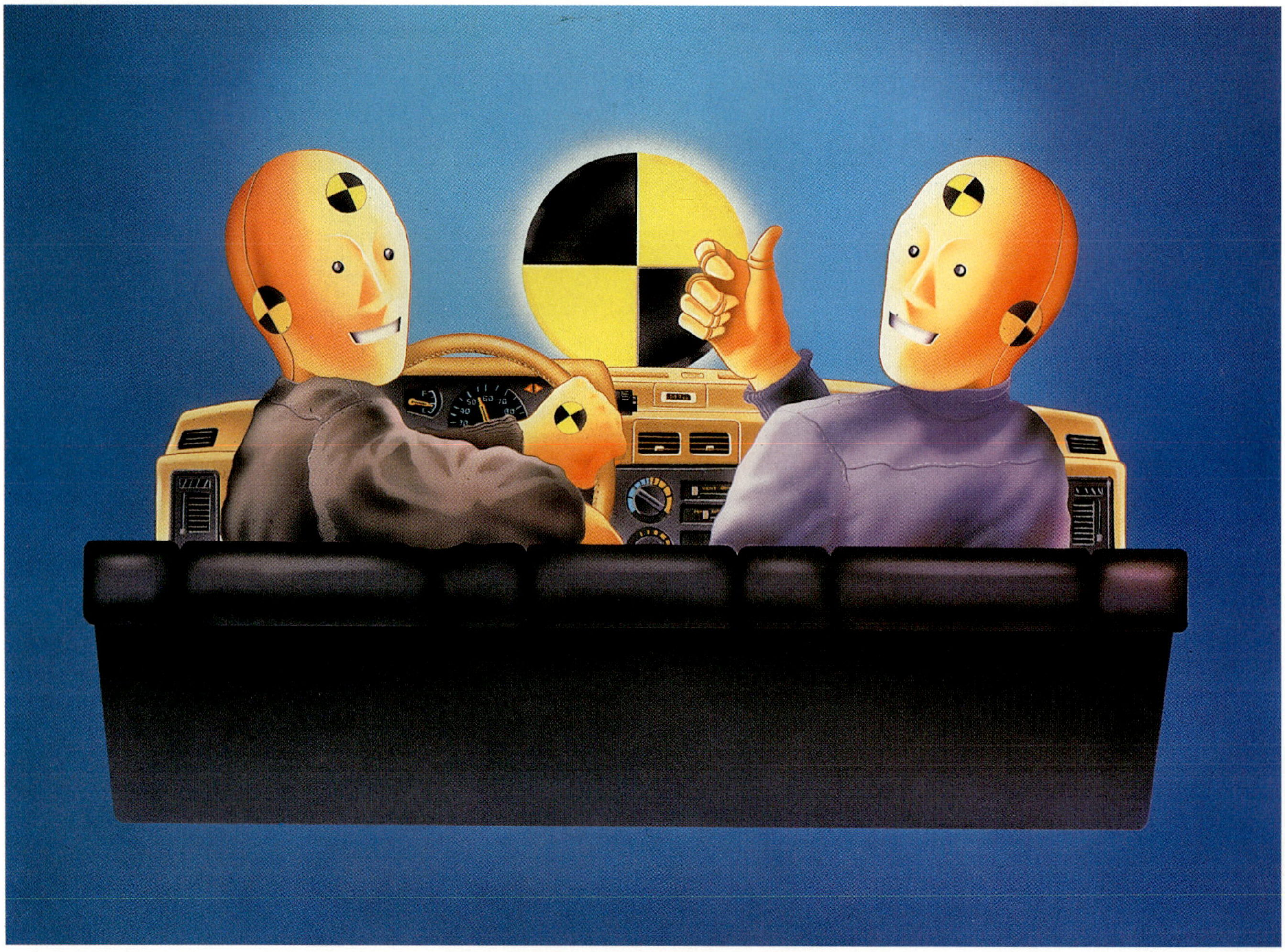

1
Artist Doug Meythaler
Title Steve Young
Art Director Kelly Russell
Usage Fine Art
Media Used Acrylic

2
Artist Doug Meythaler
Title Wrapped In Passion
Usage Fine Art
Media Used Acrylic

3
Artist Richard Mollo
Title Burning The Flag
Art Director Ken Schwarz
Usage Student Art
Media Used Acrylic

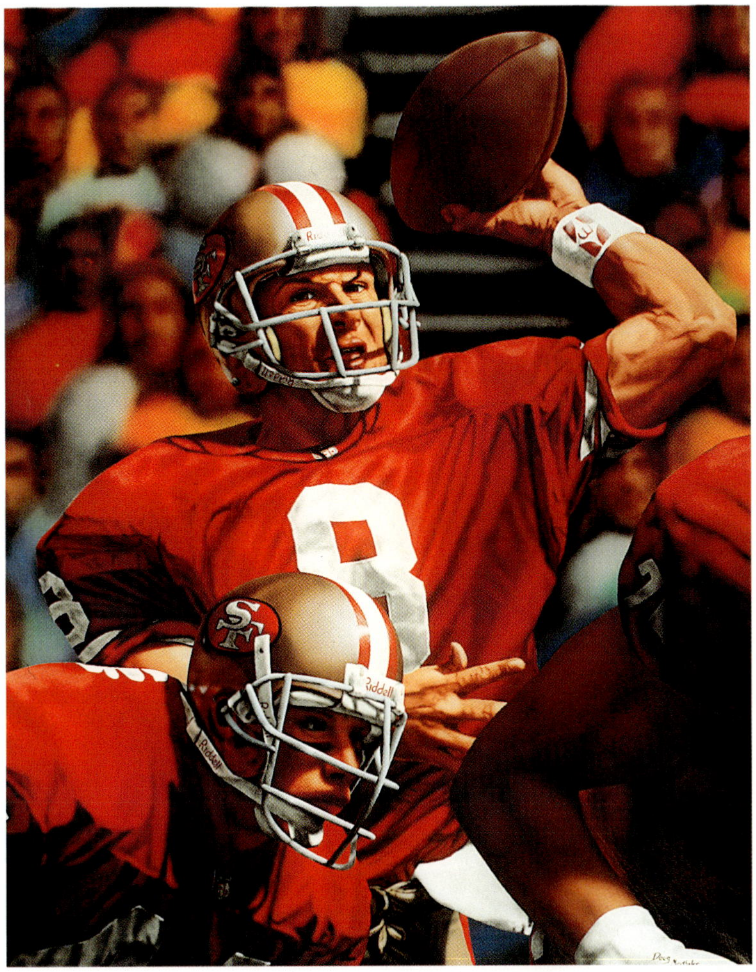

1

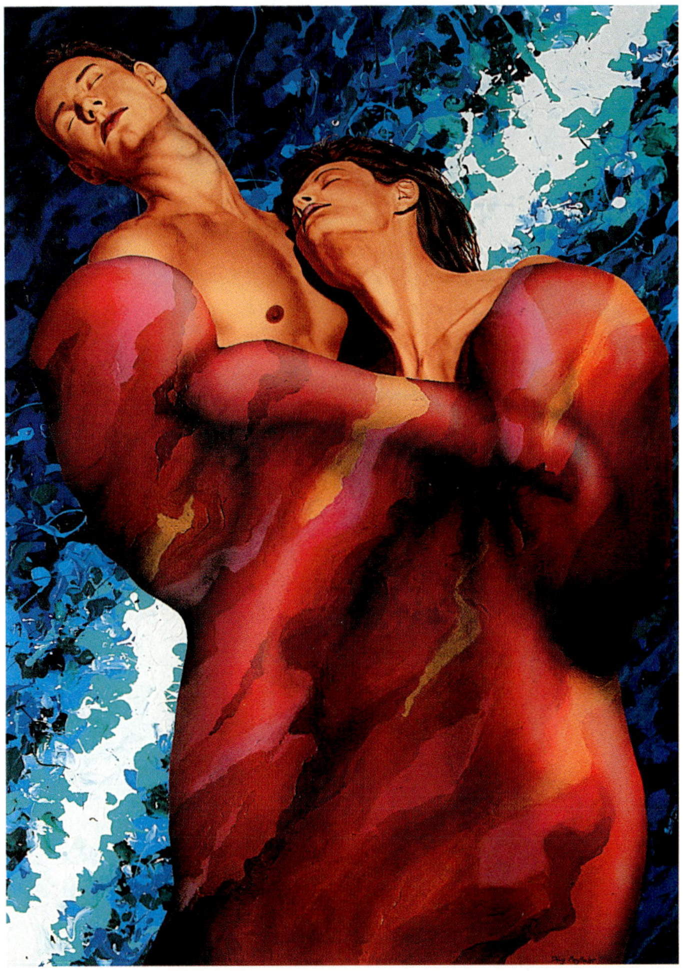

2

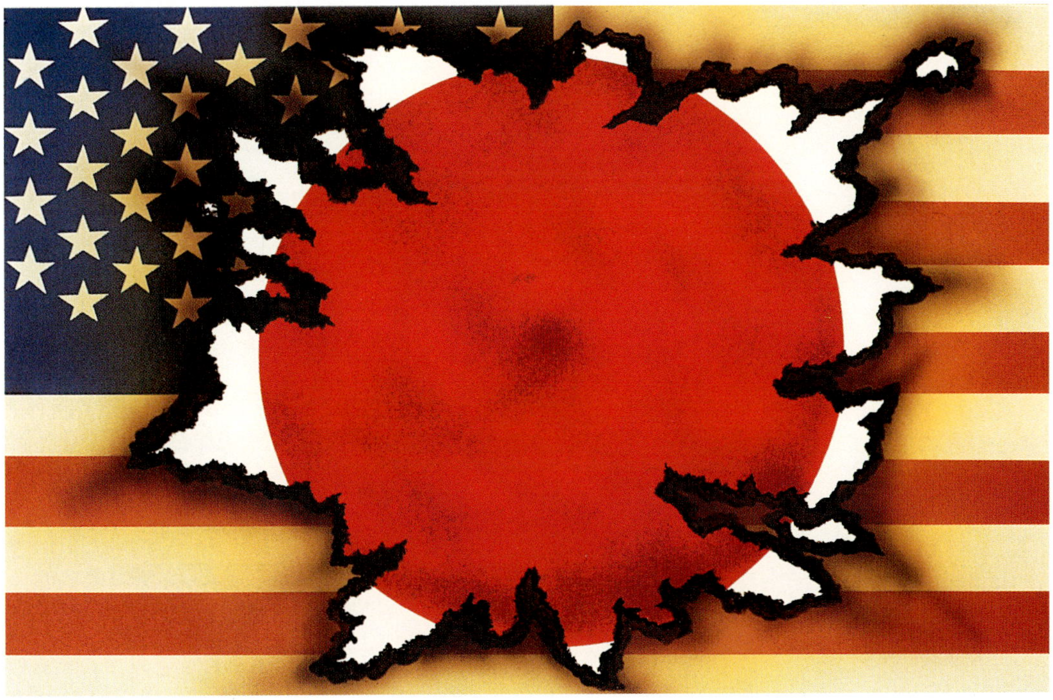

3

1
Artist Gerard Mooney
Title Speakeasy
Client Forbes
Art Director Andy Christie
Usage Magazine Illustration
Media Used Gouache

2
Artist Gerard Mooney
Title The End
Client The New Republic
Art Director Dorothy Wickenden
Usage Magazine Cover
Media Used Gouache

3
Artist Gerard Mooney
Title Shopping by Computer
Client National Home Center News
Art Director Bob Brockman
Usage Magazine Illustration
Media Used Gouache

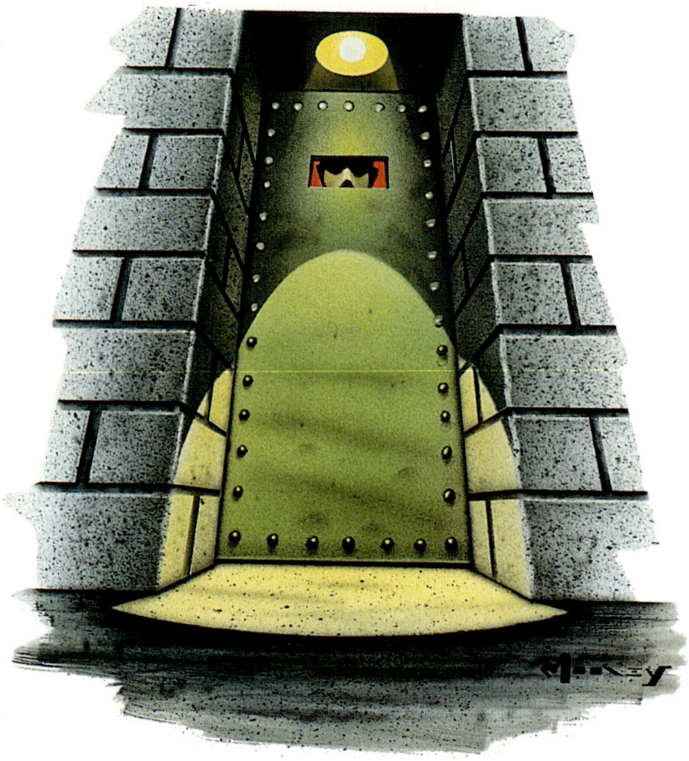

1

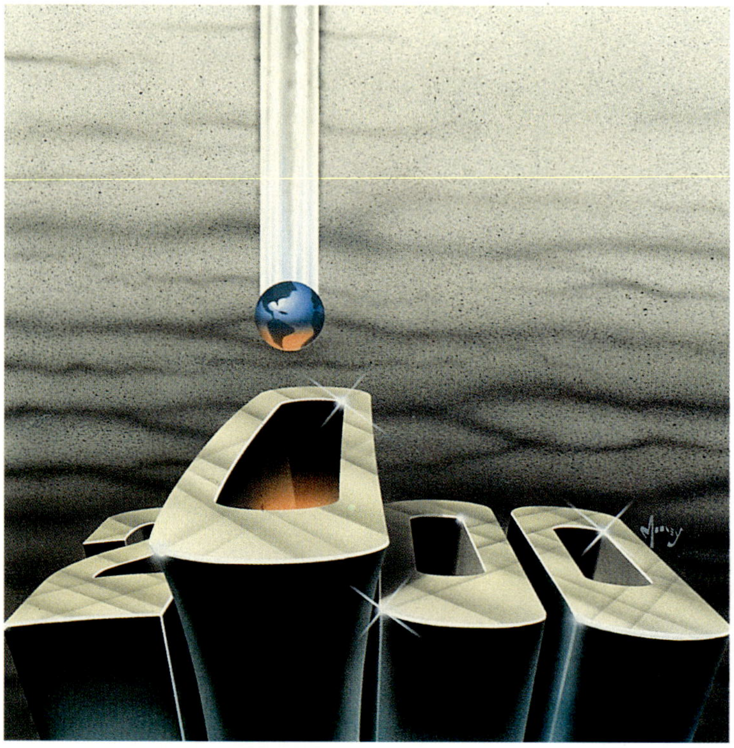

2

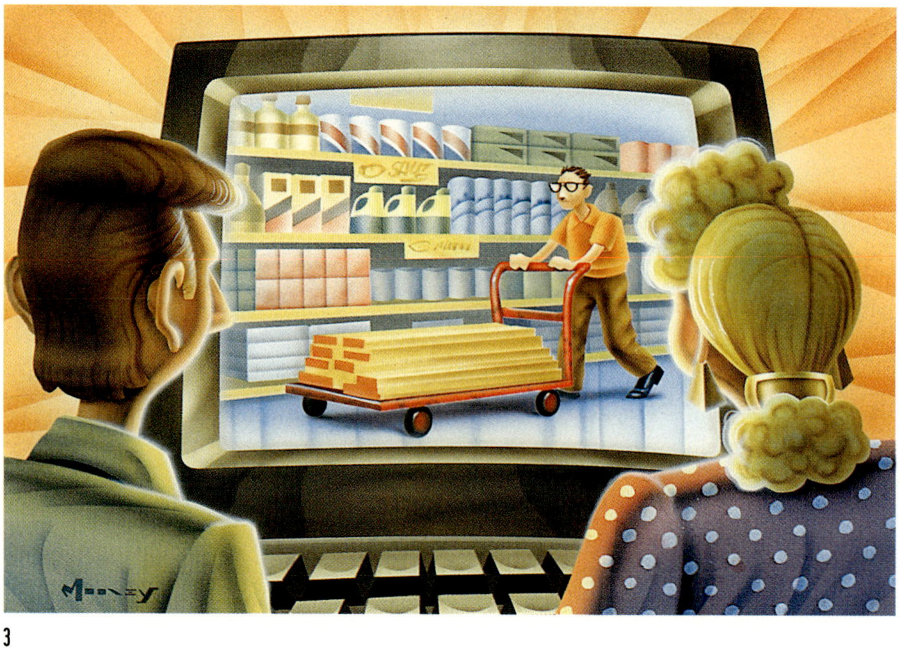

3

1
Artist Gerard Mooney
Title American Manufacturing
Client Forbes
Art Director Roger Zapke
Usage Magazine Illustration - Inside Spread
Media Used Gouache

2
Artist Gerard Mooney
Title Nothing's On
Client Cablevison Magazine
Art Director Vera Steiner
Usage Magazine Cover
Media Used Gouache

3
Artist Gerard Mooney
Title Bugbots: THe Mansect Rebellion
Client Gerard Mooney
Art Director Gerard Mooney
Media Used Gouache

1
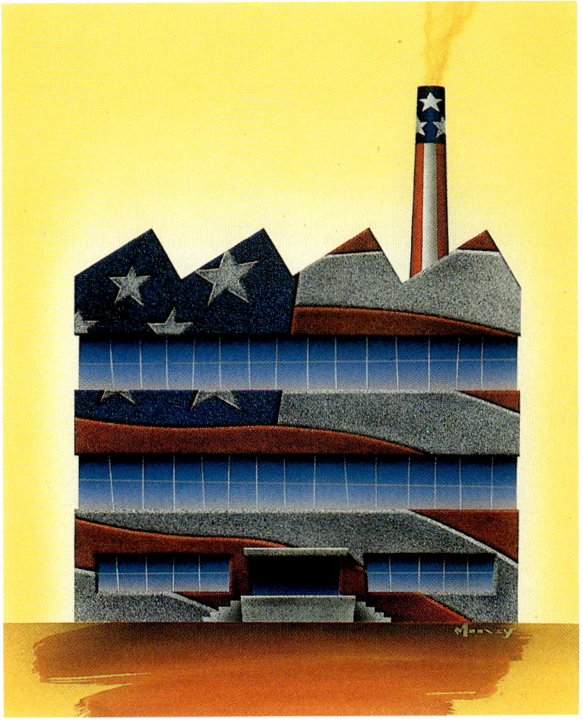

2
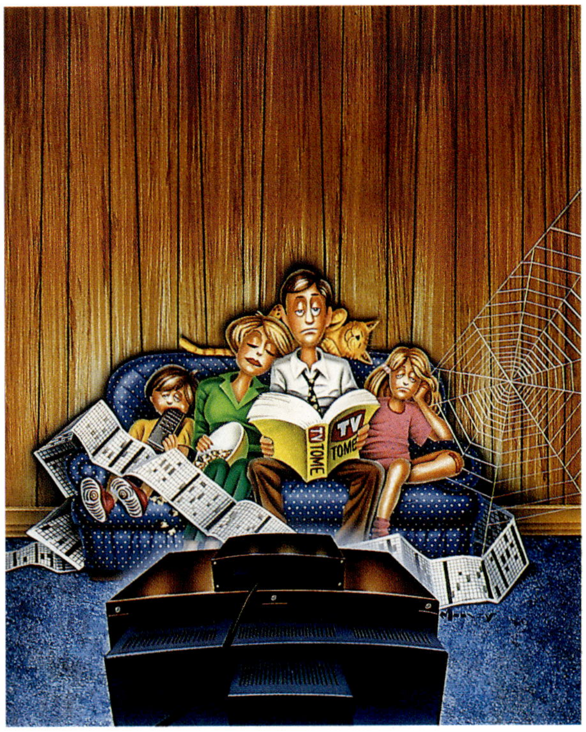

3
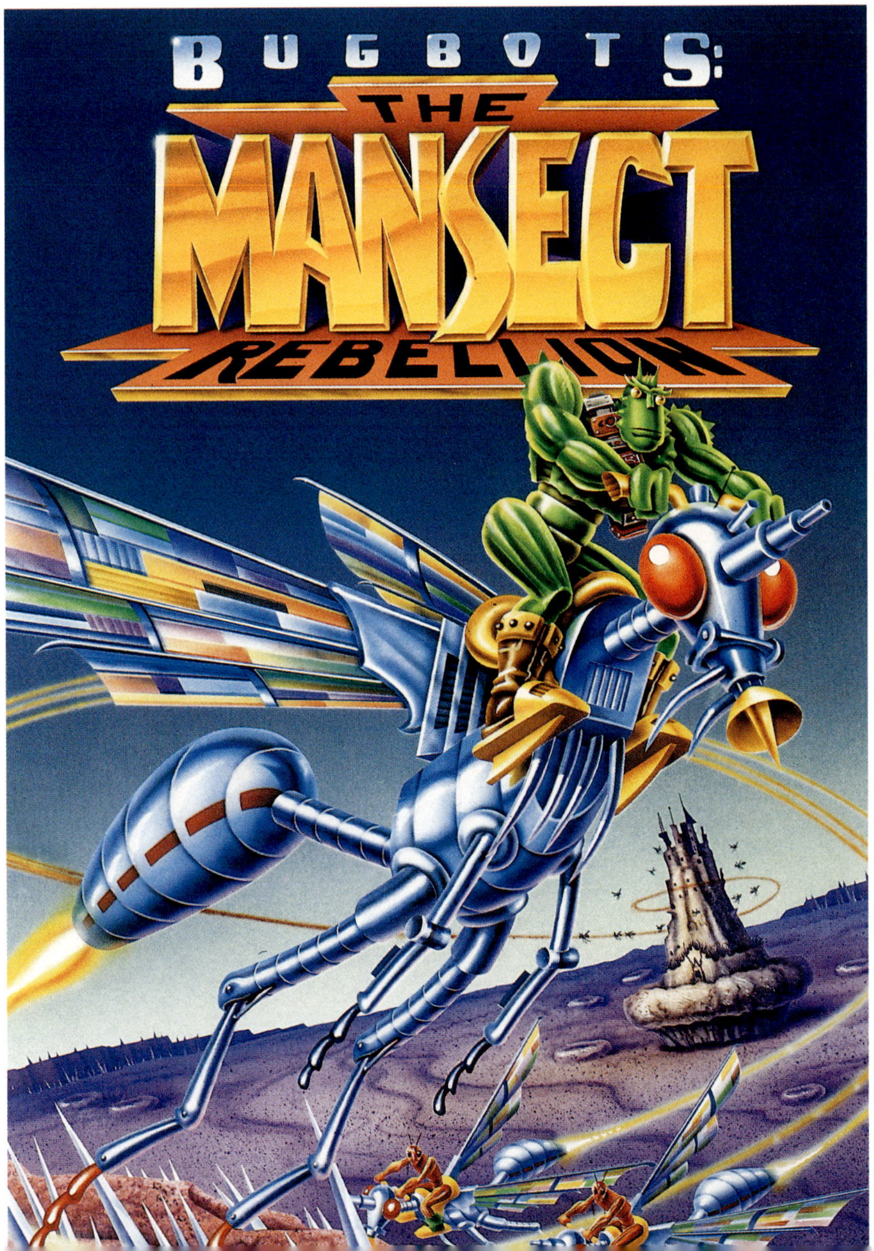

1
Artist Gerard Mooney
Title The Personal Computer
Client American Arts & Graphics
Usage Poster
Media Used Gouache

2
Artist Gerard Mooney
Title Move Over!
Client Medical Economics
Art Director Tom Darnsteadt
Usage Cover/Drug Topics
Media Used Gouache

3
Artist Gerard Mooney
Title Unlike a Virgin
Client The New Republic
Art Director Hendrik Hetzberg
Usage Magazine Cover
Media Used Gouache

4
Artist Clark Most
Usage **Album** Cover Art (Gospel Music)
Media Used Acrylic and Pencil

1

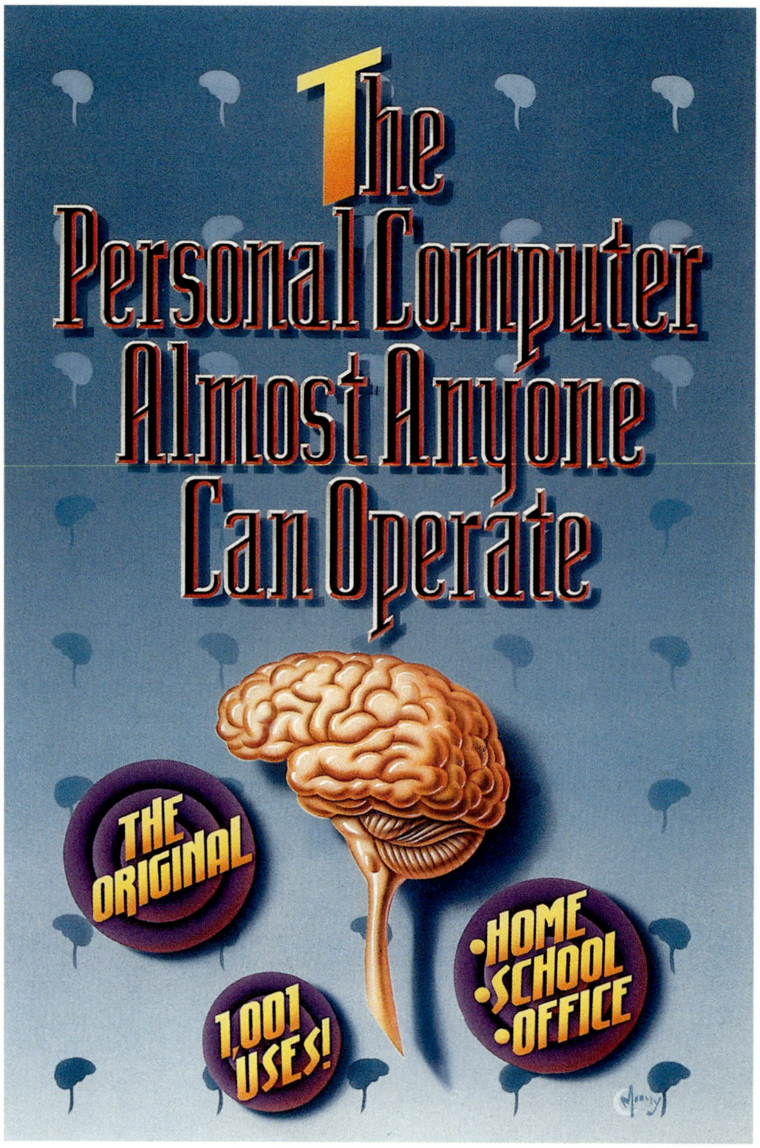

2

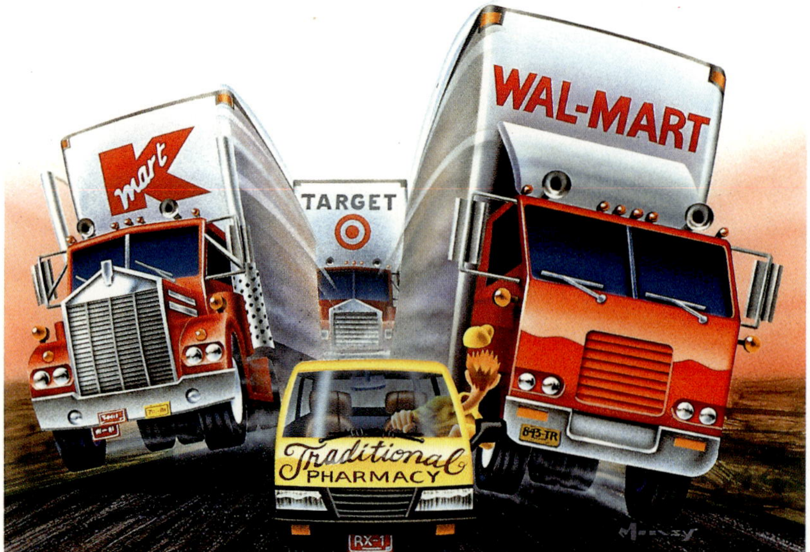

3

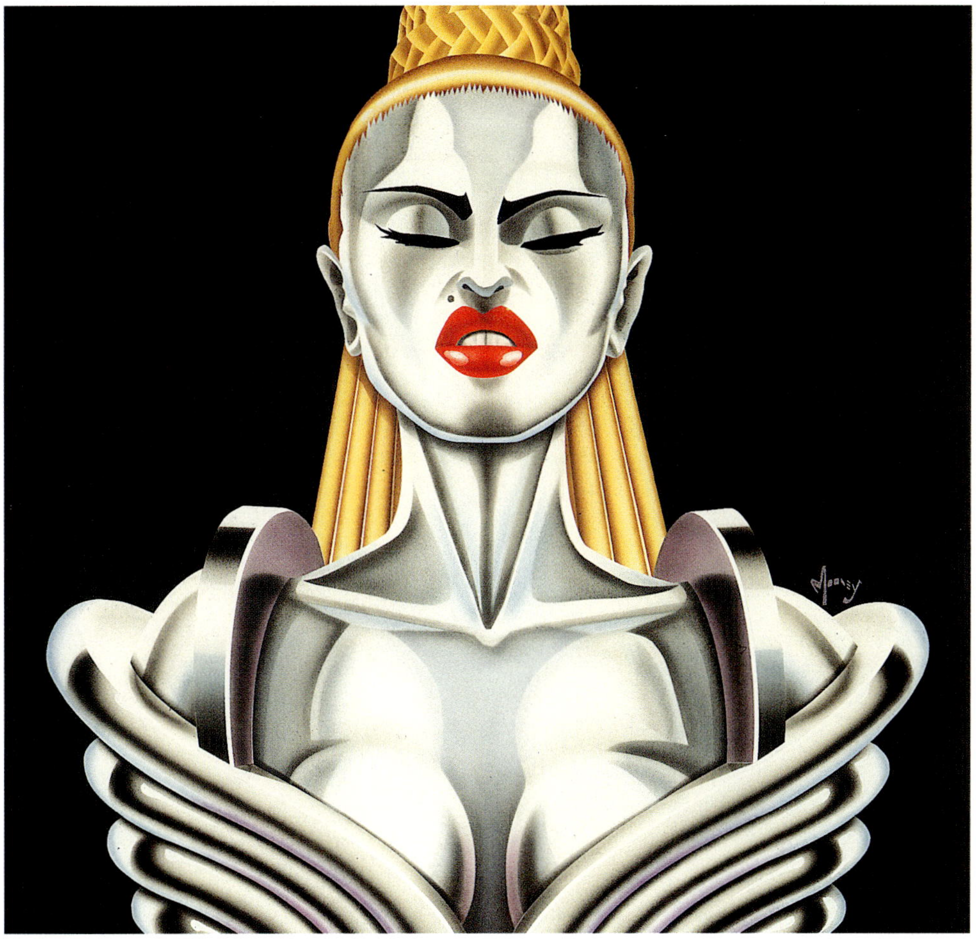

4

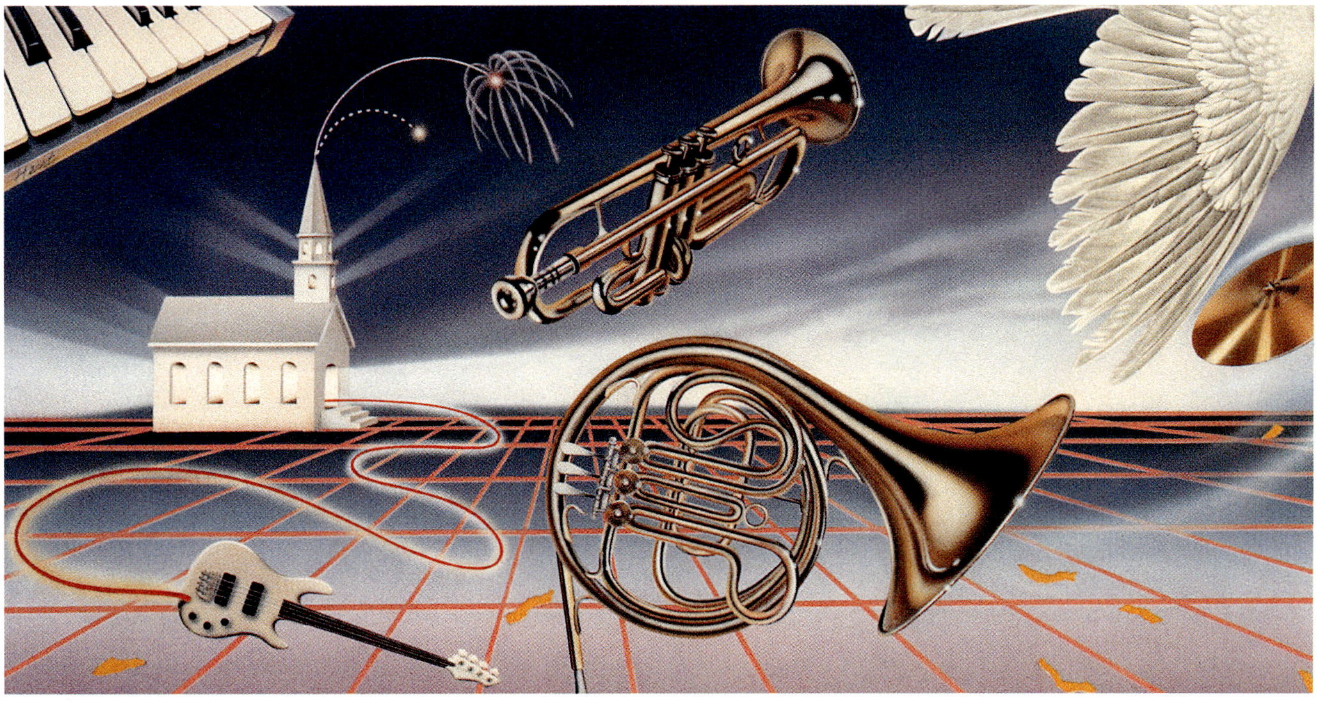

1
Artist Peggy Mozley
Title Home Sweet Home
Usage Self Promotion
Media Used Gouache

2
Artist Peggy Mozley
Title Melissa
Usage Self Promotion
Media Used Gouache

3
Artist Peggy Mozley
Usage Self Promotion
Media Used Gouache

2

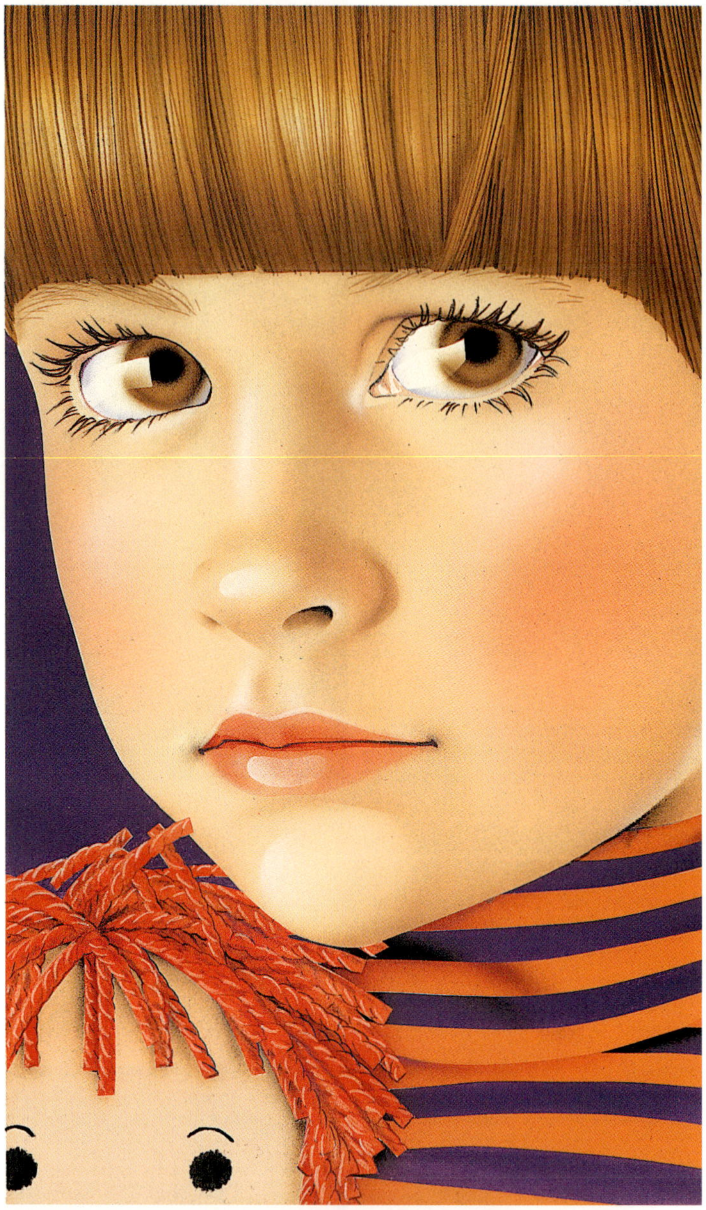

1

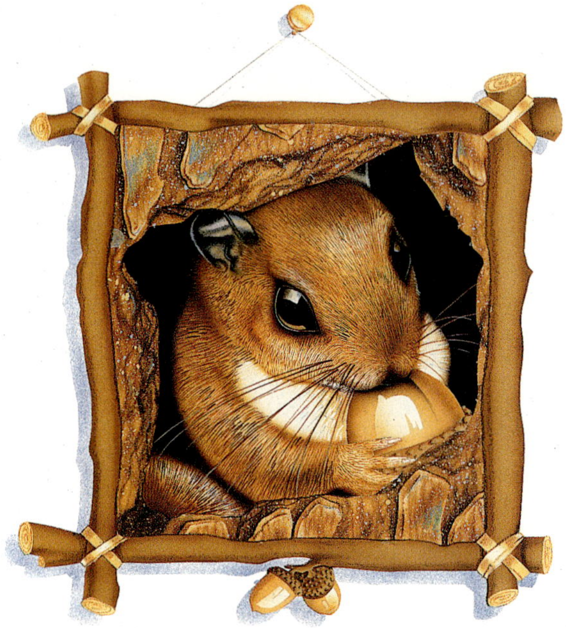

3

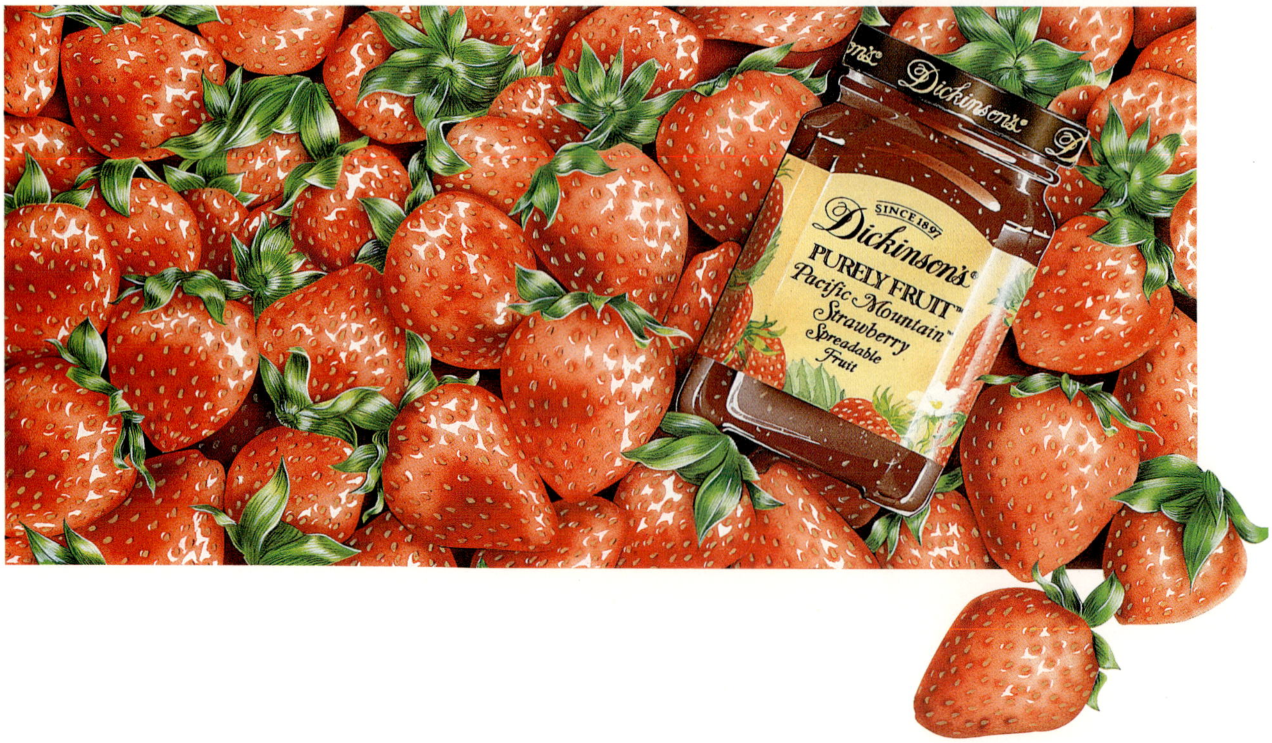

1
Artist Peggy Mozley
Title Snarling Pit Bull
Client Chamberlin's Graphics
Usage Magazine Advertisement
Media Used Gouache

2
Artist Peggy Mozley
Title American Eagle
Usage Self Promotion
Media Used Gouache

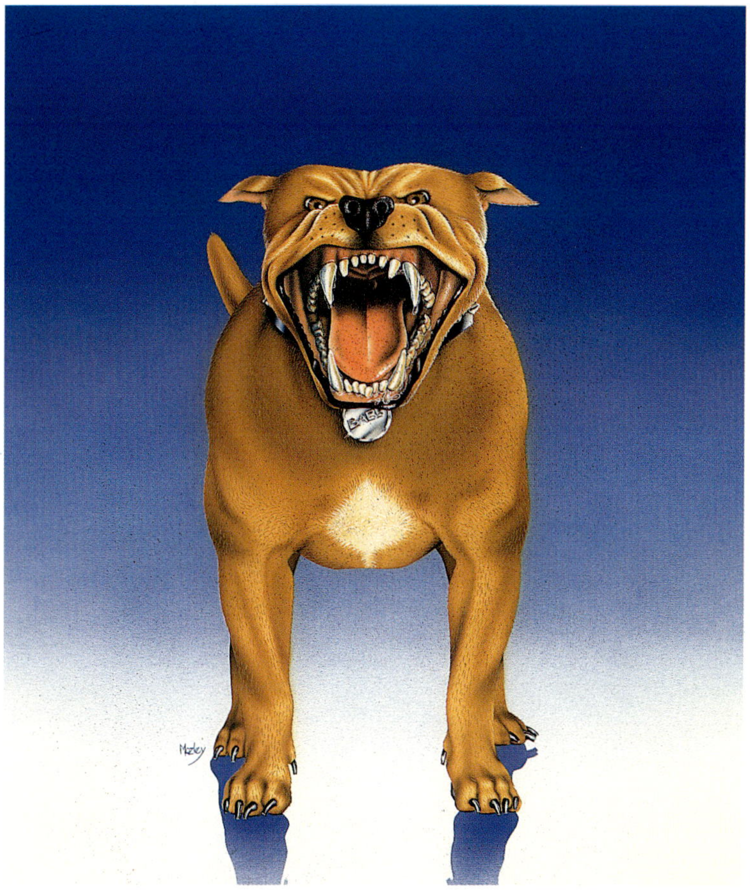

1

2

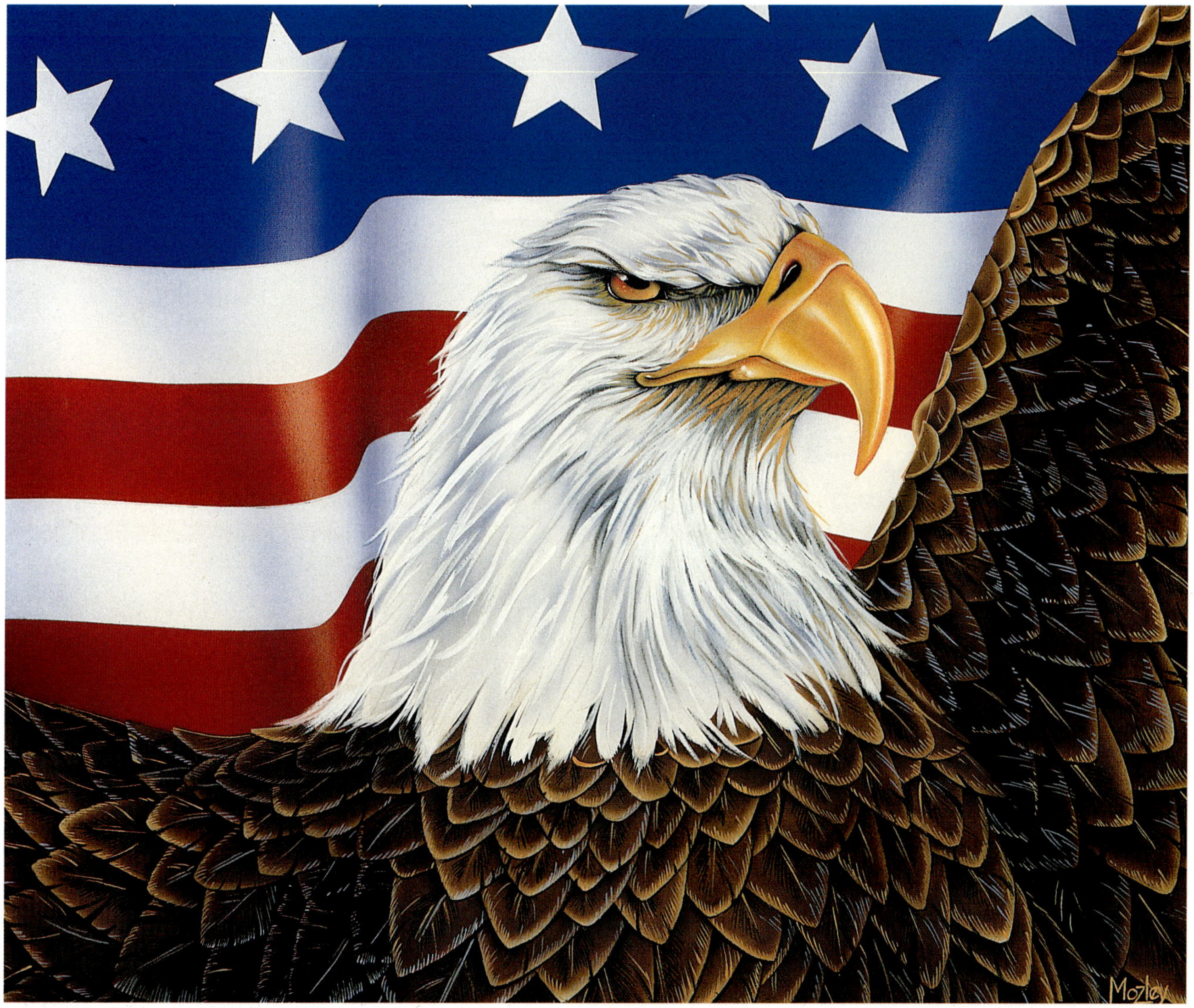

1
Artist Peggy Mozley
Title The Girl in the T-Bird
Usage Self Promotion
Media Used Gouache, Dr. Martin Inks

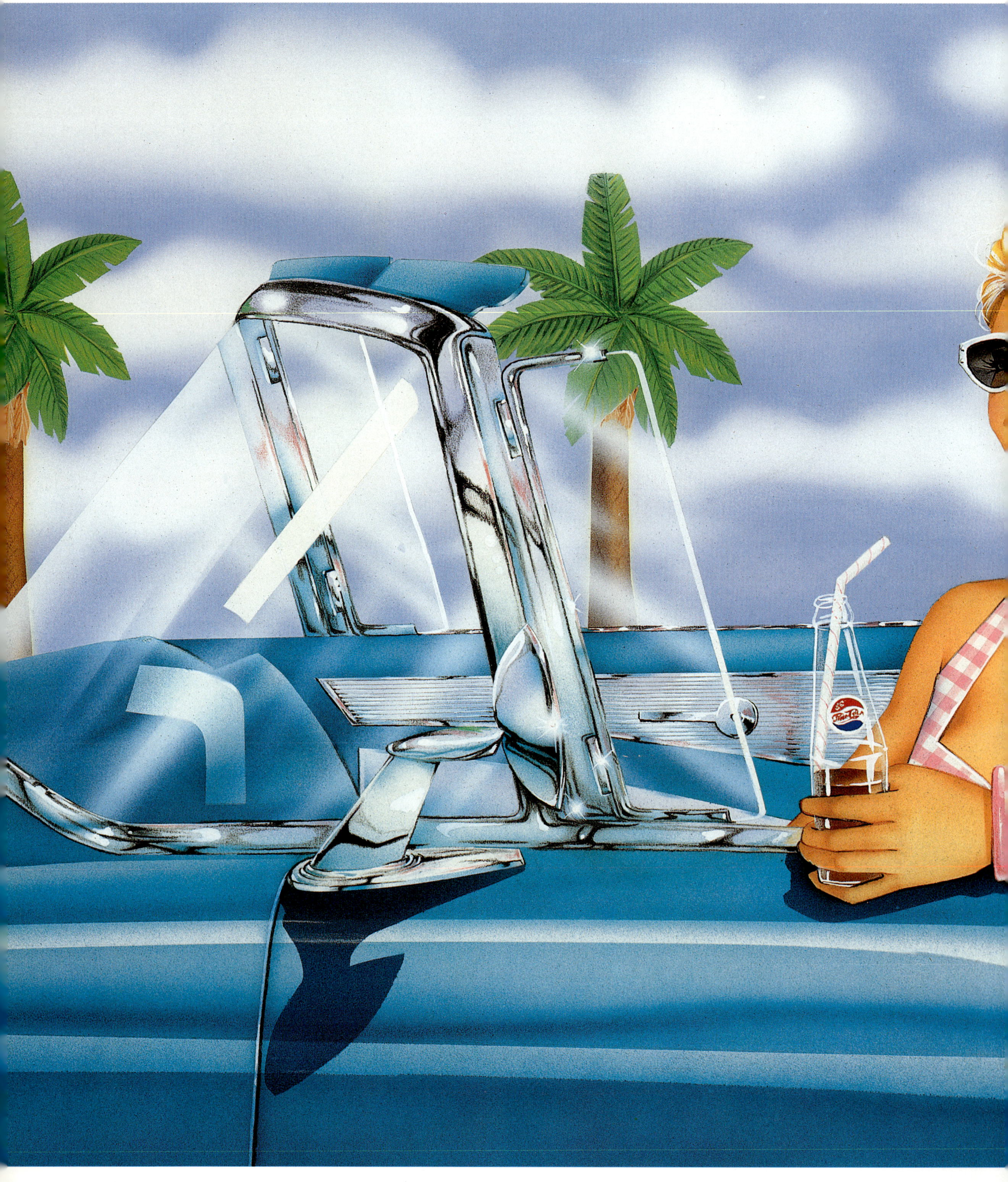

1

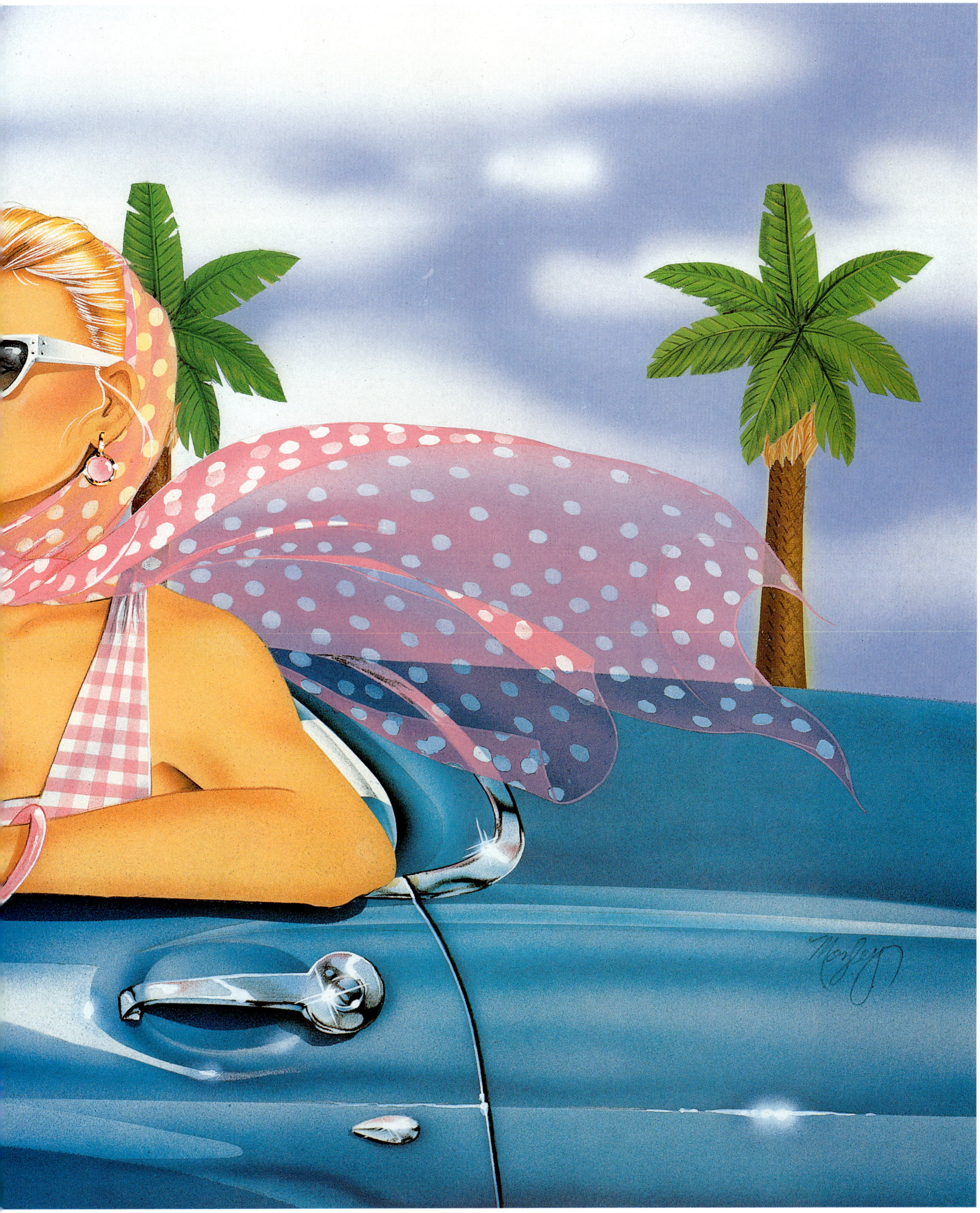

1
Artist Eric Oliver
Title Stein Studios
Usage Student Art
Media Used Acrylic

2
Artist Eric Oliver
Usage Student Art
Media Used Acrylic

3
Artist Osni Omena
Title Illustrator/Designer
Client Epic/Vision
Art Director George Grant
Usage Commercial Art
Media Used Prismacolor Pencils, Ecoline-Water Base

2

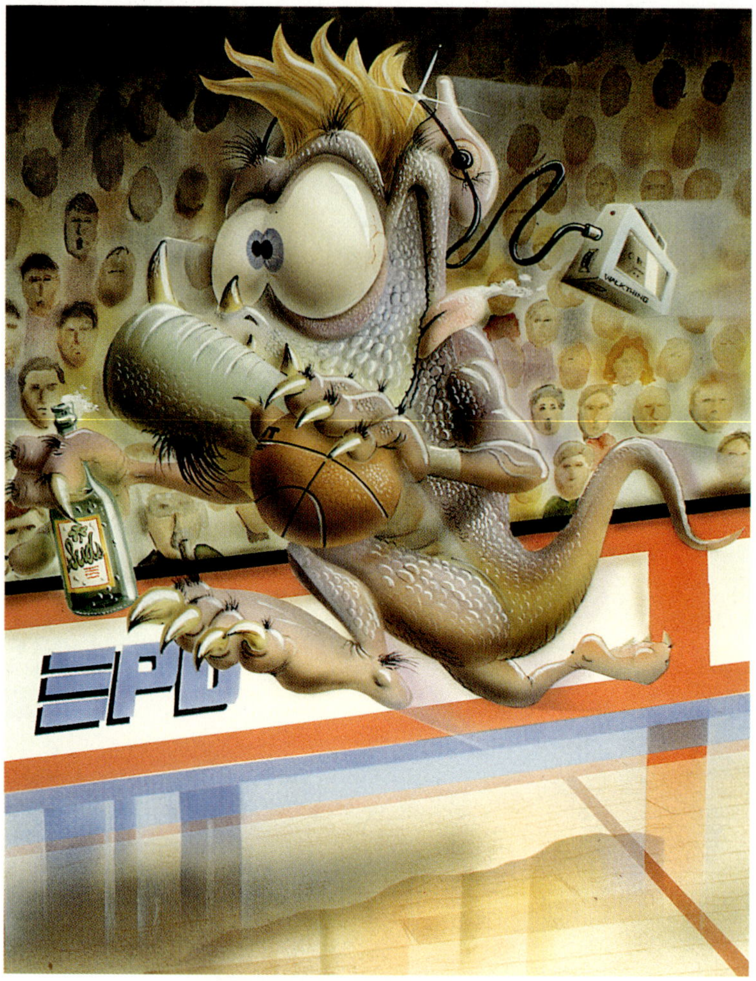

3

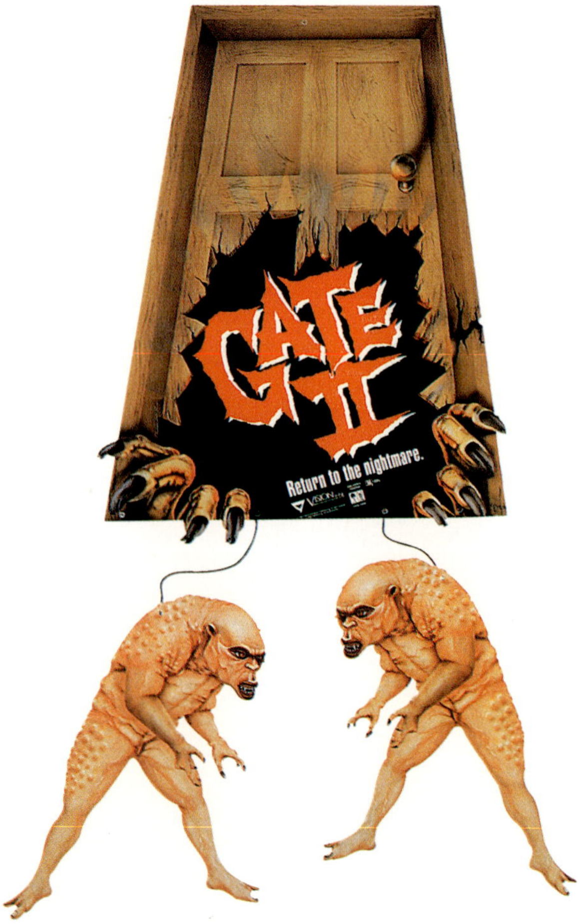

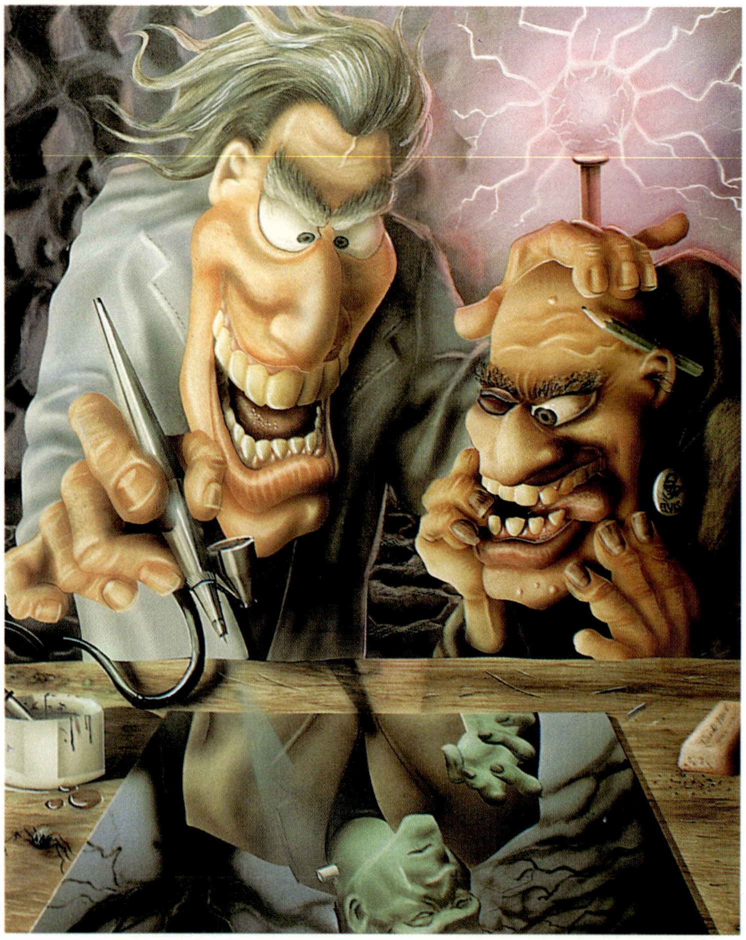

1

1
Artist Mark Otnes
Title Gun Play
Usage Self Promotion
Media Used Acrylic on Bristol

2
Artist Mark Otnes
Title Umbrella Man
Client Compuadd, Inc., Austin, Texas
Art Director Curtis Riker
Usage Print Advertisement
Media Used Acrylic on Canvas Board

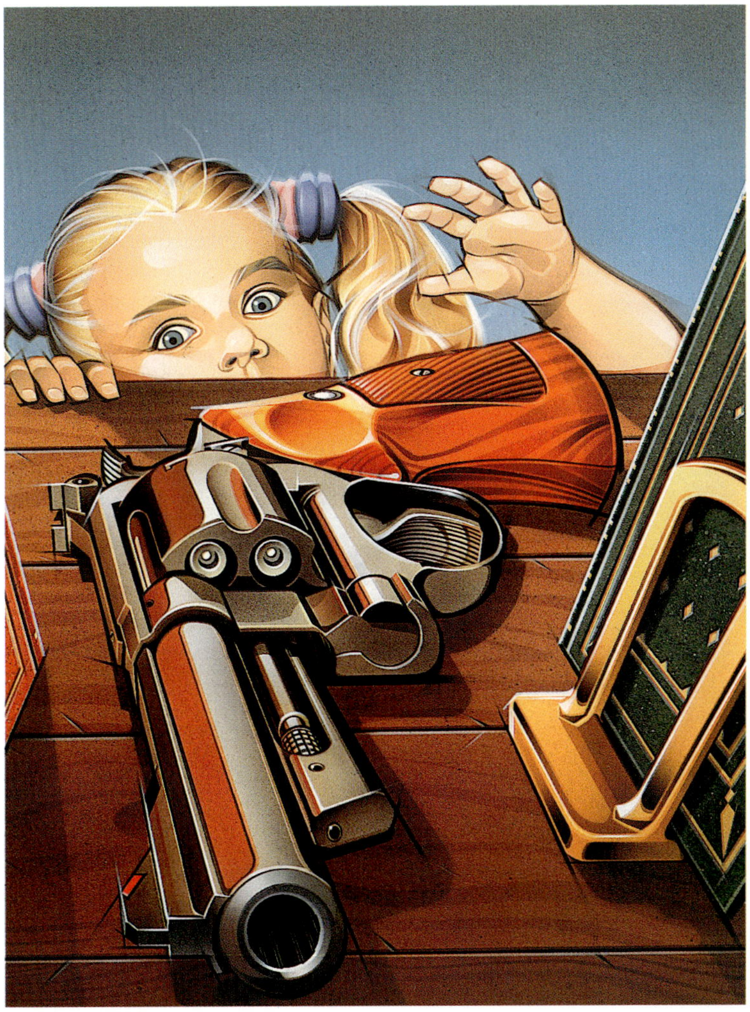

1

2

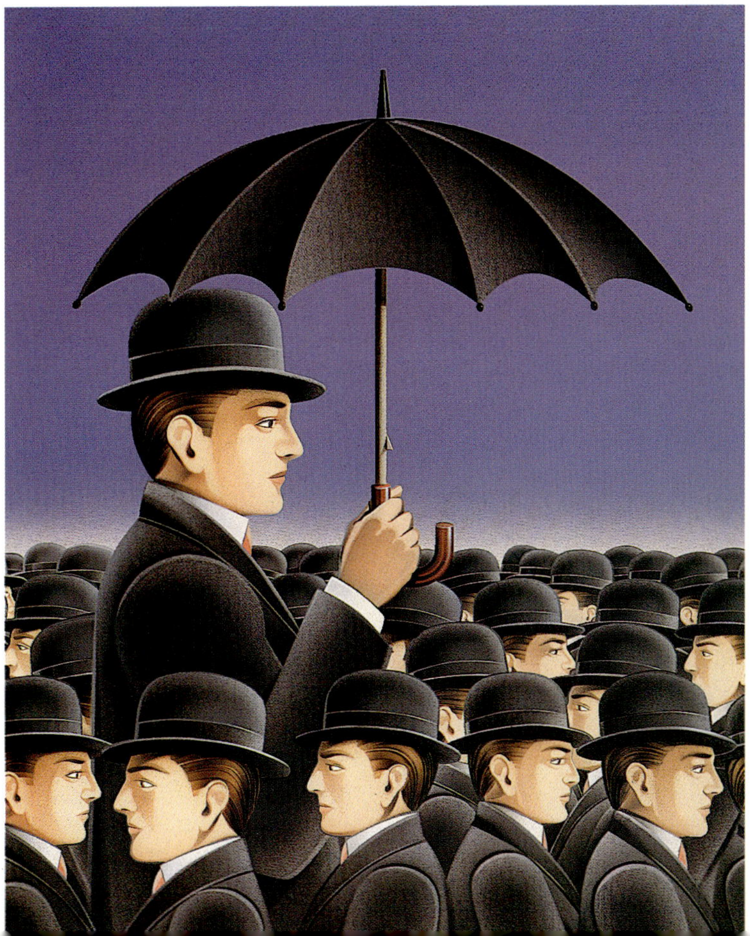

1&2
Artist Mark Otnes
Title Flying Computer Guy
Client Capital Spectrum, Inc., Austin, Texas
Art Director Curtis Riker
Usage Brochure (concerning "breaking through" output problems)
Media Used Acrylic on Bristol

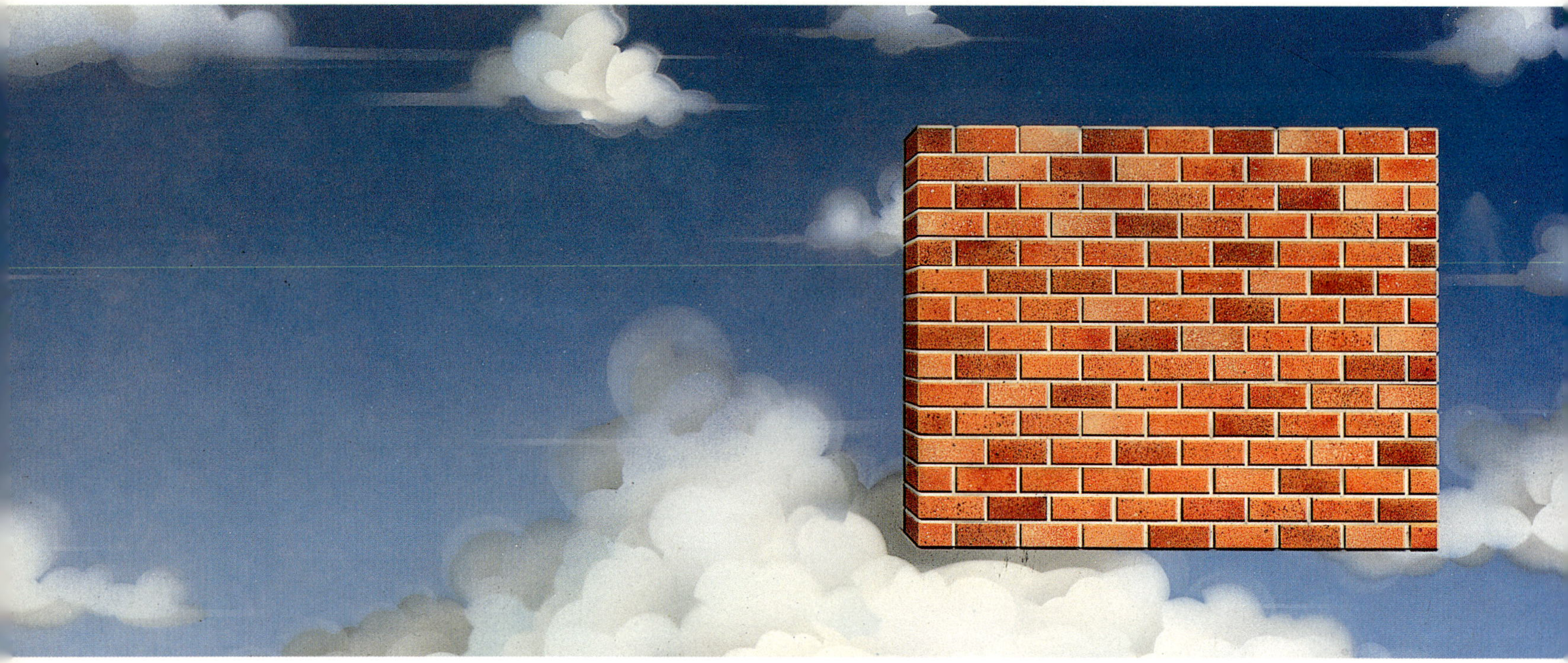

1

2

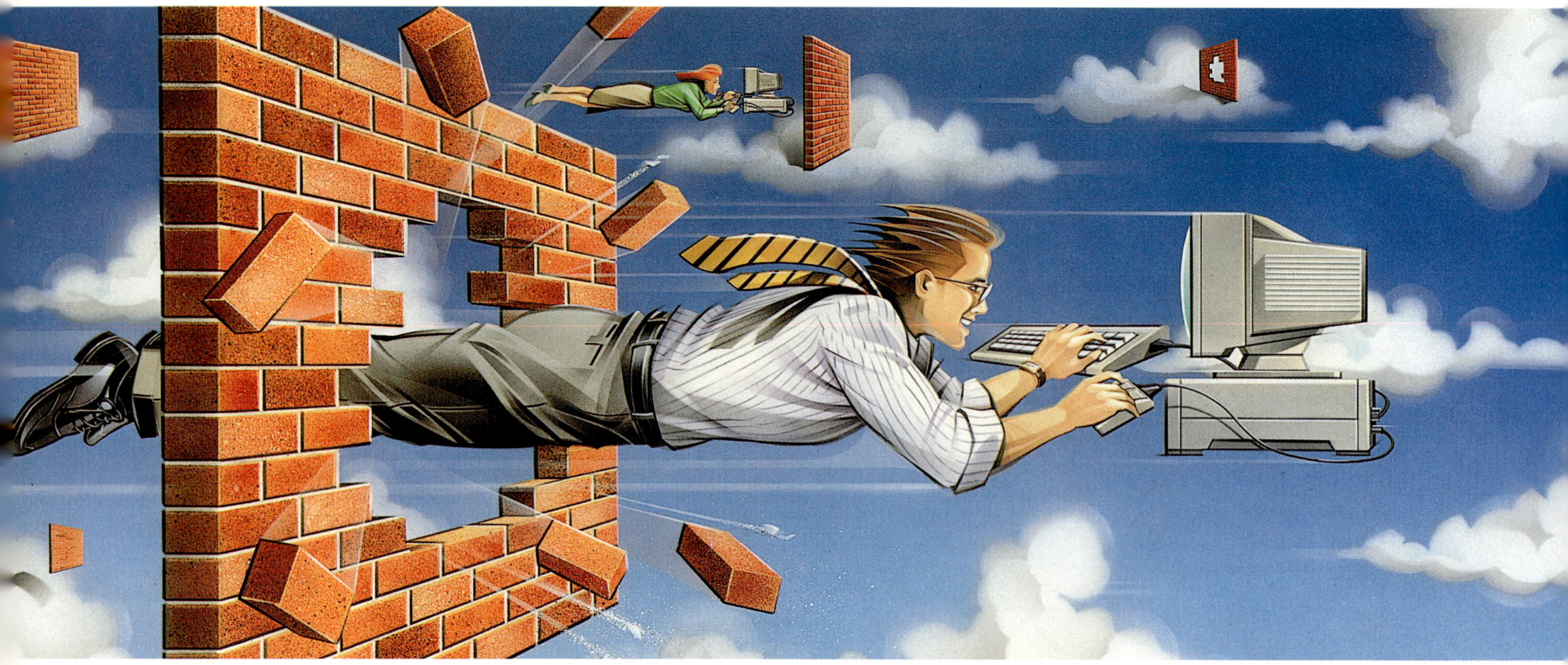

1
Artist Christopher Palmer
Title The Bath
Usage Fine Art
Media Used Acrylic on Canvas

2
Artist Christopher Palmer
Title Quiet Silence
Usage Fine Art
Media Used Acrylic on Canvas

3
Artist Christopher Palmer
Title Mother of Pearl
Usage Fine Art
Media Used Acrylic on Canvas

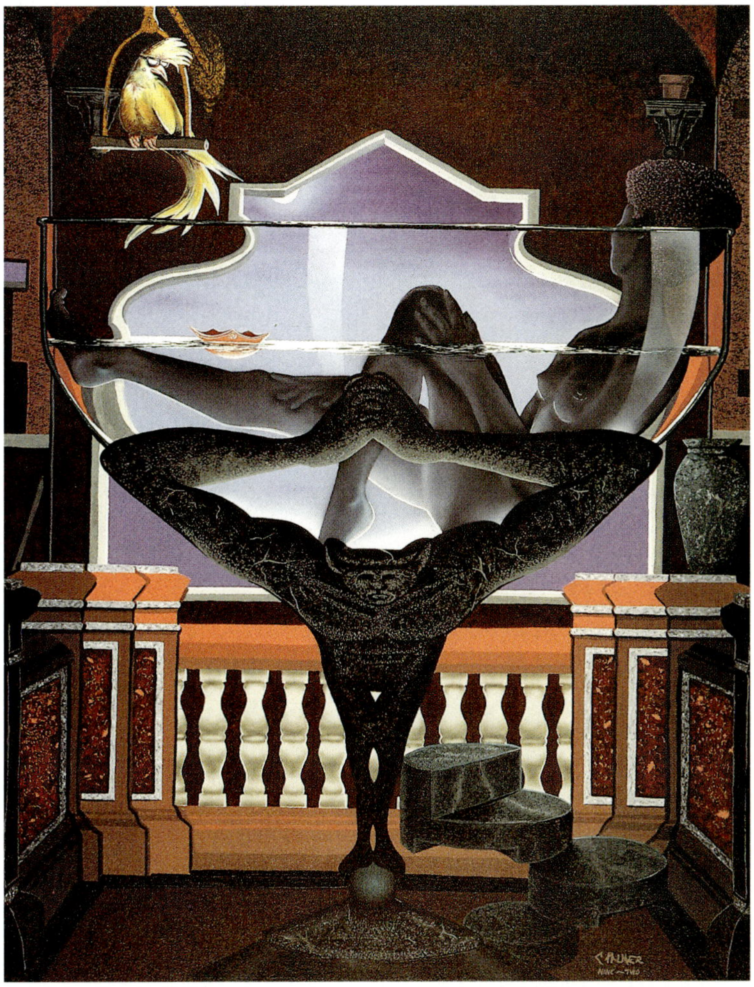

1

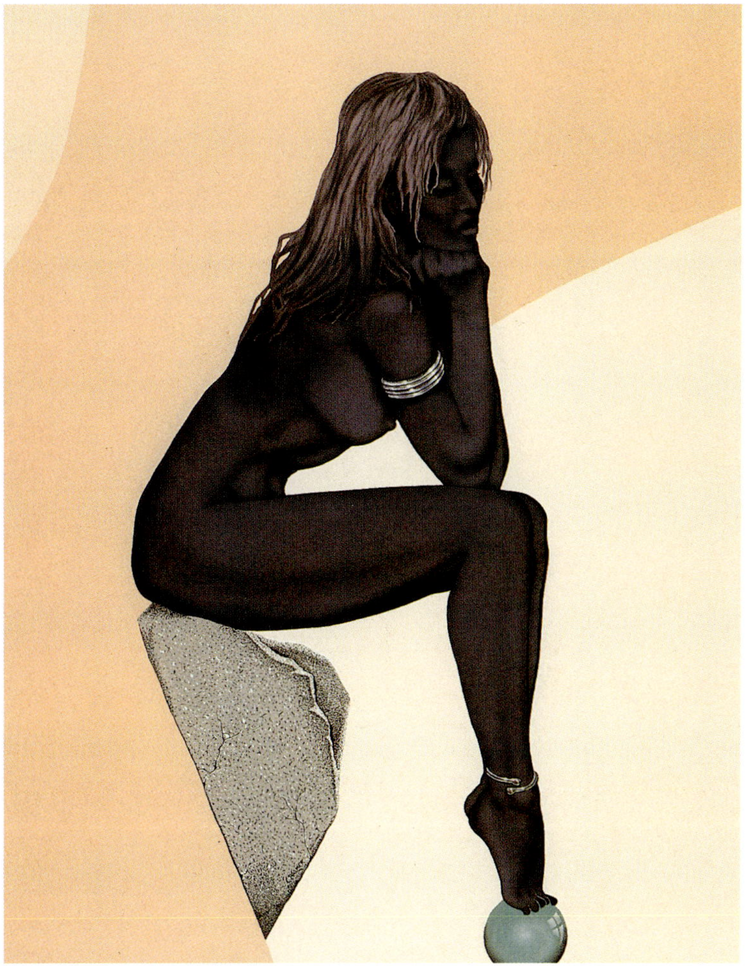

2

3

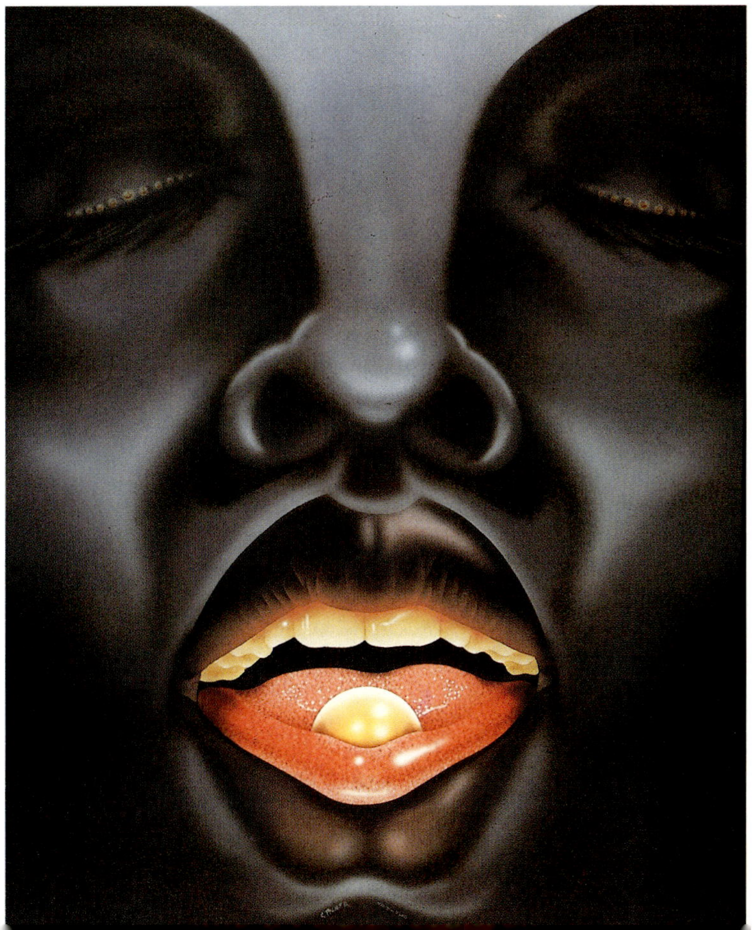

1
Artist Christopher Palmer
Title AJ's Rainy Day
Usage Fine Art
Media Used Acrylic on Canvas

2
Artist Thomas Peiffer
Title Temptation
Usage Fine Art
Media Used Acrylic, Colored Pencil

3
Artist Gary Penca
Title Tired of the Same Old Square Feet
Client Forest City Development
Art Director Brian Roach
Media Used Gouache

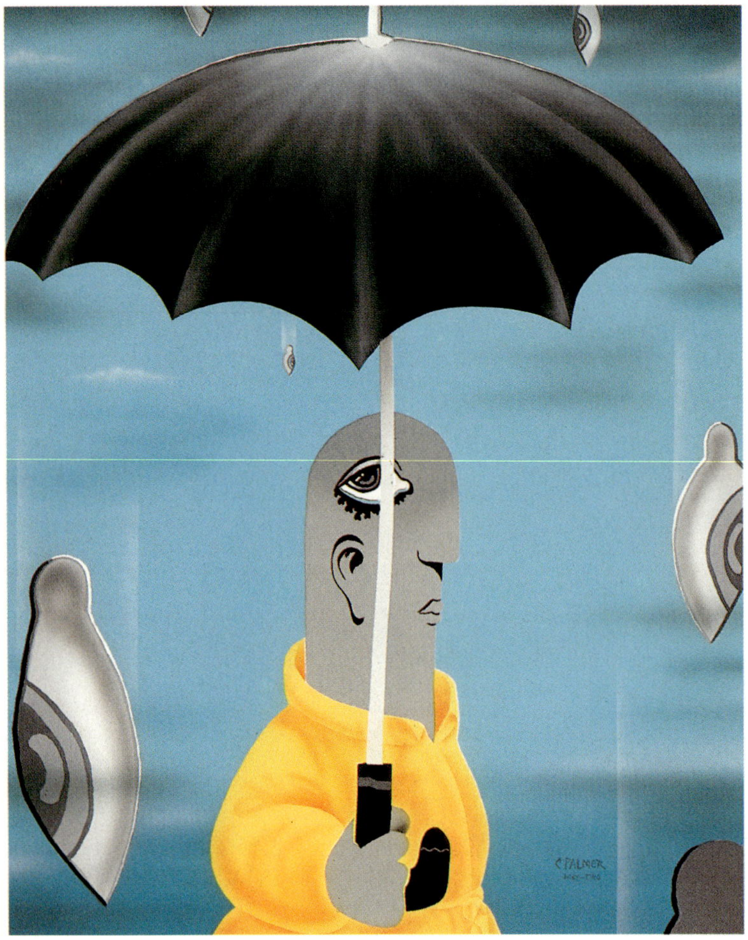

1

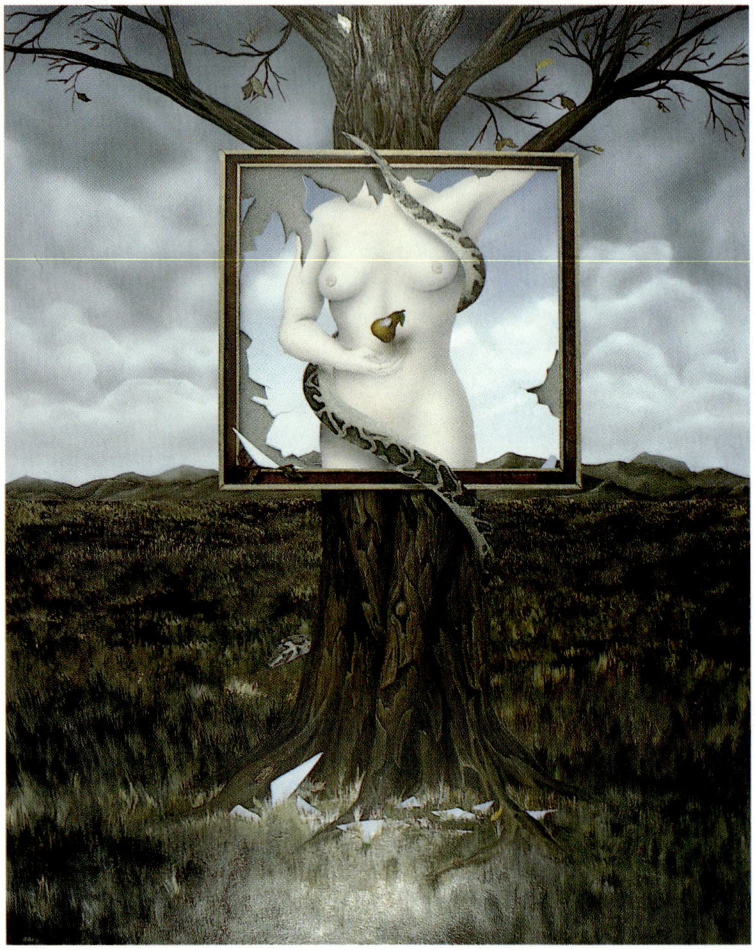

2

3

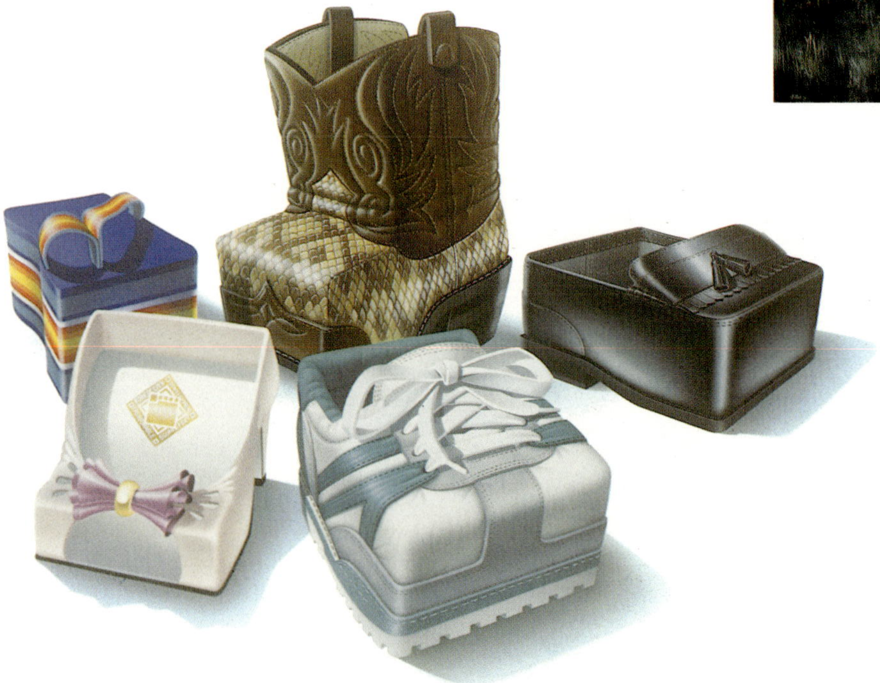

1
Artist Gary Penca
Usage Self Promotion
Media Used Gouache

2
Artist Gary Penca
Client Royal Crown Cola
Art Director Dave Rubinson
Usage 1993 Corporate Calendar
Media Used Gouache

3
Artist Gary Penca
Usage Self Promotion
Media Used Gouache

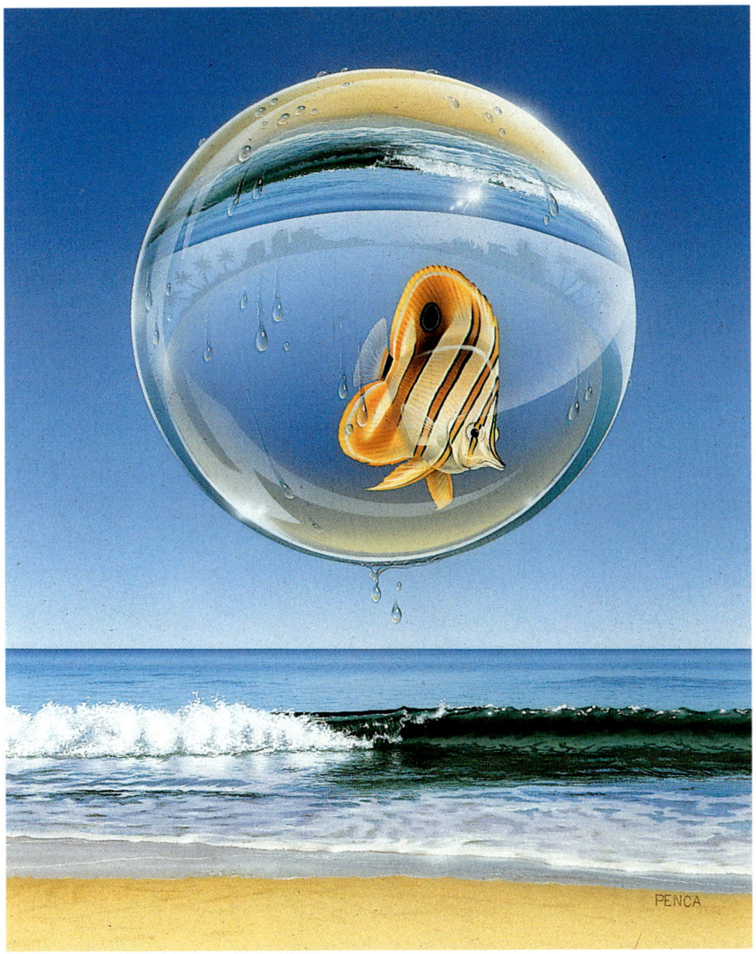

1

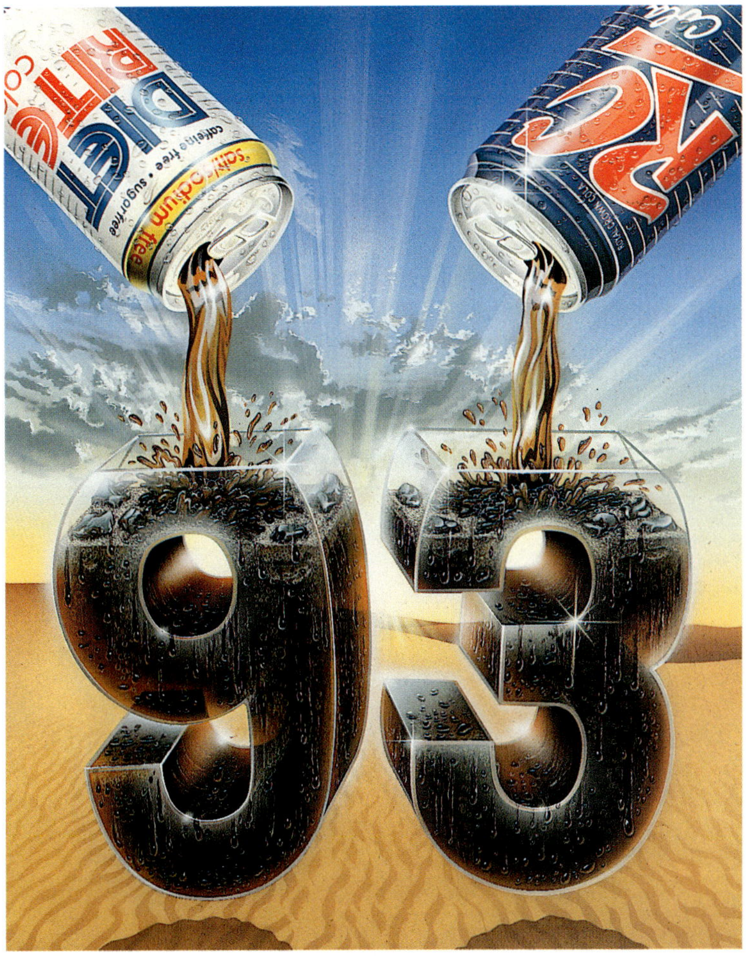

2

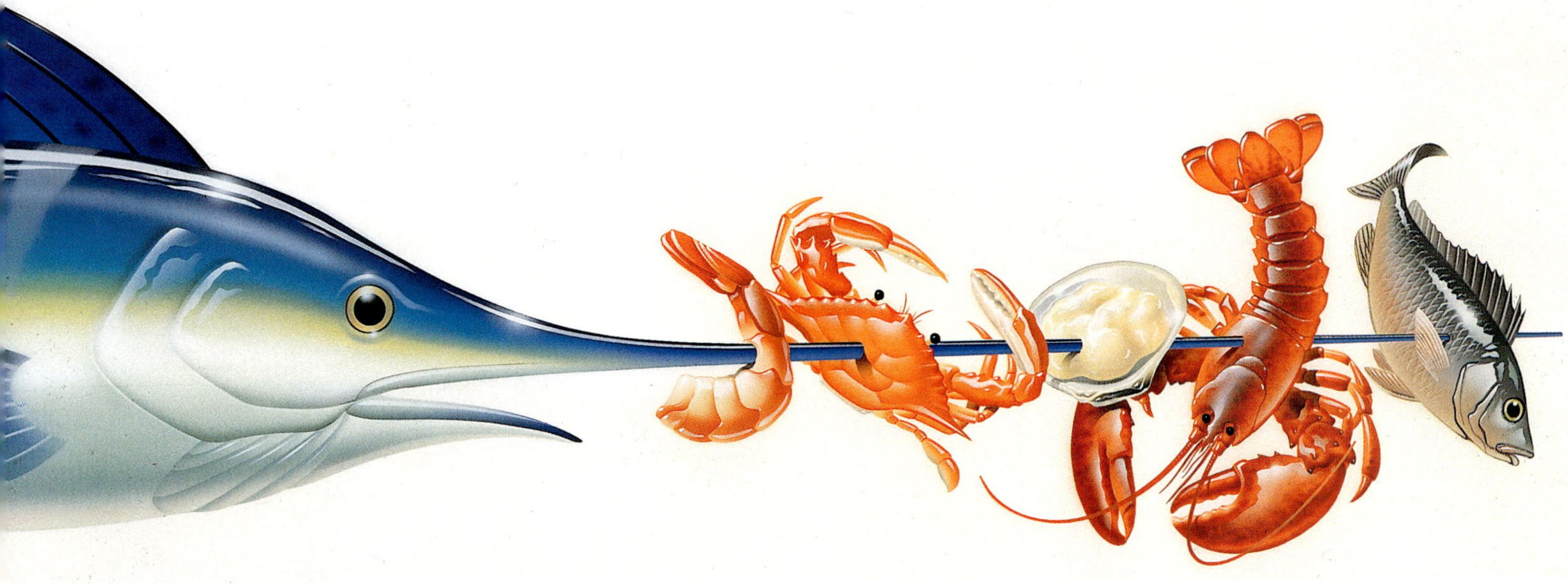

3

1

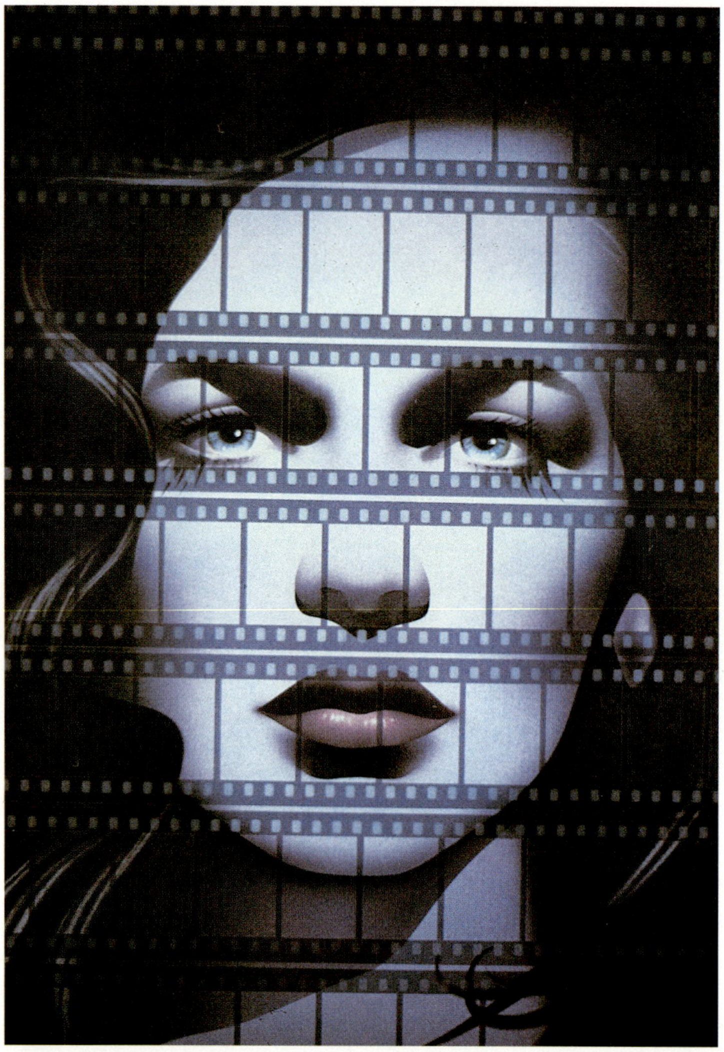

2

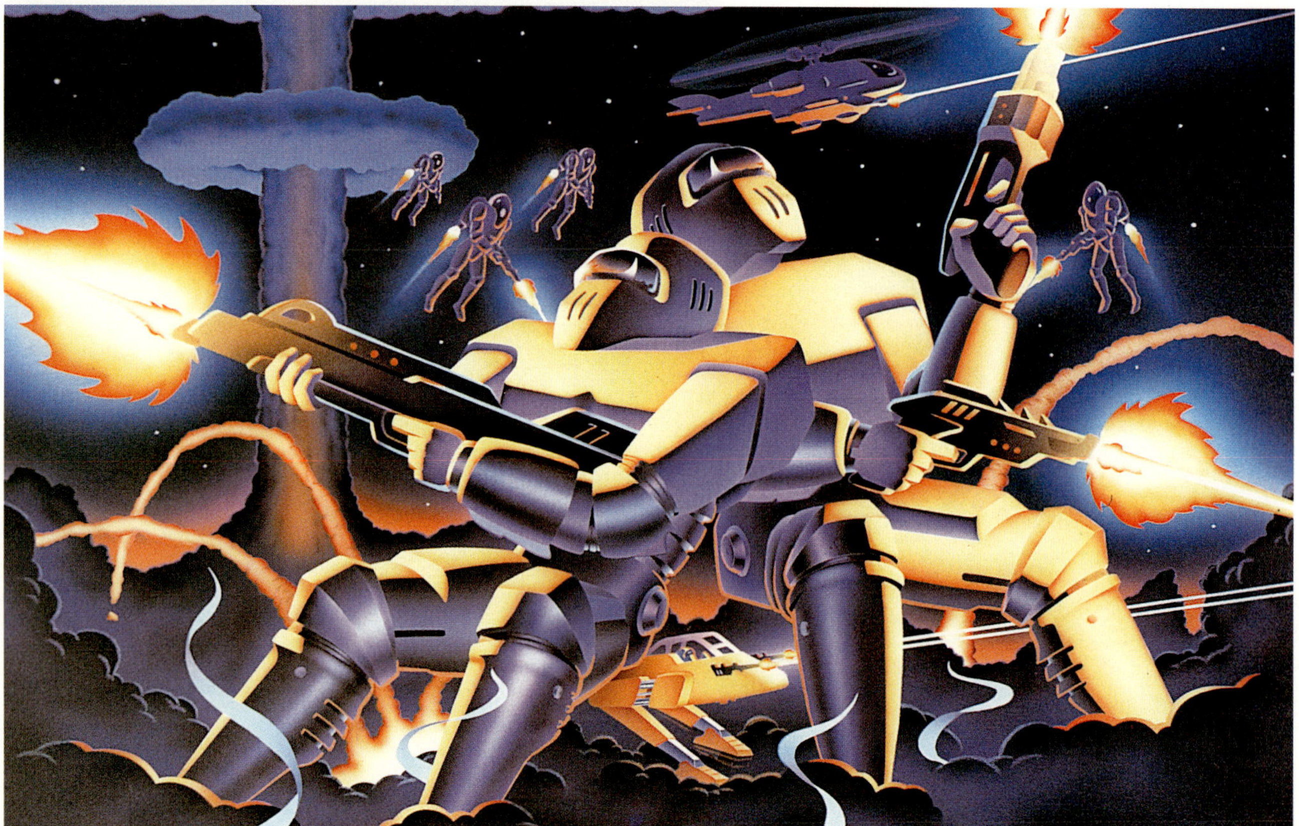

1
Artist Stephen Peringer
Title Flicker
Client Bantam Books
Art Director Amy King
Usage Commercial Art
Media Used Acrylic

2
Artist Stephen Peringer
Title Gunforce
Client Irem
Art Director Darlene Kindler
Usage Commercial Art
Media Used Acrylic

3
Artist Eric Perrotta
Art Director Eric Perrotta
Usage Commercial Art
Media Used Comart

4
Artist Eric Perrotta
Client Chess Life Magazine
Art Director Eric Perrotta
Usage Commercial Art
Media Used Comart, Iwata HP-A, Berol Colored Pencils

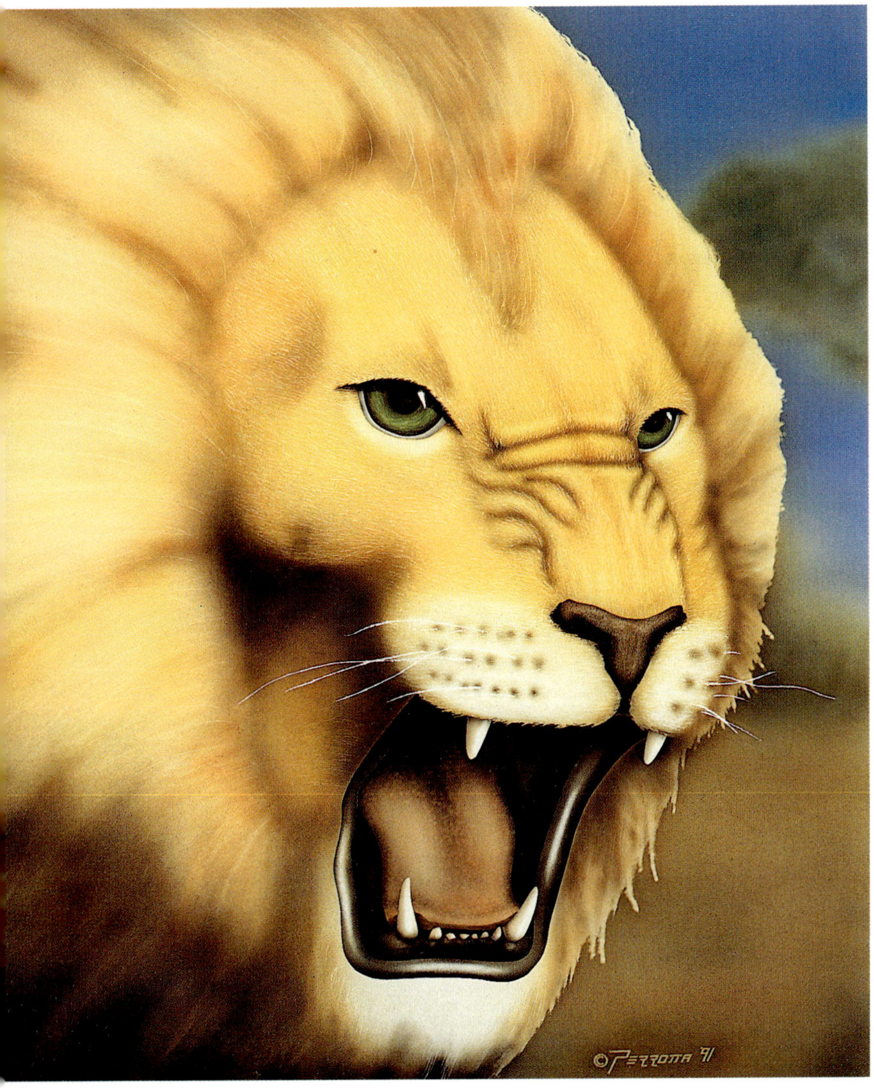

3

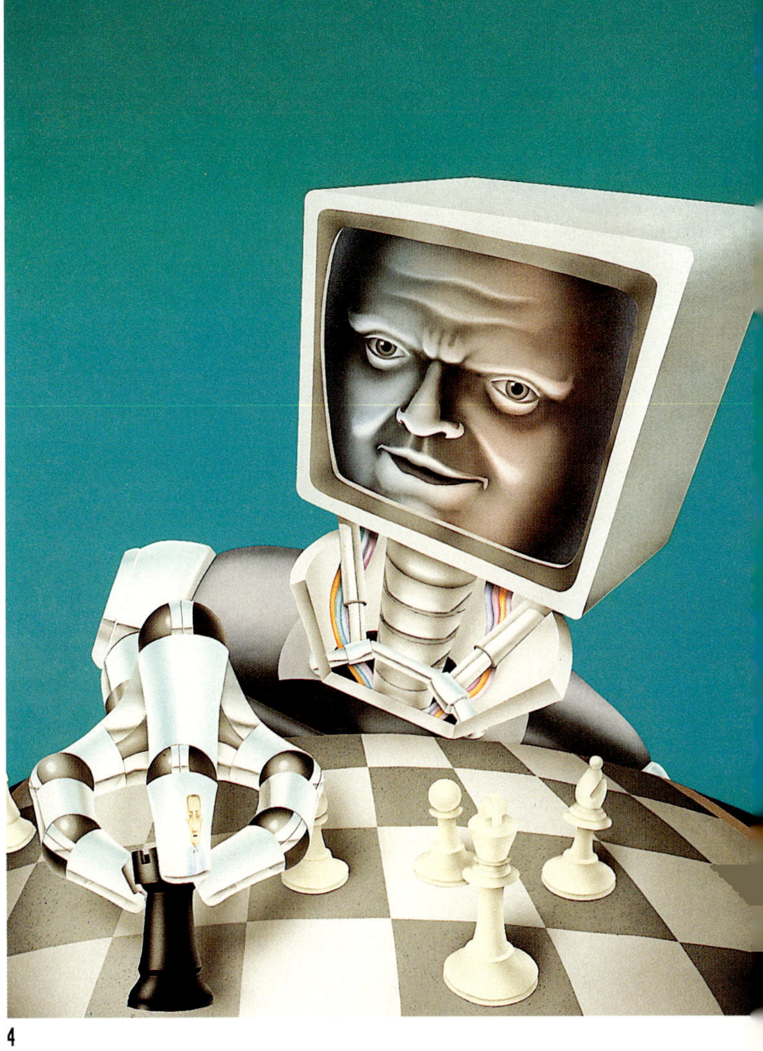

4

1
Artist Thom Petersen
Title The B-50
Usage Fine Art for Limited Edition Print
Media Used Acrylic

2
Artist Thom Petersen
Title Bonneville
Usage Fine Art
Media Used Acrylic

3
Artist Thom Petersen
Title Daze of Future's Past
Usage Fine Art
Media Used Acrylic

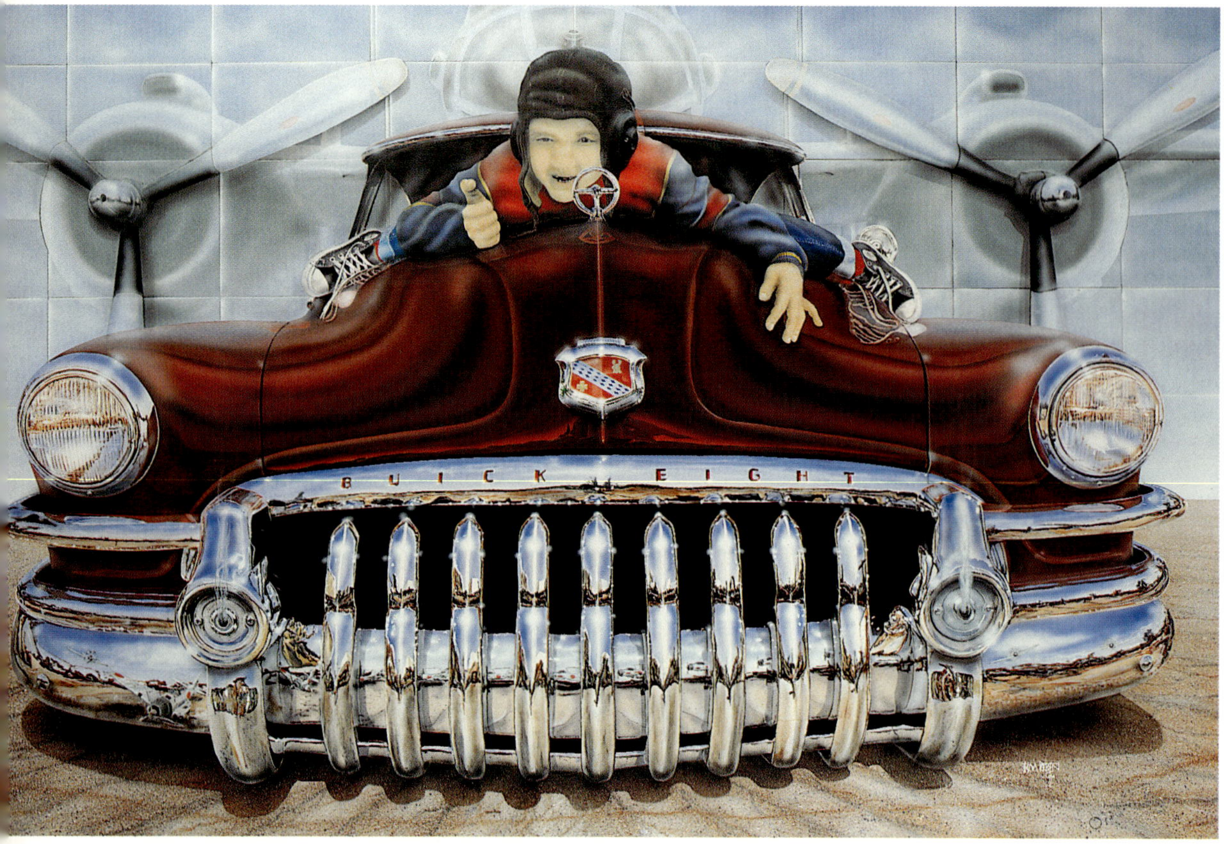

1

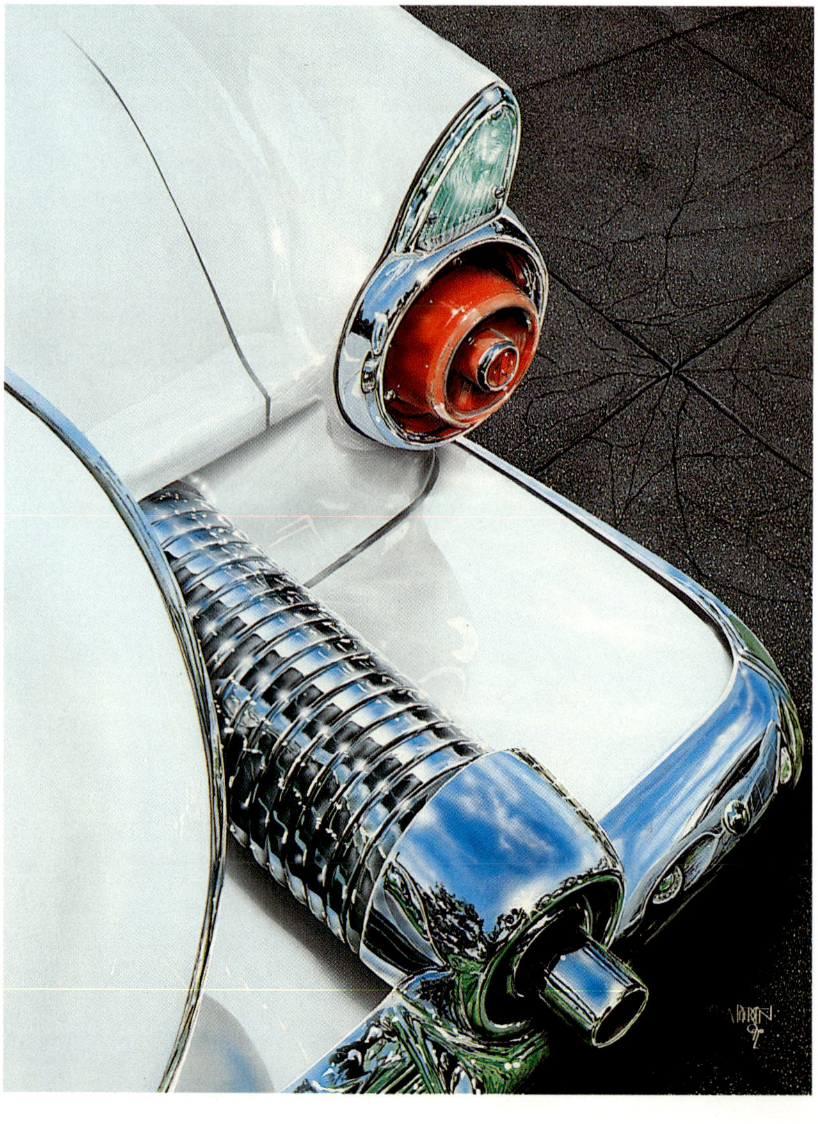

3

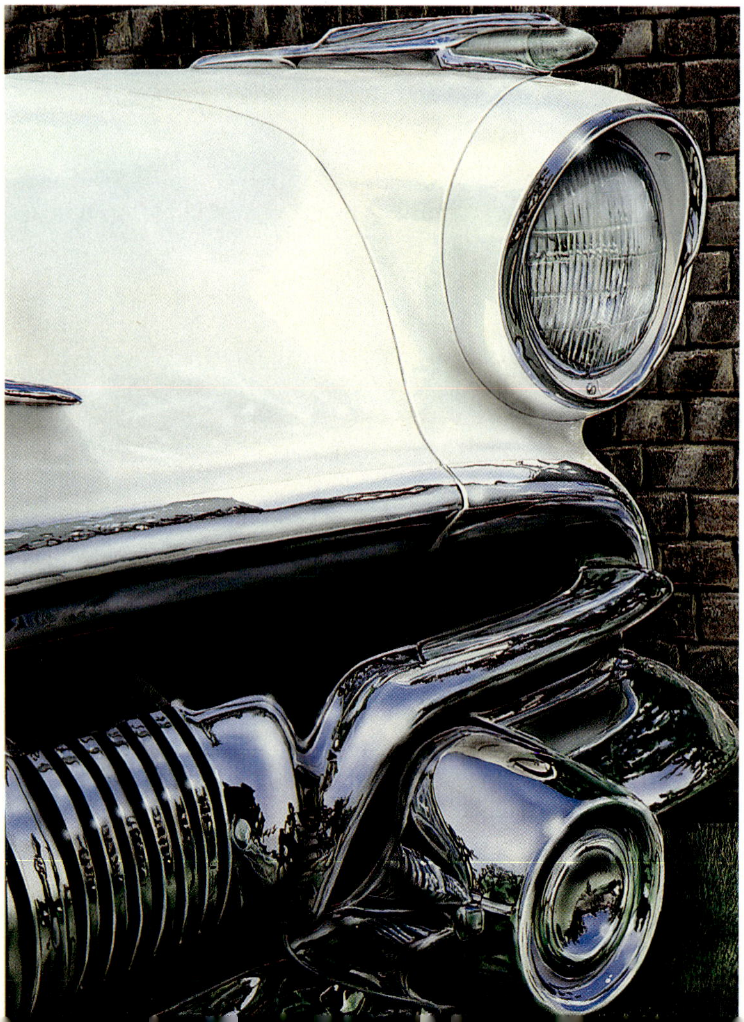

2

1
Artist Thom Petersen
Title The Patriarch
Usage Fine Art for Limited Edition Print
Media Used Acrylic

2
Artist Thom Petersen
Title Rolling Thunder
Usage Fine Art for Limited Edition Print
Media Used Acrylic

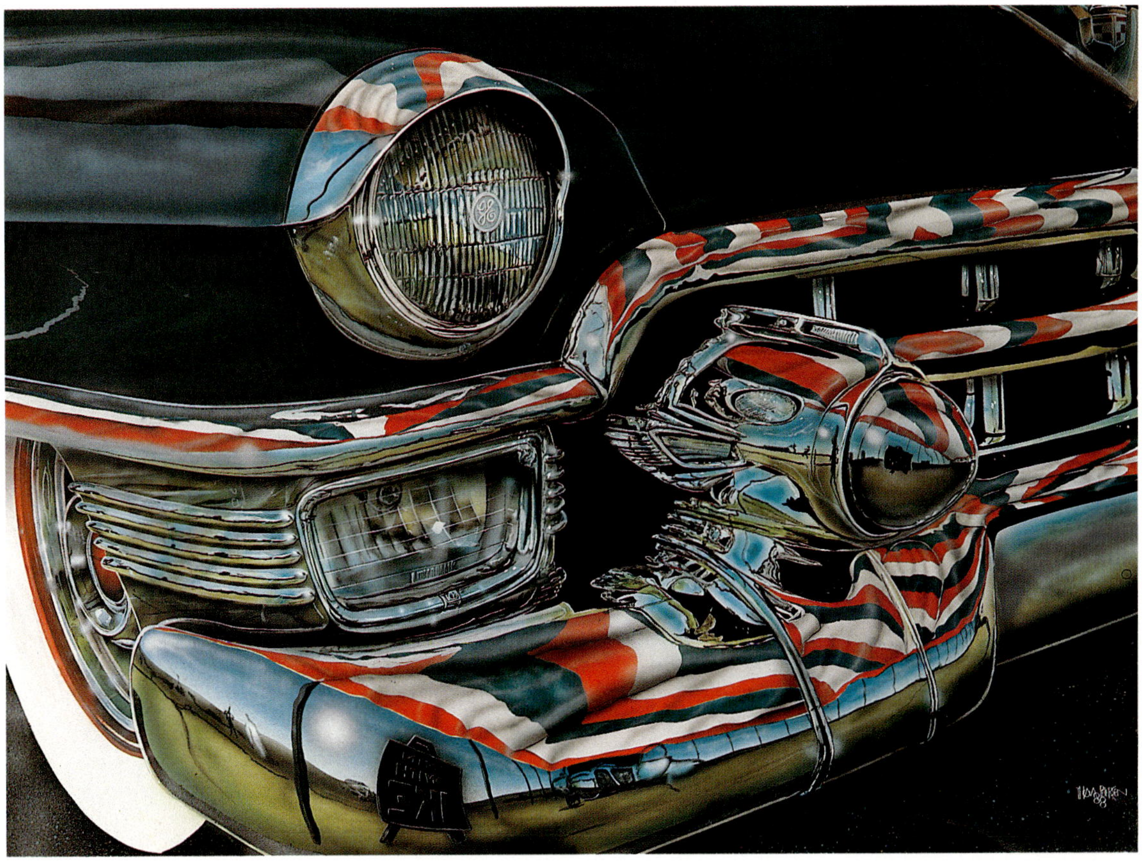

1

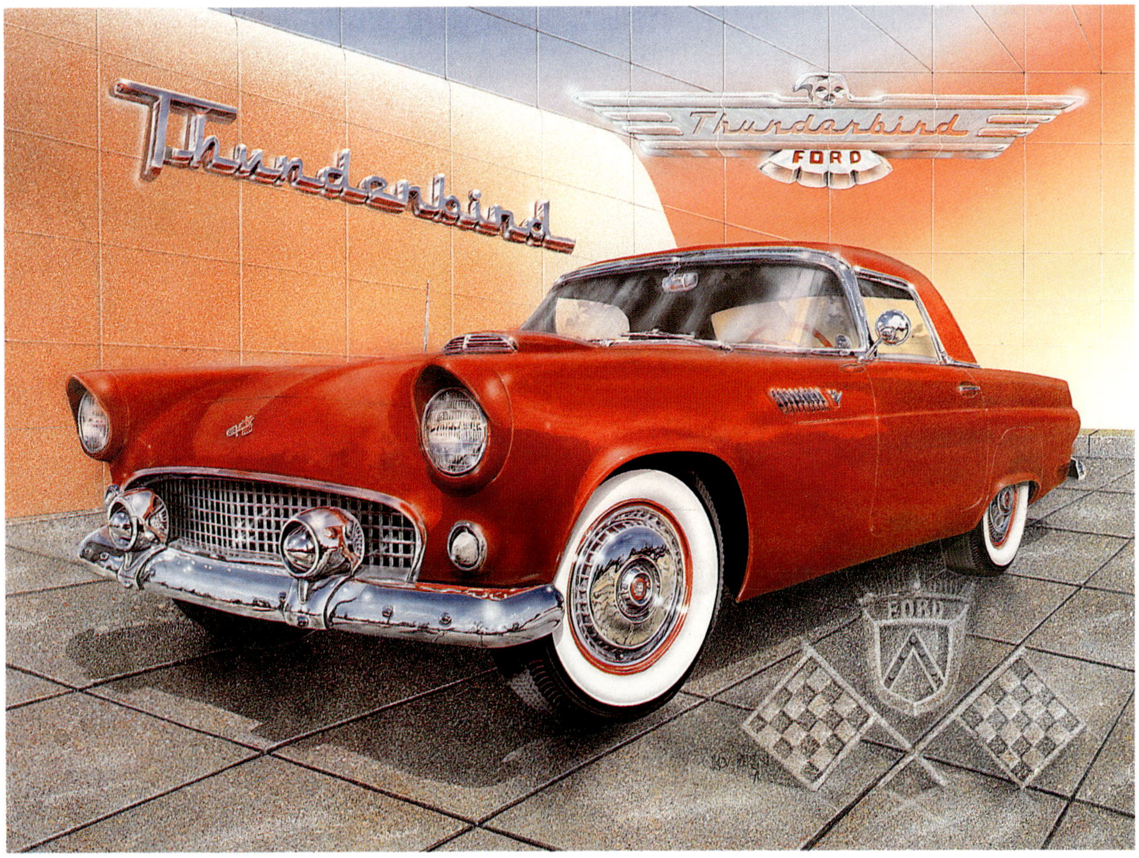

2

1
Artist Myles Pinkney
Title Wizard
Client Portal Publications
Usage Commercial Art
Media Used Gouache, Acrylic

2
Artist Oscar Quarles
Title Posing
Usage Fine Art
Media Used Watercolor, Gouache, India Ink

3
Artist Roberto Ramirez
Title Lucas
Client Self Promotion
Usage Commercial Art
Media Used Acrylic

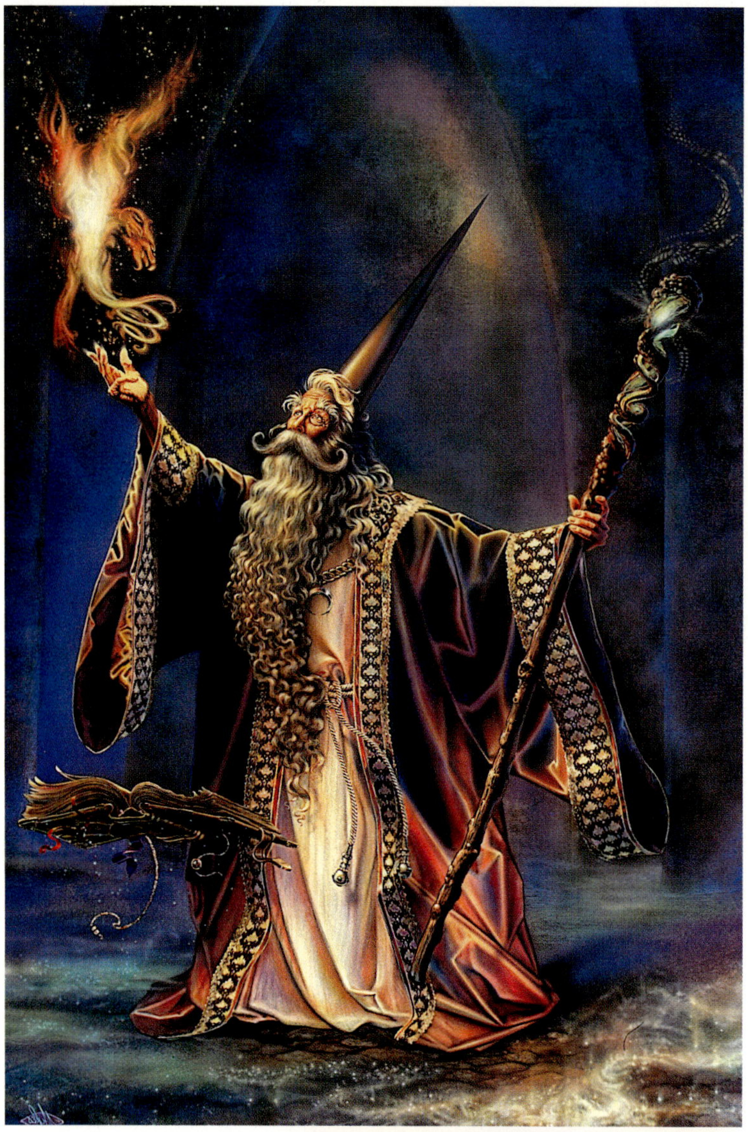

1

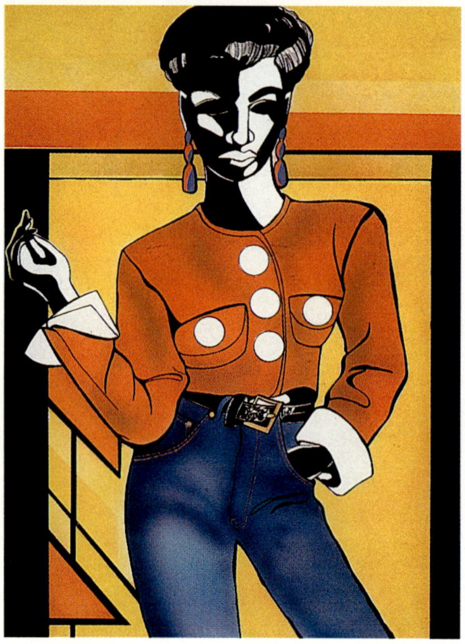

2

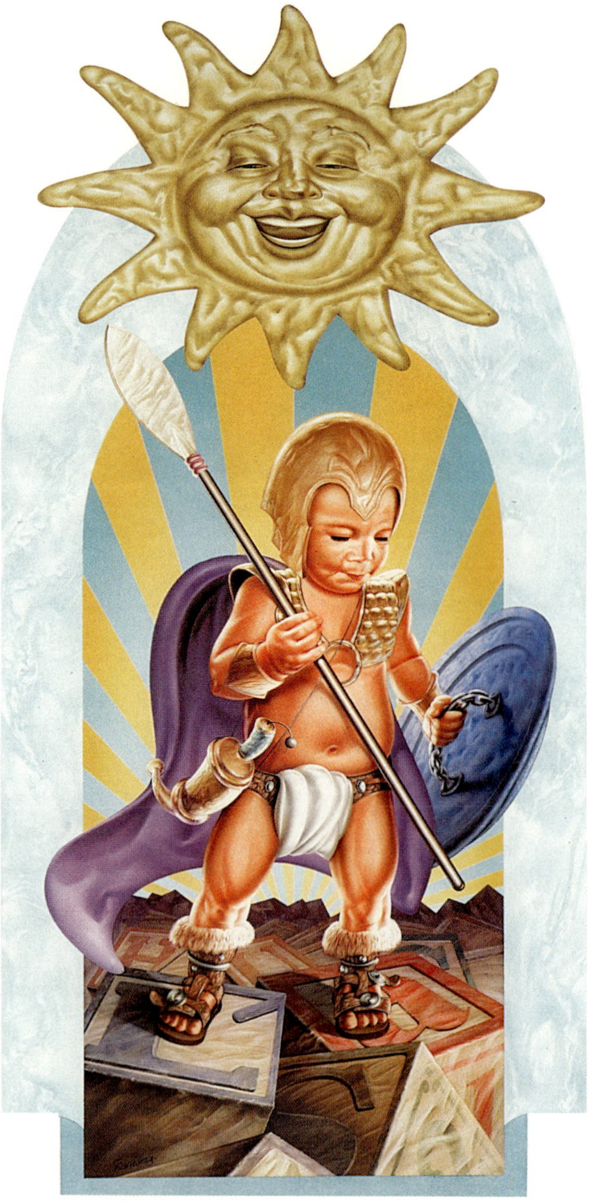

3

1
Artist Roberto Ramirez
Title Deanna
Client Self Promotion
Usage Commercial Art
Media Used Acrylic

2
Artist Kathleen Regan
Title Cocktail
Client Self Promotion
Usage Student Art
Media Used Acrylic

3
Artist Kathleen Regan
Title The Milky's Way
Client Self Promotion
Usage Student Art
Media Used Acrylic

2

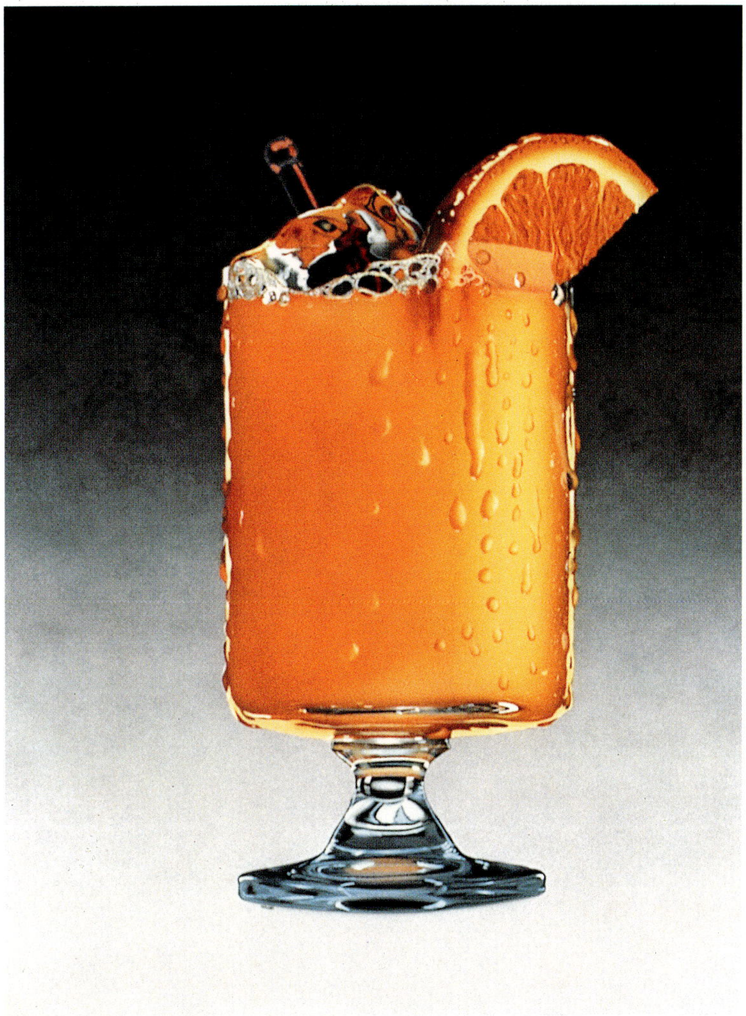

1

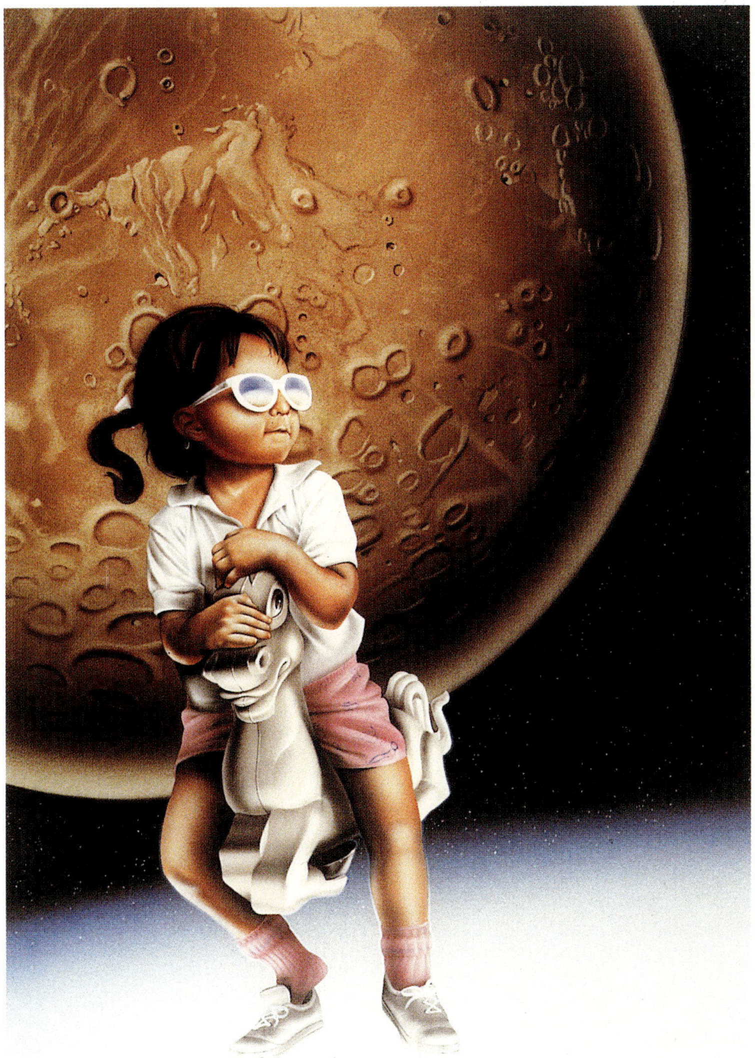

3

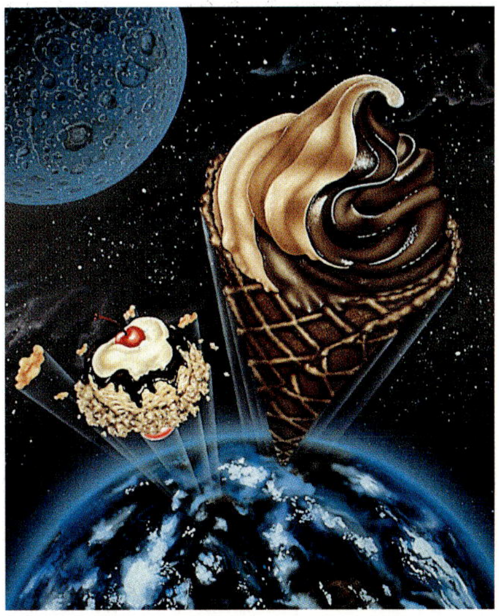

1
Artist Robert Revels
Title Father Figure
Art Director Academy of Art
Usage Student Art
Media Used Gouache, Acrylic

2
Artist Robert Revels
Title Spike
Art Director Academy of Art
Usage Student Art
Media Used Gouache, Acrylic

3
Artist Mark V. Robinson
Title 49 Buick Eight
Client Self Promotion
Usage Commercial Art
Media Used Acrylic

1

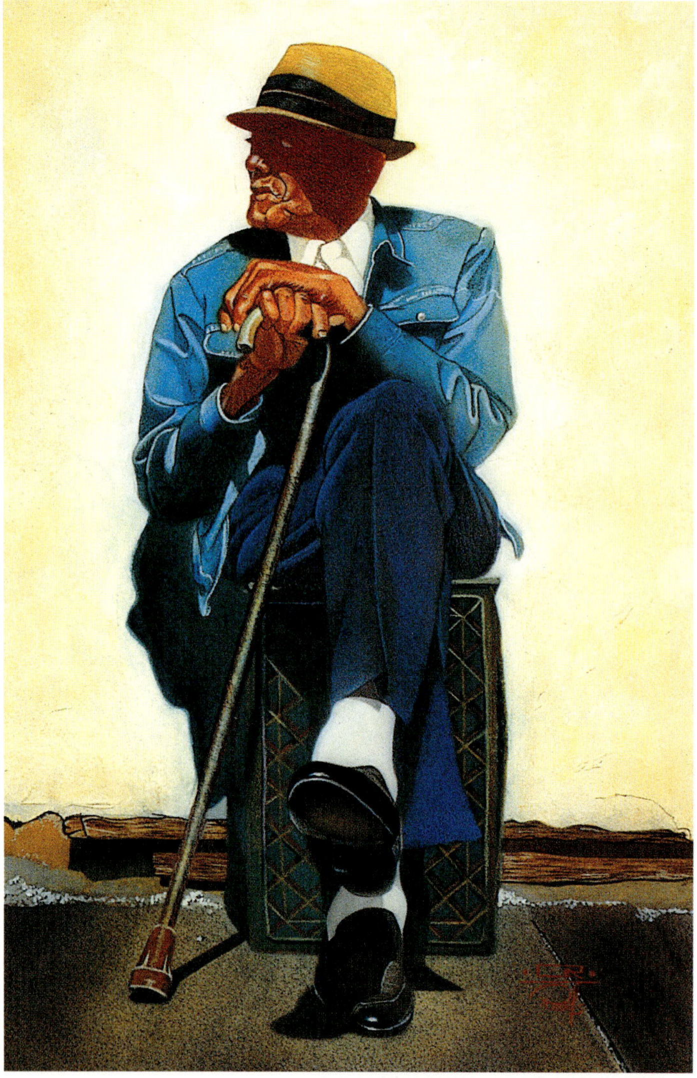

2

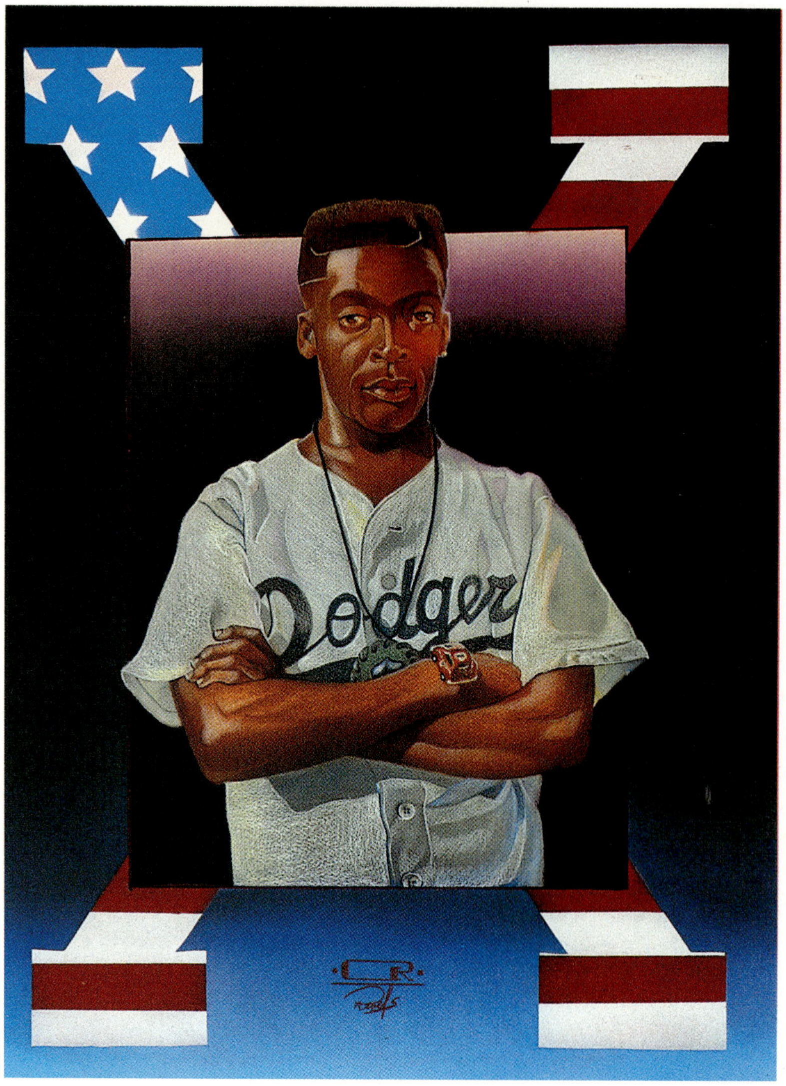

3

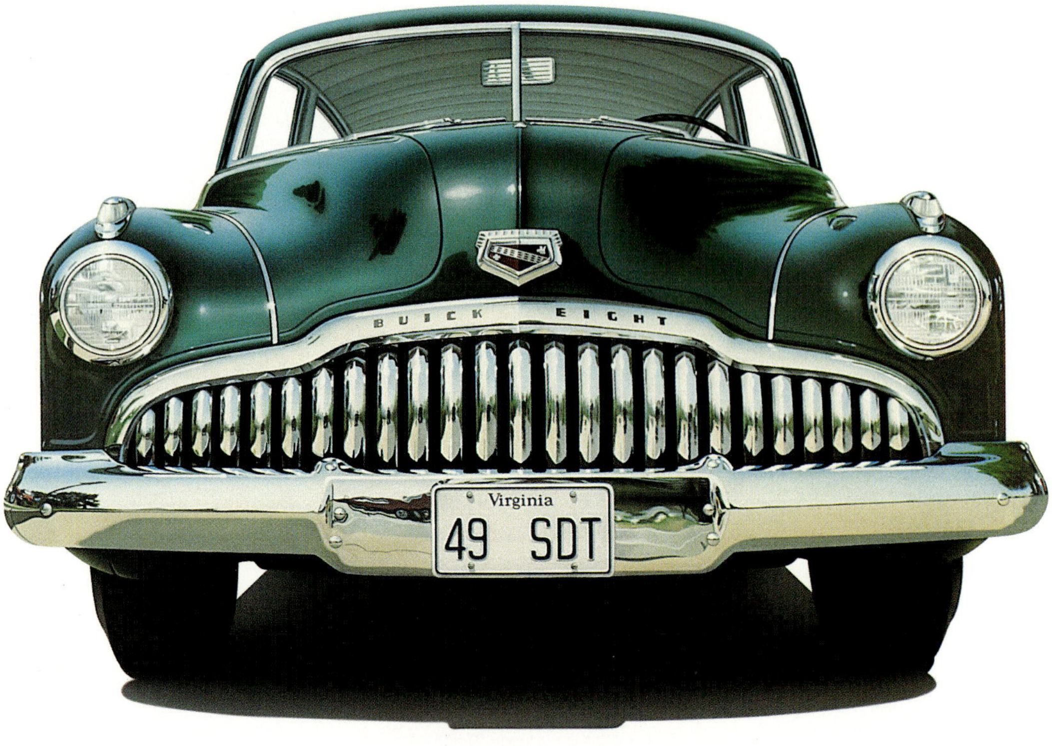

1
Artist David Salazar
Usage Fine Art
Media Used Acrylic

2
Artist Samuel Salfino III
Client Cheverolet
Art Director Moore Sports
Usage Commercial Art
Media Used Acrylic

3
Artist Samuel Salfino III
Title "Lil" Miss Muffet
Client Self Promotion
Usage Commercial Art
Media Used Acrylic

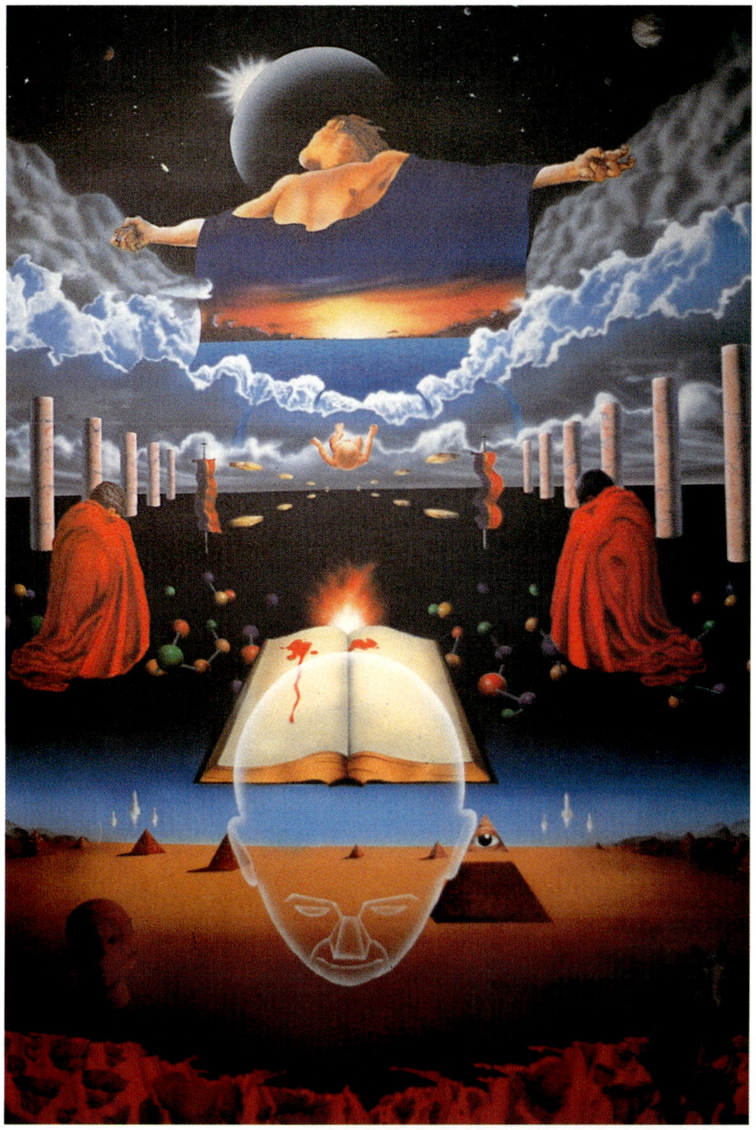

1

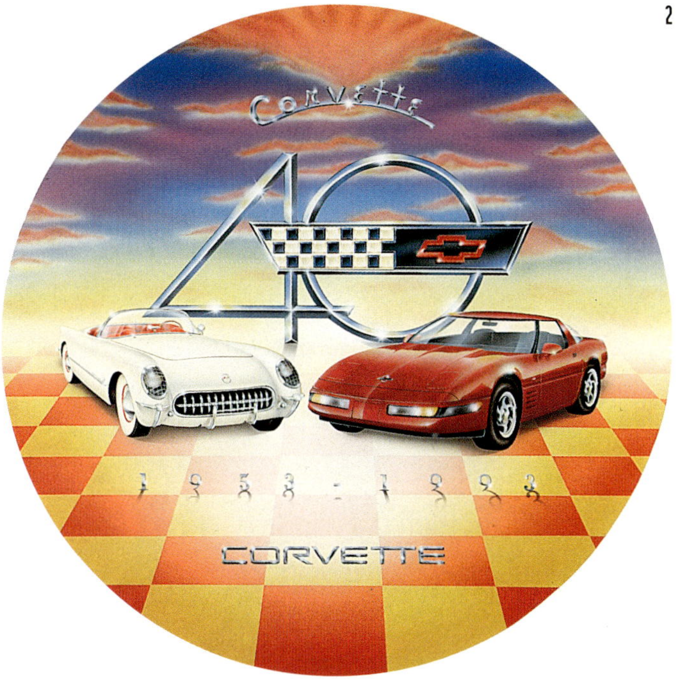

2

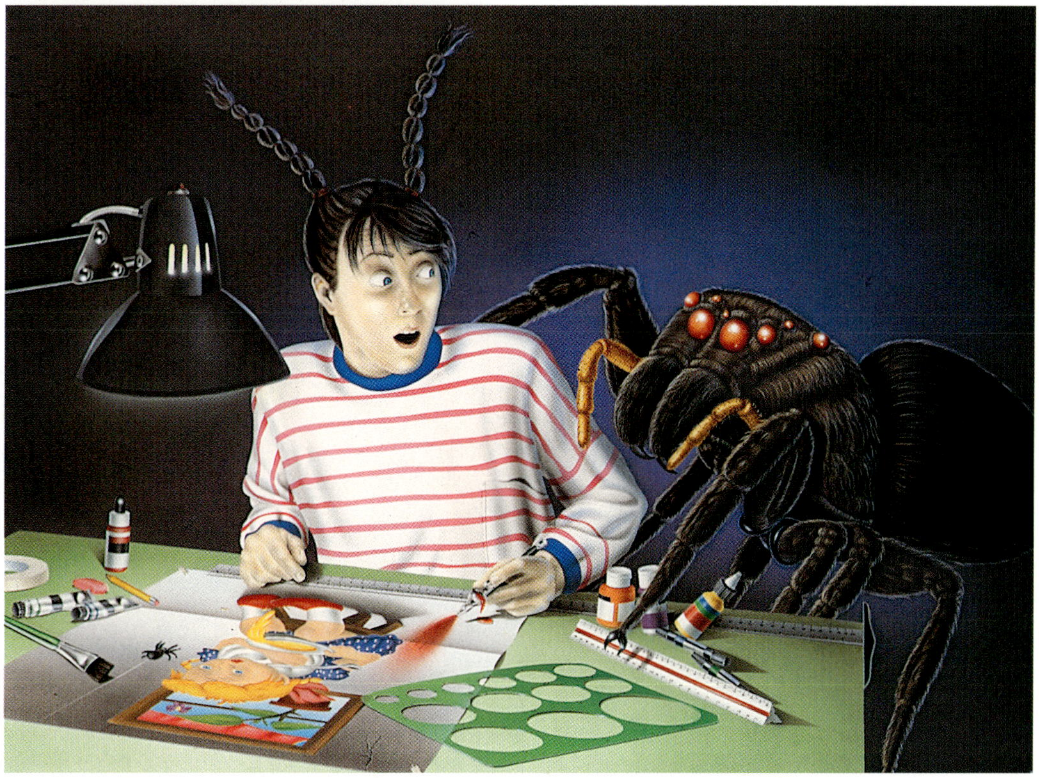

3

1
Artist Samuel Salfino III
Client Self Promotion
Usage Fine Art
Media Used Acrylic

2
Artist Samuel Salfino III
Title Day in the Park
Client Self Promotion
Usage Fine Art
Media Used Acrylic

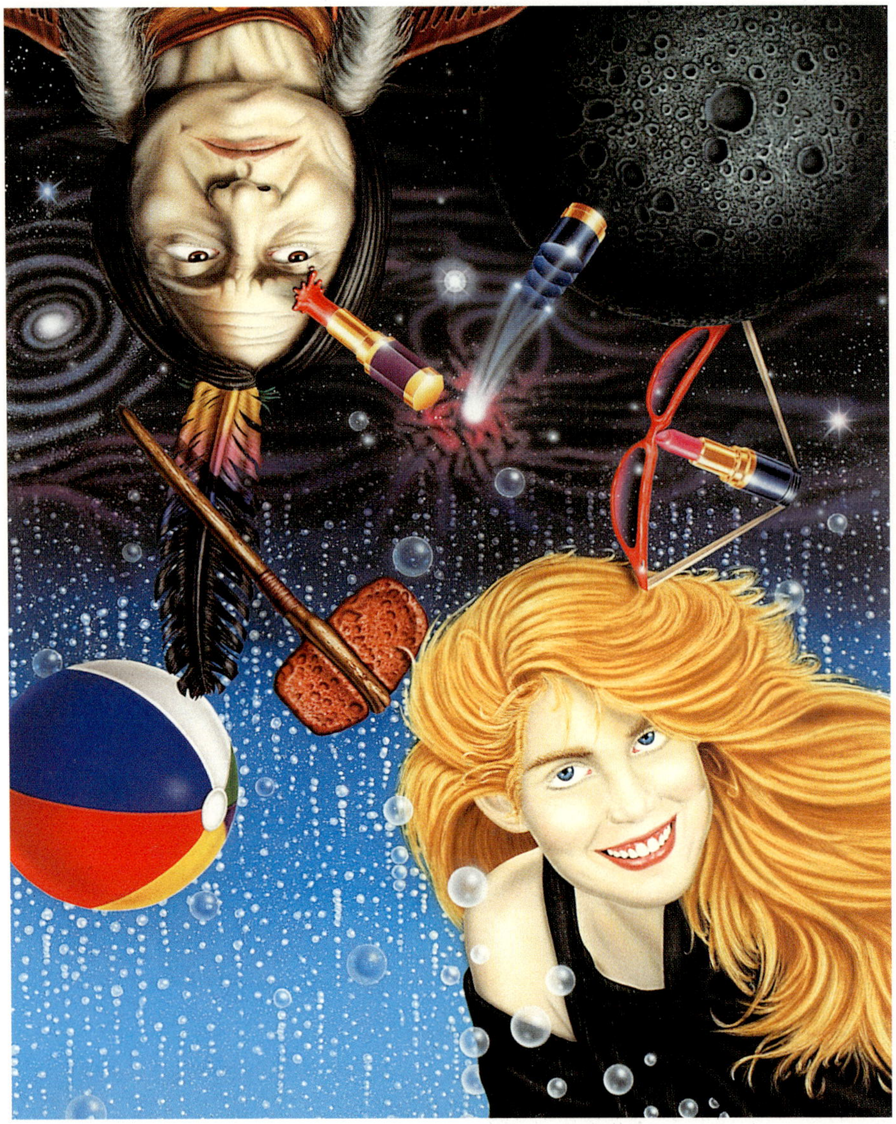

1

2

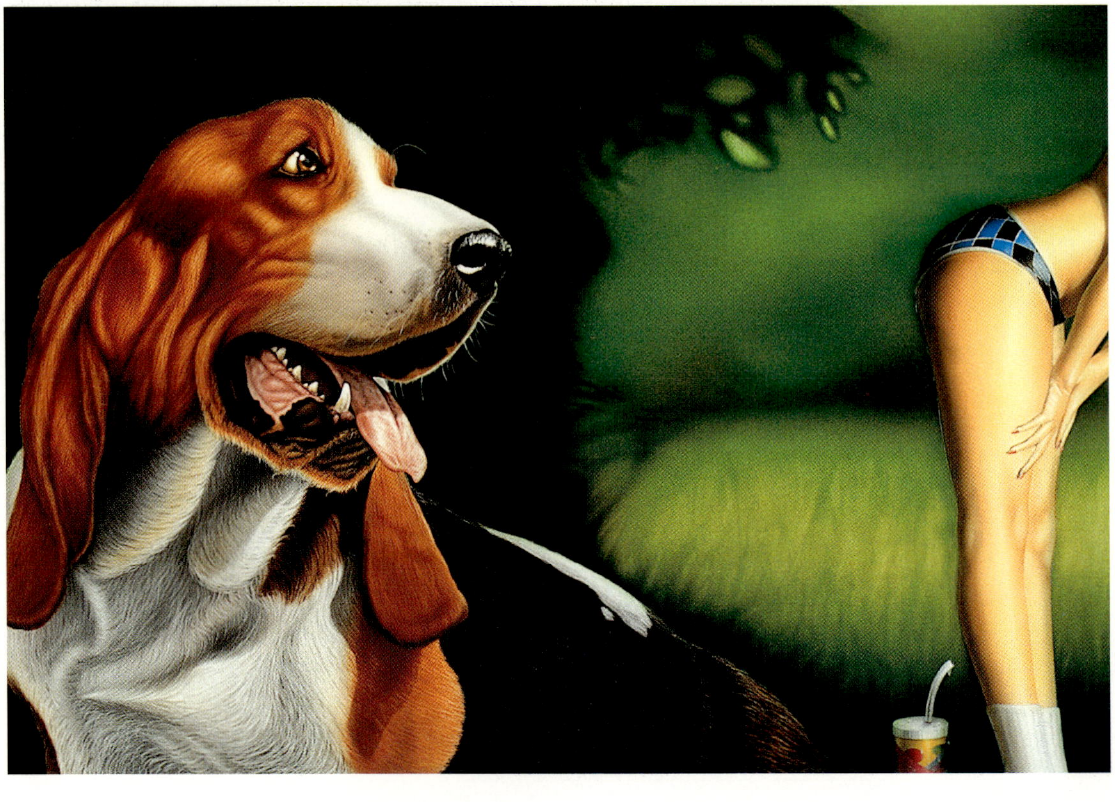

1
Artist Dr. William C. Schneider
Title Anxiety
Usage Student Art
Media Used Liquitex Acrylic

2
Artist Greg Schooley
Title Light Bulb
Client Tab/McGraw-Hill
Art Director Lori Schlosser
Usage Poster
Media Used Designer's Gouache

3
Artist Greg Schooley
Title Piano Keys
Client Tab/McGraw-Hill
Art Director Lori Schlosser
Usage Book Cover
Media Used Designer's Gouache

4
Artist Steve Shamburger
Title Batman
Client Self Promotion
Art Director Steve Shamburger
Usage Commercial Art
Media Used Acrylic, Colored Pencil

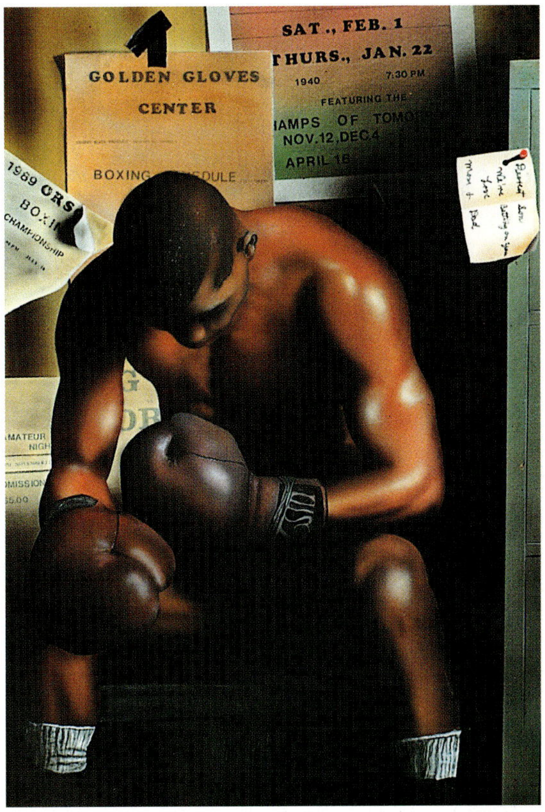

1

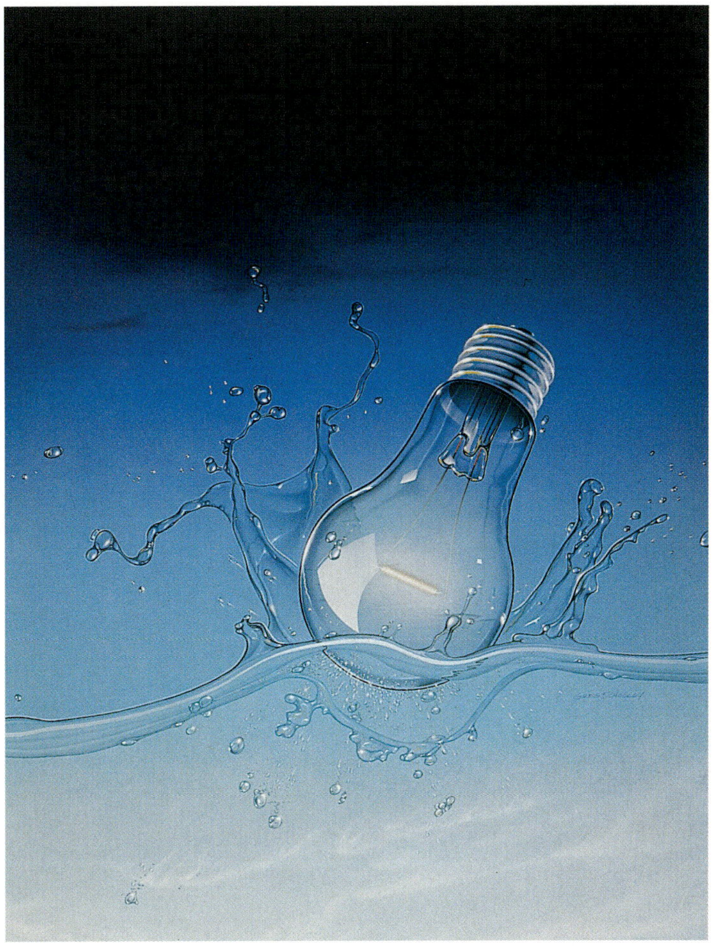

2

3

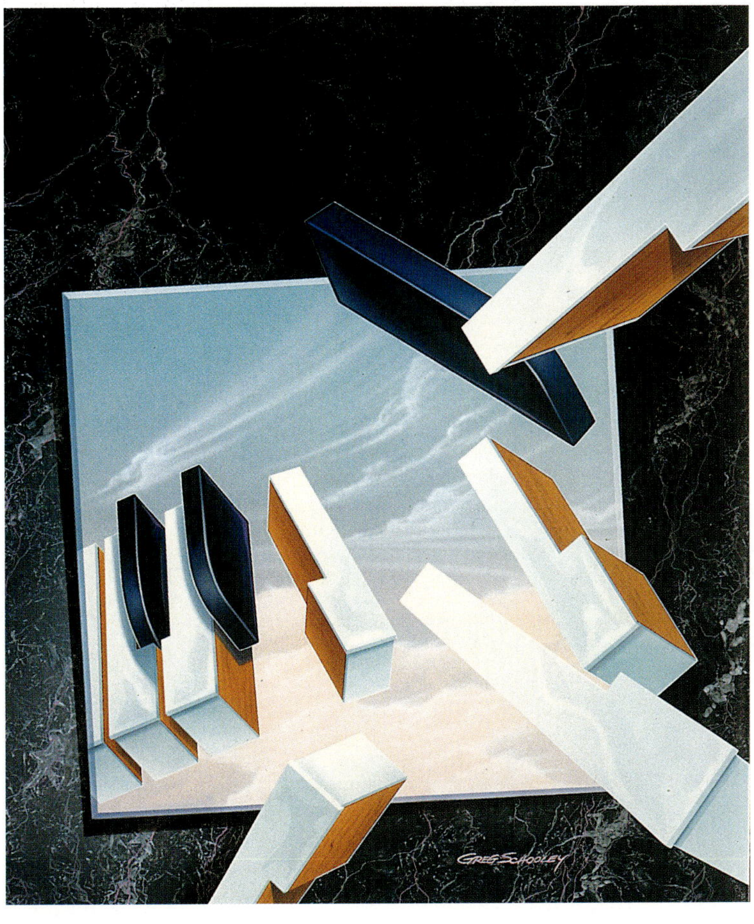

4

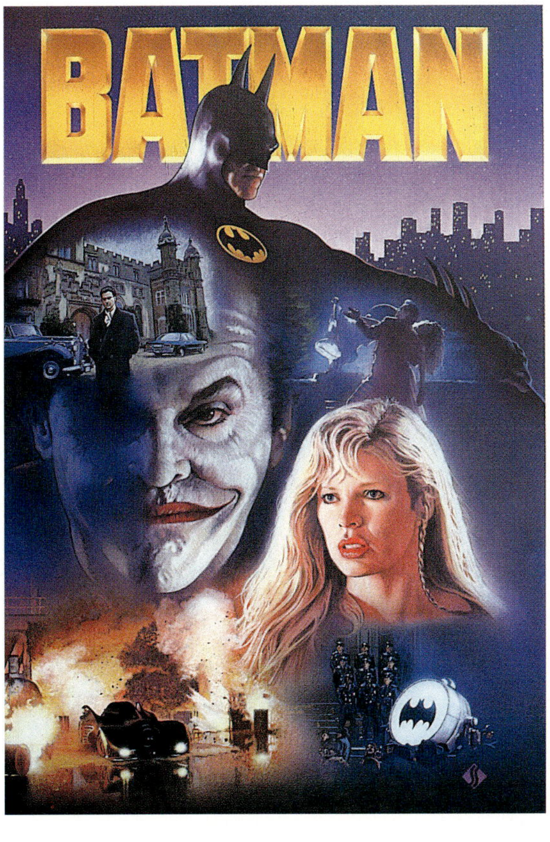

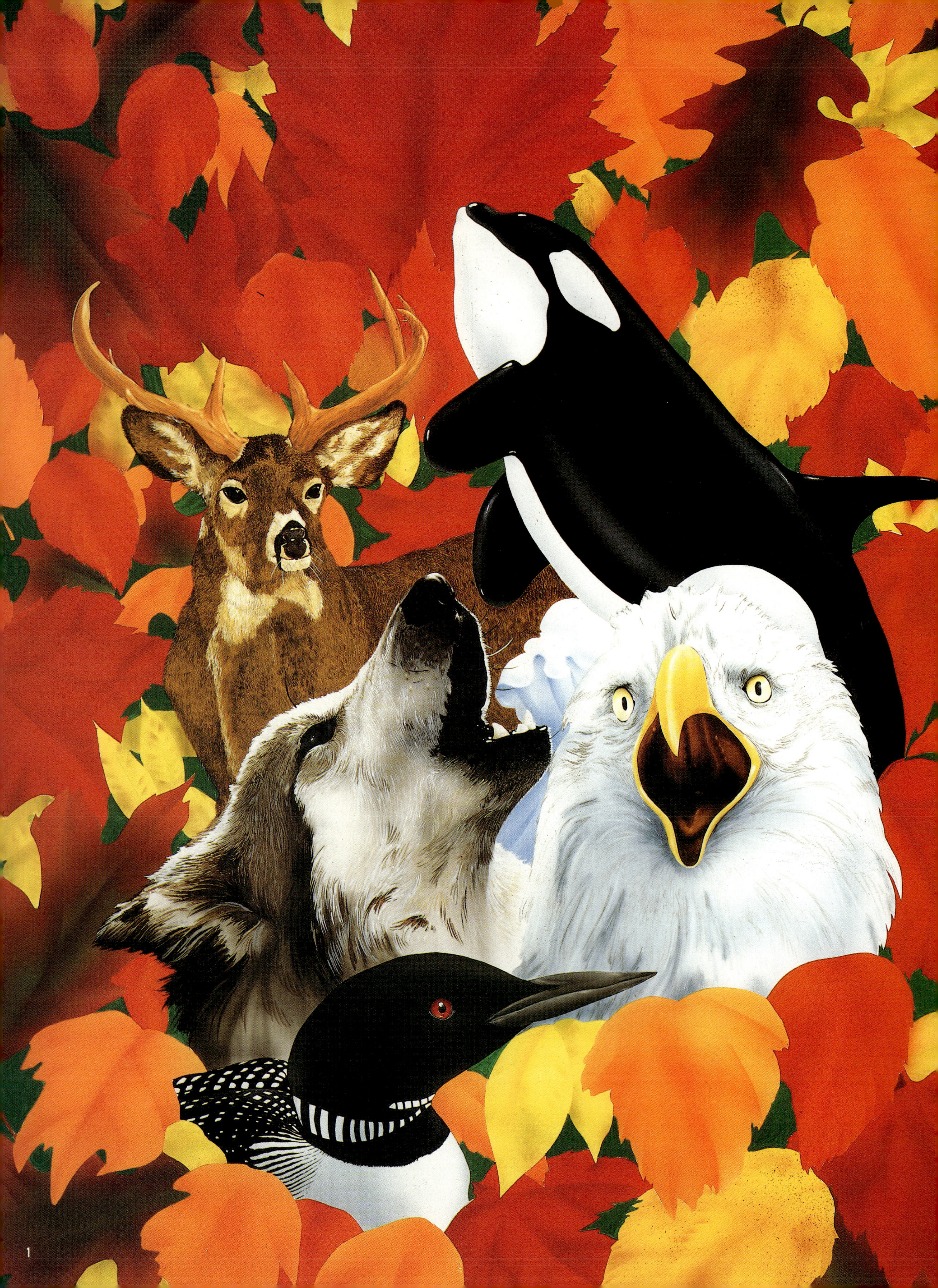

1
Artist Mary A. Shafer
Title Where the Wild Things Are
Client Northword Press, Inc.
Art Director Mary A. Schafer
Usage Point of Sale Promotion - Nature Books
Media Used Gouache, Watercolor, Ink

2
Artist Steve Singer
Title Partner
Usage Student Art
Media Used Medea Airbrush Colors

3
Artist Timothy Stafford
Title Fly Trap
Usage Student Art
Media Used Acrylic

4
Artist Timothy Stafford
Title Happy Painting
Usage Student Art
Media Used Acrylic

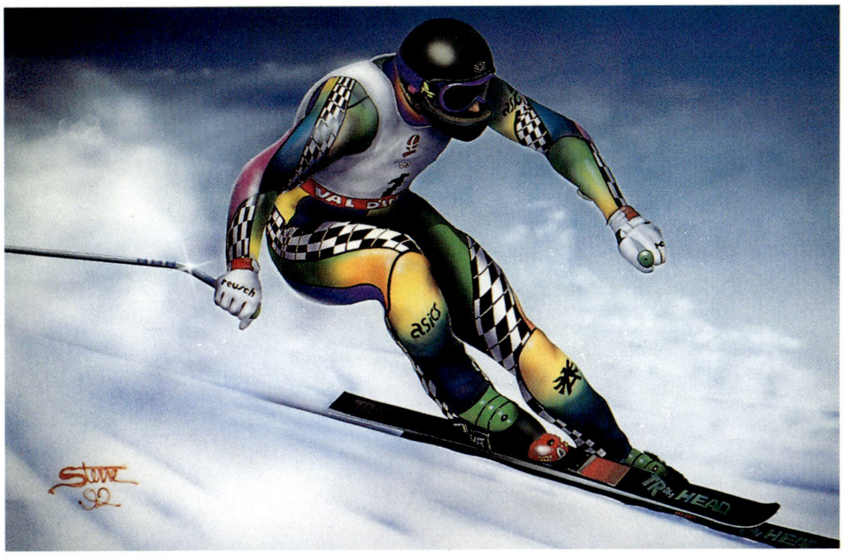
2

3
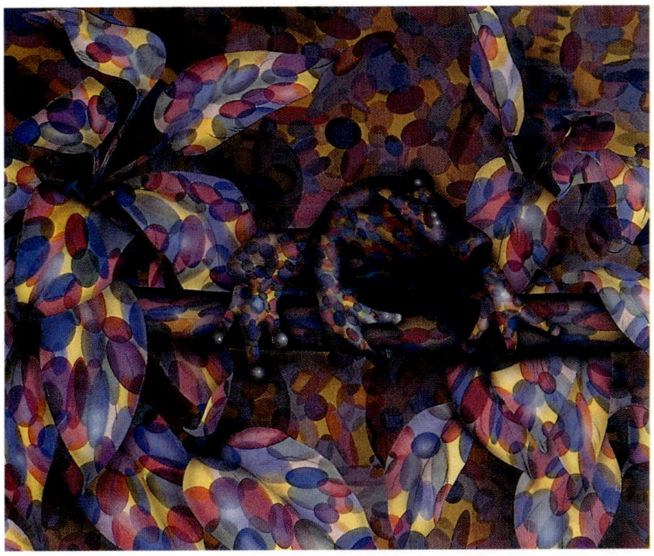

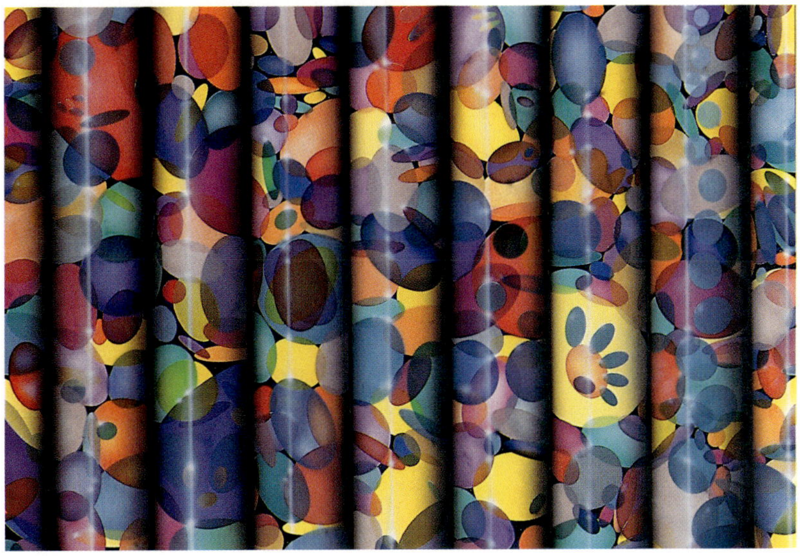
4

1
Artist William R. Stewart
Client Satellite Communications Magazine
Usage Editorial Illustration
Media Used Acrylic

2
Artist Winston Sturgen
Title Emergence from the Third World
Client Personal Creation
Usage Fine Art
Media Used Acrylic, Enamel

3
Artist Ian Suk
Title Pelagic Food Web of the Open Atlantic
Usage Technical Illustration
Media Used Acrylic

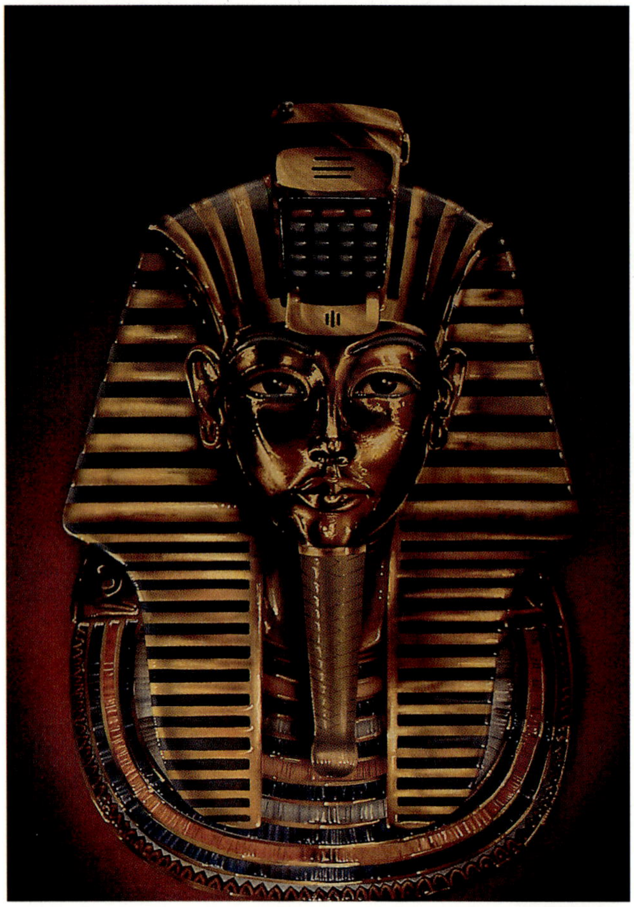

1

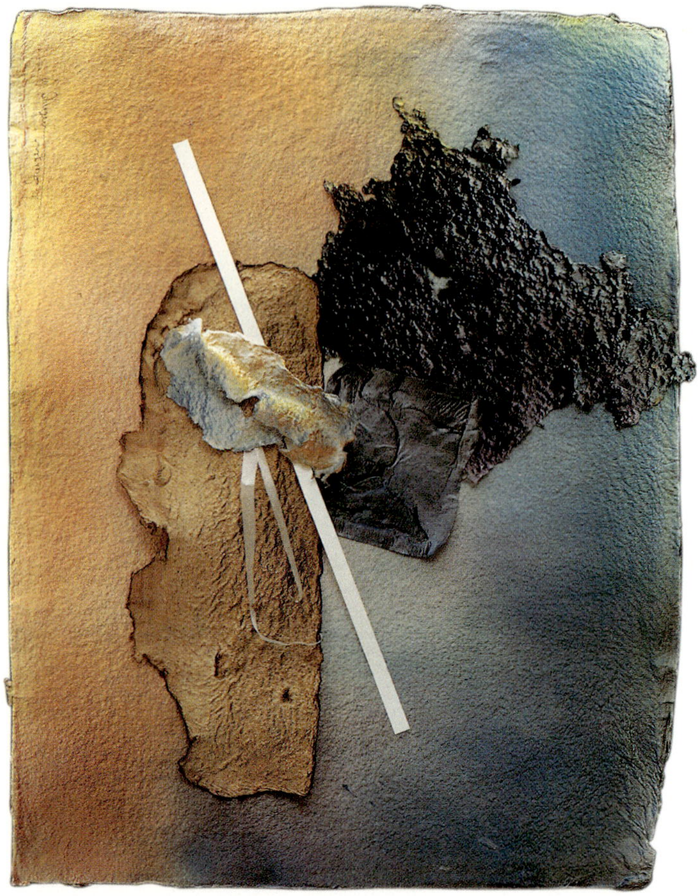

2

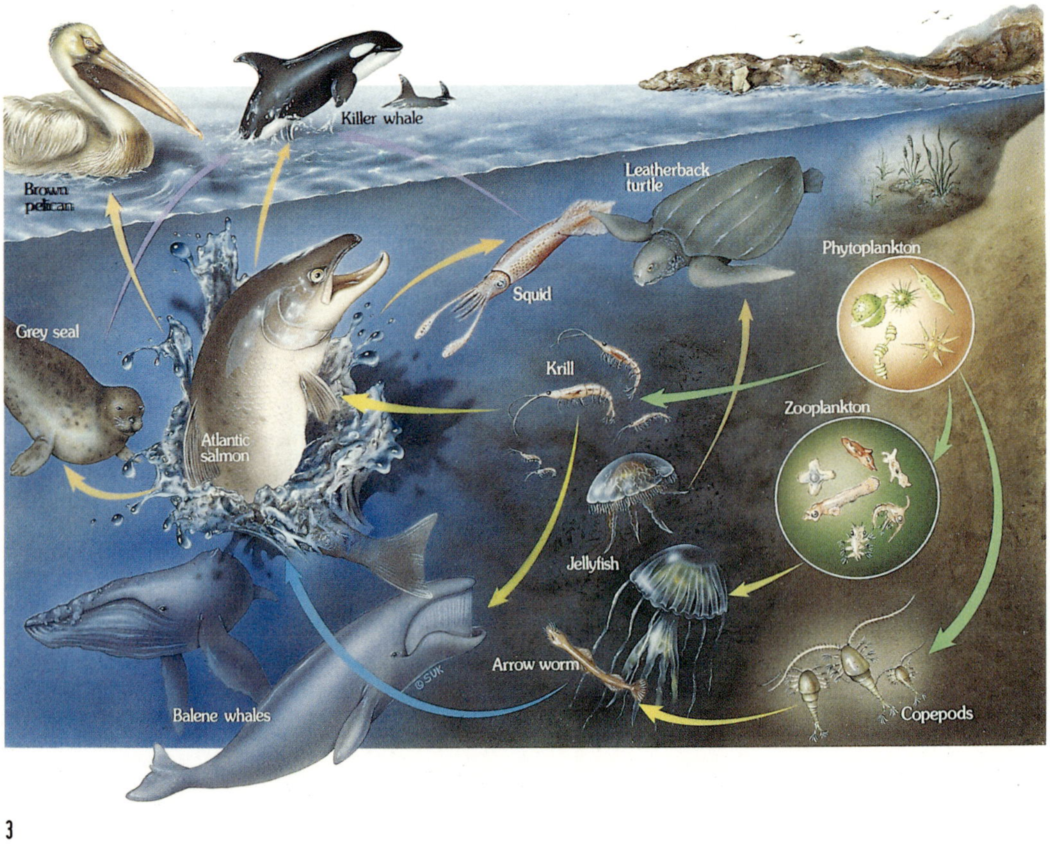

3

1
Artist Michael Takagi
Title Syvalion
Art Director Connie Viveros
Usage Commercial Art
Media Used Acrylic

2
Artist Daniel K. Tennant
Title Still Life With Cutting Board
Client Gallery Henoch
Gallery Director George H. Shechtman
Usage Fine Art
Media Used Goucahe on Museum Board

3
Artist Daniel K. Tennant
Title Still Life With Weeping Fig
Client Gallery Henoch
Art Director George H. Shechtman
Usage Fine Art
Media Used Gouache on Museum Board

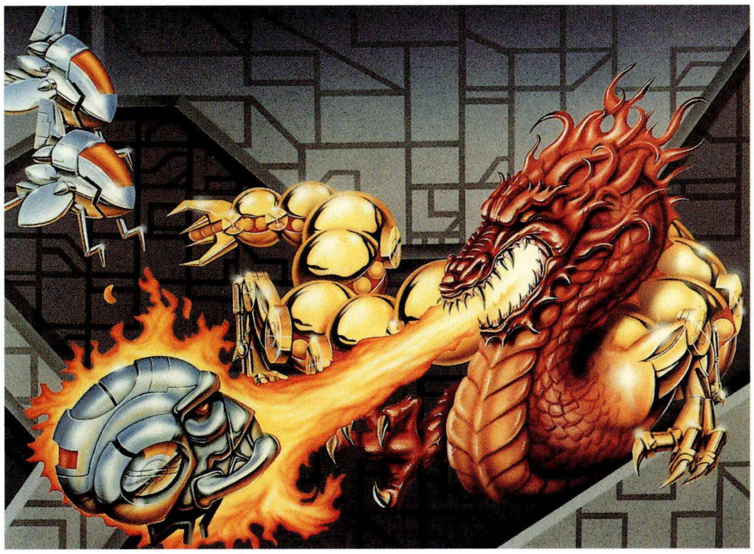

1

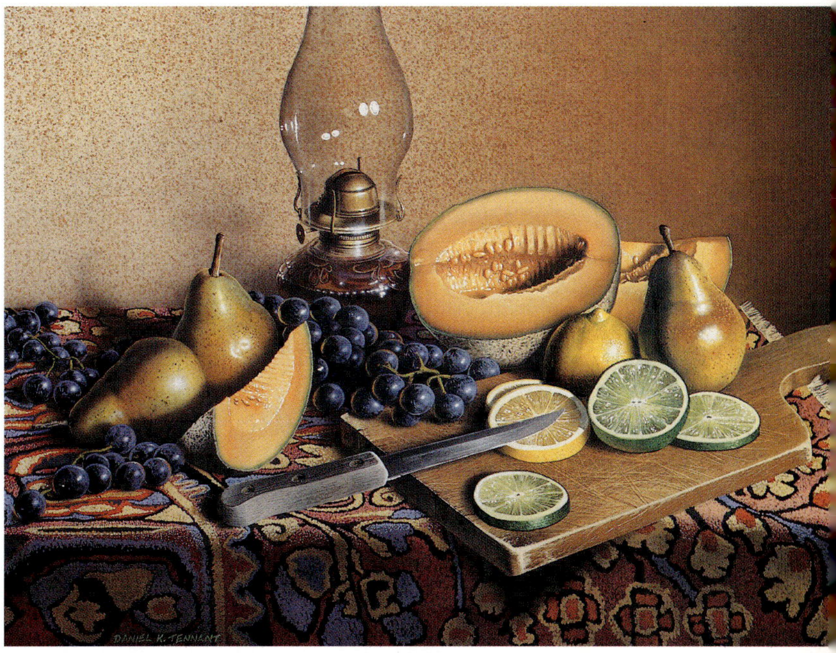

2

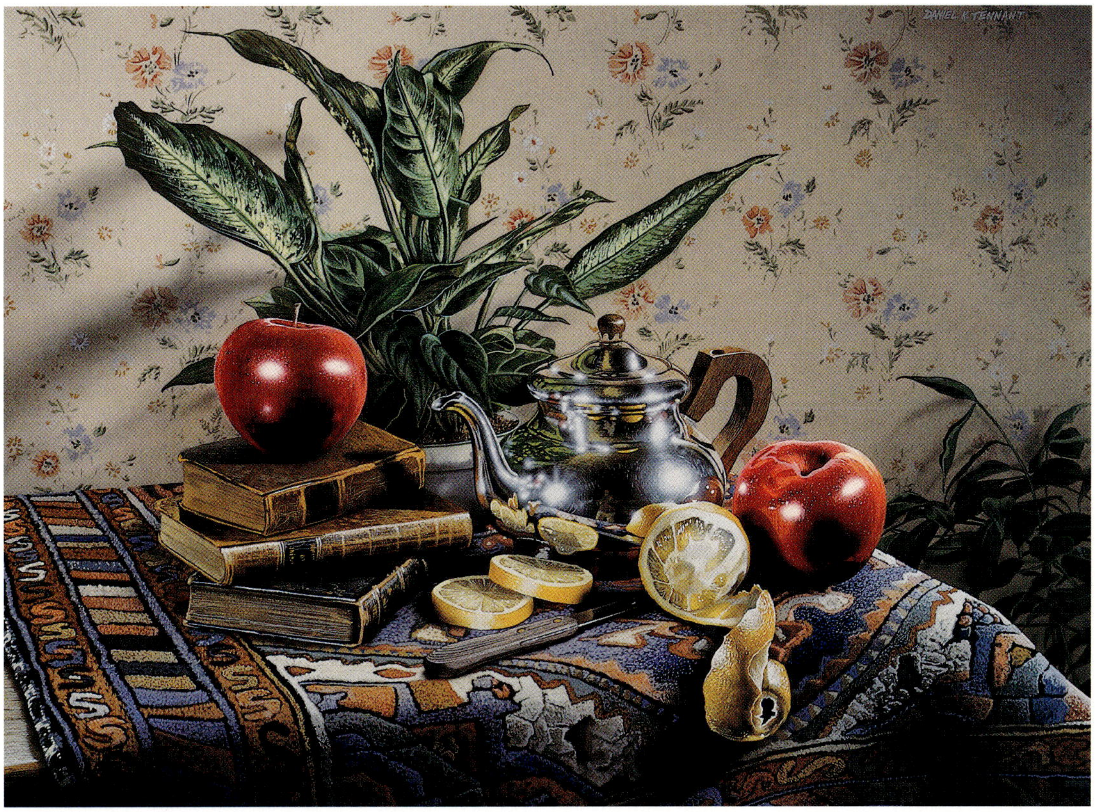

3

1
Artist Daniel K. Tennant
Title Still Life with Philodendron
Client Gallery Henoch
Gallery Director George H. Shechtman
Usage Fine Art
Media Used Gouache on Museum Board

2
Artist Daniel K. Tennant
Title Still Life with Blue Cloth
Client Gallery Henoch
Gallery Director George H. Shechtman
Usage Fine Art
Media Used Gouache on Museum Board

3
Artist Daniel K. Tennant
Title Still Life in a Book Shop
Client Gallery Henoch
Gallery Director George H. Shechtman
Usage Fine Art
Media Used Gouache on Museum Board

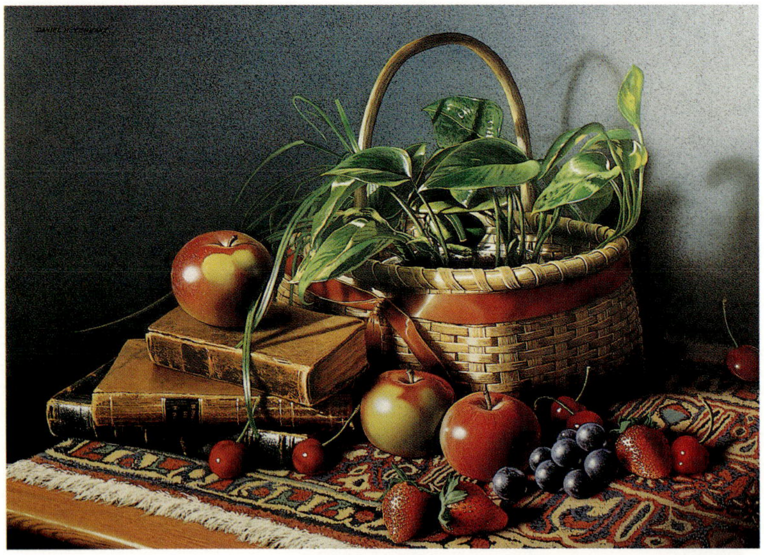

1

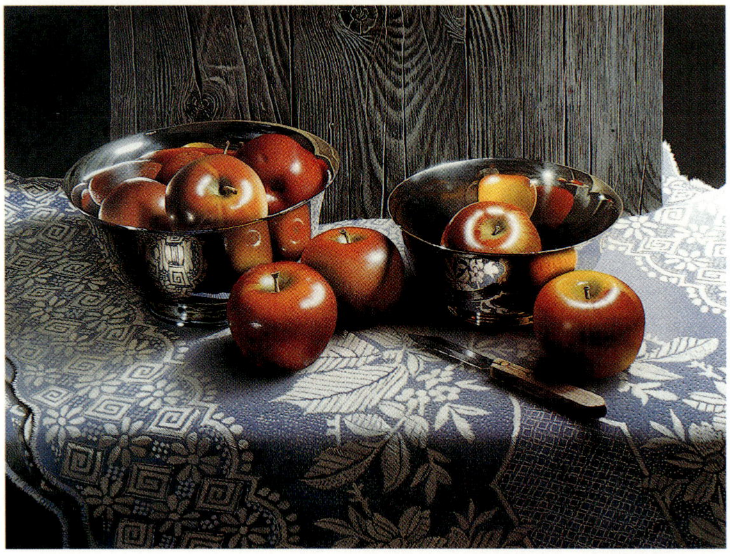

2

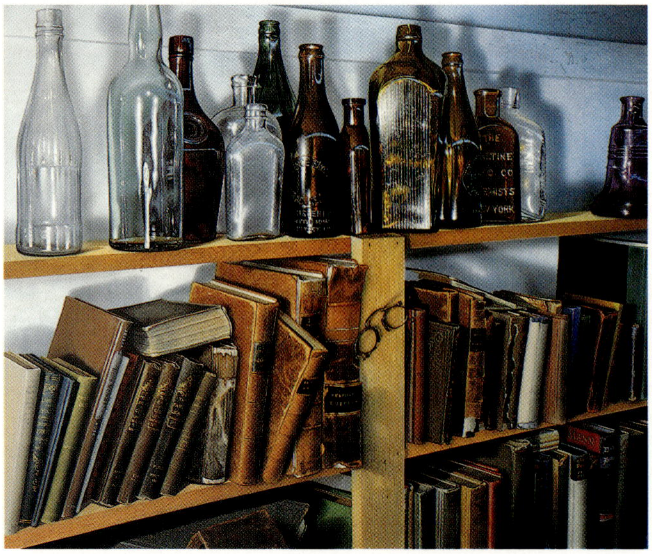

3

1
Artist Daniel K. Tennant
Title Still Life with Sundrops
Client Gallery Henoch
Gallery Director George H. Shechtman
Usage Fine Art
Media Used Gouache on Museum Board

2
Artist Daniel K. Tennant
Title Still Life with Open Book
Client Gallery Henoch
Gallery Director George H. Shechtman
Usage Fine Art
Media Used Gouache on Museum Board

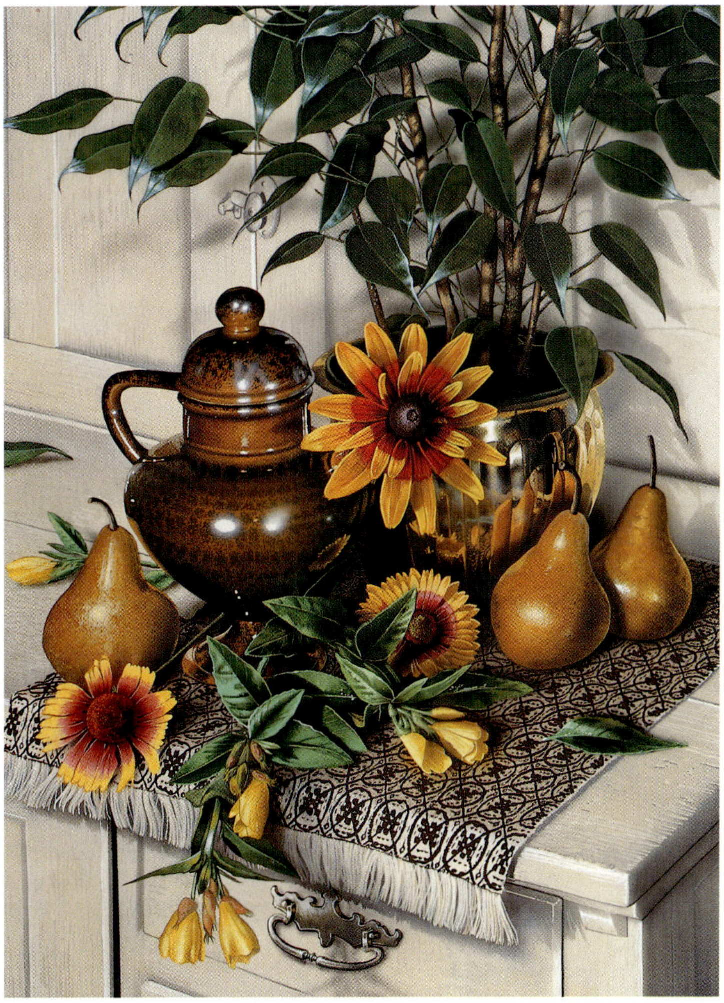
1

2
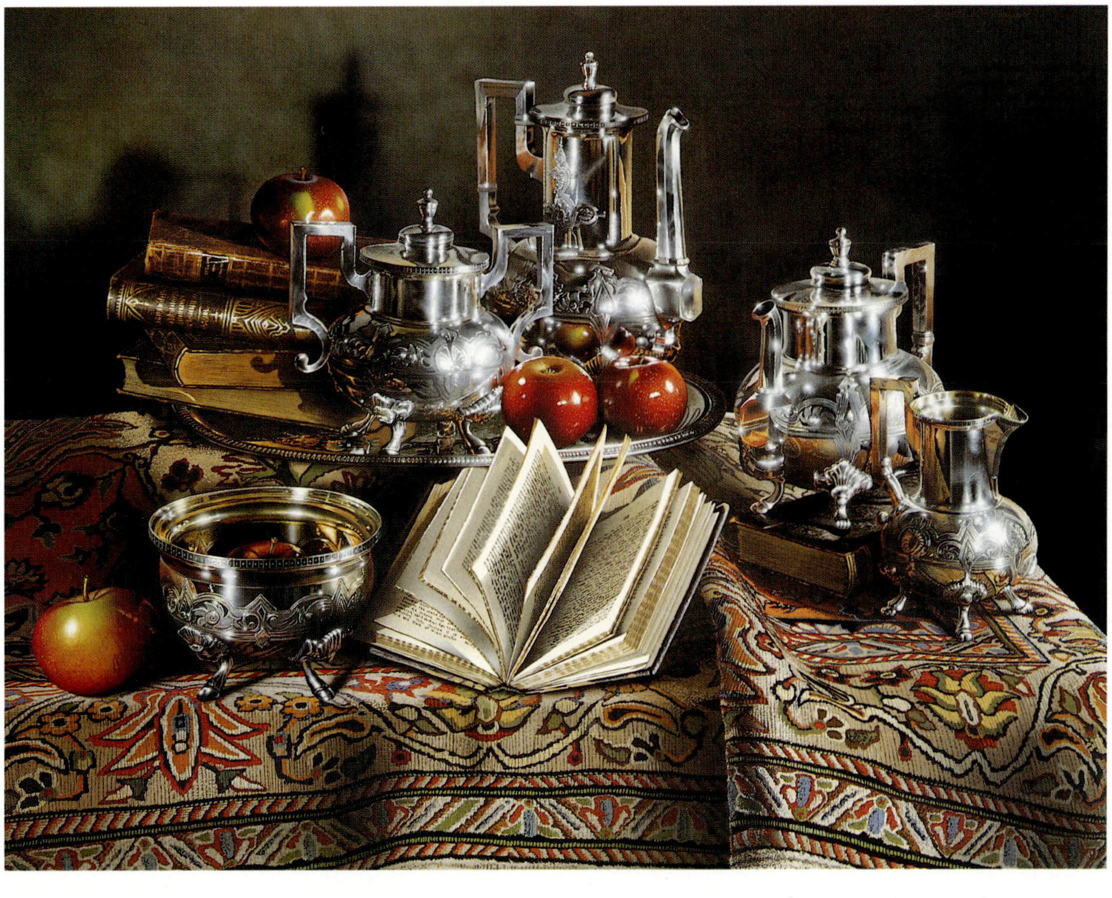

1
Artist Daniel K. Tennant
Title Still Life with Marble Table
Client Gallery Henoch
Gallery Director George H. Shechtman
Usage Fine Art
Media Used Gouache on Museum Board

2
Artist Daniel K. Tennant
Title Still Life with Strawberries
Client Gallery Henoch
Gallery Director George H. Shechtman
Usage Fine Art
Media Used Gouache on Museum Board

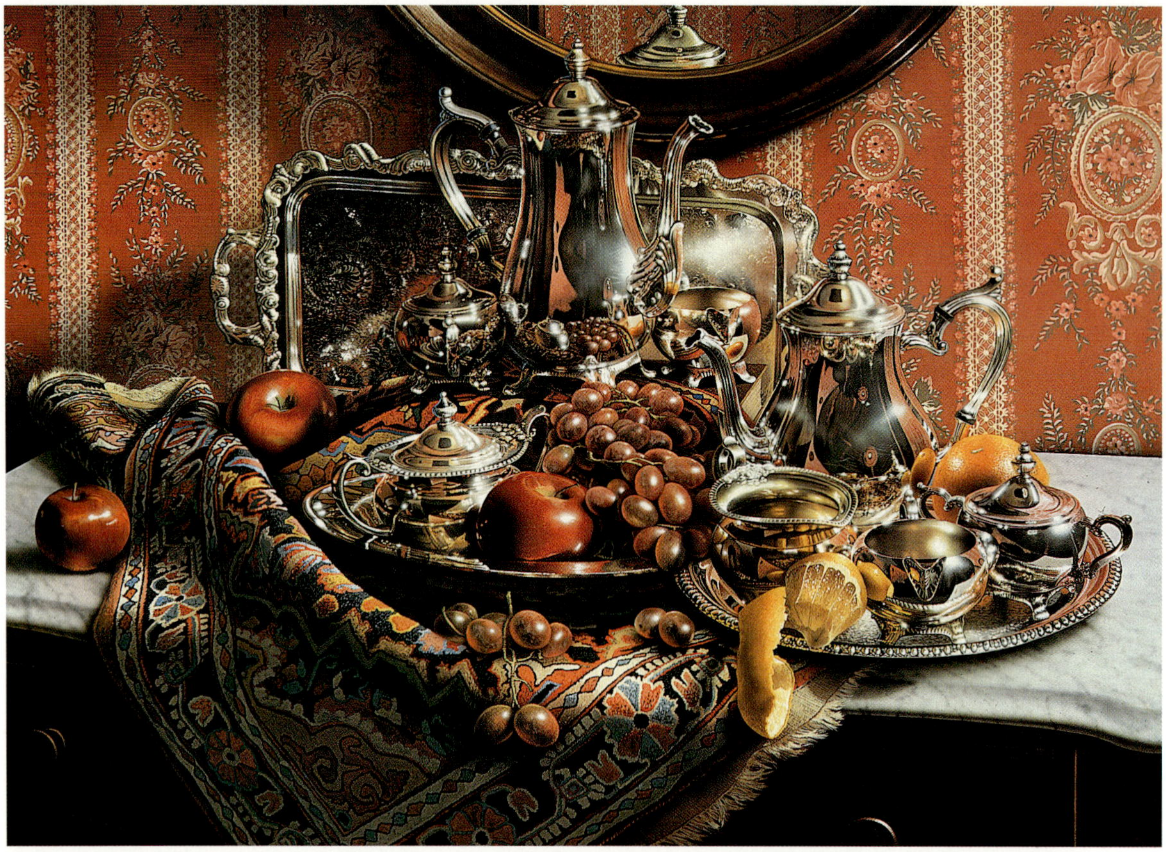

1

2

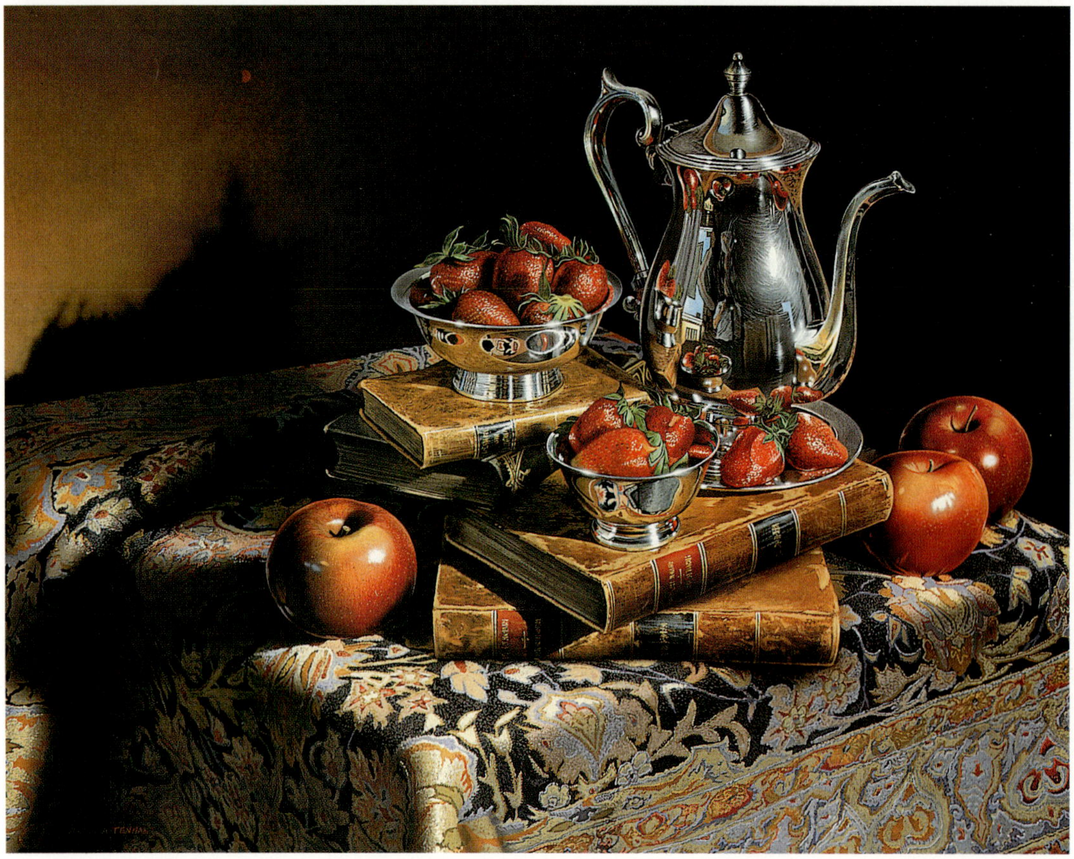

1
Artist John E. Thies
Title Senior Art Specialist
Art Director John E. Thies
Usage Commercial Art
Media Used Acrylic

2
Artist John E. Thies
Title Senior Art Specialist
Art Director John E. Thies
Usage Commercial Art
Media Used Acrylic

3
Artist John E. Thies
Title Senior Art Specialist
Client AT&T Microelectronics
Usage Technical Illustration
Media Used Comart Dyes

4
Artist John E. Thies
Title Senior Art Specialist
Client AT&T Marketing
Usage Technical Illustration
Media Used Windsor & Newton Designer's, Gouache

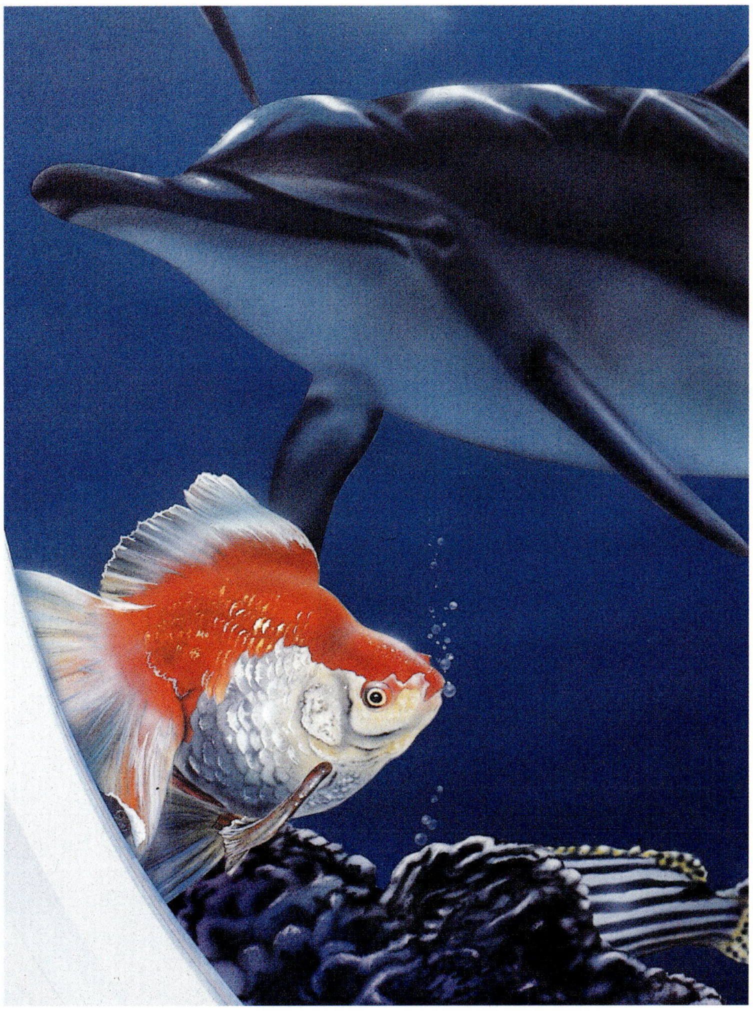
1

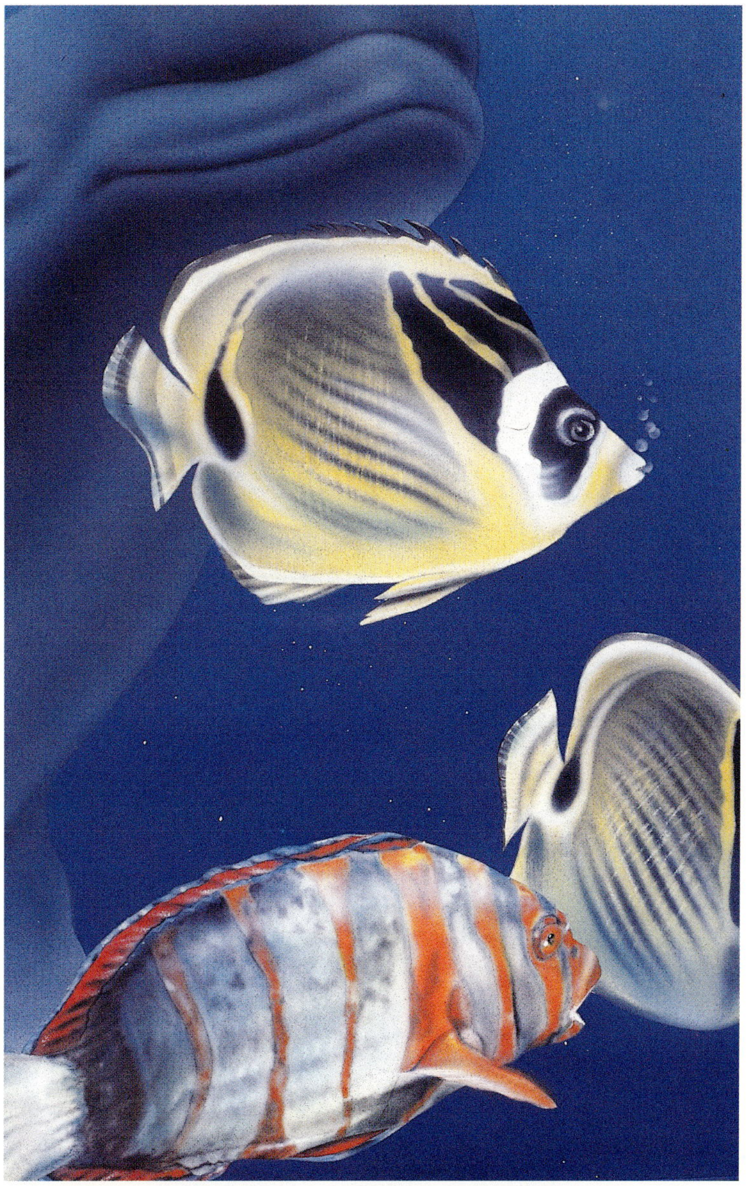
2

3
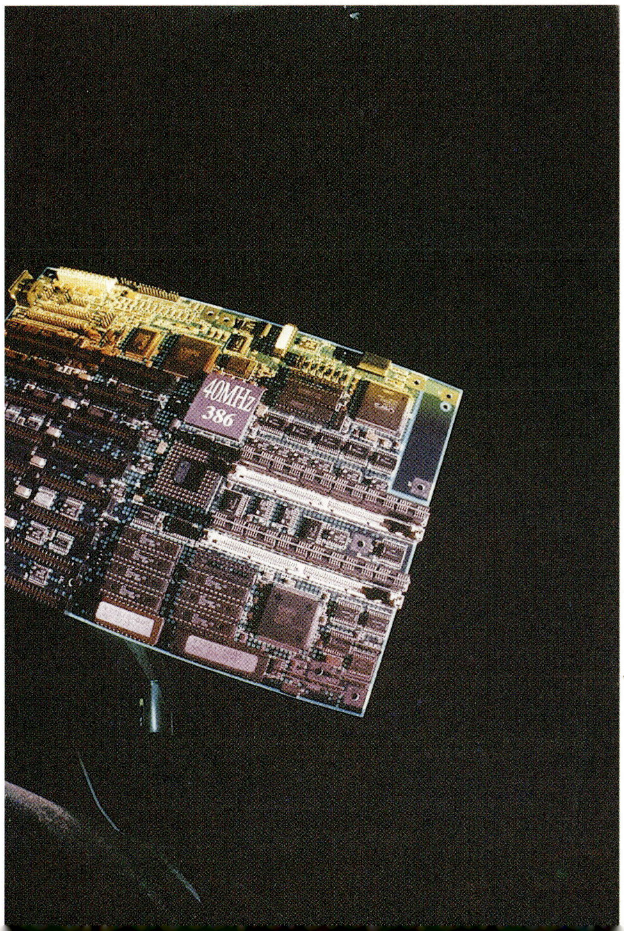

4
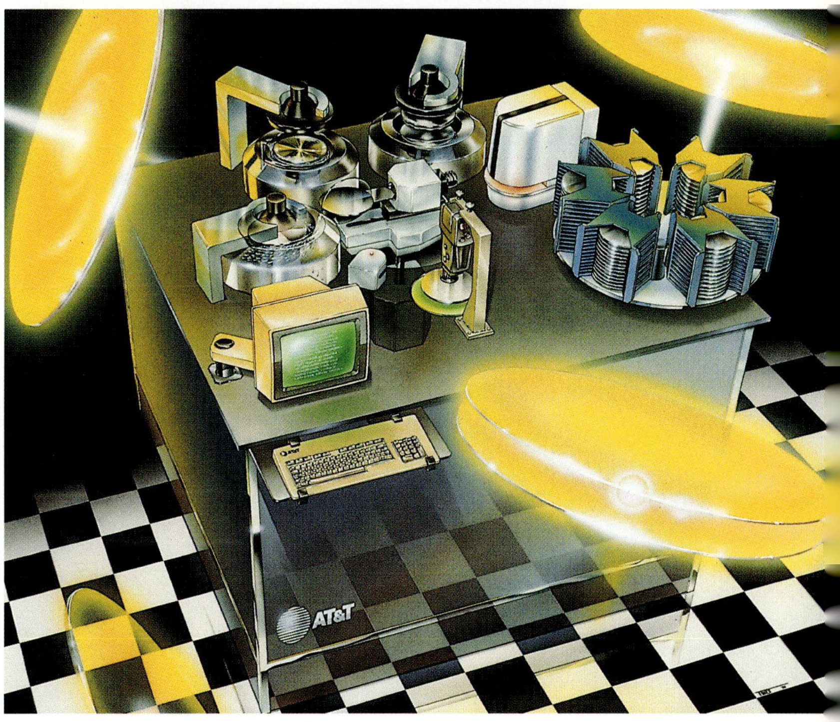

1
Artist John E. Thies
Title Senior Art Specialist
Client AT&T Microelectronics
Usage Photo-Retouching
Media Used Comart Opaque Dyes, Acrylic

2
Artist John E. Thies
Title Senior Art Specialist
Client AT&T Microelectronics
Usage Signs/Murals
Media Used Comart Dyes

3
Artist John E. Thies
Title Senior Art Specialist
Client AT&T Microelectronics Toolroom
Media Used Comart Dyes and Acrylics

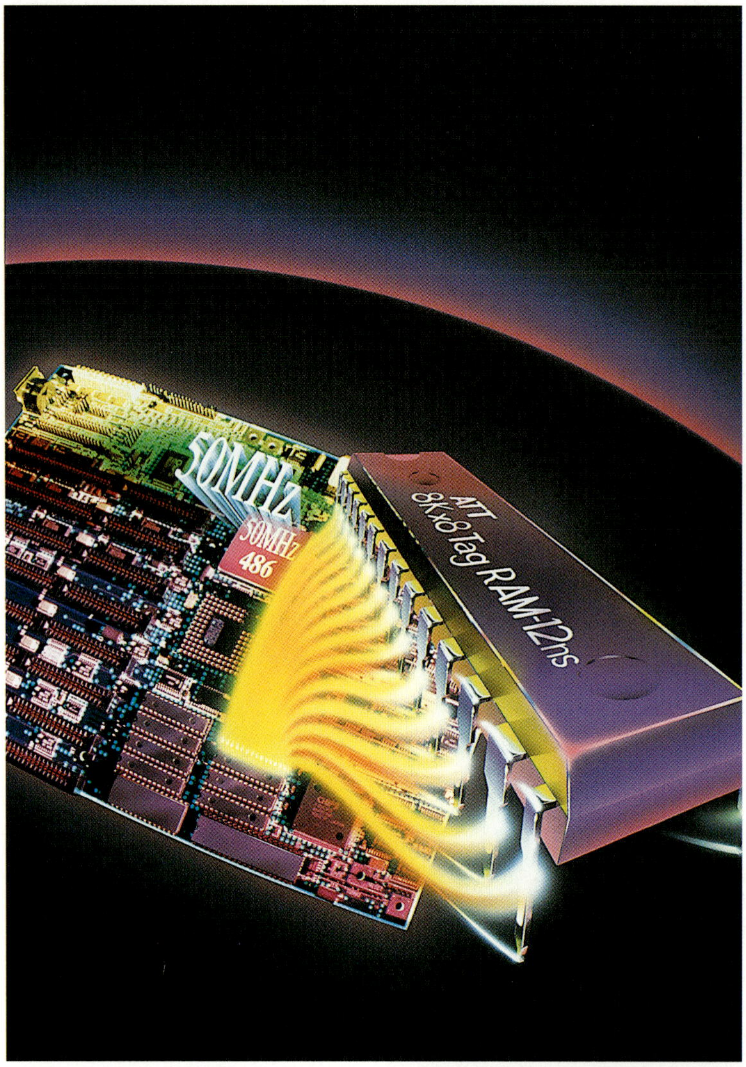

1

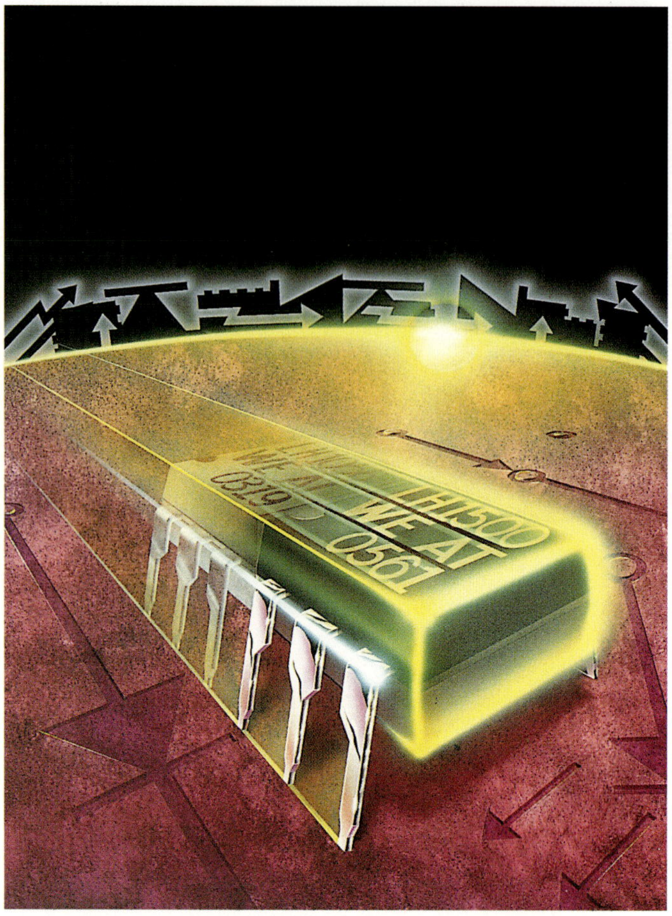

2

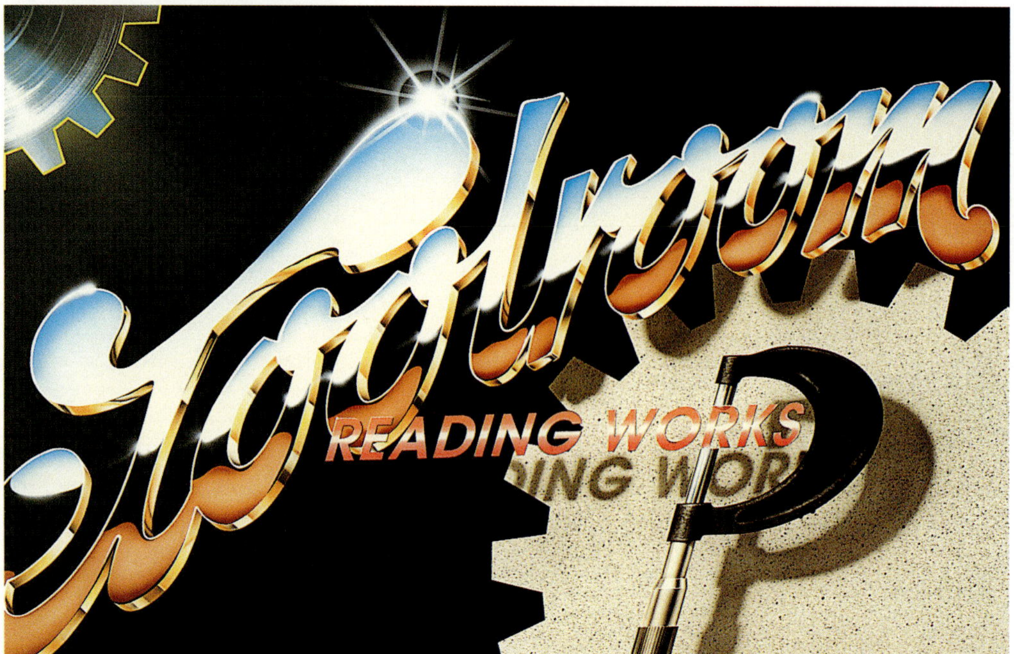

3

1
Artist Carlos Torres
Title Theatersports
Client Games Magazine
Art Director Rick Stark
Usage Editorial Illustration
Media Used Acrylic

2
Artist Carlos Torres
Title Mike Tyson
Usage Promo Piece - RSVP; N.Y. Society of Illustrators
Media Used Acrylic on Illustration Board

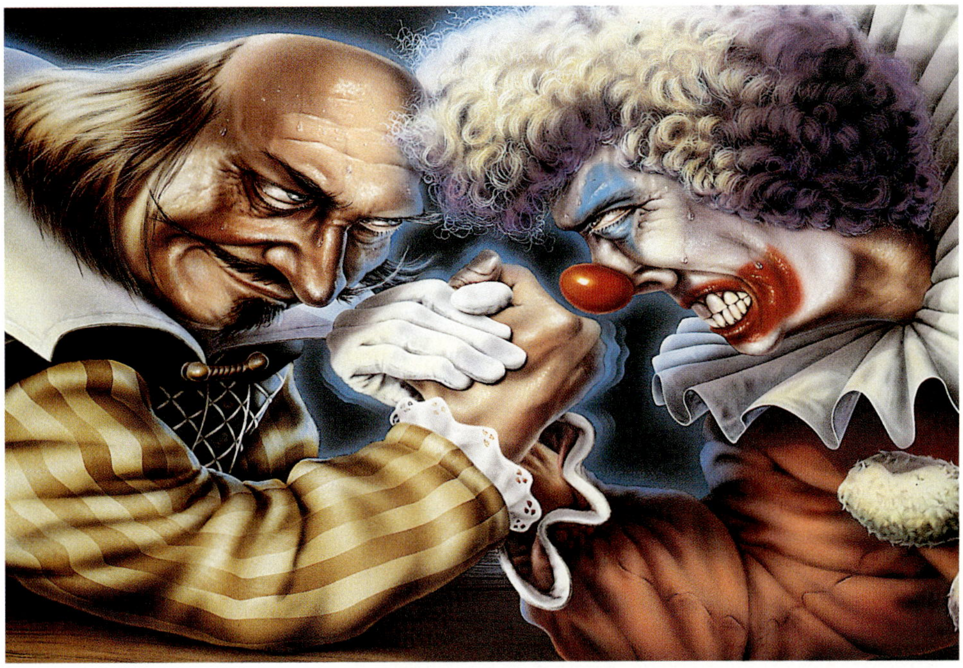

1

2

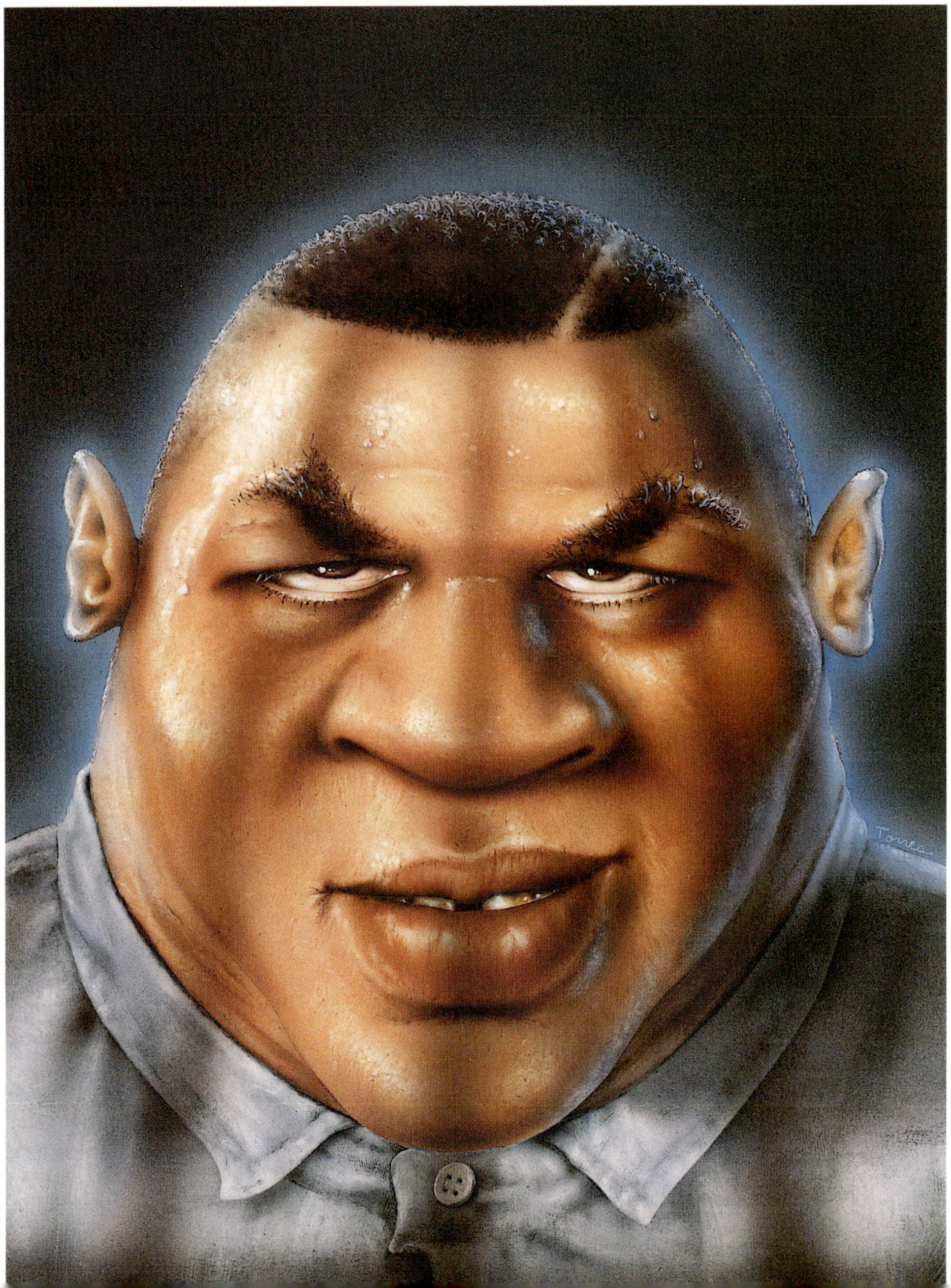

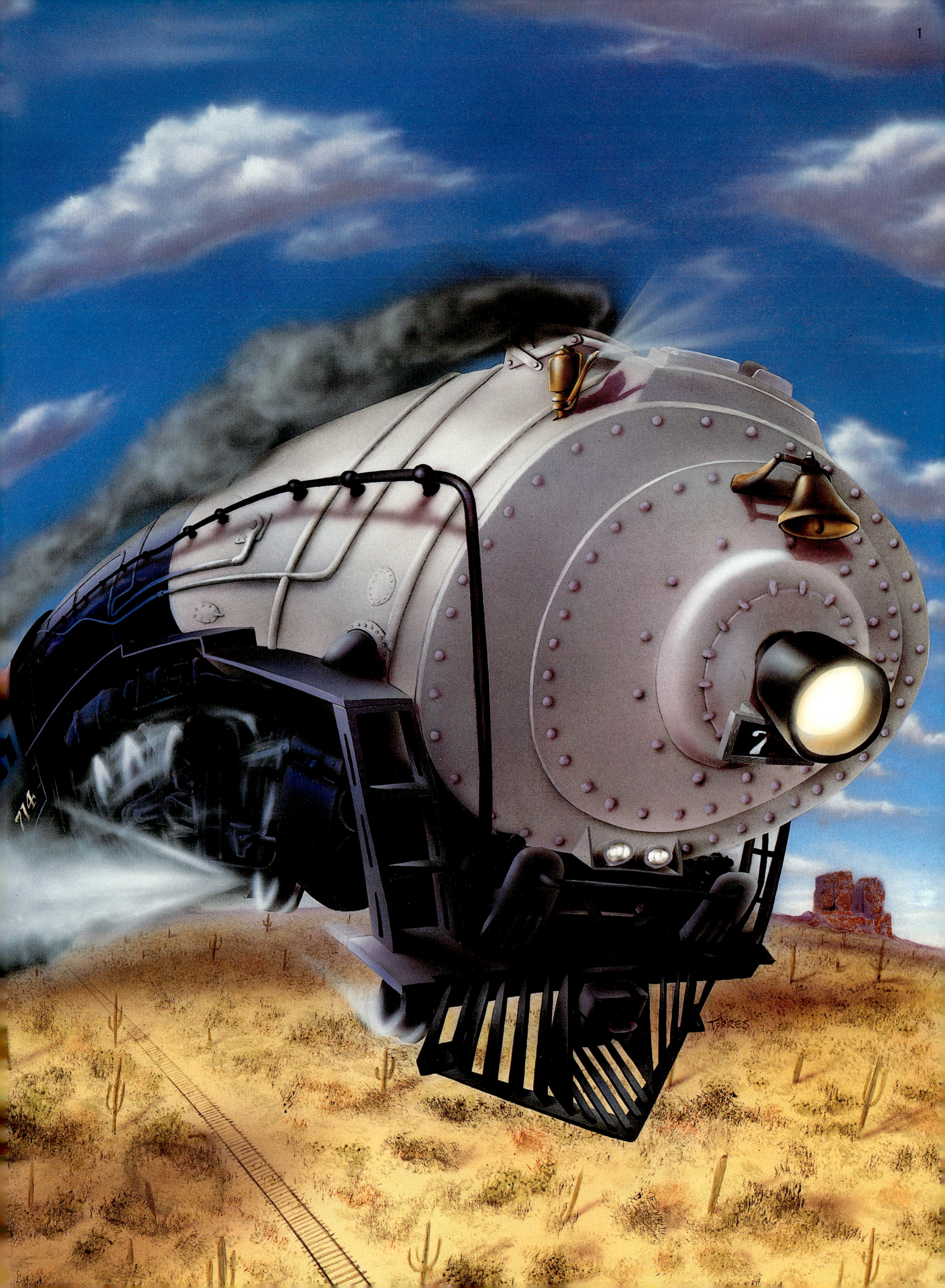
714
TORRES

1
Artist Carlos Torres
Title 4-8-4
Usage Promotional
Media Used Acrylic on Illustration Board

2
Artist Carlos Torres
Title Bill
Usage Promotional
Media Used Acrylic on Illustration Board

3
Artist Jimmie Turner
Title Miller Lite Beer
Art Director Jimmie Turner
Usage Commercial Art
Media Used Gouache

4
Artist Mark Villarta
Title I Spoke to God
Usage Student Art
Media Used Comart

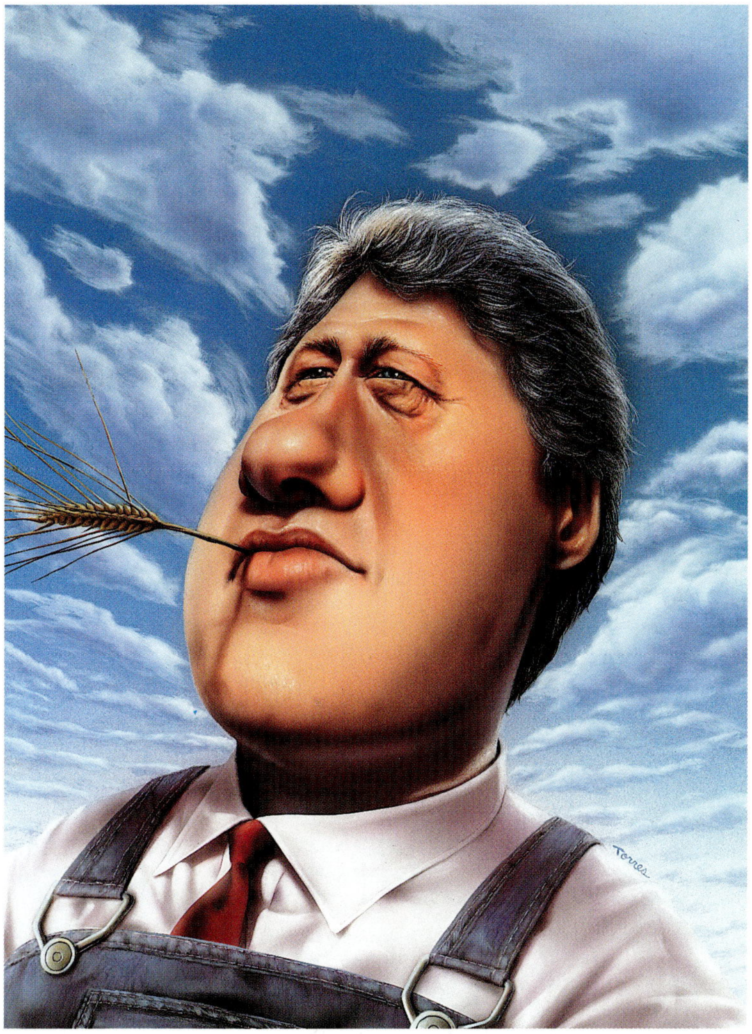

2

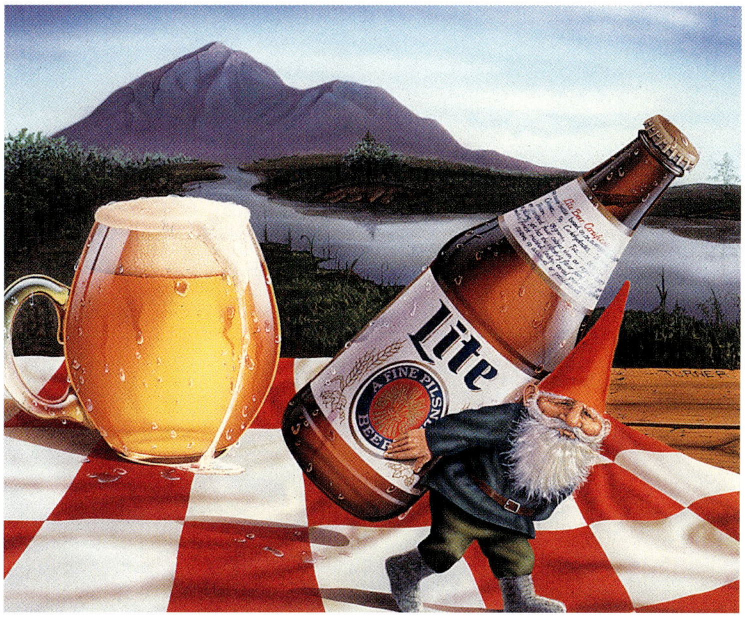

3

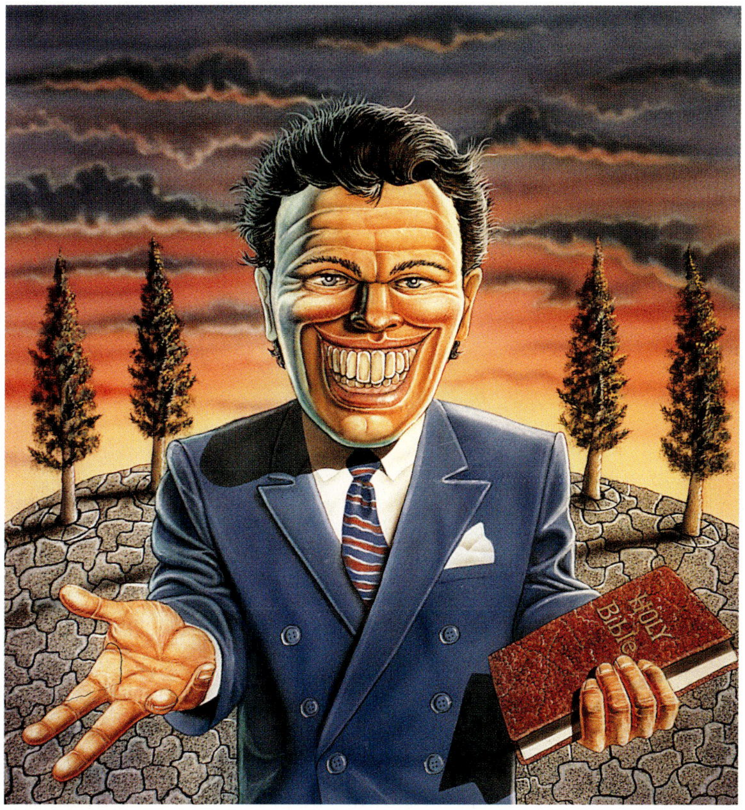

4

1
Artist Patrick C. Wanebo
Client Patrick C. Wanebo
Art Director Patrick Wanebo
Usage Student Art
Media Used Acrylic

2
Artist Tobie Warren
Title Bogie
Client Joe Kernan
Usage Fine Art
Media Used Acrylic

3
Artist Tobie Warren
Title Bono
Client Sue Donahue
Usage Fine Art
Media Used Acrylic

4
Artist Tobie Warren
Title Steven Tyler
Client Garry Willets
Usage Fine Art
Media Used Acrylic

1
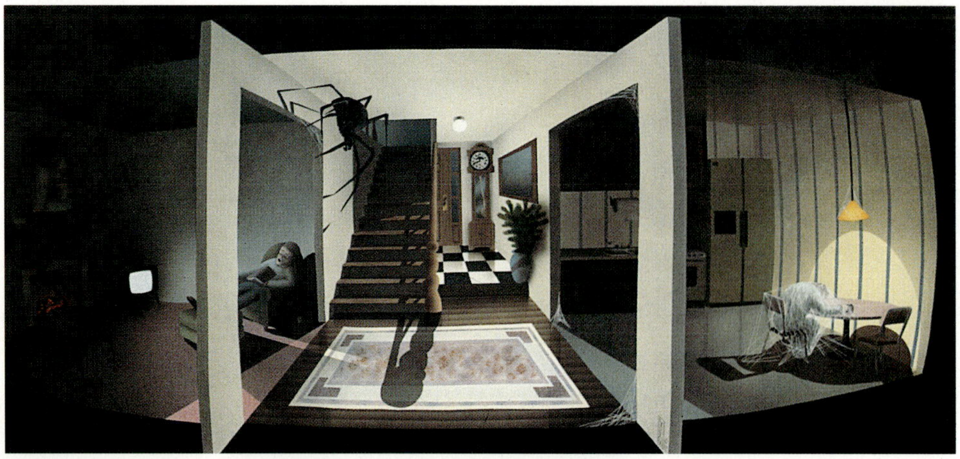

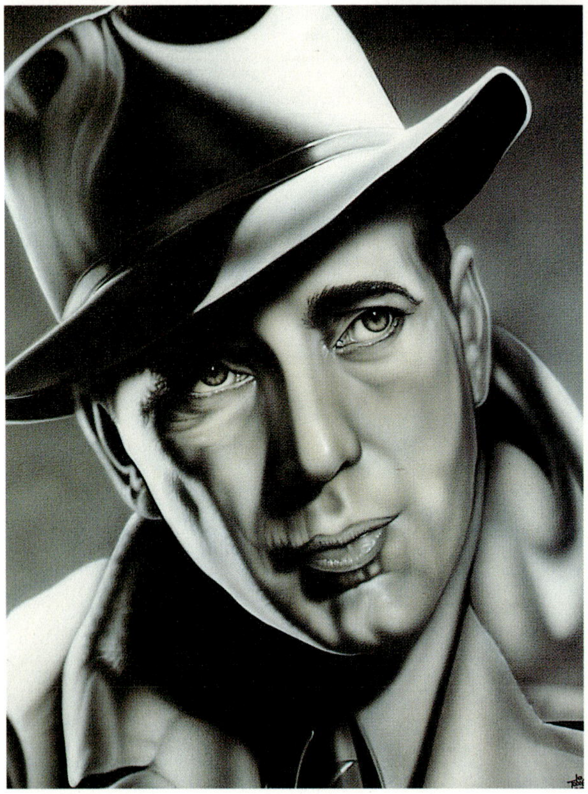

2

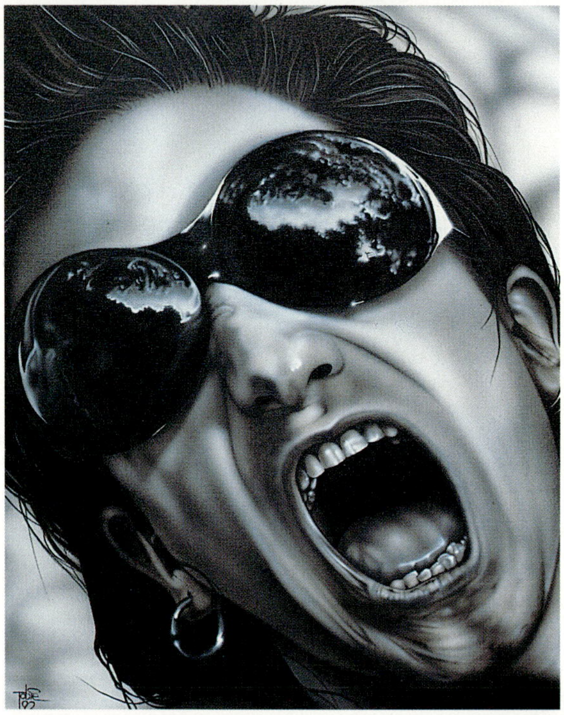

3

4
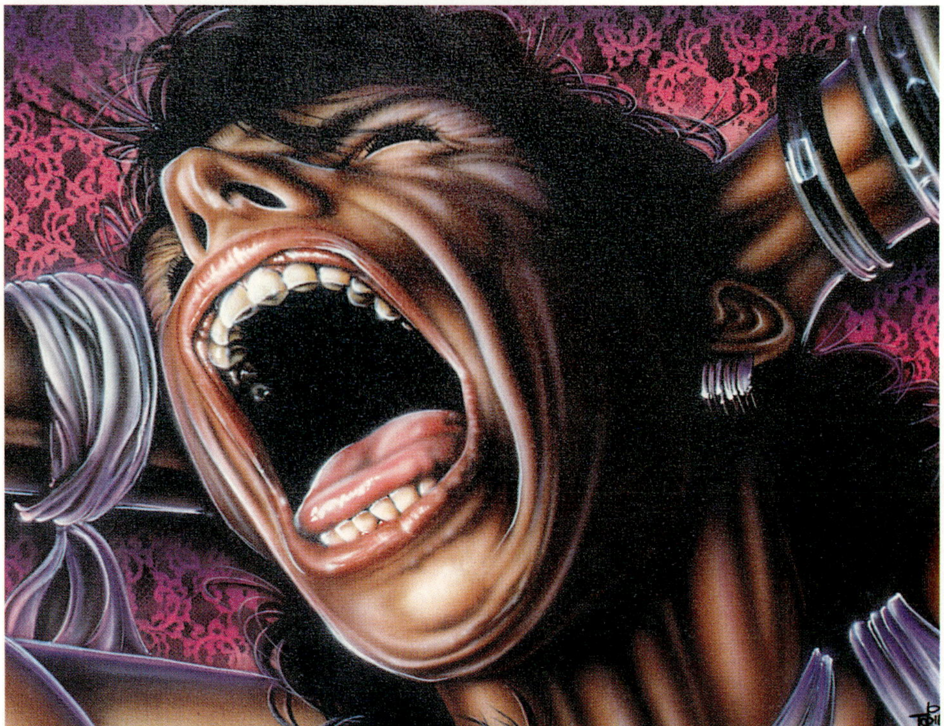

1
Artist Wayne Watford
Client Long Haymes & Carr/RJR
Art Director Inga Borgmeyer
Usage Poster
Media Used Acrylic

2
Artist Wayne Watford
Client Busch Creative
Art Director Mike Ivester
Usage Poster
Media Used Acrylic

3
Artist Wayne Watford
Usage Self Promotion
Media Used Acrylic

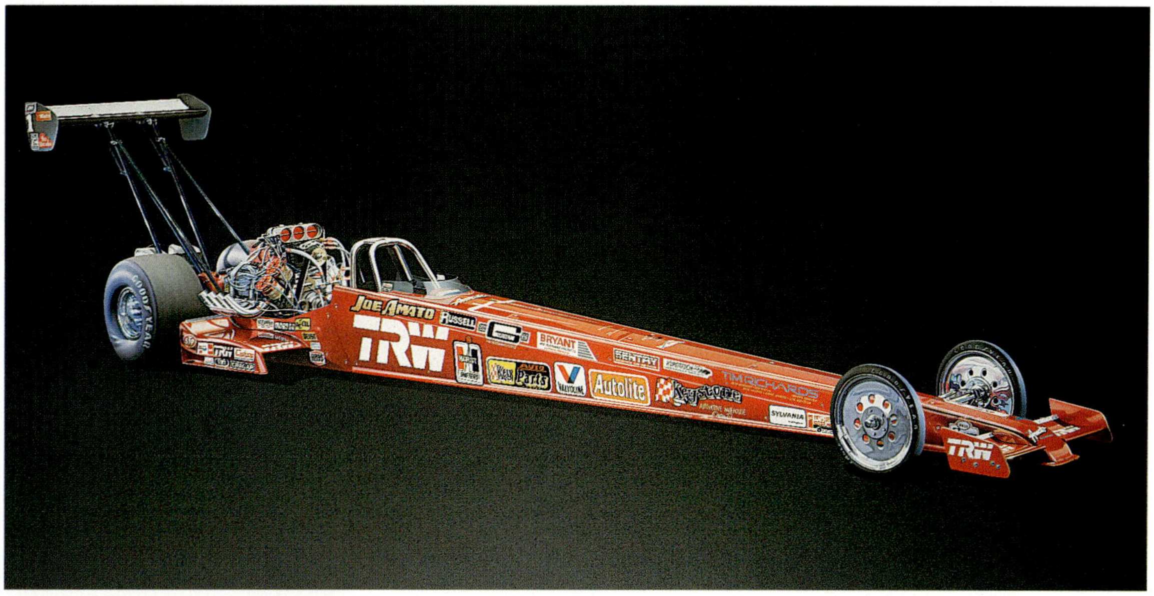

1

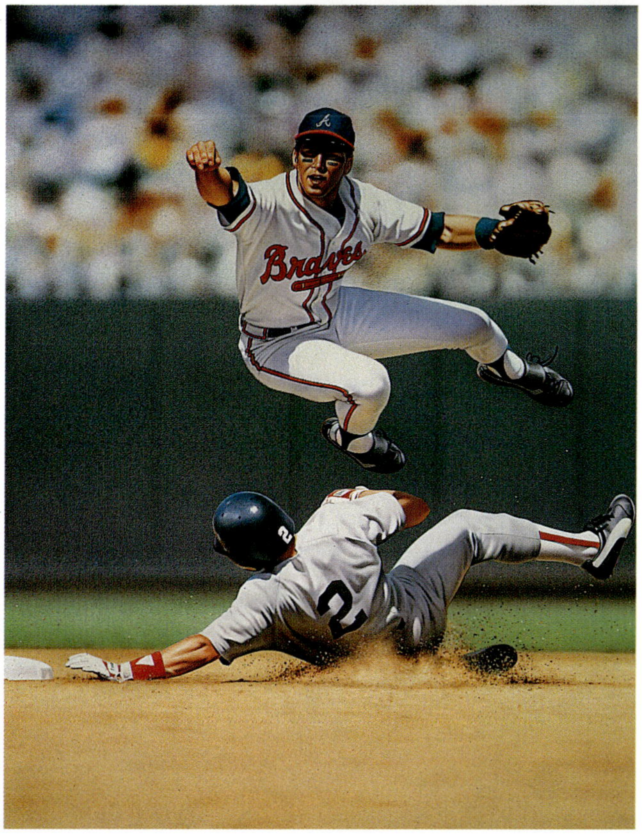

2

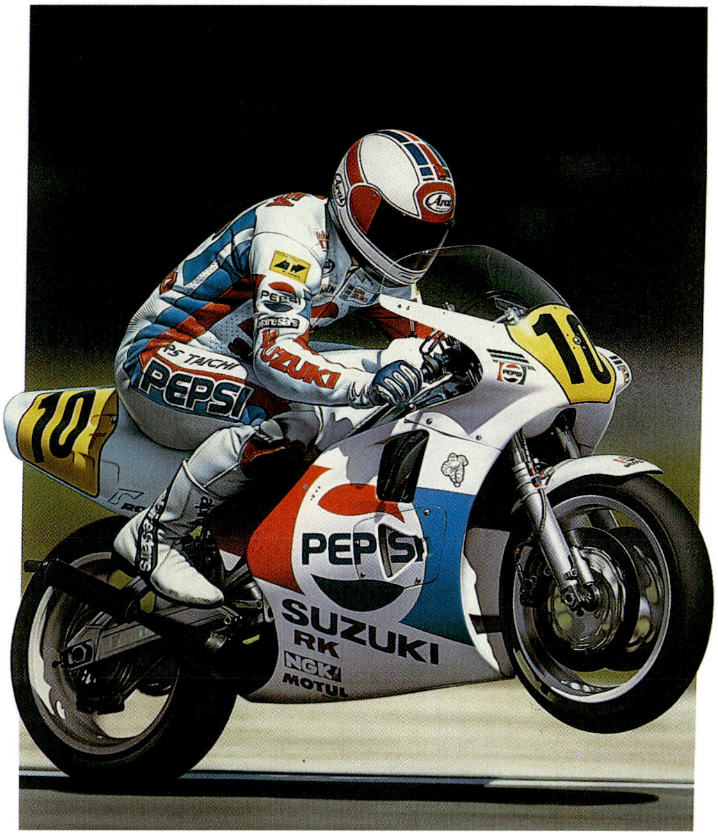

3

1
Artist Wayne Watford
Client NFL Properties
Art Director Dave Boss
Usage Poster
Media Used Acrylic

2
Artist Wayne Watford
Client Foote Cone & Belding / Orion Pictures
Art Director Steve Sonnenleiter
Usage Poster
Media Used Acrylic

3
Artist Tom Watters
Title Classroom Rules
Client BE
Usage Classroom Headers
Media Used Pen & Ink, Gouache

4
Artist Tom Watters
Title Super Sour Crackling Gum
Client Zeta
Usage Bubble Gum Package
Media Used Pen & Ink, Comart

1

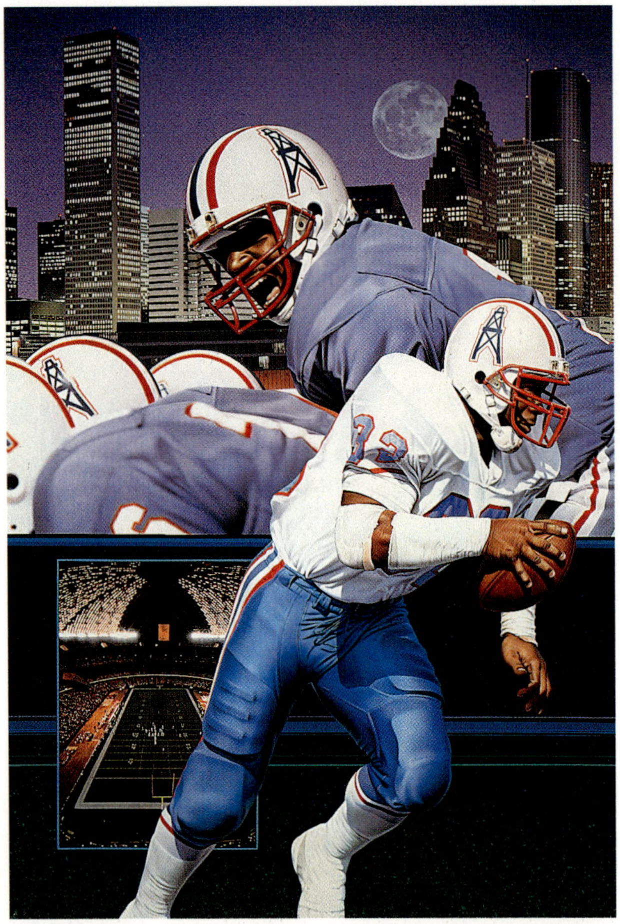

2

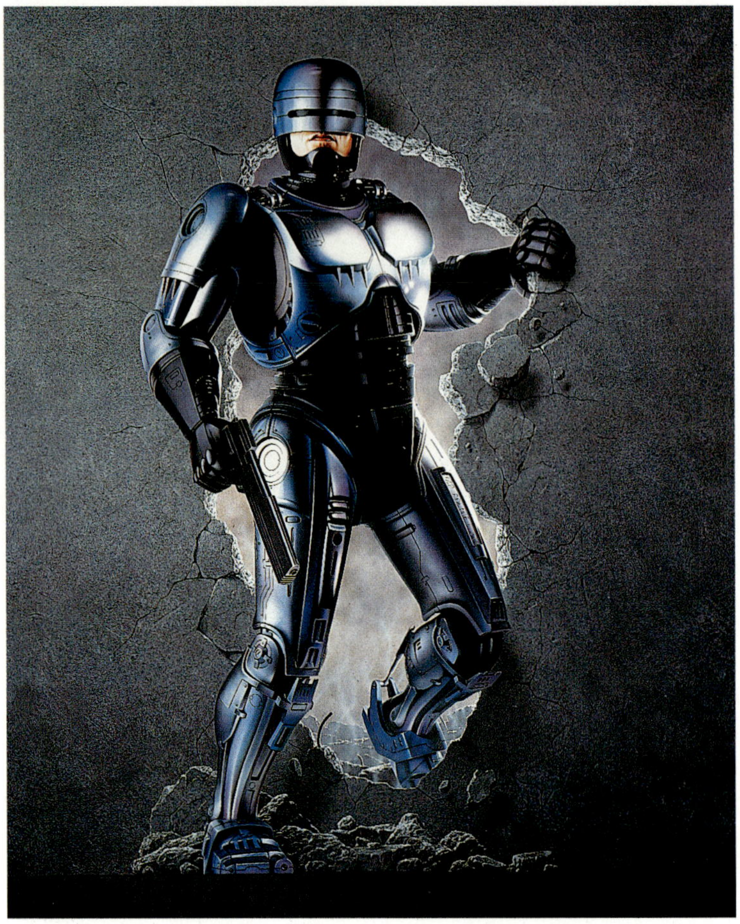

3

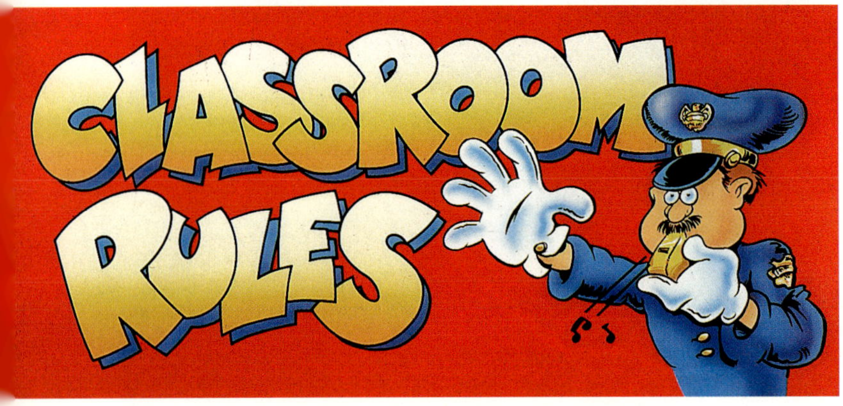

4

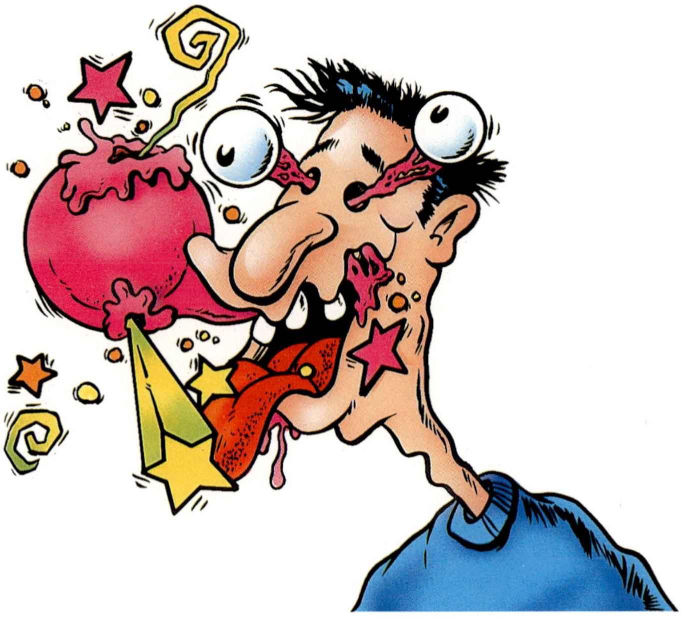

1
Artist Tom Watters
Title Trouble Trolls Logo
Client Classic Cards
Usage Trading Cards Logo
Media Used Pen & Ink, Gouache

2
Artist Tom Watters
Title Gone Fishin
Client Fasco
Usage Stationery Line
Media Used Comart, Designer's Gouache

3
Artist Michael E. Weaver
Title Crane Game Part I
Client Michael E. Weaver
Usage Commercial Art
Media Used Acrylic

4
Artist Michael E. Weaver
Title Arizona Joe
Client Michael E. Weaver
Usage Commercial Art
Media Used Acrylic

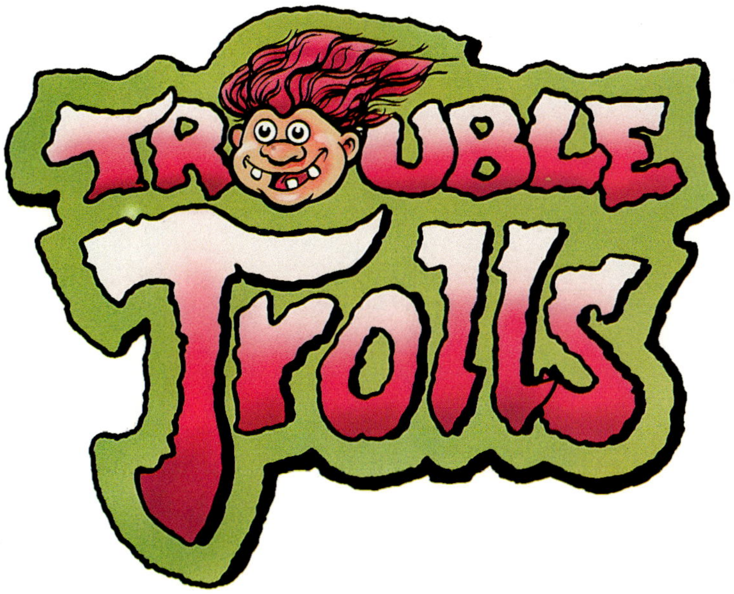

1

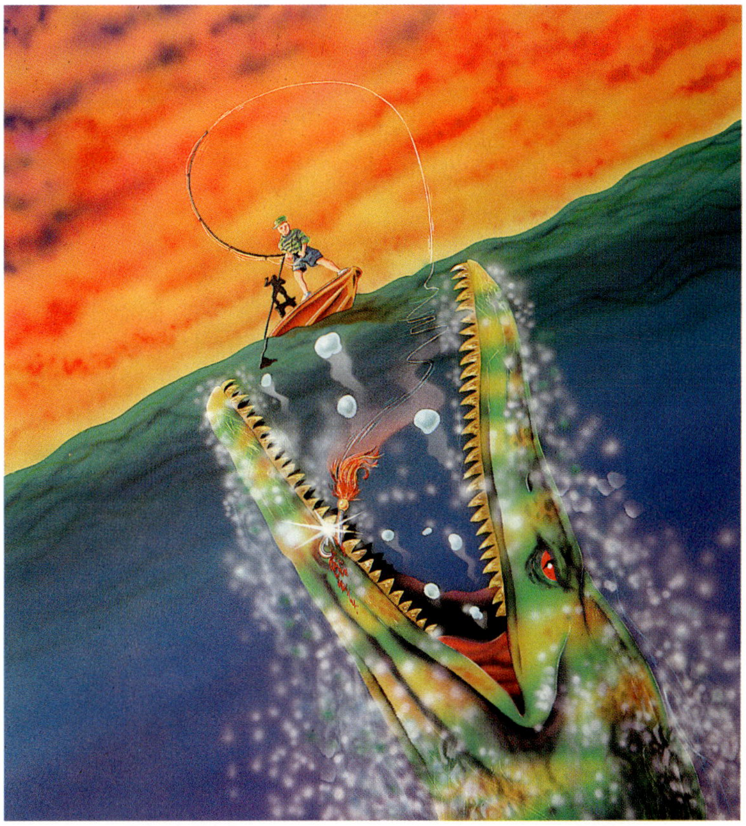
2

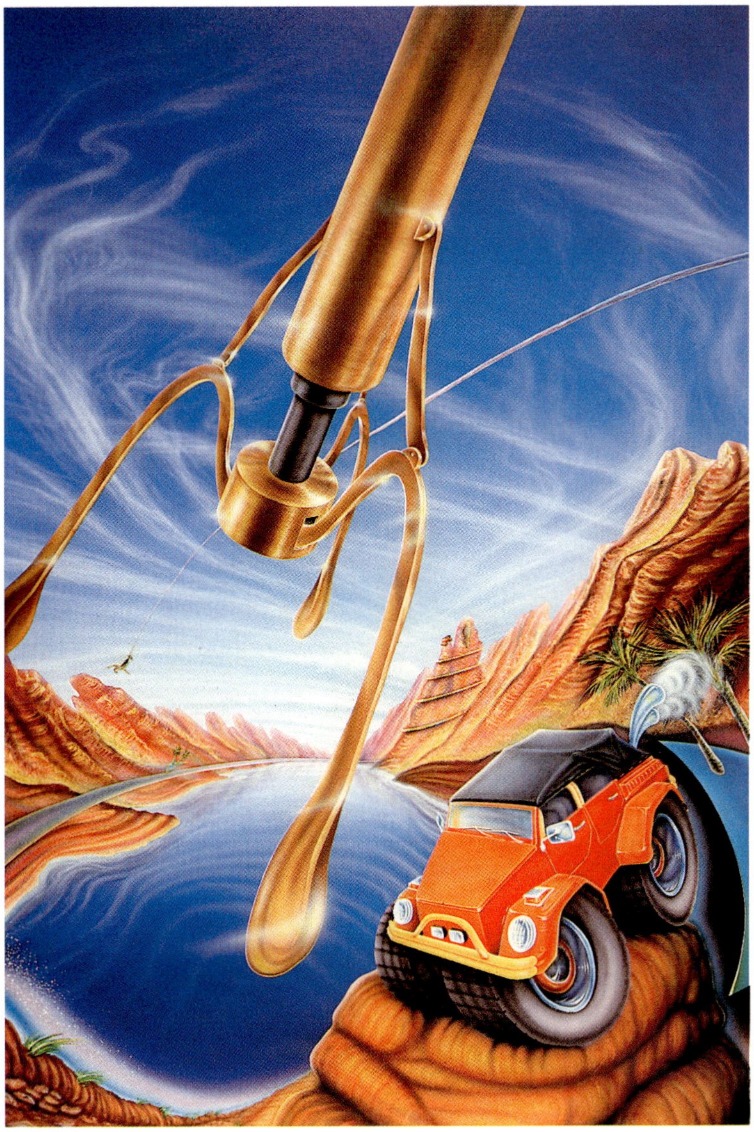
3

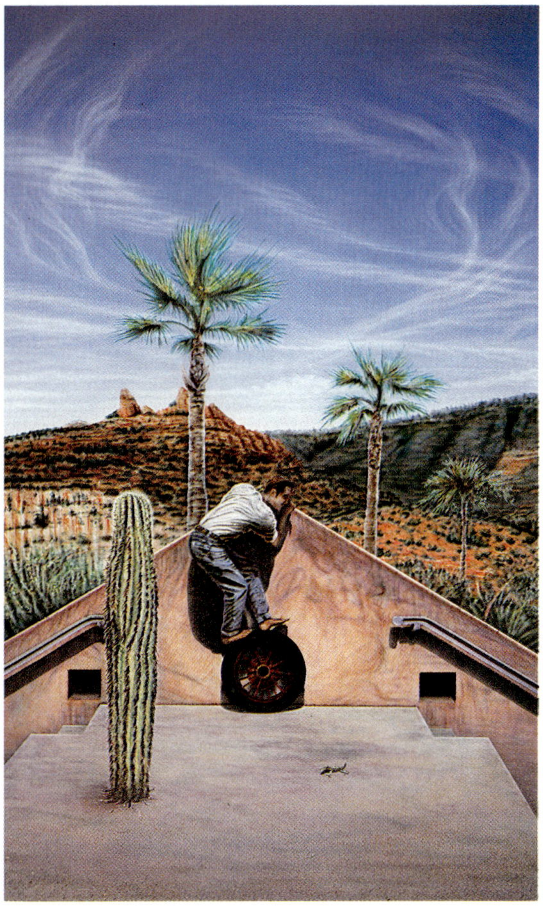
4

1
Artist Ken Westphal
Title Lethal Chickens
Client Sanofi Animal Health
Art Director John Baker
Usage Commercial Art
Media Used Liquid Acrylic

2
Artist Ken Westphal
Title I'm all ears, America
Client People Magazine
Art Director Hillie Pitzer
Usage Editorial Illustration
Media Used Liquid Acrylic

3
Artist Ken Westphal
Title Texas Chester
Client Cheetos
Art Director Brad Morgan
Usage Commercial Art
Media Used Liquid Acrylic

4
Artist June Workman
Title The Dawn of Victory
Client June Workman
Usage Fine Art
Media Used Acrylic

2

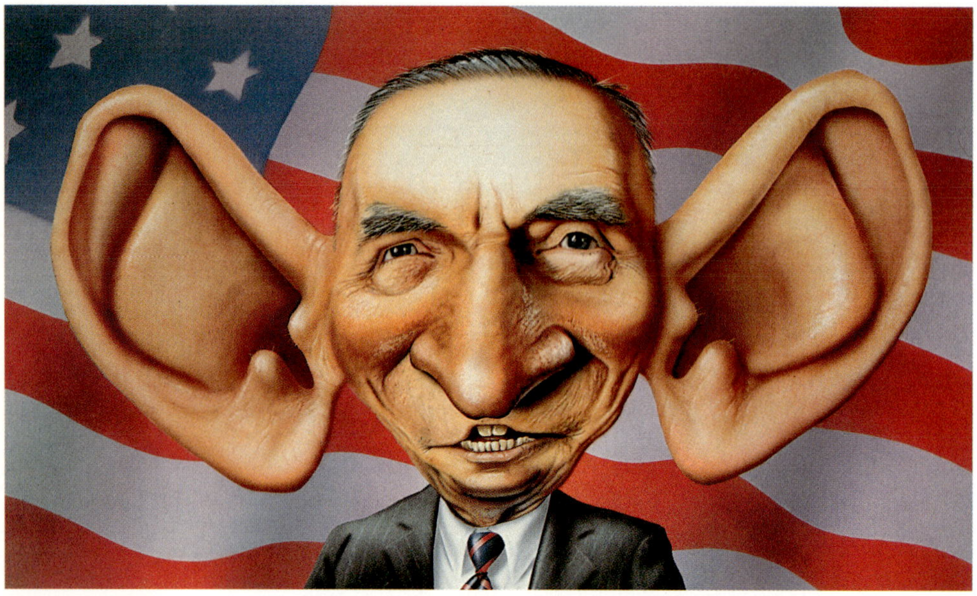

1

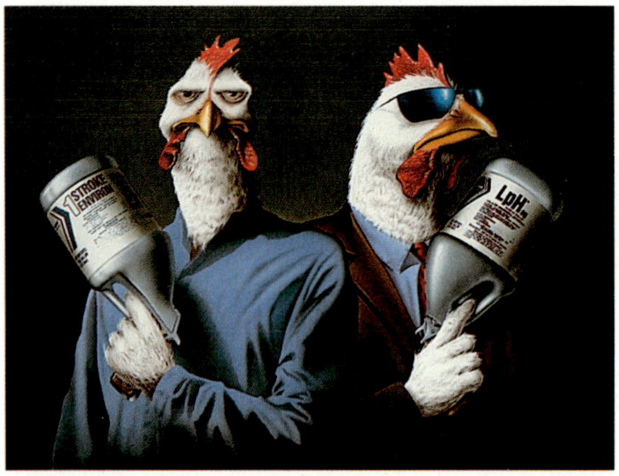

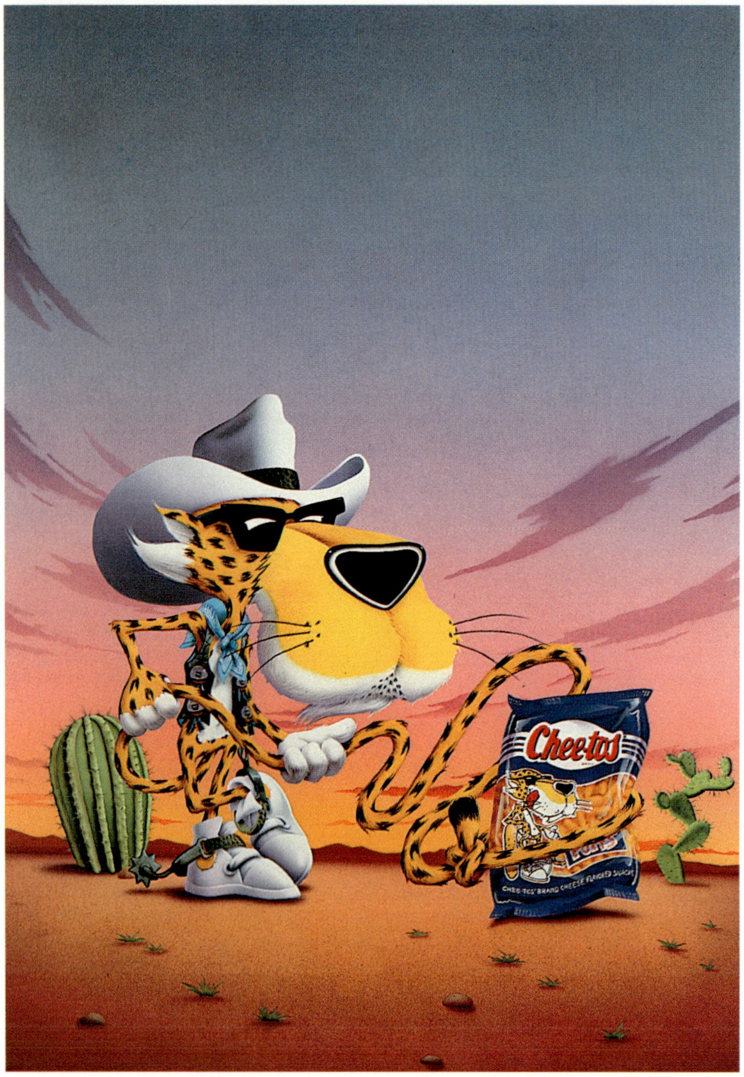

3

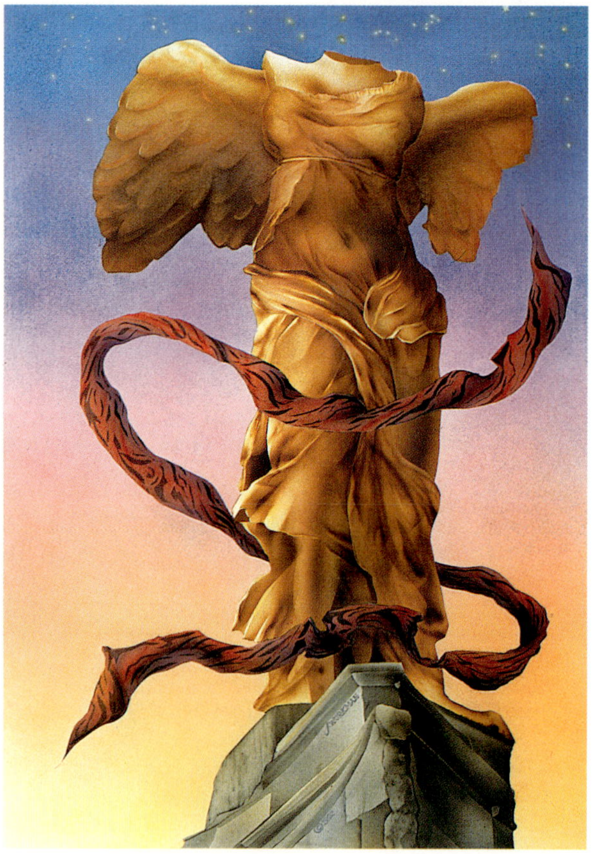

4

1
Artist June Workman
Title Rising Above
Client June Workman
Usage Fine Art
Media Used Airbrush Acrylic

2
Artist June Workman
Title Booger
Art Director June Workman
Usage Fine Art-Portrait
Media Used Acrylic

3
Artist Gary Yealdhall
Title The Hoffmans
Art Director Elvis Brook
Usage Promotional Art
Media Used Gouache

1

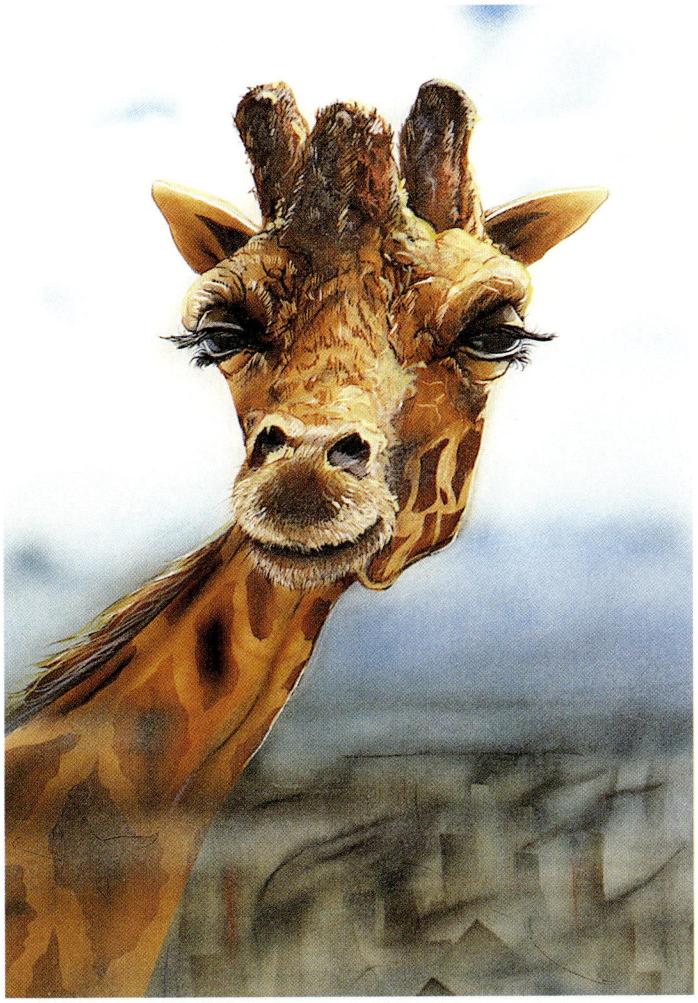

2

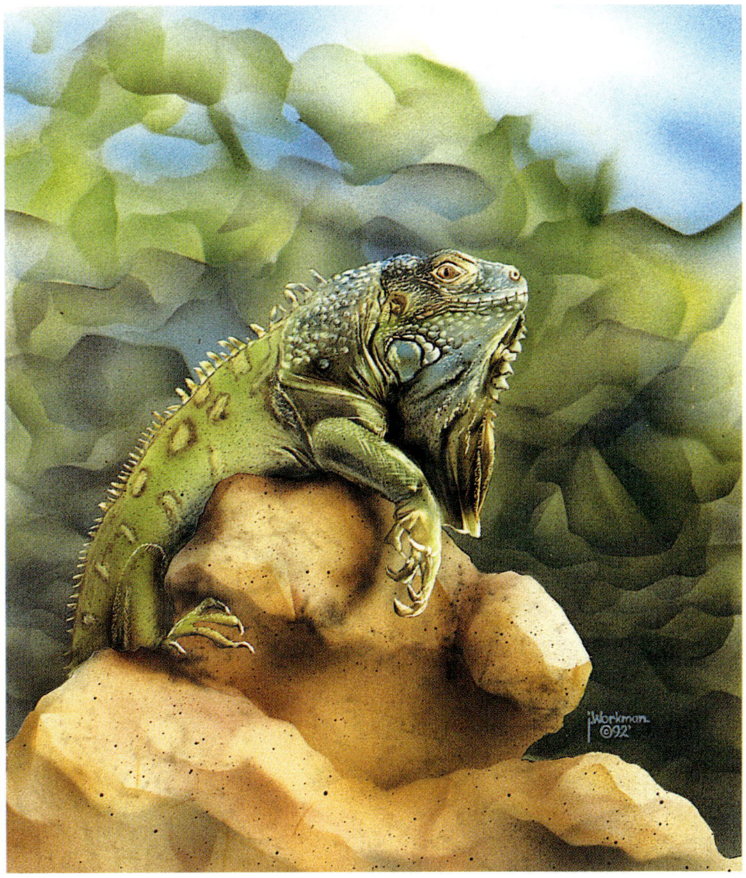

3

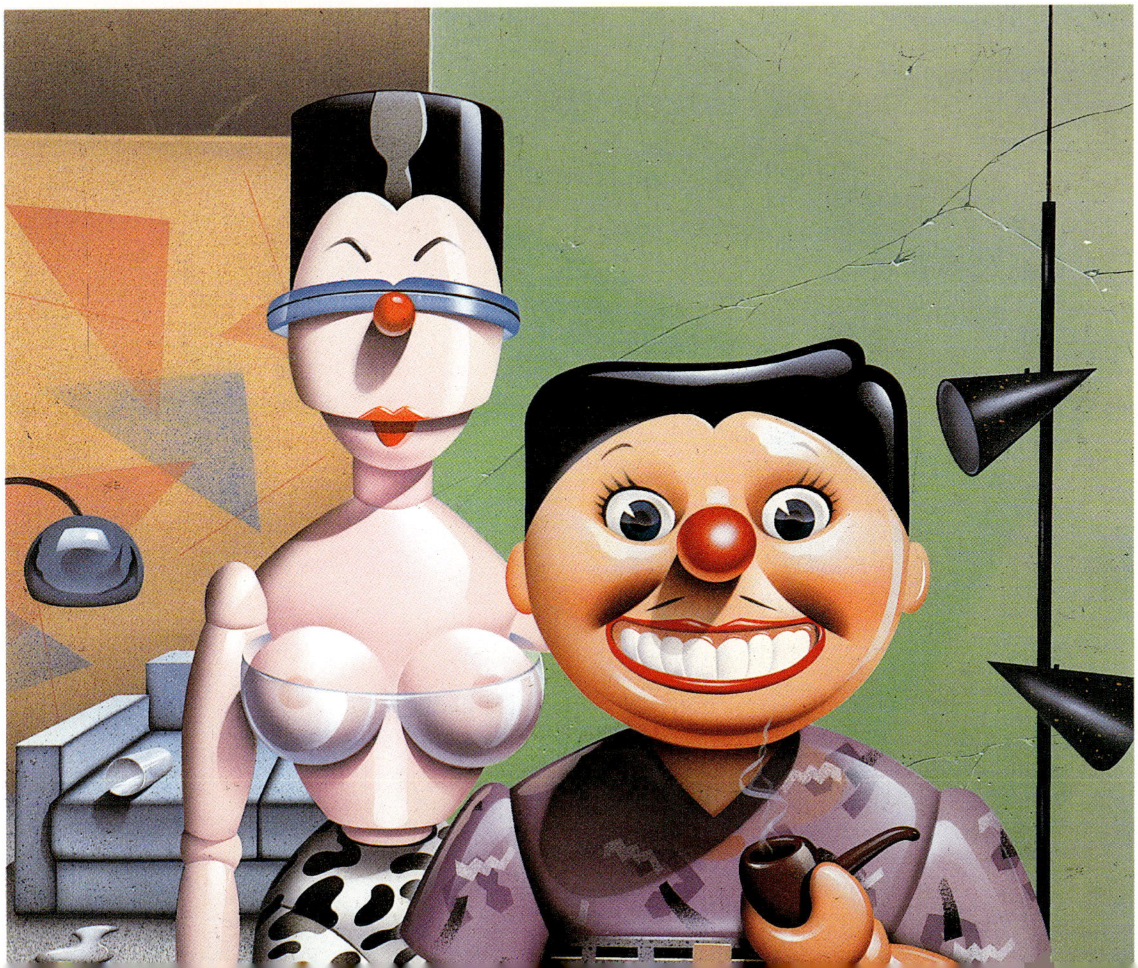

1
Artist Gary Yealdhall
Title Drive. In. Art
Usage Self Promotion
Media Used Gouache

2
Artist Gary Yealdhall
Title Santa
Usage Christmas Card
Media Used Gouache

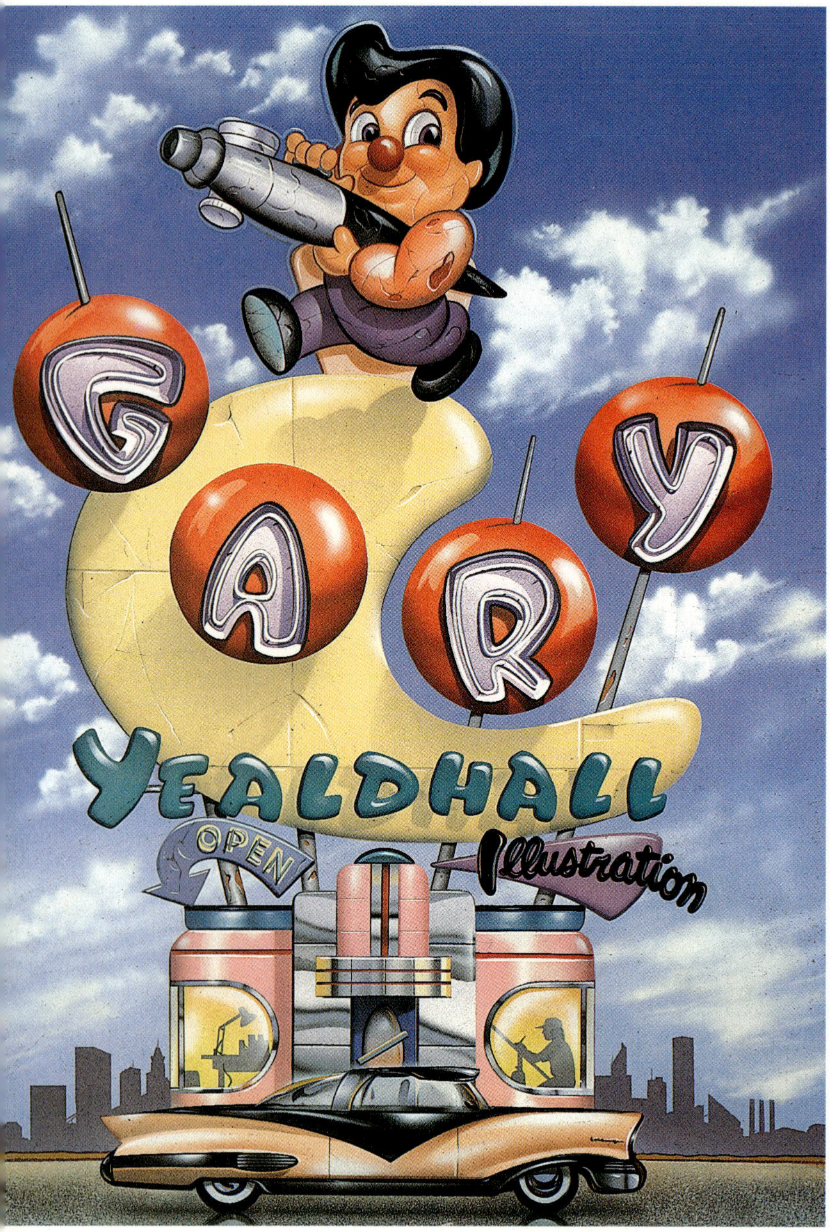

1

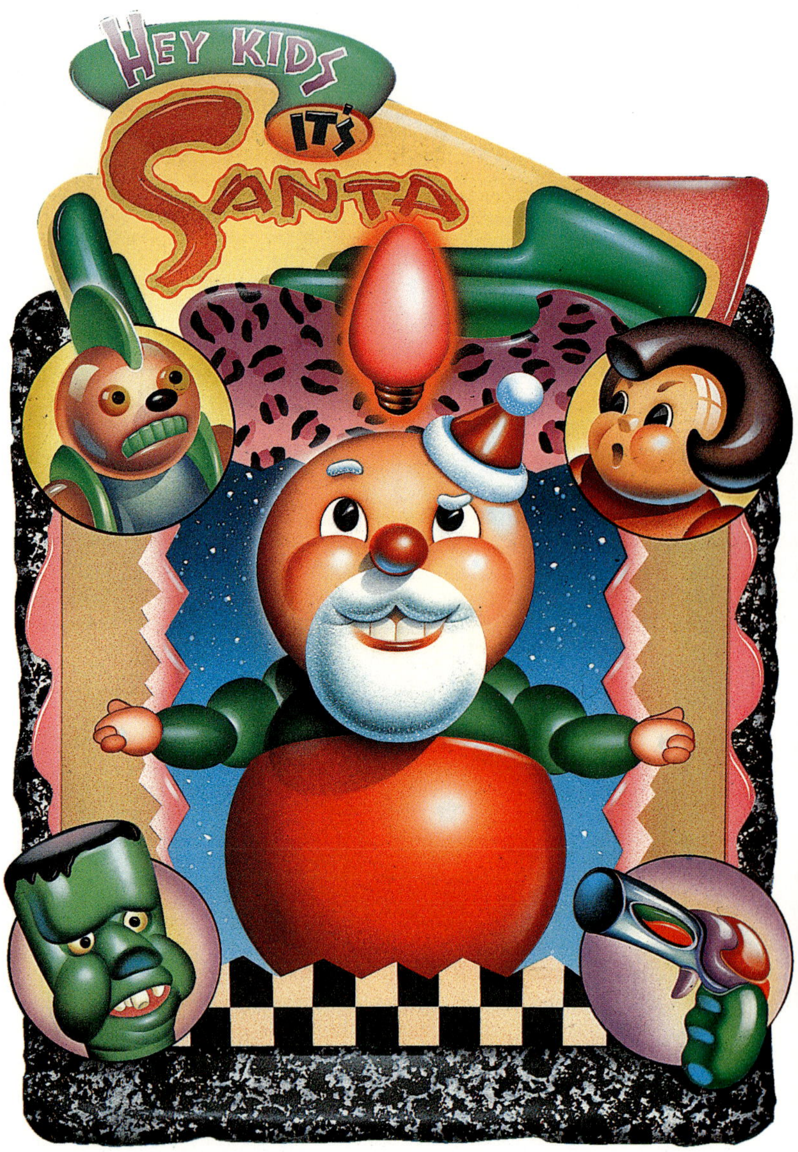

2

1
Artist Eddie Young
Title Jungle Scene
Client Educational Insights
Art Director Jamie Elliot
Usage Catalog Cover
Media Used Acrylic

2
Artist Eddie Young
Title Wonder Worker
Client Imporex International
Art Director Steve Morris
Usage T-Shirt
Media Used Acrylic

3
Artist Eddie Young
Title Metal Fingers
Client Center Stream
Art Director Ron Middlebrook
Usage Book Cover
Media Used Acrylic

1

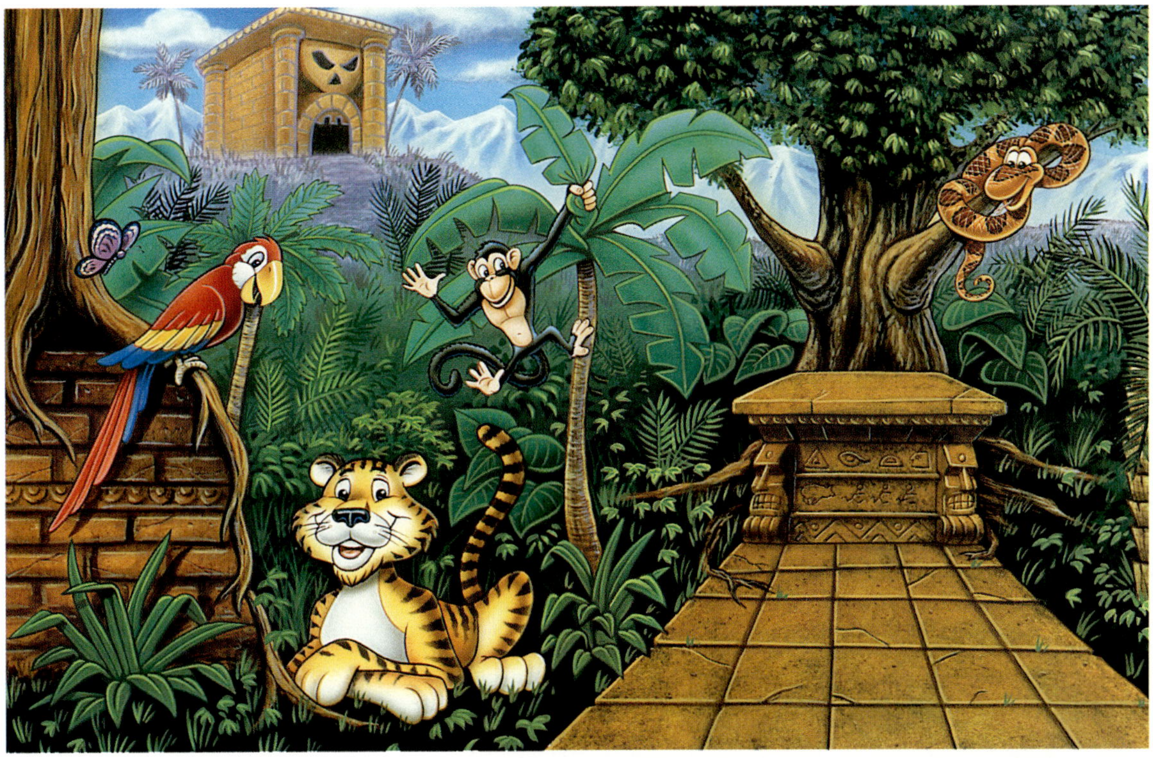

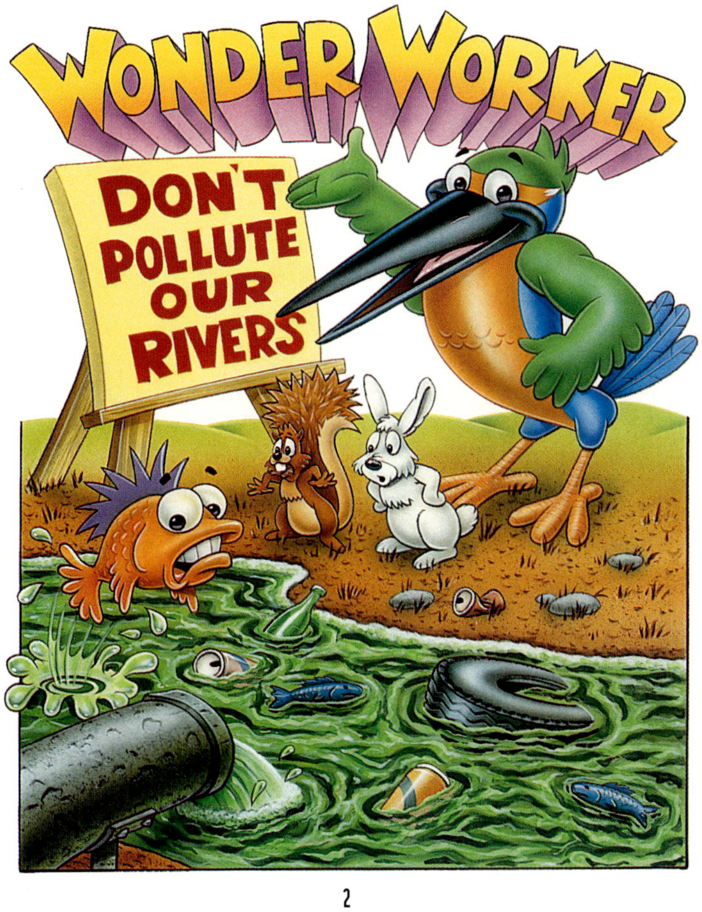

2

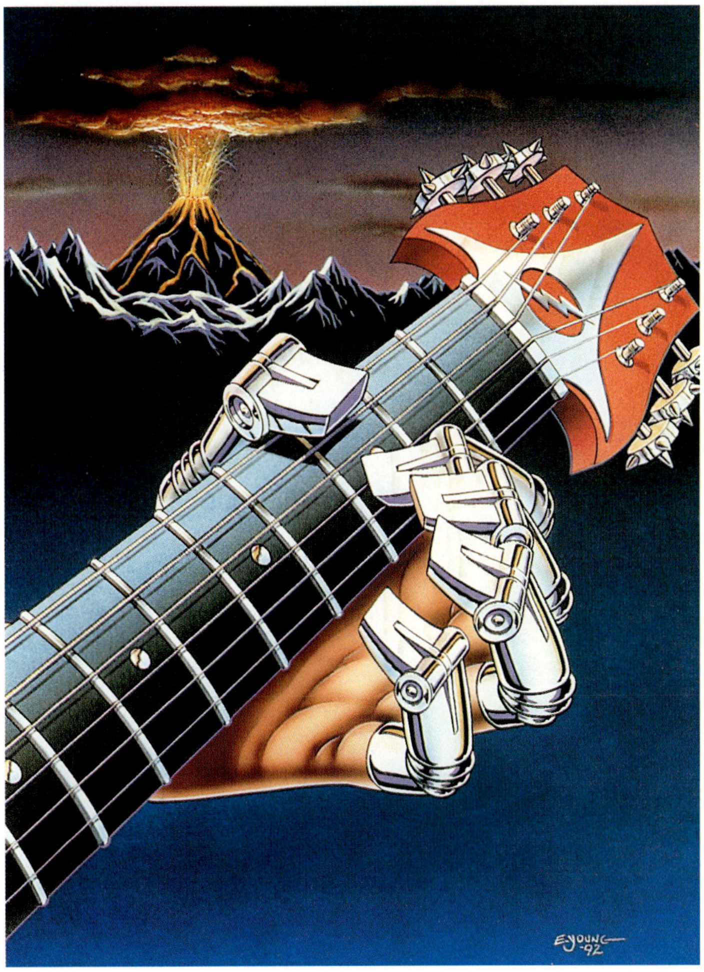

3

1
Artist Eddie Young
Title Blaster Board
Client Imporex International
Art Director Steve Morris
Usage T-Shirt
Media Used Acrylic

2
Artist Eddie Young
Title Tyrannosaurus Rocks
Client Mattel Toys
Art Director Jim Wolfe
Usage Toy Packaging
Media Used Acrylic

3
Artist Eddie Young
Title Toes on the Nose
Client Imporex International
Art Director Steve Morris
Usage T-Shirt
Media Used Acrylic

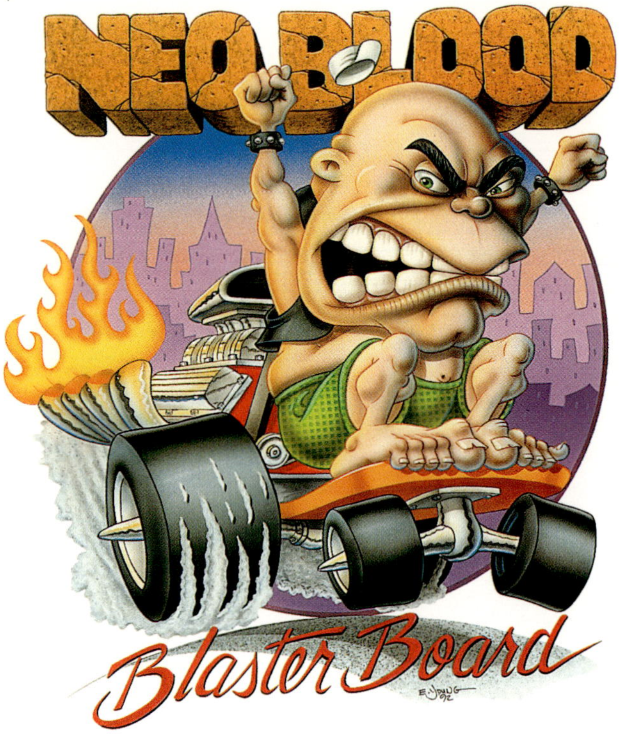

1

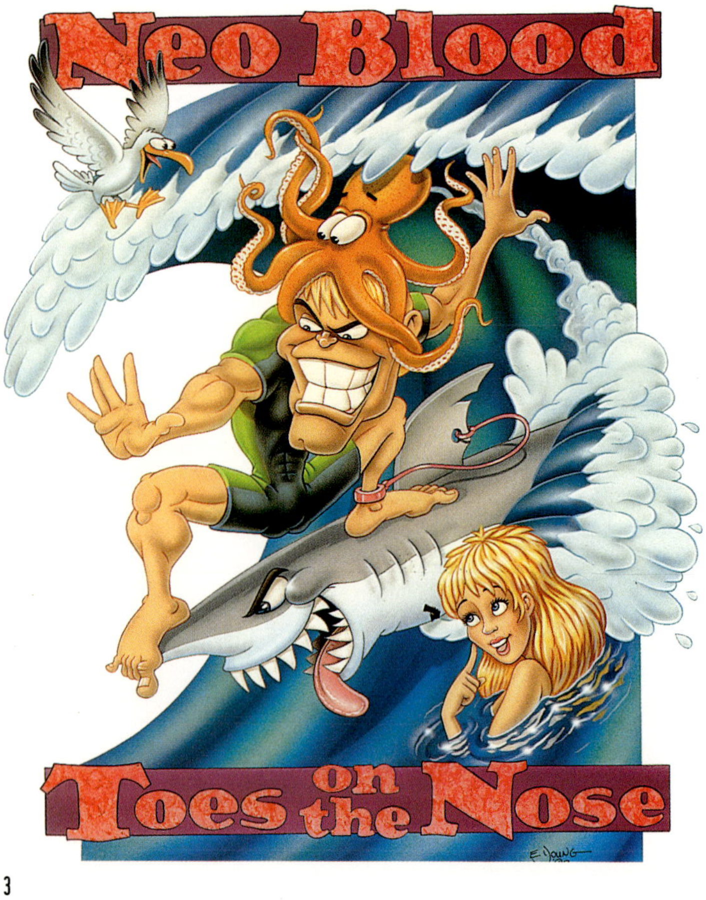

3

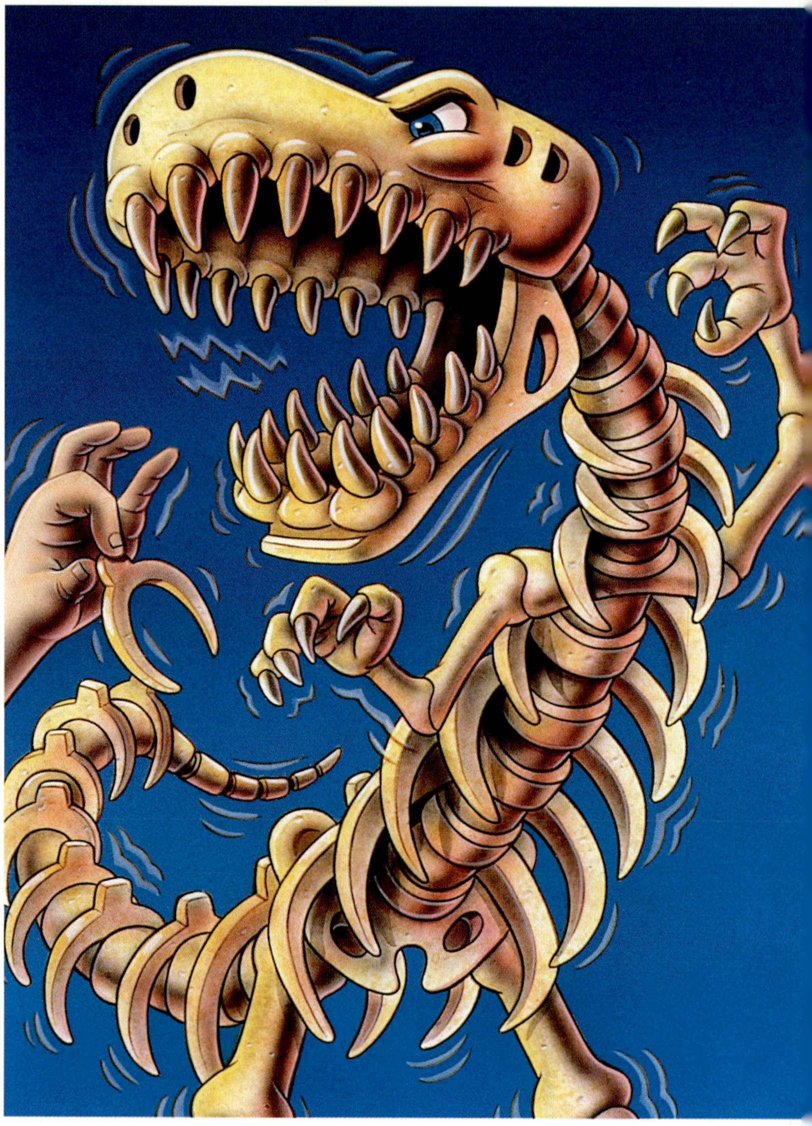

2

1
Artist Eddie Young/Scott Angle
Title Acid Rain Duane
Client Toxic Waste Zombies
Art Director Eddie Young/Scott Angle
Usage T-Shirt
Media Used Acrylic

2
Artist Eddie Young
Title King Putt
Client Hobie Sports Wear
Art Director Terri Murcia
Usage T-Shirt
Media Used Acrylic

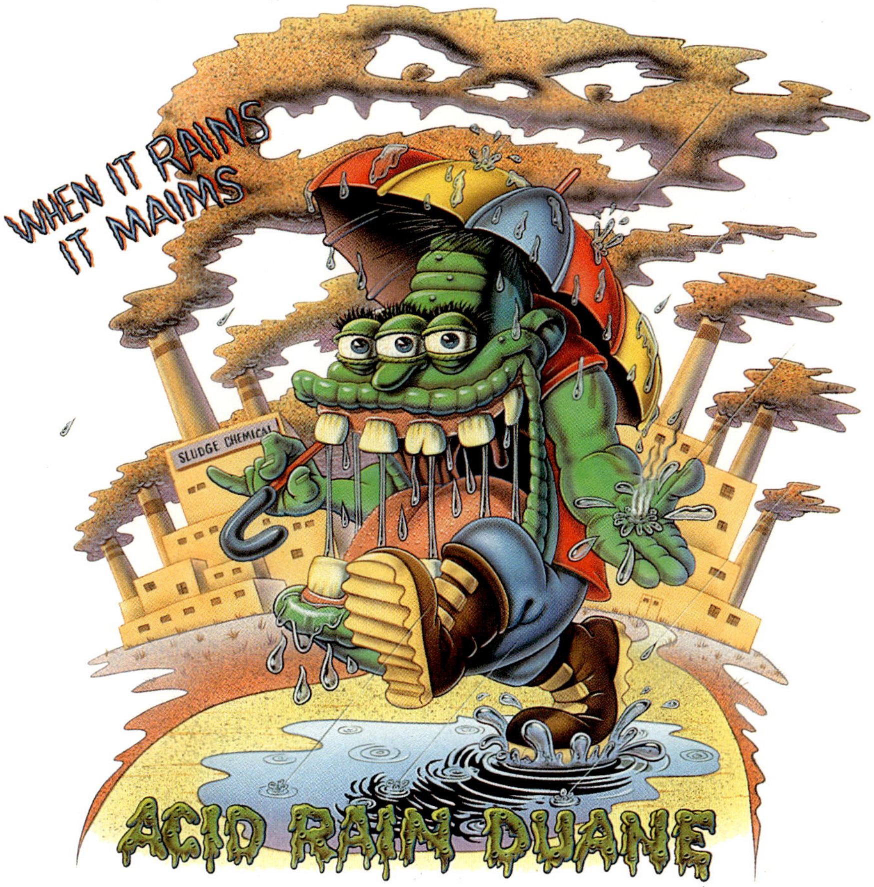

1

2

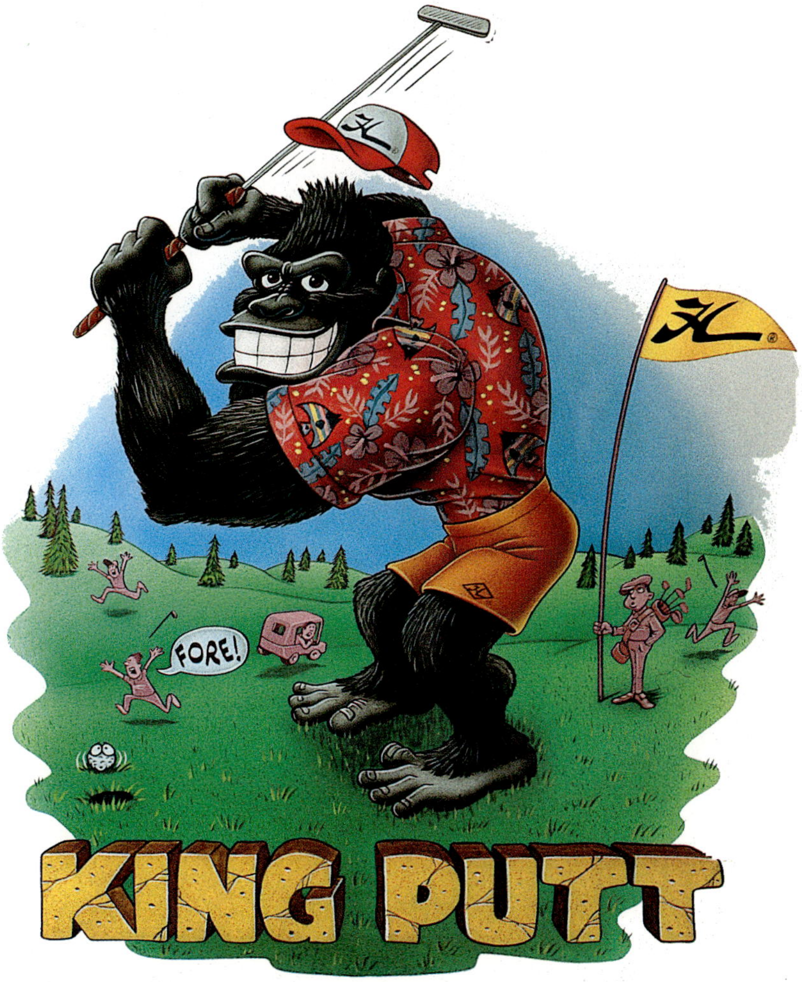

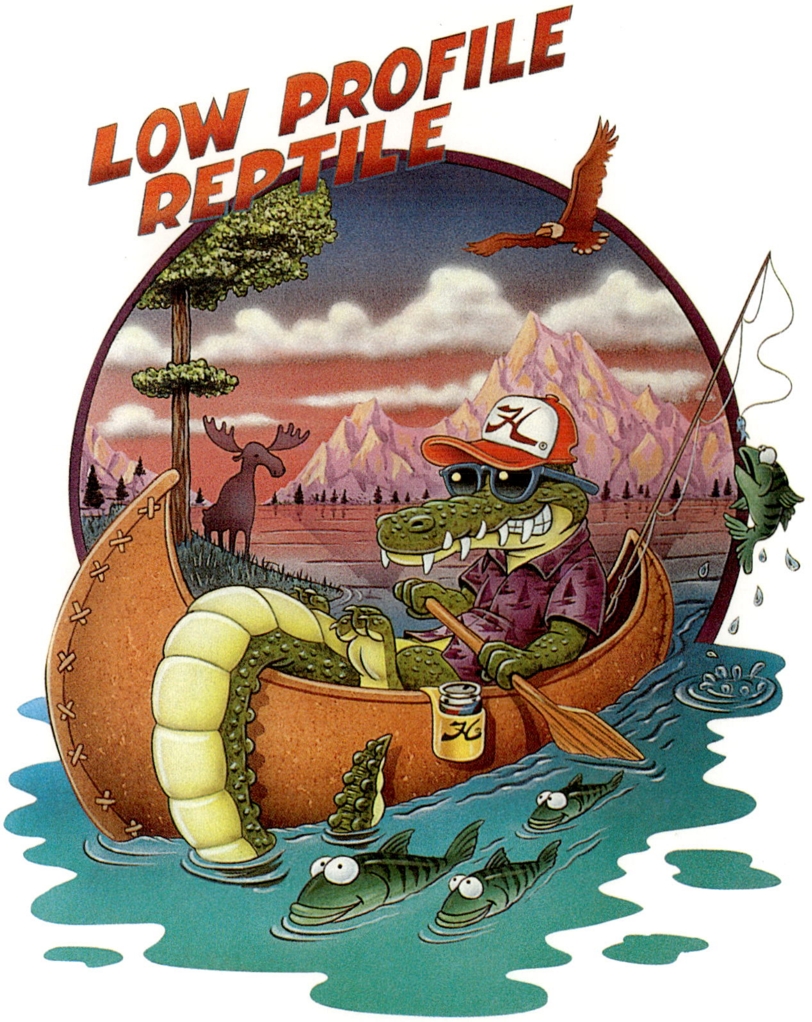

1

2

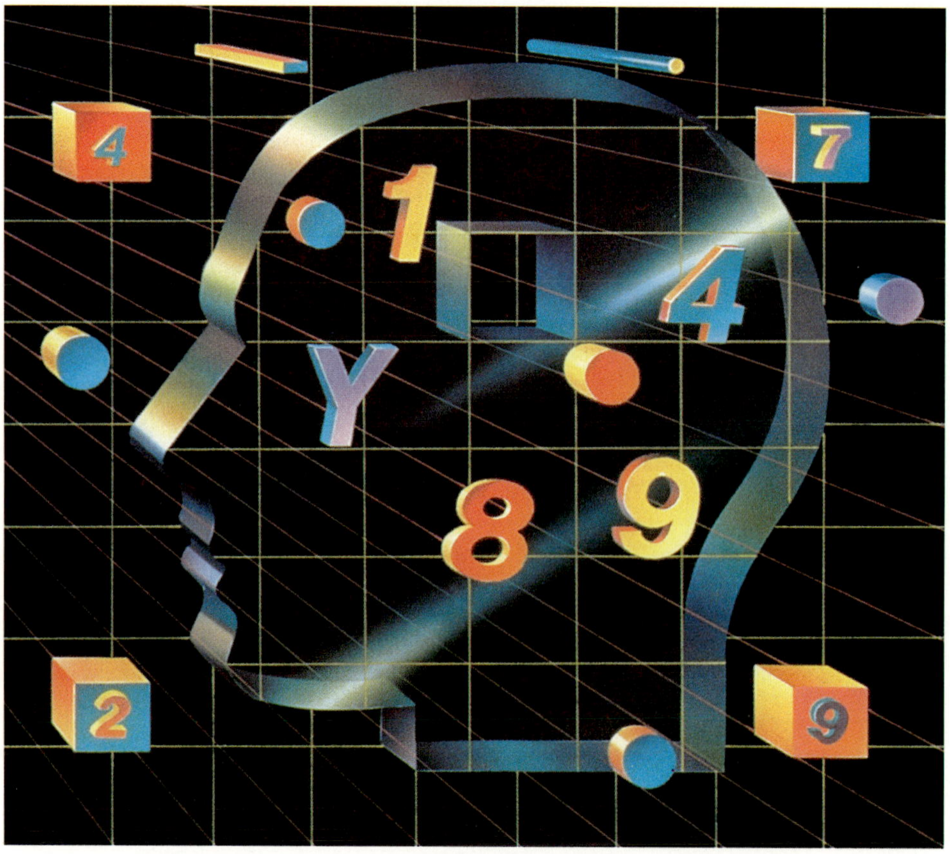

1
Artist Eddie Young
Title Low Profile Reptile
Client Hobie Sports Wear
Art Director Terri Murcia
Usage T-Shirt
Media Used Acrylic

2
Artist Andy Zito
Title Mental Data Entries
Client Texas Instruments
Art Director Andy Zito
Usage Video Game Cover
Media Used Acrylic

3
Artist Andy Zito
Title Automotive Economics 1900-1992
Client U.S. News and World Report
Art Director Greg Crossely
Usage Large Poster
Media Used Acrylic

4
Artist Andy Zito
Title Infinite Possibilities
Client Vicor
Art Director Andy Zito
Usage Advertisement
Media Used Acrylic

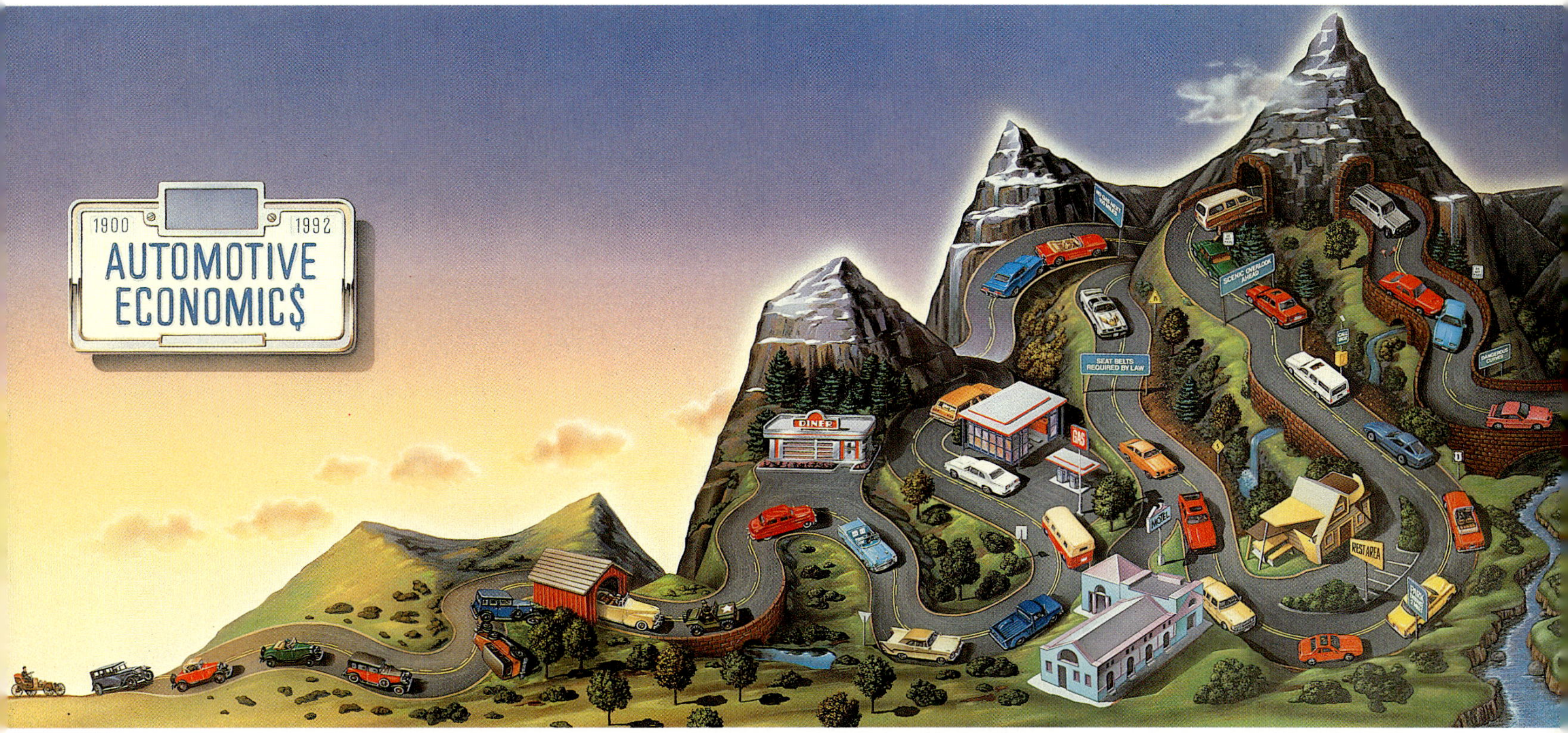

3

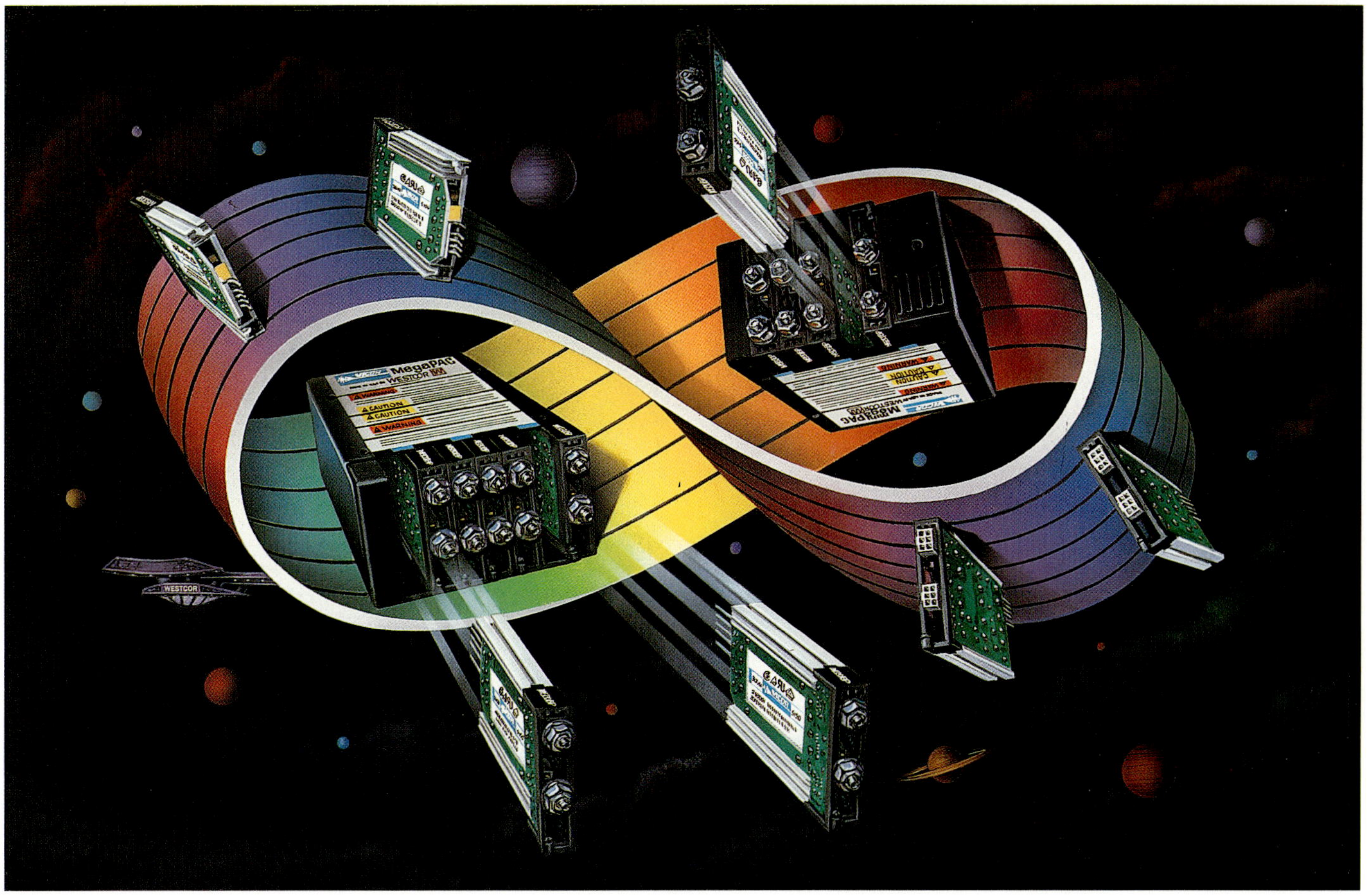

4

1
Artist Andy Zito
Title European Community - Open for Business
Client Sample
Art Director Andy Zito
Media Used Acrylic

2
Artist Andy Zito
Title Go to the Head of the Computer Class
Client Sample
Art Director Andy Zito
Media Used Acrylic

3
Artist Andy Zito
Title Putting the Pieces Together
Client CGI
Art Director Steve Martin
Usage Annual Report
Media Used Acrylic

1

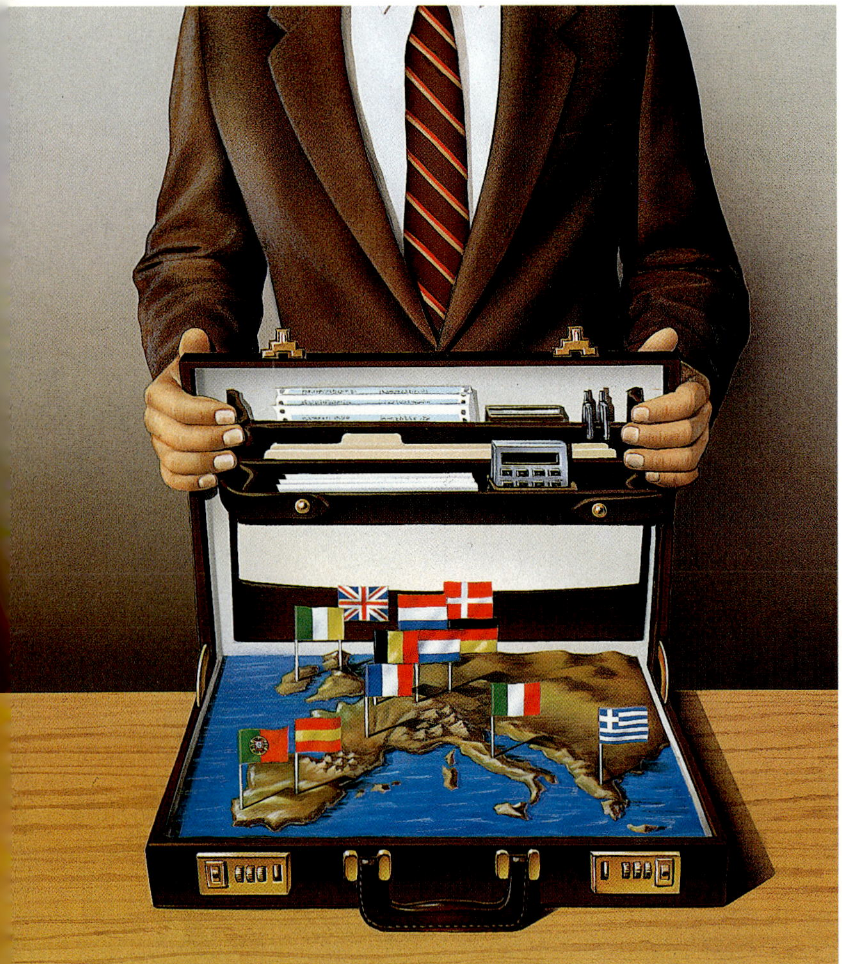

2

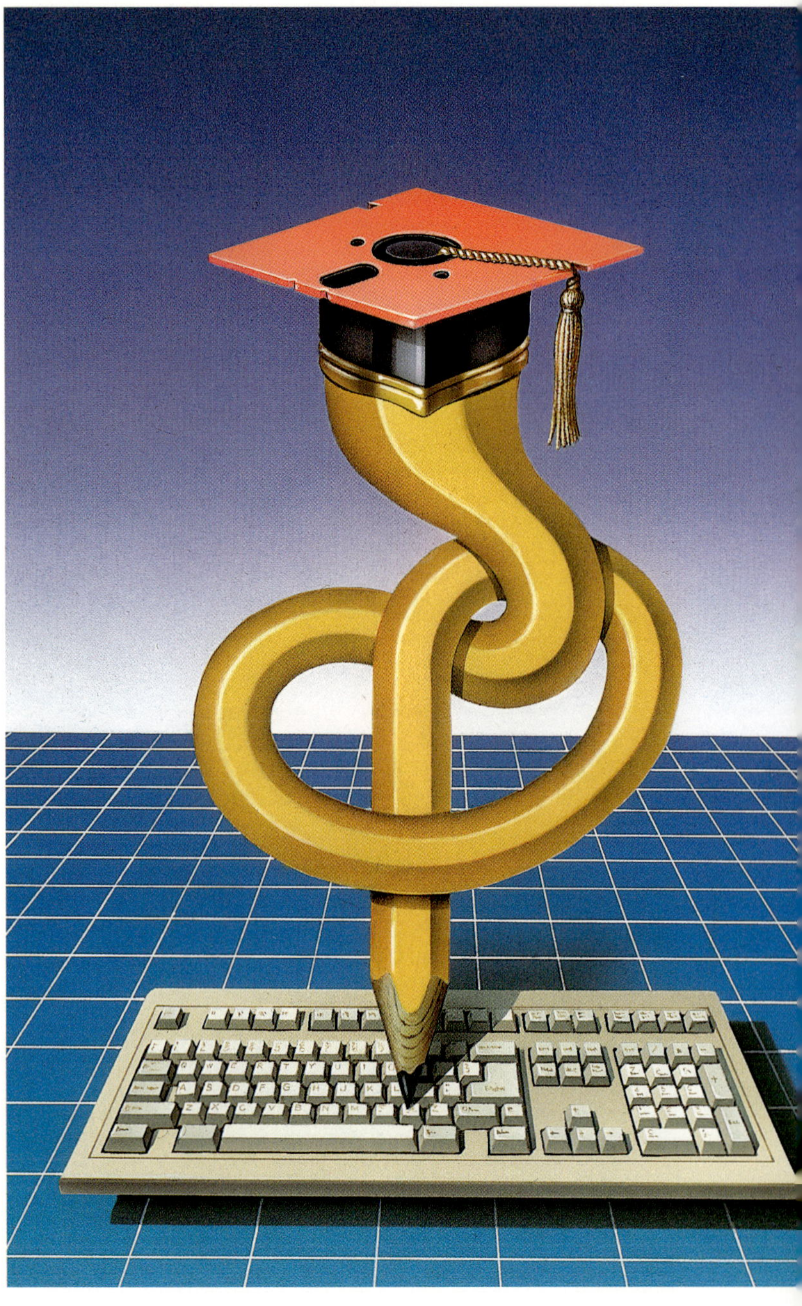

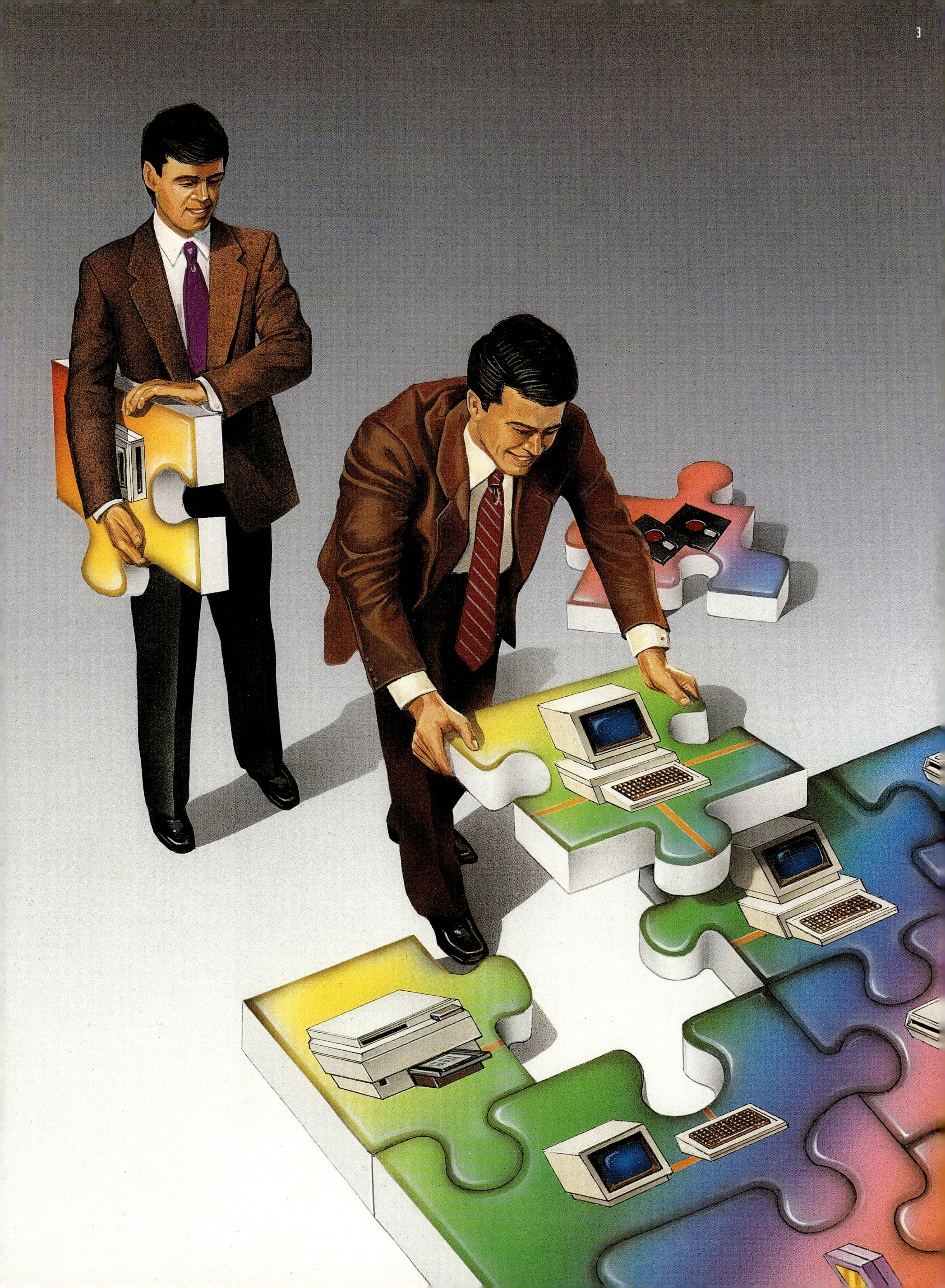

1
Artist Andy Zito
Title European Bullet Train
Client Pacific Bell Telephone
Art Director Dean Perkins
Usage Brochure
Media Used Acrylic

2
Artist Andy Zito
Title Dollar Sign Staircase
Art Director Andy Zito
Media Used Acrylic

3
Artist Boris Zlotsky
Title C - Printer . Kyocera
Client J.M.H.
Art Director Ray Aron
Usage Technical Illustration
Media Used Acrylic

1

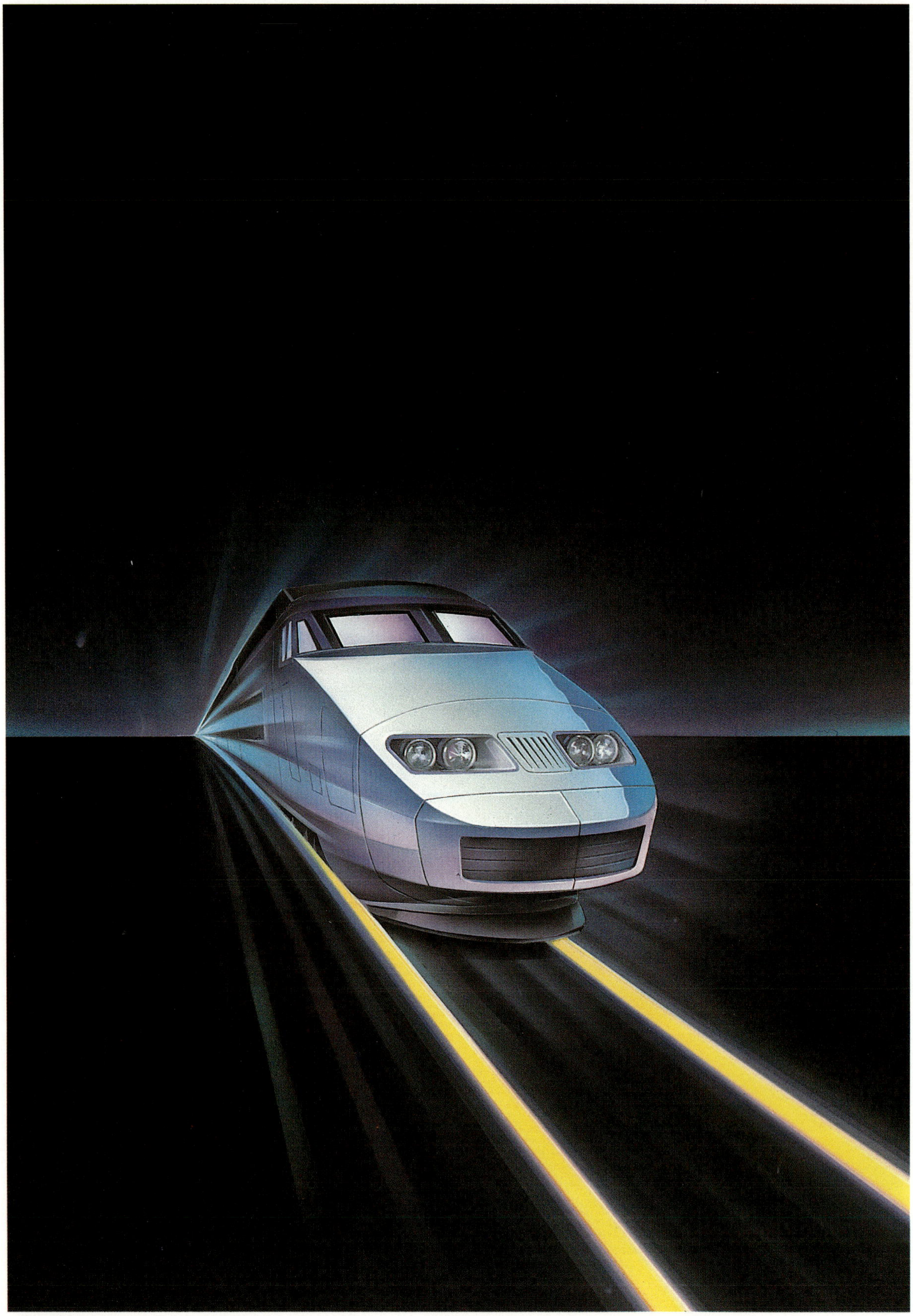

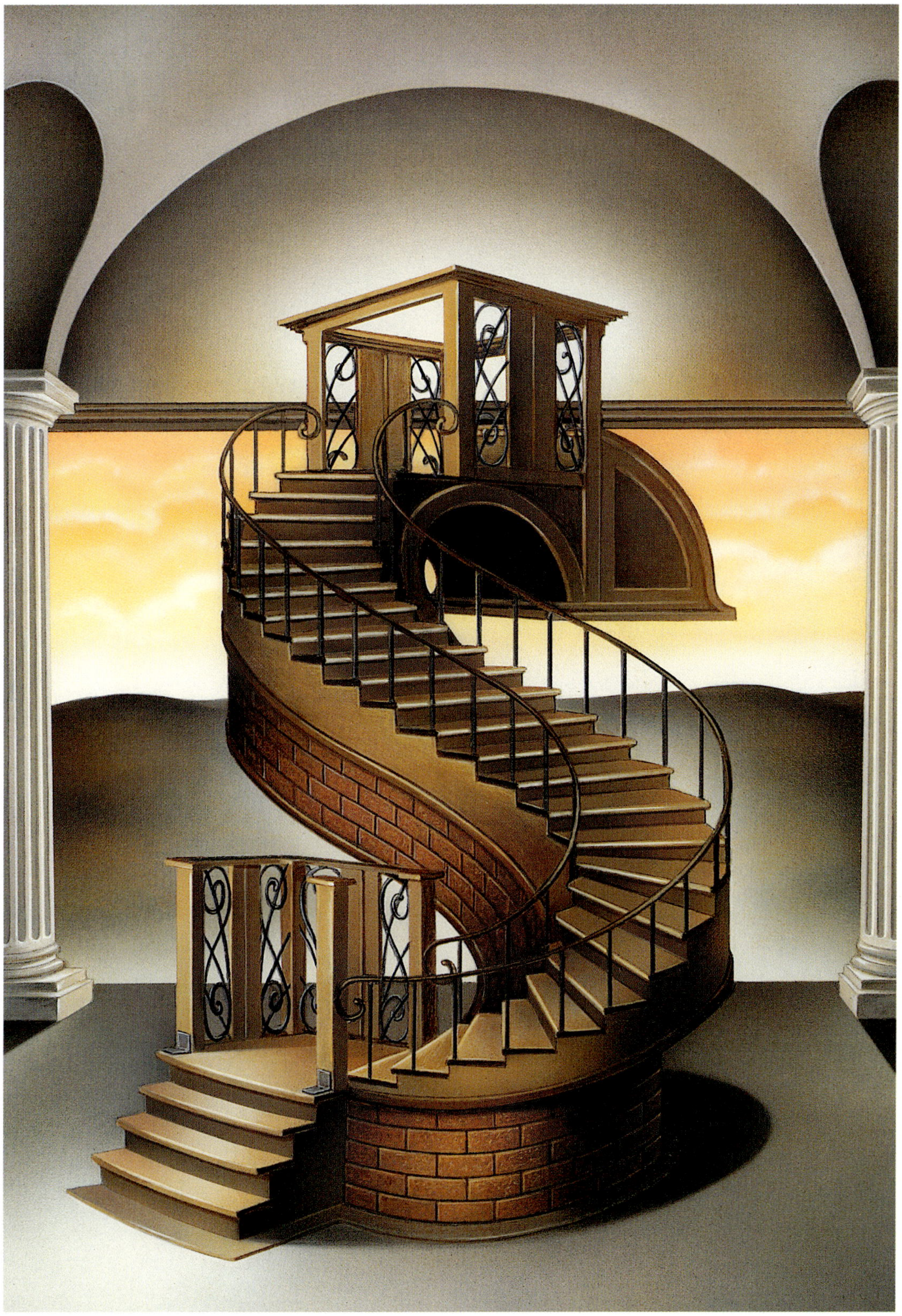

2

3

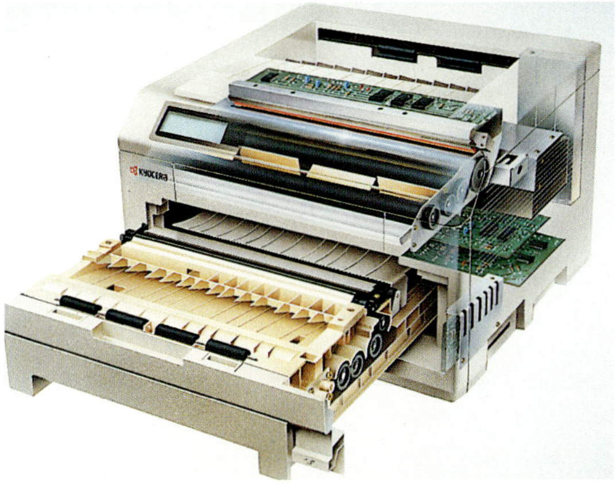

DIRECTORY

Angel
2414 South Darien Street
Philadelphia, PA 19148
215 463-7780

Lori Anzalone
35-02 Berdan Avenue
Fairlawn, NJ 07410
201 796-5588

Chris P. Apostolou
2939 Summerfield Road
Falls Church, CA 22042
703 241-0872

Craig Attebery
Atteberry Illustration & Design
1812 Wollam Street
Los Angeles, CA 90065
213 227-4120

Peter Bartczak
Clown Bank Studio
P.O. Box 7709
Santa Cruz, CA 95061
408 426-4247

Leslie Bates
3124 Nassau Road
Oceanside, NY 11572
516 764-5258

Rodino R. Bautista
1193 Bayard Drive
San Jose, CA 95122
408 297-0325

Dennis Bayuzick
4608 5th Avenue
Kenosha, WI 53140
414 654-8209

Scott Beckley
5025 Arapaho Road #502
Addison, TX 75248
214-387-5667

Doron Ben-Ami
14 Fox Run Lane
Newtown, CT 06470
203 270-7451

Mark A. Bender
930 North Lincoln Avenue
Pittsburgh, PA 15233
412 321-3266

Anita S. Bice
1009 Park Avenue
Moody, AL 35004
205 640-6168

Kurt Bittle
709 Woodsyde Circle
Bel Air, MD 21014
410 836-7255

Brian Blair
Blair Graphics
3110 N. Locust Street
Muncie, IN 47303
317 289-6331

Tim Blough
4827 31st Avenue So.
Minneapolis, MN 55417
612 724-1442

John M. Booth
Mason Graphics
2205 California NE #501
Minneapolis, MN 55418
612 789-4799

Steven Boswick
331 Oak Circle
Wilmette, IL 60091
708 251-1430

Marty Braun
265 Pleasant Avenue
Peaks Island, ME 04108
207 766-9726

Robert Brun
The Independent Pencil Company
76 State Street
Newburyport, MA 01950
508 462-1948

Todd Buck
3 Elizabeth Ct.
Lombard, IL 60148
708 627-0903

Hank Buffington
Rhode Island School of Design
5 Edna Horn Drive
Stockton, NJ 08559
609 397-0423

Lonnie Busch
Air Busch Studio
12012 Charter House Lane
St. Louis, MO 63146
314 569-1178

Thomas Cain
Thomas Cain Illustration
66 Baxter Street
Melrose, MA 02176
617 662-7705

Philip H. Campbell
546 S. Meridian Street
Studio #408
Indianapolis, IN 46225
317 359-1677

Kurt Carloni
Kurt Carloni Studio
1942 West Shore Drive
Delafield, WI 53018
414 646-3356

Martin Castillo
10164 Raincloud
El Paso, TX 79927
915 859-8352

Gary Ciccarelli
Gary Ciccarelli, Inc.
317 Elmwood
Dearborn, MI 48124
313 278-3504

Mick Coulas
Coulas Cartoons
579 Richmond Street W. #300
Toronto, Canada M5V 1Y6
416 864-1182 Ext. 235

David Crowe
David Crowe Fine Art & Graphics
1224 Winton Avenue
Studio #5
Speedway, IN 46224
317 244-2668

Tom Daly
47 East Edsall Avenue
Palisade Park, NJ 07650
201 943-1837

Richard Daskas
2720 Associates Road #C-5
Fullerton, CA 92635
714 529-1282

Ruben Deanda
4085 Harrison
Riverside, CA 92503
714 785-9371

Catherine Dittmer
401 Camberly Way
Redwood City, CA 94061
415 322-5658

Jim Durk
Durk Illustration
1853 Hastings Avenue
Downers Grove, IL 60516
708 719-9779

Jim Effler
AIR Studio, Inc.
203 East 7th Street
Cincinnati, OH 45202
513 721-1193

Dave Ekman
43726 Emile Zola Street
Lancaster, CA 93535
805 942-7112

Brian Evans
Brian Evans Illustration
1304 Ponderosa Drive
Fort Collins, CO 80521
303 482-7653

Alan Flinn
2720 East Yampa
Suite 221B
Colorado Springs, CO 80909
719 389-0182

Mark A. Fredrickson
853 South Pantano Parkway
Tucson, AZ 85710
602 722-5777

Brian Fujimori
1781 Atchison Street
Pasadena, CA 91104
818 789-9023

Pedro Gamero
c/o 118 Wyndham Drive
Portola Valley, CA 94028
415 851-9520

Mike Gardner
16 Goddard Street
Quincy, MA 02169
617 786-8454

Ben Garvie
118 Wyndham Drive
Portola Valley, CA 94028
415 851-9520

Scott T. Gee
4361 V. Vereda Rosada
Tuscon, AZ 85715
602 624-9338

Alan Giana
Giana Illustration & Design
17 Colonial Drive
Simsbury, CT 06089
203 658-2938

Gary Glover
Gary Glover Illustration
6715 Xana Way
Carlsbad, CA 92009-6023
619 471-9453

Stuart Hall
1228 West 300 South
Pingree, ID 83262
208 684-4135

Andy Hickes
315 West 23rd Street
#3A
New York, NY 10011
212 989-9023

Michael Holguin
Hickes Associates
14811 Fabius
San Antonio, TX 78248
210 492-1006

Reggie Holladay
Holladay Arts Inc.
7395 N.W. 51st Street
Lauderhill, FL 33319
305 749-9031

Tom Hoover
1748 Honeysuckle Drive
Mansfield, OH 44905
419 589-8956

Robert L. Horwath
A T & T Bell Laboratories
1713 Spruce Hills Drive
Glen Gardner, NJ 08826
908 537-7114

Ron Houghton, Jr.
Memorial Wildlife Federation
43 Opan Street
Holbrook, NY 11741
516 589-7746

Thomas J. Humpert
Thomas Humpert Studio
P.O. Box 876
Sherwood, OR 97140
503 625-3897

Michael W. Hunt, Jr.
Hunt Graphics
1516 Carol Sue Avenue
Cretna, LA 70056
800 426-1379

Stephen M. Hunter
Hellman Associates
1225 West 4th Street
Waterloo, IA 50702
319 234-7055

Greg Hurley
Hurley Design Associates
6021 Hughes Road
Lansing, MI 48911
517 394-0471

Christopher Iorillo
Double Action Studio
P.O. Box 296
Ridgefield, CT 06877
203 438-1954

Jake Jones
Naples Daily News
439 St. Andrews Boulevard.
Naples, FL 33962
813 775-6386

Albert Juarez
2900 McKinley
El Paso, TX 79930
915 565-7307

Nicholas Kendysh
6942 Sowell Avenue
Westminster, CA 92683
714 898-6832

Brian Kim
89 Red Fox Drive
Savannah, GA 31419
912 925-3274

Robert A. Kling
Funwear
461 S. Ninth Street
Miamisburg, OH 45342
859-3940

Andrew Kong Knight
21095 Gary Drive #309
Hayward, CA 94546
510 581-7292

David Kovach
1390 Sprague Street
Akron, OH 44305
216 733-9258

Dave Kuhn
7601 N. 320 E.
Albany, NY 47320
317 282-7031

Vincent Lacava
1186 Broadway #939
New York, NY 10001
212 725-8949

Andy Lackow
Aardvark Studio
7004 Boulevard East
#29-C
Guttenberg, NJ 07093
201 854-2770

Jim Langman
6784 Laird Avenue
Reynoldsburg, OH 43068
614 864-7170

Jorgen Larsson
Silver Turbo Illustrated
Agnegatan 2.
Vasteras, Sweden S-72217
46-021-141521

Pete LaSalle, Jr.
1151 Independence Avenue
St. Charles, IL 60174
708 584-9195

Samuel Laterza
Rochester Institute of Technology
34 Marberth Drive
Henrietta, NY 14467
716 334-8989

Robert Leverette
N.W. Custom Designs
36427 28th Avenue S.
Federal Way, WA 98003
206 927-3412

Jerry Lofaro
270 Lafayette Street
#308
New York, NY 10012
212 941-7936

Travis A. Louie
132-70 Pople Avenue
Flushing, NY 13355
718 353-2046

Shannon Mac Donald
29 Station Road
Bayville, NJ 08721
908 269-8154

Farley Magadia
Farley Magadia Illustration
13984 Hubbard Street
Sylmar, CA 91342
818 365-5794

Joseph Martin
4799 Warwick S.
Canfield, OH 44406
216 746-4628

Trent Martin
276 202 Hemmingford
Quebec Canada JOC 1HO
514 247-3594

Bill Mayer
240 Forkner Road
Decatur, GA 30030
404 378-0686

Craig McKay
5307 E. Knoll Court. #512
Cincinnati, OH 45239
513 541-0920

Richard O. Menchaca
106 Meredith
San Antonio, TX 78228
210 732-1124

Jim Mendillo
Scrambled Eggz Productions
70 East Main Street
Marlton, NJ 08053
609 596-6990

Doug Meythaler
Kelly Russell Studios
9103 Blaisdell Avenue S.
Bloomington, MN 55420
612 888-7735

Richard Mollo
52 Greenbrook Road
Greenbrook, NJ 08812
908 752-6409

Gerard Mooney
Gerry Mooney Studio
2 Main Street
Dobbs Ferry, NY 10522
914 693-8076

Clark Most
Heart Graphic Design
501 George Street
Midland, MI 48640
517 832-9710

Peggy Mozley
17914 Hillcrest Road
Dallas, TX 75252
214 248-2704

Eric Oliver
3456 Bosworth Avenue (UP)
Cleveland, OH 44111
216 941-5581

Osni Omena
1500 Broadway
24th Floor
New York, NY 10036
212 398-3838

Mark Otnes
4 Illini Circle
Urbana, IL 61801
217 337-1717

Christopher Palmer
Pen Point Productions
7336 S. Blackstone Avenue
Chicago, IL 60619
312 684-3753

Thomas Peiffer
22743 West Front Street
P.O. Box 36
Curtice, OH 43412
419 836-8296

Gary Penca
8335 NW 20th Street
Coral Springs, FL 33071
305 752-4699

Stephen Peringer
17808 184th Avenue NE.
Woodinville, WA 98072
206 788-5767

Eric Perrotta
E. V. Perrotta
P.O. Box 771011
Coral Springs, FL 33077
305 971-4003

Thom Peterson
2417 Homestead Street
Racine, WI 53404
414 633-2293

Myles Pinkney
The Aart Works
1355 North Union Boulevard.
Colorado Springs, CO 80909
719 635-8848

Oscar Quarles
1478 Beach Channel Drive
Apartment 3C
Far Rockaway, NY 11691
718 337-5584

Roberto Ramirez
Remirez Illustration
8804 Las Camas NE
Albuquerque, NM 87111
505 293-2943

Kathleen Regan
64 Maplecrest Drive
Pawtucket, RI 02861
401 723-1702

Robert Revels
414 88th #3
Daly City, CA 94015
992-7586

Mark V. Robinson
9050 Loreleigh Way
Fairfax, VA 22033
703 280-4123

David Salazar
6 Edgemont Drive
Daly City, CA 94015
415 588-9640

Samuel Salfino III
SSIII Illustration Studio
57 Lakeside Drive
Nutley, NJ 07110
201 667-5103

Dr. William C. Schneider
NASA
1723 Festival
Houston, TX 77062
713 488-3213

Greg Schooley
207 Bellwood Circle
Mars, PA 16046
412 776-4156

Steve Shamburger
Shamburger Illustration
6108 Newton
Overland Park, KS 66202
913 362-2787

Mary A. Shafer
HCR2 Box 183
Park Falls, WI 54552
715 583-2247

Steve Singer
S.L. Crow Co.
2161 N.W. Military Highway #313
San Antonio, TX 78213
210 344-0364

Timothy Stafford
714 7th Avenue
Belmar, NY 07719
280-9543

William R. Stewart
Cardiff Publishing
3581 S. Pitkin Cr.
Aurora, CO 80013
303 693-4508

Winston Sturgen
212 W. Broadway
P.O. Box 370
Silver City, NM 88062
505 388-3423

Ian Suk
25 Mabelle Avenue
Suite 1415
Etobicoke Ontario
Canada M9A 4Y1
416 231-9642

Michael Takagi
442 27th Avenue
San Mateo, CA 94403
415 345-7313

Daniel K.Tennant
80 Wooster Street
New York, NY 10012
212 966-6360

John E. Thies
A T & T
64 Lynn Drive
Mohrsville, PA 19541
215 939-6189

Carlos Torres
192 17th Street
Brooklyn, NY 11215
718 768-3296

Jimmie Turner
Turner Illustration
4215 Bedford
Detroit, MI 48224
313 882-2783

Mark Villarta
32210 Hall Ranch Parkway
Union City, CA 94587
510 887-0637

Patrick C. Wanebo
516 W. Deming Place #IN
Chicago, IL 60614
312 525-5425

Tobie Warren
4768 Fredonia Place
Bensailen, PA 19020
215 463-7780

Wayne Watford
2123 E. Montebello Avenue
Phoenix, AZ 85016
602 265-9030

Tom Watters
Scrambled Eggz Productions, Inc.
70 E. Main Street
Marlton, NJ 08055
609 596-6990

Michael E. Weaver
Real Art Design Group, Inc.
332 East Nottingham Road
Dayton, OH 45405
513 275 3879

Ken Westphal
Westphal Illustration
9208 Roe Avenue
Prarie Village, KS 66207
913 381-8399

June Workman
June Workman Illustration
P.O. Box 8032
Fremont, CA 94537
510 792-1449

Gary Yealdhall
110 West 25th Street
Baltimore, MD 21218
410 889-5361

Eddie Young
6108 East Pageantry Street
Long Beach, CA 90808
310 429-2513

Andy Zito
Andy Zito Visuals
135 South LaBrea Avenue
Los Angeles, CA 90036
213 931-1182

Boris Zlotsky
8 Southgate Road
Aparatment 1A
New Providence, NJ 07974
908 665-1803

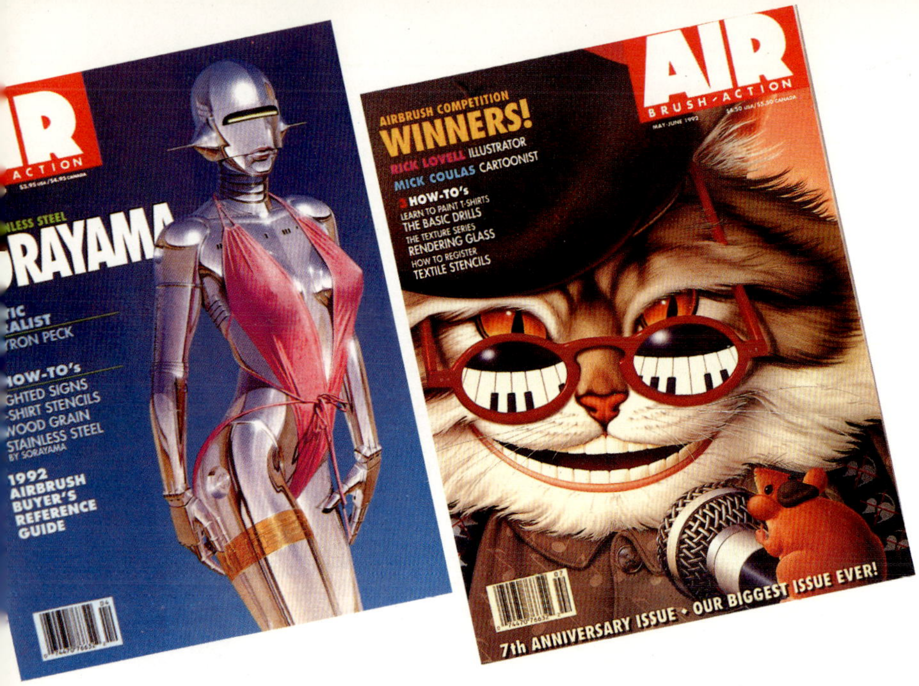

Airbrush Action Magazine

If it's happening in art, you'll read about it in *Airbrush Action*. We cover the hottest airbrush painting being done around the country today. With detailed instruction on "how-to-do-it" from some of the best artists in the industry.

We provide the most practical, up-to-date information on studio equipment, new products, and the secrets to a successful business in art. Each issue also offers innovative features on commercial illustration, T-shirt art, and sign painting, with fascinating interviews from successful artists, including Mark Fredrickson, David Kimble, Jerry LoFaro, Jürek, and Sorayama.

Subscribe to *Airbrush Action* today—it's the best magazine around for serious airheads.

One Year: U.S. $21.95, Canada $28, International $50
Two Year: U.S. $37.95, Canada $43, International $75

Learn airbrushing from the leading artists in the world.

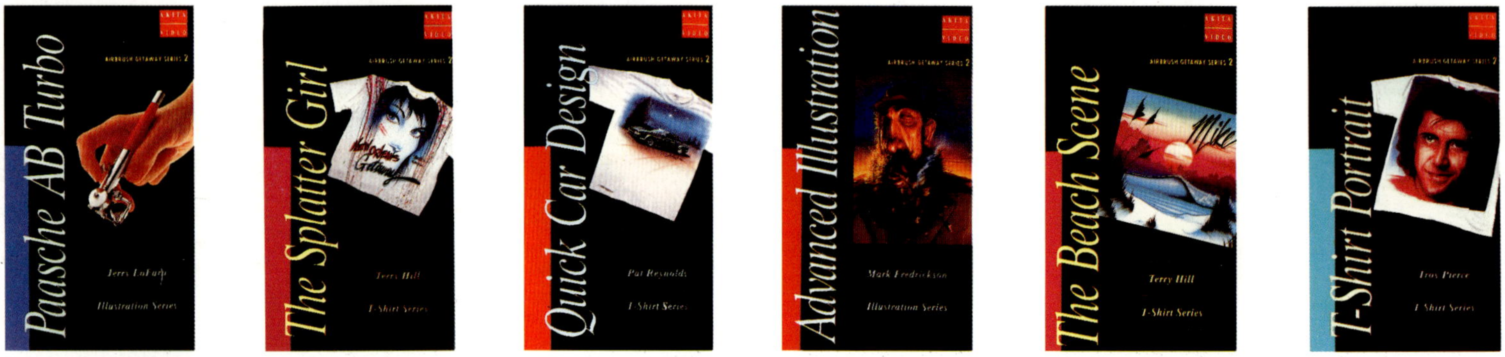

AIRBRUSH GETAWAY
Instructional Videos

Choose from over a dozen sensational how-to videos. Each tape features a top talent guiding you through an actual commercial illustration, T-shirt design or other technique—all are packed with essential information to create fabulous art in record-breaking time. Learn tips and tricks on portraits, landscapes, stenciling, loads more! Most videotapes were filmed at the popular Airbrush Getaway workshops.
Read *Airbrush Action* magazine for a current list of video titles or call for prices.
Terry Hill T-Shirt Series, License Plates with Pat Reynolds, Advanced Illustration with Mark Fredrickson, Paasche AB Turbo with Jerry LoFaro.

AIRBRUSH GETAWAY
Professional Workshops

Spend four exciting, information-packed days learning from successful, professional artists in the best airbrush seminars you'll ever attend! Airbrush Getaway workshops are held across the country—in New York, Florida, New Orleans, Dallas, Arizona, Los Angeles, Chicago, and other areas!
Call 800-232-8998 for a complete description and schedule of Getaway workshops during the next year.
FOUR-DAY WORKSHOPS: *Commercial and Technical Illustration, Signs and Custom Lettering, T-Shirt Airbrushing.* ONE-DAY CLASSES: *The Paasche AB Turbo, Intro to Airbrush Techniques, Fingernail Airbrushing.*

TO SUBSCRIBE TO *AIRBRUSH ACTION* MAGAZINE CALL:

1-800-232-8998

OR WRITE TO: AIRBRUSH ACTION, INC.
1985 SWARTHMORE AVENUE • LAKEWOOD, NJ 08701
908-364-2111 • FAX 908-367-5908